NATIONAL GEOGRAPHIC

FIELD GUIDE TO THE BIRDS OF WESTERN NORTH AMERICA

NATIONAL GEOGRAPHIC

FIELD GUIDE TO THE BIRDS OF WESTERN NORTH AMERICA

EDITED BY JON L. DUNN
AND JONATHAN ALDERFER

WASHINGTON, D.C.

Contents

Introduction

In this field guide, the division between East and West follows the general north-south line of the Rocky Mountains and incorporates state and provincial boundaries whenever possible.

In 2006, National Geographic released the fifth edition of *The Field Guide to the Birds of North America,* featuring 967 species, new artwork, and revised text reflecting the most current and accurate ornithological information. Building on that work, this volume, *The Field Guide to the Birds of Western North America,* provides annotated illustrations and detailed accounts specific to species found from the Pacific Ocean to the Rocky Mountains and adjacent portions of the Great Plains just to the east.

We adhere to the Committee on Classification and Nomenclature of the American Ornithologists' Union (AOU) for issues of taxonomy and nomenclature—English and scientific names—as determined in the seventh edition of the AOU Check-list (1997) and its eight subsequent supplements, published annually in the July issue of the AOU journal *The Auk.* There are slight differences in the taxonomy and nomenclature between the Eastern and Western editions of the North American field guide. The West guide was produced some months later than the East guide and reflects the 2008 supplement, whereas the East does not. We also follow either the American Birding Association Checklist Committee or the above-mentioned AOU committee in deciding which species to include. Apart from the list of exotics, the differences are few.

Virginia's Warbler: a species that breeds only in the western United States

The area covered in this guide (see map at left and on back cover flap) follows important topographical features but uses state, provincial, and territorial lines when possible. Coverage extends 200 nautical miles offshore. Although a companion volume, *The Field Guide to the Birds of Eastern North America,* covers birds east of the Rocky Mountains; a number of eastern species are fully covered in this guide because they are of regular occurrence as migrants (or vagrants) in western North America, even to the West Coast in most cases.

If a species is regular in the West, defined as very rare to abundant (see abundance terms, page 12), it receives full treatment in this guide. Many exotic species from other continents have been introduced into North America as game, park, or cage birds and are seen in the wild frequently. Those species that have at least some degree of establishment (e.g., Nutmeg Mannikin) are included here.

Yellow Warbler *aestiva*: a widespread North American breeder

Found in the back of this book are two appendices. The first is an illustrated list of casual and accidental species that have occurred primarily in the West or are equally rare in the East. Most of these species originate from Asia or Mexico, or they are stray seabirds. The second appendix is a brief list of primarily eastern species that are casual or accidental in the West. These species receive fuller treatment in *The Field Guide to the Birds of Eastern North America.*

Museum specimens have been an essential resource in preparing detailed and accurate illustrations for both this guide and *The National Geographic Field Guide to the Birds of North America.* We are grateful to the many institutions that have loaned specimens to the artists (see Acknowledgments, page 436).

Families

Scientists organize animal species into family groups that share certain structural or molecular characteristics. Some bird families have more than a hundred members; others only one. Characteristics within a family are helpful in identifying birds in the field. With sturdy bills, strong claws, and short legs, members of the Picidae family, for example, are easily recognized as woodpeckers.

Brief family descriptions, with information applicable to all members of the family, can be found at the beginning of each group. Additionally, a description of a smaller group within a family is sometimes provided, such as that given for the *Empidonax* flycatchers, which share some distinguishing traits.

Downy Woodpecker
Picoides pubescens

Scientific Names

Each species has a unique two-part scientific name, derived from Greek or Latin (in italics). The first part, always capitalized, indicates the genus. For example, nine members of the family Picidae are placed in the genus *Picoides*. Together with the second part of the name (the specific epithet), which is not capitalized, this identifies the species. *Picoides pubescens* is the name of one specific kind of woodpecker, commonly known as Downy Woodpecker.

Subspecies

Since the latter half of the 19th century, species have been further divided into subspecies, or *races,* when populations from different geographical regions show recognizable differences. Each subspecies bears a third scientific name, or trinomial. For instance, of the eleven recognized subspecies of the Gray Jay (*Perisoreus canadensis*), eight are resident in the West. We choose to illustrate the widespread nominate *canadensis* race, which breeds across the boreal forest to Alaska, as well as the darkest *obscurus* race of the Pacific Northwest and the very pale *capitalis* subspecies of the southern Rockies. Given the East's more uniform topography and climate, there is less geographical variation there than in the West, which has many mountain ranges, valleys, and deserts.

Polytypic:
Gray Jay

If the third part of a scientific name is the same as the second, the subspecies in question is known as the *nominate subspecies,* the type of the species originally described. The nominate subspecies of Gray Jay, *canadensis,* was named and described by Linnaeus in 1766, well before *obscurus* or *capitalis,* both of which were named and described by Robert Ridgway in 1874. For subspecies names, we have relied on the fifth edition of the AOU Check-list (1957), the last edition that treated subspecies.

For polytypic species (those having more than one subspecies) where the illustrations show mainly or entirely one subspecies, that subspecies' name appears italicized under the English name. If we include illustrations of other subspecies, those names appear next to the figures. Many species are monotypic (having no recognized subspecies), thus only the scientific binomial is used. For example, Hermit Warbler is monotypic and is simply known by the scientific name *Dendroica occidentalis.*

Monotypic:
Hermit Warbler

How to Identify Birds

Lesser Scaup *(top)* and Greater Scaup *(bottom)* are best distinguished by head shape

Field marks, a bird's physical features, are the clues by which birds are identified. They include plumage, or the bird's overall feathering; the shape of the body and its individual parts (see Parts of a Bird, page 10); and any actual markings such as bars, bands, spots, or rings. A field mark can be obvious, like a male Northern Cardinal's red plumage or a Killdeer's double breast bands. Other field marks are more subtle, such as the difference in head markings between a Clay-colored or Brewer's and a winter-plumaged Chipping Sparrow, or the difference in head shapes of Greater and Lesser Scaup.

Some plumage field marks are plainly visible only in good light, or from a certain angle, or when the bird is in flight. In this guide, the most distinctive features for each species in each plumage are usually listed first in the text account; boldface terms (e.g., ***adult female*** or ***first-winter male***) in the accounts correspond to the illustrated figures.

The most important thing when birding is *to look at the actual bird.* There will be plenty of time to consult the field guide later.

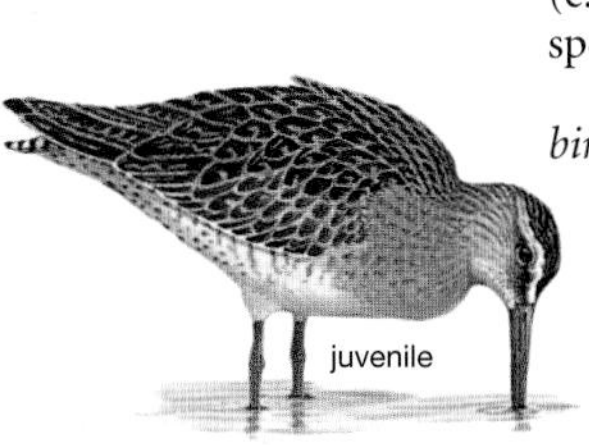

Both Short-billed *(above)* and Long-billed Dowitchers move their bills up and down like a sewing machine needle when feeding

Behavior

Behavioral traits also provide many clues to species identity. Look, for example, at a bird's flight. Is it direct or undulating? Does the bird beat its wings rapidly or slowly? Observe feeding habits too. Does the bird forage on the ground or in the treetops? Does it peck at the water or drill the mud? Consider personality clues as well. Is the bird usually visible and approachable or shy and difficult to locate? Does it hop or walk? Does it flick its tail up or drop it down?

Voice

A bird's songs and calls reveal not only its presence, but also, in many cases, its identity. Some species—particularly nocturnal or secretive birds such as owls, nightjars, and rails—are more often heard than seen. A few species are most reliably identified by voice even when they are seen well.

When birds assemble or travel in flocks, they often keep in touch with a *contact* or *flight call* that may be markedly different from their other calls. Flight calls are especially important for identifying individuals (or flocks) overhead.

Alder Flycatcher *(top)* and Willow Flycatcher *(bottom)* are best separated by song

Molt and Plumage Sequence

The regular renewal of plumage, called *molt,* is essential to a bird's ability to fly and to its overall health. A molt produces a specific plumage, and not all birds go through the same sequence of plumages. Some species have a very simple sequence of plumages from juvenile to adult: for example, most raptors molt from juvenal plumage directly into adult plumage. Other species, such as many of the gulls, take more than three years to acquire adult plumage and go through a complicated series of interim plumages. Shown in this guide are all of the most distinctive plumages likely to be encountered in the field.

House Sparrows' appearance changes with wear, not molt

The first coat of true feathers, acquired before a bird leaves the nest, is called the *juvenal plumage;* birds in this plumage are referred to as *juveniles*. True hawks and loons, as well as many other waterbirds, hold juvenal plumage well into winter. In many species, juvenal plumage is replaced in late summer or early fall by a *first-fall* or *first-winter* plumage that more closely resembles adult plumage. First-fall and any subsequent plumages that do not resemble the adult—known as *immature plumages*—may continue in a series that includes *first-spring* (when the bird is almost a year old), first-summer, and so on, until *adult plumage* is attained. When birds take several years to reach adult plumage, we label the interim plumages as *subadult* or note the specific year or season shown.

Western Tanagers undergo a complete molt from summer to late fall

In adult birds, the same annual sequence of molt and plumages is repeated throughout the bird's life. Most adults undergo a complete molt, replacing all their feathers, in late summer or early fall, after breeding. For some species this is the only molt of the year, so adults of these species have the same plumage year-round. Other species undergo a partial molt—usually involving the head, body, and some wing coverts—in late winter or early spring, resulting in a more colorful *breeding plumage* that is seen in spring and summer. For species with two annual molts, the plumage attained after breeding is referred to as the *nonbreeding* or *winter plumage.* Some changes are evident only during the brief period of courtship. In herons, for example, the colors of bill, lores, legs, and feet may change. When these colors are at their height, the birds are said to be in *high breeding plumage.* After breeding, most ducks molt into a briefly held *eclipse plumage* in which males acquire a femalelike plumage and females show little change, although some become paler and duller.

In addition, wear and fading of a bird's feathers can have a pronounced effect on its appearance. In species with a single annual molt in fall, the fresh colors exhibited right after molting are usually brighter than the faded colors seen at the end of the breeding season. For instance, Hammond's Flycatchers are brightest in fall; by the following summer, their plumage becomes worn and faded. Plumage patterns can also be affected. In certain songbirds, such as Snow Bunting or House Sparrow, the more patterned spring plumage appears as the dull tips of the fresh fall plumage gradually wear away, with very little molt involved.

Hammond's Flycatchers appear brightest in fall just after the complete molt

Often the fall molt occurs before migration, so we see these birds in fresh fall plumage even if they spend winter outside of North America. Certain species, including many shorebirds, suspend their molt during fall migration and complete it on arrival at the wintering grounds. Some species molt over a considerably longer period than others. Birds of prey, for instance, must rely on their wing feathers for successful hunting and thus molt very gradually so that only a few wing feathers are missing at any one time.

Parts of a Bird

Because the size, the shape, and the configuration of birds' various parts differ among families and species, birders should become familiar with their names and locations—bird topography. Nonpasserines are quite variable, and we give three examples: hummingbird, shorebird, and gull. Notice how the feathers overlap, and remember that a bird's posture and activity level can affect what feathers are visible.

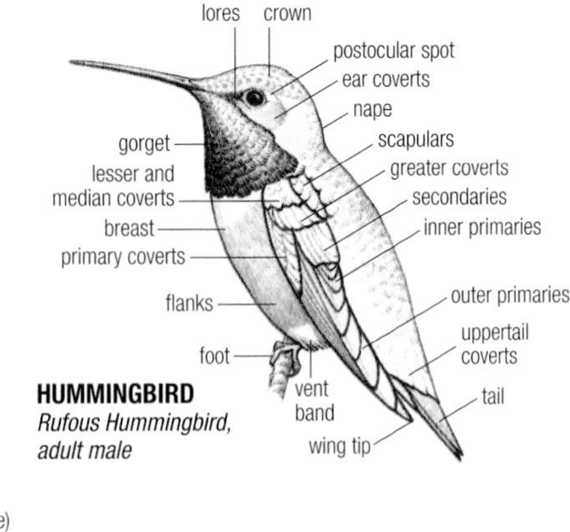

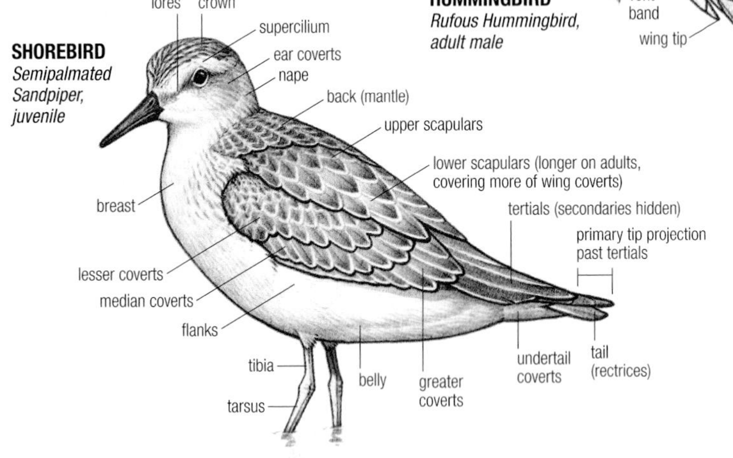

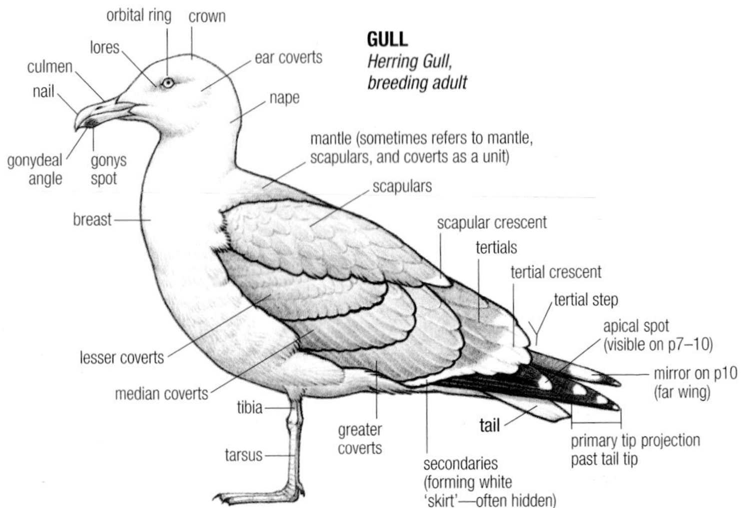

Passerines show less variation in body shape and feather organization. The Lark Sparrow example illustrates all the features of the head and wings. Many species show wing bars, formed by the pale tips of the greater and/or median coverts when the wing is folded.

UPPER WING
Lark Sparrow, adult

tertials
secondaries
scapulars
marginal coverts
lesser coverts
median coverts
greater coverts
bend of wing
carpal covert
alula
primary coverts
primaries
emargination
primary no. 1
p2
p3
p4
p5
p6
p7
p8
p9

PASSERINE
Lark Sparrow, adult

median crown stripe
lores
lateral crown stripe
supraloral
supercillium
forehead
eye stripe
upper mandible (maxilla)
ear coverts
nape
lower mandible
chin
back
throat
moustachial stripe
scapulars
submoustachial stripe
malar stripe
lesser coverts
breast spot
tertials
breast
median coverts
undertail coverts
side
greater coverts
uppertail coverts
primary coverts
flanks
belly
secondaries
primaries
tail (rectrices)
tail spots

Some feather groups can be seen only when a bird is in flight. Other feather groups have special names when they are prominently marked, such as the carpal bar seen on a Common Tern (below). Most birds have twelve tail feathers. When you observe the folded tail from below, the two outermost tail feathers are visible.

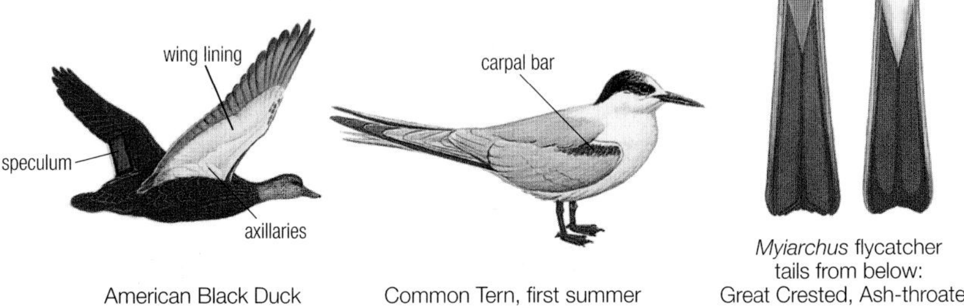

American Black Duck

Common Tern, first summer

Myiarchus flycatcher tails from below: Great Crested, Ash-throated

Plumage Variation

Barrow's x Common Goldeneye hybrid

Where adult males and females of a species are similar, we show only one. When male (♂) and female (♀) look different, we usually show both. If spring and fall, or *breeding* and *nonbreeding*, plumages differ only slightly, or if only one of these plumages is usually seen in North America, we tend to show only one figure. Juveniles and immatures are illustrated when they hold a different-looking plumage after they are old enough to be seen away from their more easily recognizable parents.

A number of species have two or more *color morphs*—variations in plumage color occurring regionally or within the same population—as is the case with Swainson's Hawk.

Some species (usually, but not always, of the same genus) occasionally breed with each other, producing *hybrid* offspring that may appear intermediate. Different subspecies also interbreed, resulting in *intergrade* individuals or populations.

Measurements

Greater *(top)* and Lesser Yellowlegs *(bottom)* are distinguishable by size

Knowing the size of a bird is important. When identifying a kinglet, for example, it helps to know that the bird in question is tiny (only about four inches long). Relative size is also significant: In mixed flocks, Greater and Lesser Yellowlegs are easily distinguished from each other by size alone.

Body length and wingspread measurements are by their nature somewhat imprecise and may vary slightly from one source to another. However, we feel that these are the most useful measurements for birders in the field. Thus, average length (L) from tip of bill to tip of tail for each species is given. Where size varies greatly within a species, either because of sex or geographical variation among subspecies, a range of smallest to largest is provided. And for large birds often seen in flight, we give the wingspan (WS), measured from wing tip to wing tip.

Abundance and Habitat

Casual: Eurasian Hobby

Abundance must be considered in relation to habitat. Under the heading **Range**, the species accounts include supplemental information about habitat, abundance, and seasonal status that cannot be shown in a single map. Some species are highly local, found only in a very specialized habitat.

The following categories of abundance—given from most to least numerous—are used in this guide: *abundant, common, fairly common, uncommon, rare,* and *very rare.* Unlike rare species, *casual* species do not occur annually in North America, but a pattern of their occurrence is apparent over decades. *Accidental* species have been seen only once or a few times in an area that is far out of their normal range. In fact, it may be decades, or even centuries, before another one is seen there again.

Accidental: Eurasian Hoopoe

Some other terms used herein include the following: *Vagrant* is a bird that is found well off its usual migration route. *Irruptive* species are erratic in their movements over much of their range.

One year they may be numerous in a given region and the next year, or even the next decade, they may be totally absent.

Range Maps

Maps are provided for all species with two general exceptions: (1) introduced species with very limited ranges that are described in the text and (2) species that do not breed in western North America and are of rare, casual, or accidental occurrence here.

On each map, range boundaries are drawn where the species ceases to be regularly seen. Keep in mind that nearly every species will be rare at the edges of its range. The map key on the back cover flap explains the colors and symbols used. Many maps in this guide have been revised to reflect the most current information.

Irruptive: Snowy Owl

Birds are not, however, bound by maps. Their ranges continually expand and contract. Irruptive species move southward in some years in large or small numbers and for great or small distances. In some species, birds leave the nesting grounds in late summer and then move northward. These post-breeding wanderers, principally young birds, will subsequently migrate southward by winter. Range maps of pelagic species, which spend most of their time over the open sea, are somewhat conjectural.

Range information is based on actual sightings and therefore depends on the number of knowledgeable and active birders in each area. There is much to learn about bird distribution in every part of North America. Participation by birders is necessary to the monitoring of expanding and contracting ranges. Breeding-bird surveys and atlas projects make a vital contribution to the general fund of information about each species. The Cornell Laboratory of Ornithology has created eBird (www.ebird.org), a website where birders can post their observations of species and add to our understanding of status and distribution.

Recent arrival:
Ruddy Ground-Dove

In the accounts of birds presently on the U.S. federal list of threatened or endangered species, we have placed the symbols **E** (endangered) or **T** (threatened). Canada also has its own list of threatened species, as do many states and provinces. Extinct species are indicated with the symbol **EX**.

How to Be a Better Birder

The time you spend studying your field guide at home will be repaid when you go out birding. In addition, a number of introductory books designed to help the beginning birder are available. One such book, *Birding Essentials,* published by National Geographic, covers all the basic skills and information.

Observing and studying birds can be an enriching, pleasurable experience with far-reaching rewards. With birding's increasing popularity, birders are becoming powerful advocates for the protection and stewardship of our natural resources. We urge you to get involved in conservation activities and to pass your knowledge and love of birds onto others.

Endangered species:
California Condor

THE EDITORS

Ducks, Geese, Swans (Family Anatidae)

Worldwide family. Web-footed, gregarious birds, ranging from small ducks to large swans. Largely aquatic, but geese, swans, and some "puddle ducks" also graze on land.

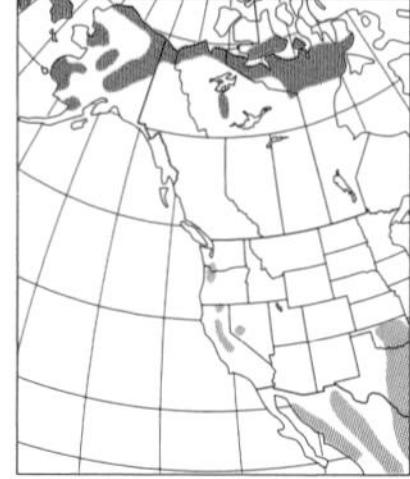

Greater White-fronted Goose *Anser albifrons*

L 28" (71 cm) Named for the distinctive white band at base of bill. Medium-size, grayish brown goose, with irregular black barring on underparts; orange feet and legs. Bill pink or orangish with whitish tip. In flight, note grayish blue wash on wing coverts and white, U-shaped rump band. Most ***immatures*** acquire white front above bill and white bill tip during first winter; acquire black belly markings by second fall; best distinguished from similar Taiga Bean Goose and Tundra Bean Goose (page 412) by bill color. Color and size vary in ***adults:*** Small, pale, Arctic tundra birds have heavy barring; taiga-breeding (central Alaska) race, *elgasi,* wintering in California's Sacramento Valley, is larger, with a larger bill, less barring on belly, and a darker, longer, thicker neck.

Voice: Call is a high-pitched, laughing *kah-lah-aluck.*

Range: Large populations found locally in Pacific states. Rare winter visitor outside mapped range in all western states and north into southern Canada. Uncommon to rare on western Great Plains.

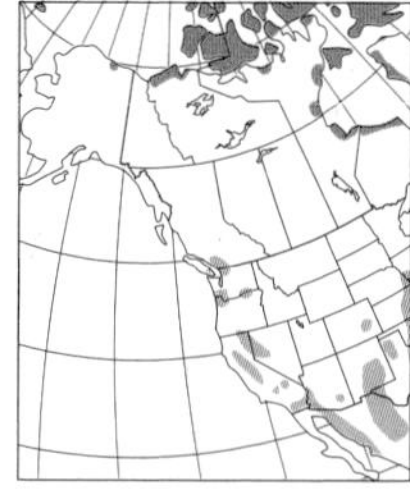

Snow Goose *Chen caerulescens L 26-33" (66-84 cm)*

Two color morphs. Adult distinguished from smaller Ross's Goose by larger, pinkish bill with black "grinning patch." Flies with slower wingbeat than Ross's; rusty stains often visible on face in summer. ***White-morph juvenile*** is grayish above, with dark bill. ***Blue-morph adult*** has mostly white head and neck, brown back, variable amount of white on underparts. Juvenile is dark bodied; distinguished from Greater White-fronted Goose by dark legs and bill and lack of white on face. Intermediates between morphs have mainly white underparts and whitish wing coverts.

Voice: Very vocal in flight, typically nasal cackling.

Range: Locally abundant. Occasionally hybridizes with Ross's Goose. "Lesser Snow Goose" (subspecies shown) is rare in winter throughout interior West outside mapped range. Blue morph is abundant in central North America; rare west of the Great Plains.

Ross's Goose *Chen rossii L 23" (58 cm)*

Stubby, triangular bill, mostly deep pinkish red with purplish blue-gray base (lacking in Snow Goose). More vertical demarcation between feathering and base of bill than Snow. Neck shorter, head rounder than Snow, white head generally lacks rusty stains. Has two color morphs: ***White-morph juvenile*** may have very pale gray wash on head, back, and flanks, but far less than juvenile white-morph Snow. Extremely rare ***blue morph*** is darker than blue-morph Snow; face and belly are white.

Voice: Like Snow Goose, but pitch is higher.

Range: Rare visitor to much of West outside mapped range; casual in Yukon and Alaska. Usually seen with Snow Geese.

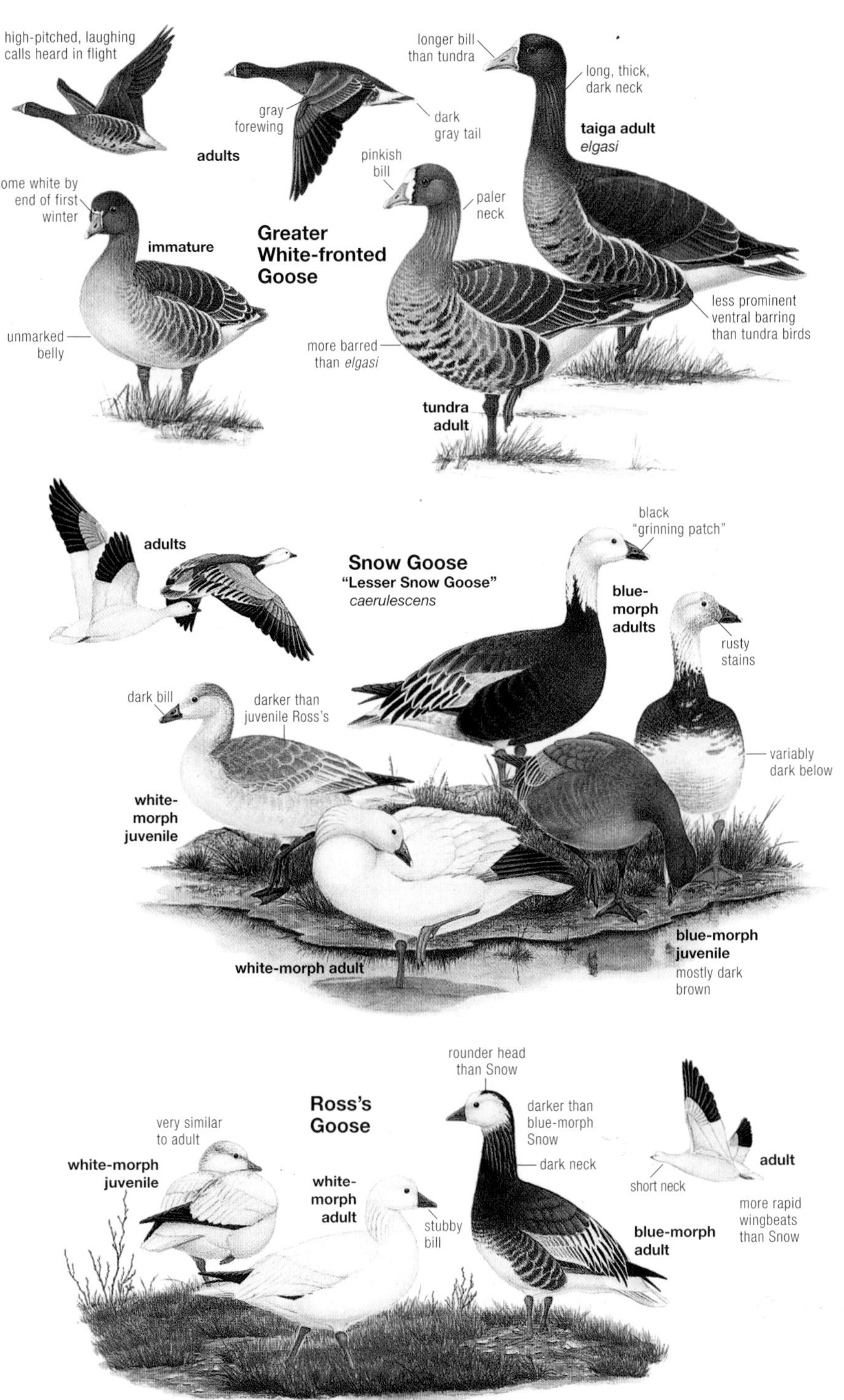

high-pitched, laughing calls heard in flight
adults
gray forewing
dark gray tail
longer bill than tundra
long, thick, dark neck
taiga adult
elgasi
pinkish bill
paler neck
some white by end of first winter
immature
Greater White-fronted Goose
unmarked belly
more barred than elgasi
less prominent ventral barring than tundra birds
tundra adult
adults
Snow Goose
"Lesser Snow Goose"
caerulescens
black "grinning patch"
blue-morph adults
rusty stains
dark bill
darker than juvenile Ross's
variably dark below
white-morph juvenile
white-morph adult
blue-morph juvenile
mostly dark brown
Ross's Goose
rounder head than Snow
darker than blue-morph Snow
dark neck
very similar to adult
white-morph juvenile
white-morph adult
stubby bill
short neck
adult
more rapid wingbeats than Snow
blue-morph adult

Brant *Branta bernicla L 25" (64 cm)*
Small, dark, stocky. Note whitish patch on side of neck. White uppertail coverts almost conceal black tail. White undertail coverts conspicuous in flight. Wings comparatively long and pointed, wingbeat rather rapid. Immature shows bold white edging to wing coverts and secondaries, and fainter neck patches than ***adult. Juvenile*** sometimes lacks neck patches. Western *nigricans,* ***"Black Brant,"*** has dark belly contrasting with whiter flanks and neck patches that meet in front. In eastern subspecies *hrota,* ***"American Brant,"*** very rare or casual on Pacific coast, pale belly, contrasting black chest; neck patches do not meet in front. ***"Gray-bellied Brant,"*** breeding on western islands of Canada's Arctic Archipelago, wintering mainly in western Washington, has gray sides, paler belly than "Black Brant," intermediate "necklace" pattern.
Voice: Call is a low, rolling, slightly upslurred *raunk-raunk.*
Range: Primarily a sea goose; flocks fly low in ragged formation and feed on aquatic plants of shallow bays and estuaries. Locally common. Western *nigricans* is regular at Salton Sea in spring and sometimes summers. Casual elsewhere in interior West.

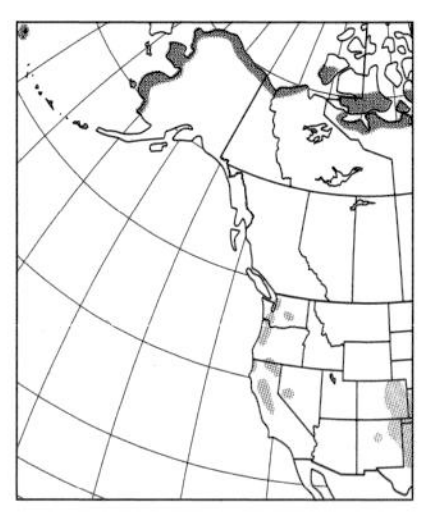

Cackling Goose *Branta hutchinsii L 23-33" (58-84 cm)*
Formerly considered part of the Canada Goose complex; smaller with rounder head and stubbier bill. Shorter neck is most obvious in flight. Four subspecies vary from smallest and darkest *minima,* breeding in southwest Alaska, to largest *taverneri,* breeding in western and northern Alaska; both winter in the Pacific states. Aleutian breeding *leucopareia,* with a prominent white neck ring (sometimes present on other subspecies), winters primarily in California's Central Valley; it has increased greatly in recent decades. Palest *hutchinsii,* intermediate in size, breeds in Canada's Arctic Archipelago and winters from southern Great Plains to western Gulf Coast region. Size of *parvipes* Canada and *taverneri* Cackling overlap; *taverneri* averages darker with stubbier bill, but identification criteria are still not adequately worked out.
Voice: Calls are higher pitched than Canada Goose.
Range: Rare to Great Basin and Arizona.

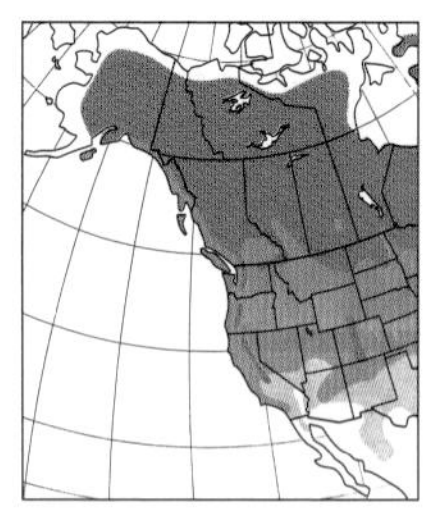

Canada Goose *Branta canadensis L 30-43" (76-109 cm)*
Our most common and familiar goose. Black head and neck marked with distinctive white "chin strap," stretching from ear to ear. In flight, shows large dark wings; white undertail coverts; white, U-shaped rump band; and long neck. The approximately seven named subspecies in North America vary in overall color and size, generally darker in West; darkest is *occidentalis,* which breeds on eastern Gulf of Alaska coast. Size decreases northward: The smallest subspecies, *parvipes* (***"Lesser Canada Goose"***), breeds from central Alaska to north-central Canada and winters mainly in central portions of U.S. with some in the Pacific states.
Voice: Call is a deep, musical *honk-a-lonk.*
Range: Flocks usually migrate in V-formations, stopping to feed in wetlands, grasslands, or agricultural areas. Breeding programs have now produced expanding populations that are resident south of mapped range and along Pacific coast.

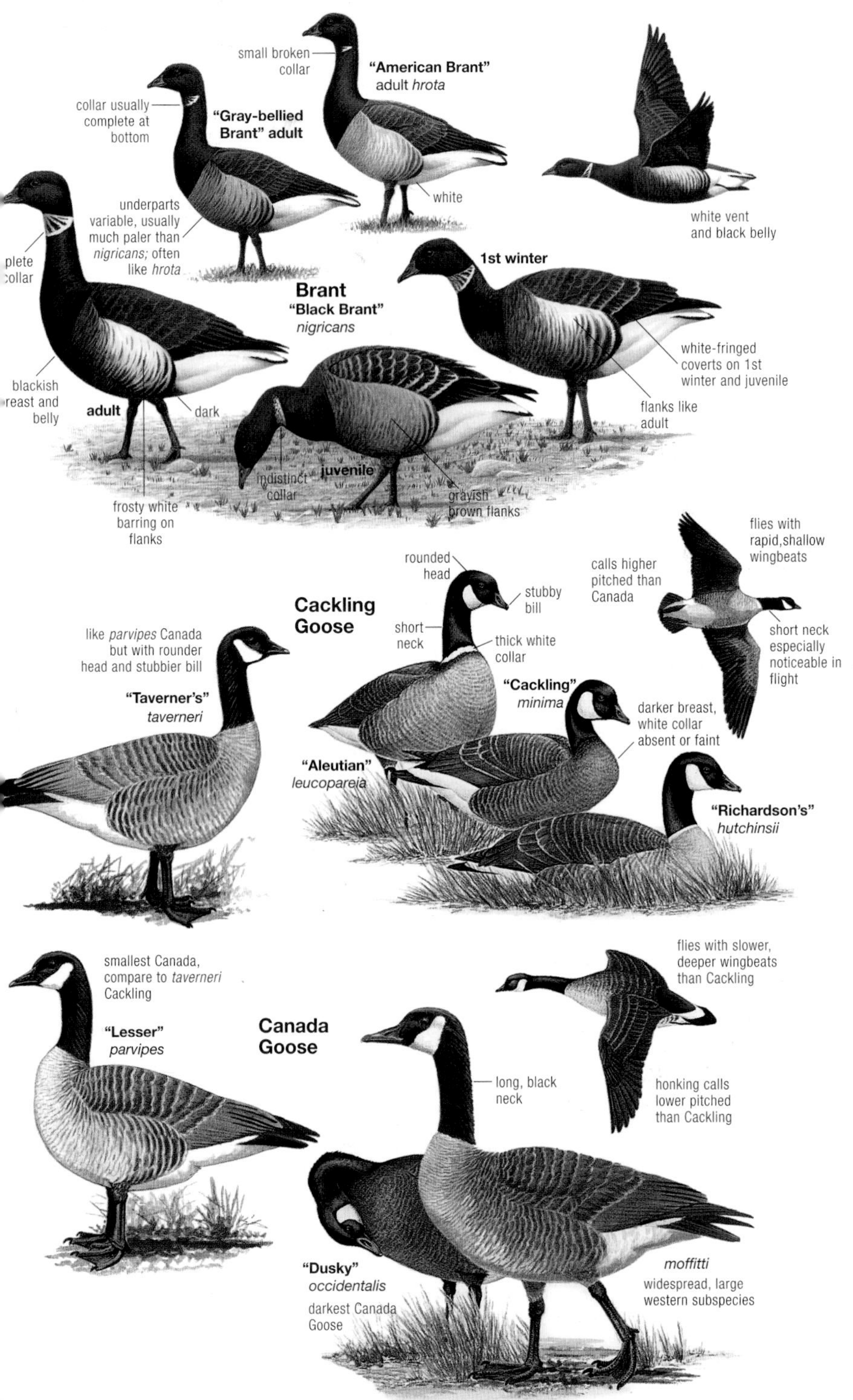
small broken collar
"American Brant"
adult hrota
collar usually complete at bottom
"Gray-bellied Brant" adult
white
white vent and black belly
underparts variable, usually much paler than nigricans; often like hrota
plete collar
1st winter
Brant
"Black Brant"
nigricans
white-fringed coverts on 1st winter and juvenile
blackish reast and belly
adult
dark
flanks like adult
indistinct collar
juvenile
grayish brown flanks
frosty white barring on flanks
rounded head
flies with rapid,shallow wingbeats
calls higher pitched than Canada
Cackling Goose
stubby bill
short neck
like parvipes Canada but with rounder head and stubbier bill
thick white collar
short neck especially noticeable in flight
"Taverner's"
taverneri
"Cackling"
minima
darker breast, white collar absent or faint
"Aleutian"
leucopareia
"Richardson's"
hutchinsii
smallest Canada, compare to taverneri Cackling
flies with slower, deeper wingbeats than Cackling
"Lesser"
parvipes
Canada Goose
long, black neck
honking calls lower pitched than Cackling
"Dusky"
occidentalis
darkest Canada Goose
moffitti
widespread, large western subspecies

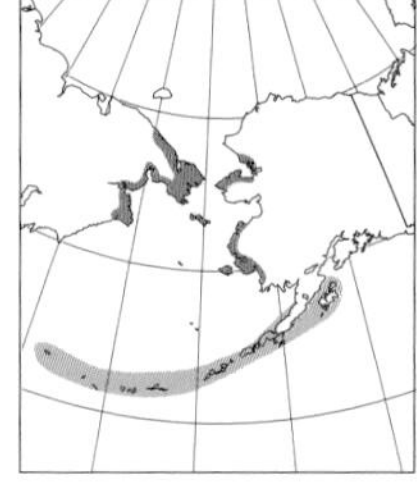

Emperor Goose *Chen canagica L 26" (66 cm)*
Fairly stocky, small goose with short, thick neck. Head and back of neck white; chin and throat black; face often stained rusty in summer. Bill pinkish; lower mandible is sometimes black. Black-and-white edging to silvery gray plumage creates a scaled effect above and below. ***Juvenile*** has dark head and bill. During first fall, acquires white flecking on head; resembles adult by winter.
Voice: Calls include a high-pitched, hoarse *kla-ha*. Less vocal than other geese.
Range: Breeds in tidewater marsh and tundra; winters on seashores, reefs. Casual south on Pacific coast to central California and inland to Sacramento Valley.

Swans

Large, long-necked birds; North American species are white overall as adults; browner immatures are difficult to identify.

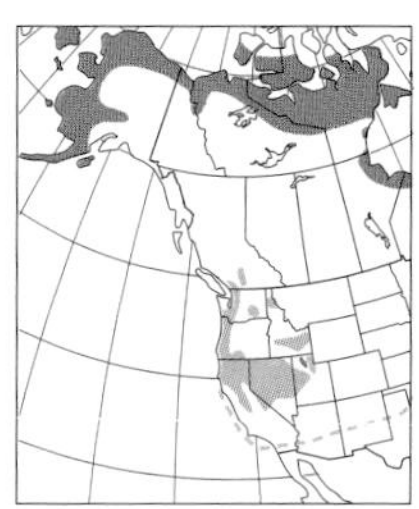

Tundra Swan *Cygnus columbianus L 52" (132 cm)*
In ***adult,*** black facial skin tapers to a point in front of eye and cuts straight across forehead; most birds have a yellow spot of variable size in front of eye. Head is rounded, bill slightly concave. In Eurasian race, ***"Bewick's Swan,"*** seen very rarely in the Pacific states, facial skin and base of bill are yellow, but usually only above the nostril; compare with Whooper Swan. ***Juvenile*** Tundra molts earlier than immature Trumpeter and Whooper Swans; appears much whiter by late winter. Immature "Bewick's" has whitish bill patch.
Voice: Call is a noisy, high-pitched whooping or yodeling.
Range: Nests on tundra or sheltered marshes; winters in flocks on shallow ponds, lakes, estuaries. Rare to uncommon in migration and winter over parts of interior U.S.

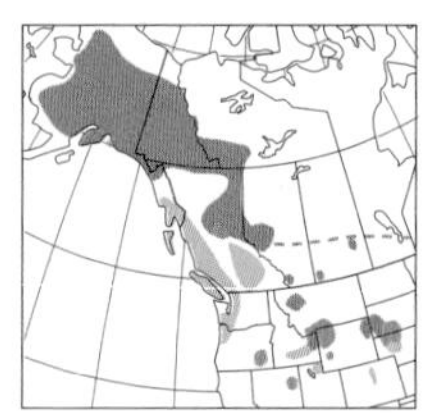

Trumpeter Swan *Cygnus buccinator L 60" (152 cm)*
Adult's black facial skin tapers to broad point at the eye, dips down in a V on forehead. Forehead slopes evenly to straight bill. ***Juvenile*** retains gray-brown plumage through first spring.
Voice: Common call is a single or double *honk* like an old car horn.
Range: Locally fairly common in breeding areas. Reintroduced into parts of former range and introduced elsewhere. Rare in winter south to California and casual in Southwest.

Whooper Swan *Cygnus cygnus L 60" (152 cm)*
Eurasian species closely related to Trumpeter Swan. Large yellow patch on lores and bill usually extends in a point to the nostrils; compare with "Bewick's Swan." Forehead slopes evenly to the straight bill. ***Juvenile*** retains dusky plumage through first winter; by first fall, bill attains whitish patches in same shape as adult's bill patch.
Voice: Common call is a buglelike double note.
Range: Regular winter visitor to outer and central Aleutians; has bred on Attu Island. Casual elsewhere in northwestern North America (south to northern California).

appears
stocky in
flight
white tail
Emperor
Goose
white head
and neck
adult
extensive
black throat
juvenile
dusky head
and neck
scaly pattern
overall
more concave
shape than
Trumpeter
white feathering cuts
straight across forehead
size of yellow
lore spot variable,
absent on some
eye
stands out
extensive yellow
at base of bill
squared off
juvenile
Tundra Swan
columbianus
adult
"Bewick's Swan"
adult
bewickii
Whooper
Swan
Trumpeter
Swan
extensive yellow
extends forward
in a point
pinkish gray
forms same
shape in adult
adult
juvenile
white forms
V-shape
on forehead
retains darker
plumage later in
inter than Tundra
juvenile
adult

Whistling-Ducks

Named for their whistling calls, these gooselike ducks have long legs and long necks. Their wingbeats are slower than those of ducks, faster than those of geese.

Fulvous Whistling-Duck *Dendrocygna bicolor*

L 20" (51 cm) Rich tawny color overall; back darker, edged with tawny. Dark stripe along hindneck is continuous in female, usually broken in male. Bill and legs dark. Whitish rump band conspicuous in flight.

Voice: Call is a squealing *pe-chee.*

Range: Forages in marshes, shallow waters; seldom found in trees; often dives to feed. More active at night than day. Nearly extirpated in the West. Formerly had a rather extensive breeding range in California. In recent decades, regular occurrence restricted to California's Imperial Valley, but has largely disappeared even there since about 2000 and now very rare. Casual elsewhere in California and Southwest, and some birds may be of questionable origin.

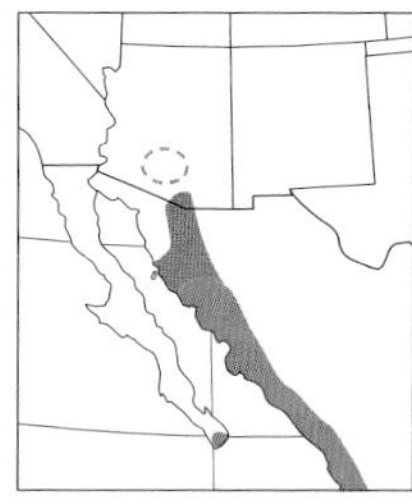

Black-bellied Whistling-Duck *Dendrocygna autumnalis*

L 21" (53 cm) Gray face with white eye ring, red bill. Legs red or pink; belly, rump, and tail black. White wing patch shows as broad white stripe in flight. ***Juvenile*** is paler, with gray bill.

Voice: Call is a high-pitched, four-note whistle.

Range: Casual west to southeastern California and to New Mexico and west Texas. Inhabits wetlands; nests and perches in trees, nest boxes.

Perching Ducks

These surface-feeding, woodland ducks are equipped with sharp claws for perching in trees. They nest in tree cavities or nest boxes.

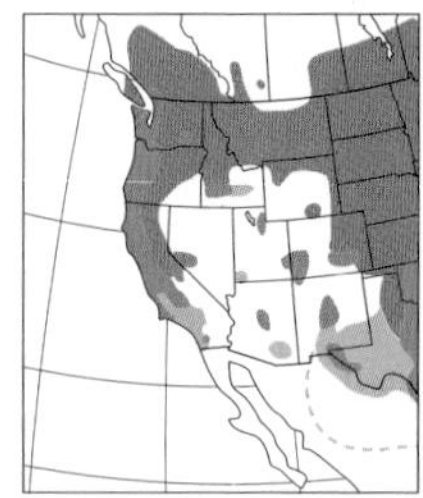

Wood Duck *Aix sponsa L 18½" (47 cm)*

Male's glossy, colorful plumage and sleek crest are distinctive. Head pattern and bill colors are retained in drab eclipse plumage. ***Female*** identified by short crest and large, white, teardrop-shaped eye patch; compare with female Mandarin Duck (page 44). ***Juvenile*** resembles female but is spotted below. In all plumages, flight profile is distinctive: large head with bill angled downward; long, squared-off tail.

Voice: Male gives soft, upslurred whistle when swimming; female's squealing flight call is a rising *oo-eek.*

Range: Fairly common in open woodlands near water. Rare during winter throughout most of breeding range. Generally rare in southwestern deserts; casual in southeastern California. Also casual to southeast Alaska.

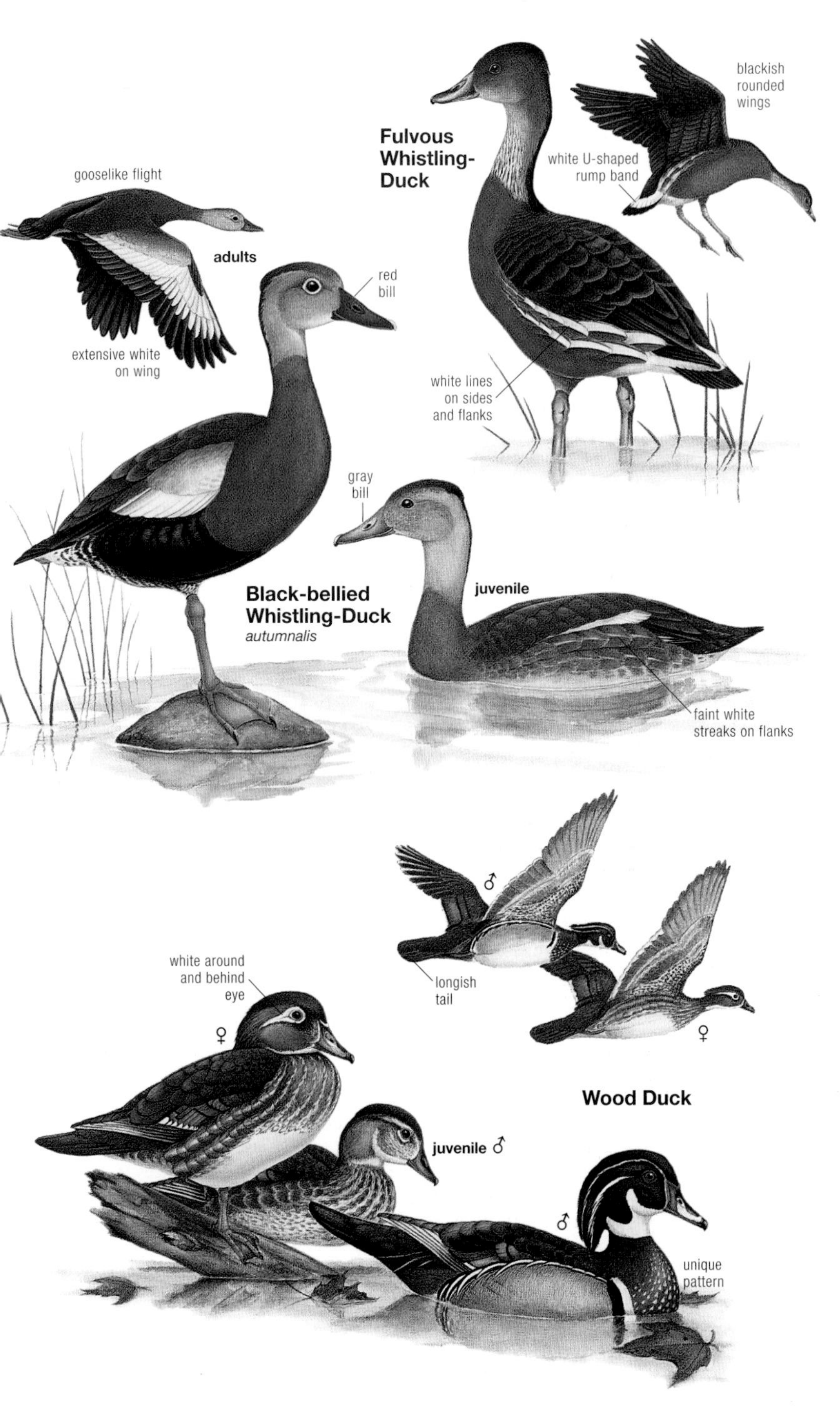

blackish rounded wings
Fulvous Whistling-Duck
white U-shaped rump band
gooselike flight
adults
red bill
extensive white on wing
white lines on sides and flanks
gray bill
juvenile
Black-bellied Whistling-Duck
autumnalis
faint white streaks on flanks
♂
longish tail
♀
white around and behind eye
♀
Wood Duck
juvenile ♂
♂
unique pattern

Dabbling Ducks

Surface-feeding members of the genus *Anas:* the familiar "puddle ducks" of freshwater shallows and, chiefly in winter, salt marshes. Dabblers feed by tipping, tail up, to reach aquatic plants, seeds, and snails. They require no running start to take off but spring directly into flight. Most species show a distinguishing swatch of bright color, the speculum, on the secondaries. Many are known to hybridize.

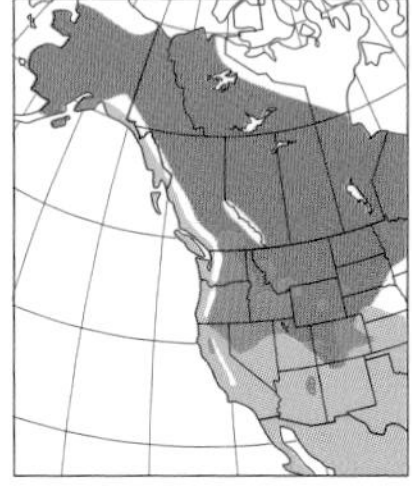

American Wigeon *Anas americana L 19" (48 cm)*
Male's white forehead and cap are conspicuous in mixed flocks foraging in fields, marshes, and shallow waters; in flight, identified by mainly white wing linings and, in ***adult male,*** by large white patches on upperwing. Wing patches are grayish on ***adult female*** and immature. Female lacks white on head, closely resembles gray-morph female Eurasian Wigeon; distinguishing field marks in flight are female American's white wing linings and contrast between gray throat and brown breast; Eurasian female's throat and breast are of uniform color.
Voice: Male gives piercing three-note whistle; female call is a much lower single-syllable *quack.*
Range: Common. Rare to Aleutians and Bering Sea islands.

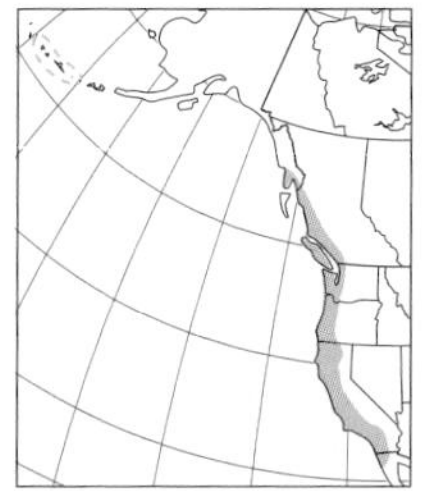

Eurasian Wigeon *Anas penelope L 20" (51 cm)*
Dark rufous head and gray back and sides make males conspicuous in flocks of American Wigeons; dusky wing linings are distinctive in all plumages. Hybridizes regularly with American Wigeon. ***Adult male*** has reddish brown head and neck with creamy crown; large white patches on upperwings. Many fall males retain some brown eclipse feathers but show distinctive reddish head. ***Immature male*** begins to acquire adult head and breast color but retains some brown juvenal plumage, particularly on forewing, similar to American Wigeon. ***Gray-morph female*** more closely resembles female American. ***Rufous morph*** has a more reddish head.
Voice: Male gives a whistled *wheeooo,* like American Wigeon, but with two, not three, syllables and even higher pitched.
Range: Rare but regular winter visitor along West Coast and coastal valleys. Rarer still in the interior West. Regular migrant in western Alaska; a few winter in Aleutians.

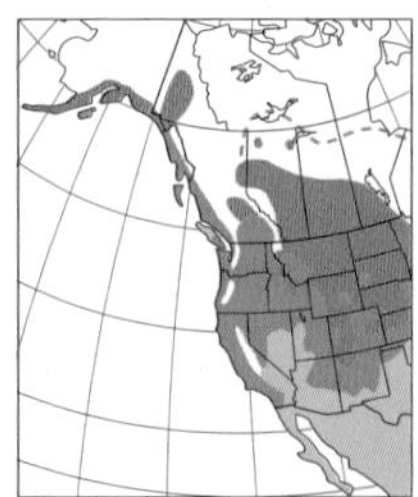

Gadwall *Anas strepera L 20" (51 cm)*
Male is mostly gray, with white belly, black tail coverts, pale chestnut on wings. ***Female***'s mottled brown plumage resembles female Mallard (next page), but belly is white, forehead steeper, upper mandible gray with orange sides. Both sexes have white inner secondaries that may show as small patch on swimming bird and identify the species in flight.
Voice: Male's single-syllable call is loud and nasal; female's is a Mallard-like *quack.*
Range: Rather common overall; uncommon in Yukon and Alaska, casual to western and northern Alaska.

American Wigeon
adult ♂
white under-
wing coverts
and axillaries
♀
white or
buffy white
crown
adult ♂
eclipse
adult ♂
♀
gray face contrasts
with cinnamon-buff
chest
bluish gray bill
with dark tip
head and chest
uniform in color
most with
rusty cast
rufous morph ♀
gray-morph
♀
Eurasian
Wigeon
dusky underwings
and axillaries
adult ♂
gray-
morph ♀
cream
rufous
adult ♂
immature ♂
steep
forehead
Gadwall
en line of
ange on
des of bill
♀
♂
small white
speculum
patch
♂
black
undertail
coverts
white belly
♀

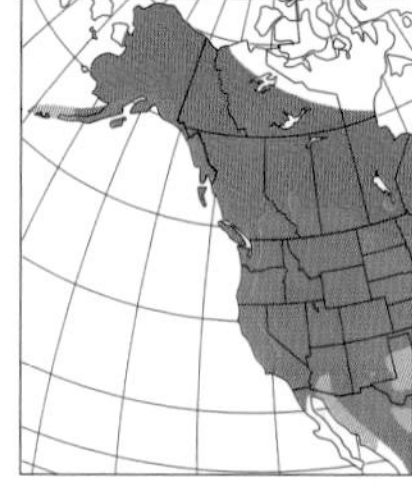

Mallard *Anas platyrhynchos L 23" (58 cm)*
Male readily identified by metallic green head and neck, yellow bill, narrow white collar, chestnut breast. Black central tail feathers curl up. Both sexes have white tail, white underwings, bright blue speculum with both sides bordered in white. ***Female***'s mottled plumage resembles other *Anas* species; look for orange bill marked with black. Juvenile and ***eclipse male*** resemble female but bill is dull olive. Mallards in central Mexico, formerly considered a separate species, "Mexican Duck," *diazi*, are darker, lack distinctive male plumage; their bills are unmarked dull greenish (males) to orange with darker blotches (female). It is believed that mainly ***intergrades*** occur in the southwestern U.S., from southeast Arizona to southwestern Texas.
Voice: Male gives a *quack* and a rasping *kreep*; female gives a series of *quack* notes.
Range: Frequents a wide variety of shallow-water environments. Abundant and widespread. Feral and domestic birds are permanent residents, often found on park ponds. These birds are slightly discolored (probably largely as a result of hybridization) and/or misshapen and are usually excessively tame.

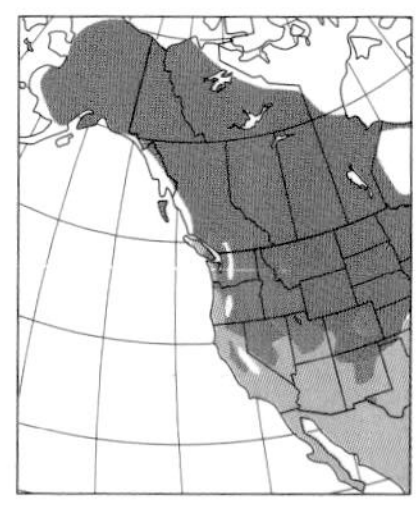

Northern Shoveler *Anas clypeata L 19" (48 cm)*
Large, spatulate bill, longer than head, identifies both sexes. ***Male*** distinguished by green head, white breast, and brown sides; in early ***fall*** has a white crescent on each side of face, like Blue-winged Teal (page 28). ***Female***'s grayish bill is tinged with orange on cutting edges and lower mandible. In flight, both sexes show blue forewing patch.
Voice: Male gives a two-syllable nasal call; female gives a *quack*.
Range: Common to abundant in the West; rare to uncommon in western Alaska. Found in marshes, ponds, and bays; often in large numbers on sewage ponds.

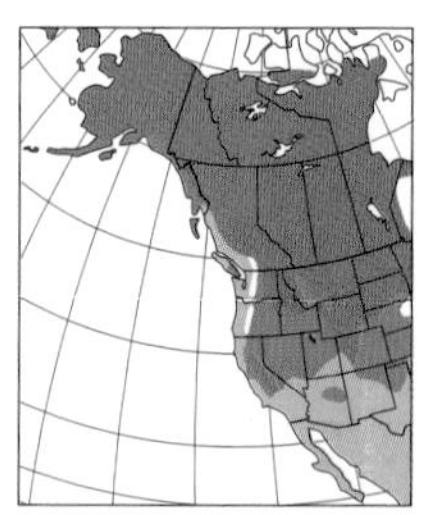

Northern Pintail *Anas acuta ♂L 26" (66 cm) ♀L 20" (51 cm)*
Male's chocolate brown head tops long, slender white neck, the white extending in a thin line onto head. Black central tail feathers extend far beyond rest of long, wedge-shaped tail. ***Female*** is mottled brown, paler on head and neck; bill uniformly grayish. In both sexes, flight profile shows long neck; slender body; long, pointed wings; dark speculum bordered in white on trailing edge. In flight, female's mottled brown wing linings contrast with white belly; long, wedge-shaped tail lacks male's extended feathers.
Voice: Male gives a soft whistled one- (usually) to three-syllable call, often quite suggestive of the male Green-winged Teal's call; the female gives one *quack* or a series of weak, hoarse *quack* notes.
Range: A common, widespread duck, found in marshes and open areas with ponds and lakes; in winter often feeds in grainfields. Much more common in West than in East. Rare in winter north to southern Alaska. Very rare breeder south of mapped range.

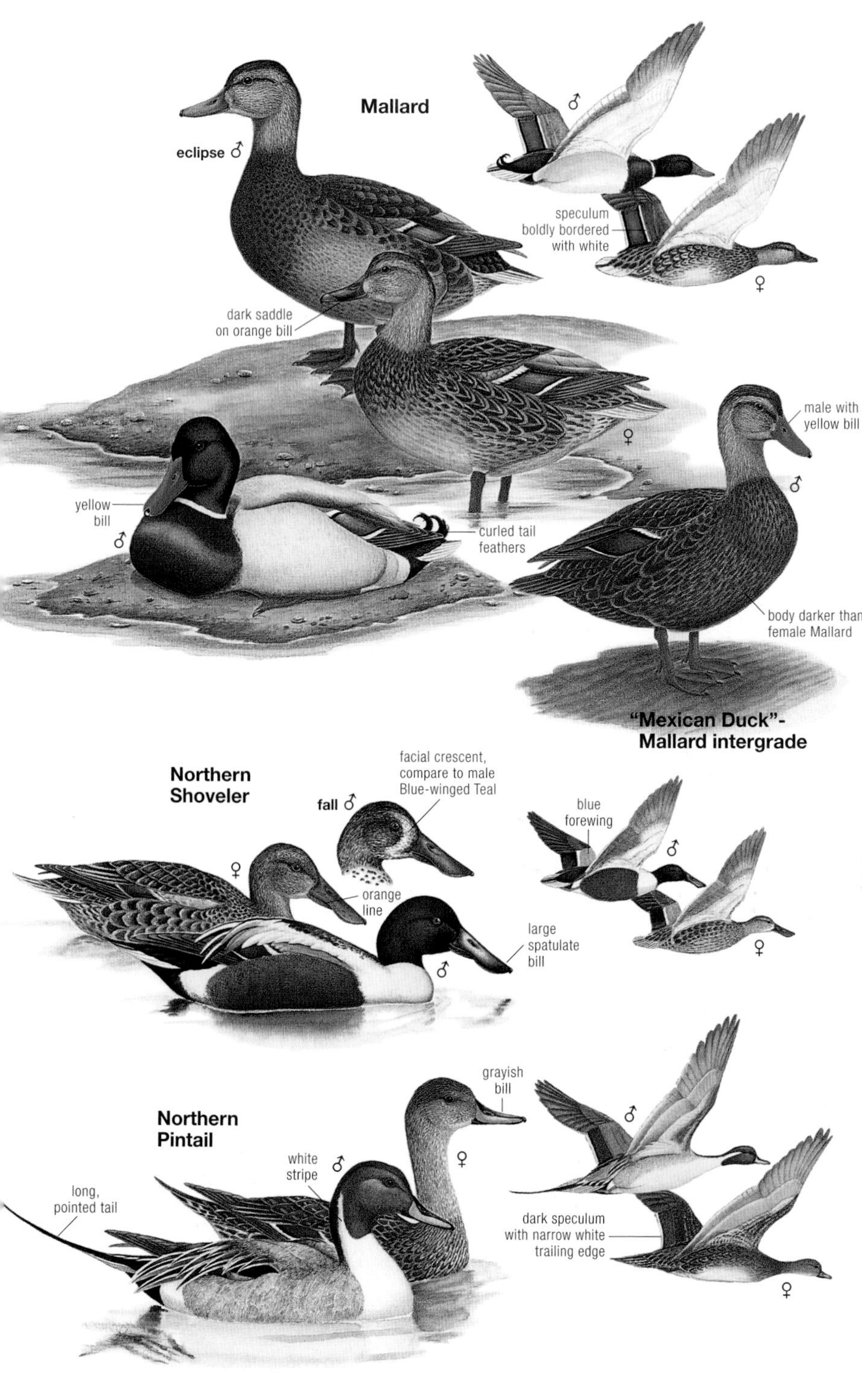
Mallard
eclipse ♂
♂
speculum
boldly bordered
with white
♀
dark saddle
on orange bill
male with
yellow bill
♀
♂
yellow
bill
♂
curled tail
feathers
body darker than
female Mallard
"Mexican Duck"-
Mallard intergrade
Northern
Shoveler
facial crescent,
compare to male
Blue-winged Teal
fall ♂
blue
forewing
♂
♀
orange
line
large
spatulate
bill
♂
♀
Northern
Pintail
grayish
bill
♂
white
stripe
♂
♀
long,
pointed tail
dark speculum
with narrow white
trailing edge
♀

Falcated Duck *Anas falcata L 19" (48 cm)*

East Asian species. Named for ***male***'s long, falcated (sickle-shaped) tertials that overhang tail. Both sexes are chunky, with large head. ***Female***'s all-dark bill distinguishes her from female wigeons (page 22) and Gadwall; note slight bump on back of head. In flight, both sexes show a broad, dark speculum bordered in white.

Voice: Generally silent away from breeding grounds.

Range: Very rare visitor to the western Aleutians; casual to Pribilofs and from West Coast region.

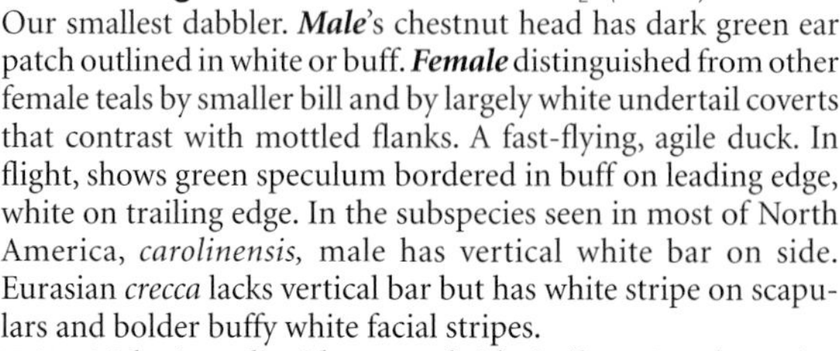

Green-winged Teal *Anas crecca L 14½" (37 cm)*

Our smallest dabbler. ***Male***'s chestnut head has dark green ear patch outlined in white or buff. ***Female*** distinguished from other female teals by smaller bill and by largely white undertail coverts that contrast with mottled flanks. A fast-flying, agile duck. In flight, shows green speculum bordered in buff on leading edge, white on trailing edge. In the subspecies seen in most of North America, *carolinensis,* male has vertical white bar on side. Eurasian *crecca* lacks vertical bar but has white stripe on scapulars and bolder buffy white facial stripes.

Voice: Male gives a liquid *preep* or *krick,* similar to Northern Pintail; female gives a weak, high-pitched *quack.*

Range: Nests in marshes and on tundra; winters in a variety of wetland habitats. Very rare breeder south of mapped range. Eurasian *crecca* is fairly common on the Aleutians and Pribilofs; uncommon to rare elsewhere on Bering Sea islands, and very rare elsewhere on West Coast. Was formerly considered a separate species, the Common Teal; some (e.g., British Ornithologists' Union) have resplit these two.

Baikal Teal *Anas formosa L 17" (43 cm)*

Asian species. ***Adult male***'s intricately patterned head is distinctive. Long, dropping dark scapulars are edged in rufous and white. Gray sides are set off front and rear by vertical white bars. ***Female*** similar to smaller female Green-winged Teal, but tail appears a bit longer; note distinct face pattern with a well-defined white spot at base of bill and white throat that angles up to rear of eye. Distinct eyebrow is bordered by darker crown. "Female" birds with ***bridle*** marking may be immature males. In flight, Baikal's underwing is like Green-winged but has more extensive and darker leading edge. Green speculum has an indistinct cinnamon-buff inner border.

Voice: Males give a deep chuckling three-syllable call; females give a low *quack.*

Range: Winters from China to Japan. Huge numbers have been found very locally recently in South Korea. After several decades of decline, Asian populations appear to have rebounded recently with a corresponding increase of records from western Alaska (St. Paul Island, Pribilofs, and western Aleutian Islands), and primarily in fall, and two other records on West Coast (Washington and California). Records away from Pacific region may be of escapes.

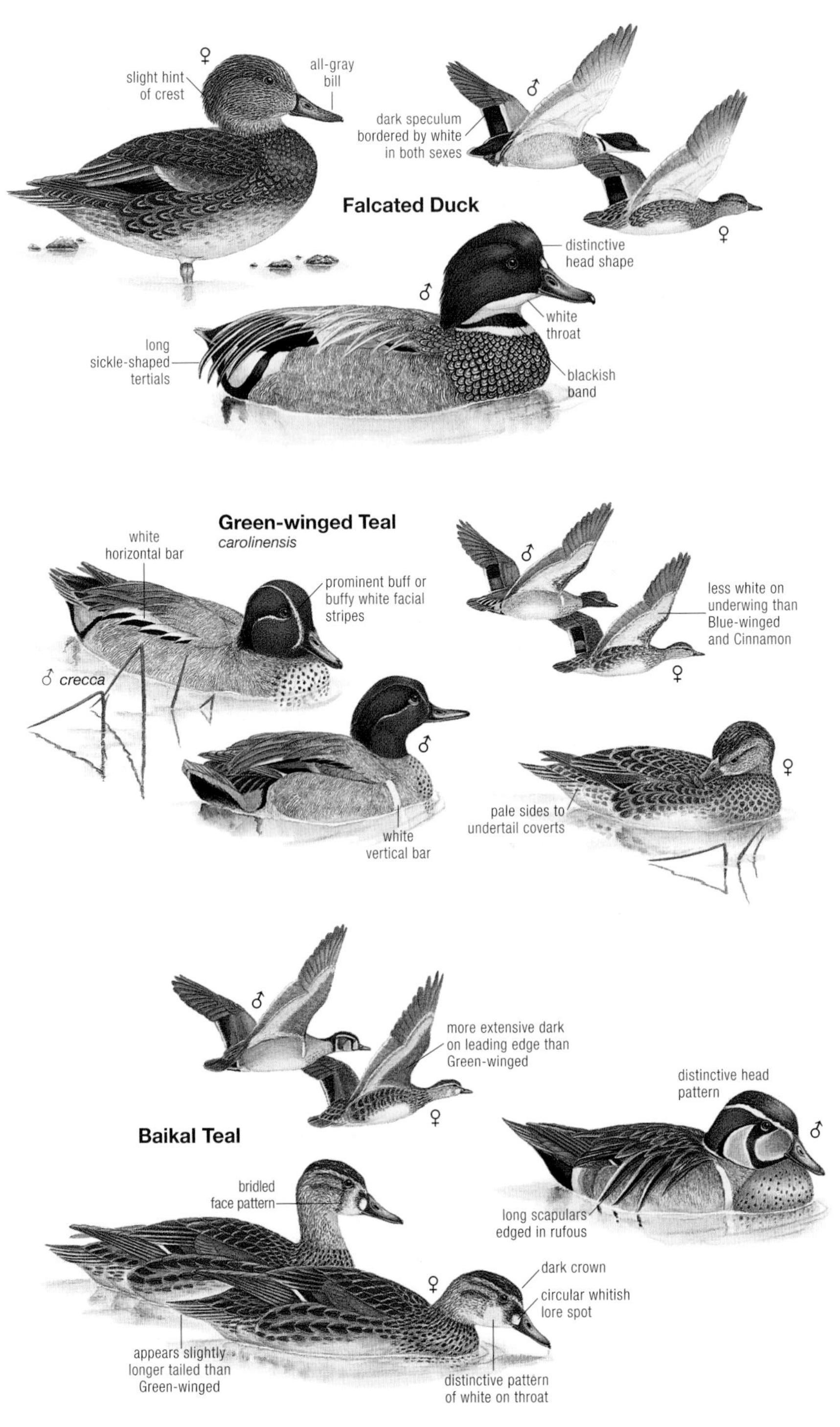

♀
slight hint of crest
all-gray bill
♂
dark speculum bordered by white in both sexes
♀
Falcated Duck
distinctive head shape
♂
white throat
long sickle-shaped tertials
blackish band
Green-winged Teal
carolinensis
white horizontal bar
prominent buff or buffy white facial stripes
♂ crecca
♂
less white on underwing than Blue-winged and Cinnamon
♀
♂
♀
pale sides to undertail coverts
white vertical bar
♂
more extensive dark on leading edge than Green-winged
♀
distinctive head pattern
♂
Baikal Teal
bridled face pattern
long scapulars edged in rufous
♀
dark crown
circular whitish lore spot
appears slightly longer tailed than Green-winged
distinctive pattern of white on throat

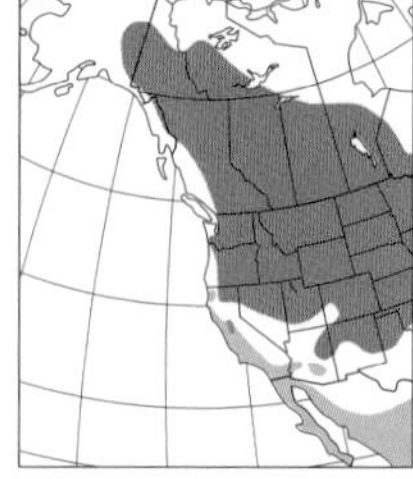

Blue-winged Teal *Anas discors L 15½" (39 cm)*

Violet-gray head with white crescent on each side identifies ***male.*** ***Female*** distinguished from smaller female Green-winged Teal (page 26) by larger bill, more heavily spotted undertail coverts, yellowish legs. Compare also with female Cinnamon Teal; note Blue-winged's grayer plumage, smaller bill, and bolder facial markings, including whiter lore and more prominent, broken eye ring. Male in eclipse plumage resembles female. In flight, wing patterns of both sexes match those of Cinnamon. On males of both species, white bar at near edge of forewing is much broader than in females.

Voice: Male gives a high, whistled *peeu*; female gives a nasal *quack*.

Range: Fairly common in marshes and on ponds and lakes in open country. Uncommon on the West Coast. Casual to northern Alaska, very rare breeder south of mapped range.

Cinnamon Teal *Anas cyanoptera L 16" (41 cm)*

Cinnamon head, neck, and underparts identify ***male. Female*** closely resembles female Blue-winged Teal but plumage is a richer brown; lore spot, eye line, and broken eye ring less distinct; bill longer and more spatulate. Compare also with Green-winged Teal (page 26). Young birds and males in eclipse plumage resemble female. Males more than a couple of months old have red-orange eyes; Blue-winged's eyes are dark. Wing pattern is almost identical to Blue-winged. Known to interbreed with Blue-winged Teal.

Voice: Male gives a chattering call; female gives a nasal *quack*.

Range: Common in marshes, ponds, and lakes. Casual to Alaska and northwestern Canada.

Garganey *Anas querquedula L 15½" (39 cm)*

Old World species. Prominent whitish edge to tertials is an important field mark in swimming birds; head shape is less rounded than Blue-winged and Cinnamon Teal; bill appears a bit larger than Blue-winged. ***Male***'s bold white eyebrows separate dark crown, red-brown face; in flight, shows gray-blue forewing and green speculum bordered fore and aft with white. Wing pattern is retained when male acquires femalelike supplemental plumage, held into winter. ***Female*** has strong facial pattern: dark crown, pale eyebrow, dark eye line, white lore spot bordered by a second dark line; note also dark bill and legs, dark undertail coverts. Larger and paler overall than female Green-winged Teal (page 26). In flight, female shows gray-brown forewing, dark green speculum bordered in white. Note pale gray inner webs of primaries, visible in flight from above.

Voice: Male gives a dry rattling call; female gives a *quack* note.

Range: Rare migrant on western Aleutians mostly in fall; very rare on Pribilofs and in Pacific states in spring and hall (has wintered in California); casual elsewhere in western North America. Fewer records over past 15 years. Asian populations, at least in some areas, have plummeted recently.

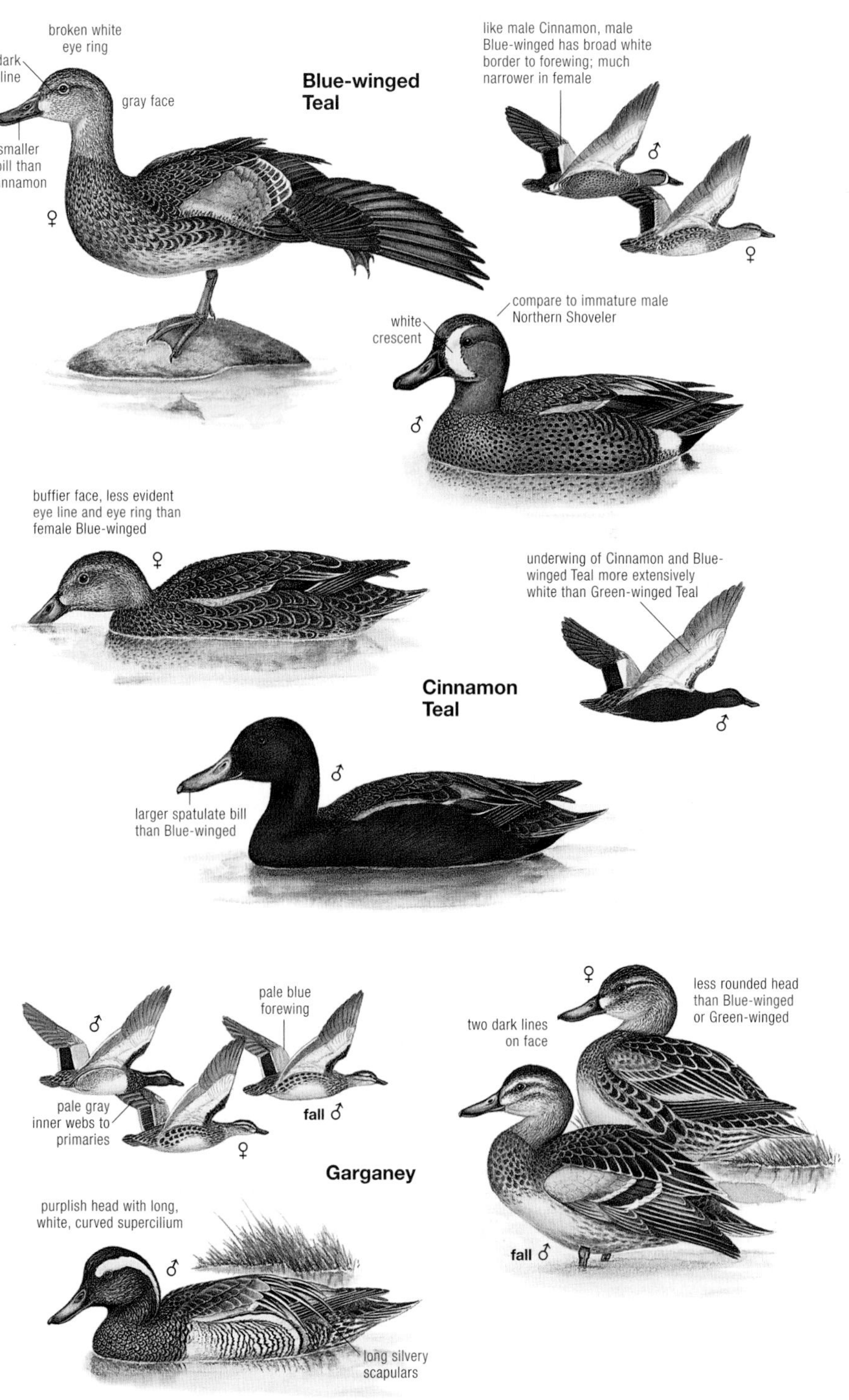

broken white eye ring
dark
e line
gray face
smaller bill than Cinnamon
♀
Blue-winged Teal
like male Cinnamon, male Blue-winged has broad white border to forewing; much narrower in female
♂
♀
compare to immature male Northern Shoveler
white crescent
♂
buffier face, less evident eye line and eye ring than female Blue-winged
♀
underwing of Cinnamon and Blue-winged Teal more extensively white than Green-winged Teal
Cinnamon Teal
♂
♂
larger spatulate bill than Blue-winged
pale blue forewing
♂
pale gray inner webs to primaries
fall ♂
♀
Garganey
♀
less rounded head than Blue-winged or Green-winged
two dark lines on face
fall ♂
purplish head with long, white, curved supercilium
♂
long silvery scapulars

Pochards

Diving ducks of the genus *Aythya* have legs set far back and far apart, which makes walking awkward. Heavy bodies require a running start on water for takeoff. Various species hybridize. Always carefully check potential vagrants to make sure they are not hybrids.

Canvasback *Aythya valisineria L 21" (53 cm)*

Forehead slopes to long, black bill. ***Male***'s head and neck are chestnut, back and sides whitish. ***Female*** and eclipse male have pale brown head and neck, pale brownish gray back and sides. In flight, whitish belly contrasts with dark breast, dark undertail coverts. Wings lack contrasting pale stripe of smaller Common Pochard and Redhead. Migrating flocks fly in irregular V-formations or in lines.

Voice: Mostly silent, except during display.

Range: Locally common in marshes, lakes, and bays; feeds in flocks; has decreased substantially but decline has stabilized.

Common Pochard *Aythya ferina L 18" (46 cm)*

Eurasian species. Resembles Canvasback in plumage and head shape. Bill similar to Redhead's but dark at base and tip, gray in center. Gray on upperparts immediately distinguishes ***female*** from female Redhead and Ring-necked Duck. In flight, wings show gray stripe along trailing edge.

Voice: Mostly silent, except during display.

Range: Rare migrant to Pribilofs and to western and central Aleutians; accidental elsewhere in Alaska and in southern California.

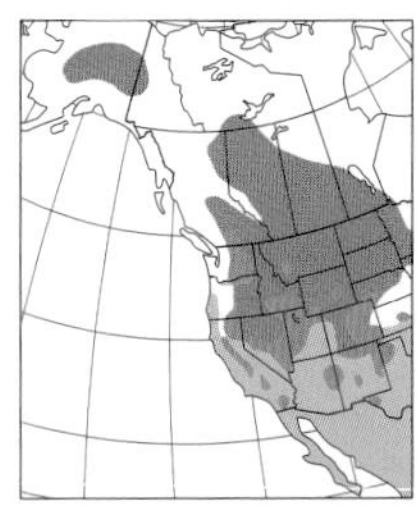

Redhead *Aythya americana L 19" (48 cm)*

Rounded head and shorter, tricolored bill separate this species from Canvasback. Bill is mostly pale blue (male) or slate (female), with narrow white ring bordering black tip. ***Male***'s back and sides are smoky gray. ***Female*** and eclipse male are tawny brown, with slightly darker crown, pale patch bordering black bill tip; compare to female Greater and Lesser Scaup (next page) and female Ring-necked Duck. Redheads in flight show gray stripe on trailing edge of wings.

Voice: Mostly silent, except during display.

Range: Locally common in marshes, ponds, and lakes. Uncommon and local along much of West Coast.

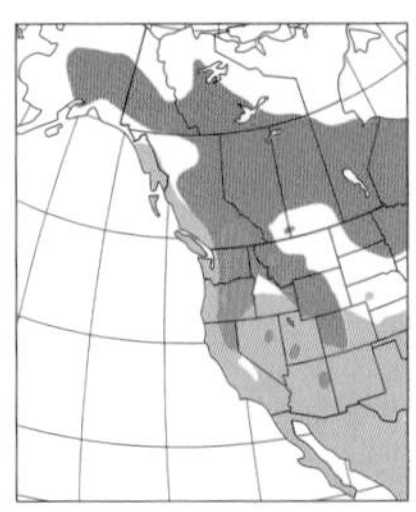

Ring-necked Duck *Aythya collaris L 17" (43 cm)*

Peaked head; bold white ring near tip of bill. ***Male*** has second white ring at base of bill; white crescent separates black breast from gray sides. Narrow cinnamon collar is often hard to see in the field. ***Female*** has dark crown, white eye ring; may have a pale line extending back from eye; face is mainly gray. In flight, all plumages show a gray stripe on secondaries.

Voice: Mostly silent, except during display.

Range: Fairly common in freshwater marshes and on woodland ponds and lakes; during winter, found also in southern coastal marshes. May breed south or winter north of mapped range.

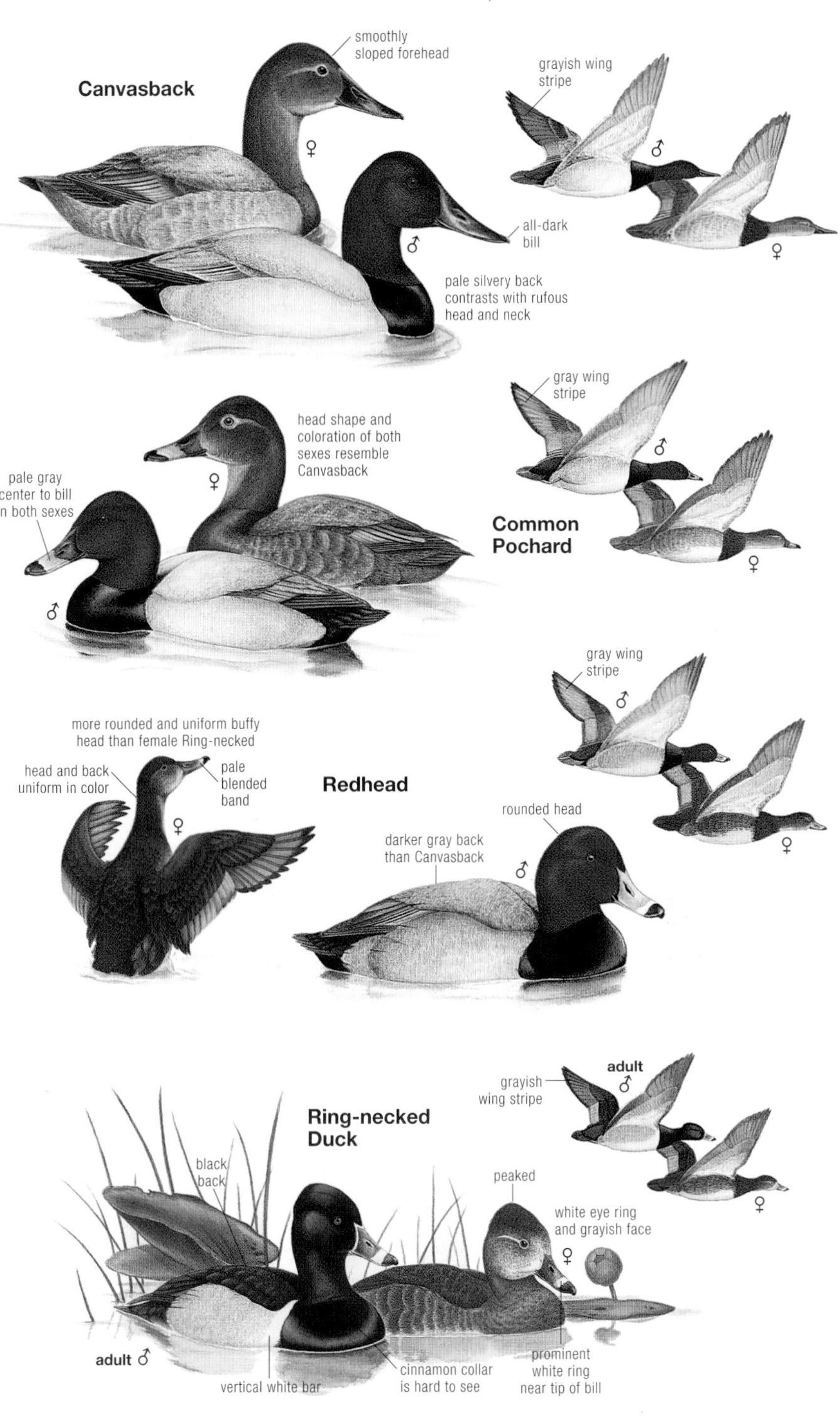

Canvasback
smoothly sloped forehead
♀
♂
all-dark bill
pale silvery back contrasts with rufous head and neck
grayish wing stripe
♂
♀
head shape and coloration of both sexes resemble Canvasback
pale gray center to bill in both sexes
♀
♂
gray wing stripe
♂
Common Pochard
♀
gray wing stripe
♂
♀
more rounded and uniform buffy head than female Ring-necked
head and back uniform in color
pale blended band
♀
Redhead
rounded head
darker gray back than Canvasback
♂
adult ♂
grayish wing stripe
♀
Ring-necked Duck
black back
peaked
white eye ring and grayish face
♀
adult ♂
vertical white bar
cinnamon collar is hard to see
prominent white ring near tip of bill

Tufted Duck *Aythya fuligula L 17" (43 cm)*
Old World species. Head is rounded; crest distinct in ***male,*** smaller in ***female*** and immatures; may be absent in eclipse male. Gleaming white sides further distinguish male from male Ring-necked Duck. ***First-winter male*** has grayer sides but lacks the white crescent conspicuous in male Ring-necked. Female is blackish brown above; lacks white eye ring and distinct white bill ring of female Ring-necked. Bills of both male and female Tufted have a wide black tip. Some females also have a small white area at base of bill. In flight, all plumages show a broad white stripe on secondaries and extending onto primaries. May hybridize with scaup, especially Greater Scaup.
Voice: Mostly silent, except during display.
Range: Small numbers found, mostly in migration in western and central Aleutians and on the Pribilofs. Very rare elsewhere in Alaska and down the West Coast, where mostly found in winter; casual elsewhere in the West. Found on ponds, rivers, bays, often with Ring-necked Ducks and especially scaup.

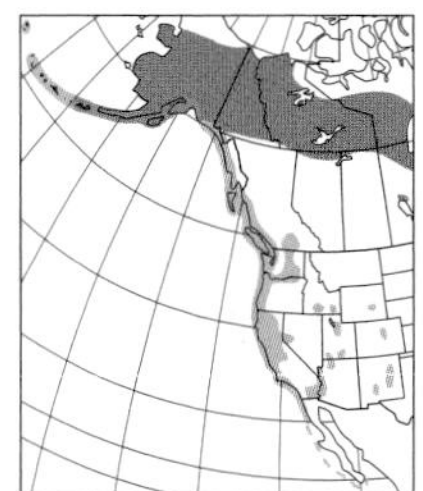

Greater Scaup *Aythya marila L 18" (46 cm)*
Larger size and smoothly rounded head help distinguish this species from Lesser Scaup. In close view, note Greater Scaup's slightly larger bill with wider black tip. ***Male*** averages paler on back and flanks; in good light, head may show a green gloss. In both species, ***female*** has bold white patch at base of bill. Some female Greaters, especially in spring and summer, have a paler head with a distinct whitish ear patch—as do some Lessers in summer. In flight, Greater typically shows a bold white stripe on secondaries and well out onto primaries, unlike Lesser.
Voice: Mostly silent, except during display.
Range: Locally common; found on large, open lakes and bays and on inshore ocean waters. Migrates and winters in small or large flocks, often with Lesser Scaup. Mostly rare to uncommon in southern California and over much of the interior West.

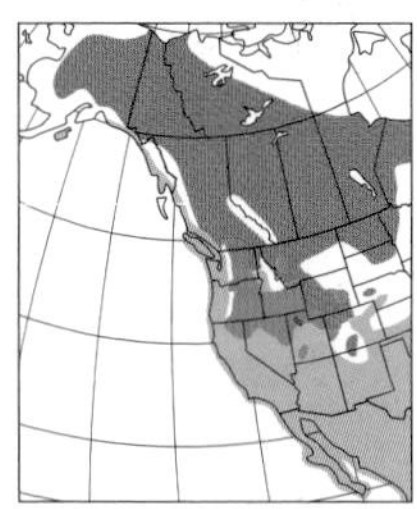

Lesser Scaup *Aythya affinis L 16½" (42 cm)*
Smaller size and peaked crown help distinguish from Greater Scaup. In close view, note Lesser Scaup's slightly smaller bill with smaller black tip. In good light, ***male***'s head may show a purple gloss, sometimes mixed with green. ***Female*** is brown overall, with bold white patch at base of bill. In some females, especially in spring and summer, head is paler, with whitish ear patch less distinct than female Greater Scaup. In flight, Lesser Scaup shows bold white stripe on secondaries only.
Voice: Mostly silent, except during display.
Range: Common; breeds in marshes, small lakes, and ponds. In winter, found in large flocks on sheltered bays, inlets, and lakes; sometimes sheltered inshore ocean waters. Rare breeder south of mapped range.

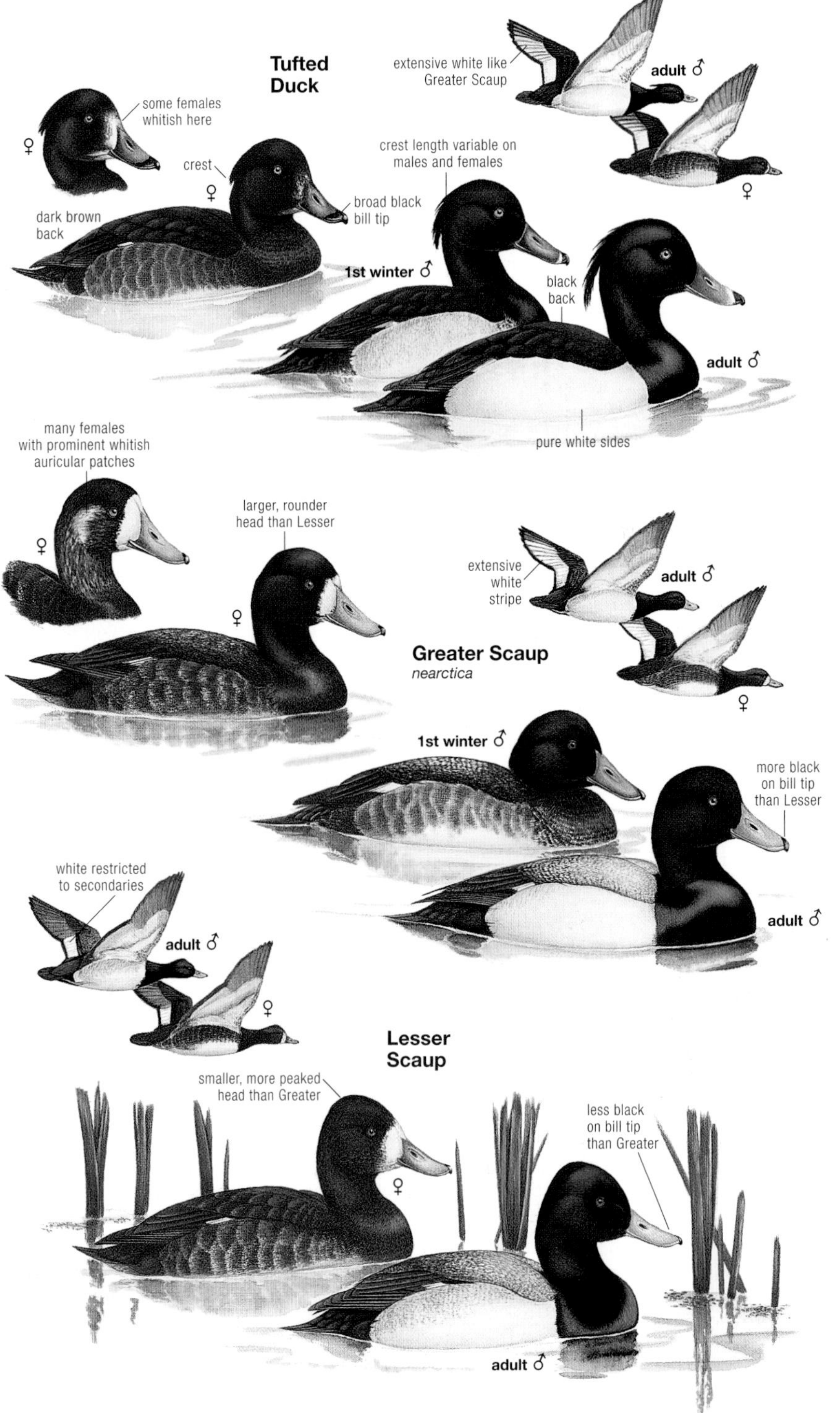
Tufted Duck
extensive white like Greater Scaup
adult ♂
♀
some females whitish here
♀
crest
♀
broad black bill tip
dark brown back
crest length variable on males and females
1st winter ♂
black back
adult ♂
pure white sides
many females with prominent whitish auricular patches
♀
larger, rounder head than Lesser
♀
extensive white stripe
adult ♂
♀
Greater Scaup
nearctica
1st winter ♂
more black on bill tip than Lesser
adult ♂
white restricted to secondaries
adult ♂
♀
Lesser Scaup
smaller, more peaked head than Greater
♀
less black on bill tip than Greater
adult ♂

Common Eider *Somateria mollissima* L 24" (61 cm)
Female distinguished from female King Eider by larger size, sloping forehead, and evenly barred sides and scapulars. Feathering extends along sides of bill to or beyond nostril, with minimal feathering on top of bill. Western North American race is *v-nigrum.* ***Adult male***'s head pattern is distinctive. Most show a thin black V on throat; bill color is orange-yellow. ***Eclipse*** and first-winter male are dark; first-winter has white on breast; full adult plumage is attained by fourth winter. Female is brownish in coloration. In flight, adult male shows solid white back and wing coverts.
Voice: Mostly silent, except during display.
Range: Locally common on shallow bays, rocky shores. Accidental to south on coast to southern British Columbia, Washington, and northernmost California.

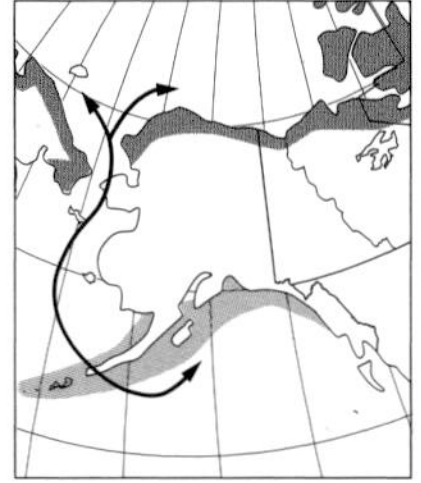

King Eider *Somateria spectabilis* L 22" (56 cm)
Female distinguished from female Common Eider by smaller size, more rounded head, and crescent or V-shaped markings on sides and scapulars. Feathering extends only slightly along sides of bill but extensively down the top, making bill look stubby. ***Male***'s head pattern is distinctive. In flight, shows partly black back, black wings with white patches. ***First-winter male*** has brown head, pinkish or buffy bill, buffy eye line; lacks white wing patches; full adult plumage attained by third winter.
Voice: Mostly silent, except during display; croaking notes in flight.
Range: Common on tundra and coastal waters in northern part of range; casual on West Coast; accidental inland.

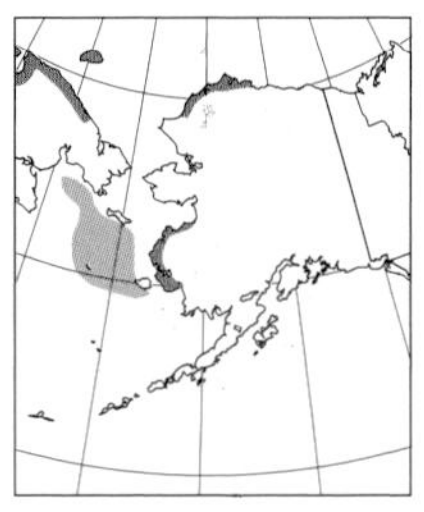

Spectacled Eider *Somateria fischeri* **T** L 21" (53 cm)
Male has green head with white, black-bordered eye patches and orange bill. In flight, black breast separates adult male from other eiders, smaller size from Common Eider. Drab ***female*** has fainter spectacle pattern; bill is gray-blue; feathering extends far down upper mandible.
Voice: Largely silent, even on breeding grounds.
Range: Uncommon and declining; found on coastal tundra near lakes and ponds. Large flocks winter in openings in ice pack on Bering Sea. Accidental on Aleutians and in British Columbia.

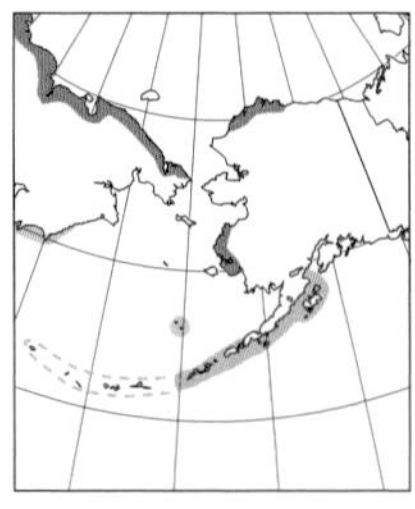

Steller's Eider *Polysticta stelleri* **T** L 17" (43 cm)
Greenish head tufts, black eye patch, chin, and collar identify ***male. Female*** is dark cinnamon brown with pale eye ring, unfeathered dark bill. In flight, adults, immature males, and some immature females show blue speculum bordered fore and aft in white.
Voice: Mostly silent, except during display.
Range: Found along rocky coasts; nests on inland grassy areas or tundra. Winters casually south to northern California coast. Numbers greatly reduced over recent decades.

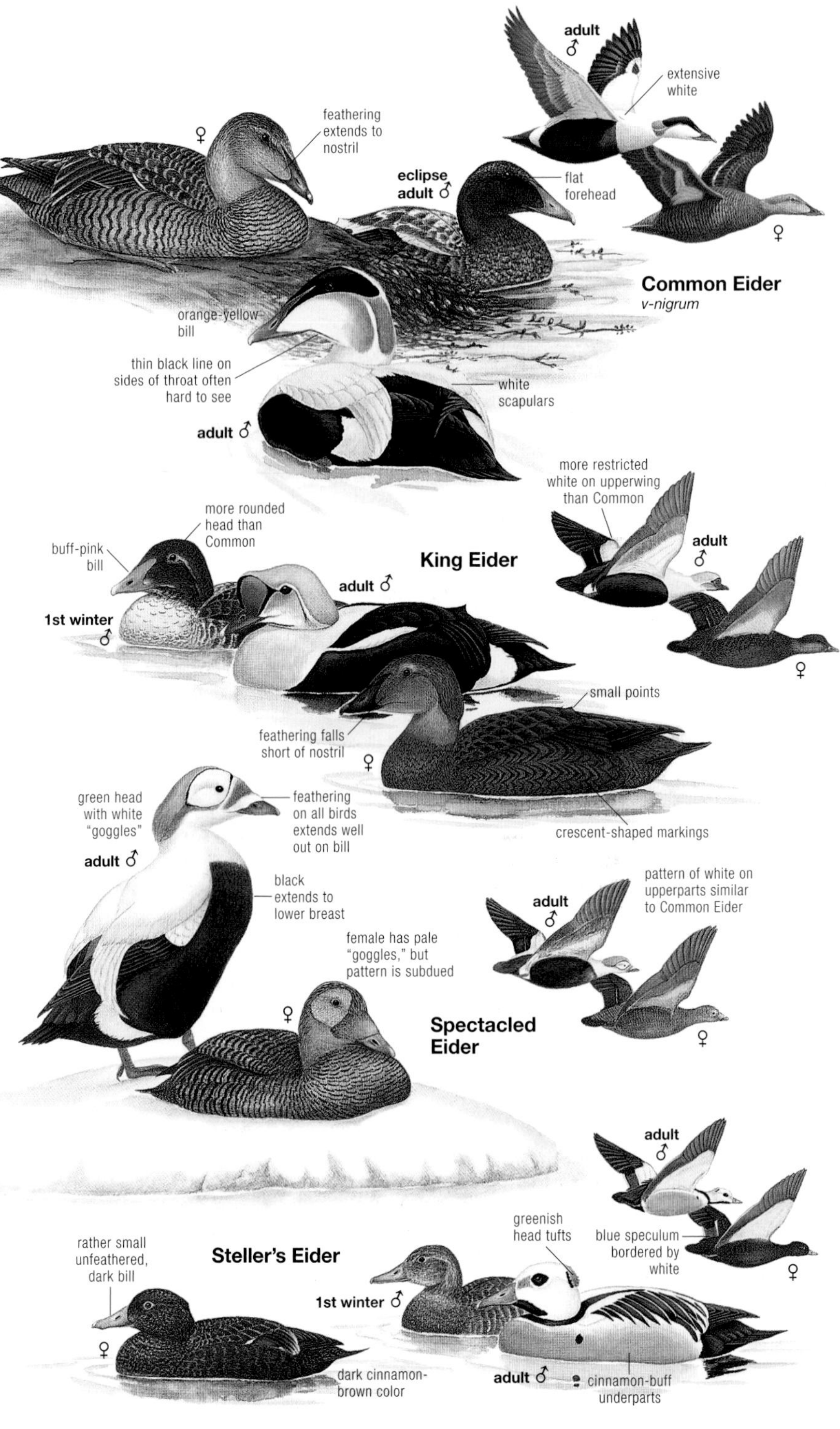
adult ♂
extensive white
♀
feathering extends to nostril
eclipse adult ♂
flat forehead
♀
Common Eider
v-nigrum
orange-yellow bill
thin black line on sides of throat often hard to see
white scapulars
adult ♂
more restricted white on upperwing than Common
more rounded head than Common
buff-pink bill
King Eider
adult ♂
adult ♂
1st winter ♂
♀
small points
feathering falls short of nostril
♀
green head with white "goggles"
feathering on all birds extends well out on bill
crescent-shaped markings
adult ♂
black extends to lower breast
pattern of white on upperparts similar to Common Eider
adult ♂
female has pale "goggles," but pattern is subdued
♀
Spectacled Eider
♀
adult ♂
greenish head tufts
blue speculum bordered by white
rather small unfeathered, dark bill
Steller's Eider
♀
1st winter ♂
♀
dark cinnamon-brown color
adult ♂
cinnamon-buff underparts

Sea Ducks

Stocky, short-necked diving ducks, most species breed in the far north and migrate in large, compact flocks to and from their coastal wintering grounds.

Surf Scoter *Melanitta perspicillata L 20" (51 cm)*

Male's black plumage sets off colorful bill, white eye, white patch on forehead and nape; forehead is sloping, not rounded. ***Female*** is brown, with dark crown; usually has two white patches on each side of face, one primary vertical and one more horizontal; feathering extends down top of bill only. Adult female and ***first-winter male*** may have whitish nape patch. All juveniles have whitish belly, usually white face patches. In flight, more uniform color of underwings helps distinguish Surf from Black Scoter; also orangish, not dark, legs and feet.

Voice: Mostly silent, except during display.

Range: Common; nests on tundra and in wooded areas near water. Rare inland migrant, chiefly in fall; also a few in winter. Small numbers of nonbreeders oversummer in winter range.

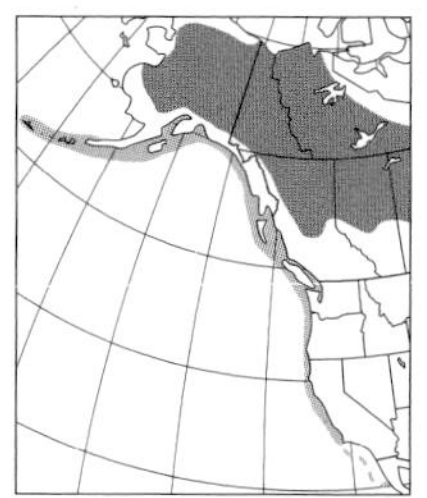

White-winged Scoter *Melanitta fusca L 21" (53 cm)*

White secondaries, conspicuous in flight, may show as a small white patch on swimming bird. Forehead slightly rounded. Feathering extends almost to nostrils on top and sides of bill. ***Female*** and juveniles lack contrasting dark crown and paler face of other scoters; white oval-shaped facial patches are distinct on juveniles, often indistinct on adult female. Juveniles and immatures are whitish below. ***Adult male*** has black knob at base of colorful bill, crescent-shaped white patch below white eye, brownish flanks. Black-flanked adult male Asian *stejnegeri,* casual to western Alaska (recorded from St. Lawrence Island and near Nome), has more obvious nasal hook, different bill color pattern, and longer white slash behind eye; females and juvenile males very similar to *deglandi.*

Voice: Mostly silent, except during display.

Range: Fairly common on inland lakes in breeding season, coastal areas in winter. Very rare inland migrant, chiefly in fall.

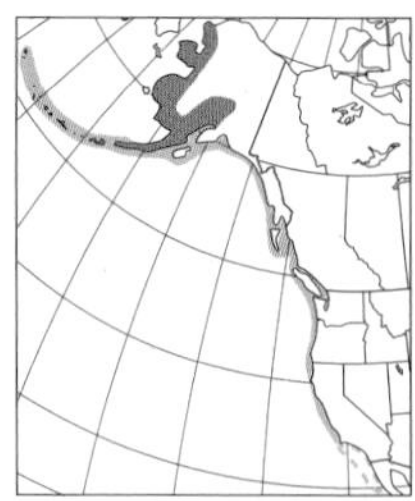

Black Scoter *Melanitta nigra L 19" (48 cm)*

Male is black, with yellow-orange knob at base of dark bill. ***Female***'s dark crown and nape contrast with pale face and throat; feathering does not extend onto bill. In both, forehead is rounded. In flight, adult male's blackish wing linings contrast with paler flight feathers. Juveniles resemble females but are whitish on belly; ***first-winter male*** has some yellow at base of bill by winter.

Voice: Most vocal of the scoters. Drakes call even in winter; most frequent call is a prolonged and plaintive whistle.

Range: Nests on tundra. Casual in western interior; most records in late fall.

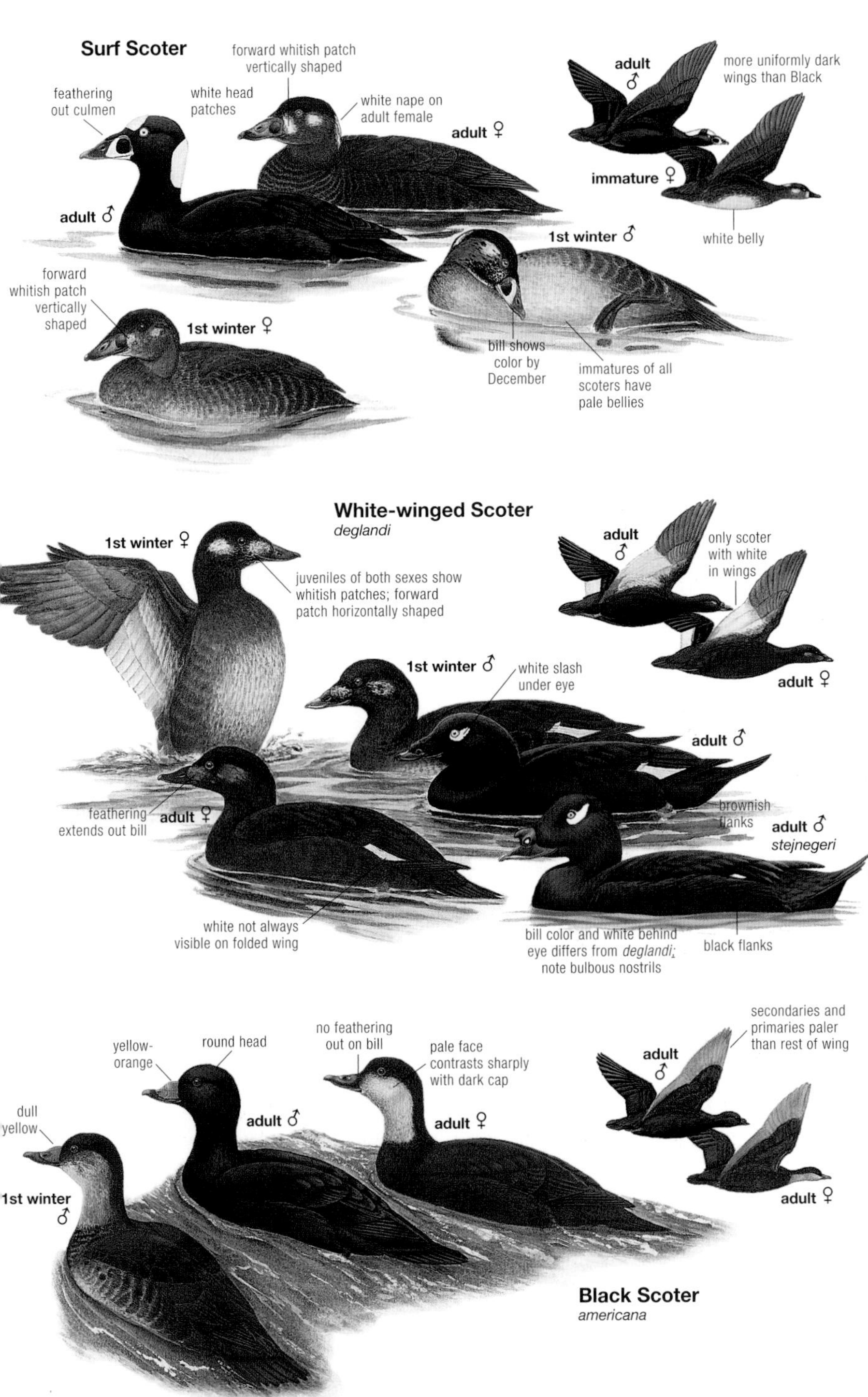

Surf Scoter
feathering out culmen
white head patches
forward whitish patch vertically shaped
white nape on adult female
adult ♀
adult ♂
adult ♂
more uniformly dark wings than Black
immature ♀
white belly
1st winter ♂
forward whitish patch vertically shaped
1st winter ♀
bill shows color by December
immatures of all scoters have pale bellies
White-winged Scoter
deglandi
1st winter ♀
juveniles of both sexes show whitish patches; forward patch horizontally shaped
adult ♂
only scoter with white in wings
adult ♀
1st winter ♂
white slash under eye
adult ♂
feathering extends out bill
adult ♀
brownish flanks
adult ♂
stejnegeri
white not always visible on folded wing
bill color and white behind eye differs from deglandi; note bulbous nostrils
black flanks
yellow-orange
round head
no feathering out on bill
pale face contrasts sharply with dark cap
secondaries and primaries paler than rest of wing
adult ♂
dull yellow
adult ♂
adult ♀
adult ♀
1st winter ♂
Black Scoter
americana

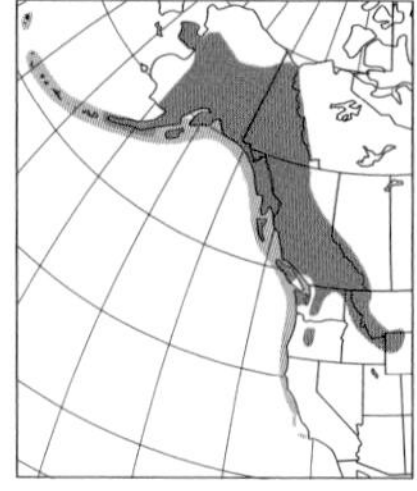

Harlequin Duck *Histrionicus histrionicus L 16½" (42 cm)*
Small duck, with rounded head and stubby bill. ***Male***'s colorful plumage appears dark at a distance. ***Female*** has three white spots on each side of head. Juvenile resembles adult female. Flight is rapid and low. Compare female in flight with female Bufflehead.

Voice: Male's call is a high-pitched nasal squeaking, but mostly silent, except during breeding season.

Range: Locally common on rocky coasts; moves inland along swift streams for nesting; substantial numbers of nonbreeders summer along the coast. Very rare, mostly in winter, south to coastal southern California; casual in western interior south of breeding range. Formerly nested in the Sierra Nevada up through the 1920s; sightings in the 1970s and 1980s offer hope of eventual recolonization.

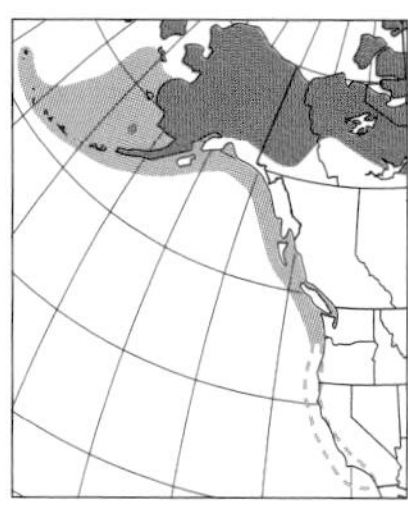

Long-tailed Duck *Clangula hyemalis*
♂L 22" (56 cm) ♀16" (41 cm) Formerly Oldsquaw. ***Male***'s long tail is conspicuous in flight, may be submerged in swimming bird. Male in winter and spring is largely white; breast and back dark brown, scapulars pearl gray; stubby bill shows pink band. By late spring, male becomes mostly dark, with pale facial patch, bicolored scapulars; acquires paler crown and shorter, buff-edged scapulars in later, supplemental molt. Molt into full eclipse plumage continues until early fall. ***Female*** lacks long tail; bill is dark; plumage whiter in winter, darker in summer. First-fall birds are even darker. Long-taileds are identifiable at some distance by their swift, careening flight. Both sexes show uniformly dark underwings.

Voice: Loud, yodeling, three-part calls, heard all year.

Range: Very uncommon to rare but regular south of Washington. Very rare in the interior. Most records are in fall; casual in winter; has remained into summer at Salton Sea.

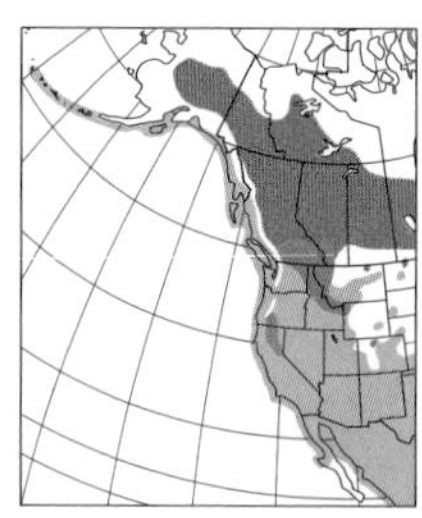

Bufflehead *Bucephala albeola L 13½" (34 cm)*
A small duck with a large, puffy head, steep forehead, short bill. ***Male*** is glossy black above, white below, with large white patch on head. ***Female*** is duller, with small, elongated white patch on each side of head. ***First-winter male*** and male in eclipse resemble female. In flight, males show white patch across entire wing; female has white patch only on inner secondaries.

Voice: Mostly silent; sounds made during display comparatively feeble in comparison to related goldeneyes.

Range: Generally common. Nests in woodlands near small lakes and ponds. During migration and winter, found also on sheltered bays, rivers, and lakes. Very rare in western Alaska. Casual breeder south of mapped range.

Harlequin Duck

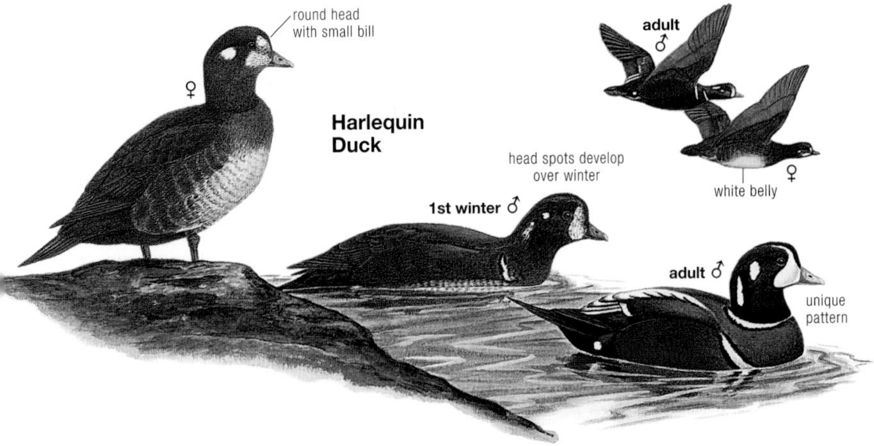

round head
with small bill
♀
adult
♂
head spots develop
over winter
1st winter ♂
white belly
♀
adult ♂
unique
pattern

Long-tailed Duck

1st winter ♂
males have
pink band
small
bill
early summer
adult ♂
long,
pointed tail
winter
adult
♂
dark wings
1st fall ♀
winter adult ♂
variably
white on
face
females have
grayish bills
winter ♀
winter ♀

Bufflehead

adult
♂
♀
extensive white
head pattern
adult ♂
small
dark bill
1st winter ♂
white
cheek spot
♀

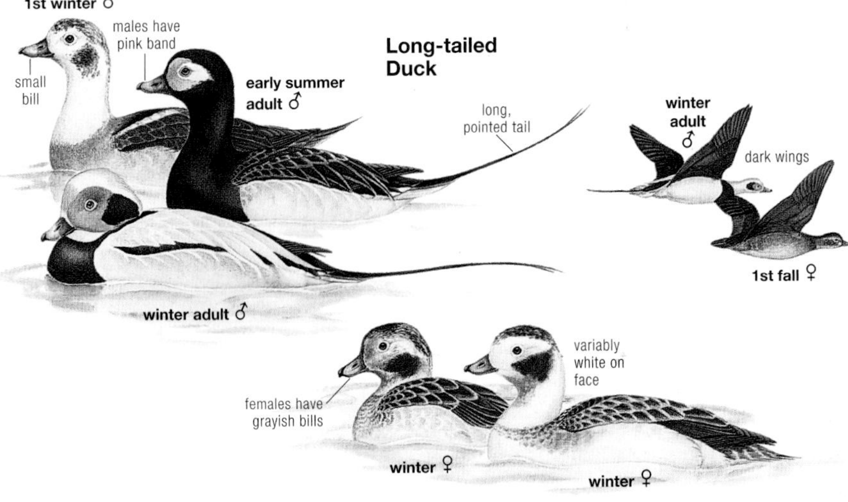

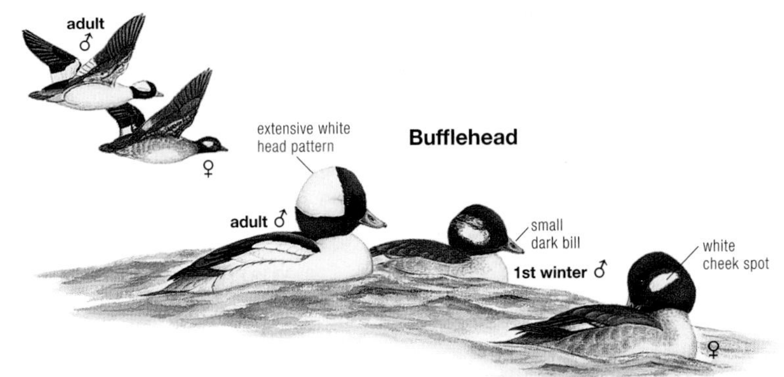

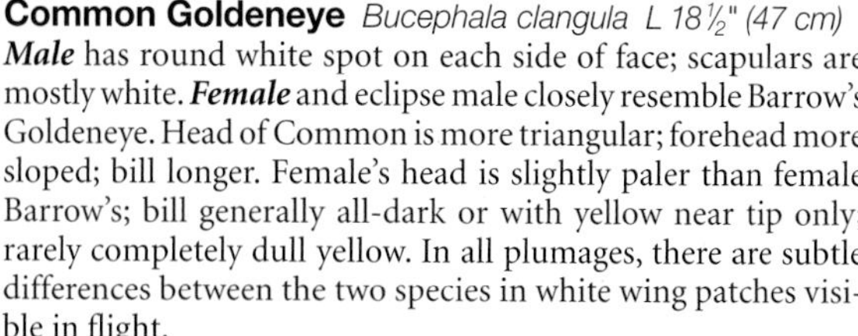

Common Goldeneye *Bucephala clangula L 18½" (47 cm)*
Male has round white spot on each side of face; scapulars are mostly white. ***Female*** and eclipse male closely resemble Barrow's Goldeneye. Head of Common is more triangular; forehead more sloped; bill longer. Female's head is slightly paler than female Barrow's; bill generally all-dark or with yellow near tip only; rarely completely dull yellow. In all plumages, there are subtle differences between the two species in white wing patches visible in flight.
Voice: Generally silent except in flight, when wings produce a whistling sound. Drakes produce a double-noted harsh, rasping, high-pitched call when throwing head back in elaborate display; female gives a grunting note.

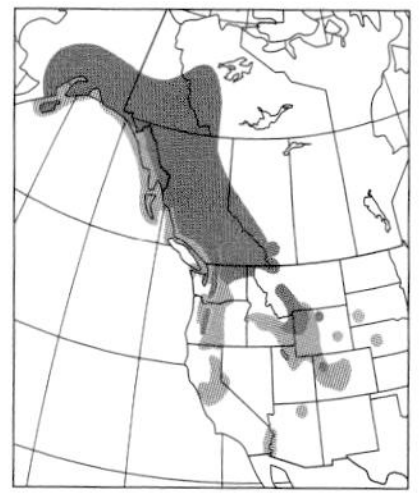

Barrow's Goldeneye *Bucephala islandica L 18" (46 cm)*
Male has white crescent on each side of face; white patches on scapulars show on swimming bird as a row of spots; dark color of back extends forward in a bar partially separating white breast from white sides. ***Female*** and male in eclipse plumage closely resemble Common Goldeneye. Puffy, oval-shaped head, steep forehead, and stubby, triangular bill help identify Barrow's. Adult female's head is slightly darker than female Common; bill mostly yellow, except in young females, which may have only a yellow band near tip of bill. In all plumages, white wing patches visible in flight differ subtly between the two species. ***Hybrids*** between the two goldeneye species occur.
Voice: Generally silent except in flight, when wings produce a whistling sound. During display (less elaborate than Common), drake gives an *e-eng* call; female gives a grunting note.
Range: Both goldeneyes summer on open lakes and small ponds; winter in sheltered coastal areas, inland lakes, and rivers. Overall, Barrow's is much less common. Winters in small numbers with large numbers of Common Goldeneye below Parker Dam on Colorado River; otherwise very rare or casual in the the Southwest, southern California, and the Aleutians. Formerly nested on western slope of the Sierra Nevada (until mid-1930s).

Mergansers

Long, thin, serrated bills help these divers catch fish, crustaceans, and aquatic insects. Mergansers in flight show pointed wings.

Smew *Mergellus albellus L 16" (46 cm)*
Eurasian species. Bill is dark and relatively short. In ***female,*** white throat and lower face contrast sharply with reddish brown head and nape. ***Adult male*** is white with black markings; black-and-white wings are conspicuous in flight.
Voice: Generally silent.
Range: Rare migrant to western and central Aleutians; casual on Pribilofs; accidental in winter in Pacific states.

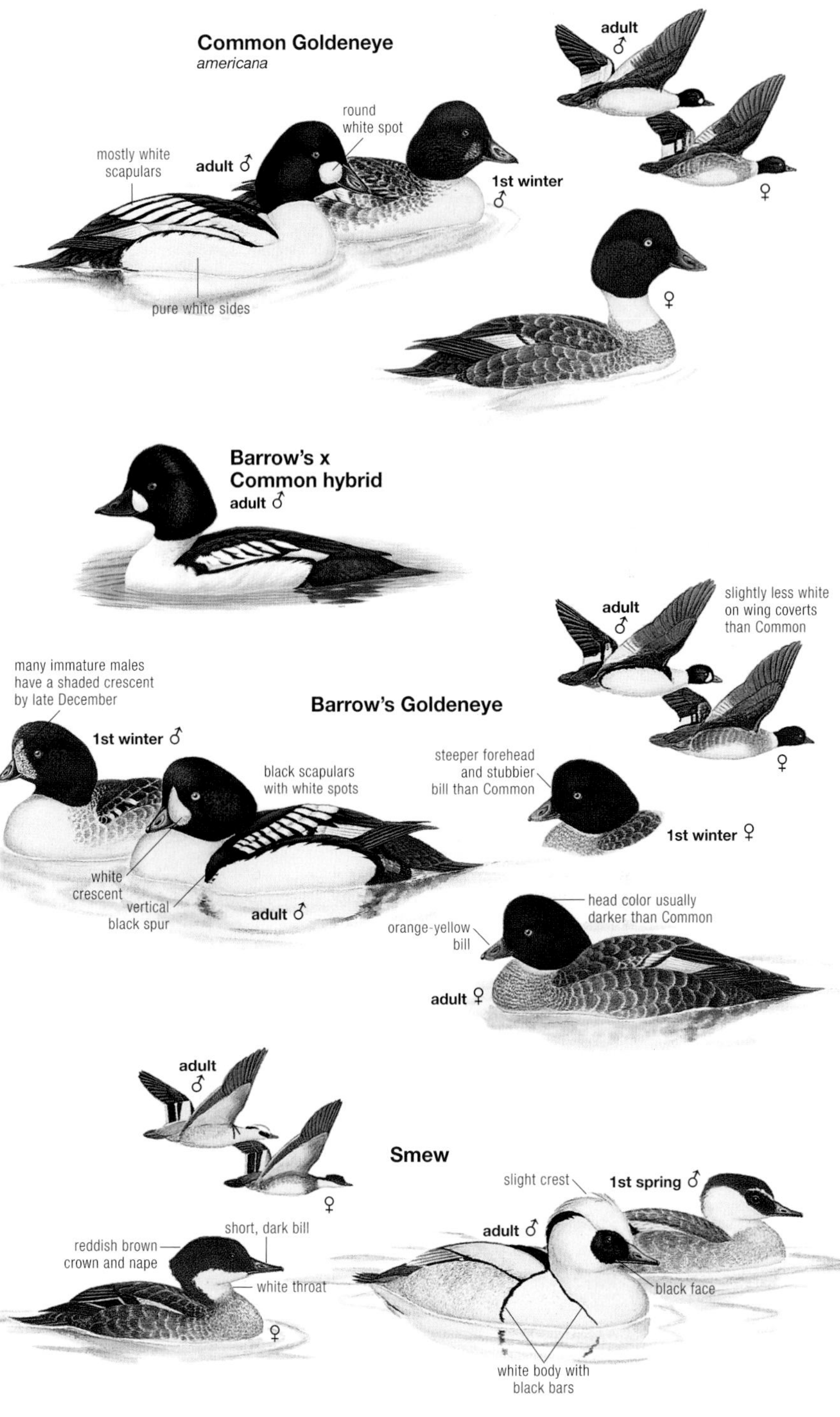

Common Goldeneye
americana
adult ♂
round
white spot
mostly white
scapulars
adult ♂
1st winter
♂
♀
pure white sides
♀
Barrow's x
Common hybrid
adult ♂
adult
♂
slightly less white
on wing coverts
than Common
many immature males
have a shaded crescent
by late December
Barrow's Goldeneye
♀
1st winter ♂
steeper forehead
and stubbier
bill than Common
black scapulars
with white spots
1st winter ♀
white
crescent
vertical
black spur
adult ♂
head color usually
darker than Common
orange-yellow
bill
adult ♀
adult
♂
Smew
♀
slight crest
1st spring ♂
short, dark bill
reddish brown
crown and nape
adult ♂
white throat
black face
♀
white body with
black bars

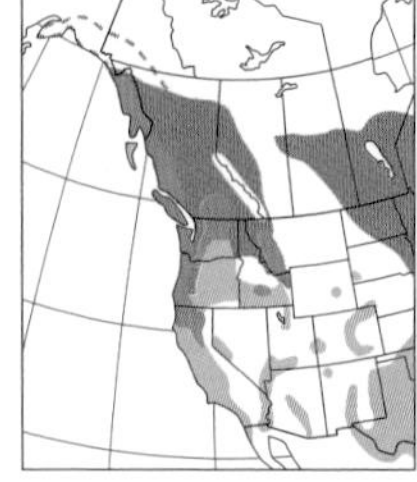

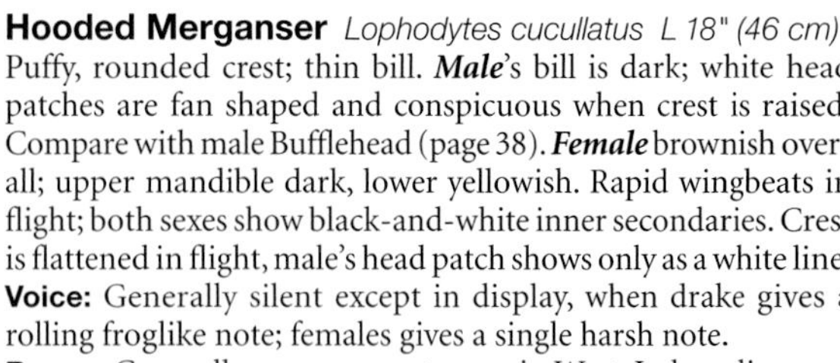

Hooded Merganser *Lophodytes cucullatus L 18" (46 cm)*
Puffy, rounded crest; thin bill. ***Male***'s bill is dark; white head patches are fan shaped and conspicuous when crest is raised. Compare with male Bufflehead (page 38). ***Female*** brownish overall; upper mandible dark, lower yellowish. Rapid wingbeats in flight; both sexes show black-and-white inner secondaries. Crest is flattened in flight, male's head patch shows only as a white line.
Voice: Generally silent except in display, when drake gives a rolling froglike note; females gives a single harsh note.
Range: Generally uncommon to rare in West. In breeding season, found on woodland ponds, rivers, and backwaters. Winters chiefly on fresh or brackish water. Casual to central Alaska.

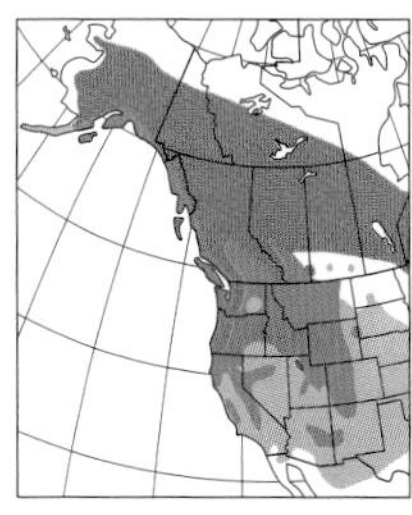

Common Merganser *Mergus merganser L 25" (64 cm)*
Large duck with long, slim neck and thick-based, hooked, red bill. White breast and sides, often tinged with pink, and lack of crest distinguish ***male*** from Red-breasted Merganser. ***Female***'s bright chestnut, crested head and neck contrast sharply with white chin, white breast. Adult male in flight shows white patch on upper surface of entire inner wing, partially crossed by a single black bar. Eclipse male resembles female but retains wing pattern. Female's white inner secondaries and greater coverts are partially crossed by a black bar. Old World ***"Goosander"*** (nominate *merganser*), recorded from western Aleutians, Pribilofs and St. Lawrence Island; lacks dark bar on wing. Note different bill shape. As in all species on this page, young male resembles adult female, but may show some darkening on face by spring.
Voice: Generally silent except in display, when drake gives single bell-like calls. Both sexes give single harsh calls.
Range: Nests in woodlands near lakes and rivers; in winter, sometimes also found on brackish water, rarely salt water.

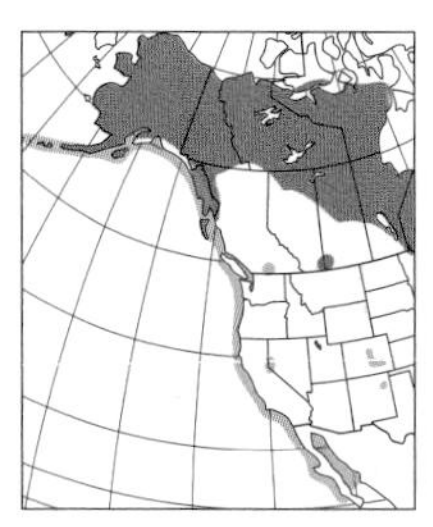

Red-breasted Merganser *Mergus serrator L 23" (58 cm)*
Shaggy double crest, white collar, and streaked breast distinguish ***male*** from male Common Merganser. ***Female***'s head and neck are duller than female Common; chin and foreneck whitish. Adult male in flight shows white patch on upper surface of inner wing, partly crossed by two black bars. Eclipse male resembles female but retains male wing pattern. Female's white inner secondaries and greater coverts are crossed by a single black bar. Smaller size and thinner bill help distinguish Red-breasted Merganser in mixed flocks.
Voice: Generally silent except in display, when drake gives various notes, including mewing calls; female gives various harsh calls.
Range: Nests in woodlands near fresh water or in sheltered coastal areas; prefers brackish or salt water in winter. Generally uncommon (mostly in migration) in western interior. As in many species of waterfowl, small numbers of nonbreeders over summer in winter range.

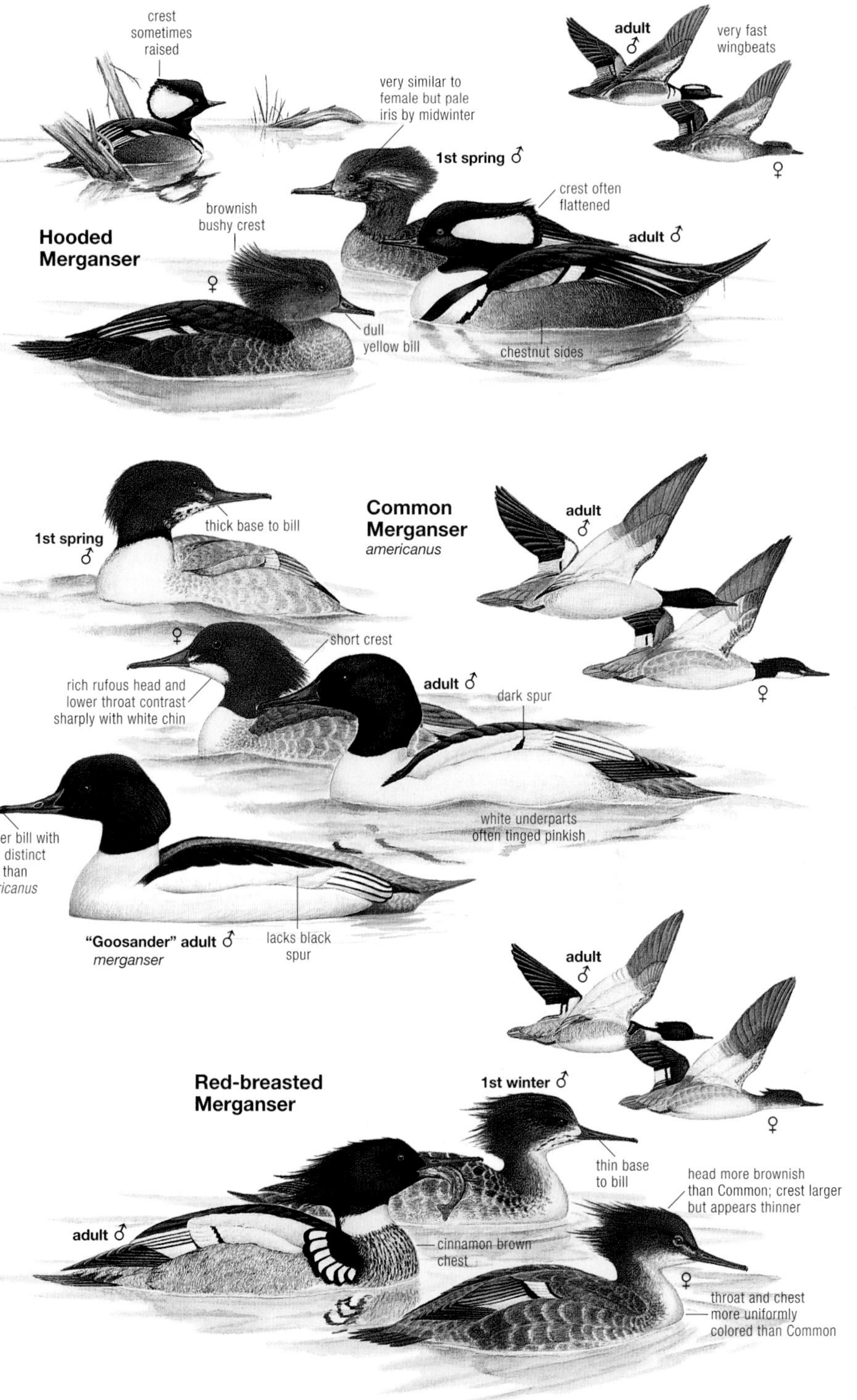

crest
sometimes
raised
adult ♂
very fast
wingbeats
very similar to
female but pale
iris by midwinter
1st spring ♂
♀
crest often
flattened
brownish
bushy crest
Hooded
Merganser
adult ♂
♀
dull
yellow bill
chestnut sides
thick base to bill
Common
Merganser
americanus
adult ♂
1st spring ♂
♀
short crest
rich rufous head and
lower throat contrast
sharply with white chin
adult ♂
dark spur
♀
white underparts
often tinged pinkish
ier bill with
e distinct
k than
ricanus
"Goosander" adult ♂
merganser
lacks black
spur
adult ♂
Red-breasted
Merganser
1st winter ♂
♀
thin base
to bill
head more brownish
than Common; crest larger
but appears thinner
adult ♂
cinnamon brown
chest
♀
throat and chest
more uniformly
colored than Common

Stiff-tailed Ducks

Long, stiff tail feathers serve as a rudder for this diving duck. Highly aquatic, these ducks are rarely seen on land and are reluctant to fly.

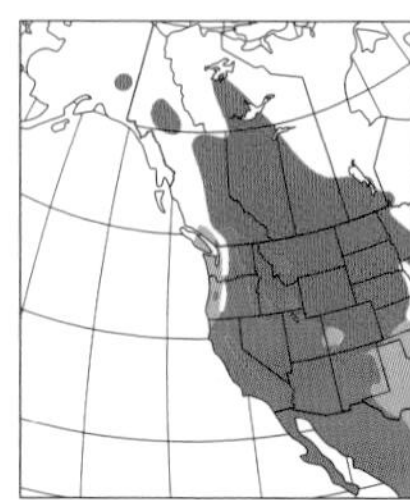

Ruddy Duck *Oxyura jamaicensis L 15" (38 cm)*
Small but chunky, with large head, broad bill, long tail, often cocked up. ***Male***'s white cheeks are conspicuous both in ***breeding*** plumage and in dull ***winter*** plumage. In ***female,*** single dark line crosses cheek. Young resemble female through first winter.
Voice: Mostly silent. During display, male produces soft ticking and popping sounds.
Range: Common; nests in dense vegetation of freshwater wetlands. During migration and winter, found on lakes, bays, and salt marshes. Rare breeder in east-central Alaska.

Exotic Waterfowl

Many waterfowl species are brought into North America from other continents for zoos and private collections. Escapes are frequent. The species shown here are among those seen most frequently.

Ruddy Shelduck *Tadorna ferruginea L 26" (66 cm)*
Afro-Eurasian species often kept in captivity.

Common Shelduck *Tadorna tadorna L 25" (64 cm)*
Eurasian species. Female smaller, lacks knob on bill.

Egyptian Goose *Alopochen aegyptiacus L 27" (68 cm)*
African species. Widespread escape. Note white wing patches.

Graylag Goose *Anser anser L 34" (86 cm)*
Eurasian species, progenitor of most domestic geese. Compare wild type to Greater White-fronted Goose (page 14).

Bar-headed Goose *Anser indicus L 30" (76 cm)*
Asian species. Fairly common in zoos and private collections.

Mandarin Duck *Aix galericulata L 16" (41 cm)*
Asian species. Compare female to female Wood Duck (page 20).

Mute Swan *Cygnus olor L 60" (152 cm)*
Prominent black knob at base of orange bill. Juvenile may be white or brownish; bill gray with black base.
Range: Very small numbers on lakes and ponds in parks locally in West; occasionally seen in wilder settings.

Muscovy Duck *Cairina moschata L 26-33" (66-84 cm)*
Tropical species. Coloration of wild birds largely black, but many domestics are partly or largely white.
Range: Tame escaped birds found in parks in West.

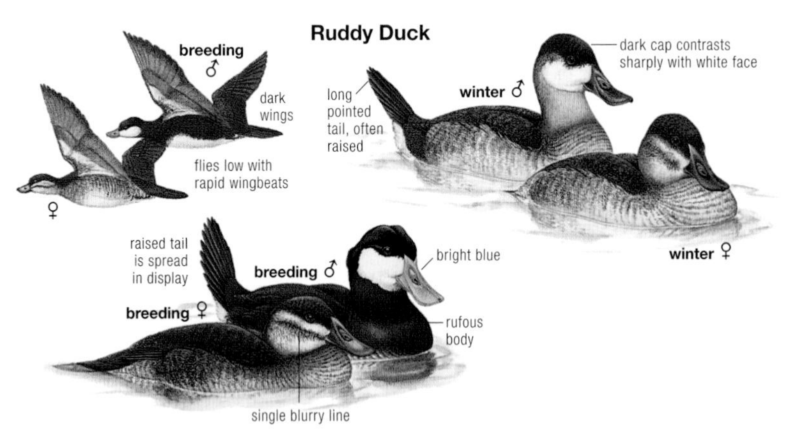

Ruddy Shelduck

adult ♂

adult ♂

Common Shelduck

Egyptian Goose

adults

Graylag Goose

wild type

domestic type

Bar-headed Goose

adult

Mandarin Duck

♀

♂

compare to female Wood Duck

Mute Swan

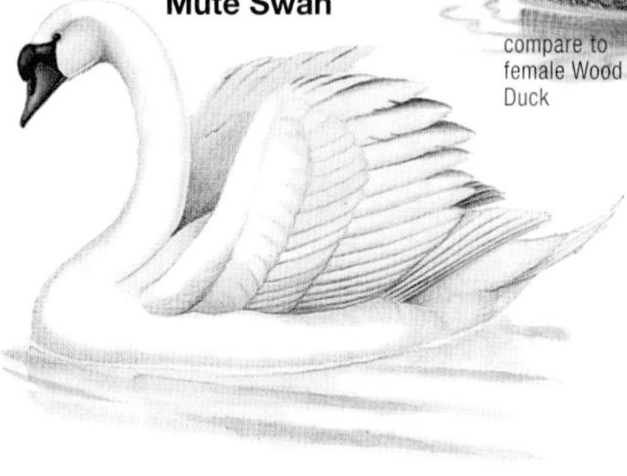

adult ♂

Muscovy Duck

Ducks in Flight

Perching and Stiff-tailed Ducks

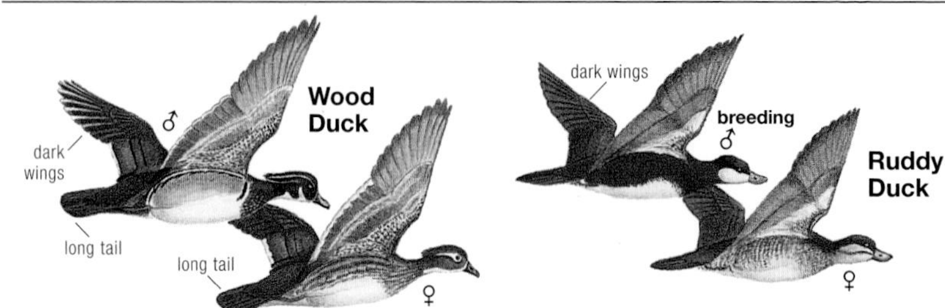

Dabbling Ducks

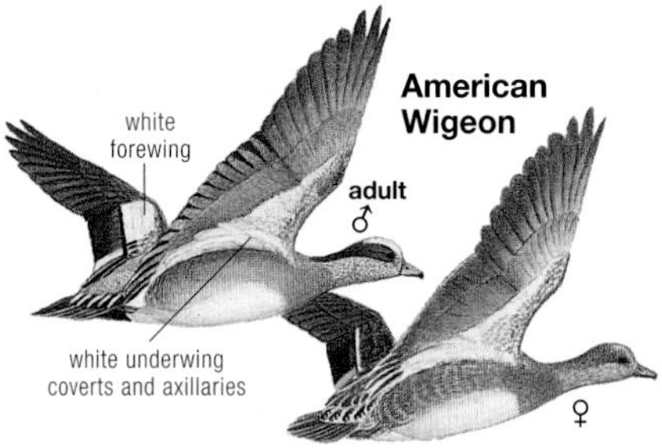

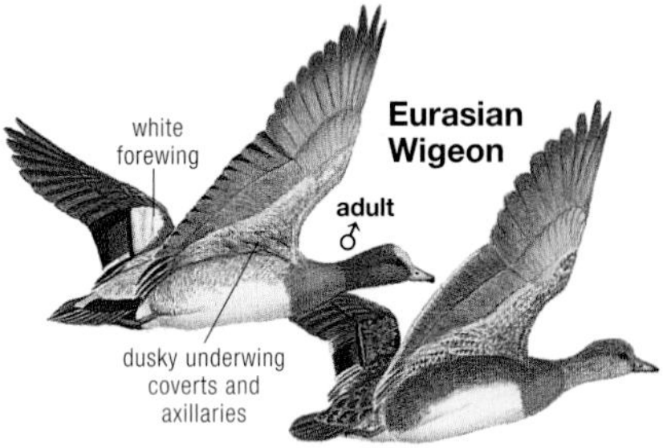

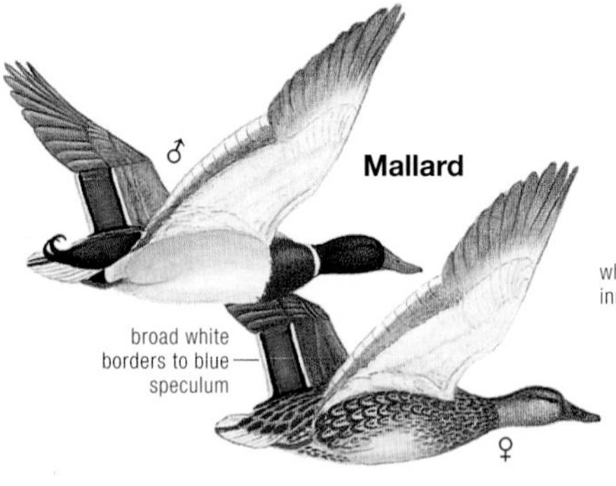

American Wigeon

white forewing

adult ♂

white underwing coverts and axillaries

♀

Eurasian Wigeon

white forewing

adult ♂

dusky underwing coverts and axillaries

Mallard

♂

broad white borders to blue speculum

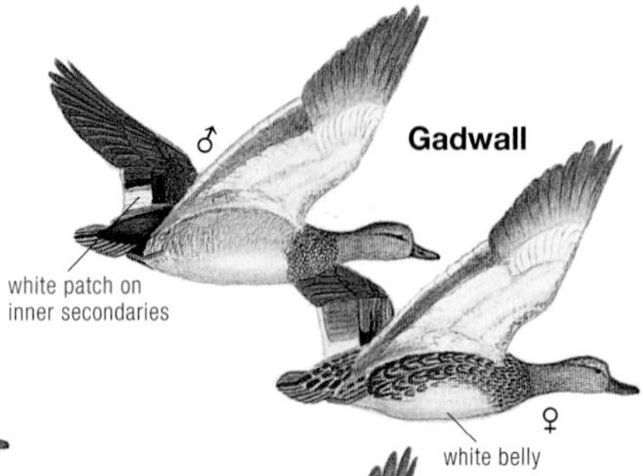

♀

Gadwall

♂

white patch on inner secondaries

♀

white belly

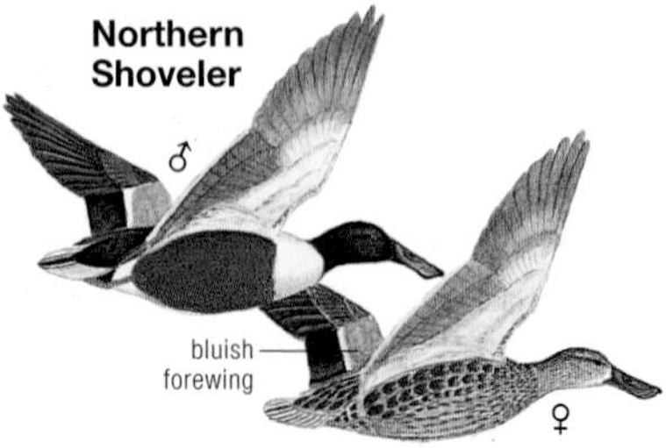

Northern Shoveler

♂

bluish forewing

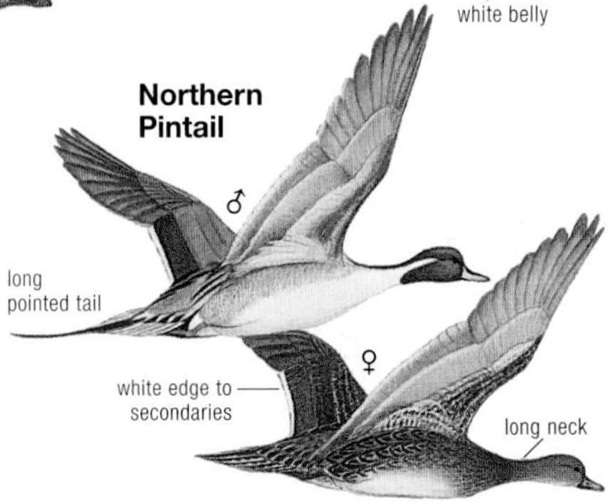

♀

Northern Pintail

♂

long pointed tail

♀

white edge to secondaries

long neck

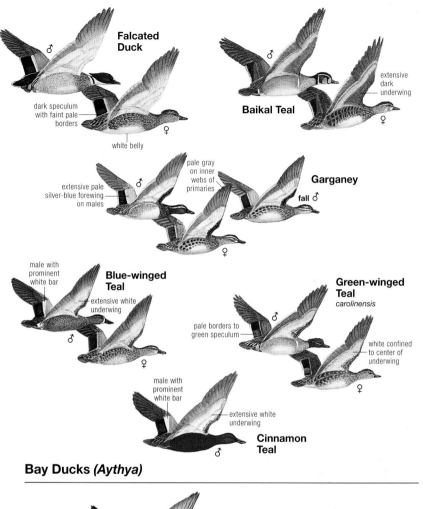

Falcated Duck

♂

dark speculum with faint pale borders

white belly

♀

Baikal Teal

♂

extensive dark underwing

♀

Garganey

extensive pale silver-blue forewing on males

♂

pale gray on inner webs of primaries

fall ♂

♀

Blue-winged Teal

male with prominent white bar

extensive white underwing

♂

♀

Green-winged Teal

carolinensis

pale borders to green speculum

♂

white confined to center of underwing

♀

male with prominent white bar

extensive white underwing

Cinnamon Teal

♂

Bay Ducks *(Aythya)*

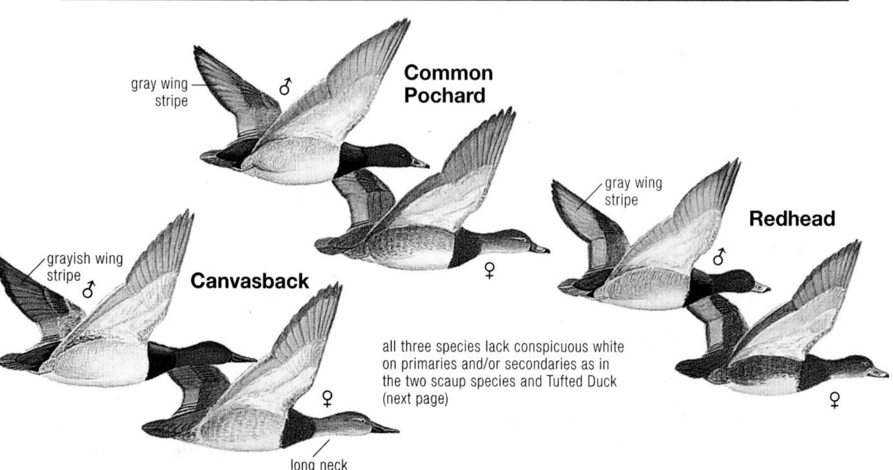

Ducks in Flight

Bay Ducks *(Aythya),* continued

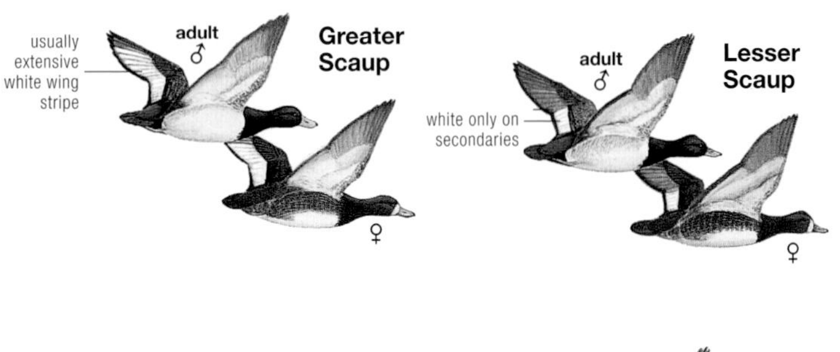
usually extensive white wing stripe
adult ♂
Greater Scaup
♀
white only on secondaries
adult ♂
Lesser Scaup
♀

extensive and bold white wing stripe
adult ♂
Tufted Duck
♀

grayish stripe
adult ♂
Ring-necked Duck
♀

Eiders

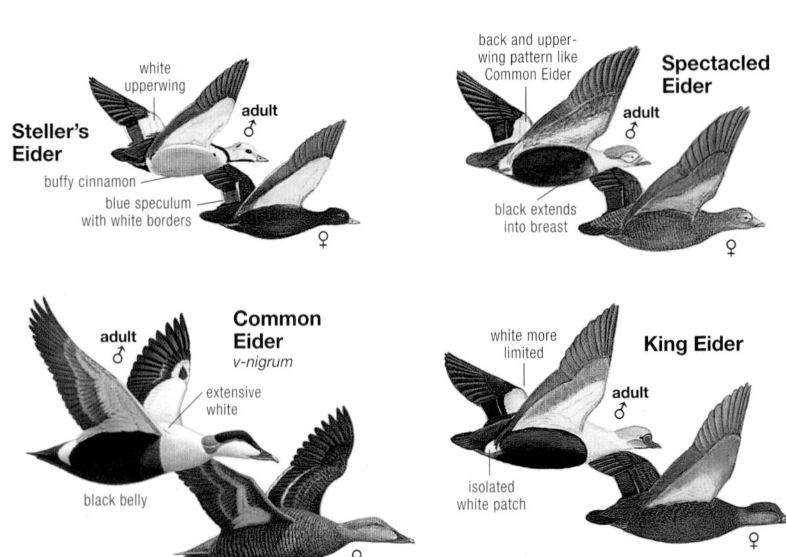
white upperwing
adult ♂
Steller's Eider
buffy cinnamon
blue speculum with white borders
♀
back and upper-wing pattern like Common Eider
Spectacled Eider
adult ♂
black extends into breast
♀
adult ♂
Common Eider
v-nigrum
extensive white
black belly
♀
white more limited
King Eider
adult ♂
isolated white patch
♀

Sea Ducks

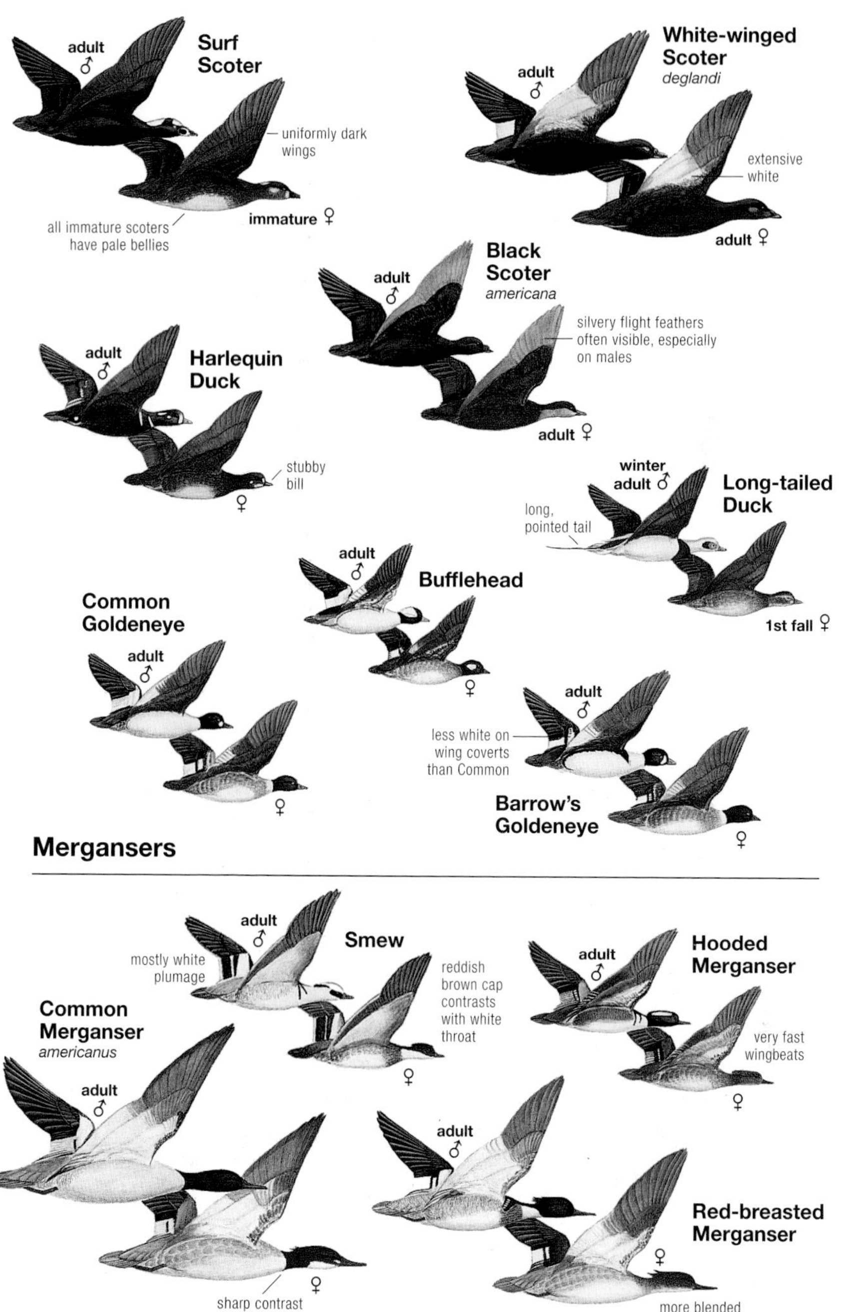

Surf Scoter
adult ♂
uniformly dark wings
immature ♀
all immature scoters have pale bellies
White-winged Scoter
deglandi
adult ♂
extensive white
adult ♀
Black Scoter
americana
adult ♂
silvery flight feathers often visible, especially on males
adult ♀
Harlequin Duck
adult ♂
stubby bill
♀
Long-tailed Duck
winter adult ♂
long, pointed tail
1st fall ♀
Bufflehead
adult ♂
♀
Common Goldeneye
adult ♂
♀
Barrow's Goldeneye
adult ♂
less white on wing coverts than Common
♀
Mergansers
Smew
adult ♂
mostly white plumage
reddish brown cap contrasts with white throat
♀
Hooded Merganser
adult ♂
very fast wingbeats
♀
Common Merganser
americanus
adult ♂
sharp contrast
♀
Red-breasted Merganser
adult ♂
♀
more blended neck pattern

Partridges, Grouse, Turkeys, Old World Quail

(Family Phasianidae)

Ground dwellers with feathered nostrils, short, strong bills, and short, rounded wings. Flight is brief but strong. Males perform elaborate courting displays. In some species, birds gather at the same strutting grounds, known as leks, every year.

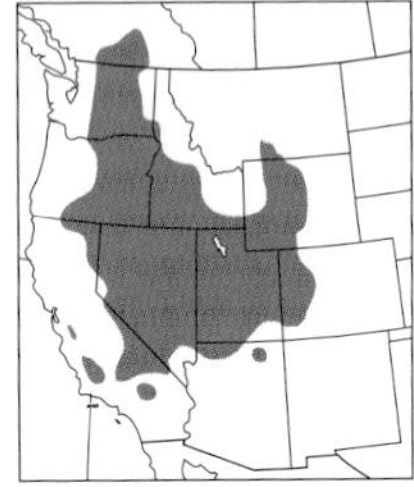

Chukar *Alectoris chukar L 14" (36 cm)*
Old World species. Gray-brown above; flanks boldly barred black and white; buffy face, throat outlined in black; gray breast; buff belly; chestnut outer tail feathers, best seen in flight just prior to landing. Red bill, legs. Males slightly larger with small leg spurs. ***Juvenile*** smaller, mottled; lacks bold black markings.
Voice: Calls include a series of loud, rapid *chuck chuck chuck* notes and a shrill *whitoo* alarm note.
Range: Introduced in North America as a game bird in the 1930s. Now established in rocky, arid mountains of West. Except in spring, feeds in coveys of 5 to 40 birds.

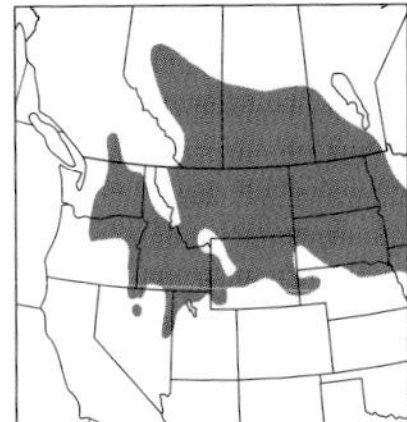

Gray Partridge *Perdix perdix L 12½" (32 cm)*
Grayish brown with rusty face and throat, paler in ***female. Male*** has dark chestnut patch on belly; patch smaller or absent in females. Flanks barred with reddish brown; outer tail feathers rusty.
Voice: Calls include a hoarse *kee-uck,* likened to a rusty gate.
Range: Widely introduced from Europe in early 1900s. Has declined over many parts of North American range. Inhabits open farmlands, grassy fields. In fall, forms coveys of 12 to 15 birds.

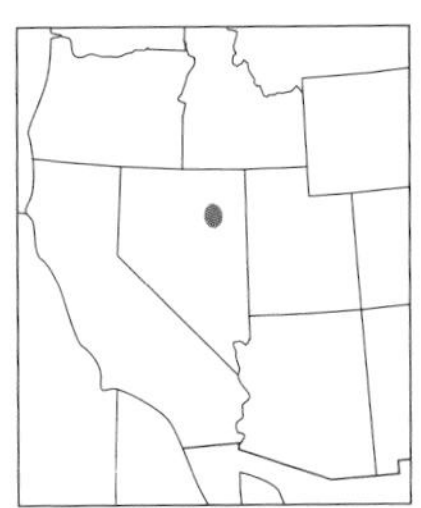

Himalayan Snowcock *Tetraogallus himalayensis*
L 28" (71 cm) Large, gray-brown overall, with tan streaking above. Whitish face and throat, outlined with chestnut stripes; undertail coverts white. Note white in wing in flight. ***Male*** almost identical to female, except female slightly smaller, lacks spurs, has buffier forehead and grayer area around eye. Inhabits mountainous terrain; flies downhill in the morning, then walks back up, feeding.
Voice: Calls include various clucks and cackles while feeding; one advertising call suggestive of Long-billed Curlew (male's call rises, female's descends).
Range: Asian species, successfully established (introduced 1963) only at high elevations in Nevada's Ruby Mountains.

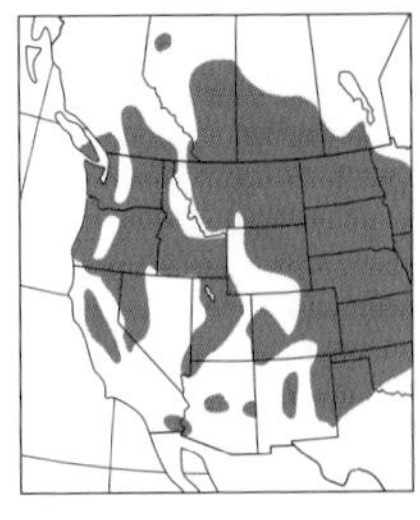

Ring-necked Pheasant *Phasianus colchicus*
♂L 33" (84 cm) ♀L 21" (53 cm) Introduced from Asia, this large, flashy bird has a long, pointed tail and short, rounded wings. ***Male*** is iridescent bronze overall, mottled with brown, black, and green; head varies from dark, glossy green to purplish, with fleshy red eye patches and iridescent ear tufts. Often shows a broad white neck ring. ***Female*** is buffy overall, much smaller and duller than male.
Voice: Male's territorial call is a loud, penetrating *kok-cack.*
Range: Locally fairly common. Found in open country, farmlands, brushy areas, woodland edges. A group of subspecies with white wing coverts (not shown) established in parts of the West.

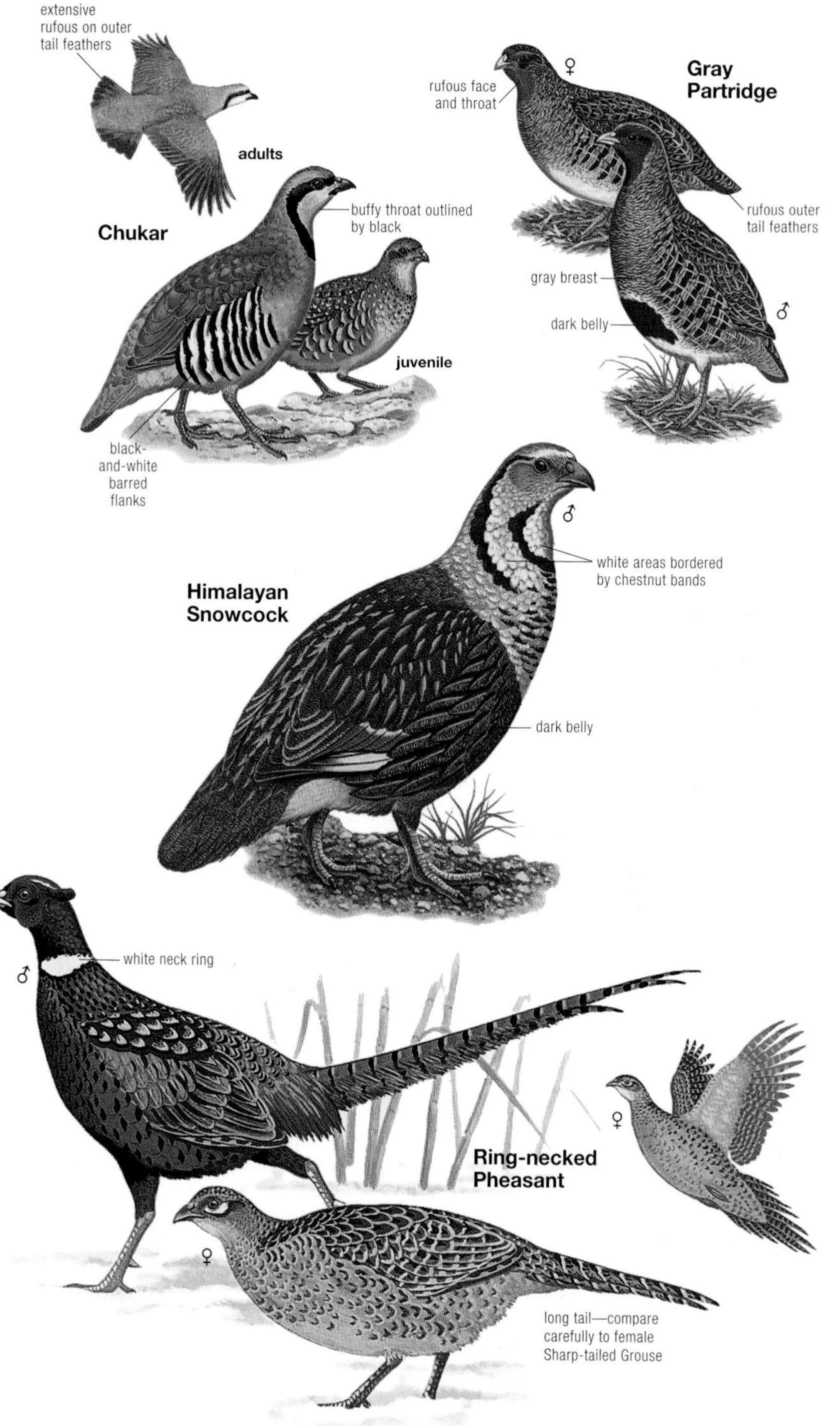
extensive
rufous on outer
tail feathers
adults
Chukar
buffy throat outlined
by black
juvenile
black-
and-white
barred
flanks
♀
Gray
Partridge
rufous face
and throat
rufous outer
tail feathers
gray breast
dark belly
♂
♂
white areas bordered
by chestnut bands
Himalayan
Snowcock
dark belly
white neck ring
♂
♀
Ring-necked
Pheasant
♀
long tail—compare
carefully to female
Sharp-tailed Grouse

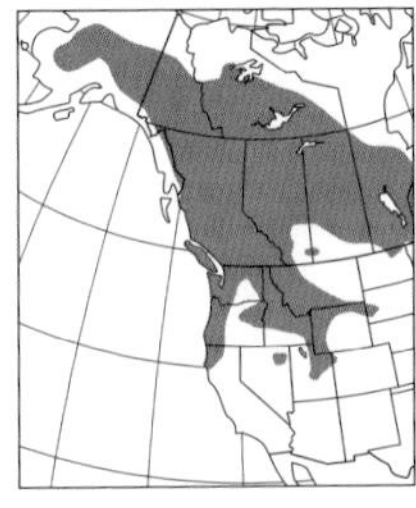

Ruffed Grouse *Bonasa umbellus L 17" (43 cm)*
Small crest; black ruff on sides of neck, usually inconspicuous; banded tail with wide dark band near tip, incomplete in ***female.*** The two color ***morphs, red*** and ***gray,*** are most apparent by tail color. Red morphs predominate in the humid Pacific Northwest; gray morphs elsewhere in West. Seven subspecies are found in the West.
Voice: In spring, ***male*** displays by raising ruff and crest, fans tail, and beats wings to make a hollow, accelerating, drumming noise.
Range: Uncommon in deciduous and mixed woodlands. Introduced in northeastern Nevada.

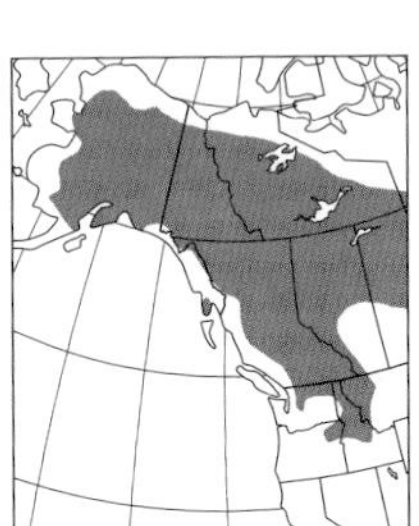

Spruce Grouse *Falcipennis canadensis L 16" (41 cm)*
Male has dark throat and breast, edged with white; red eye combs. Over most of range, both sexes have black tail with chestnut tip. Birds of the northern Rockies and Cascades, ***"Franklin's Grouse,"*** *franklinii,* have white spots on uppertail coverts; male's tail is all-dark. In all subspecies, ***females*** have two color ***morphs, red*** and ***gray;*** resemble female Sooty and Dusky Grouse but are smaller and have black barring and white spots below.
Voice: Both sexes give soft, low, croaking notes. Female's high-pitched call is thought to be territorial. In courtship display, male spreads his tail, erects the red eye combs, and rapidly beats his wings. In territorial flight display, male flutters upward on shallow wingstrokes; "Franklin's Grouse" ends this performance by beating his wings together, making a clapping sound.
Range: Widespread but easily overlooked; inhabits coniferous forests. Frequents roadsides, especially in fall.

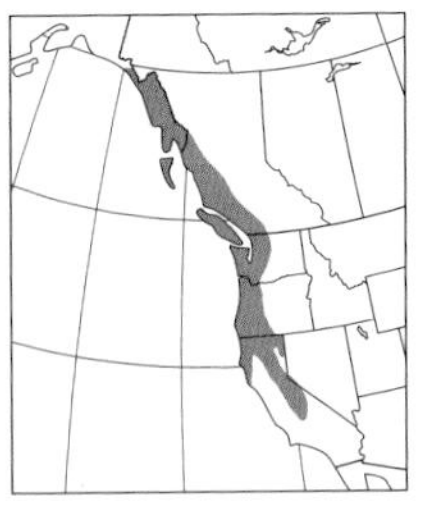

Sooty Grouse *Dendragapus fuliginosus L 20" (51 cm)*
Formerly (with Dusky Grouse) known as Blue Grouse. ***Male***'s sooty gray plumage sets off yellow-orange eye comb. On neck, white-based feathers cover an inflatable bare yellow sac. Female is mottled brown above, with plain gray belly. On both sexes, the 18 tail feathers are round and tipped with gray. Chicks are yellowish.
Voice: Male display call is series of loud low hoots audible at considerable distance, usually delivered from perch in tree.
Range: Inhabits coniferous forest but will forage at meadow edges. Believed extirpated from mountains of southern California.

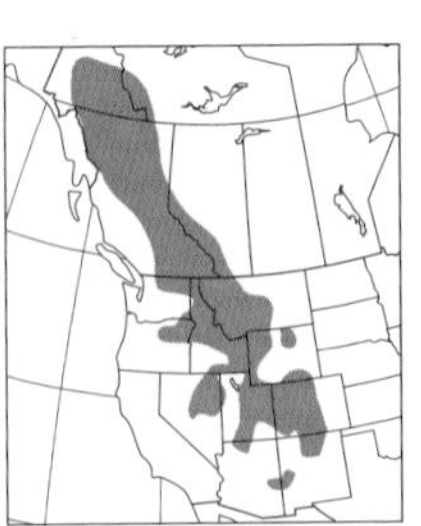

Dusky Grouse *Dendragapus obscurus L 20" (51 cm)*
All plumages similar to Sooty Grouse, but paler overall; closed tail squarer (less graduated), the 20 tail feathers are more square tipped. Northern subspecies (*richardsonii* and *pallidus*) largely or completely lack the gray terminal band. ***Male***'s neck sac is purplish and smoother, with broader white-feathered border than Sooty. Chicks are grayish. Male's display, usually from ground, often involves low fluttering or making short circular flights, then strutting with tail fanned, body tipped forward, head drawn in, wings dragging.
Voice: Male's display call, usually given from ground, is softer and lower pitched than Sooty and audible only at close range.
Range: Often prefers more open forest than Sooty; sometimes found in sagebrush. Range almost entirely separate from Sooty; hybrids recorded from interior of British Columbia.

male with
solid band
crest
red-morph ♂
Ruffed
Grouse
red-morph ♀
displaying
gray-morph ♂
female with
broken band
red comb
gray-
morph ♀
red-morph ♀
Spruce
Grouse
white
tips
rufous tail
band
♂
"Franklin's
Grouse"
franklinii
♂
Dusky Grouse
northern
races lack
gray tail
band
northern
Rockies ♂
richardsonii
broad gray
tail band
Sooty Grouse
purple
air sac
coastal ♂
fuliginosus
yellow
air sac
southern
Rockies ♀
obscurus

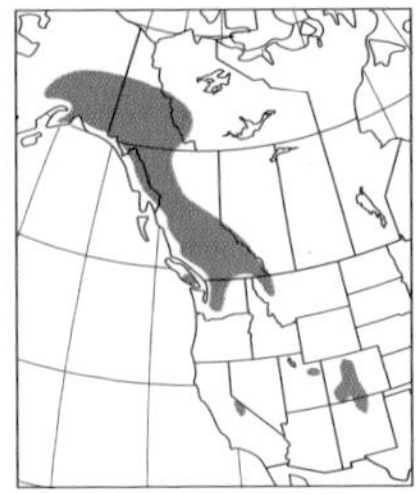

White-tailed Ptarmigan *Lagopus leucura L 12½" (32 cm)*
As with all ptarmigans, legs and feet are feathered and plumage is molted three times a year, matching seasonal changes in habitat. Distinguished from other ptarmigans in all seasons by white tail. ***Winter*** bird is white except for small dark bill and eyes and red eye combs. In ***summer,*** body is mottled blackish or brown with white belly, wings, and tail. Spring and ***fall molts*** give a patchy appearance.
Voice: Calls include a henlike clucking and soft, low hoots.
Range: Locally common on rocky alpine slopes, high meadows. Small numbers have been successfully introduced in the central Sierra Nevada, Wallowa, and Uinta Mountains and on Pike's Peak. Reintroduced into northern New Mexico. Extirpated from Wyoming. Moves to slightly lower elevations during severe weather. May form flocks in fall and winter.

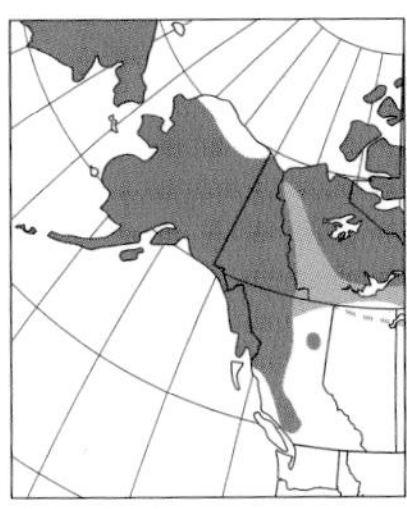

Rock Ptarmigan *Lagopus muta L 14" (36 cm)*
Mottled ***summer*** plumage is black, dark brown, or grayish brown; ***male*** generally lacks the reddish tones of male Willow Ptarmigan. There are many recognized subspecies, with color variations according to geography. In ***winter*** plumage, ***male*** has a black line from bill through eye, lacking in male Willow. Acquires breeding plumage later in spring than Willow. In both sexes, bill and overall size are slightly smaller than Willow. ***Female*** is otherwise difficult to distinguish from Willow. Plumage is patchy white during spring and fall molts. Both species retain white wings and black tail year-round.
Voice: Calls include low growls and croaks and noisy cackles.
Range: Common on high, rocky slopes and tundra. In breeding season, generally prefers higher and more barren habitat than Willow. May form flocks in fall and winter. Accidental on Queen Charlotte Islands, British Columbia, in spring.

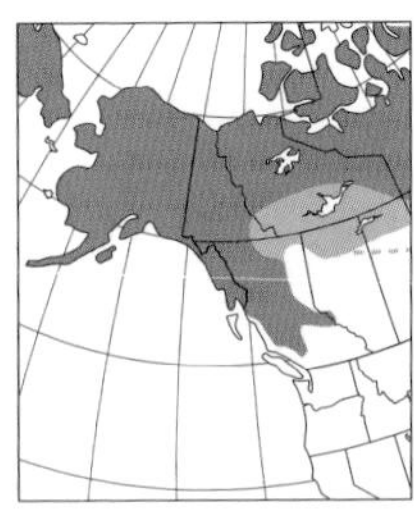

Willow Ptarmigan *Lagopus lagopus L 15" (38 cm)*
Largest ptarmigan. Mottled ***summer*** plumage of ***male*** is generally redder than Rock Ptarmigan. White ***winter*** plumage lacks the black eye line of male Rock Ptarmigan; bill and overall size are slightly larger in Willow Ptarmigan. ***Female*** is otherwise difficult to distinguish from Rock Ptarmigan. Both species retain white wings and black tail year-round. Plumage is patchy white during ***spring*** and fall ***molts.***
Voice: Calls include low growls and croaks, noisy cackles. In courtship and territorial displays, male utters a raucous *go-back go-back go-backa go-backa go-backa.* Ptarmigans' red eye combs can be concealed or raised during courtship and aggression.
Range: Common on tundra, especially in thickets of willow and alder. In breeding season, generally prefers wetter, brushier habitat than Rock. May form flocks in fall and winter.

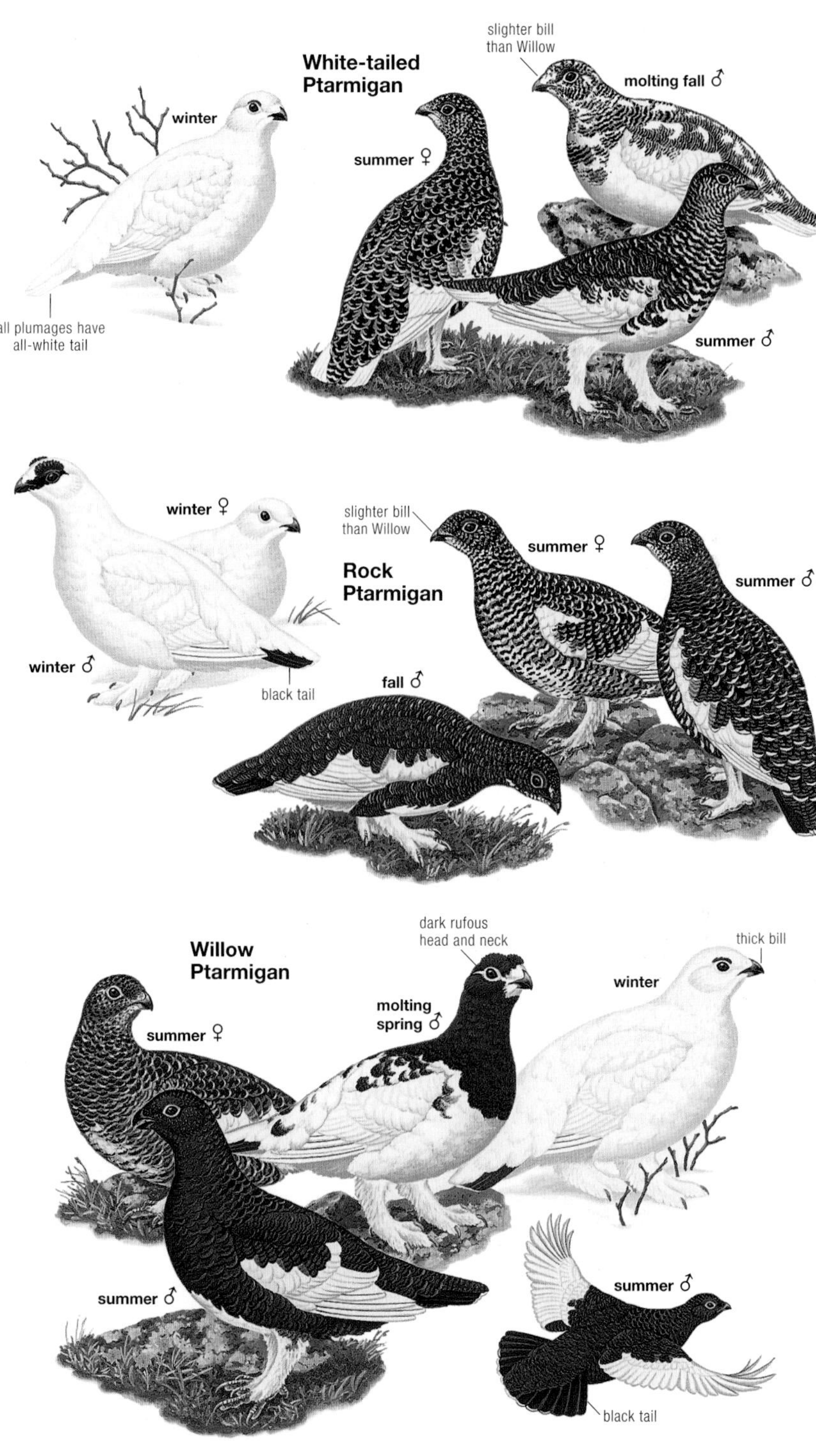
White-tailed Ptarmigan
slighter bill than Willow
molting fall ♂
winter
summer ♀
all plumages have all-white tail
summer ♂
winter ♀
slighter bill than Willow
summer ♀
Rock Ptarmigan
summer ♂
winter ♂
black tail
fall ♂
Willow Ptarmigan
dark rufous head and neck
thick bill
winter
molting spring ♂
summer ♀
summer ♂
summer ♂
black tail

Greater Prairie-Chicken *Tympanuchus cupido*

L 17" (43 cm) Heavily barred with dark brown, cinnamon, and pale buff above and below. Short, rounded tail is all-dark in ***male*** and is barred in ***female.*** Male has fleshy yellow-orange eye combs. Both sexes have elongated dark neck feathers, longer in males and erected during courtship to display inflated golden neck sacs.

Voice: Courting males make a deep *oo-loo-woo* sound known as "booming," like blowing over top of an empty bottle.

Range: Uncommon, local, and declining. Found in areas of natural tallgrass prairie interspersed with cropland. In West, found only in northeastern Colorado. Has declined greatly over range as a whole. In West formerly common in southeastern Alberta, disappearing by the mid-1930s; last recorded 5 March 1972.

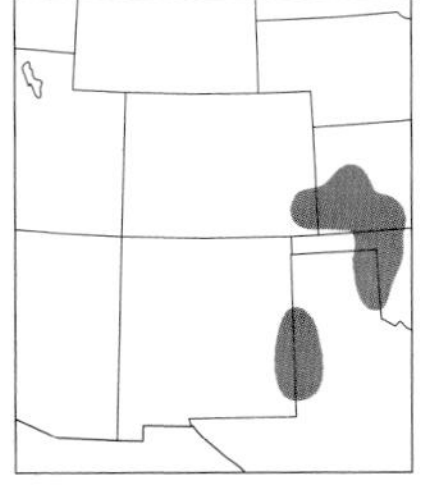

Lesser Prairie-Chicken *Tympanuchus pallidicinctus*

L 16" (41 cm) Resembles Greater Prairie-Chicken (ranges do not overlap), but slightly smaller, paler, less heavily barred below. Courting ***male*** displays dull orange-red neck sacs and erects dark neck tufts.

Voice: Male's "booming" sound slightly higher pitched than Greater Prairie-Chicken.

Range: Uncommon, local, and declining over most of range; found in sagebrush and shortgrass prairie country, especially where shinnery oak grows.

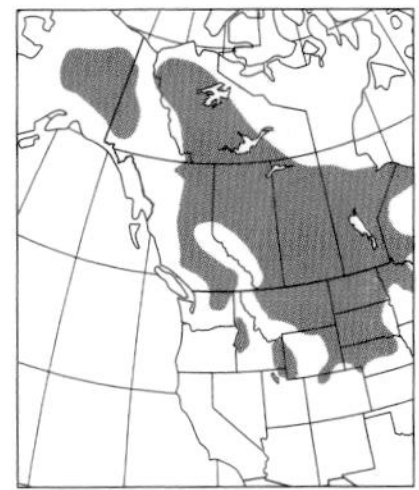

Sharp-tailed Grouse *Tympanuchus phasianellus*

L 17" (43 cm) Similar to prairie-chickens, but underparts are scaled and spotted; tail is mostly white and pointed; yellowish eye combs are less prominent. Compare with female Ring-necked Pheasant (page 50), which is larger and has a longer tail, warmer color, and less patterning below. Birds are darkest in Alaska and northern Canada (standing figure), palest in the plains (flying figure). ***Male***'s purplish neck sacs are inflated during courtship display.

Voice: Male's courting notes include cackling and a single, low *coo-oo* call accompanied by the rattling of wing quills.

Range: Inhabits grasslands, sagebrush, woodland edges, clearcuts, and river canyons. Overall rare in western U.S. Formerly found south to northeastern California, Utah, and northern New Mexico. Extirpated from entire southern part of range in West. The subspecies *columbianus* was formerly found south to Oregon (extirpated by 1970s; reintroductions attempted), northeast California (extirpated by 1915), Nevada (extirpated by late 20th century, reintroductions attempted) and northeast New Mexico (sightings of flocks in 1920s). In western Oklahoma panhandle *jamesi* was present until about 1932. Declining and in serious jeopardy in all other areas of West south of Canadian border (both *columbianus* and adjacent subspecies to east, *jamesi*). Where ranges overlap, can hybridize with Greater Prairie-Chicken or Dusky Grouse.

Greater
Prairie-Chicken
short, square
black tail
displaying ♂
♀
orange
air sacs
Lesser
Prairie-Chicken
♀
displaying ♂
weaker barring
than Greater
Prairie-Chicken
reddish
air sacs
pointed tail shorter
than female
Ring-necked Pheasant
displaying ♂
Sharp-tailed
Grouse
♀
grayish plumage
heavily mottled and
barred with dark

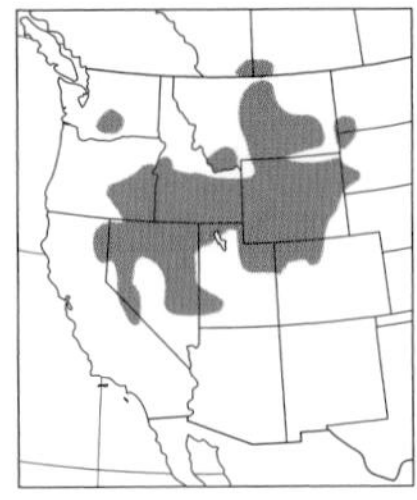

Greater Sage-Grouse *Centrocercus urophasianus*
♂L 28" (71 cm) ♀L 22" (56 cm) Blackish belly, long, pointed tail feathers, and large size are distinctive. ***Male*** is larger than ***female*** and has yellow eye combs, black throat and bib, and large white ruff on breast. In flight, dark belly, absence of white outer tail feathers, and larger size distinguish it from Sharp-tailed Grouse; from female Ring-necked Pheasant by grayer coloration and dark belly patch. ***Displaying male*** fans tail and rapidly inflates and deflates air sacs.
Voice: When displaying, male gives gulping, popping sounds. Both sexes give cackling calls.
Range: Uncommon and local; declining. Found in sagebrush areas of foothills and plains; also at high elevations above tree line in some areas (e.g., White Mountains of California and Nevada).

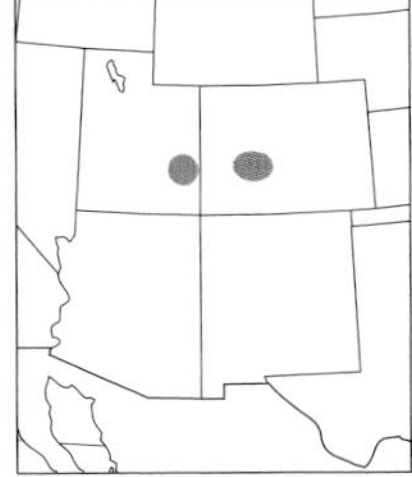

Gunnison Sage-Grouse *Centrocercus minimus*
♂L 22" (56 cm) ♀L 18" (46 cm) Distinguished from Greater Sage-Grouse by smaller size and more strongly white-banded tail. Longer, denser filoplumes are erected to form a distinct, recurved crest on ***displaying male.***
Voice: Male's display call is lower pitched and more uniform than Greater Sage-Grouse.
Range: Small, threatened population in south-central Colorado and southeastern Utah is geographically isolated from Greater Sage-Grouse.

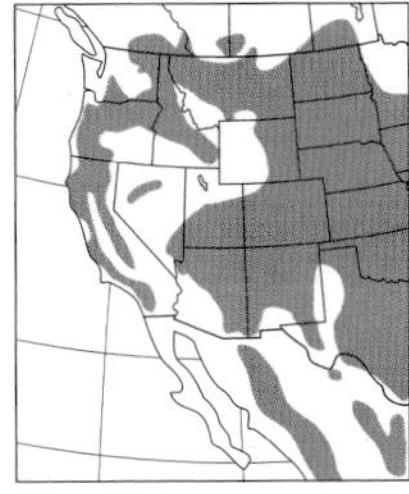

Wild Turkey *Meleagris gallopavo*
♂L 46" (117 cm) ♀L 37" (94 cm) Largest game bird in North America; slightly smaller, more slender than the domesticated bird. Usually seen in flocks. ***Male*** has dark, iridescent body, flight feathers barred with white, red wattles, blackish breast tuft, spurred legs; bare-skinned head is blue and pink. Tail, uppertail coverts, and lower rump feathers are tipped with chestnut on eastern birds, buffy white on western birds. ***Female*** and immature are smaller and duller than male, often lack breast tuft. Of the races seen in North America, *silvestris* predominates in the East, *merriami* in the West. Birds from Kansas to Mexico (*intermedia*) are intermediate with buffy tips to the uppertail coverts.
Voice: In spring a male's gobbling call may be heard a mile away.
Range: Birds of the open forest (often partial to oaks in West) and forest openings, Wild Turkeys forage mostly on the ground for seeds, nuts, acorns, and insects. At night they roost in trees. Historically, native *merriami* was found in the mountains from central Colorado south to southeastern Arizona, southern New Mexico, and west Texas (Guadalupe Mountains). Extirpated from many areas but restocked in much of its former range and widely introduced in other areas. However, these restockings and introductions also involve other subspecies and intergrades between subspecies, especially *intermedia*.

rather
uniform-colored
tail feathers
larger crest than
Greater Sage-Grouse
Gunnison
Sage-Grouse
white-banded
tail
displaying ♂
displaying ♂
Greater Sage-Grouse
♂
♀
graduated,
pointed tail
♀
black belly
patch
unfeathered
reddish head
♂
displaying ♂
Wild
Turkey
western
merriami
♀
unfeathered
gray head

New World Quail (Family Odontophoridae)

Scientific evidence has recently placed the New World Quail in their own family. All have chunky bodies and crests or head plumes. In North America, most live in the West.

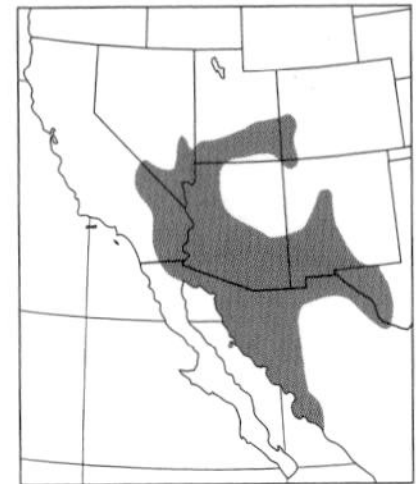

Gambel's Quail *Callipepla gambelii L 11" (28 cm)*

Grayish above; prominent teardrop-shaped plume or double plume. Distinguished from California by chestnut sides and crown, lack of scaling on underparts. ***Male*** has dark forehead, black throat, black belly patch. Smaller ***juvenile*** is tan and gray with pale mottling and streaking. Shows less scaling and streaking than darker California juvenile; nape and throat grayer. Sometimes ***hybridizes*** with Scaled (next page) and California where ranges overlap.

Voice: Calls include varied grunts and cackles and a plaintive *qua-el;* loud, querulous *chi-ca-go-go* call is similar to California Quail but higher pitched and usually has four notes.

Range: Common in desert scrublands, usually near permanent water source. Gregarious; in fall and winter, forms large coveys. Introduced populations exist in Idaho, in Colorado, and on California's San Clemente Island.

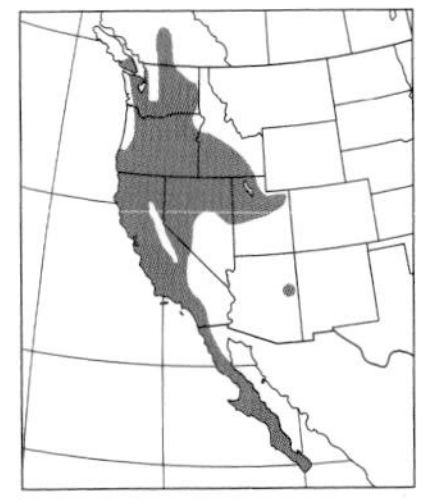

California Quail *Callipepla californica L 10" (25 cm)*

Gray and brown above; prominent teardrop-shaped plume or double plume. Scaly-looking underparts, brown sides and crown separate California from Gambel's. Body color varies from grayish, seen over most of range, to brown in coastal mountains of California; extremes shown here in ***females. Male*** has pale forehead, black throat, chestnut belly patch. ***Juvenile*** is smaller; resembles Gambel's juvenile, but darker, with traces of scaling on underparts.

Voice: Calls include varied grunts and cackles; loud, emphatic *chi-ca-go* call is similar to Gambel's but lower pitched and usually has three notes rather than four.

Range: Common in woodlands, brushy foothills, stream valleys, usually near permanent water source. Gregarious; in fall and winter, assembles in large coveys. Most populations in northern portion of range in Utah and Arizona are introduced.

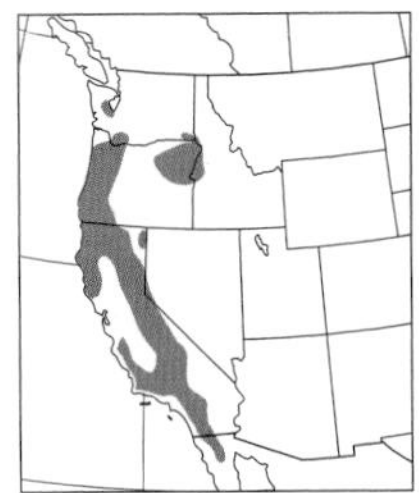

Mountain Quail *Oreortyx pictus L 11" (28 cm)*

Gray and brown above, with two long, thin head plumes that often appear to be one plume. Gray breast; chestnut sides boldly barred with white; chestnut throat outlined in white. Sexes alike; female has shorter head plumes. Amount of brown and gray in upperparts varies among races; birds of humid coastal Northwest browner, interior subspecies grayer. ***Juvenile*** smaller, grayer underparts, longer plumes than Gambel's or California Quail juveniles.

Voice: Male's mating call, a loud, clear, descending *quee-ark*; both sexes give whistled notes.

Range: Uncommon to fairly common, but declining in parts of range; in chaparral, brushy ravines, open woodlands, mountain slopes. Nonmigratory but partly descends to lower altitudes in winter. Gregarious, forms small coveys in fall and winter. Secretive; best seen in late summer in family groups along roadsides.

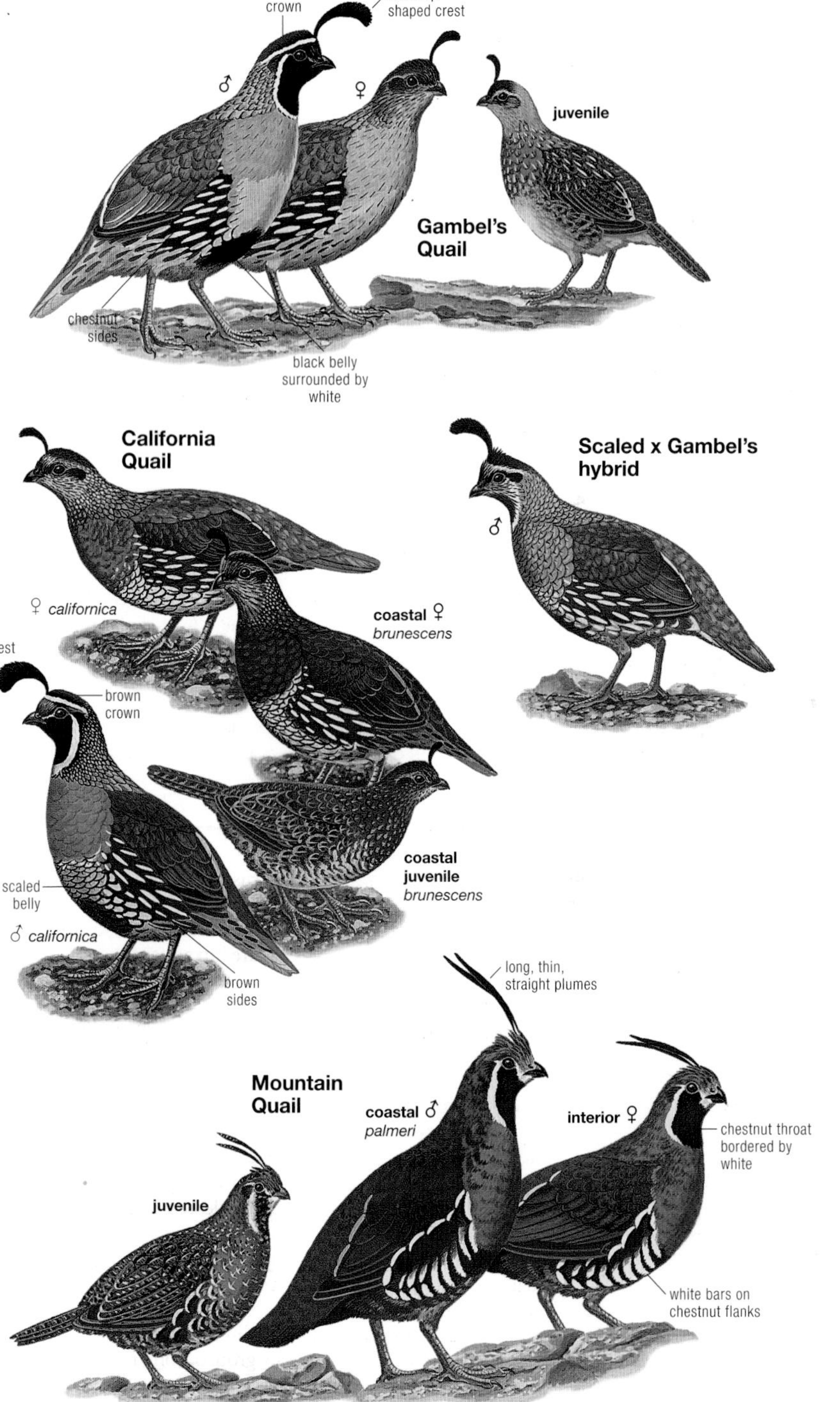
chestnut crown
teardrop-shaped crest
♂
♀
juvenile
Gambel's Quail
chestnut sides
black belly surrounded by white
California Quail
♀ californica
coastal ♀ brunescens
eardrop-
haped crest
brown crown
scaled belly
♂ californica
brown sides
coastal juvenile brunescens
Scaled x Gambel's hybrid
♂
long, thin, straight plumes
Mountain Quail
coastal ♂ palmeri
interior ♀
chestnut throat bordered by white
juvenile
white bars on chestnut flanks

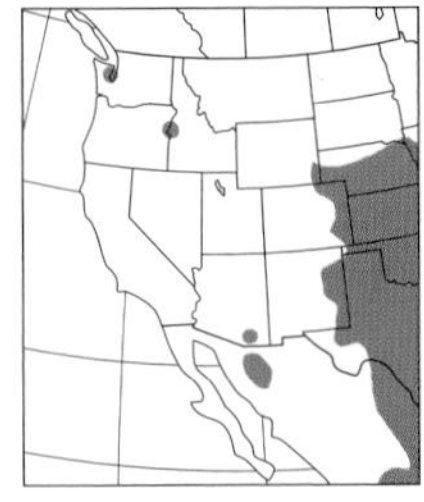

Northern Bobwhite *Colinus virginianus* L 9 ¾" (25 cm)
Mottled, reddish brown quail with short gray tail. Flanks are striped with reddish brown. Throat and eye stripe are white in ***male,*** buffy in ***female. Juvenile*** is smaller and duller. The subspecies found in eastern portion of West, *taylori* on the western Plains and *texanus* from southeastern New Mexico and west Texas, are paler than eastern subspecies.
Voice: Male's call is a rising, whistled *bob-white,* heard chiefly in late spring and summer; whistled *hoy* call is heard year-round. Also soft clucking notes.
Range: Uncommon in brushlands, field edges, agricultural land, and open woodlands; feeds and roosts in coveys except during nesting season. Declining in many areas. The population in the Northwest is introduced, as are some populations in eastern Colorado. ***"Masked Bobwhite,"*** *ridgwayi* (**E**), which was formerly found from southeastern Arizona to central Sonora, Mexico, was eliminated from the U.S. part of its range by the early 1900s. Reintroduced in 1970 from Mexico (Sonora) to Altar Valley in southeastern Arizona, it remains endangered. Male has black throat and cinnamon underparts.

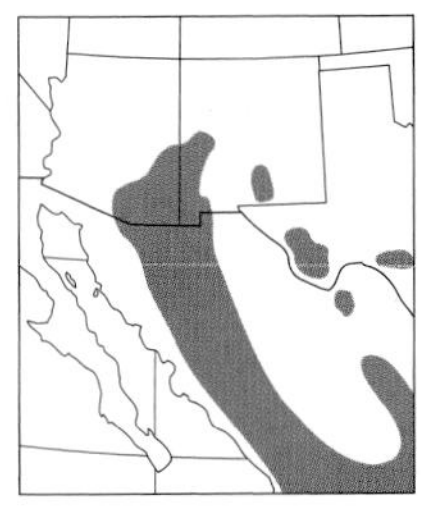

Montezuma Quail *Cyrtonyx montezumae* L 8 ¾" (22 cm)
Plump, short-tailed, round-winged quail. ***Male*** has distinctive facial pattern and rounded pale brown crest on back of head. Back and wings are mottled black, brown, and tan; breast is dark chestnut; sides and flanks are dark gray with white spots. ***Female*** is mottled pinkish brown below with less distinct head markings. ***Juvenile*** smaller and paler, has dark spotting on underparts.
Voice: Call given by male in breeding season is a loud, quavering, descending whistle; female gives multisyllabic whistles on one pitch.
Range: Uncommon, secretive, and local in grassy undergrowth of open juniper-oak or pine-oak woodlands on semiarid mountain slopes. Recently rediscovered in Chisos Mountains of southwestern Texas.

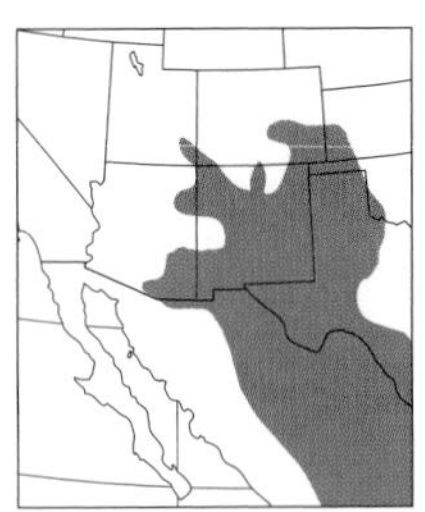

Scaled Quail *Callipepla squamata* L 10" (25 cm)
Grayish quail with conspicuous white-tipped crest. Bluish gray breast and mantle feathers have dark edges, creating a shingled or scaly-pattern effect. Female's crest is buffy and smaller. ***Juvenile*** resembles adult but is more mottled above, with less conspicuous scaling.
Voice: During breeding season, both sexes give a location call when separated, a low, nasal *chip-churr,* accented on the second syllable.
Range: Fairly common; found on barren mesas and plateaus, in semidesert scrublands, and in grasslands with mixed scrub; often frequents roadsides. In fall, forms coveys. Recent records of unknown origin in southern Utah and southwestern Colorado.

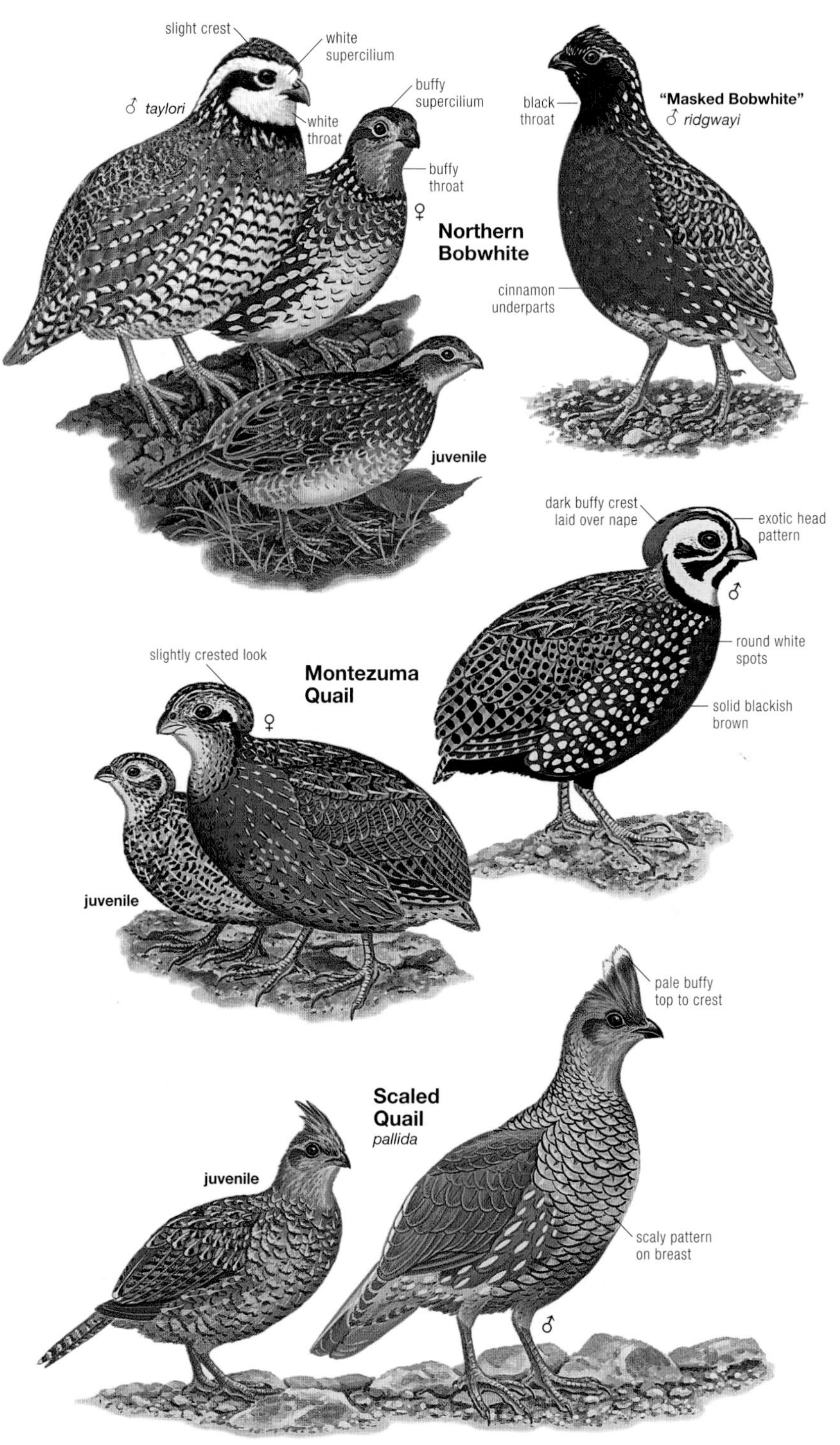
slight crest
white supercilium
♂ taylori
white throat
buffy supercilium
buffy throat
♀
Northern Bobwhite
juvenile
black throat
"Masked Bobwhite"
♂ ridgwayi
cinnamon underparts
dark buffy crest laid over nape
exotic head pattern
♂
round white spots
solid blackish brown
slightly crested look
Montezuma Quail
♀
juvenile
pale buffy top to crest
Scaled Quail
pallida
juvenile
scaly pattern on breast
♂

Loons (Family Gaviidae)

In all species, juvenal-like plumage is held through the first summer.

Red-throated Loon *Gavia stellata L 25" (64 cm)*

Thin bill often appears slightly upturned; tends to hold head tilted up. ***Breeding adult*** with gray head; brick red throat patch that appears dark in flight; dark brown upperparts with no contrasting white patches on scapulars as in all other loons in breeding plumage. ***Winter adult*** has sharply defined white on face, extensive white spotting on back. ***Juvenile***'s head grayish brown; throat may have dull red markings. In all plumages, white on flanks extends a bit on sides of rump, similar to Arctic. In flight, shows smaller head and feet than Common and Yellow-billed; wingbeat quicker; often flies with drooping neck, unlike other loons.

Voice: Flight call, heard on breeding grounds, is a rapid, gooselike *kak-kak-kak.*

Range: Migrates coastally; casual inland during migration, winter. Small numbers of nonbreeders oversummer in winter range.

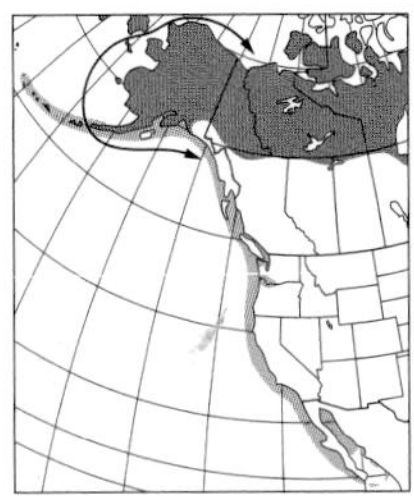

Pacific Loon *Gavia pacifica L 26" (66 cm)*

In all plumages, has dark flanks, with no white extending upward on sides of rump. Bill is slim and straight; head smoothly rounded and held level. ***Breeding adult***'s head and nape are pale gray; white stripes on sides of neck show only moderate contrast; throat's iridescent purple patch, sometimes washed with green, usually appears black unless seen clearly on swimming bird. ***Juvenile***'s crown and nape are slightly paler than back, unlike Common Loon (next page); in juveniles and ***winter adults,*** dark cap extends to eye. Winter adults and most juveniles have a thin, brown "chin strap," though it may be faint in juveniles. Compare to juvenile Red-throated Loon, with which this this species is sometimes confused. In flight, resembles Common, but head and feet are smaller.

Voice: On breeding grounds gives various yodeling calls.

Range: A coastal and offshore migrant; often migrates in small to moderate-size flocks. Rare inland during migration and winter.

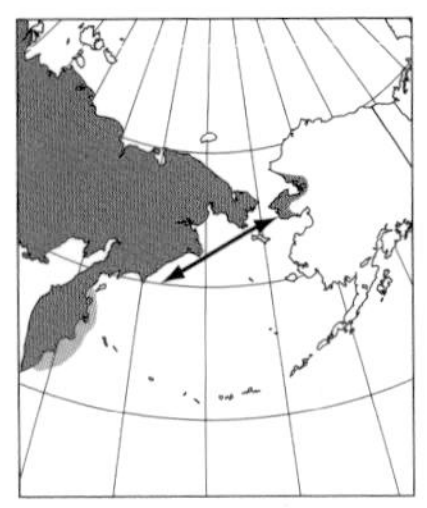

Arctic Loon *Gavia arctica L 28" (73 cm)*

Old World species. Larger than Pacific Loon, with less rounded head; best distinguished in all plumages from Pacific by more extensive white on flanks, coming up over sides of rump. Visibility of white area depends on how buoyantly the bird is swimming. When diving, often only a small white rump patch is evident. At rest, Arctic Loon shows much more white; note Pacific can also show some white. Nape in ***breeding adult*** is darker, and black-and-white stripes are bolder, than Pacific; white stripes on face connect more to sides of neck; greenish on throat very hard to see.

Voice: On breeding grounds, yodeling calls are deeper than Pacific.

Range: Large Asian race, *viridigularis,* breeds in northwestern Alaska. Seen in migration in coastal western Alaska, especially at St. Lawrence Island. Casual elsewhere on West Coast mostly in winter; accidental inland (Colorado).

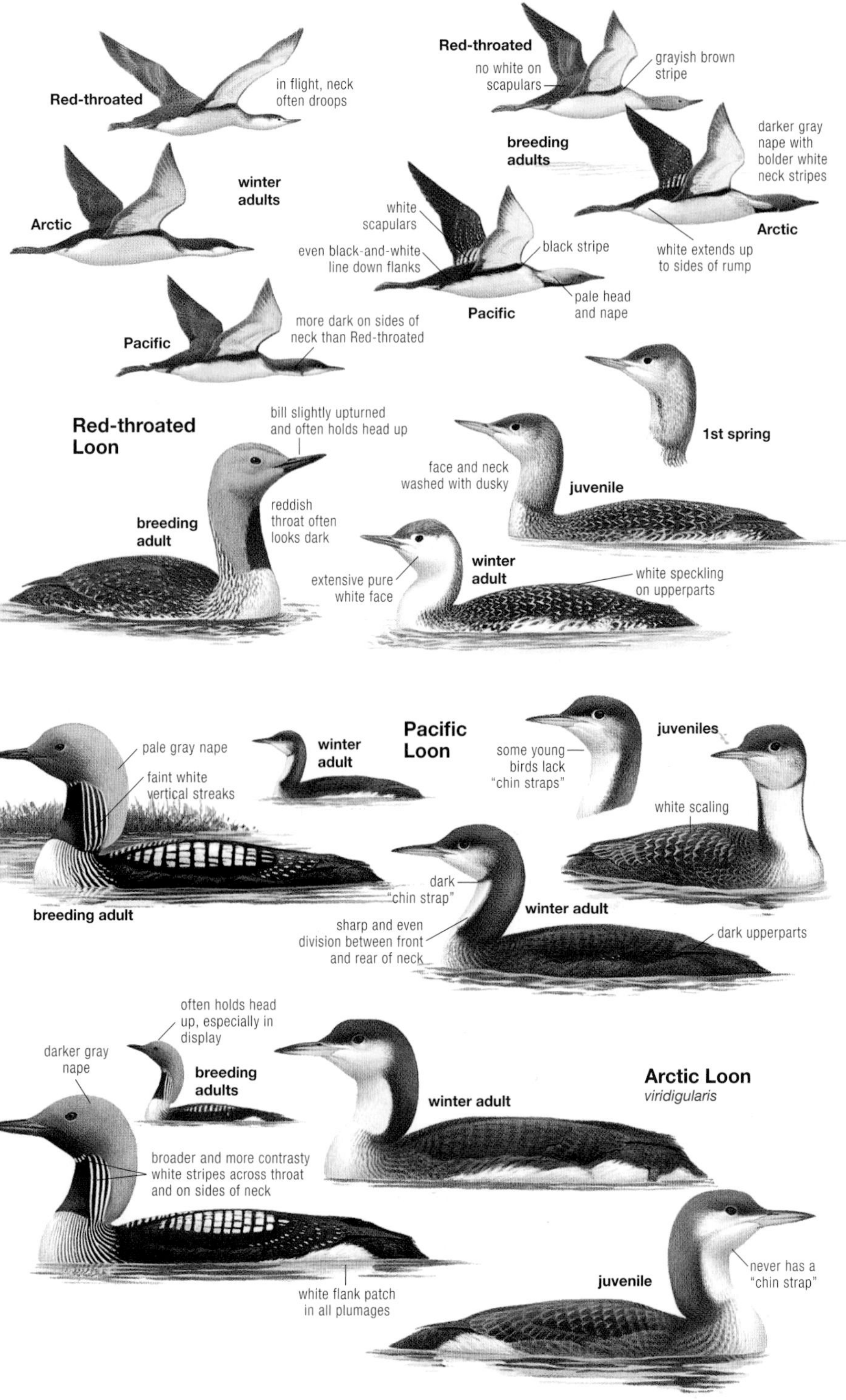
Red-throated
in flight, neck often droops
Arctic
winter adults
Pacific
more dark on sides of neck than Red-throated
Red-throated
no white on scapulars
grayish brown stripe
breeding adults
darker gray nape with bolder white neck stripes
Arctic
white scapulars
even black-and-white line down flanks
black stripe
white extends up to sides of rump
pale head and nape
Pacific
Red-throated Loon
bill slightly upturned and often holds head up
reddish throat often looks dark
breeding adult
1st spring
face and neck washed with dusky
juvenile
extensive pure white face
winter adult
white speckling on upperparts
pale gray nape
faint white vertical streaks
winter adult
Pacific Loon
some young birds lack "chin straps"
juveniles
white scaling
breeding adult
dark "chin strap"
winter adult
sharp and even division between front and rear of neck
dark upperparts
often holds head up, especially in display
darker gray nape
breeding adults
winter adult
Arctic Loon
viridigularis
broader and more contrasty white stripes across throat and on sides of neck
white flank patch in all plumages
never has a "chin strap"
juvenile

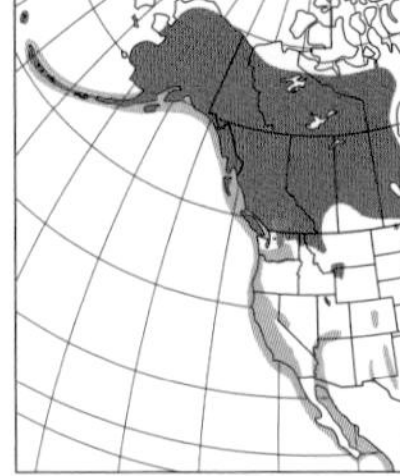

Common Loon *Gavia immer L 32" (81 cm)*

Large, thick-billed loon with slightly curved culmen. Bill is black in ***breeding*** plumage, blue-gray in ***winter adults*** and ***juveniles,*** but the culmen remains dark. In winter plumage, crown and nape are darker than back; dark on nape extends around sides of neck, but note the white indentation above this. In winter adults the white extends up and around the eye; the face pattern is more blended in juveniles. Forehead is steep, crown is peaked at front. Holds head level. Juvenile Common and Yellow-billed Loons have whitish scalloping on their scapulars, distinguishing them from the plainer backed winter adults. Juvenal plumage is kept through most of the winter, with a partial molt in spring. Most winter adults retain at least a few spotted coverts, often visible on swimming birds. Full adult breeding plumage is not acquired until nearly three years of age. Under most conditions, Common and Yellow-billed fly quite high above the water when migrating, while the other loon species fly lower. Note their slower wingbeats and the paddle-shaped feet that are usually visible beyond the tail. In flight, large head and feet help distinguish Common from Arctic, Pacific, and Red-throated Loons (flight figures previous page).

Voice: Loud yodeling calls delivered on water and in flight are heard all year, but most often on breeding grounds.

Range: Fairly common; nests on lakes. Migrates overland as well as coastally. Winters mainly in coastal waters or on large, ice-free inland bodies of water. Small numbers of nonbreeders oversummer in winter range. Generally rare in Southwest due to lack of appropriate habitat.

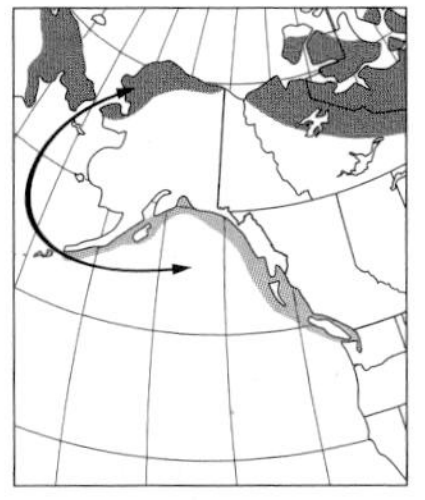

Yellow-billed Loon *Gavia adamsii L 34" (86 cm)*

Breeding adult has straw yellow bill, usually longer than Common Loon; culmen is straight, giving bill a slightly uptilted look; head often tilted back, which enhances this effect. Crown is peaked at front and rear, giving a subtle double-bump effect. Bill is duskier at the base in ***winter adults*** and ***juveniles,*** but always shows strong yellow cast toward the tip, including the culmen (dark in Common). Note also pale face and distinct, variably shaped dark mark behind eye; eye is smaller, back and crown are paler and browner than Common. As with Common, full adult breeding plumage is not acquired until nearly three years of age.

Voice: Calls are similar to Common.

Range: Breeds on tundra lakes and rivers. Migrates coastally; very rare south of Canada on West Coast, where it is recorded annually south to northern California, mostly in winter, and casually to southern California. Very rare to casual inland in West in migration and winter.

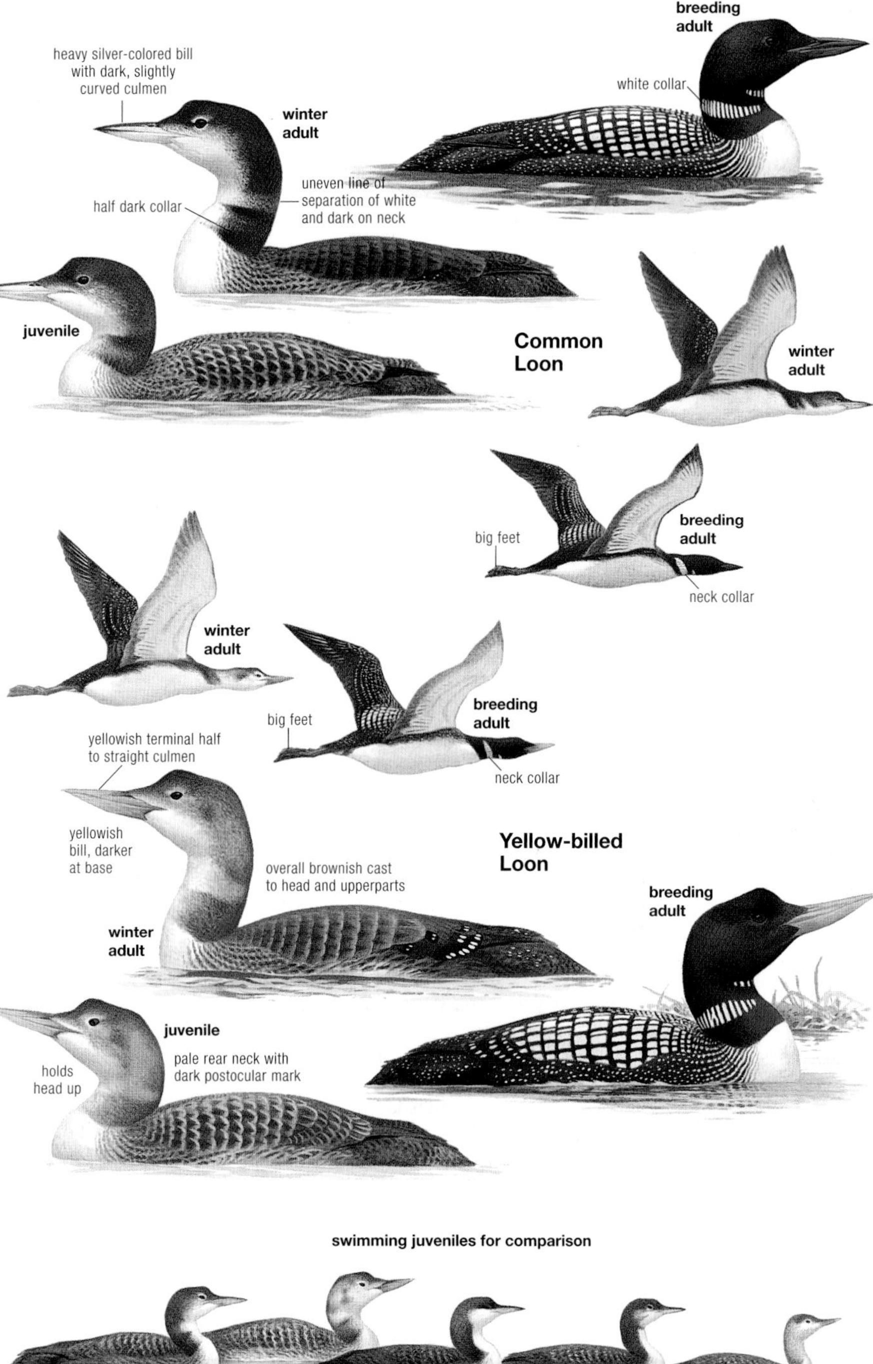
breeding
adult
heavy silver-colored bill
with dark, slightly
curved culmen
white collar
winter
adult
uneven line of
separation of white
and dark on neck
half dark collar
juvenile
Common
Loon
winter
adult
big feet
breeding
adult
neck collar
winter
adult
big feet
breeding
adult
yellowish terminal half
to straight culmen
neck collar
yellowish
bill, darker
at base
Yellow-billed
Loon
overall brownish cast
to head and upperparts
breeding
adult
winter
adult
juvenile
pale rear neck with
dark postocular mark
holds
head up
swimming juveniles for comparison
Common
Yellow-billed
Arctic
Pacific
Red-throated

Grebes (Family Podicipedidae)

A worldwide family of aquatic diving birds. Lobed toes make them strong swimmers. Grebes are infrequently seen on land or in flight.

Pied-billed Grebe *Podilymbus podiceps L 13½" (34 cm)*

Breeding adult is brown overall, with black ring around stout, whitish bill; black chin and throat; pale belly. ***Winter*** birds lose bill ring; chin is white, throat tinged with pale rufous. ***Juvenile*** resembles winter adult but throat is much redder, eye ring absent, head and neck streaked with brown and white. First-winter birds lack streaking; throat is duller. A short-necked, big-headed, stocky grebe. In flight, shows almost no white on wing.

Voice: On breeding grounds gives distinctive, loud series of gulping notes.

Range: Nests around marshy ponds and sloughs; sometimes hides from intruders by sinking until only its head shows. Common but not gregarious. Winters on fresh or salt water. Casual to southern Alaska.

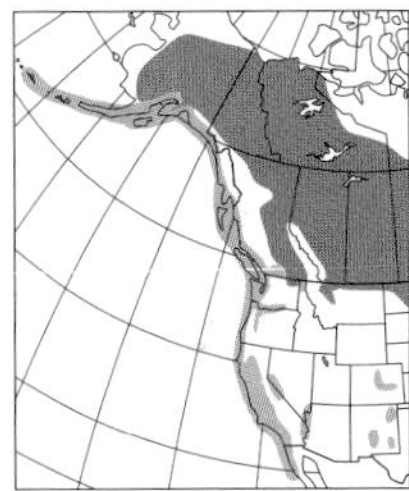

Horned Grebe *Podiceps auritus L 13½" (34 cm)*

Breeding adult has chestnut foreneck, golden "horns." In ***winter*** plumage, white cheeks and throat contrast with dark crown and nape; some are dusky on lower foreneck. Black on nape narrows to a thin stripe. All birds show a pale spot in front of eye. In flight (next page), white secondaries show as patch on trailing edge of wing. Bill is short and straight, thicker than Eared Grebe's and often shows pale tip; neck is thicker too, crown flatter. Most often confused when in transitional plumage in early spring. Smaller size and shorter, dark bill most readily separate winter Horned from Red-necked Grebe.

Voice: Generally silent except on breeding grounds, where it gives descending two-syllable nasal notes. Other notes given in a series in duet.

Range: Breeds on lakes and ponds. Winters mostly on salt water but also a few on ice-free lakes inland. Regular in small numbers in Aleutians; casual to other Bering Sea islands.

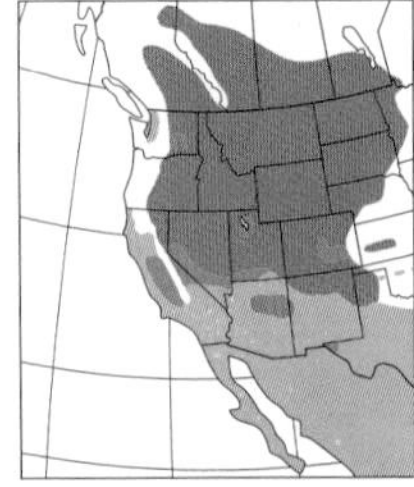

Eared Grebe *Podiceps nigricollis L 12½" (32 cm)*

Breeding adult has blackish neck, golden "ears" fanning out behind eye. In ***winter*** plumage, throat is variably dusky; cheek dark; whitish on chin extends up as a crescent behind eye; compare with Horned Grebe. Note also Eared Grebe's longer, thinner bill; thinner neck; more peaked crown. Lacks pale spot in front of eye. Generally rides higher in the water than Horned, exposing fluffy white undertail coverts. In flight, white secondaries show as white patch on trailing edge of wing.

Voice: Most vocal on the breeding grounds; most frequent is a rising, whistled note.

Range: Nests on freshwater lakes. Huge concentrations of fall migrants may concentrate at several interior sites. Accidental to interior Alaska.

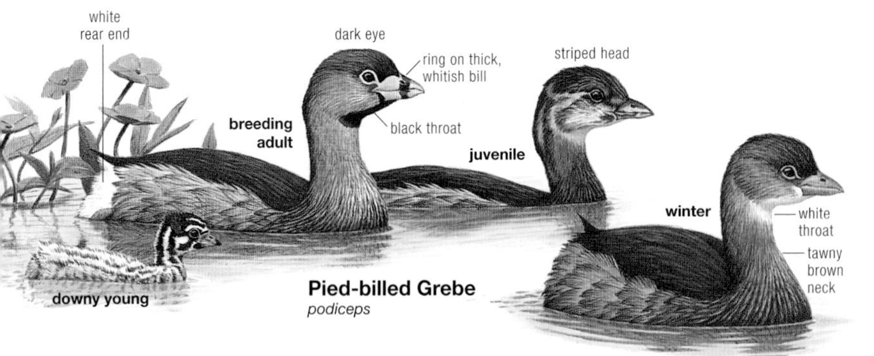

Pied-billed Grebe
podiceps

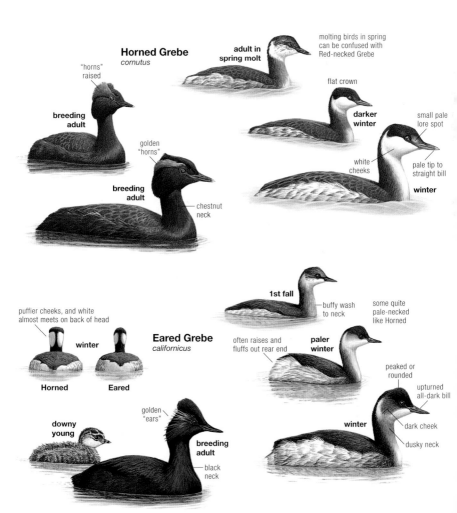

Horned Grebe
cornutus

adult in spring molt

molting birds in spring can be confused with Red-necked Grebe

"horns" raised

breeding adult

flat crown

darker winter

small pale lore spot

golden "horns"

white cheeks

pale tip to straight bill

winter

breeding adult

chestnut neck

1st fall

buffy wash to neck

some quite pale-necked like Horned

puffier cheeks, and white almost meets on back of head

winter

Eared Grebe
californicus

often raises and fluffs out rear end

paler winter

Horned **Eared**

peaked or rounded

upturned all-dark bill

golden "ears"

downy young

winter

dark cheek

breeding adult

dusky neck

black neck

Red-necked Grebe *Podiceps grisegena L 20" (51 cm)*
Large grebe with heavy, tapered, mostly yellowish bill almost as long as the head. ***Breeding adult***'s whitish throat and cheeks contrast with reddish foreneck. In ***winter*** plumage, throat is dusky, white of chin extends onto rear of face in a crescent. ***First-winter*** bird has rounder head, darker bill, paler eye; lacks strong facial crescent. ***Juvenile*** has striped head. In flight, Red-necked Grebe shows a white leading and trailing edge on inner wing; thick neck is often held slouched down. Generally solitary.
Voice: Calls, usually heard only on breeding grounds, include a *crick-crick* note and drawn out braying calls.
Range: Breeds on shallow lakes; winters mostly along coast. Rare in interior south of northern tier of states; rare to very rare over much of the rest of interior West and coastal southern California; casual to Southwest.

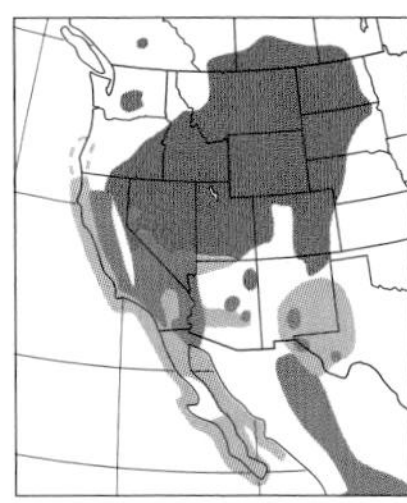

Clark's Grebe *Aechmophorus clarkii L 25" (64 cm)*
Resembles Western Grebe but bill is orange; back and flanks are paler; black cap does not extend to eye in ***breeding*** plumage; ***downy young*** are paler. In ***winter adult,*** lore region acquires more dark color, pattern looks more like Western; best distinction, then, is bill color. In flight, Clark's Grebe's white wing stripe is more extensive than Western. Both species have an elaborate courtship that includes both sexes rising out of the water and rushing forward in almost perfect synchronization. Formerly considered one species with Western; hybrids are sometimes noted, are undoubtedly more frequent than reported.
Voice: Call is a single, two-syllabled, upslurred *kree-eek* note.
Range: Limits of range in both species are not well known; Clark's occupies same general area and habitat as Western but is much less common in northern and eastern part of range.

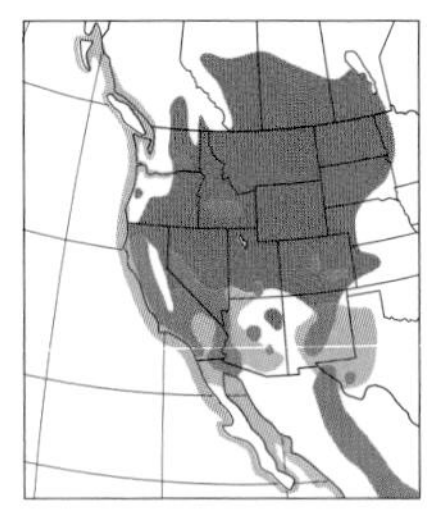

Western Grebe *Aechmophorus occidentalis L 25" (64 cm)*
Large grebe, with striking black-and-white plumage, a long, thin neck, and a long bill. Resembles Clark's Grebe but bill is greenish yellow; black cap extends to include eyes; back and flanks are darker; ***downy young*** are darker. In ***winter adult,*** lore region acquires more whitish color, and pattern can closely resemble winter Clark's. In flight, Western's white wing stripe is less extensive than Clark's. Like Clark's, gregarious. The two species often occur together.
Voice: Call is a loud, two-note *crick-kreek.*
Range: Nests in reeds along broad, freshwater lakes. Winters on seacoasts and sheltered bays and large inland bodies of water. Occupies same general range and habitat as Clark's but greatly predominates in northern and eastern part of range. Casual north to the Yukon.

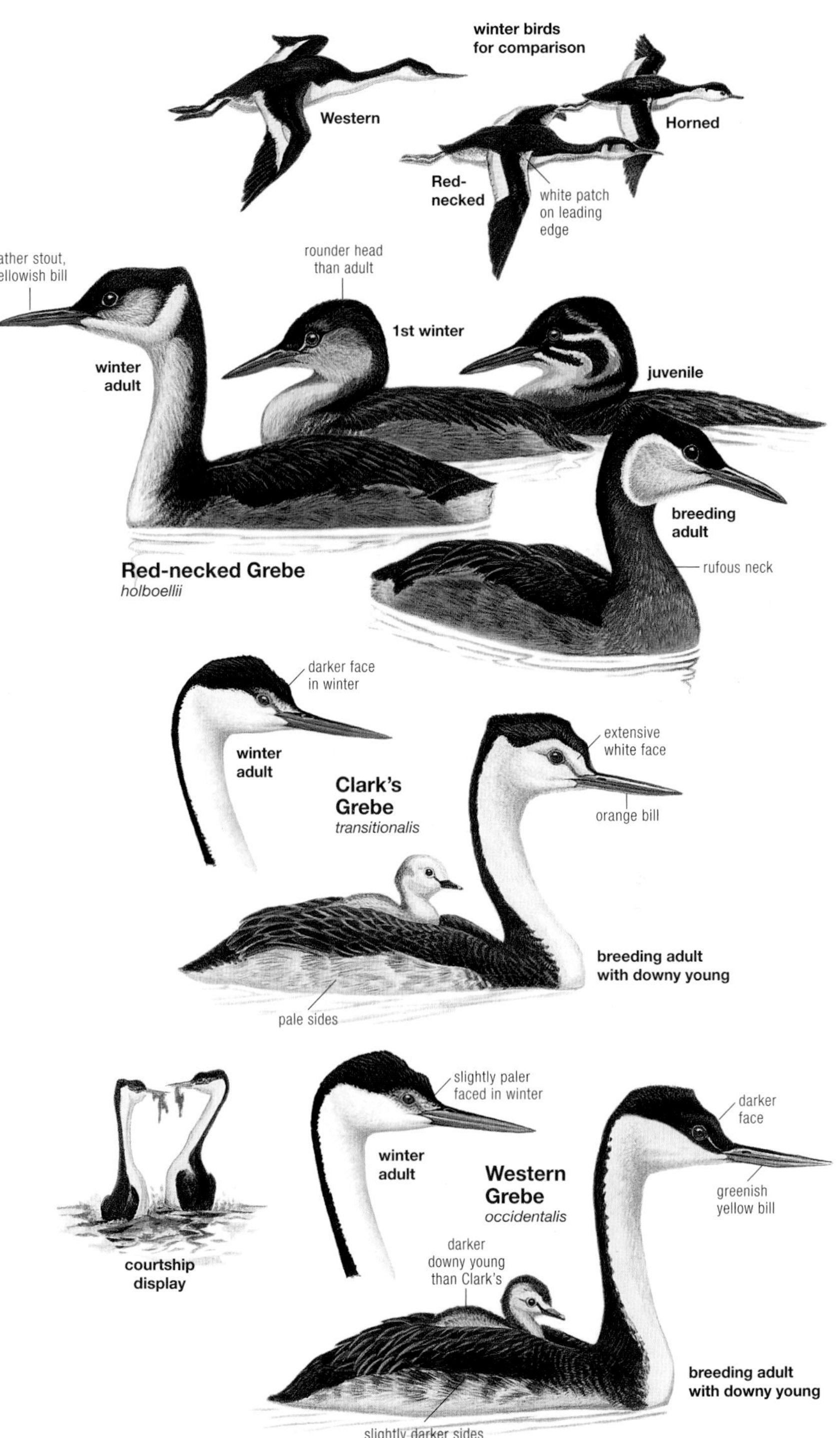

winter birds
for comparison
Western
Horned
Red-
necked
white patch
on leading
edge
rather stout,
yellowish bill
rounder head
than adult
1st winter
juvenile
winter
adult
breeding
adult
rufous neck
Red-necked Grebe
holboellii
darker face
in winter
winter
adult
extensive
white face
Clark's
Grebe
transitionalis
orange bill
breeding adult
with downy young
pale sides
slightly paler
faced in winter
darker
face
courtship
display
winter
adult
Western
Grebe
occidentalis
greenish
yellow bill
darker
downy young
than Clark's
breeding adult
with downy young
slightly darker sides

Albatrosses (Family Diomedeidae)

Gliding on extremely long narrow wings, these largest of seabirds spend most of their lives at sea, alighting on the water when becalmed or when feeding on squid, fish, and refuse. Pelagic; most species nest in colonies on oceanic islands; pairs mate for life. Largely silent at sea. A number of species, especially those in Southern Hemisphere, are threatened by long-line fishing.

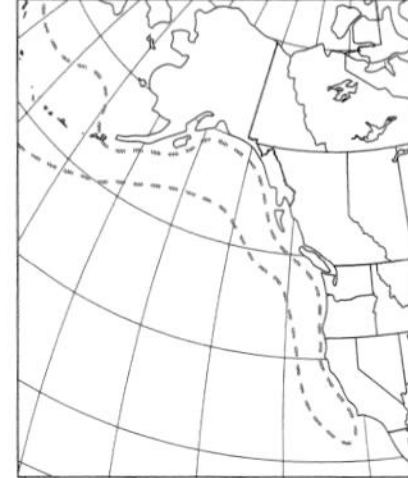

Short-tailed Albatross *Phoebastria albatrus* E

L 36" (91 cm) WS 85-91" (215-230 cm) Large size, but best field mark is the long and massive pink bill (initially dark on very young juveniles) with pale bluish tip. Dark humerals and pale feet distinctive in post-juvenal plumages. ***Adult*** is mostly white, with golden wash on head. ***Juvenile*** is blackish brown, except for traces of white below and behind eye and on chin. Older juvenile has more white around bill; compare with Black-footed Albatross. ***Subadult*** shows white forehead and face, dark cap; acquires white patches on scapulars and inner secondary coverts; with age becomes progressively white, but retains dark hindneck. Full adult plumage takes more than a decade to acquire, but can breed in subadult plumages.

Range: Common until end of 19th century, then decimated, and on verge of extinction by 1930s. Very small numbers of breeders reappeared on Torishima Island, beginning in 1951. Now protected and population slowly recovering—global population believed to number about 2,000. Presently breeds on Torishima (most) and Minami-kojima Islands off southern Japan. Still very rare to rare, but sightings are increasing in North Pacific off North America from central Bering Sea to California. The great majority of these sightings are of juveniles and subadults.

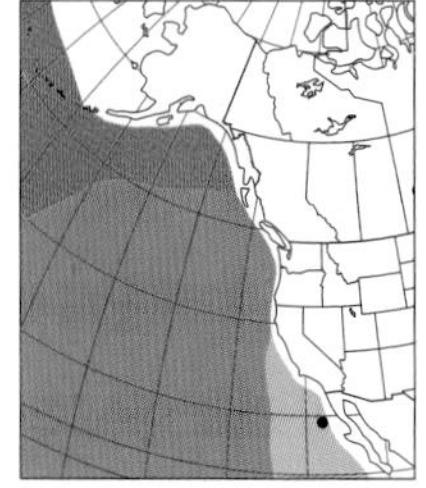

Laysan Albatross *Phoebastria immutabilis*

L 32" (81 cm) WS 77-80" (195-203 cm) Back, upperwing blackish brown, except for white flash in primaries; underwings with black margins and variable internal markings. Note blurry dark mark surrounding eye; pinkish bill. Adults and juveniles similar. Occasionally hybridizes with Black-footed Albatross.

Range: Most numerous spring through early fall off Alaska; rare to uncommon off West Coast from late fall through spring. Casual inland in winter and spring; most records from southeastern California in spring; accidental from southwestern Arizona. Breeds mainly on Hawaiian Islands; small colonies recently established in the Revillagigedo Archipelago and Isla Guadalupe, Mexico.

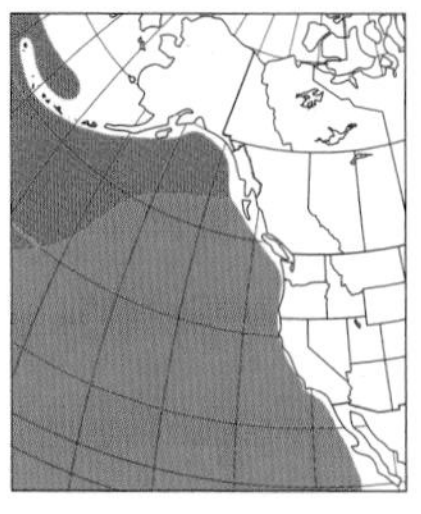

Black-footed Albatross *Phoebastria nigripes*

L 32" (81 cm) WS 80" (203 cm) Mostly dark in all plumages. White area around bill is more extensive on ***old*** birds; reduced or absent on immatures. Most birds of all ages have dark undertail coverts. Some ***adults*** have white undertail coverts, and white may extend onto belly; these can be confused with subadult Short-tailed, but lack white upperwing patches, have thinner, shorter, darker bills.

Range: Seen year-round off West Coast; most common in spring and summer. Breeds mainly on Hawaiian Islands; declining.

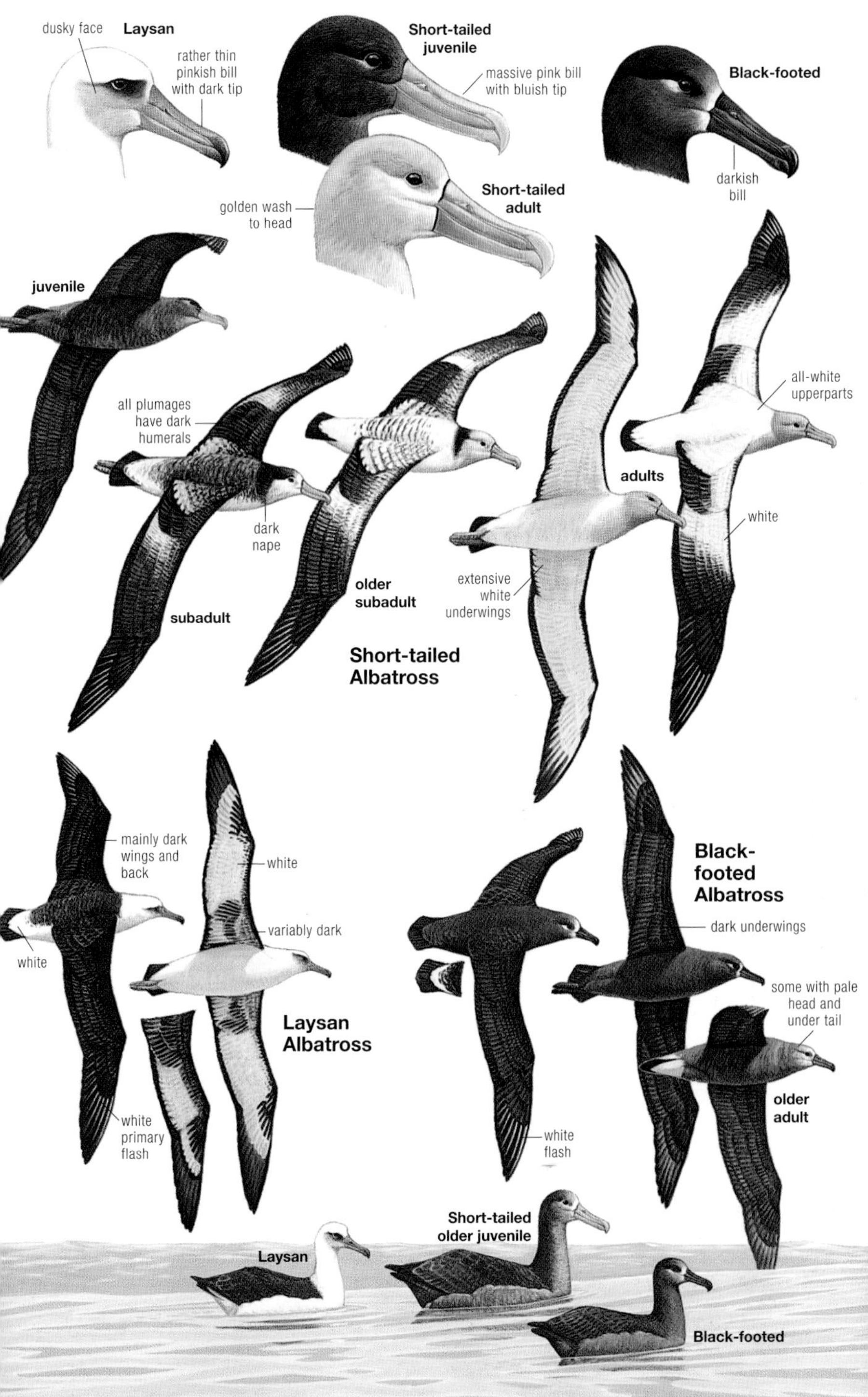
dusky face
Laysan
rather thin pinkish bill with dark tip
Short-tailed juvenile
massive pink bill with bluish tip
Black-footed
darkish bill
golden wash to head
Short-tailed adult
juvenile
all plumages have dark humerals
dark nape
subadult
older subadult
adults
all-white upperparts
white
extensive white underwings
Short-tailed Albatross
mainly dark wings and back
white
white
variably dark
Laysan Albatross
white primary flash
Black-footed Albatross
dark underwings
some with pale head and under tail
older adult
white flash
Short-tailed older juvenile
Laysan
Black-footed

Shearwaters, Petrels (Family Procellariidae)

These pelagic seabirds, rarely seen from shore, fly with rapid wingbeats and stiff-winged glides. Their bills have nostril tubes. Most species are generally silent at sea.

Murphy's Petrel *Pterodroma ultima*

L 16" (41 cm) WS 38" (97 cm) Dark brownish gray color with faint dark M-pattern on back, wedge-shaped tail, and white underwing flash; white most conspicuous below bill; legs and feet pink. Compare to dark-morph Northern Fulmar. The similar but larger Solander's Petrel (*P. solandri*), reported off California and Washington (no accepted records) and well documented in Russia west of Attu Island, has heavier bill with equal or more white above bill than below; prominent dark primary covert tips.

Range: Breeds on remote central South Pacific islands. Uncommon spring visitor off California coast; recorded at least north to Washington.

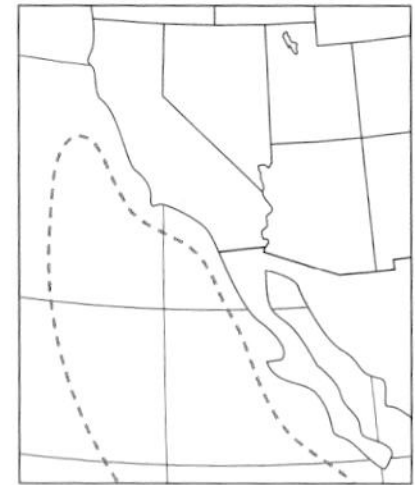

Cook's Petrel *Pterodroma cookii*

L 10 ¾" (27 cm) WS 26" (66 cm) This and Stejneger's (page 414) considered part of the *Cookilaria* petrel subgenus. They are smaller and more acrobatic than the larger *Pterodroma* petrels. All show a dark M across the dorsal surface. Cook's has long wings and rather short tail. Grayish above with blackish eye patch. Note mainly white underwings and dark M across upperwings. White on outer tail feathers and dark tip to central tail feathers can be hard to see.

Range: Breeds on islands off New Zealand. Found well off California coast from spring through late fall, where it is the most numerous *Pterodroma* petrel. Casual off Aleutians and on the Salton Sea in summer.

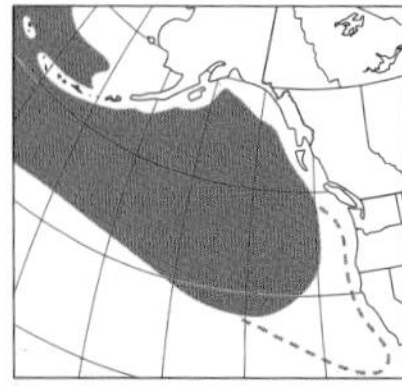

Mottled Petrel *Pterodroma inexpectata*

L 14" (36 cm) WS 32" (81 cm) White throat, breast, and vent contrast with rest of mostly gray underparts. Shows prominent black bar on otherwise white underwings; dark M across upperwings.

Range: Breeds on islands off New Zealand. Regular well off southern Alaska and Aleutians in summer and fall; rare and irregular well off the West Coast, chiefly in late fall.

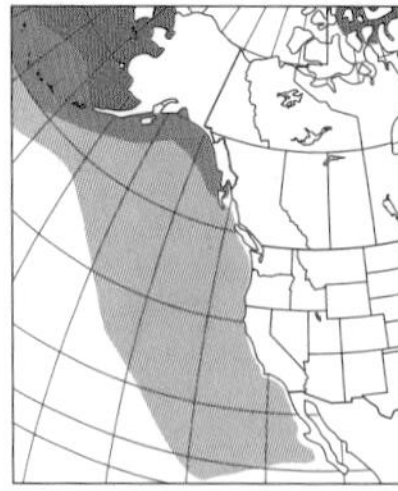

Northern Fulmar *Fulmarus glacialis*

L 19" (48 cm) WS 42" (107 cm) ***Light morphs*** predominate in Bering Sea; ***dark morphs*** farther south; both winter off West Coast. Pacific subspecies (*rodgersii*) has a more slender bill; shows greater variation in color morphs (darker dark morphs and paler lights), and darker tail contrasts with rump. ***Intermediates*** of all shades are frequent. Distinguished from gulls by short, thick bill with nostril tubes and shearwater-like flight; from shearwaters by thick, yellow bill, stockier shape, and rounder wings.

Range: Common and increasing. Within winter range, numbers fluctuate annually; some nonbreeders oversummer.

silver
primary flash
dark primary
coverts
forehead
mostly dark
white chin
Murphy's
Petrel
dark
M-pattern
above
extensive
white
underwing
Cook's
Petrel
gray
dark tip
white outer
tail feather
Mottled
Petrel
dark
M-pattern
above
extensive
gray belly
thick
black
bar
intermediate
morph
Northern
Fulmar
rodgersii
white flash on
inner primaries
light
morph
Pacific birds have dark
tails that contrast with
paler rump
dark
morph
uniformly
dark
light
morph
variable, some
individuals even paler
light
morph

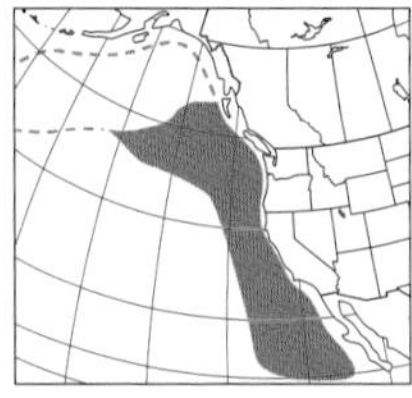

Flesh-footed Shearwater *Puffinus carneipes*

L 17" (43 cm) WS 41" (104 cm) Dark above and below except for pale flight feathers, distinctive pale pink base of bill. Compare especially with Sooty Shearwater, which has whitish wing linings, all-dark bill, less languid flight.

Range: Breeds on islands off Australia and New Zealand. Winters (our summer) in North Pacific; rare off West Coast.

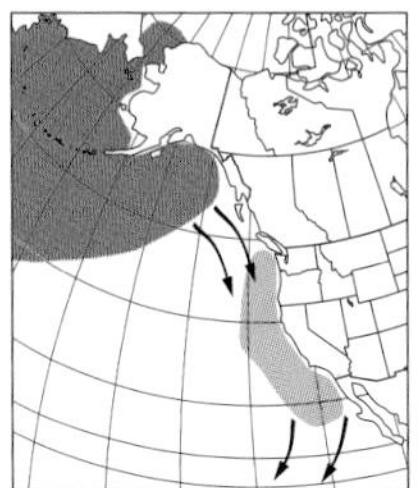

Short-tailed Shearwater *Puffinus tenuirostris*

L 17" (43 cm) WS 39" (99 cm) Plumage variable. Usually dark overall, but often with pale wing linings like Sooty Shearwater; white is more evenly distributed, when present, forming a panel. Has shorter bill than Sooty, slightly steeper forehead, more rounded crown. Some birds, unlike Sooty, have pale throat and dark-capped appearance.

Range: Breeds in Australia. Winters (during our summer) in North Pacific to Alaska, especially west of Kodiak Island, west through the Aleutians and Bering Sea. Seen along West Coast from British Columbia to California during southward migration in fall and winter.

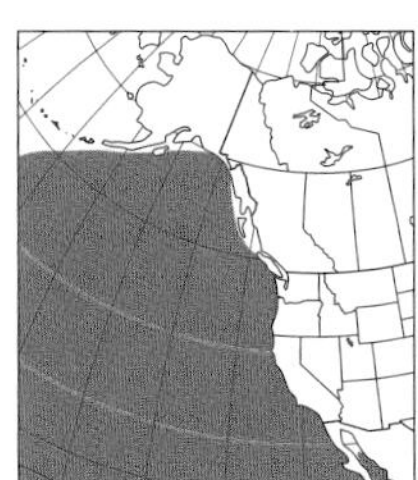

Sooty Shearwater *Puffinus griseus*

L 18" (46 cm) WS 40" (101 cm) Whitish underwing coverts contrast with overall dark plumage. Flies with fast wingbeats and, except when it is windy, short glides. Almost identical to Short-tailed Shearwater. White on underwings usually most prominent on primary coverts.

Range: Breeds in Southern Hemisphere. Abundant off West Coast, often seen from shore in large numbers between late spring and early fall. Small numbers present in winter. Accidental inland to southeastern California and southwestern Arizona.

IDENTIFYING: Sooty and Short-tailed Shearwaters These two abundant, medium-sized dark shearwaters present a real identification challenge in the Pacific. Their plumage is similar, and most of the traits used to separate them are subjective. Key field marks are the shape and coloration of the head and bill, and the underwing pattern.

Short-tailed is a smaller bird overall, and its bill is shorter and more slender. Sooty's longer bill is thicker at the base and tip (with a "pinched in" center) and has a more prominent nail. Short-tailed, which sometimes has a dark cap, often appears paler throated and rounder headed.

On Short-tailed, the underwing averages darker than Sooty, but there is much individual variation. Any bird with completely dark or smoky underwings is a strong candidate for Short-tailed. On birds with paler underwings, check the location of the pale feathers. On Sooty, the underwing primary coverts are usually the palest area of the underwing; on Short-tailed the primary coverts are dusky and the palest area is closer to the body on the secondary coverts. These details can be difficult to determine in various lighting conditions, and in such cases, it may be best to identify an individual by evaluating photographs. Flight styles are variable, but some believe that Short-tailed has a more buoyant flight style.

Short-tailed is abundant in its summer range in Alaska—at least west of Kodiak Island, and including the waters off the Aleutians and the entire Bering Sea. Small numbers are found in fall and winter off the West Coast. Sooty is abundant off the West Coast in spring and summer and common north to and including the Kodiak Island region.

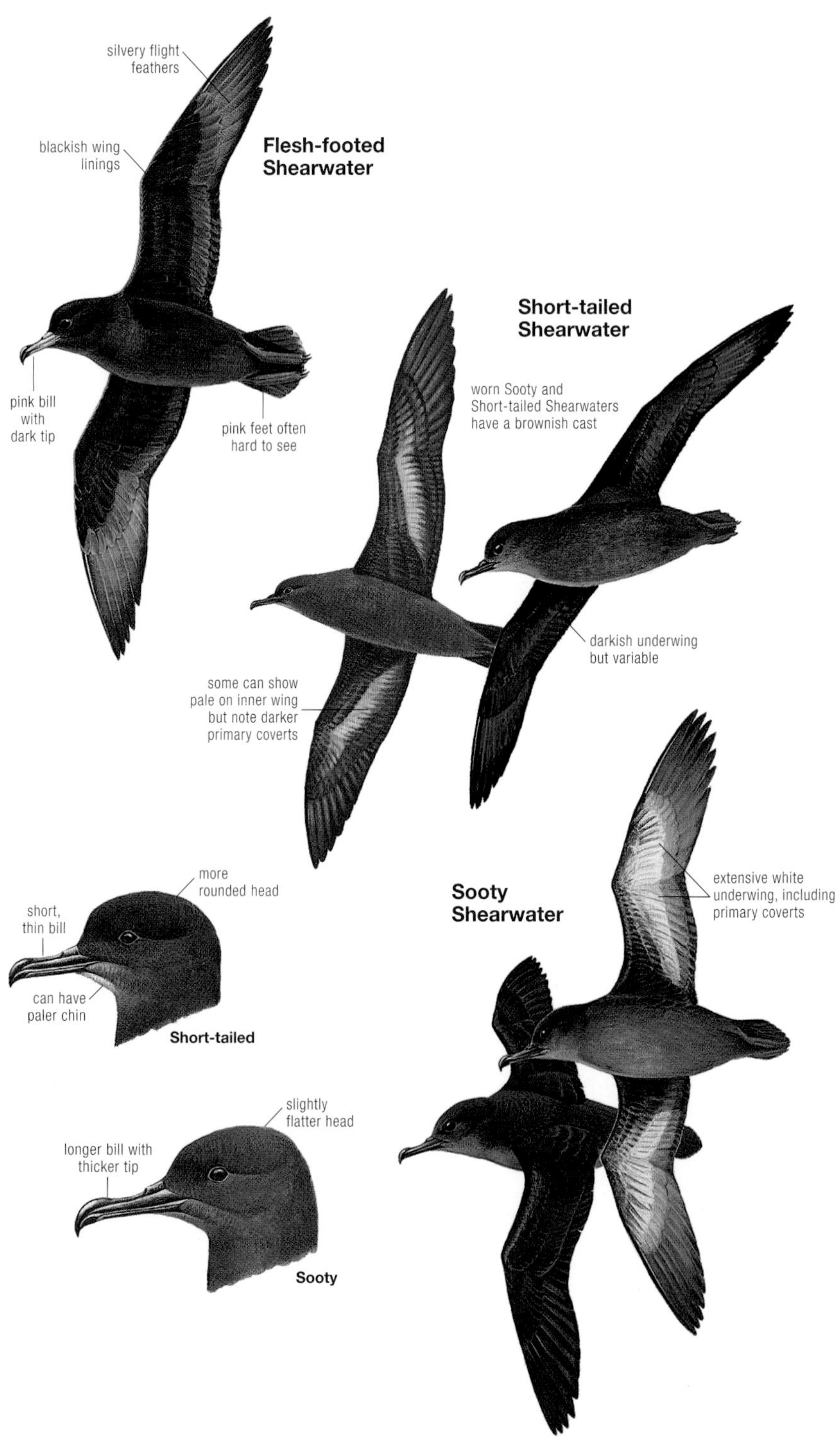
silvery flight feathers
blackish wing linings
Flesh-footed Shearwater
pink bill with dark tip
pink feet often hard to see
Short-tailed Shearwater
worn Sooty and Short-tailed Shearwaters have a brownish cast
darkish underwing but variable
some can show pale on inner wing but note darker primary coverts
more rounded head
short, thin bill
can have paler chin
Short-tailed
Sooty Shearwater
extensive white underwing, including primary coverts
slightly flatter head
longer bill with thicker tip
Sooty

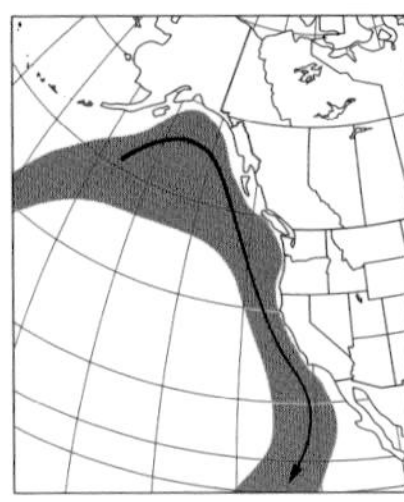

Buller's Shearwater *Puffinus bulleri*

L 16" (41 cm) WS 40" (102 cm) Gleaming white below, including wing linings. Gray above, with a darker cap and a long, dark, wedge-shaped tail. Dark bar across leading edge of upperwing extends across back, forming a distinct M. Flight is graceful, buoyant, with long periods of gliding.

Range: Breeds on islands off New Zealand. Irregular off West Coast during southward migration in late summer and fall. Most common from Washington to central California; rarer north (regular off southern Alaska) and south. Accidental inland at north end of Salton Sea on 6 Aug. 1966.

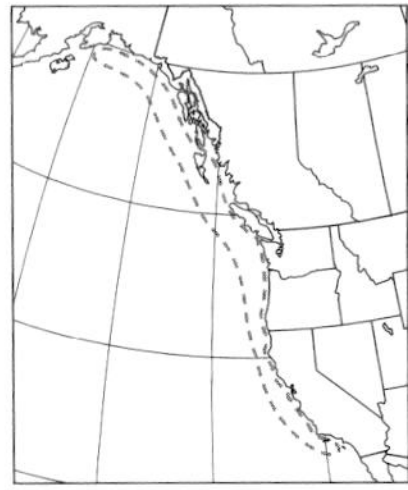

Manx Shearwater *Puffinus puffinus*

L 13½" (34 cm) WS 33" (84 cm) Blackish above, white below with white wing linings. Compared to Black-vented, Manx is darker above and much cleaner white below, including pure white undertail coverts; it has the pale wrapping around the dark ear coverts; and its flight is more buoyant.

Range: Most breed on islands around United Kingdom. Winter off eastern South America. Rare, mostly in summer and fall off West Coast north to Alaska and nesting may yet be proven on an offshore island or islet.

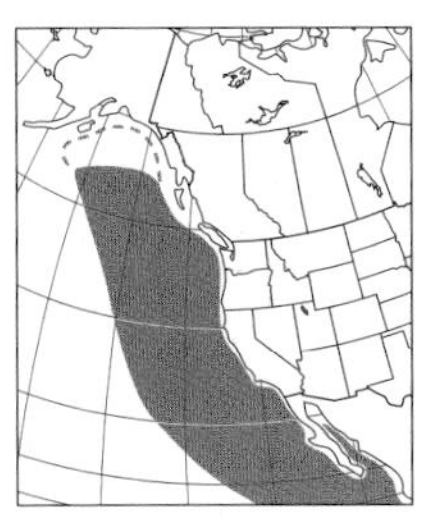

Pink-footed Shearwater *Puffinus creatopus*

L 19" (48 cm) WS 43" (109 cm) Uniformly blackish brown above; white wing linings and underparts are variably mottled (sight records of much darker birds than illustrated); pink bill and feet distinctive at close range. Flies with slower wingbeats and more soaring than Sooty Shearwater (previous page). Spring birds of this and other Southern Hemisphere species may be in heavy ***molt,*** often resulting in whitish wing bars and odd wing shape.

Range: Breeds on islands off Chile; winters (our summer) in the northern Pacific. Common from spring through fall; rare throughout the rest of the year. Rare off southeast Alaska.

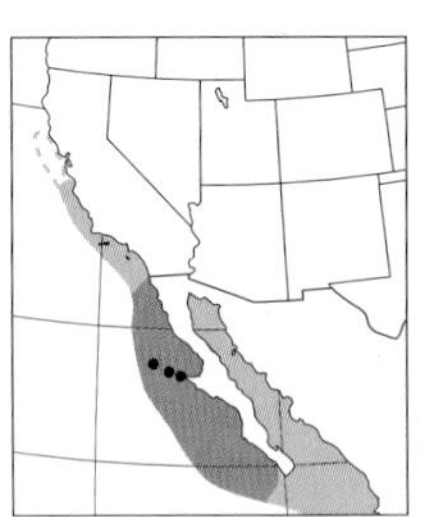

Black-vented Shearwater *Puffinus opisthomelas*

L 14" (36 cm) WS 34" (86 cm) Dark brown above, white below, with dark undertail coverts. Variable dusky mottling on sides of breast, often extending across entire breast.

Range: Seen primarily off the coast of California from Aug. to May. Black-vented is an inshore species and is often visible from shore in large flocks; much rarer well out to sea. Nests chiefly on islands off Mexico's Baja peninsula. Strictly casual north of central California to southwestern British Columbia. Formerly considered a subspecies of the Atlantic species Manx Shearwater, which is rare.

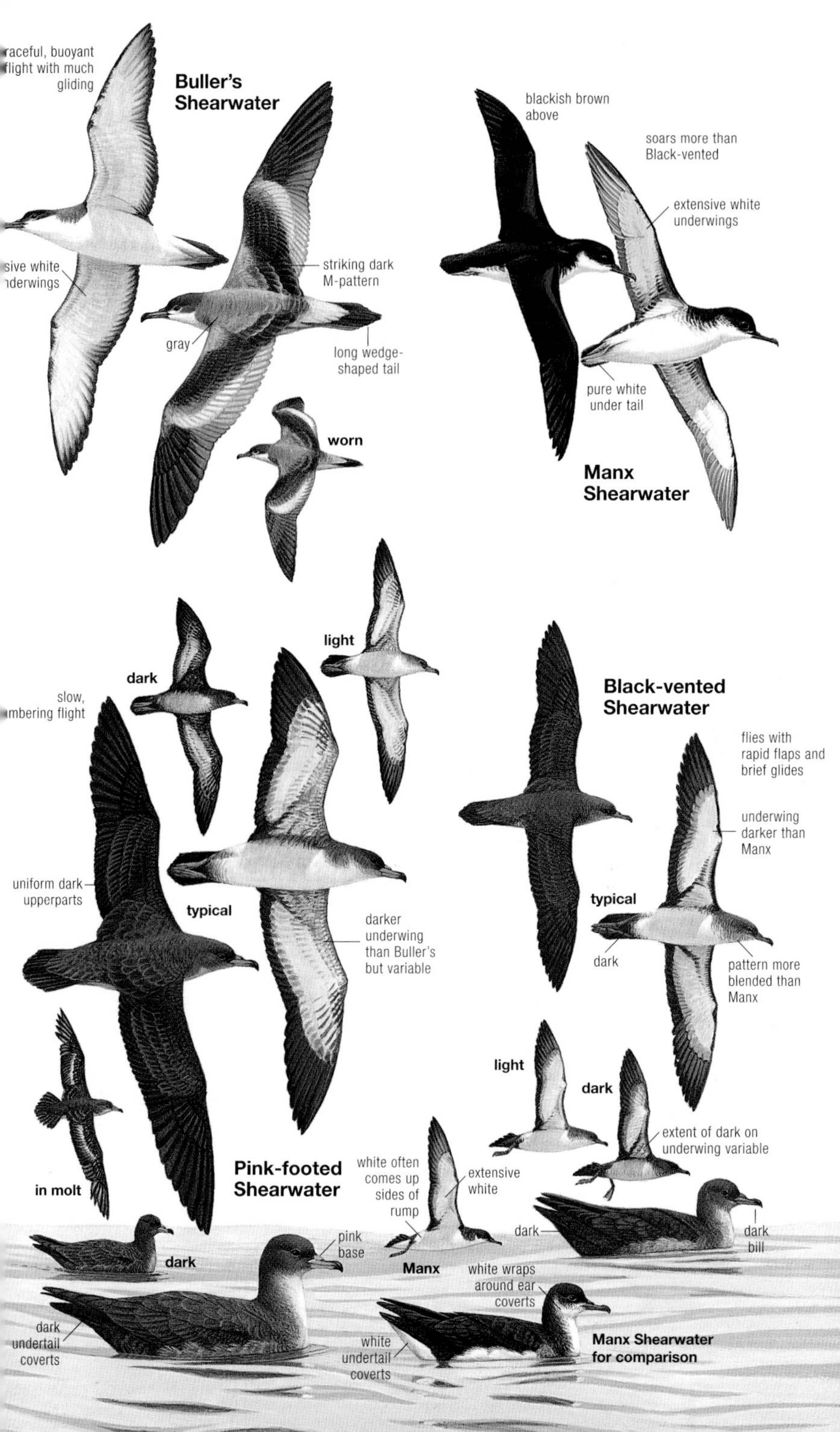
raceful, buoyant
flight with much
gliding
Buller's
Shearwater
sive white
nderwings
striking dark
M-pattern
gray
long wedge-
shaped tail
worn
blackish brown
above
soars more than
Black-vented
extensive white
underwings
pure white
under tail
Manx
Shearwater
light
dark
slow,
mbering flight
Black-vented
Shearwater
flies with
rapid flaps and
brief glides
underwing
darker than
Manx
uniform dark
upperparts
typical
darker
underwing
than Buller's
but variable
typical
dark
pattern more
blended than
Manx
light
dark
extent of dark on
underwing variable
in molt
Pink-footed
Shearwater
white often
comes up
sides of
rump
extensive
white
dark
dark
bill
dark
pink
base
Manx
white wraps
around ear
coverts
dark
undertail
coverts
white
undertail
coverts
Manx Shearwater
for comparison

Storm-Petrels (Family Hydrobatidae)

These small seabirds hover close to the water, pattering across water to pluck up small fish and plankton. Some species follow ships. Identification is often difficult. Flight behavior helps to distinguish the various species but can vary deceptively depending on weather. Silent at sea.

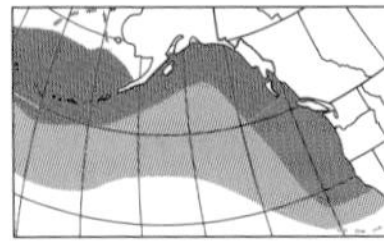

Fork-tailed Storm-Petrel *Oceanodroma furcata*
L 8½" (22 cm) WS 18" (46 cm) Distinctively bluish gray above, pearl gray below. Note also dark eye patch and wing linings.
Range: Rare off southern California.

Wilson's Storm-Petrel *Oceanites oceanicus*
L 7¼" (18 cm) WS 16" (41 cm) Flies with shallow, fluttery wingbeats. Short rounded wings; long legs; rounded tail. Often hovers to feed, pattering its yellow-webbed feet on the water. Bold white rump band extends onto undertail coverts.
Range: Rare off California (fall); casual off Washington.

Leach's Storm-Petrel *Oceanodroma leucorhoa*
L 8" (20 cm) WS 18" (46 cm) Distinctive erratic flight, with deep strokes of long, pointed wings. In close view, note dusky line dividing white rump band on most birds. No white is visible on flanks of sitting bird. Brown overall, with pale wing stripes and forked tail. Amount of white on rump varies geographically; a few birds seen off southern California have dark rumps.
Range: Fairly common well off Pacific coast; casual on Salton Sea.

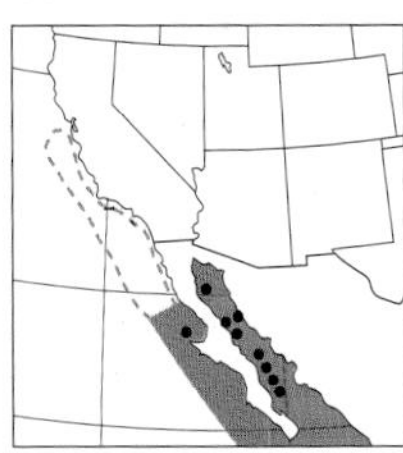

Least Storm-Petrel *Oceanodroma microsoma*
L 5¾" (15 cm) WS 15" (38 cm) Our smallest storm-petrel; deep wingbeats suggestive of the much larger Black Storm-Petrel. Blackish brown overall. Short tailed; appears almost tailless in flight; often confused with molting Ashy Storm-Petrels.
Range: Irregular; off southern California in late summer and fall; in peak years, a few to central California; casual to interior Southwest.

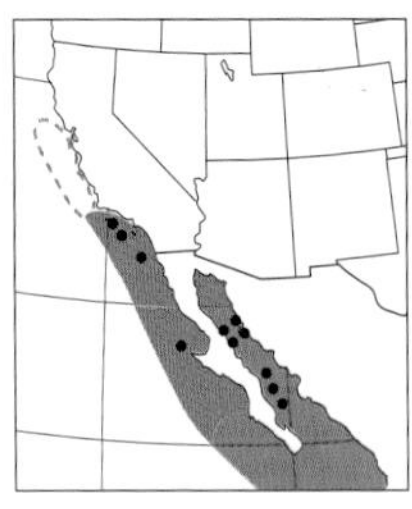

Black Storm-Petrel *Oceanodroma melania*
L 9" (23 cm) WS 19" (48 cm) Large and blackish brown overall with pale bar on upperwing. Slow, deep wingbeats and larger size distinguish Black from paler Ashy and from dark-rumped individuals of Leach's.
Range: Breeds off Baja California and in Gulf of California; small colony in vicinity of Santa Barbara Island. Fairly common off southern California from late spring; by late summer north to Monterey Bay. Casual inland.

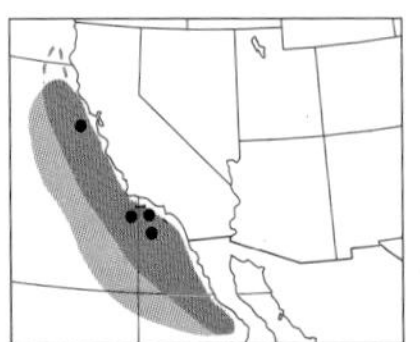

Ashy Storm-Petrel *Oceanodroma homochroa*
L 8" (20 cm) WS 17" (43 cm) Distinguished from larger Black Storm-Petrel by rapid, shallow wingbeats and overall paler, grayer appearance and longer tail.
Range: Fairly common most of the year; rare in winter. Breeds on islands off central and southern California.

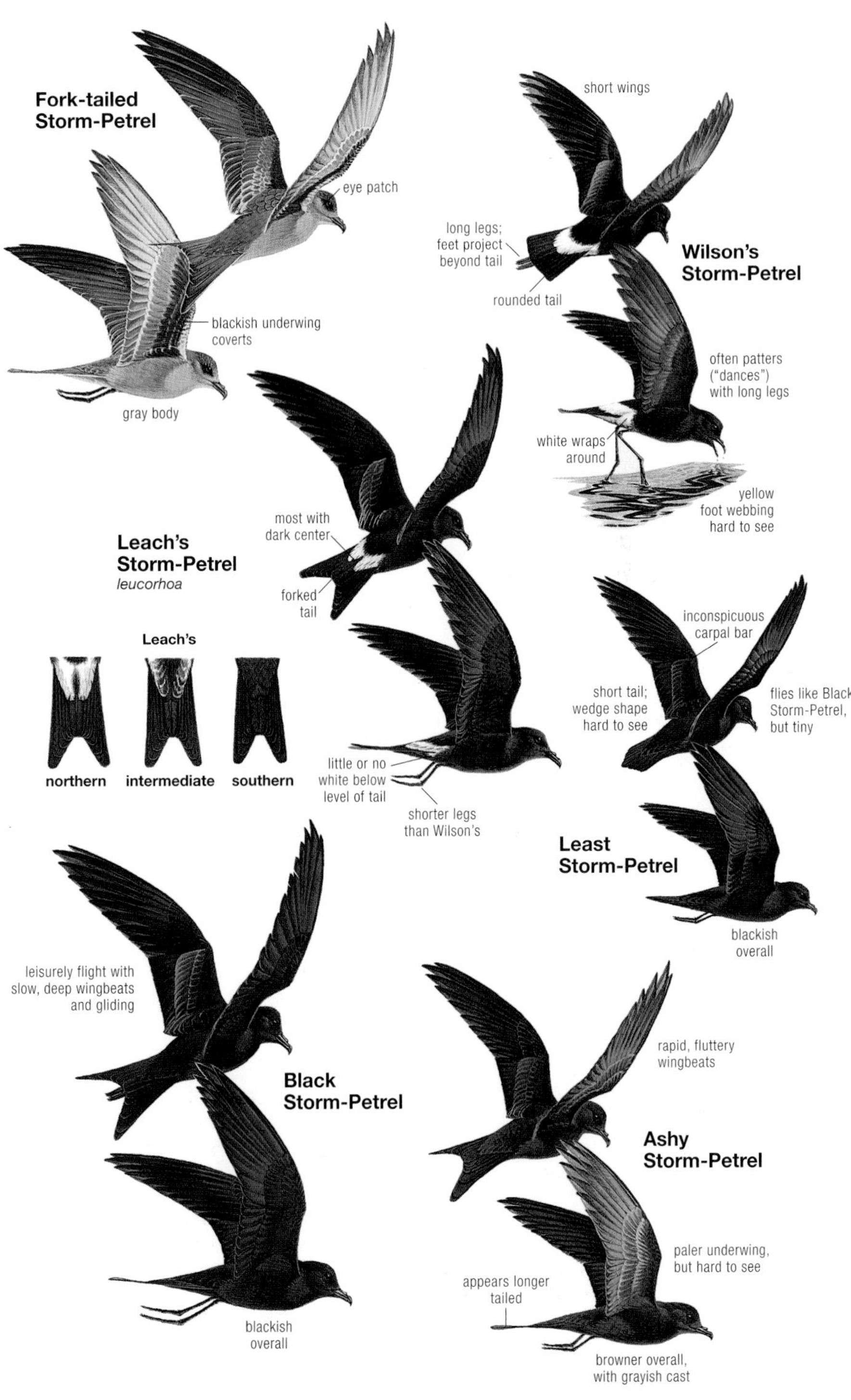

Fork-tailed Storm-Petrel
eye patch
blackish underwing coverts
gray body
short wings
long legs; feet project beyond tail
rounded tail
Wilson's Storm-Petrel
often patters ("dances") with long legs
white wraps around
yellow foot webbing hard to see
most with dark center
Leach's Storm-Petrel
leucorhoa
forked tail
Leach's
northern
intermediate
southern
little or no white below level of tail
shorter legs than Wilson's
inconspicuous carpal bar
short tail; wedge shape hard to see
flies like Black Storm-Petrel, but tiny
Least Storm-Petrel
blackish overall
leisurely flight with slow, deep wingbeats and gliding
Black Storm-Petrel
blackish overall
rapid, fluttery wingbeats
Ashy Storm-Petrel
paler underwing, but hard to see
appears longer tailed
browner overall, with grayish cast

Frigatebirds (Family Fregatidae)

These large, dark seabirds have the longest wingspan, in proportion to weight, of all birds. Silent at sea.

Magnificent Frigatebird *Fregata magnificens*

L 40" (102 cm) WS 90" (229 cm) Long, forked tail; long, narrow wings. ***Male*** is glossy black; orange-red throat pouch becomes bright red when inflated in courtship display. ***Female*** is blackish brown, with white at center of underparts. ***Juveniles*** show varying amount of white on head and underparts; require four to six years to reach adult plumage. Frigatebirds skim the sea, snatching up food from surface; also harass other birds in flight, forcing them to disgorge food.

Range: Very rare at Salton Sea and north along California coast, casual farther north, mostly in summer; many fewer records in recent decades.

Tropicbirds (Family Phaethontidae)

Long central tail feathers identify adults. Usually seen far out at sea, where they are mostly silent.

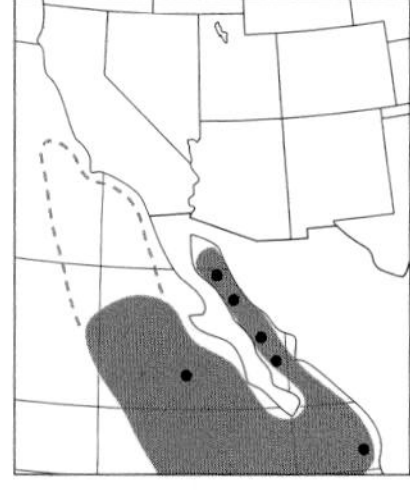

Red-billed Tropicbird *Phaethon aethereus*

L 40" (102 cm) WS 44" (112 cm) Tropical species. Flies with rapid, stiff, shallow wingbeats, unlike other tropicbirds, whose flight is more ternlike. ***Adult*** has red bill, black primaries and primary coverts, barring on back and wings, white tail streamers. ***Juvenile*** has black collar; lacks streamers; tail tipped with black; barring on upperparts finer than other young tropicbirds. Also bill is yellowish but soon becomes orange-red.

Range: Rare well off southern California coast chiefly in late summer and early fall. Accidental in southeast California.

Boobies, Gannets (Family Sulidae)

High-diving seabirds that plunge into water. Gregarious, nesting in colonies on small islands. The rest of the year, gannets roost at sea, boobies primarily on land. Mostly silent at sea.

Masked Booby *Sula dactylatra*

L 32" (81 cm) WS 62" (158 cm) Proportionately, the shortest tailed booby. ***Adult*** distinctive with yellow bill and extensive black facial skin; black tail; and solid black trailing edge to wing. On ***juvenile,*** note more white on underwing than all plumages of Blue-footed and Brown Booby, with contrasting dark median primary coverts and most with pale collar. ***Subadult*** has paler head and broader collar; note yellow on bill. See also Nazca Booby (page 416), which is similar in all plumages but is still not definitely recorded for U.S. waters.

Range: Very rare or casual to coastal and offshore California.

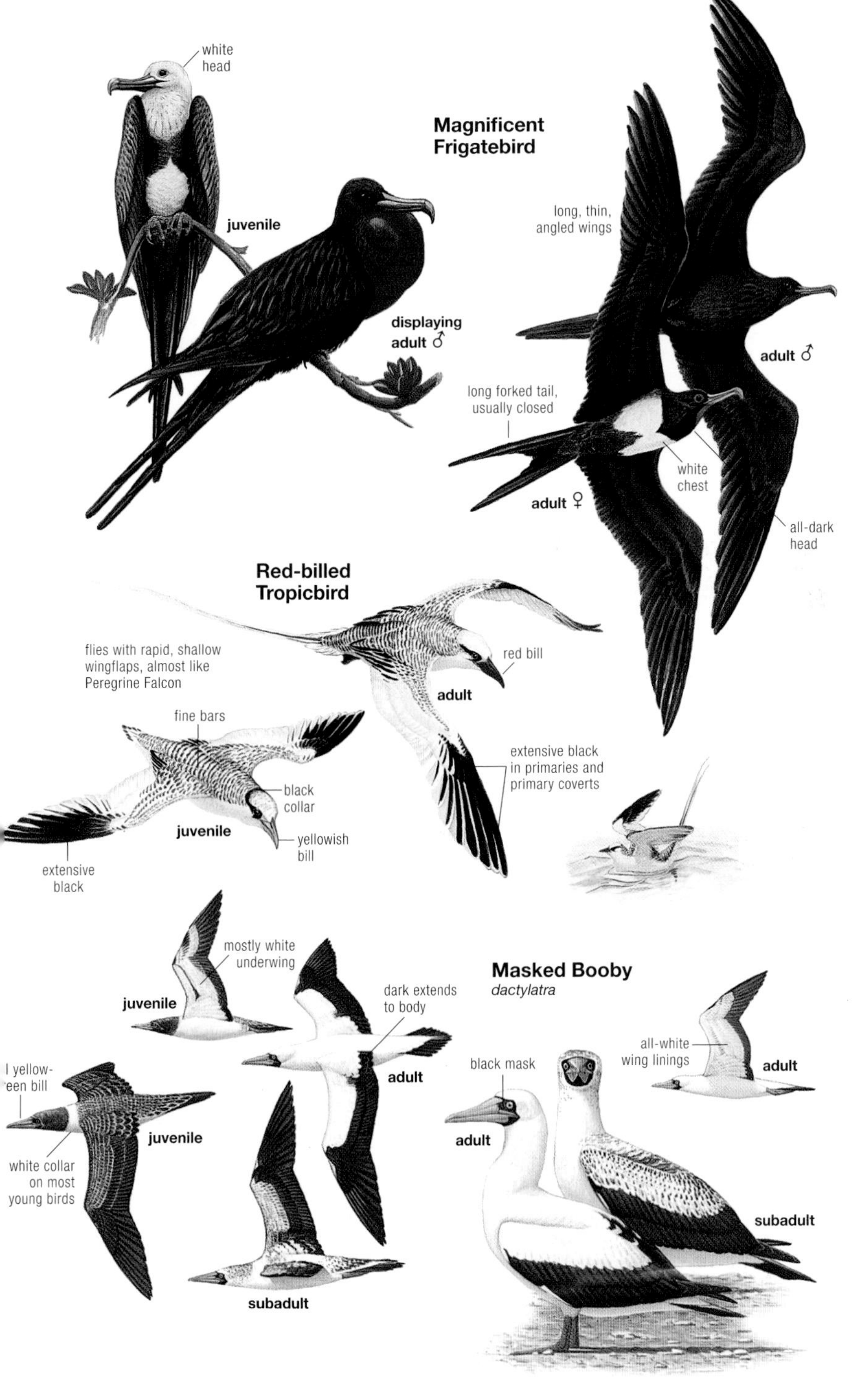

white head
Magnificent Frigatebird
juvenile
displaying adult ♂
long, thin, angled wings
adult ♂
long forked tail, usually closed
white chest
adult ♀
all-dark head
Red-billed Tropicbird
flies with rapid, shallow wingflaps, almost like Peregrine Falcon
red bill
adult
fine bars
extensive black in primaries and primary coverts
black collar
juvenile
yellowish bill
extensive black
mostly white underwing
Masked Booby
dactylatra
juvenile
dark extends to body
all-white wing linings
black mask
adult
adult
adult
juvenile
white collar on most young birds
subadult
subadult

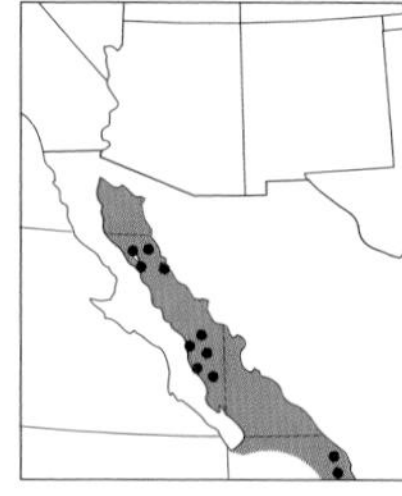

Blue-footed Booby *Sula nebouxii*

L 32" (81 cm) WS 62" (158 cm) Feet bright blue in adults, darker in young; long, attenuated bill is dark bluish gray. ***Adult*** has streaked head, whitish patches on upper back and uppertail coverts. Note also white-fringed scapulars and pale iris. ***Juvenile*** has darker head and neck; compare with immature Masked Booby, which has an even darker neck and usually a pale contrasting collar; note also pale dorsal patches, all-dark underwing primary coverts and the darker and differently shaped bill.

Range: Breeds on islands in Gulf of California. Very rare and irregular to inland California and southwestern Arizona in late summer and fall (most to Salton Sea). Casual to California coast; accidental to Washington. Absent in U.S. most years; formerly occurred somewhat more regularly.

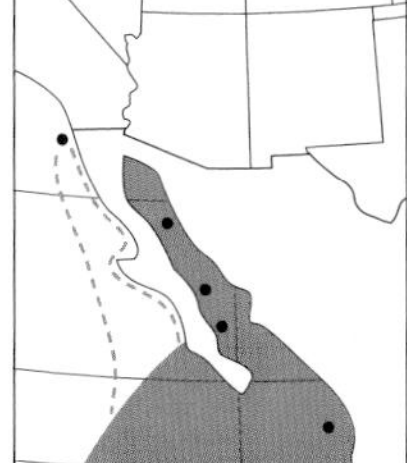

Brown Booby *Sula leucogaster*

L 30" (76 cm) WS 57" (145 cm) West Mexican race is *brewsteri.* ***Adult male*** distinctive with white on head and neck. ***Adult female*** with dark brown head, like adults of other races. Both sexes show sharp contrast with white belly, underwing coverts. Adult female's bill, facial skin (except dark spot in lores), legs, and feet bright yellow; male's soft parts washed with grayish green, throat bluish. ***Juveniles*** dark brown, with little or no apparent contrast between breast and belly; underwing muted; legs and feet variably colored, often dusky gray, sometimes yellowish to yellowish flesh. ***Subadults*** show white on belly and sharp line of contrast with darker neck.

Range: Widespread breeder in western Mexico with isolated population off northern Baja California on Islas Coronados. Rare, but increasing, along coast of San Diego County. Very rare along remainder of California coast. Casual north to Washington and to the interior Southwest; most records are for the Salton Sea.

Red-footed Booby *Sula sula*

L 28" (71 cm) WS 60" (152 cm) Tropical species. Smallest booby, with rounded head. All ***adults*** show bright coral red feet, and blue and pink at base of bill. Four principal morphs occur: ***brown morph, white-tailed brown morph, white morph,*** and ***black-tailed white morph;*** note that white morphs have black primaries, secondaries, scapulars, and underwing median primary coverts. The adult Masked Booby has black lower scapulars, a black mask, white underwing primary coverts, and a yellow bill. All ***juveniles*** and ***subadults*** are brownish overall, sometimes with a grayish cast, with darker chest band, with mainly dark underwings and flesh pink legs and feet. Separate with care from juvenile Brown Booby, which is a darker chocolate brown color and lacks any pink on the bill base; note also the flatter head shape of Brown Booby. Subadult Red-faced has a brighter, pinkish-based bill.

Range: Breeds on Hawaiian Islands (*rubipes*) and off western Mexico (*websteri*) on Revillagigedo Islands (nearly all white morphs) and Clipperton Island (mostly brown morphs), fewer on Islas Tres Marias and Isla Isabel. Casual on and off the California coast. Some 15 records, through 2003, mostly late spring to late fall.

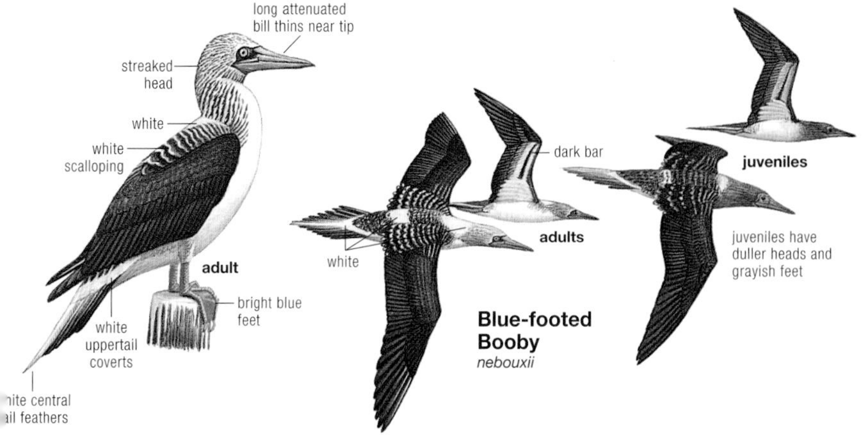

Blue-footed Booby
nebouxii

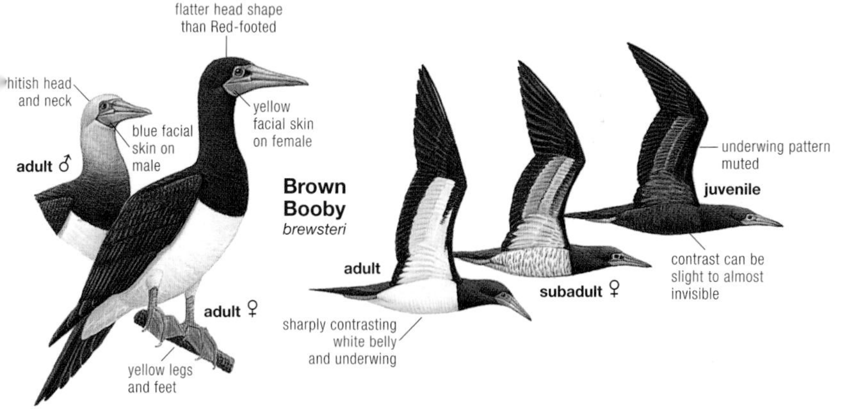

long attenuated bill thins near tip

streaked head

white

white scalloping

adult

bright blue feet

white uppertail coverts

ite central
ail feathers

white

dark bar

adults

juveniles

juveniles have duller heads and grayish feet

Brown Booby
brewsteri

flatter head shape than Red-footed

hitish head and neck

blue facial skin on male

adult ♂

yellow facial skin on female

adult ♀

yellow legs and feet

adult

sharply contrasting white belly and underwing

subadult ♀

underwing pattern muted

juvenile

contrast can be slight to almost invisible

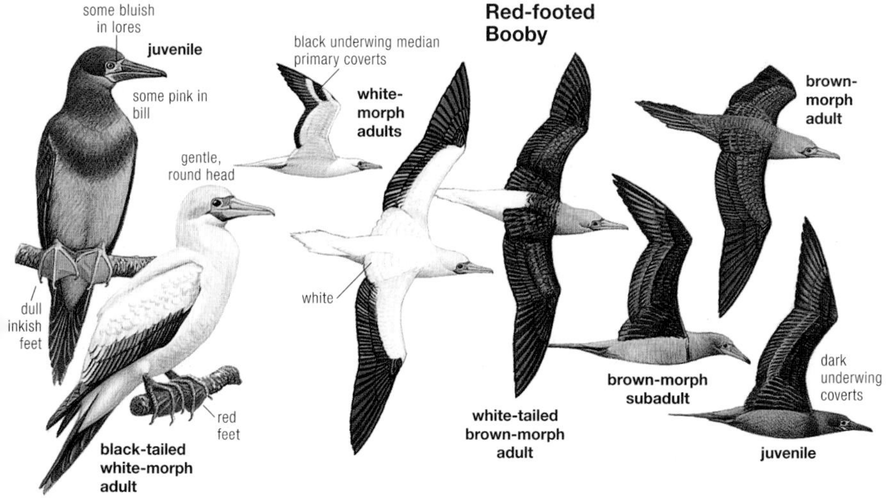

Red-footed Booby

some bluish in lores

juvenile

some pink in bill

dull inkish feet

gentle, round head

red feet

black-tailed white-morph adult

black underwing median primary coverts

white-morph adults

white

white-tailed brown-morph adult

brown-morph adult

brown-morph subadult

dark underwing coverts

juvenile

Pelicans (Family Pelecanidae)

These large, heavy waterbirds have massive bills and huge throat pouches used as dip nets to catch fish. In flight, they hold their heads drawn back. Mostly silent away from breeding grounds.

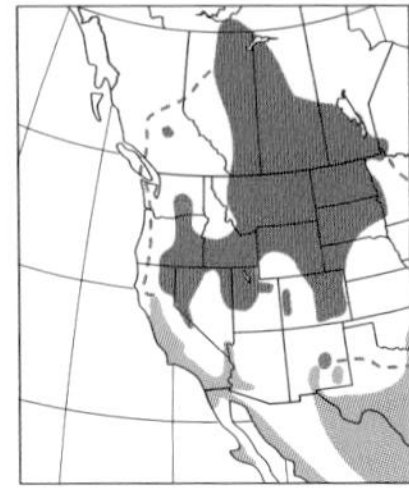

American White Pelican *Pelecanus erythrorhynchos*
L 62" (158 cm) WS 108" (274 cm) White, with black primaries and outer secondaries. ***Breeding adult*** has pale yellow crest; bill is bright orange, usually with a fibrous plate on upper mandible. Plate is shed after eggs are laid; crown and nape become grayish. Juvenile is white with brownish wash on head, neck, and lesser coverts; soft parts more dully colored. White Pelicans do not dive for food but dip their bills into the water while swimming. Usually found in flocks.
Range: Nonbreeding birds are seen in summer throughout area enclosed by dashed line on map. Accidental north to Alaska.

Brown Pelican *Pelecanus occidentalis* **E**
L 48" (122 cm) WS 84" (213 cm) ***Nonbreeding adult*** has white head and neck, often washed with yellow; grayish brown body; blackish belly. In ***breeding*** plumage, hindneck is dark chestnut; yellow patch appears at base of foreneck. On West Coast race, *californicus* (shown here), gular pouch is bright red in breeding plumage. Molt during incubation and ***chick feeding*** produces speckled head and foreneck. Adult eye color is light except during chick feeding, when it darkens. Juvenile is grayish brown above, tipped with pale buff; underparts whitish. ***Immatures*** are browner; acquire adult plumage by third year. Dives from the air after prey, capturing fish in its pouch.
Range: Large numbers annually move north to Salton Sea after breeding; in some years small numbers to Southwest too, where normally very rare. Casual elsewhere in interior West. Rare to southwestern British Columbia, casual to southeast Alaska.

Cormorants (Family Phalacrocoracidae)

Dark birds with set-back legs; long, hooked bill; and colorful bare facial skin and throat pouch. Dive from the surface for fish. May briefly soar; may swim partially submerged. Mostly silent away from breeding grounds.

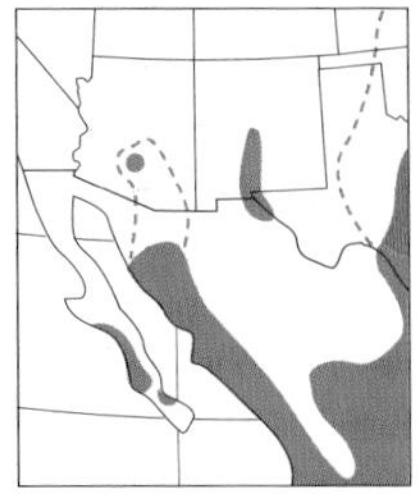

Neotropic Cormorant *Phalacrocorax brasilianus*
L 26" (66 cm) WS 40" (102 cm) Small, long-tailed cormorant with white-bordered, yellow-brown or dull yellow throat pouch that tapers to a sharp point behind bill. ***Breeding adult*** acquires short white plumes on sides of neck. Distinguished from Double-crested (next page) by smaller size, longer tail, and smaller, angled throat pouch that usually does not extend around eye. Neotropic ***juveniles*** overall browner than adults, particularly on underparts.
Range: Found at marshy ponds or shallow inlets near perching stumps, snags. Fairly common along Rio Grande in New Mexico; regular to Arizona; causal to southeastern California, Colorado.

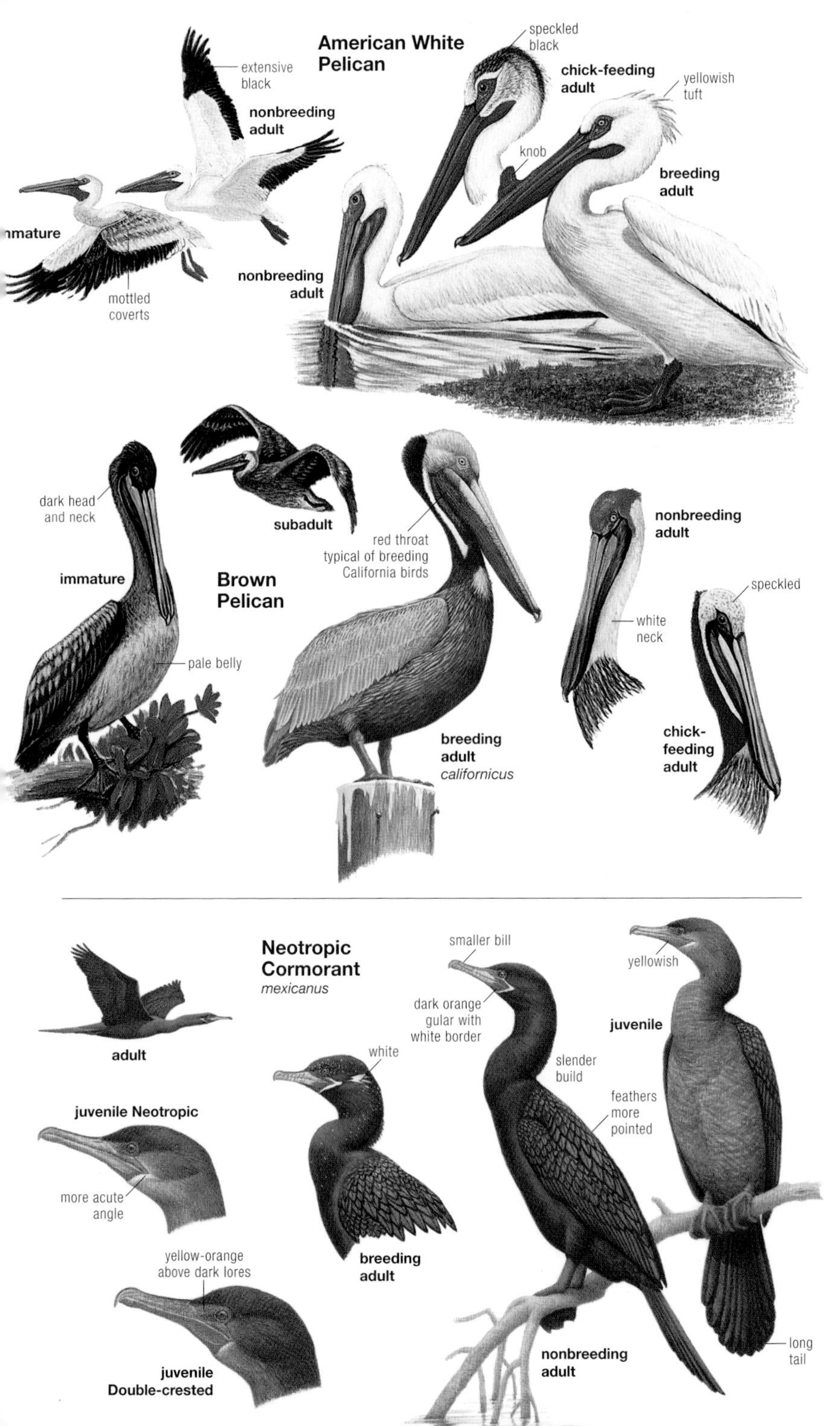
American White Pelican
extensive black
nonbreeding adult
speckled black
chick-feeding adult
yellowish tuft
knob
breeding adult
nmature
mottled coverts
nonbreeding adult
dark head and neck
subadult
immature
Brown Pelican
red throat typical of breeding California birds
nonbreeding adult
speckled
white neck
pale belly
breeding adult californicus
chick-feeding adult
Neotropic Cormorant mexicanus
smaller bill
yellowish
dark orange gular with white border
juvenile
adult
white
slender build
feathers more pointed
juvenile Neotropic
more acute angle
breeding adult
yellow-orange above dark lores
juvenile Double-crested
long tail
nonbreeding adult

Pelagic Cormorant *Phalacrocorax pelagicus*

L 26" (66 cm) WS 39" (99 cm) ***Adult*** is dark and glossy overall; bill dark. Smaller and slenderer than other western cormorants. ***Breeding adult*** has tufts on crown and nape; fine white plumes on sides of neck; white patches on flanks. Distinguished from Red-faced Cormorant by darker and less extensive red facial skin and lack of yellow in bill. ***Juvenile*** uniformly dark brown; closely resembles young Red-faced, but note dark bill and smaller size. Pelagic distinguished in flight from Brandt's by smaller head, slimmer neck, smaller overall size, and disproportionately longer tail. Its bill is thinner and different in color than Red-faced. Less gregarious than other species. Breeds in smaller colonies.

Range: Despite name, rare out over open ocean. Accidental to inland California (Mono County).

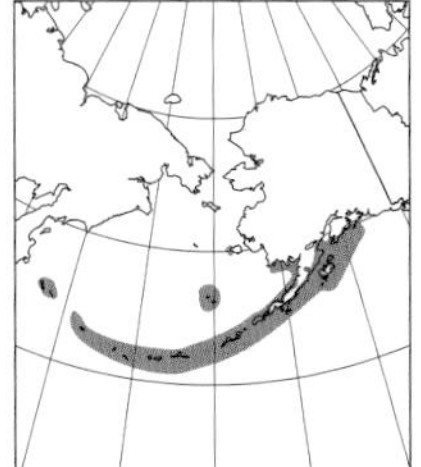

Red-faced Cormorant *Phalacrocorax urile*

L 31" (79 cm) WS 46" (117 cm) Heavier and paler bill distinguishes all ages from Pelagic Cormorant. In ***adult,*** dull brown wings contrast with glossy upperparts; more uniform in Pelagic. Extensive yellow on bill with bluish at base. Facial skin is red and becomes enlarged and brighter in the ***breeding*** season. ***Juvenile*** is uniformly dark brown, with pale yellowish gray bill. More gregarious than Pelagics.

Range: Nests in colonies on the ledges of steep coastal cliffs and on rocky sea islands, alongside gulls, murres, and auklets.

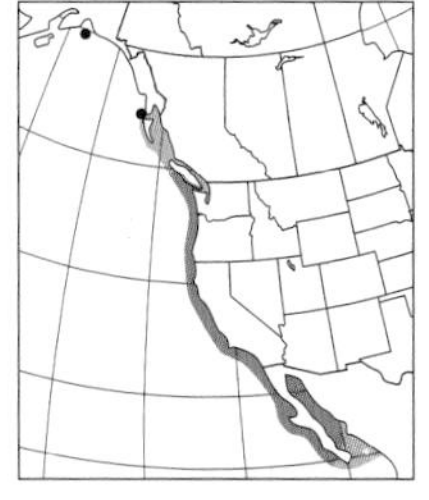

Brandt's Cormorant *Phalacrocorax penicillatus*

L 35" (89 cm) WS 48" (122 cm) A band of pale buffy feathers bordering the throat pouch identifies all ages. Throat pouch becomes bright blue in ***breeding*** plumage; head, neck, and scapulars acquire fine, white plumes. ***Juvenile*** is dark brown above, slightly paler below. In all ages, appears more uniformly dark above than Double-crested Cormorant; wings and tail are shorter. Head and bill are larger than Pelagic Cormorant.

Range: Common and gregarious; often fishes in large flocks; flies in long lines between feeding and roosting grounds. Much more likely to be seen over open ocean than Pelagic Cormorant. Very rare in southeast Alaska. Accidental to inland California.

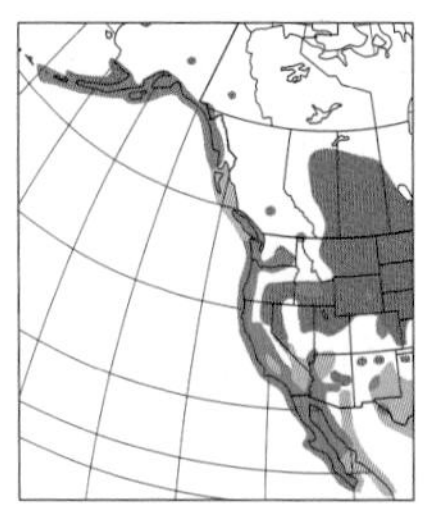

Double-crested Cormorant *Phalacrocorax auritus*

L 32" (81 cm) WS 52" (132 cm) Large, rounded throat pouch is orangish year-round. ***Breeding adult*** has a tuft curving back on either side of its head from behind eyes. Tufts are largely white in western birds. ***Juvenile*** is brown above, variably pale below, but usually palest on upper breast and neck. Immatures sometimes have pouch edged with white, which can cause confusion with Neotropic Cormorant (previous page). Among West Coast cormorants, Double-crested's kinked neck is distinctive in flight; its wings are also longer and more pointed than Brandt's and Pelagic.

Range: Common and widespread; found along coasts, inland lakes, and rivers. Breeding populations in the interior have greatly increased in the last several decades. Nonbreeders regularly found oversummering in winter range.

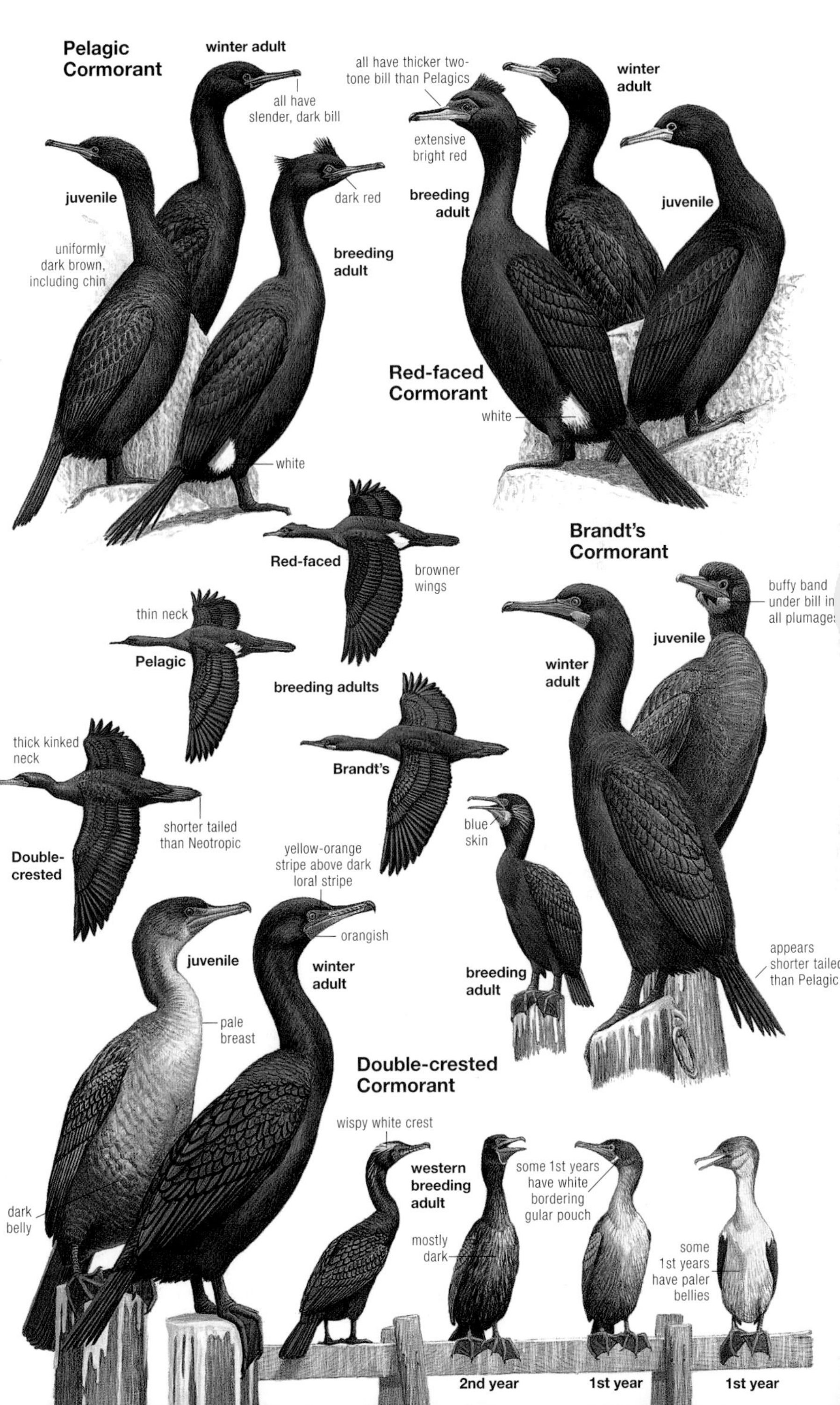
Pelagic Cormorant
winter adult
all have slender, dark bill
juvenile
uniformly dark brown, including chin
dark red
breeding adult
white
all have thicker two-tone bill than Pelagics
extensive bright red
breeding adult
winter adult
juvenile
Red-faced Cormorant
white
Red-faced
browner wings
thin neck
Pelagic
breeding adults
Brandt's
Brandt's Cormorant
buffy band under bill in all plumages
juvenile
winter adult
thick kinked neck
shorter tailed than Neotropic
Double-crested
yellow-orange stripe above dark loral stripe
orangish
blue skin
breeding adult
appears shorter tailed than Pelagic
juvenile
winter adult
pale breast
Double-crested Cormorant
dark belly
wispy white crest
western breeding adult
mostly dark
some 1st years have white bordering gular pouch
some 1st years have paler bellies
2nd year
1st year
1st year

Herons, Bitterns, Allies (Family Ardeidae)

Wading birds; most have long legs, neck, and bill for stalking food in shallow water. Graceful crests and plumes adorn some species in breeding season.

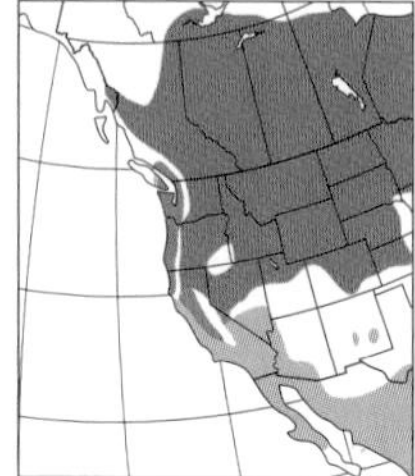

American Bittern *Botaurus lentiginosus*

L 28" (71 cm) WS 42" (107 cm) Mottled brown upperparts and brownish neck streaks. Contrasting dark flight feathers are conspicuous in flight; note also that wings are longer, narrower, and more pointed, not rounded as in night-herons. ***Juvenile*** lacks neck patches. When alarmed, may freeze with bill pointing up.

Voice: Distinctive spring and early summer ***song,*** *oonk-a-lunk,* is most often heard at dusk in dense marsh reeds; also gives a nasal *arrk* call in flight.

Range: Uncommon and declining; casual breeder south of mapped range.

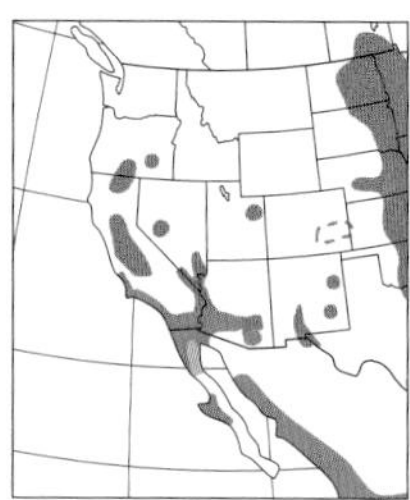

Least Bittern *Ixobrychus exilis L 13" (33 cm) WS 17" (43 cm)*

Buffy inner wing patches identify this small, rather secretive heron as it fleshes briefly from dense marsh cover. When alarmed, it may freeze with bill pointing up. In ***male*** back and crown are black; in ***female*** they are browner. ***Juvenile*** resembles female but has more prominent streaking on back and breast.

Voice: Calls include a series of harsh *kek* notes; song, a softer short series of *ku* notes, is heard only on breeding grounds.

Range: Rare to fairly common. May breed sporadically beyond mapped range. Migrants are rarely detected.

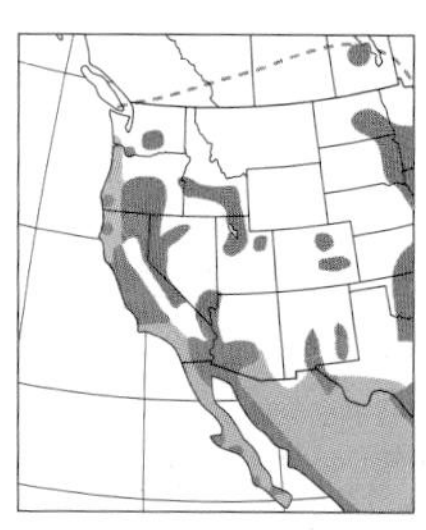

Great Egret *Ardea alba L 39" (99 cm) WS 51" (130 cm)*

Large white heron with heavy yellow bill, blackish legs and feet. In ***breeding*** plumage, long plumes trail from back, extending beyond tail. In immature and ***nonbreeding adult,*** bill and leg colors are duller, plumes absent. Distinguished from most other white herons by large size; from white morph of the larger Great Blue Heron by black legs and feet.

Voice: Occasional deep croaks.

Range: Common in wetlands and wet fields. Partial to open habitats for feeding; stalks prey slowly, methodically. Occasionally breeds far north of usual range. Post-breeding wanderers reach far north of mapped breeding range. Asian *modesta* has reached central and western Aleutians.

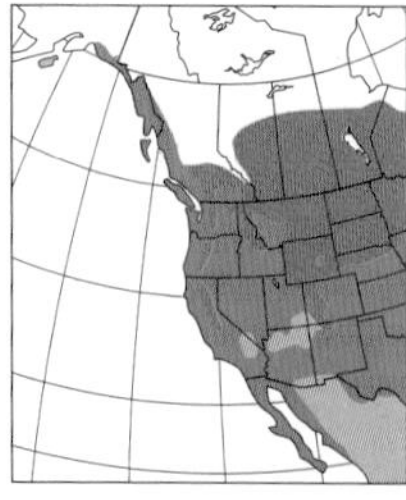

Great Blue Heron *Ardea herodias*

L 46" (117 cm) WS 72" (183 cm) Large, gray-blue heron; black stripe extends above eye; white foreneck is streaked with black. ***Breeding adult*** has yellowish bill and ornate plumes on head, neck, and back. Nonbreeding adult lacks plumes; bill is yellower. ***Juvenile*** has black crown, no plumes.

Voice: Occasional deep croaks.

Range: Common. A few winter far north into breeding range. Wanderers reach well north of mapped range.

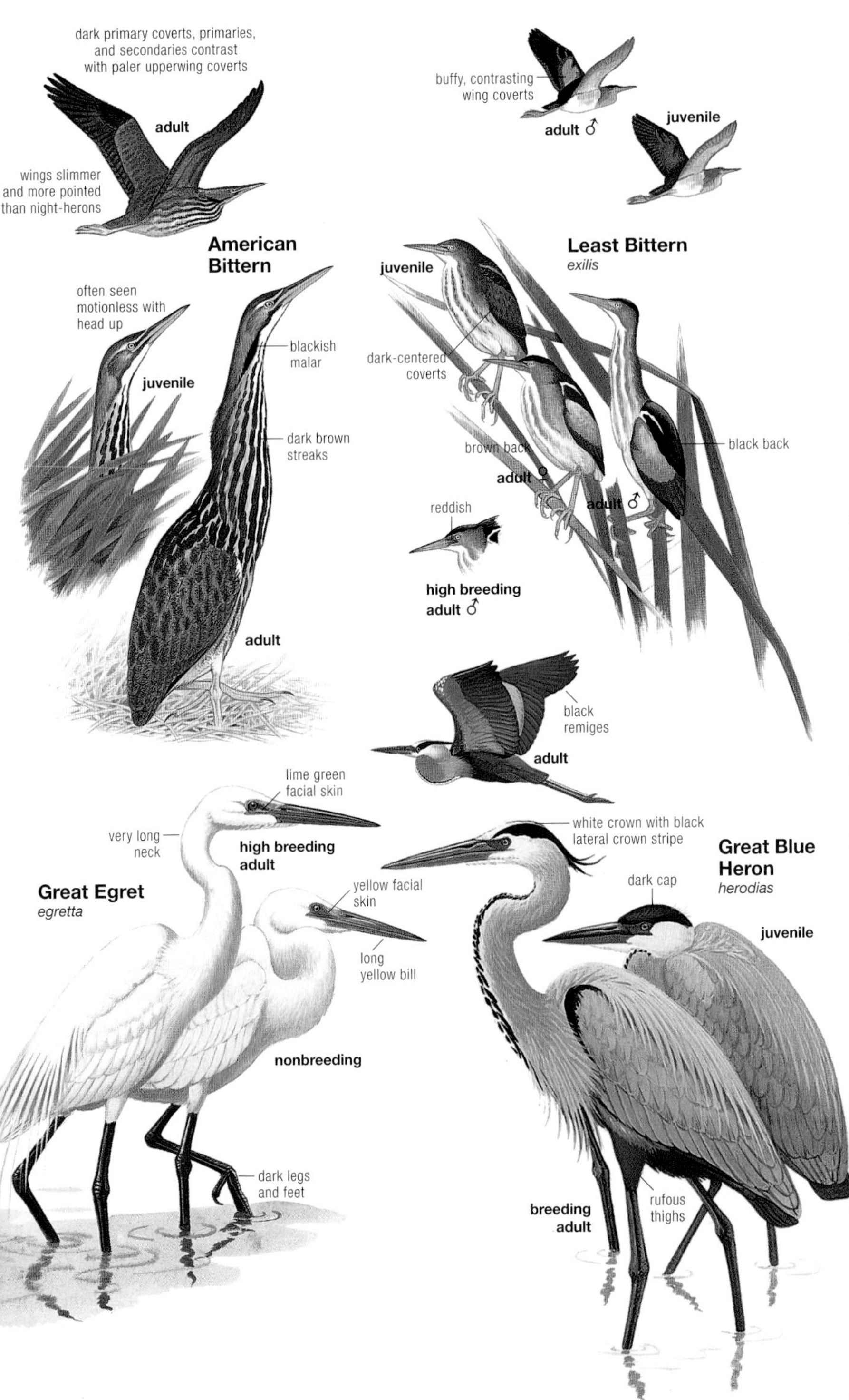
dark primary coverts, primaries, and secondaries contrast with paler upperwing coverts
adult
wings slimmer and more pointed than night-herons
American Bittern
often seen motionless with head up
juvenile
blackish malar
dark brown streaks
adult
buffy, contrasting wing coverts
adult ♂
juvenile
Least Bittern
exilis
juvenile
dark-centered coverts
brown back
adult ♀
adult ♂
black back
reddish
high breeding adult ♂
black remiges
adult
lime green facial skin
very long neck
high breeding adult
Great Egret
egretta
yellow facial skin
long yellow bill
nonbreeding
dark legs and feet
white crown with black lateral crown stripe
Great Blue Heron
herodias
dark cap
juvenile
rufous thighs
breeding adult

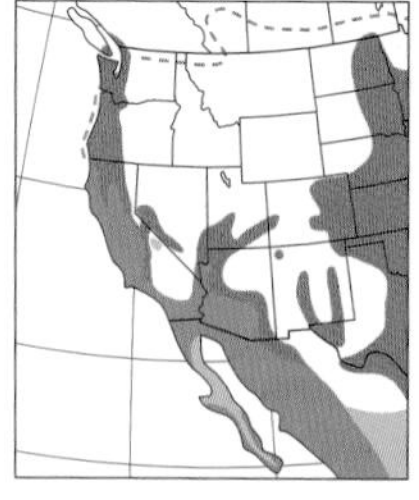

Green Heron *Butorides virescens*

L 18" (46 cm) WS 26" (66 cm) Small, chunky, with short legs. Back and sides of ***adult***'s neck deep chestnut; green on upperparts mixed with blue-gray. Dark crown feathers, sometimes raised to form shaggy crest. ***Juvenile*** browner above; underparts heavily streaked.

Voice: Common call is a loud, sharp *kyowk.*

Range: Fairly common, but usually solitary; found in a variety of habitats, but prefers streams, ponds, and marshes with woodland cover; often perches in trees. A few winter north of resident limit.

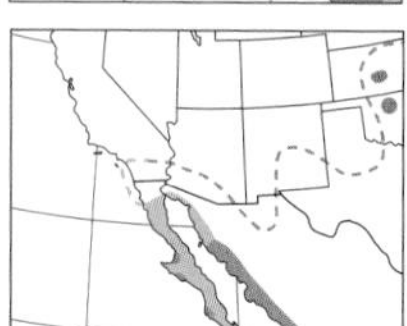

Tricolored Heron *Egretta tricolor*

L 26" (66 cm) WS 36" (91 cm) White belly and foreneck contrast with mainly dark blue upperparts; bill long and slender. ***Juvenile*** has chestnut hindneck and wing coverts.

Range: Rare but regular on southern California coast, chiefly in winter; casual in the Southwest and elsewhere in interior.

Little Blue Heron *Egretta caerulea*

L 24" (61 cm) WS 40" (102 cm) Slate blue overall. During most of the year, plumage, head, and neck are dark purple; legs and feet dull green. In high ***breeding*** plumage, head and neck become reddish purple, legs and feet black. ***Juvenile*** easily confused with immature Snowy Egret; note Little Blue Heron's dull yellow legs and feet; two-toned bill with thicker, gray base and dark tip; mostly grayish lores; and, often, narrow, dusky primary tips. During first spring, juvenile's white plumage begins gradual ***molt*** to adult plumage. Little Blue Herons are slow, methodical feeders in freshwater ponds, lakes, and marshes and coastal saltwater wetlands.

Range: A few breed in coastal San Diego County. Very rare to Southwest. Casual north on the West Coast to southern British Columbia and elsewhere in interior.

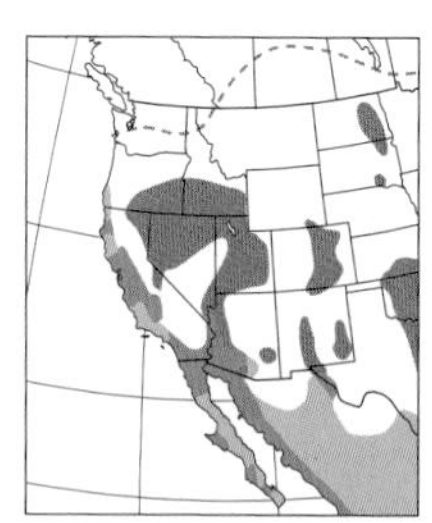

Snowy Egret *Egretta thula L 24" (61 cm) WS 41" (104 cm)*

White with slender black bill, yellow eyes, black legs, bright golden yellow feet. Graceful plumes on head, neck, and back (where they curve upward) are striking in ***breeding adult.*** In ***high breeding*** plumage, lores turn red, feet orange. Nonbreeding plumage similar but plumes shorter; also note yellow on backs of legs. ***Juvenile*** resembles nonbreeding adult, but lacks plumes and shows some bluish gray at base of lower mandible. Active feeders.

Voice: Low, raspy note, mostly at nest site.

Range: Common in wetland habitats. Rare north of mapped range.

Reddish Egret *Egretta rufescens*

L 30" (76 cm) WS 46" (117 cm) Only ***dark morph*** recorded from West. Lurches while feeding, dashing about with wings spread in a canopy. ***Breeding adult*** has shaggy plumes on rufous head, neck. Bill is pink with black tip; legs cobalt blue. Nonbreeding plumage varies, but in general duller, with shorter plumes, dark bill. ***Juvenile*** largely grayish; some pale cinnamon on neck; bill dark.

Range: Rare to coastal southern California and Salton Sea; casual elsewhere in West.

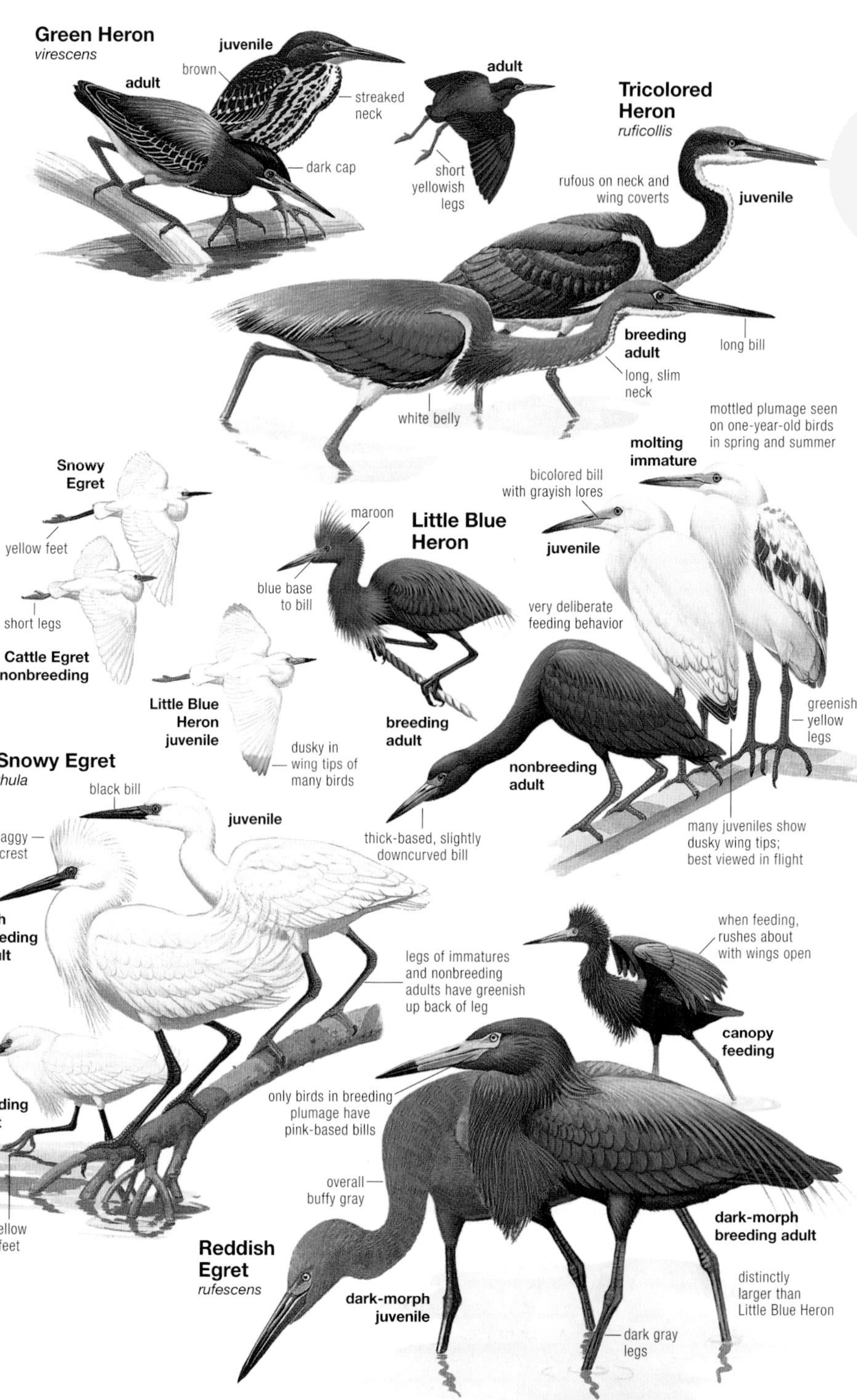
Green Heron
virescens
juvenile
brown
streaked neck
adult
dark cap
adult
short yellowish legs
Tricolored Heron
ruficollis
rufous on neck and wing coverts
juvenile
breeding adult
long bill
long, slim neck
white belly
mottled plumage seen on one-year-old birds in spring and summer
molting immature
bicolored bill with grayish lores
juvenile
Snowy Egret
yellow feet
short legs
Cattle Egret nonbreeding
maroon
Little Blue Heron
blue base to bill
very deliberate feeding behavior
Little Blue Heron juvenile
breeding adult
greenish yellow legs
dusky in wing tips of many birds
Snowy Egret
thula
black bill
juvenile
nonbreeding adult
crest
thick-based, slightly downcurved bill
many juveniles show dusky wing tips; best viewed in flight
when feeding, rushes about with wings open
legs of immatures and nonbreeding adults have greenish up back of leg
canopy feeding
only birds in breeding plumage have pink-based bills
overall buffy gray
feet
dark-morph breeding adult
Reddish Egret
rufescens
distinctly larger than Little Blue Heron
dark-morph juvenile
dark gray legs

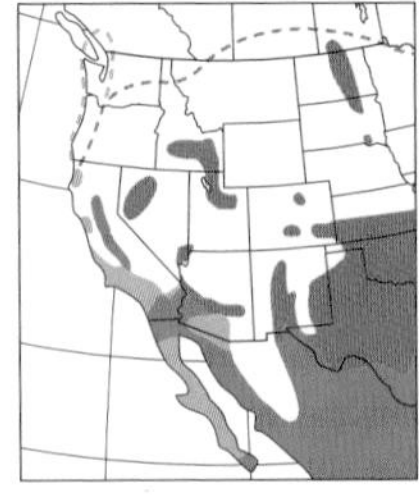

Cattle Egret *Bubulcus ibis L 20" (51 cm) WS 36" (91 cm)*
Old World species. Small, stocky white heron with large, rounded head; note throat feathering extends far out on bill. ***Breeding adult*** is adorned with orange-buff plumes on crown, back, and foreneck. At height of breeding season, bill is red-orange, lores purplish, legs pinkish. Nonbreeding adult has short yellow bill, yellowish legs. Juvenile's bill is black; begins to turn yellow in late summer; resembles nonbreeding adult. Often seen among livestock in fields, feeding on insects. In flight (previous page), resembles Snowy, but Cattle is smaller, with shorter bill and legs and faster wingbeats.
Voice: Mostly silent.
Range: Came to South America from Africa, spread to Florida in the early 1950s, reached California by the mid-1960s. In spring, summer, and especially fall into early winter, wanders well north of breeding range. Casual to southeast Alaska. Larger, longer-necked, cinnamon-headed (in breeding plumage) *coromandus* from Asia is accidental from Agattu, Aleutians (one found dead on 19 June 1988); *coromandus* flies with slower wingbeats than nominate *ibis*.

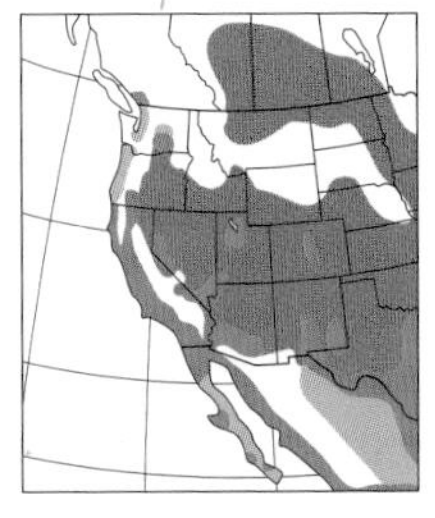

Black-crowned Night-Heron *Nycticorax nycticorax*
L 25" (64 cm) WS 44" (112 cm) Stocky, with short neck and legs. ***Adult*** has black crown and back; white hindneck plumes longest in breeding season. In high breeding plumage, legs turn bright pink. ***Juvenile*** distinguished from young Yellow-crowned by stockier shape, thicker neck, browner upperparts with bolder white spotting; paler, less contrasting face with smaller eyes; longer, thinner bill with mostly pale lower mandible. In flight, legs barely extend past tail. Full adult plumage not acquired until third year. Mainly nocturnal feeder. Typically roosts in trees.
Voice: Calls include a low, harsh *woc,* more guttural than Yellow-crowned Night-Heron.
Range: Fairly common to common. Casual to Alaska, including to the western Aleutians; these individuals likely nominate *nycticorax* from Eurasia.

Yellow-crowned Night-Heron *Nyctanassa violacea*
L 24" (61 cm) WS 42" (107 cm) ***Adult*** has buffy white crown, black face with white cheeks; acquires head plumes in breeding season. ***Juvenile*** distinguished from young Black-crowned Night-Heron by grayer upperparts with less conspicuous white spotting; longer neck; stouter, mostly dark bill (although recently fledged juveniles have some yellow at bill base); and larger eyes. In flight, its legs extend well beyond its tail and it shows darker flight feathers and trailing edge on wings. Overall less stocky than Black-crowned with thinner and more pointed wings. Full adult plumage is acquired in third year.
Voice: Calls include a short *woc,* higher and less harsh than Black-crowned Night-Heron.
Range: A few have been found breeding in the San Diego area. Casual elsewhere on California coast and to Southwest.

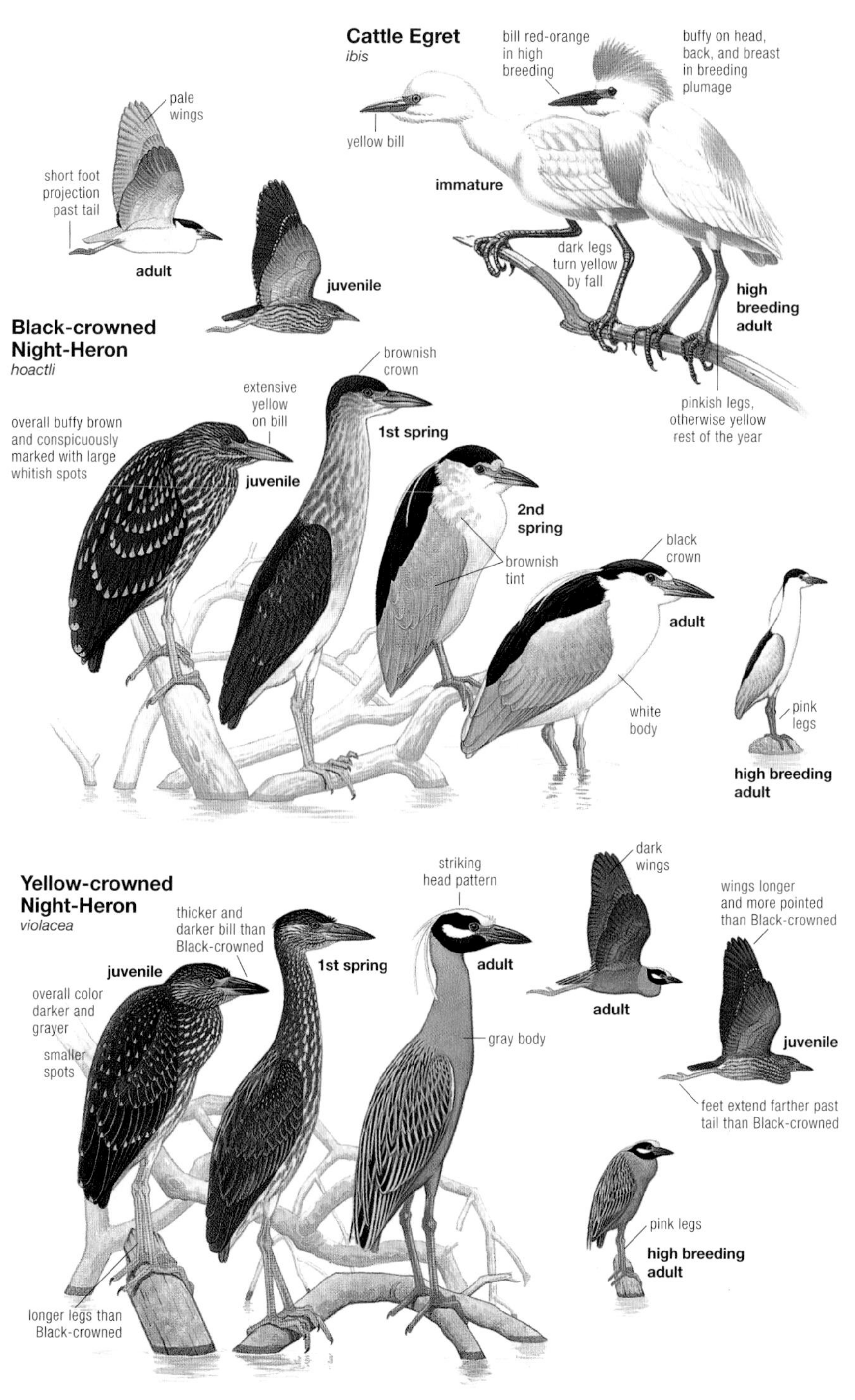
Cattle Egret
ibis
bill red-orange in high breeding
buffy on head, back, and breast in breeding plumage
yellow bill
immature
dark legs turn yellow by fall
high breeding adult
pinkish legs, otherwise yellow rest of the year
pale wings
short foot projection past tail
adult
juvenile
Black-crowned Night-Heron
hoactli
brownish crown
extensive yellow on bill
1st spring
overall buffy brown and conspicuously marked with large whitish spots
juvenile
2nd spring
brownish tint
black crown
adult
white body
pink legs
high breeding adult
Yellow-crowned Night-Heron
violacea
striking head pattern
dark wings
thicker and darker bill than Black-crowned
1st spring
adult
wings longer and more pointed than Black-crowned
juvenile
overall color darker and grayer
smaller spots
adult
gray body
juvenile
feet extend farther past tail than Black-crowned
pink legs
high breeding adult
longer legs than Black-crowned

Ibises, Spoonbills (Family Threskiornithidae)

Gregarious, heronlike birds, these long-legged waders feed with long, specialized bills: slender and curved downward in ibises, wide and spatulate in spoonbills.

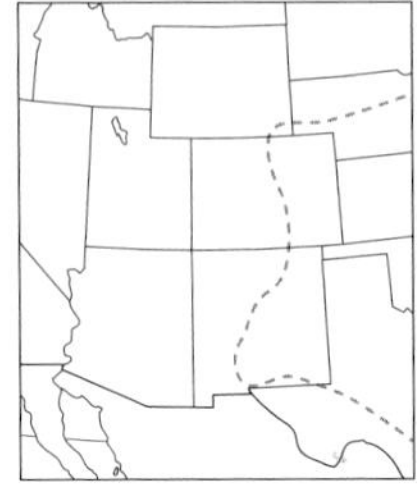

Glossy Ibis *Plegadis falcinellus L 23" (58 cm) WS 36" (91 cm)*

Breeding adult's chestnut plumage is glossed with green or purple; looks all-dark at a distance. Distinguished from White-faced Ibis by brown eye, gray-green legs with red joints, and lack of distinct white border to bare facial skin. Blue edge to gray facial skin does not extend behind eye or under chin. ***Winter adult*** like White-faced, but gray facial skin partially bordered by blue line. ***Juvenile*** closely resembles juvenile White-faced, but note gray facial skin and at least trace of blue line on most; adult breeding plumage acquired in second spring. Identification of a Glossy should be made cautiously as hybrids (with White-faced) are not infrequent.

Voice: Low grunts, especially when flushed.

Range: A recent visitor from East, and now annual. Recorded through much of West; most records are from California and New Mexico. No winter records yet. Increase in West reflects great increase in records in Texas and on Great Plains.

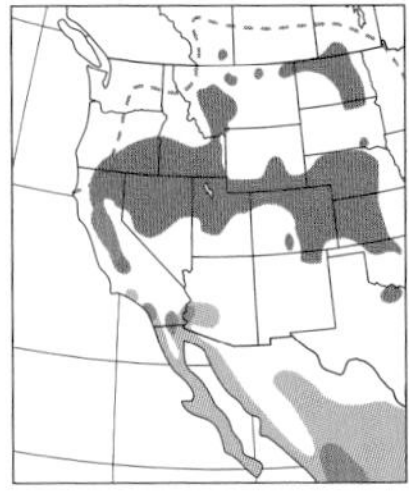

White-faced Ibis *Plegadis chihi*

L 23" (58 cm) WS 36" (91 cm) ***Breeding adult*** distinguished from Glossy Ibis, with which it sometimes hybridizes, by bronzer tones in chestnut plumage, reddish bill, red eye, mostly red legs, and white feathered border around pinkish red facial skin; border extends behind eye and under chin. ***Winter adult*** plumage is like Glossy, but lacks pale blue line from eye to bill; facial skin is pale pink. ***Juvenile*** closely resembles juvenile Glossy until winter, when facial skin turns pinkish; look for lack of blue line (or a hint of white border) and reddish tinge to eye.

Voice: Low grunts, especially when flushed.

Range: Breeds in freshwater marshes. Rare but regular north to Washington, casually farther.

Storks (Family Ciconiidae)

Large, long-legged birds that fly with slow beats of their long, broad wings, soaring and circling like hawks.

Wood Stork *Mycteria americana* **E**

L 40" (102 cm) WS 61" (155 cm) Black flight feathers and tail contrast with white body. ***Adult*** has bald, blackish gray head; thick, dusky, downcurved bill. ***Juvenile***'s head is feathered largely with grayish brown; bill is yellow.

Voice: Occasional grunts.

Range: Now an uncommon post-breeding summer visitor to south end of Salton Sea. Formerly much more numerous and regular on southern California coast; now casual there and elsewhere in Southwest. Accidental north to British Columbia.

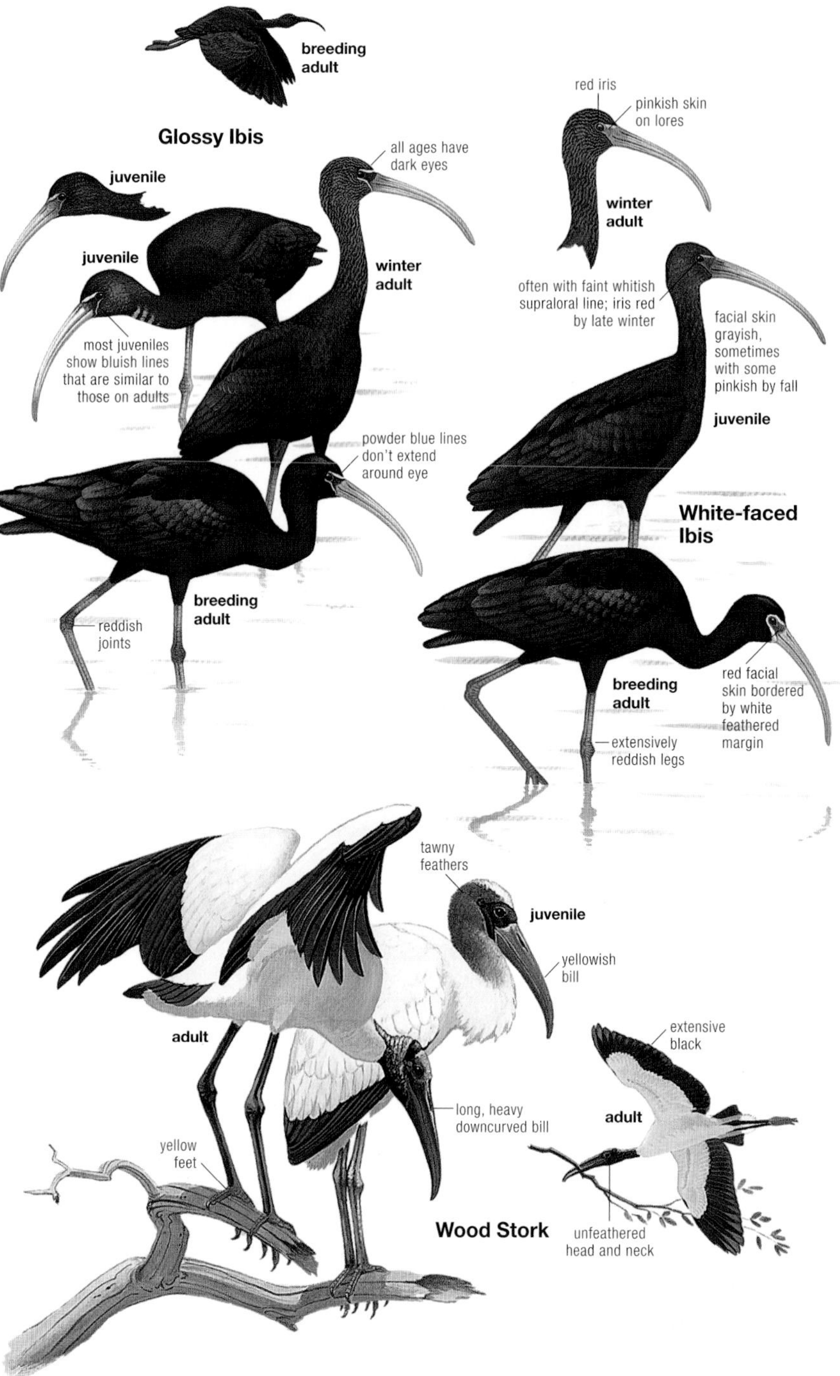
breeding adult
Glossy Ibis
juvenile
all ages have dark eyes
juvenile
winter adult
most juveniles show bluish lines that are similar to those on adults
powder blue lines don't extend around eye
breeding adult
reddish joints
red iris
pinkish skin on lores
winter adult
often with faint whitish supraloral line; iris red by late winter
facial skin grayish, sometimes with some pinkish by fall
juvenile
White-faced Ibis
breeding adult
red facial skin bordered by white feathered margin
extensively reddish legs
tawny feathers
juvenile
yellowish bill
adult
extensive black
adult
long, heavy downcurved bill
yellow feet
Wood Stork
unfeathered head and neck

New World Vultures (Family Cathartidae)

Small, unfeathered head and hooked bill aid in consuming carrion.

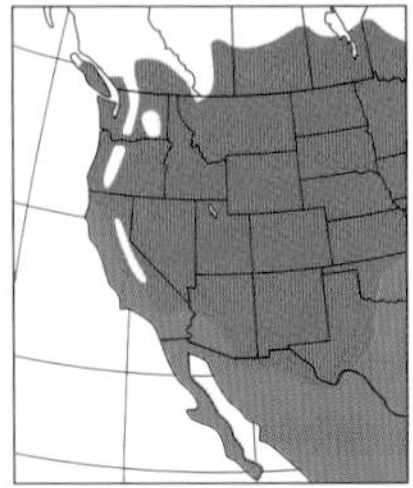

Turkey Vulture *Cathartes aura*
L 27" (69 cm) WS 69" (175 cm) In flight, rocks side to side with little flapping (flaps are rather deep and slow) and wings held upward in a shallow V; dark wing linings contrast with silvery flight feathers. Rather long tailed. ***Adult*** has red head, white bill, brown legs; ***juvenile***'s head and bill are dark, legs are paler. Feeds chiefly on carrion and refuse.
Voice: Generally silent. Occasional hisses and kissing notes heard, usually at nesting site.
Range: Common in mapped range. Casual to Alaska and northwestern Canada.

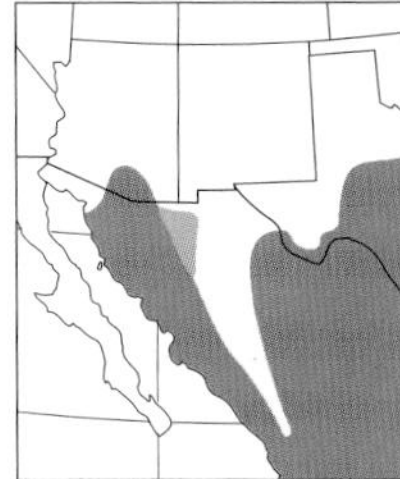

Black Vulture *Coragyps atratus*
L 25" (64 cm) WS 57" (145 cm) In flight, shows large white patches at base of primaries. Tail is shorter than Turkey Vulture; wings shorter and broader; legs white; feet usually extend to edge of tail or beyond. Flight includes rapid flapping and short glides, usually with wings flat. Gregarious and aggressive, but less efficient at spotting carrion than Turkey Vulture, which, unlike Black Vulture, also has a well-developed sense of smell.
Voice: Generally silent. Occasional hisses, barks, and groans heard, most often at nesting site.
Range: Generally uncommon in mapped range in Arizona and along Rio Grande in west Texas. Accidental in southwest New Mexico even though present in numbers nearby in Chihuahua, Mexico. Casual to northern California. Accidental in eastern Colorado and, remarkably, to British Columbia and the southern Yukon.

California Condor *Gymnogyps californianus* **E**
L 47" (119 cm) WS 108" (274 cm) Huge size distinctive. ***Adult*** has white wing linings, orange head; ***juvenile***'s wing linings mottled, head dusky. Soars on flat wings, without flapping, in search of large carrion.
Voice: Usually silent. Occasional hisses and grunting notes heard.
Range: Last wild birds captured in Apr. 1987. Before that, found in arid foothills and mountains of southern and central California. Historically found north to Columbia River (early 1800s) and south to northern Baja California until 1937. Decline to near extinction caused largely by lead poisoning and illegal shooting. Recently reintroduced in California and northern Baja California and introduced in northern Arizona. Population in wild now about 100; 100 more in captivity.

Turkey Vulture
adults
soars on slight dihedral; wingflaps are slow and deep
long tail
two-toned underwings
reddish head
adult
grayish
juvenile
soars on flat wings; wingflaps are rapid and shallow
adult
extensive white base to outer primaries
pale grayish legs
short tail
Black Vulture
wings are long, broad, and of rather uniform width
unlike Turkey Vulture soars with no distinct dihedral
whitish wing linings
juvenile
orange head
California Condor
adult
huge size
white wing linings contrast with black flight feathers
adult
short tail
white tips to greater coverts and white on edges of secondaries visible from above
adult

Hawks, Kites, Eagles, Allies (Family Accipitridae)

Worldwide family of diurnal birds of prey, with hooked bills and strong talons.

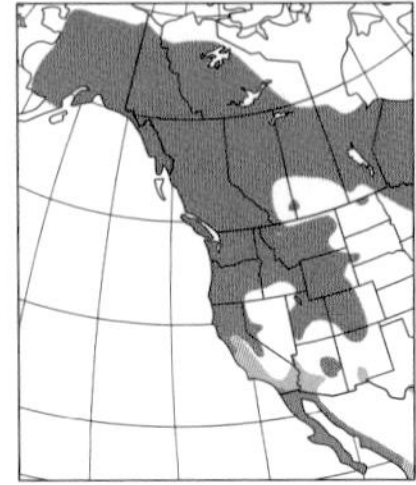

Osprey *Pandion haliaetus*

L 22-25" (56-64 cm) WS 58-72" (147-183 cm) Dark brown above, white below, with white head, prominent dark eye stripe. Females average darker streaking on neck; ***juvenal*** plumage fringed with pale buff above. In flight, long, narrow wings are bent back at "wrist," dark carpal patches conspicuous; wings slightly arched in soaring. Eats mostly fish; hovers over water, dives down, then plunges feetfirst to snatch prey.

Voice: Call is a series of loud, whistled *kyew* notes.

Range: Nests near fresh or salt water. Bulky nests are built in trees, on sheds, poles, docks, and special platforms. Conservation programs successful and now fairly common.

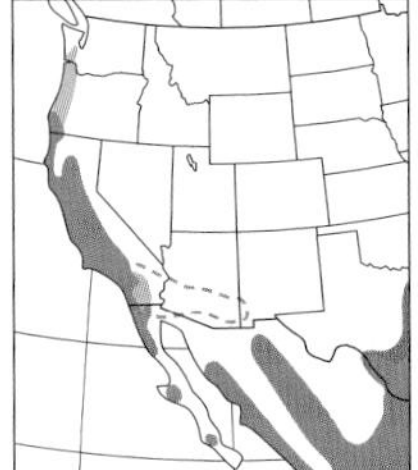

White-tailed Kite *Elanus leucurus*

L 16" (41 cm) WS 42" (107 cm) Long, pointed wings; long tail. White underparts and mostly white tail distinguish ***adults*** from similar Mississippi Kite. Compare also with male Northern Harrier (page 106). ***Juvenile***'s underparts and head are lightly streaked with rufous, which rapidly fades. In all ages, black shoulders show in flight as black leading edge of inner wings from above, small black patches from below. Hovers while hunting, unlike any other North American kite. Eats mainly rodents and insects.

Voice: Calls include various whistled notes.

Range: Populations fluctuate. Fairly common in grasslands, farmlands. Often forms winter roosts of more than a hundred birds. Rare to California's Channel Islands. Casual well north of mapped range to British Columbia and Wyoming.

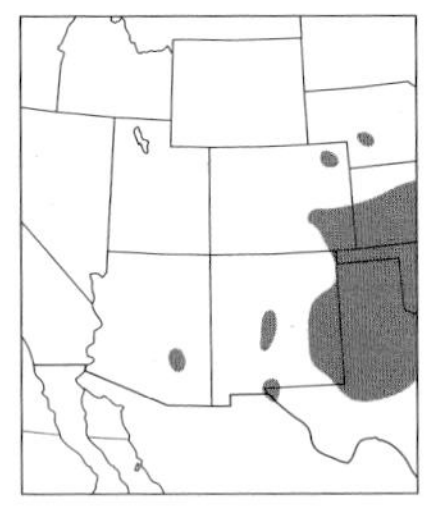

Mississippi Kite *Ictinia mississippiensis*

L 14½" (37 cm) WS 35" (89 cm) Long, pointed wings with first primary distinctly shorter; long, flared tail. Dark gray above, paler below, with pale gray head, averaging paler on ***male. Female*** with white shaft on outer tail feather and often whitish in vent region. White secondaries show in flight as white wing patch. Black tail readily distinguishes Mississippi from White-tailed Kite. Compare also with male Northern Harrier (page 106); note Mississippi never hovers. ***Juvenile*** is heavily streaked and spotted, with pale bands on tail, but pattern and overall darkness highly variable on underparts, underwings, and tail. ***First-summer bird*** (page 118) more like adult but retains juvenal flight feathers. At all ages, may be confused with Peregrine Falcon (page 118); compare wing and tail shapes. Mississippi captures and eats its prey, mainly insects, on the wing. Gregarious; often hunts in groups, nests in loose colonies.

Voice: A downslurred whistle, given mainly on breeding grounds.

Range: Breeds in towns on western plains and very locally in central New Mexico and southeastern Arizona. Casual west to Nevada and California. Winters in South America.

Osprey
carolinensis

long, angled wings
dark "wrist"
pale wing linings
barred flight feathers
gull-like flight
adult

bold dark eye stripe
uniformly dark above
adult

prominent pale tips
juvenile

White-tailed Kite
majusculus

habitually hovers when foraging
dark spot
long whitish tail
adults

juvenile
buffy on chest

black shoulders
adult

Mississippi Kite

never hovers
adult ♂
whitish secondary patch

dark wings
adult ♀
black tail

juvenile
banded tail held through 1st summer

pale gray head
adult ♂

Eagles

These three species, our largest diurnal birds of prey, share a soaring behavior—on the lookout for prey—although their preferred food differs. Bald and Golden Eagles are widespread in the West, whereas White-tailed Eagle barely enters into western Alaska from Asia.

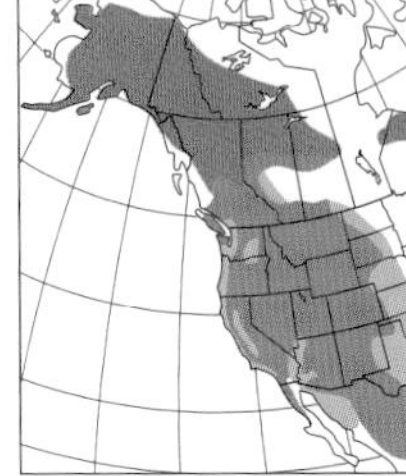

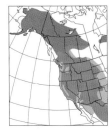

Golden Eagle *Aquila chrysaetos*

L 30-40" (76-102 cm) WS 80-88" (203-224 cm) Brown, with variable yellow to tawny brown wash over back of head and neck; bill mostly horn colored; tail faintly barred. Tawny greater upperwing coverts form a bar. ***Juvenile,*** seen in flight from below, shows white patches at base of primaries, white tail with distinct dark terminal band. Compare with juvenile Bald Eagle, with its larger head, shorter tail, and underwing pattern. ***Adult*** plumage acquired in four years. Often soars with wings slightly uplifted.

Voice: Mostly silent away from nest.

Range: Uncommon to fairly common in the West. Inhabits mountainous or hilly terrain, hunting over open country for small mammals, snakes, birds, and carrion. Also found in valleys and on plains, especially in migration and winter. Nests on cliffs or in trees.

White-tailed Eagle *Haliaeetus albicilla*

L 26-35" (66-89 cm) WS 72-94" (183-239 cm) Short, wedge-shaped white tail. Plumage mottled; head may be very pale and appear white at a distance; undertail coverts are dark, unlike subadult and adult Bald Eagles. ***Juvenile***'s tail has variable dark mottling and darker underwing than Bald Eagle.

Voice: Generally silent away from nest.

Range: Flies over northern Eurasia and Greenland in diminishing numbers. Very rare visitor to western Aleutians, especially Attu Island, where it has nested. Accidental Kiska Island, central Aleutians. One well-documented record of an adult on St. Lawrence Island.

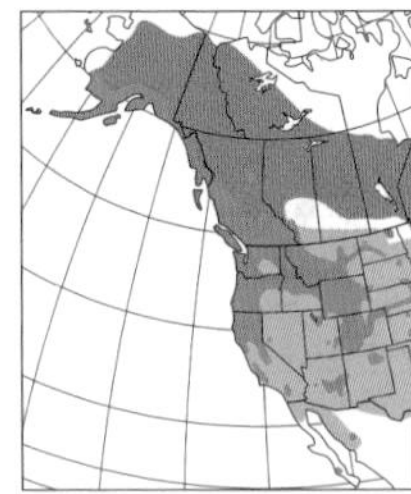

Bald Eagle *Haliaeetus leucocephalus* **T**

L 31-37" (79-94 cm) WS 70-90" (178-229 cm) ***Adults*** readily identified by white head and tail, large yellow bill. ***Juvenile*** mostly dark, may be confused with juvenile Golden Eagle; compare blotchy white on underwing coverts, axillaries, and tail with Golden's more sharply defined pattern; note also Bald's disproportionately larger head, shorter tail. Shorter neck and longer tail than White-tailed; Steller's Sea-Eagle (page 417) has longer, wedge-shaped tail. Flat-winged soar distinguishes young Bald from Turkey Vulture (page 98). Bald requires four or five years to reach full adult plumage.

Voice: A variety of calls, including a series of high-pitched twitterings or whistles.

Range: Seen most often on seacoasts or near rivers and lakes. Feeds mainly on fish in breeding season, regularly on carrion, on injured waterfowl, and on roadkill in winter. Nests in tall trees or on cliffs. Most common in Alaska; fairly common in the Northwest; fairly common to rare over much of the rest of the West. Most numerous around large bodies of water.

Golden Eagle
canadensis
golden nape
adult
adult
dark or faintly barred tail
juvenile
short head projection
whitish wing patch
whitish tail base
underwing darker than immature Bald Eagle
White-tailed Eagle
juvenile
dark undertail coverts
pale blond head
adult
short, whitish wedge-shaped tail
uvenile
2nd year
whitish
nderwing
verts and
axillaries
longer head projection than Golden
Bald Eagle
3rd
year
larger bill than Golden
juvenile
white head
adults
white tail
tail shorter than Golden

Accipiters

Comparatively long tails and short, rounded wings give these woodland hawks great agility. Flight is several quick wingbeats and a glide. The three species in North America are confusingly similar. They are generally silent, except at the nest site; Cooper's Hawk is usually the most vocal.

Sharp-shinned Hawk *Accipiter striatus*

L 10-14" (25-36 cm) WS 20-28" (51-71 cm) Distinguished from Cooper's Hawk by shorter, squared tail (often appears notched when folded), thinner legs, and smaller head and neck. ***Adult*** lacks Cooper's strong contrast between crown and back. ***Juveniles*** are whitish below, some streaked with brown (like Cooper's), others spotted with reddish brown. Note also the pale eyebrows, narrow white tip on tail, entirely white undertail coverts, less tawny head than other accipiters. In flight (see also page 119), again compare smaller head and proportionately shorter tail than Cooper's; wingbeats quick and choppy, slower on Cooper's. Preys chiefly on small birds, often at feeders.

Range: Fairly common over much of its range; found in mixed woodlands. Migrates singly or in loose groups.

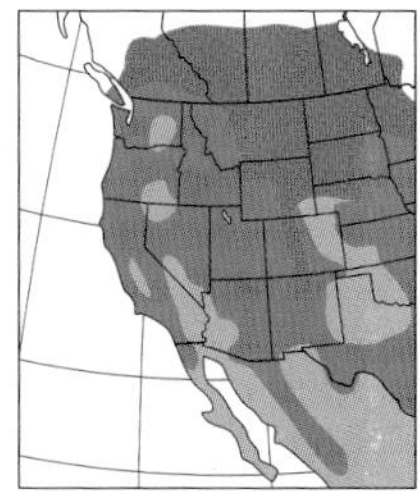

Cooper's Hawk *Accipiter cooperii*

L 14-20" (36-51 cm) WS 29-37" (74-94 cm) Distinguished from Sharp-shinned Hawk by longer, rounded tail, larger head, and, in ***adult,*** stronger contrast between back and crown. ***Juvenile*** has whitish or buffy underparts with fine streaks on breast, streaking reduced or absent on belly; tawny rufous color on head is much richer, white tip on tail is broader, than Sharp-shinned; undertail coverts entirely white. Note that some juveniles may have a pale eyebrow like Sharp-shinned. In flight (see also page 119), again compare larger head and longer tail. Preys largely on songbirds, often at feeders, and some small mammals. Often perches on telephone poles, unlike Sharp-shinned.

Range: Inhabits broken woodlands or streamside groves, especially deciduous. Also found in residential areas. Usually migrates singly.

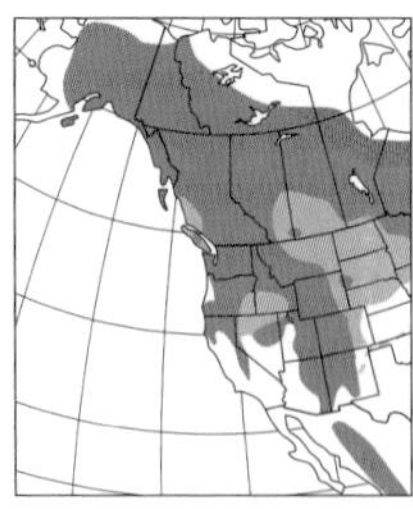

Northern Goshawk *Accipiter gentilis*

L 21-26" (53-66 cm) WS 40-46" (102-117 cm) Conspicuous eyebrow, flaring behind eye, separates ***adult***'s dark crown from blue-gray back. Underparts, white with dense gray barring, appear gray at a distance; wedge-shaped tail with fluffy undertail coverts. Note disproportionately shorter tail, longer wings, than Cooper's Hawk. ***Juvenile*** is brown above, buffy below, with thick, blackish brown streaks, heaviest on flanks; tail has wavy dark bands bordered with white; undertail coverts usually have dark streaks. In flight (see also page 119), note tawny bar on upperwing on greater secondary coverts. Juvenile also can be confused with Gyrfalcon (page 116) and Red-shouldered Hawk (page 108).

Range: Inhabits deep, conifer-dominated, mixed woodlands; preys on birds and mammals as large as hares. Strictly casual outside of mapped range in West.

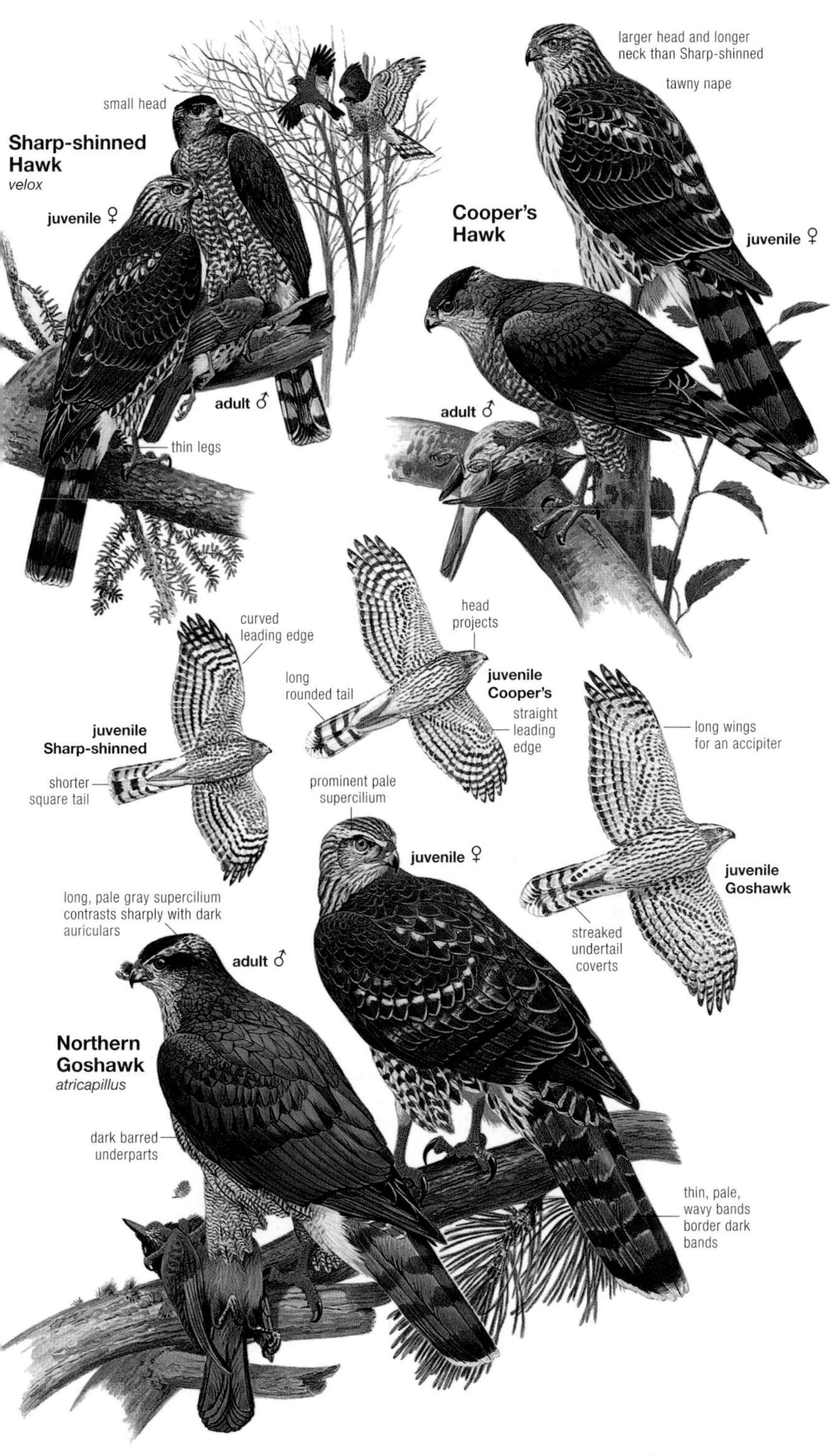
small head
Sharp-shinned Hawk
velox
juvenile ♀
adult ♂
thin legs
larger head and longer neck than Sharp-shinned
tawny nape
Cooper's Hawk
juvenile ♀
adult ♂
curved leading edge
head projects
long rounded tail
juvenile Cooper's
straight leading edge
juvenile Sharp-shinned
shorter square tail
long wings for an accipiter
prominent pale supercilium
juvenile ♀
juvenile Goshawk
long, pale gray supercilium contrasts sharply with dark auriculars
adult ♂
streaked undertail coverts
Northern Goshawk
atricapillus
dark barred underparts
thin, pale, wavy bands border dark bands

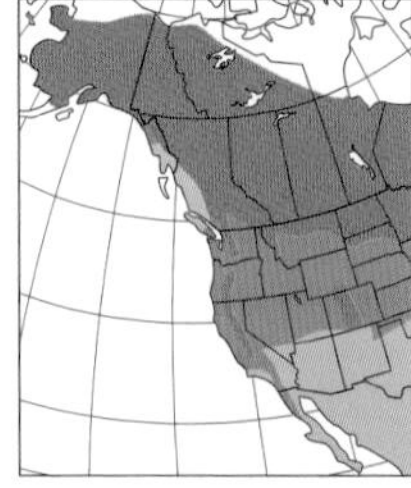

Northern Harrier *Circus cyaneus*

L 16-20" (41-51 cm) WS 38-48" (97-122 cm) White uppertail coverts and owl-like facial disk distinctive in all plumages. Body slim; wings long and narrow with somewhat rounded tips; tail long. ***Adult male*** is grayish above; mostly white below with variable chestnut spotting; has black wing tips and black tips to secondaries. ***Female*** is brown above, whitish below with heavy brown streaking on breast and flanks, lighter streaking and spotting on belly. ***Juvenile*** resembles adult female but cinnamon below, fading to creamy buff by spring; streaked only on the breast; wing linings are cinnamon, distinctly darker on inner half. Harriers perch low and usually fly close to the ground, with wings upraised.

Voice: Occasionally gives a high-pitched, downslurred call; also a series of *keee* notes when agitated.

Range: Fairly common in wetlands, open fields, and tundra. Very local as breeder in southern part of range.

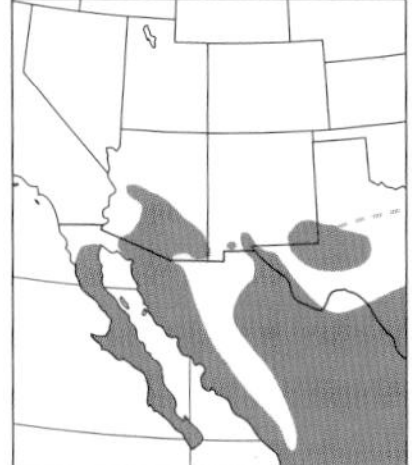

Harris's Hawk *Parabuteo unicinctus*

L 21" (53 cm) WS 46" (117 cm) Chocolate brown overall, with chestnut shoulder, leggings, and wing linings; white at base and tip of long tail; rounded wing tips. ***Juvenile*** is heavily streaked below; chestnut shoulder patches are less distinct. Gregarious; hunts in small, cooperative groups.

Voice: Call is a harsh, grating *eeaarrr.*

Range: May straggle north and west of mapped range, but many may be escapes. Inhabits semiarid woodland.

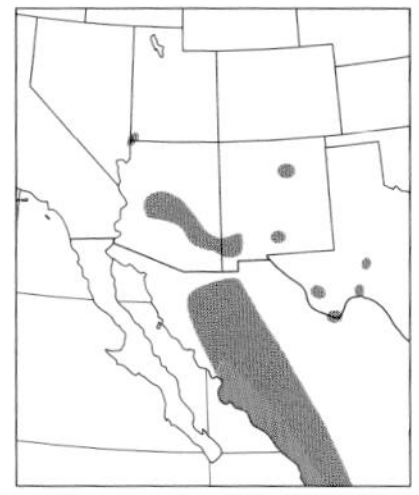

Common Black-Hawk *Buteogallus anthracinus*

L 21" (53 cm) WS 50" (127 cm) Wings broad and rounded; tail short and broad. ***Adult*** blackish overall; tail has broad white band. Legs and cere orange-yellow. Zone-tailed Hawk has broader wings and tail; larger bill; more orange-yellow in lore region. ***Juvenile*** has strong face pattern; heavily streaked underparts; many-banded tail; buffy wing panel visible from above and below.

Voice: Call is a series of loud whistles.

Range: Found along waterways. Rare, local, very rare in southern Utah and Nevada; casual in California and Colorado.

Buteos

High-soaring hawks, amongst easiest of birds of prey to spot.

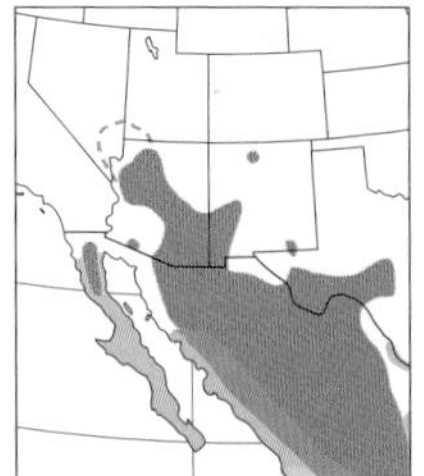

Zone-tailed Hawk *Buteo albonotatus*

L 20" (51 cm) WS 51" (130 cm) Grayish black overall, with barred flight feathers. Legs and cere yellow. Slimmer winged than Common Black-Hawk; longer tail, variably banded according to sex and age. Flies like Turkey Vulture. Compare Zone-tailed's banded tail; smaller bill; yellow cere; larger, feathered head. ***Juvenile*** has grayish tail, some white flecking on breast.

Voice: Call is a squealing whistle.

Range: Uncommon; found in mesa and mountain country, often near watercourses; drops from low glide on small birds, rodents, lizards, and fish. Rare in southern California.

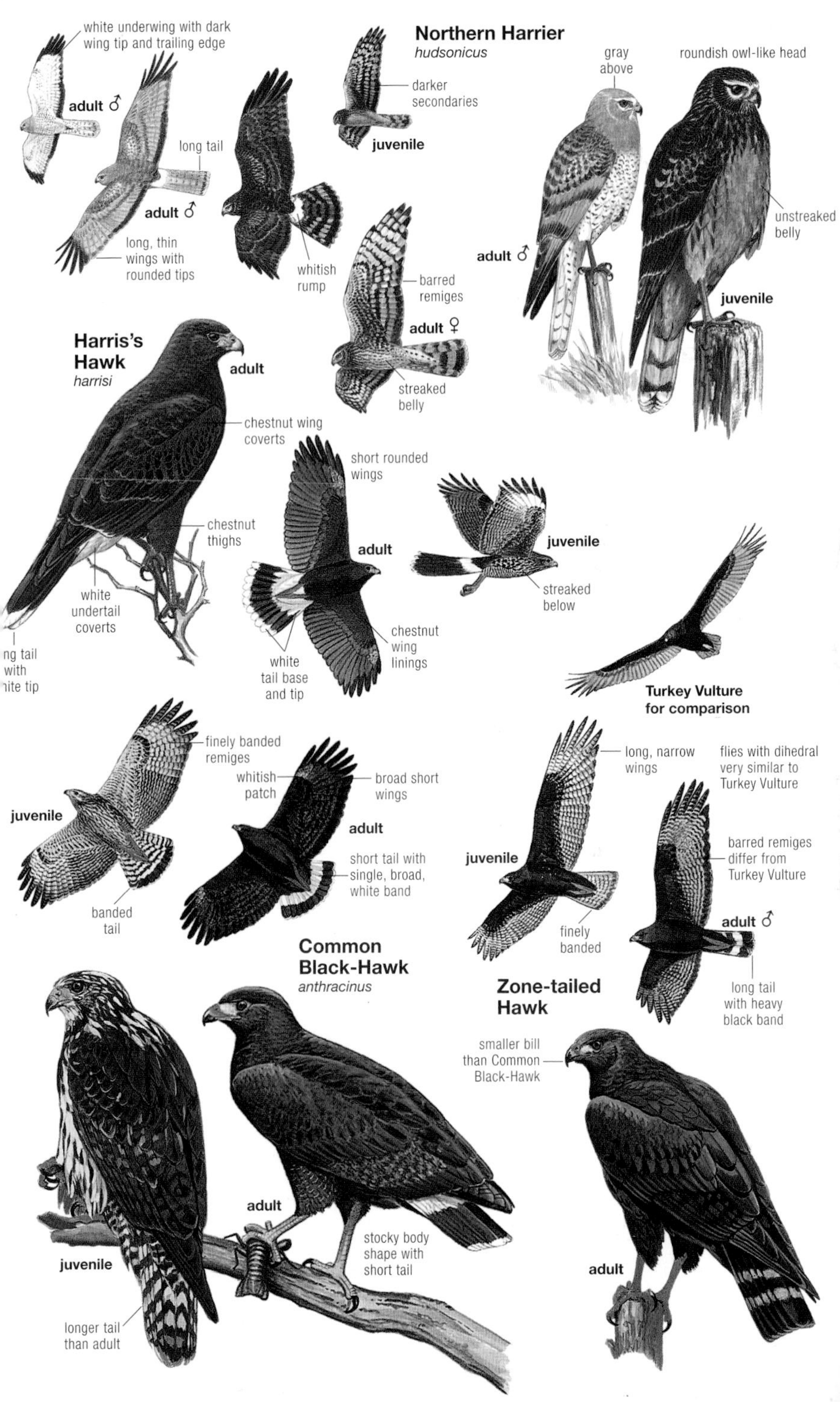

Northern Harrier
hudsonicus
white underwing with dark wing tip and trailing edge
adult ♂
long tail
adult ♂
long, thin wings with rounded tips
whitish rump
darker secondaries
juvenile
barred remiges
adult ♀
streaked belly
gray above
roundish owl-like head
unstreaked belly
adult ♂
juvenile
Harris's Hawk
harrisi
adult
chestnut wing coverts
chestnut thighs
white undertail coverts
ng tail with ite tip
short rounded wings
adult
white tail base and tip
chestnut wing linings
juvenile
streaked below
Turkey Vulture for comparison
juvenile
finely banded remiges
banded tail
whitish patch
broad short wings
adult
short tail with single, broad, white band
Common Black-Hawk
anthracinus
juvenile
long, narrow wings
finely banded
flies with dihedral very similar to Turkey Vulture
barred remiges differ from Turkey Vulture
adult ♂
long tail with heavy black band
Zone-tailed Hawk
adult
juvenile
longer tail than adult
stocky body shape with short tail
smaller bill than Common Black-Hawk
adult

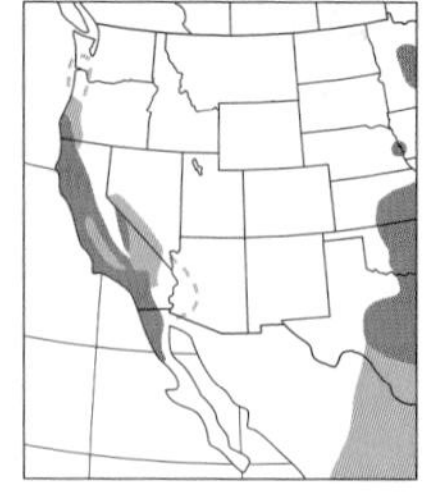

Red-shouldered Hawk *Buteo lineatus*

L 15-19" (38-48 cm) WS 37-42" (94-107 cm) Relatively long tailed and long legged. In flight, shows pale crescent at base of primaries. ***Adult*** has reddish shoulders and wing linings and extensive pale spotting above. ***Juvenile*** *elegans* is overall rather dark and has adultlike features, including some rufous on shoulders and wing linings. Flight of *elegans* is accipiter-like, with quick wingbeats.
Voice: Call, evenly spaced series of clear, high *kee-ah* or *kah* notes.
Range: Found in moist, mixed woodlands. All Pacific birds are *elegans*; nominate *lineatus* is casual on western Great Plains.

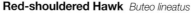

Broad-winged Hawk *Buteo platypterus*

L 16" (41 cm) WS 34" (86 cm) Pointed wing tips; white underwings have dark borders; tail has broad black and white bands. Wings broad, more pointed than Red-shouldered Hawk; wing linings buffy or white; tail shorter, broader. Wingbeats slower than in *elegans* race. ***Juvenile*** typically has black moustachial streak; dark-bordered underwings, indistinct bands on tail; very similar to juvenile eastern Red-shouldered but paler below; may have a pale area at base of primaries but lack the distinct pale crescent. Rare ***dark morph*** breeds in western and central Canada.
Voice: Call, heard on breeding and winter grounds, is a thin, shrill, slightly descending whistle: *pee-teee.*
Range: Outside of western Canada breeding range, a rare migrant in the West, when most often seen at favored hawk-watching spots. Casual in winter in coastal California.

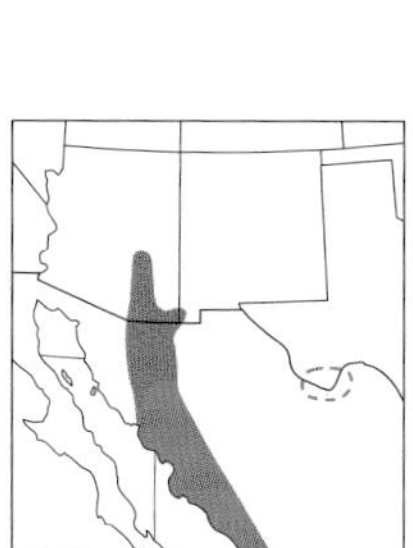

Gray Hawk *Buteo nitidus* *L 17" (43 cm) WS 35" (89 cm)*

Gray upperparts, gray-barred underparts and wing linings, and rounded wing tips distinguish Gray from Broad-winged Hawk. Flight is accipiter-like: with rapid, shallow wingbeats. ***Juvenile*** resembles juvenile Broad-winged, but has much longer tail projection, stronger face pattern with outlined white cheek, and white, U-shaped rump band; dark trailing edge on wings is smaller or absent. Gray Hawk inhabits deciduous growth along streams.
Voice: Calls include a loud, descending whistle.
Range: Tropical species; local nester along streams in southeastern Arizona. Rare along Rio Grande in west Texas and in southwestern New Mexico.

Short-tailed Hawk *Buteo brachyurus*

L 15½" (39 cm) WS 35" (89 cm) Small hawk with two color morphs. Secondaries seen from below are darker than primaries. ***Light morph*** has dark helmet and underwing resembling Swainson's Hawk (page 132), wings and tail are shorter, broader; lacks chest band. ***Adult*** has wide, dark subterminal tail band; of equal width on juveniles. Faint streaks on sides of light morph; spotted with white on wing linings and underparts on dark-morph juveniles. Most often seen in flight.
Voice: Mostly silent away from nest site.
Range: A few found recently in summer in coniferous mountains of southeastern Arizona (has nested Chiricahuas) and the Animas Mountains of southwestern New Mexico.

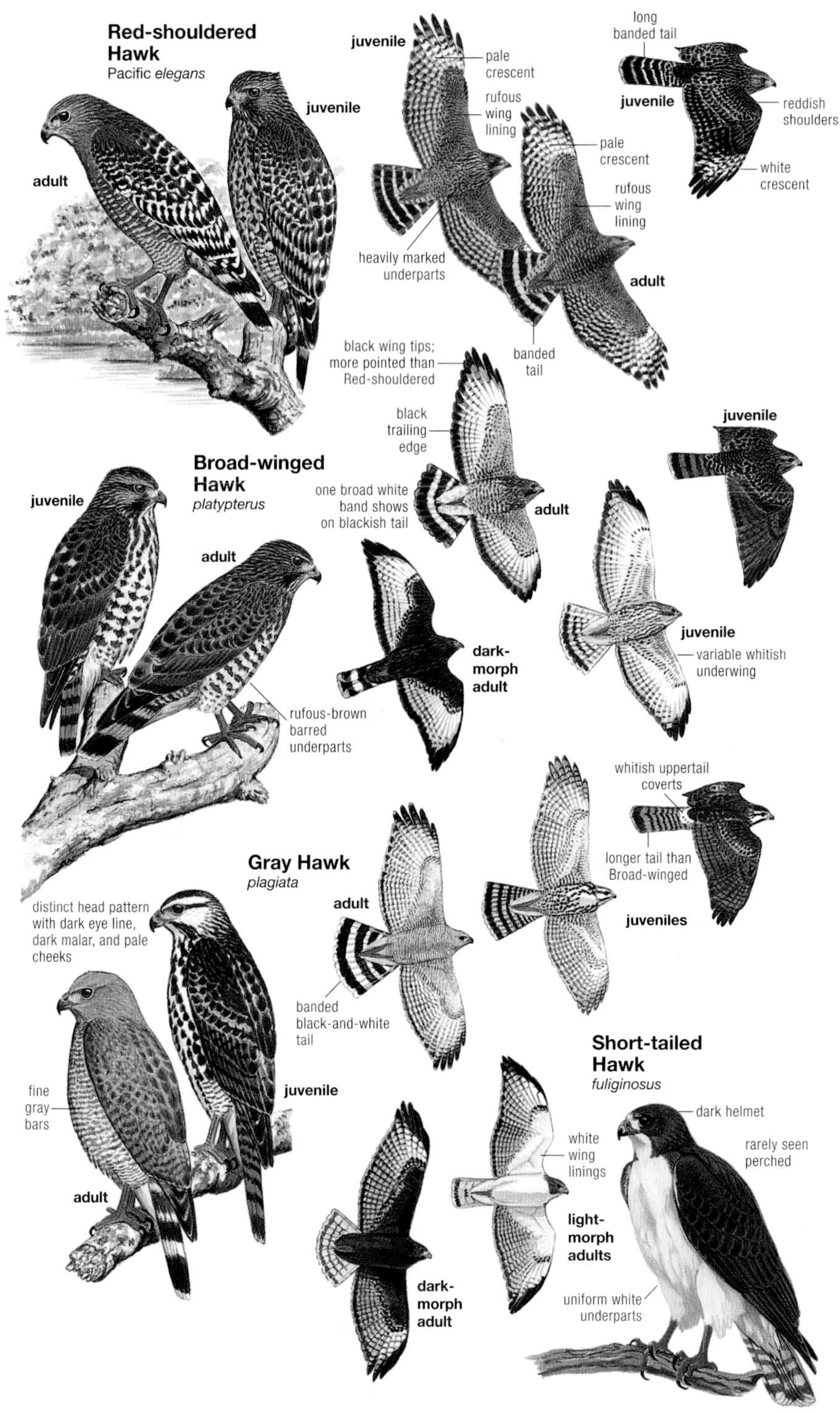
Red-shouldered Hawk
Pacific elegans
adult
juvenile
juvenile
pale crescent
rufous wing lining
heavily marked underparts
pale crescent
rufous wing lining
adult
banded tail
long banded tail
juvenile
reddish shoulders
white crescent
black wing tips; more pointed than Red-shouldered
black trailing edge
one broad white band shows on blackish tail
adult
juvenile
Broad-winged Hawk
platypterus
juvenile
adult
rufous-brown barred underparts
dark-morph adult
juvenile
variable whitish underwing
Gray Hawk
plagiata
adult
banded black-and-white tail
juveniles
whitish uppertail coverts
longer tail than Broad-winged
distinct head pattern with dark eye line, dark malar, and pale cheeks
fine gray bars
adult
juvenile
Short-tailed Hawk
fuliginosus
dark-morph adult
white wing linings
light-morph adults
dark helmet
rarely seen perched
uniform white underparts

Red-tailed Hawk *Buteo jamaicensis*

L 22" (56 cm) WS 50" (127 cm) Our most common buteo; wings broad and fairly rounded; plumage extremely variable. Looks heavy billed, unlike Rough-legged (next page) and Swainson's Hawks. Variable pale mottling on scapulars contrasts with dark mantle, often forming a broad-sided V on perched birds. Most ***adults*** show a belly band of dark streaks on whitish underparts; dark bar on leading edge of underwing, contrasting with paler wing linings (see also page 120). Note reddish upper tail; paler red under tail. Some pale breeding birds on the Great Plains designated as *krideri,* known as ***"Krider's Red-tailed,"*** have paler upperparts and whitish tail with pale reddish wash; in flight, shows pale rectangular patches at base of primaries on upperwing. Many southwestern birds of the *fuertesi* race (not shown) lack belly band and have entirely light underparts. Widespread dark and ***rufous morphs*** of western race, *calurus,* have dark wing linings and underparts, obscuring the bar on leading edge and belly band; tail is dark reddish above. In *harlani,* ***"Harlan's Hawk,"*** formerly considered a separate species, dark morph has dusky white tail, diffuse blackish terminal band; shows some white streaking on its dark breast; may lack scapular mottling; rare *harlani* light morph has typical tail pattern, but plumage resembles *krideri.* "Harlan's Hawk" breeds in Alaska and east to northwestern Canada; winters primarily in central U.S.; very small numbers in interior West. ***Juveniles*** of all morphs except *harlani* have gray-brown tails with many blackish bands; otherwise heavily streaked and spotted with brown below. Preys on rodents.

Voice: Distinctive call is a harsh, descending *keeeeer.*

Range: Habitat variable: woods with nearby open land; also plains, prairie groves, and desert.

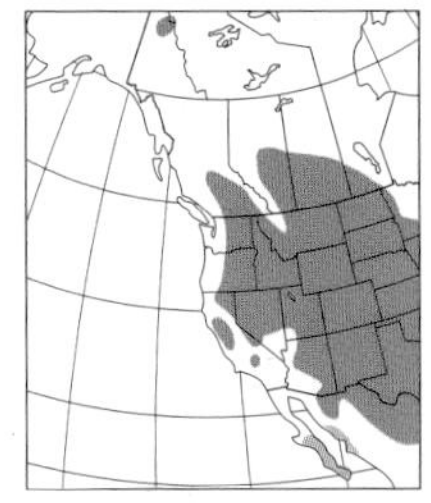

Swainson's Hawk *Buteo swainsoni*

L 21" (53 cm) WS 52" (132 cm) Distinguished from most other buteos by long, narrow, pointed wings; plumage is extremely variable. Lacks Red-tailed Hawk's pale mottling on scapulars; bill is smaller. All but darkest birds show contrast between paler wing linings and dark flight feathers; most show pale uppertail coverts. In ***light morph,*** whitish or buffy white wing linings contrast with darkly barred brown flight feathers (see also page 120); dark bib; underparts otherwise whitish to pale buff. ***Dark-morph*** bird is dark brown with white undertail coverts; shows less sharp contrast between wing linings and flight feathers; darkest birds show none. Compare with first-year White-tailed Hawk. ***Intermediate*** colorations between light and dark morphs include a rufous morph. Intermediate and ***light-morph juveniles*** have dark moustachial stripe and conspicuous whitish eyebrows that meet on the forehead; variable streaking below, very heavy on dark morphs. Show less contrast between wing linings and flight feathers than adult birds (page 120). Swainson's soars over open plains and prairie with uptilted wings in teetering, vulturelike flight.

Voice: A drawn-out scream, usually heard near nest site.

Range: Gregarious; usually migrates in large flocks. Winters chiefly in South America; rarely in California's Central Valley.

heavy bill
whitish on scapulars
juvenile
calurus
"Harlan's Hawk"
adult harlani
whitish spots on breast
ypical
dult
alurus
Red-tailed Hawk
brownish banded tail
rufous tail
pale head
adult dark-morph
calurus
whitish base to tail
dark patagial bar
"Krider's Red-tailed"
adult krideri
uniform pale underparts
paler rufous tail
adult
fuertesi
adult rufous-morph
calurus
aller bill than Red-tailed
light-morph juvenile
long, narrow pointed wings
often with darker lateral reast patches
dark-morph adult
whitish underwing coverts contrast with dark flight feathers
Swainson's Hawk
light-morph adult
brown breast band
broad dark subterminal band
light-morph adult
intermediate-morph adult

Rough-legged Hawk *Buteo lagopus*

L 21" (53 cm) WS 53" (135 cm) Long, white tail with dark band or bands distinctive; bill small. Thin legs are feathered to the toes; feathering barred in adults, unbarred in juveniles. ***Adult male*** has multibanded tail with a broad blackish subterminal band. ***Adult female***'s tail is brown toward tip with a thin, black subterminal band. ***Juvenile*** has a single broad, brown tail band. Wings are long, fairly narrow. Seen in flight from above, white at base of tail is conspicuous; small white patches at base of primaries on upperwings. In light morph, pale head contrasts with darker back and dark belly band, especially in females and immatures. Adult male has darker breast markings that may create a bib effect; belly is paler. Observe square, black carpal patches at the "wrists" of the wings. ***Dark morph*** is less common. Often hovers while hunting.

Voice: During breeding season gives a soft, plaintive courting whistle. Alarm call is a loud screech or squeal.

Range: Inhabits open country; also seen at marshes in winter. Numbers and southern limit of winter range vary annually.

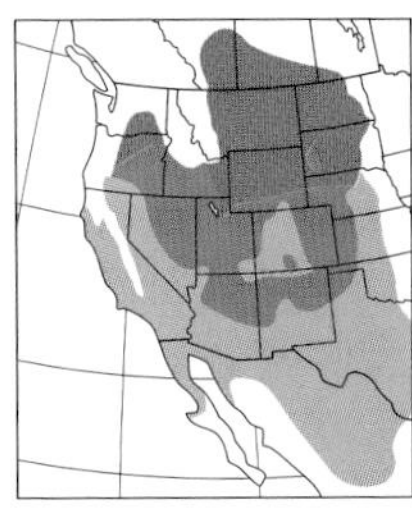

Ferruginous Hawk *Buteo regalis*

L 23" (58 cm) WS 56" (142 cm) Pale head; extended "gape line" goes back under eye; tail a mixture of pale rust, white, gray. Wings long, broad, pointed; note large, white, crescent-shaped patches on upperwing. ***Adult*** shows rusty color on back and shoulders; rusty leggings form a conspicuous V against whitish underparts spotted with rufous. Rare ***dark morph*** varies from dark rufous to dark brown, with dark undertail coverts. Absence of dark tail bands separates it from dark-morph Rough-legged. ***Juvenile*** lacks rusty leggings and is less rufous above; resembles "Krider's" type of Red-tailed (previous page), but wings longer and more pointed. Often hovers when hunting or soars in a dihedral. Often sits on ground.

Voice: Gives harsh alarm calls, *kree-a,* chiefly in breeding season.

Range: Inhabits dry, open areas. Accidental to British Columbia.

Caracaras, Falcons (Family Falconidae)

Falcons are distinguished from hawks by their long wings, which are bent back at the "wrist" and, except in the Crested Caracara, narrow and pointed. Females are larger than males.

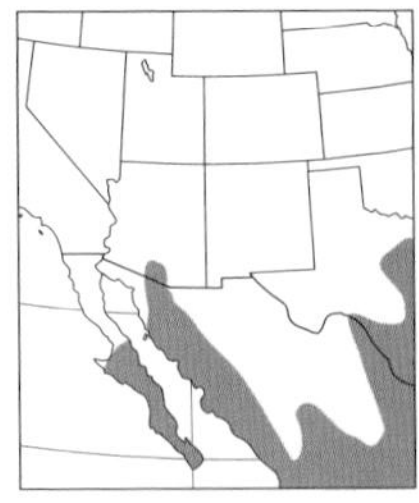

Crested Caracara *Caracara cheriway* T

L 23" (58 cm) WS 50" (127 cm) Large head, long neck, long legs. Blackish brown overall, with white throat and neck and red-orange to yellow bare facial skin; underparts barred with black. ***Juvenile*** is browner; upperparts edged and spotted with buff; underparts streaked with buff, unlike ***adult*** barring; second-year plumage closer to adult. In flight, shows whitish patches near ends of rounded wings. Flapping, ravenlike flight; soars with flat wings.

Voice: Calls include a low rattle and a single *wuck* note.

Range: Inhabits open brushlands. Rare in southern Arizona; casual in southern New Mexico and west Texas. Other records in West of debatable origin. Numerous recent records for California.

Rough-legged Hawk
sanctijohannis
squarish carpal patch
adult ♀
small bill
adult ♂
dark-morph adult ♂
juvenile
juvenile with pale head and blackish belly
feathered tarsus
white tail base with broad, black subterminal band
adult males with multiple blackish bands at tail base
juveniles whiter below than adults
juvenile
Ferruginous Hawk
variable rufous feathering in underwing coverts
pale head
dark-morph adult
extended gape
whitish tail lacks bands
adults
adult
all show broad whitish crescents
rufous underparts
blackish cap
pink facial skin
rufous leggings
slight crest
barred white chest
adult
Crested Caracara
juvenile
black belly
adults
conspicuous white patches
long white-based tail

Aplomado Falcon *Falco femoralis* **E**

L 15-16½" (38-42 cm) WS 31-40" (79-102 cm) In flight, often hovers; long, pointed wings and long, banded tail resemble young Mississippi Kite (page 188); underwings are dark, with pale trailing edge. Note slate gray crown, boldly marked head. Pale eyebrows join at back of head. Dark patches on sides sometimes extend across breast. ***Juvenile*** is cinnamon below with a streaked breast, and browner above.

Range: Once found in open grasslands and deserts from southern Texas to southeastern Arizona. Disappeared by the early 20th century. Birds seen in New Mexico and west Texas from 1990s were probably from a small extant population in northern Chihuahua, Mexico, but recent releases of captives in New Mexico and west Texas complicate the situation.

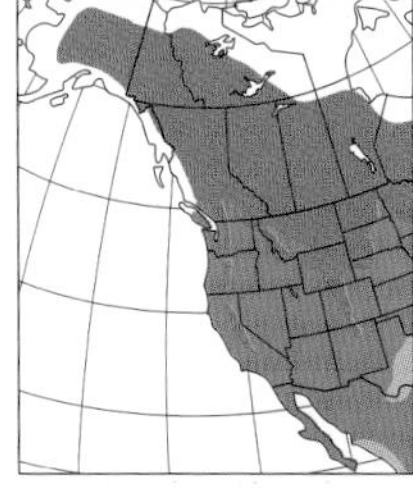

American Kestrel *Falco sparverius*

L 10½" (27 cm) WS 23" (58 cm) Smallest and most common of our falcons. Identified by russet back and tail, double black stripes on white face. Seen in flight from below, ***adult*** shows pale underwings, and ***male*** has a distinctive row of white, circular spots on trailing edge of wings. Male also has blue-gray wing coverts; compare with Merlin. ***Juvenile male*** more marked below than adult male. Often perches on telephone wires; frequently bobs its tail.

Voice: Call is a shrill *killy killy killy.*

Range: Found in open country and in cities; feeds on insects, reptiles, and small mammals and birds, hovering over prey before plunging.

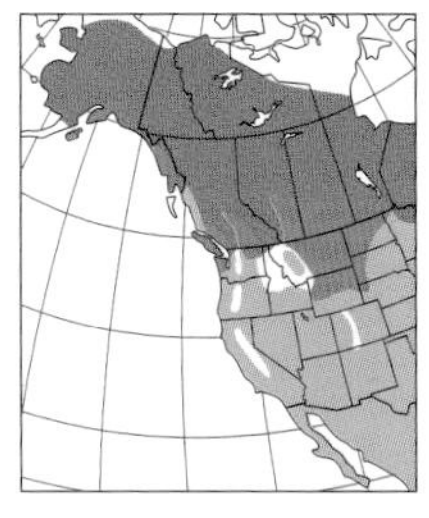

Merlin *Falco columbarius L 12" (31 cm) WS 25" (64 cm)*

Adult male is gray-blue above; ***female*** and juvenile usually dark brown. Merlins lack the strong facial markings and russet upperparts of kestrels, and have broader wings than American Kestrel. Plumage varies geographically from the very dark race, *suckleyi,* of the Pacific Northwest to the pale *richardsonii* that breeds on northern Great Plains from southern Canada to northern U.S. A few *suckleyi* winter to southern California; this race has dark cheeks and narrow, incomplete tail bands. All *richardsonii* have pale cheeks; male is paler blue-gray above; female and juvenile are pale brown, the latter with wide, pale tail bands; winter to southern Great Plains, a few to the Great Basin and Pacific states. The widespread nominate, *columbarius,* which breeds in the taiga region, is intermediate in plumage; western *columbarius* average slightly paler than eastern. In flight, strongly barred tail distinguishes Merlin from the much larger Peregrine and Prairie Falcons (next page). Underparts and underwings darker than kestrels, particularly in *suckleyi* and *columbarius,* and head larger. Powerful flyer; does not hover. Catches birds in flight by a sudden burst of speed rather than by diving. Also eats large insects and small rodents.

Voice: Silent except near nest site, when it gives shrill notes.

Range: Nests in open woods or wooded prairies; otherwise found in a variety of habitats. Generally uncommon throughout West.

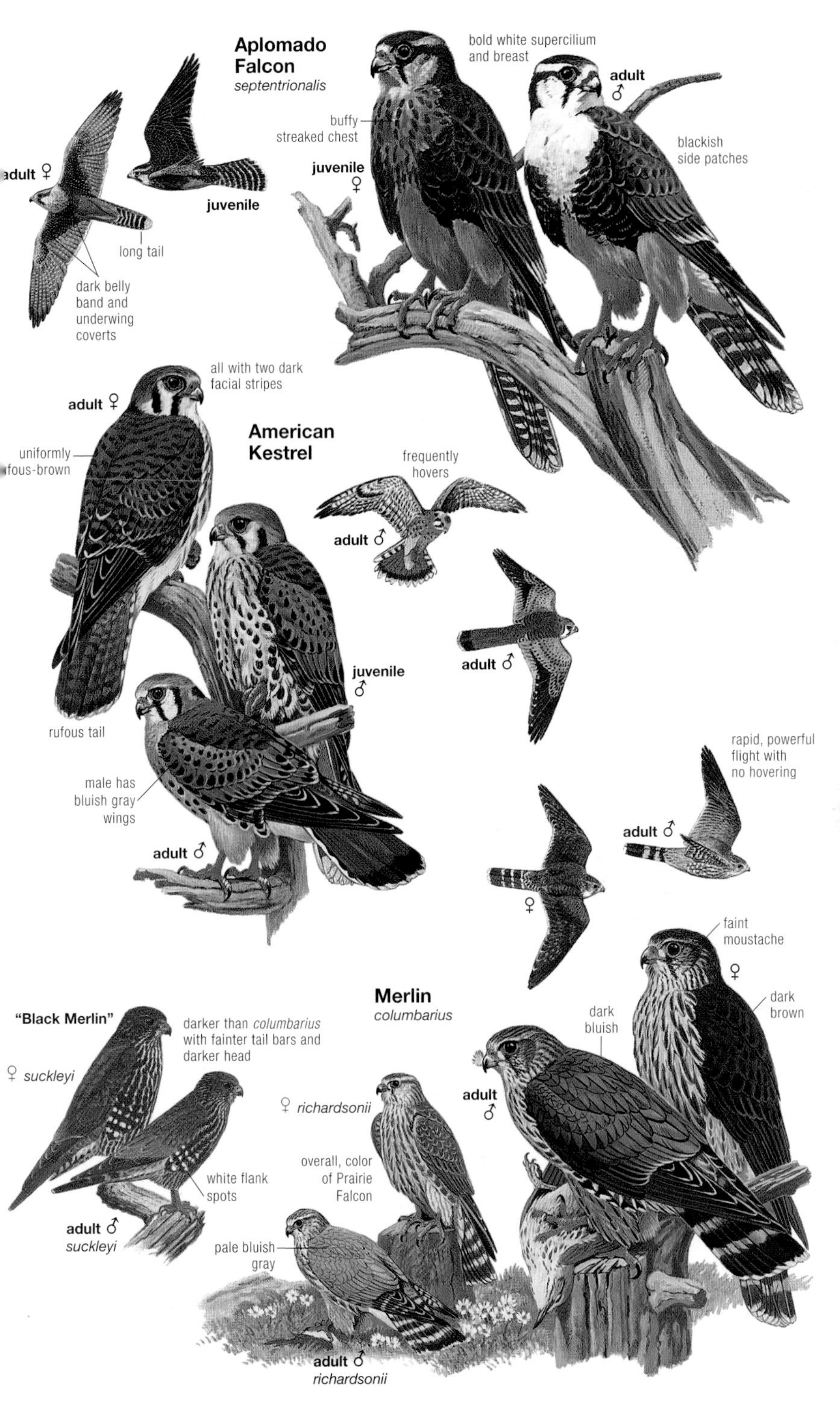

Aplomado Falcon
septentrionalis
bold white supercilium and breast
adult ♂
buffy streaked chest
juvenile ♀
blackish side patches
adult ♀
juvenile
long tail
dark belly band and underwing coverts
all with two dark facial stripes
adult ♀
American Kestrel
uniformly rufous-brown
frequently hovers
adult ♂
adult ♂
juvenile ♂
rufous tail
male has bluish gray wings
adult ♂
rapid, powerful flight with no hovering
adult ♂
♀
faint moustache
♀
Merlin
columbarius
dark brown
dark bluish
"Black Merlin"
darker than columbarius with fainter tail bars and darker head
♀ suckleyi
adult ♂
♀ richardsonii
overall, color of Prairie Falcon
white flank spots
adult ♂ suckleyi
pale bluish gray
adult ♂ richardsonii

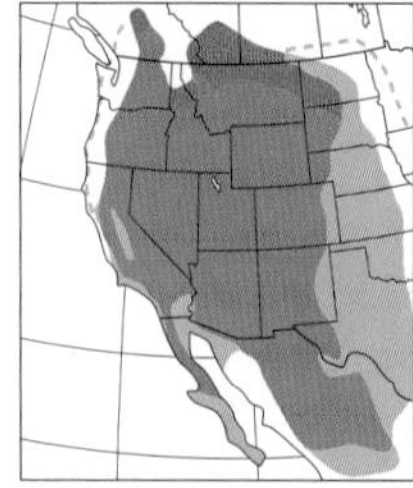

Prairie Falcon *Falco mexicanus*

L 15½-19½" (39-50 cm) WS 35-43" (89-109 cm) Pale brown above; creamy white and heavily spotted below. Brown crown, dark moustachial, and broad pale area below and behind eye; facial markings narrower and plumage paler overall than Peregrine Falcon. Compare also with female and juvenile male Merlin (previous page), especially subspecies *richardsonii.* In flight, all ages show distinctive dark axillaries and dark bar on wing lining, broader on female. Juvenile is streaked below (not spotted) and darker above; bluish cere. Preys chiefly on birds and small mammals.

Voice: Mostly silent.

Range: Inhabits dry, open country. Uncommon to fairly common.

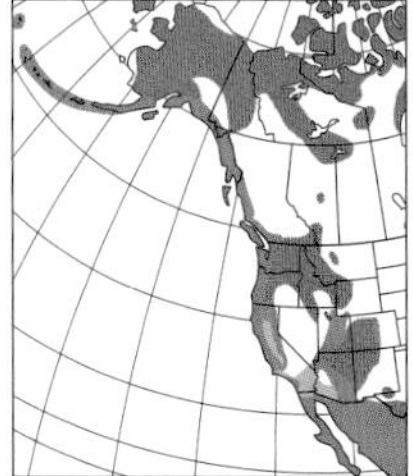

Peregrine Falcon *Falco peregrinus*

L 16-20" (41-51 cm) WS 36-44" (91-112 cm) Crown and nape black; black wedge extends below eye, forming a distinctive helmet, absent in Prairie Falcon and smaller Merlin (previous page). Tail is shorter than Prairie; wing tips almost reach the end; also lacks dark bar and axillaries on underwings. Plumage varies from pale in highly migratory subspecies *tundrius* breeding in the North to very dark in *pealei,* found from Queen Charlotte Islands to the Aleutians, some in winter down West Coast. In *pealei,* the largest race, adult has heavy spotting on whitish breast, underparts very dark. Intermediate *anatum* race, the nesting race over most of the West, has thickest moustachial stripe; ***adult*** shows rufous wash below; ***juvenile*** is dark brownish above, underparts heavily streaked. Juvenile *tundrius* has a pale eyebrow and larger pale area on side of face; underparts more finely streaked.

Voice: Gives harsh *cack* notes when agitated at nest site.

Range: Inhabits open wetlands; preys chiefly on birds. Nests on cliffs, but now established also in cities; nests on bridges, tall buildings. Use of pesticides severely reduced populations of breeding *anatum* in West. The banning of these toxins and restocking programs led to rebounding populations. Overall, it appears that *tundrius* is scarce in the West.

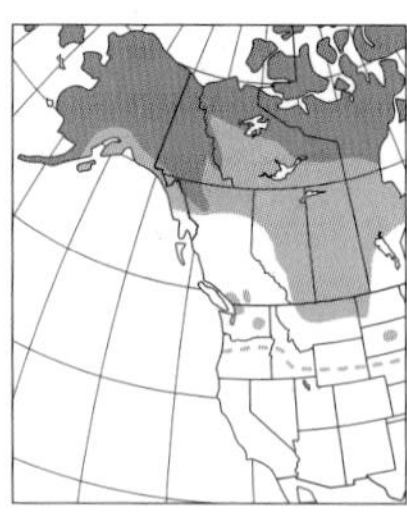

Gyrfalcon *Falco rusticolus*

L 20-25" (51-64 cm) WS 50-64" (127-163 cm) Heavily built; wings broader based than other falcons. ***Adult*** has yellow-orange eye ring, cere, and legs (bluish gray in juveniles). Tail broad and tapered, may be barred or unbarred; in perched bird, tail extends far beyond wing tips, unlike other falcons. Compare also with Northern Goshawk (page 104). Plumages vary from ***white morph*** to ***gray morph,*** to very ***dark morph,*** with paler gray morphs intermediate between typical gray and white. Facial markings range from none on white morph to all-dark cheeks on dark morph. Juveniles of white and gray morphs are much browner above; ***juveniles*** of gray and dark morphs show darker wing linings and paler flight feathers. Flies with slow, powerful wingbeats. Preys chiefly on birds.

Voice: Gives harsh *cack* notes when agitated at nest site.

Range: Uncommon; for breeding, inhabits open tundra near rocky outcrops and cliffs. Winters irregularly south to dashed line on map. Casual to central California and northeastern Colorado.

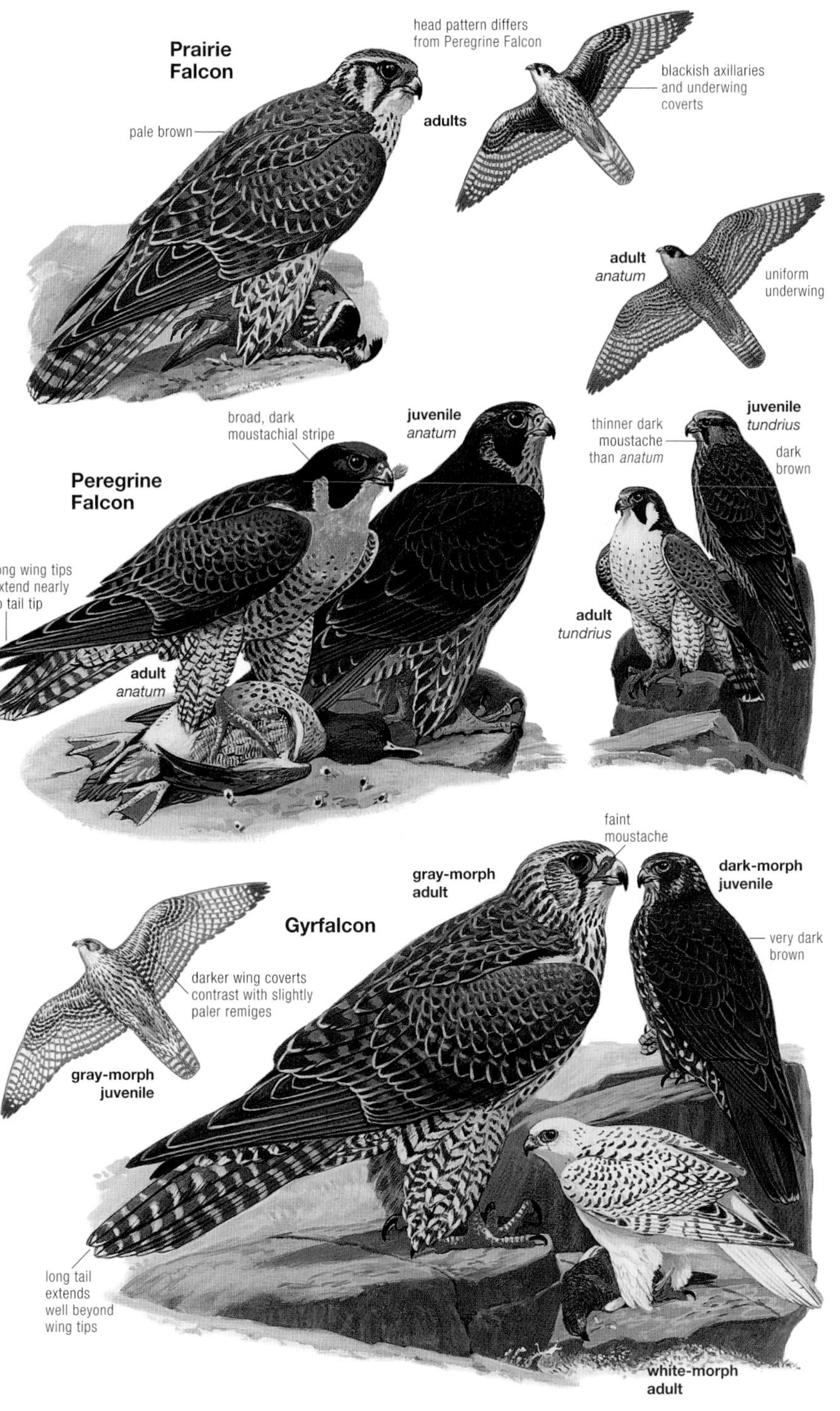
Prairie Falcon
head pattern differs from Peregrine Falcon
blackish axillaries and underwing coverts
pale brown
adults
adult anatum
uniform underwing
broad, dark moustachial stripe
juvenile anatum
thinner dark moustache than anatum
juvenile tundrius
dark brown
Peregrine Falcon
long wing tips extend nearly to tail tip
adult tundrius
adult anatum
faint moustache
gray-morph adult
dark-morph juvenile
Gyrfalcon
very dark brown
darker wing coverts contrast with slightly paler remiges
gray-morph juvenile
long tail extends well beyond wing tips
white-morph adult

Female Hawks in Flight

Kites

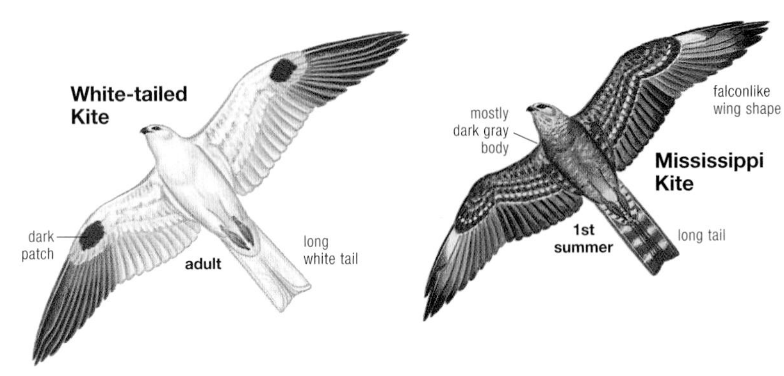

Falcons

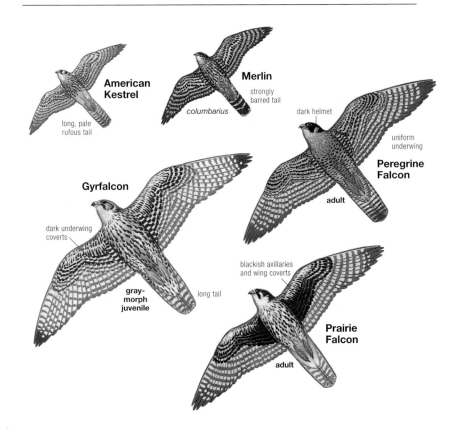

American Kestrel
long, pale rufous tail

Merlin
strongly barred tail
columbarius

dark helmet
uniform underwing
Peregrine Falcon
adult

Gyrfalcon
dark underwing coverts
gray-morph juvenile
long tail

blackish axillaries and wing coverts
Prairie Falcon
adult

Accipiters, Harrier, Smaller Buteos

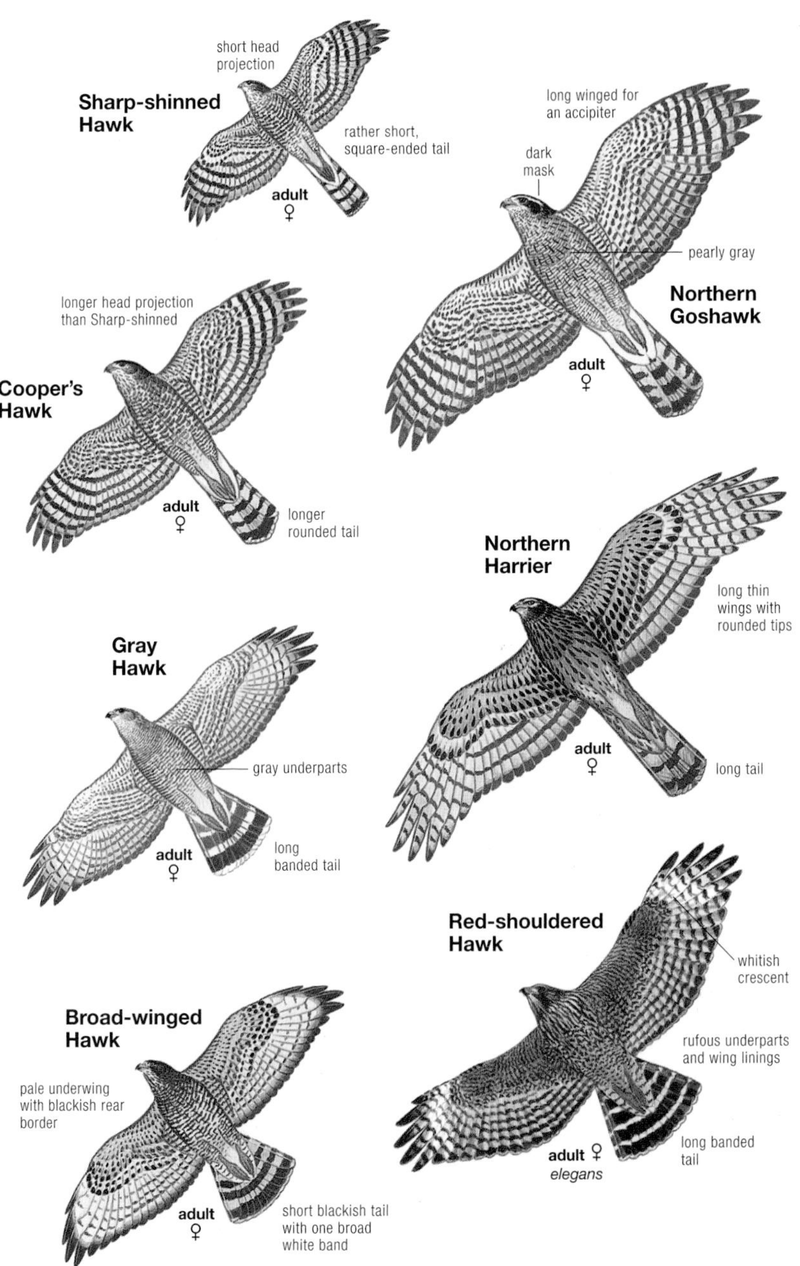

short head
projection
Sharp-shinned
Hawk
rather short,
square-ended tail
adult
♀
long winged for
an accipiter
dark
mask
pearly gray
Northern
Goshawk
adult
♀
longer head projection
than Sharp-shinned
Cooper's
Hawk
adult
♀
longer
rounded tail
Northern
Harrier
long thin
wings with
rounded tips
adult
♀
long tail
Gray
Hawk
gray underparts
adult
♀
long
banded tail
Red-shouldered
Hawk
whitish
crescent
rufous underparts
and wing linings
long banded
tail
adult ♀
elegans
Broad-winged
Hawk
pale underwing
with blackish rear
border
adult
♀
short blackish tail
with one broad
white band

Female Hawks in Flight

Larger Buteos, Black-Hawk

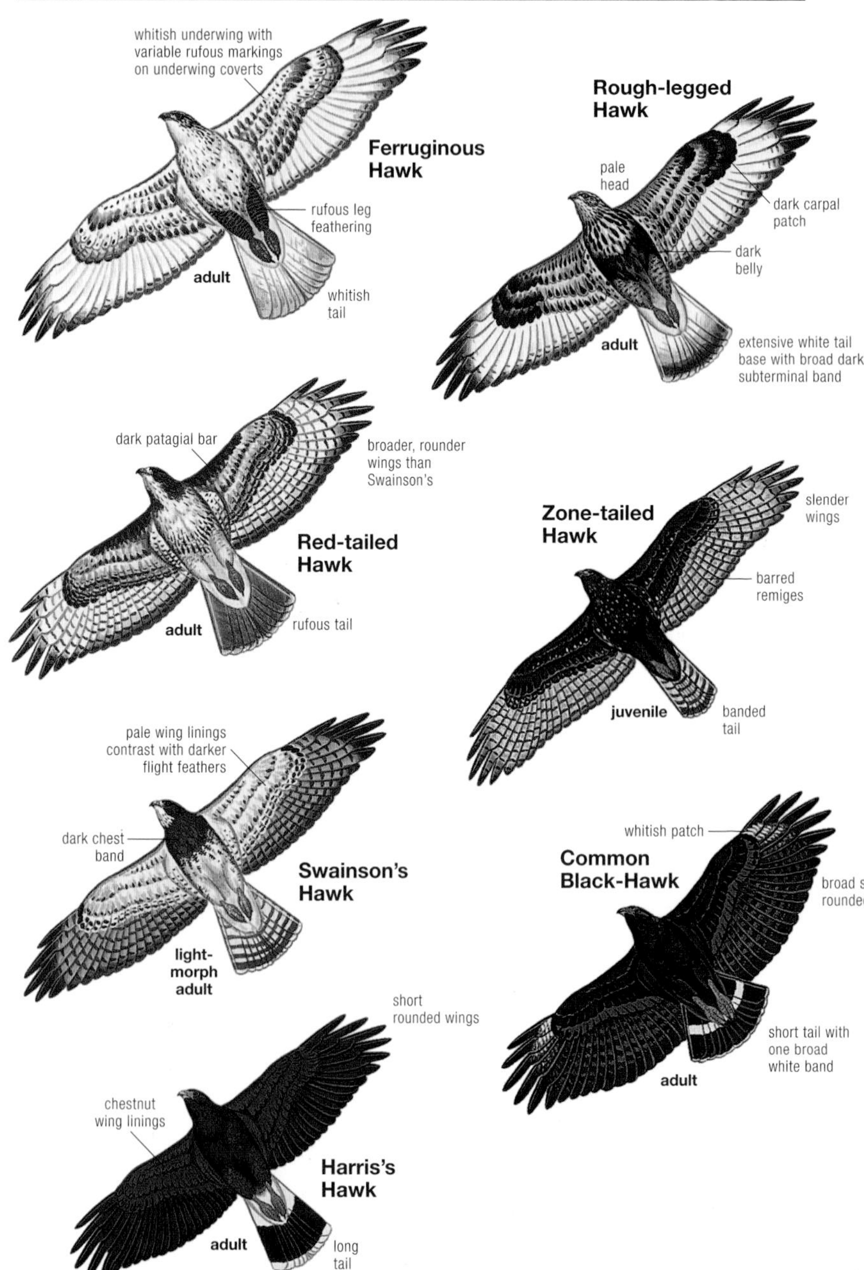
whitish underwing with variable rufous markings on underwing coverts
Ferruginous Hawk
rufous leg feathering
adult
whitish tail
Rough-legged Hawk
pale head
dark carpal patch
dark belly
adult
extensive white tail base with broad dark subterminal band
dark patagial bar
broader, rounder wings than Swainson's
Red-tailed Hawk
adult
rufous tail
Zone-tailed Hawk
slender wings
barred remiges
juvenile
banded tail
pale wing linings contrast with darker flight feathers
dark chest band
Swainson's Hawk
light-morph adult
whitish patch
Common Black-Hawk
broad
rounded
short tail with one broad white band
adult
short rounded wings
chestnut wing linings
Harris's Hawk
adult
long tail

Osprey, Eagles, Caracara

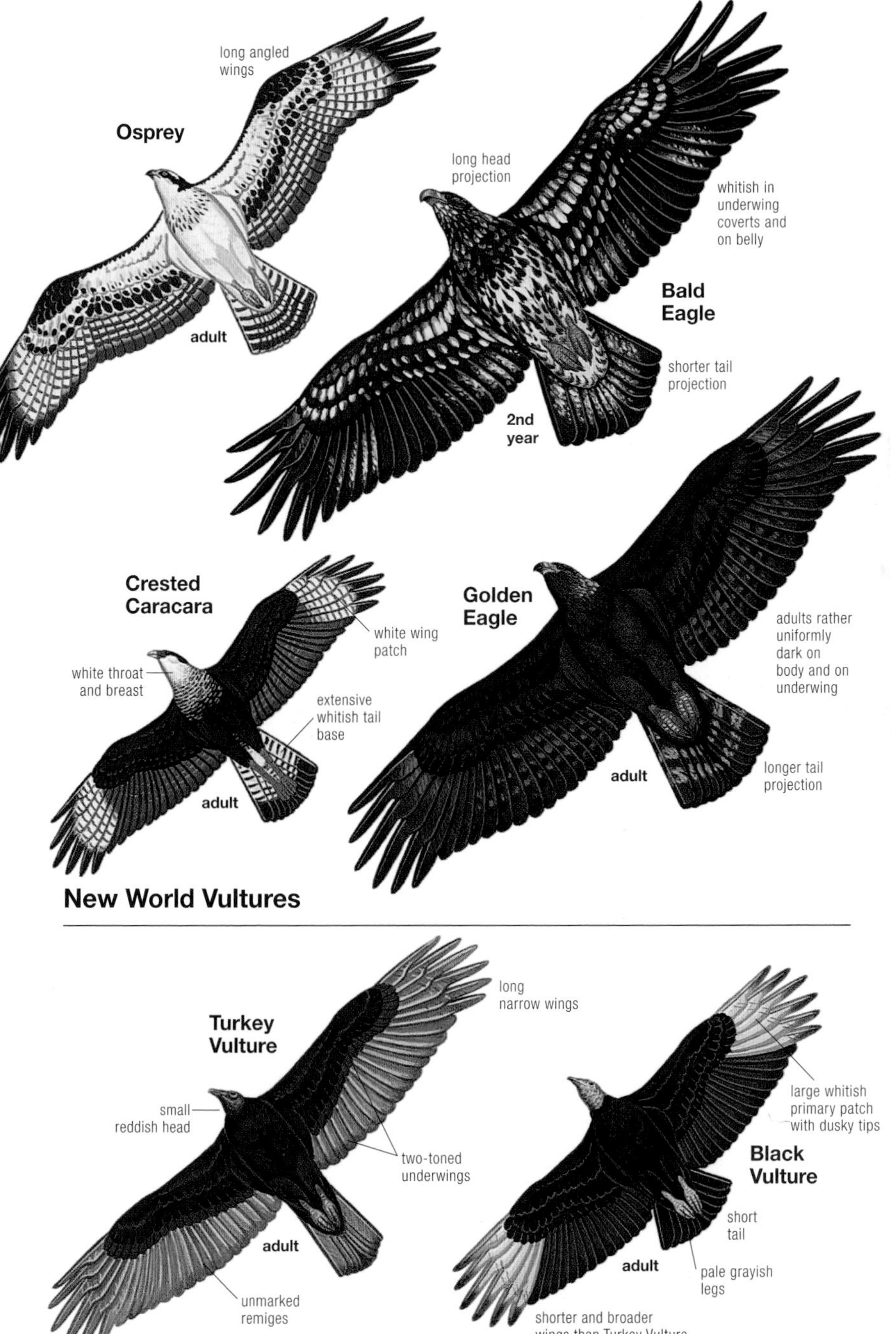

long angled wings
Osprey
adult
long head projection
whitish in underwing coverts and on belly
Bald Eagle
shorter tail projection
2nd year
Crested Caracara
white wing patch
white throat and breast
extensive whitish tail base
adult
Golden Eagle
adults rather uniformly dark on body and on underwing
adult
longer tail projection
New World Vultures
long narrow wings
Turkey Vulture
small reddish head
two-toned underwings
adult
unmarked remiges
large whitish primary patch with dusky tips
Black Vulture
short tail
adult
pale grayish legs
shorter and broader wings than Turkey Vulture

Rails, Gallinules, Coots (Family Rallidae)

These marsh birds have short tails and short, rounded wings. Most species are local and secretive. Some, especially the rails, are identified chiefly by call and habitat.

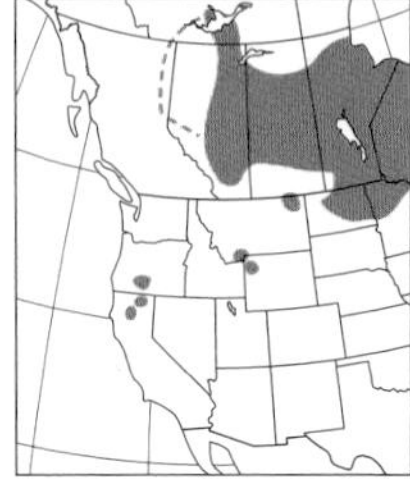

Yellow Rail *Coturnicops noveboracensis L 7¼" (18 cm)*

Small, dark, very secretive; tawny yellow above with dark stripes crossed by white bars. In flight, shows an extensive white patch on trailing edges of wings. Bill short, thick, and yellowish. Compare with juvenile Sora, which is not as black above and has upperparts streaked, not barred, with white.

Voice: Distinctive call, heard chiefly in breeding season, a four- or five-note *tick-tick, tick-tick-tick* in alternate twos or twos and threes, sounds like tapping two pebbles together.

Range: Rare in the West. Breeds in grassy marshes, damp fields. Winters in brackish or salt marshes.

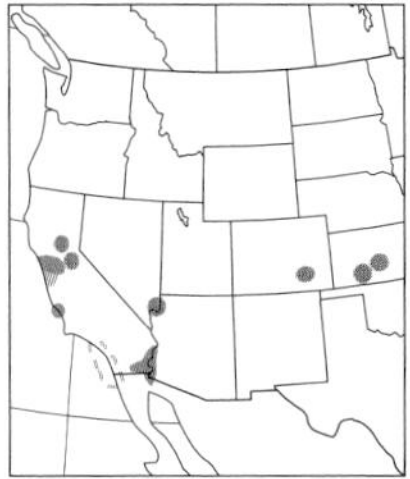

Black Rail *Laterallus jamaicensis L 6" (15 cm)*

Very small, extremely secretive. Overall blackish with white speckling and barring, chestnut nape; small dark bill. Newly hatched juveniles of other rails resemble Black Rail.

Voice: Distinctive call, heard chiefly in breeding season, is a repeated *kik-kee-do* or *kik-kee-derr;* sometimes four notes: *kik-kik-kee-do.* Most vocal in the middle of the night.

Range: Uncommon and local; inhabits marshes and swamps. Range speculative; declining in some coastal areas.

Clapper Rail *Rallus longirostris L 14½" (37 cm)*

Large; cinnamon underparts, grayish edges on brown-centered back feathers. West Coast races such as *levipes* (**E**) slightly brighter than *yumanensis* (**E**) of Colorado River and the Salton Sea.

Voice: Song is a series of ten or more dry *kek kek kek* notes. Call is a rapid series of grunt calls given year-round.

Range: Uncommon and local in coastal salt marshes; populations have declined since introduction of the Red Fox. Also found locally in Southwest from southern Nevada to central Arizona.

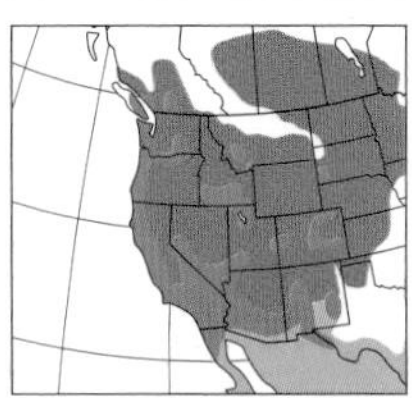

Virginia Rail *Rallus limicola L 9½" (24 cm)*

Similar to Clapper Rail but smaller; cheeks grayer; wings richer chestnut. ***Juvenile*** shows extensive black.

Voice: Territorial song is *kid kid kidick kidick;* common call, heard year-round, is a descending series of *oink* notes.

Range: Fairly common but a bit secretive; found in freshwater and brackish marshes and wetlands. Casual north to southeast Alaska.

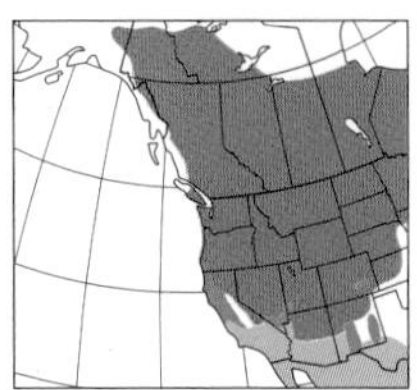

Sora *Porzana carolina L 8¾" (22 cm)*

Short, yellowish, thick bill. ***Breeding adult*** coarsely streaked above; face and center of throat and breast are black.

Voice: Calls, heard year-round, are a descending whinny and a high-pitched *keek;* whistled *ker-whee* heard on breeding grounds.

Range: Common in freshwater and brackish marshes; also found in saltwater marshes during migration and winter.

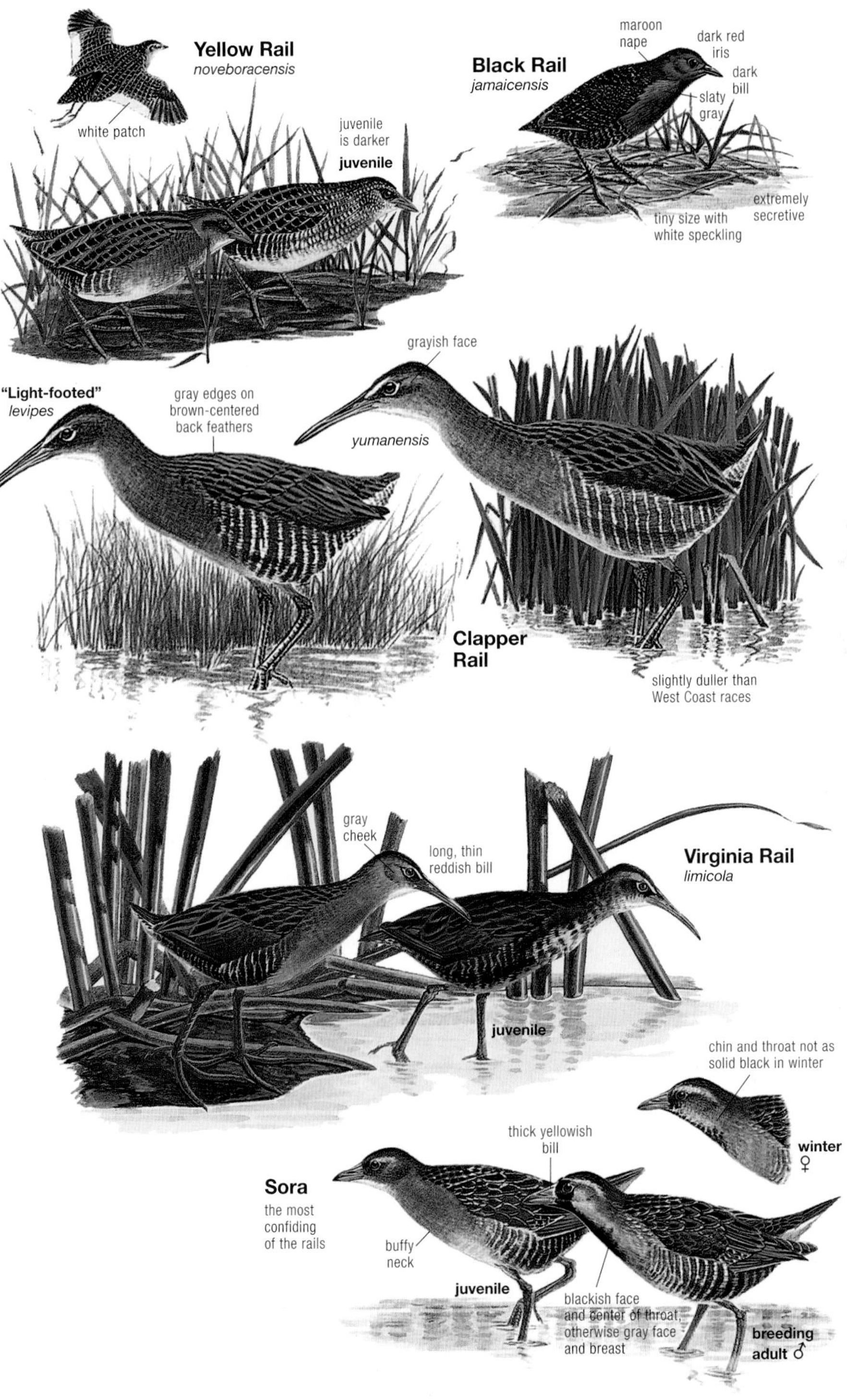
Yellow Rail
noveboracensis
white patch
juvenile
is darker
juvenile
Black Rail
jamaicensis
maroon
nape
dark red
iris
dark
bill
slaty
gray
extremely
secretive
tiny size with
white speckling
"Light-footed"
levipes
gray edges on
brown-centered
back feathers
grayish face
yumanensis
Clapper
Rail
slightly duller than
West Coast races
gray
cheek
long, thin
reddish bill
Virginia Rail
limicola
juvenile
chin and throat not as
solid black in winter
winter
♀
thick yellowish
bill
Sora
the most
confiding
of the rails
buffy
neck
juvenile
blackish face
and center of throat,
otherwise gray face
and breast
breeding
adult ♂

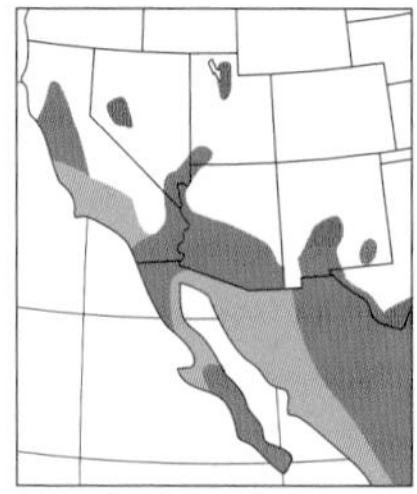
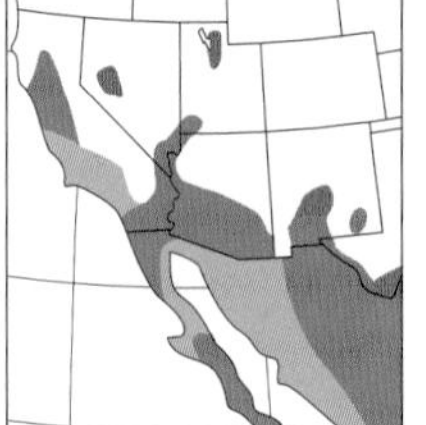

Common Moorhen *Gallinula chloropus* *L 14" (36 cm)*
Black head and neck, with red forehead shield, red bill with yellow tip. Back brownish olive; underparts slate; white along flanks is diagnostic. Outer undertail coverts white, inner ones black. Legs and feet yellow. ***Juvenile*** is paler, browner; throat whitish; bill and legs dusky. ***Winter adult*** has brownish facial shield and usually a brownish bill with dusky yellow tip.
Voice: A high *keek;* also a series of nasal clucking notes.
Range: Uncommon to common in freshwater marshes, ponds, placid rivers. Casual north to British Columbia and Montana.

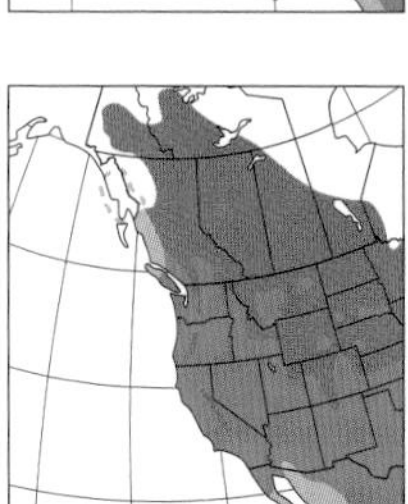

American Coot *Fulica americana* *L 15½" (39 cm)*
Overall blackish, darker on head and neck; outer undertail coverts white. Whitish bill has dark subterminal band; note reddish brown forehead shield. Leg color ranges from greenish gray in ***juvenile*** birds to yellow or orangish in adults. Toes are lobed, unlike gallinules. Juvenile is quite pale; by first winter more like adult, but still paler, with whitish feather tips, especially below. In flight, distinctive white trailing edge on most of wing. Often dives to feed.
Voice: A high *keek;* also a series of nasal clucking notes.
Range: Common to abundant. Nests in freshwater marshes, in wetlands, or near lakes and ponds; winters in both fresh and salt water, often in large flocks; also grazes on golf courses and park lawns. Rare north to Alaska.

Cranes (Family Gruidae)

Tall birds with long necks and legs. Tertials droop over the rump in a "bustle" that distinguishes cranes from herons. Cranes fly with their necks fully extended and circle in thermals like raptors. Courtship includes a frenzied, leaping dance.

Sandhill Crane *Grus canadensis*
L 34-48" (86-122 cm) WS 73-90" (185-229 cm) Races vary in size: northern nominate race smallest; more southerly *tabida* largest; *rowani* is intermediate. ***Adult*** is gray, with dull red skin on crown and lores; whitish chin, cheek, and upper throat; and slaty primaries. ***Juvenile*** lacks red patch; head and neck vary from pale to tawny; gray body is irregularly mottled with brownish red; full adult plumage reached after two and a half years. Great Blue Heron (page 90), sometimes confused with Sandhill Crane, lacks bustle. Preening with muddy bills, cranes may stain feathers of upper back, lower neck, and breast with ferrous solution in mud.
Voice: Common call is a trumpeting, rattling *gar-oo-oo,* audible for more than a mile. Young birds give a wholly different, cricket-like call.
Range: Locally common; breeds on tundra and in marshes and grasslands. In winter, regularly feeds in dry fields, returning to shallow water at night. Migrating flocks fly at great heights, sometimes too high to be seen from the ground.

Common Moorhen
cachinnans
breeding adult
red bill with yellow tip
bronze-brown back
juvenile
darker bill
winter adult
thin whitish stripe
red skin
whitish bill
juvenile
some lack dark top to shield
variant
American Coot
americana
lobed feet
swims like a duck most of the time
red crown
cranes have
tial "bustles"
juvenile
Sandhill Crane
rowani
adult
neck extended in flight
stained adult
adult
dark dusky remiges

Lapwings, Plovers (Family Charadriidae)

These compact birds run and stop abruptly when foraging. Shape and behavior identify plovers in general.

Black-bellied Plover *Pluvialis squatarola L 11½" (29 cm)*
Black-and-white ***breeding male*** has frosty crown and nape, white belly region; ***female*** averages less black. ***Winter*** and ***juvenile*** birds distinguished from Pacific and American Golden-Plovers by larger size, larger bill, and grayer plumage (including crown); underparts streaked rather than softly barred, but note that juvenile can be speckled with gold above. In flight, shows black axillaries and white uppertail coverts, barred white tail, and bold white wing stripe.
Voice: Call is a drawn-out, three-note whistle, the second note lower pitched.
Range: Nests on Arctic tundra. Common at Salton Sea; uncommon to rare elsewhere in interior.

American Golden-Plover *Pluvialis dominica L 10¼" (26 cm)* Smaller, with a smaller bill than Black-bellied Plover; wing stripe is indistinct, and underwings are smoky gray with no black in axillaries; no contrasting white rump. Note the approximately four evenly spaced primary tips. ***Breeding male*** shows broad white patches on sides of neck; underparts otherwise black. ***Female*** has less black but retains general pattern, including white bulging out on sides of neck.
Voice: Flight call is a shrill *ku-wheep.*
Range: Mar. arrivals on Gulf Coast in winter plumage; breeding plumage slowly acquired on migration north, but of the few seen in West in spring, most are in or mostly in winter plumage. Overall a rare migrant, mostly in fall, in West; in fall, nearly all are ***juveniles.*** Winters in South America.

Pacific Golden-Plover *Pluvialis fulva L 9¾" (25 cm)*
Similar to American, but shorter primary tip projection with three, not four, staggered primary tips, the outer two close together; bill appears thicker, legs longer. ***Breeding male*** has less extensive white on sides of neck than American; white continues down sides and flanks; undertail coverts whiter; slightly larger gold markings above. ***Female*** has less black below. ***Juveniles*** and ***winter*** birds typically appear brighter than American.
Voice: Call, a loud, rich *chu-wheet.*
Range: Breeds from northern Russia to western Alaska. Winters from southern Asia to Pacific islands; a few on West Coast and in California's Central Valley and the Imperial Valley. Casual elsewhere in western portion of the interior West. Some adults migrate earlier in fall than American Golden-Plovers. In Alaska, American Golden-Plovers favor less vegetated slopes, whereas Pacific Golden-Plovers in western Alaska favor the coast and river valleys.

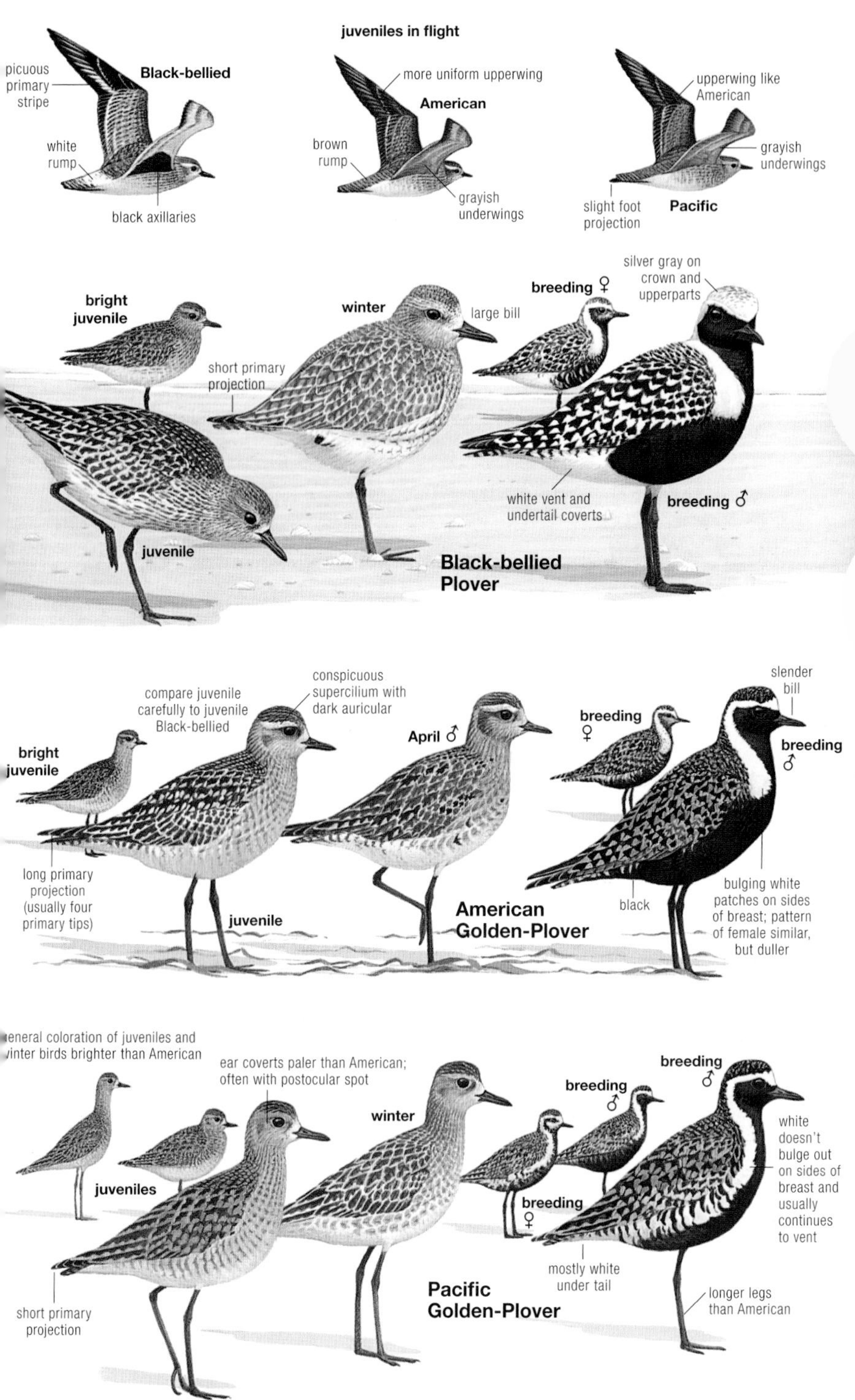
juveniles in flight
picuous
primary
stripe
Black-bellied
white
rump
black axillaries
more uniform upperwing
American
brown
rump
grayish
underwings
upperwing like
American
grayish
underwings
slight foot
projection
Pacific
bright
juvenile
winter
large bill
breeding ♀
silver gray on
crown and
upperparts
short primary
projection
white vent and
undertail coverts
breeding ♂
juvenile
Black-bellied
Plover
compare juvenile
carefully to juvenile
Black-bellied
conspicuous
supercilium with
dark auricular
slender
bill
bright
juvenile
April ♂
breeding
♀
breeding
♂
long primary
projection
(usually four
primary tips)
juvenile
American
Golden-Plover
black
bulging white
patches on sides
of breast; pattern
of female similar,
but duller
eneral coloration of juveniles and
vinter birds brighter than American
ear coverts paler than American;
often with postocular spot
breeding
♂
breeding
♂
winter
juveniles
breeding
♀
white
doesn't
bulge out
on sides of
breast and
usually
continues
to vent
short primary
projection
mostly white
under tail
Pacific
Golden-Plover
longer legs
than American

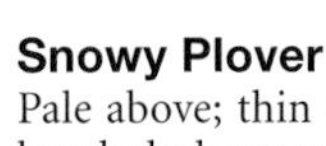

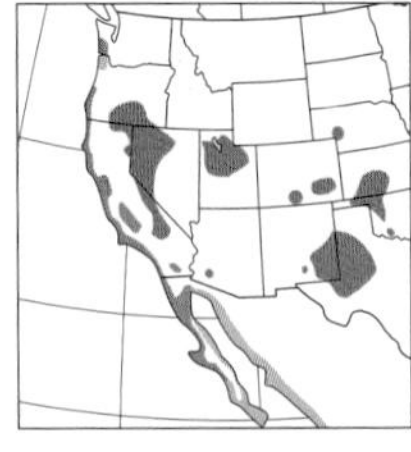

Snowy Plover *Charadrius alexandrinus L 6¼" (16 cm)*
Pale above; thin dark bill; dark or grayish legs; partial breast band; dark ear patch. ***Females*** and ***juveniles*** resemble Piping Plover; note Snowy Plover's thinner bill, darker legs.
Voice: Calls include a low *krut* and a soft, whistled *ku-wheet.*
Range: Inhabits barren sandy beaches and flats and around edges of alkali lakes. Generally uncommon; western subspecies, *nivosus,* is threatened (**T**). Accidental to western Alaska and the Yukon.

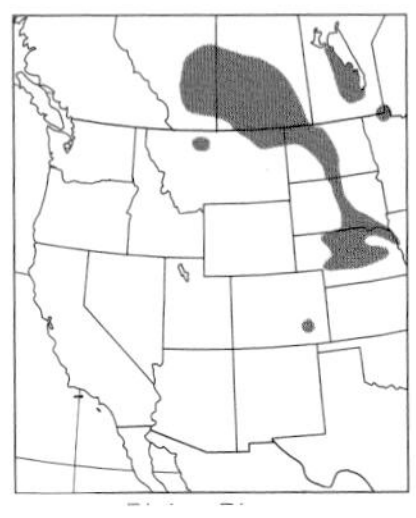

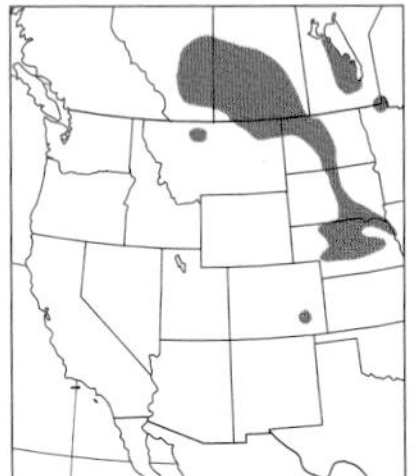

Piping Plover *Charadrius melodus* **E** *L 7¼" (18 cm)*
Very pale above; orange legs; pale rump conspicuous in flight. In ***breeding*** plumage, shows dark narrow breast band, usually complete in Great Plains and Midwest subspecies, *circumcinctus,* but sometimes incomplete, especially in ***female.*** In ***winter,*** bill is all-dark. Distinguished from Snowy Plover by thicker bill, paler back; legs are brighter than Semipalmated Plover.
Voice: Distinctive call is a clear *peep-lo.*
Range: Breeds on sandy shores of lakes, mostly alkali. Uncommon to rare in western breeding range. Subspecies *circumcinctus* winters on Gulf Coast. Casual migrant on western Great Plains and western states, where it has wintered in coastal California.

Semipalmated Plover *Charadrius semipalmatus*
L 7¼" (18 cm) Dark back distinguishes this species from Piping and Snowy Plovers; bill much smaller than Wilson's Plover. At very close range, Semipalmated shows partial webbing between toes. ***Breeding male*** often lacks white above eye; shows orangish eye ring. ***Juvenile***'s legs darker than adult's legs.
Voice: Distinctive call is a whistled, upslurred *chu-weet;* song is a series of same.
Range: Common on beaches, lakeshores, and tidal flats; seen throughout the West in migration.

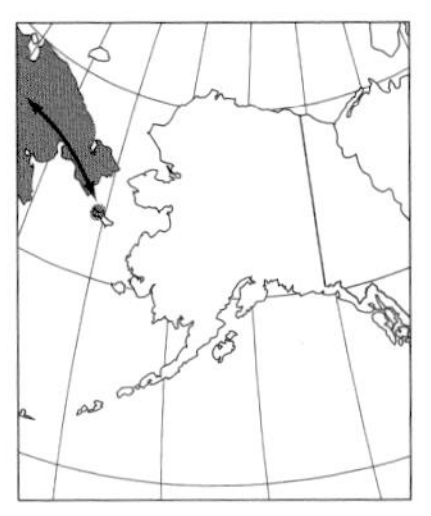

Common Ringed Plover *Charadrius hiaticula*
L 7½" (19 cm) Almost identical to Semipalmated Plover; best distinguished by voice. Breast band averages slightly broader in center than Semipalmated. White eyebrow is more distinct; orbital ring is partial or lacking altogether; webbing between toes less extensive. Bill is slightly longer, of more even thickness, and shows more orange at base; black on face meets bill where mandibles join.
Voice: Call is a soft, fluted *pooee;* song, delivered in display flight, is a series of these notes.
Range: Casual migrant on Alaska's Aleutian and Pribilof islands (most records are in fall); regular in small numbers, and occasionally breeds on St. Lawrence Island.

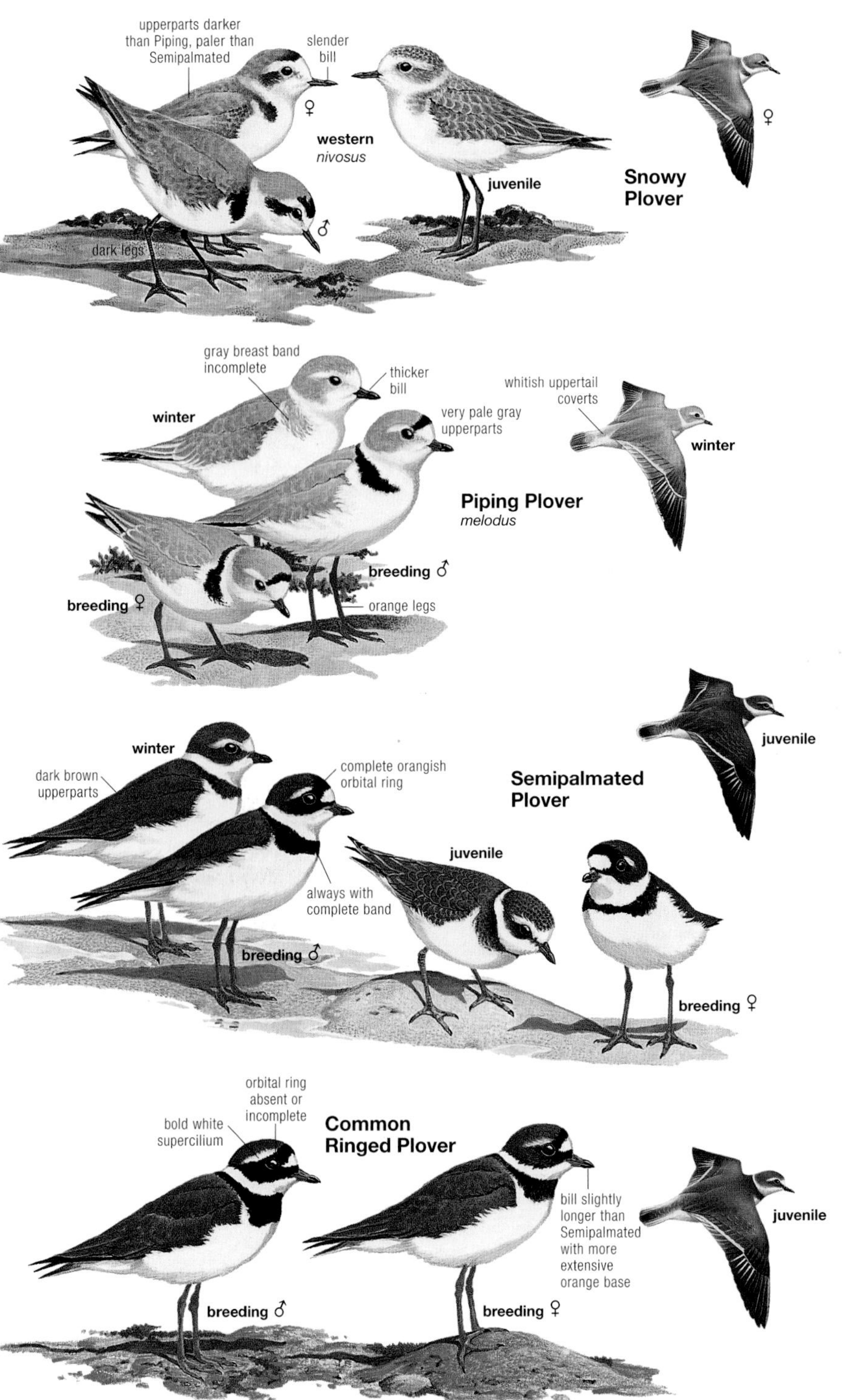
upperparts darker than Piping, paler than Semipalmated
slender bill
♀
western
nivosus
juvenile
♀
Snowy Plover
♂
dark legs
gray breast band incomplete
thicker bill
winter
very pale gray upperparts
whitish uppertail coverts
winter
Piping Plover
melodus
breeding ♂
breeding ♀
orange legs
juvenile
winter
dark brown upperparts
complete orangish orbital ring
Semipalmated Plover
juvenile
always with complete band
breeding ♂
breeding ♀
orbital ring absent or incomplete
bold white supercilium
Common Ringed Plover
bill slightly longer than Semipalmated with more extensive orange base
juvenile
breeding ♂
breeding ♀

Lesser Sand-Plover *Charadrius mongolus L 7½" (19 cm)*
Asian species. Bright rusty red breast; black-and-white facial pattern. ***Female*** is duller. ***Juvenile*** has broad buffy wash across breast; edged with buff above. In ***winter*** birds, underparts are white except for broad grayish patches on sides of breast.
Voice: Gives a hard and rather grating nonmusical *tirrick.*
Range: Rare but regular migrant on Aleutians and on islands off western Alaska; casual along West Coast in fall. Casual western and northwestern Alaska, where it has bred on a few occasions.

Killdeer *Charadrius vociferus L 10½" (27 cm)*
Double breast bands are distinctive. Bright reddish orange rump is visible in flight. Downy young have only one breast band.
Voice: Distinctive loud, piercing call, *kill-dee* or *dee-dee-dee.*
Range: Common in grassy fields and on shores. Nests on open ground, usually on gravel. May form loose flocks and linger into early winter in summer range. Vagrant north of breeding range. A very early spring migrant (by late Feb.).

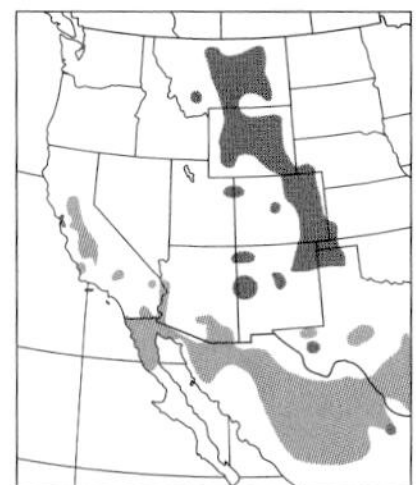

Mountain Plover *Charadrius montanus L 9" (23 cm)*
In ***breeding*** plumage, unbanded white underparts separate this plover from all other brown-backed plovers. Buffy tinge on breast is more extensive in ***winter*** plumage; compare with winter American Golden-Plover (page 126). In flight, Mountain Plover shows white underwings; American Golden-Plover's underwings are grayish.
Voice: Calls heard on breeding grounds include low, drawn-out whistles and harsh notes. In migration and winter, gives a harsh *krrr* note.
Range: Inhabits plains; local and declining in many areas. Gregarious in winter; usually found on short grassy or bare dirt fields, but also in migration found on alkali flats in association with water. Rare migrant over much of West. Casual in Pacific Northwest. Formerly bred north to southern Canada.

Eurasian Dotterel *Charadrius morinellus L 8¼" (21 cm)*
Eurasian species, very approachable. Whitish band on lower breast is somewhat obscured in young and ***winter*** birds. Bold white eyebrow extends around entire head. Unlike other plovers, ***females*** are darker and more richly colored than males. ***Juvenile*** is dark above and striped and tinged with buff, and buffy below. With a pale chest band and whitish undertail coverts.
Voice: Often silent, but flight call is a soft and rolling, descending note.
Range: Very rare, sporadic breeder in northwestern Alaska; casual along West Coast in fall. There is a single winter record in the Imperial Valley of California (with Mountain Plovers) and another in northwestern Baja California.

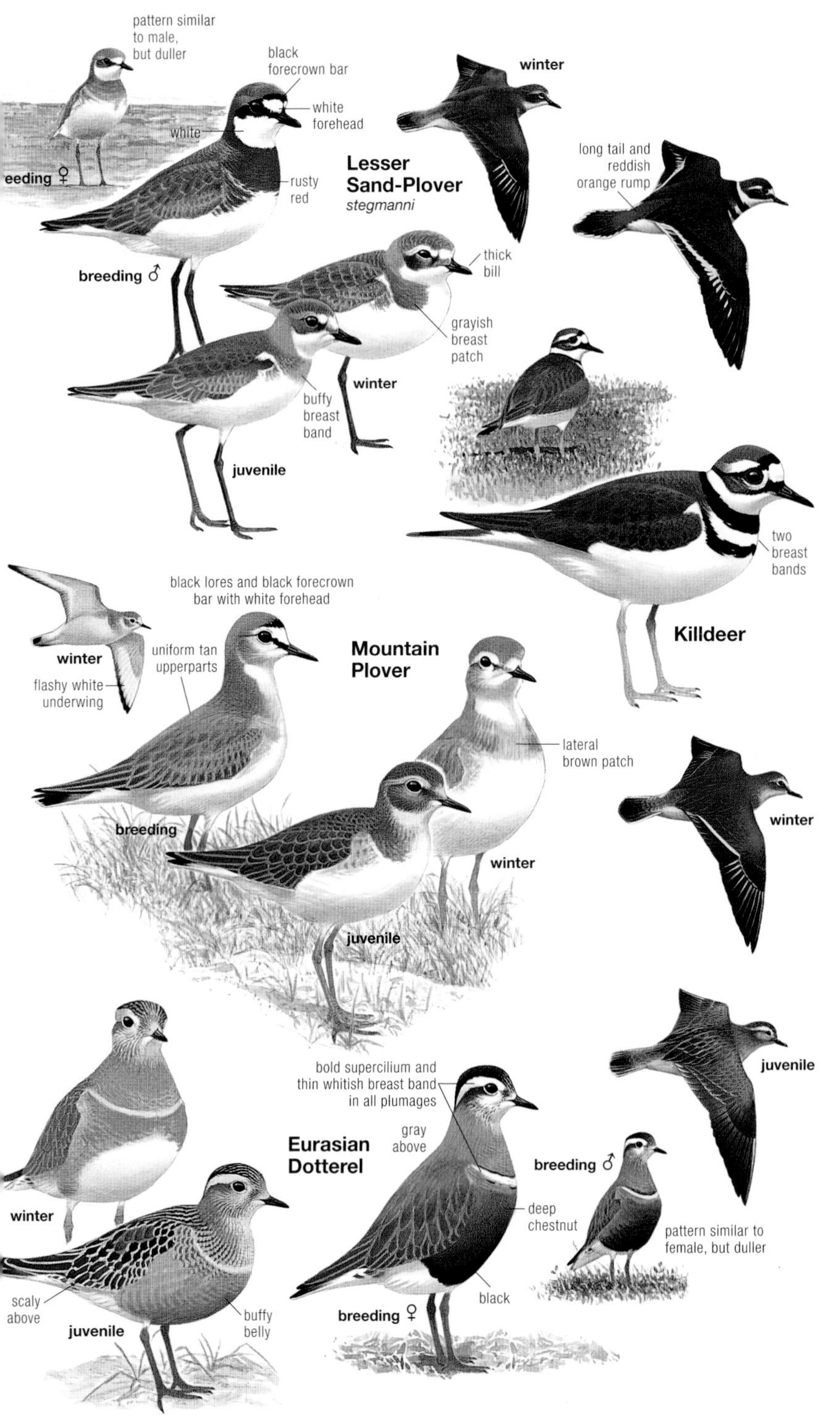
pattern similar
to male,
but duller
eeding ♀
black
forecrown bar
white
forehead
white
rusty
red
Lesser
Sand-Plover
stegmanni
breeding ♂
winter
long tail and
reddish
orange rump
thick
bill
grayish
breast
patch
buffy
breast
band
winter
juvenile
two
breast
bands
Killdeer
black lores and black forecrown
bar with white forehead
winter
flashy white
underwing
uniform tan
upperparts
Mountain
Plover
lateral
brown patch
winter
breeding
winter
juvenile
bold supercilium and
thin whitish breast band
in all plumages
juvenile
gray
above
Eurasian
Dotterel
breeding ♂
winter
deep
chestnut
pattern similar to
female, but duller
scaly
above
juvenile
buffy
belly
breeding ♀
black

Oystercatchers (Family Haematopodidae)

These chunky shorebirds have laterally flattened, heavy bills that can reach into mollusks and pry the shells open; they also probe sand for worms and crabs.

American Oystercatcher *Haematopus palliatus*
L 18½" (47 cm) Large red-orange bill. Black head and dark brown back; white wing and tail patches, white underparts. Juvenile appears scaly above; dark tip on bill is kept through first year. Feeds in small, noisy flocks on coastal beaches and mudflats.
Voice: Like Black Oystercatcher.
Range: Resident along west coast of Mexico. Very rare to coastal southern California, where many show some degree of hybridization with Black Oystercatcher. Most in northern Baja California show some limited blackish flecking in the white areas of the underparts, typical of the northwest race, *frazari,* from this region. Accidental inland.

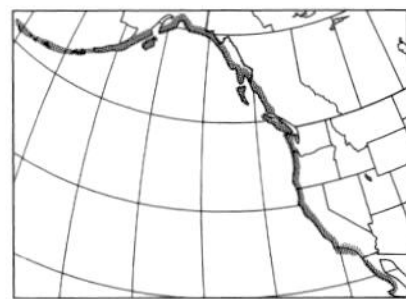

Black Oystercatcher *Haematopus bachmani*
L 17½" (45 cm) Large red-orange bill, all-dark body, pinkish legs. On immatures, outer half of bill is dusky during first year.
Voice: Call is a loud whistled *queep* given singly or in a series.
Range: Resident on rocky shores and islands along the Pacific coast.

Stilts, Avocets (Family Recurvirostridae)

Sleek and graceful waders with long, slender bills and spindly legs. Two species inhabit North America.

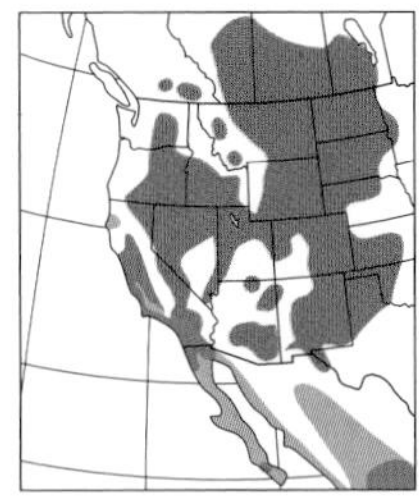

American Avocet *Recurvirostra americana L 18" (46 cm)*
Black-and-white above, white below; head and neck rusty in breeding plumage, gray in winter. ***Juveniles*** have cinnamon wash on head and neck. Avocets feed by sweeping their bills from side to side through the water. ***Male***'s bill is longer, straighter than ***female***'s.
Voice: Common call is a loud *wheet.*
Range: Fairly common on shallow ponds, marshes, and lakeshores. Casual north to southern Alaska.

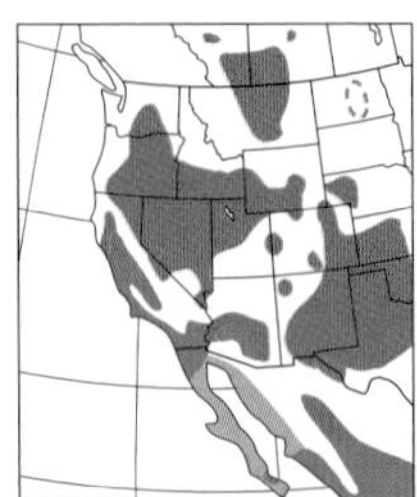

Black-necked Stilt *Himantopus mexicanus L 14" (36 cm)*
Male's glossy black back and bill contrast sharply with white underparts, long red or pink legs. Female is browner on back. ***Juvenile*** is brown above, with buffy edgings.
Voice: Common call is a loud *kek kek kek.*
Range: Breeds and winters in a wide variety of wet habitats. Breeding range is spreading north.

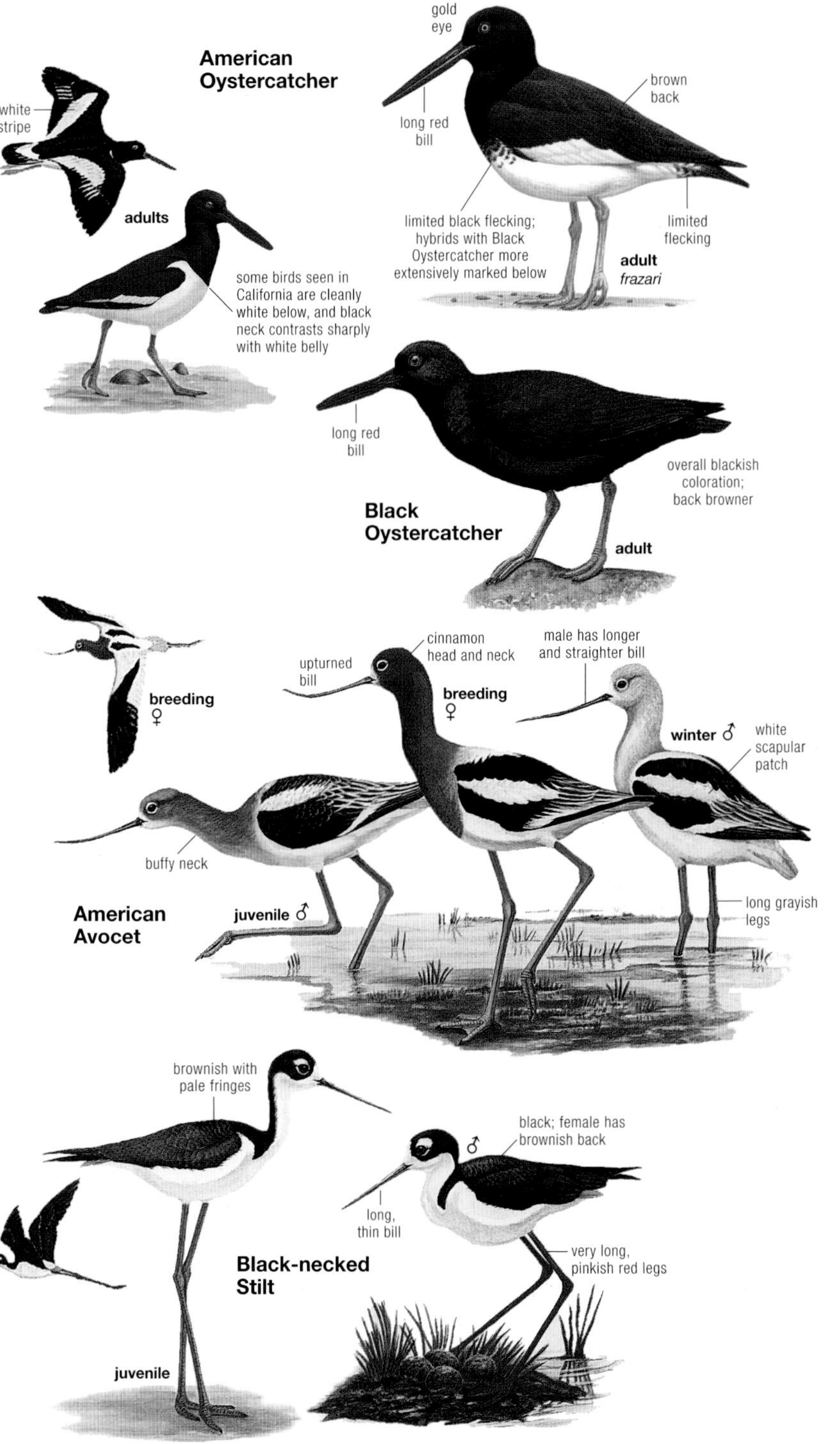
American Oystercatcher
d white
g stripe
adults
some birds seen in California are cleanly white below, and black neck contrasts sharply with white belly
gold eye
long red bill
brown back
limited black flecking; hybrids with Black Oystercatcher more extensively marked below
limited flecking
adult
frazari
long red bill
overall blackish coloration; back browner
Black Oystercatcher
adult
breeding ♀
upturned bill
cinnamon head and neck
breeding ♀
male has longer and straighter bill
winter ♂
white scapular patch
buffy neck
American Avocet
juvenile ♂
long grayish legs
brownish with pale fringes
black; female has brownish back
♂
long, thin bill
very long, pinkish red legs
Black-necked Stilt
juvenile

Sandpipers, Phalaropes, Allies (Family Scolopacidae)

The majority of these shorebirds have three distinct plumages. Most begin molting to winter plumage as they near or reach their winter grounds.

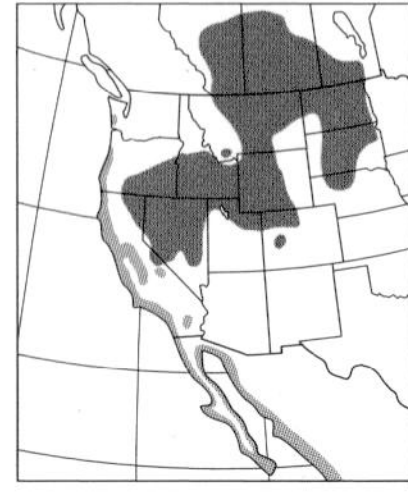

Willet *Tringa semipalmata L 15" (38 cm)*
Large, plump, and grayish overall with grayish legs. In flight, note black-and-white wing pattern. Two subspecies, but only *inornata* known for West. Marked irregularly with blackish and dark gray above and below in ***breeding*** plumage. In ***winter*** pale gray above. whitish below. ***Juvenile*** similar, but browner and edged above.
Voice: Territorial call is *pill-will-willet*. Other raucous calls given year-round, all averaging higher pitched in the nominate race.
Range: Nests in prairie interior marshes. Uncommon interior migrant, except at Salton Sea, where common. Some nonbreeders summer on coast.

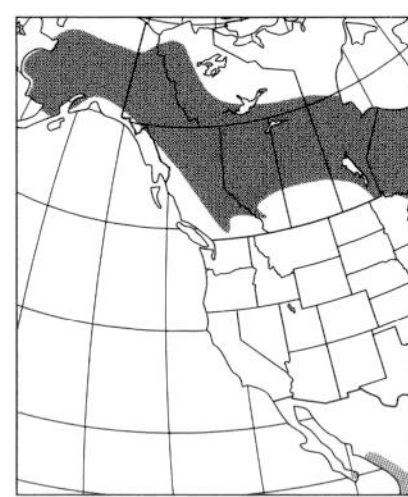

Solitary Sandpiper *Tringa solitaria L 8½" (22 cm)*
Dark brown above, heavily spotted with buffy white. White below; lower throat, breast, and sides streaked with blackish brown. Bolder white eye ring and shorter, olive legs distinguish Solitary Sandpiper from Lesser Yellowlegs (page 136). In flight, shows dark central tail feathers, white outer feathers barred with black. Underwing is dark. Often keeps wings raised briefly after alighting; on the ground, often bobs its tail. Generally seen singly or in small flocks.
Voice: Calls include a shrill *peet-weet*.
Range: Rare spring and uncommon fall migrant west of Rockies. Fairly common at shallow backwaters, pools, small estuaries.

Common Sandpiper *Actitis hypoleucos L 8" (20 cm)*
Eurasian species. ***Breeding adult*** brown above with dark barring and streaking; white below; upper breast finely streaked. ***Juvenile*** and winter birds resemble Spotted Sandpiper. Note Common's longer tail; in juvenile, barring on edge of tertials extends along the entire feather. In flight, shows longer white wing stripe, longer white trailing edge; wingbeats not as shallow and rapid.
Voice: Call in flight is a shrill, piping *twee-wee-wee.*
Range: Rare migrant, usually in spring, on western Aleutians (has nested once on Attu Island), Pribilofs, St. Lawrence Island; casual to central Aleutians and Seward Peninsula.

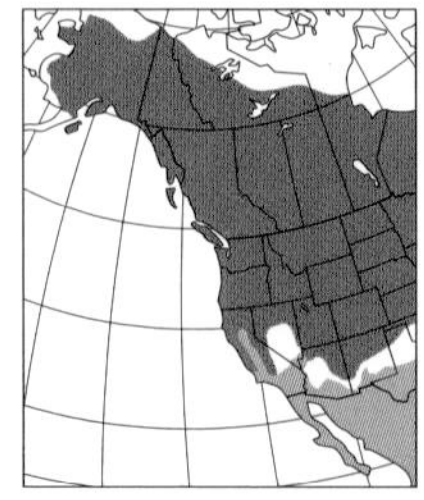

Spotted Sandpiper *Actitis macularius L 7½" (19 cm)*
Striking in ***breeding*** plumage, with barred upperparts, spotted underparts, mostly pink bill. In ***winter,*** brown above, white below, sometimes with a few spots in vent region. ***Juvenile*** similar but with barred wing coverts; tertials plain but barred near tip. Both Spotted and Common Sandpipers fly with stiff, rapid, fluttering wingbeats. On the ground, both nod and teeter constantly.
Voice: Calls include a shrill *peet-weet* and, in flight, a series of *weet* notes, lower pitched than the calls of Solitary Sandpiper.
Range: Common; found along streams, ponds, lakes. Generally seen singly; may form small flocks in migration.

Willet
inornata

striking wing pattern in flight

winter

stout bill of moderate length

irregular dark markings above

irregular markings below

plainer and paler upperparts

breeding

juvenile

winter

Sandpipers

Solitary Sandpiper
solitaria

white eye ring

juvenile

breeding

dark grayish brown breast

short greenish legs

darkish underwings

breeding

dark center to tail with barred outer tail feathers

dark lateral breast patches

barred tertials

longer tail than Spotted

breeding

juvenile

juvenile

longer wings with bolder white wing stripe than Spotted

Common Sandpiper

dark lateral breast patches

1st winter

juvenile

Spotted Sandpiper

flies with rapid, shallow, stiff wingbeats

barred wing coverts

heavily spotted underparts

juvenile

pink bill with dark tip

breeding

mostly plain tertials, except near tip

Lesser Yellowlegs *Tringa flavipes L 10½" (27 cm)*
Legs yellow to rarely orange. Smaller than Greater Yellowlegs; all-dark bill is shorter, thinner, and straighter. In ***breeding*** plumage, not nearly as heavily as marked as Greater Yellowlegs, especially on sides and flanks. ***Juvenile*** and ***winter*** birds are overall darker than Greater; juvenile Lessers are washed with grayish brown across the neck and lack the streaks that are present in Greater. A more sedate feeder than Greater, leisurely picks at prey from a more vertical position.
Voice: Call is one to three *tew* notes, higher than Greater; individual notes more clipped and all on one pitch. On nesting grounds, like Greater, often perches in trees and yelps at intruders.
Range: Overall uncommon (common on western Great Plains) in West, especially in spring (more numerous in fall). Nests on tundra or in woodland. Most winter in South America, a few in U.S.

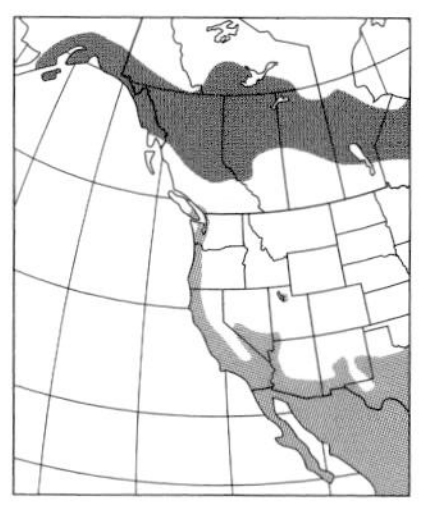

Greater Yellowlegs *Tringa melanoleuca L 14" (36 cm)*
Legs yellow to orange. Larger than Lesser Yellowlegs; bill longer, stouter, often slightly upturned, and two-toned in all plumages except breeding. In ***breeding*** plumage, throat and breast are heavily streaked; sides and belly are spotted and barred with black; bill is all-black. In ***juvenile*** the neck is distinctly streaked. Behavior is more active than Lesser Yellowlegs, often racing about with extended neck while pursuing prey (often very small fish).
Voice: Call is a loud, slightly descending series of three or more *tew* notes.
Range: Fairly common; nests on muskeg, winters in wetland habitats. Compared to Lesser, Greater is overall a later fall migrant and is much more capable of wintering at cold interior locations.

Common Greenshank *Tringa nebularia L 13½" (34 cm)*
Common Eurasian species. In plumage and structure resembles Greater Yellowlegs, but less heavily streaked; legs are greenish. In flight, white wedge extends up the middle of back.
Voice: Typical flight call is a loud *tew-tew-tew,* very much like Greater Yellowlegs, but the notes are all on one pitch.
Range: Annually visits western Alaska in spring: rare to Aleutian and Pribilof Islands; casual to St. Lawrence Island; casual in fall. Accidental to northwestern California.

Wood Sandpiper *Tringa glareola L 8" (20 cm)*
Eurasian species. Dark upperparts are heavily spotted with buff; prominent whitish supercilium. In flight, distinguished from Green Sandpiper (page 419) by paler wing linings, smaller white rump patch, more densely barred tail. Bill is straight like Green, but shorter. Compare also to Solitary Sandpiper (previous page).
Voice: Common call is a loud, sharp whistling of three or more notes, vaguely similar to the call of Long-billed Dowitcher.
Range: Fairly common spring and uncommon fall migrant and occasional breeder on the outer Aleutians; uncommon to rare on the Pribilofs; rare on St. Lawrence Island. Accidental to British Columbia and California.

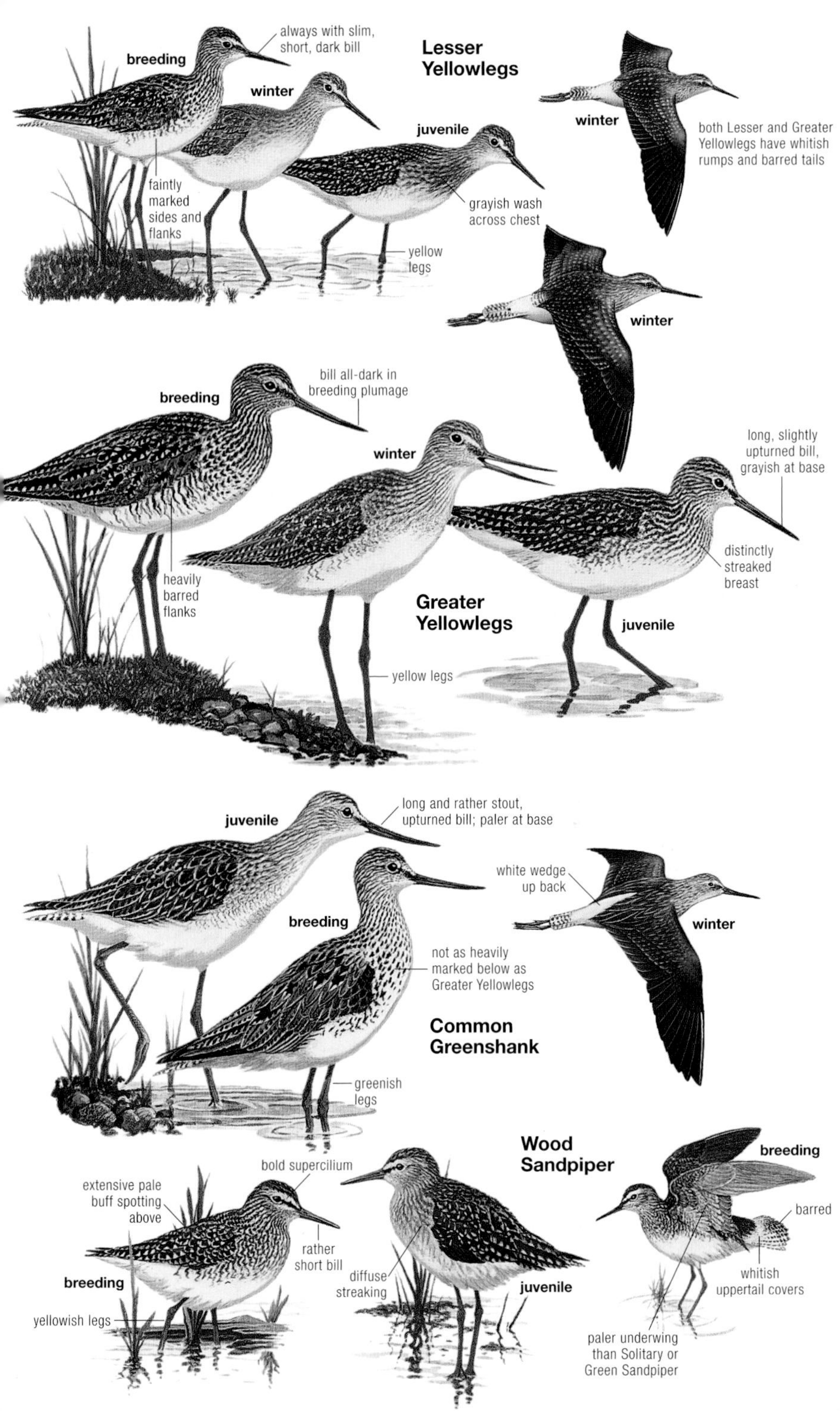
Lesser Yellowlegs
breeding
always with slim, short, dark bill
winter
juvenile
faintly marked sides and flanks
grayish wash across chest
yellow legs
winter
both Lesser and Greater Yellowlegs have whitish rumps and barred tails
winter
breeding
bill all-dark in breeding plumage
winter
long, slightly upturned bill, grayish at base
distinctly streaked breast
heavily barred flanks
Greater Yellowlegs
juvenile
yellow legs
juvenile
long and rather stout, upturned bill; paler at base
white wedge up back
winter
breeding
not as heavily marked below as Greater Yellowlegs
Common Greenshank
greenish legs
Wood Sandpiper
breeding
bold supercilium
extensive pale buff spotting above
rather short bill
breeding
diffuse streaking
juvenile
barred
whitish uppertail covers
yellowish legs
paler underwing than Solitary or Green Sandpiper

Spotted Redshank *Tringa erythropus L 12½" (32 cm)*
Eurasian species. Long bill with red-based lower mandible, droops at tip. ***Breeding adult*** is black overall with white spots above; legs dark red to blackish. Many underparts variably marked with white. ***Juvenile*** is brownish gray and is heavily barred and spotted below. ***Winter*** birds are pale gray above, spotted with white on coverts and tertials. Some fall North American sightings involve young birds in transitional plumage. Both plumages show brighter orange legs. In flight, shows white wedge on back and white wing linings.
Voice: Loud call, a loud rising *chu-weet,* closely resembles Semipalmated Plover, and is completely unlike any other *Tringa.*
Range: Very rare to casual spring and fall visitor to Aleutian and Pribilof Islands; casual on West Coast during migration and winter; accidental elsewhere.

Wandering Tattler *Tringa incana L 11" (28 cm)*
Uniformly dark gray above; white eyebrow flecked with gray; bill dark, legs dull yellow. Often teeters and bobs as it feeds. In ***breeding*** plumage, underparts are heavily barred. ***Juvenile*** and ***winter*** birds have only a dark gray wash over breast, sides, and flanks; juvenile has pale spots above. Closely resembles Gray-tailed Tattler; best distinguished by voice.
Voice: Call, a rapid series of clear, hollow whistles, all on one pitch.
Range: Breeds chiefly on gravelly stream banks. Winters on rocky coasts. Generally seen singly or in small groups. Casual inland during migration.

Gray-tailed Tattler *Tringa brevipes L 10" (25 cm)*
Asian species. Closely resembles Wandering Tattler; upperparts are slightly paler; barring on underparts finer and less extensive; whitish eyebrows are more distinct and meet on forehead. Diagnostic shorter nasal groove hard to see in field. ***Juvenile*** has less extensive gray on underparts; white flanks and belly; more pale spotting above. Best distinction is voice.
Voice: Common call is a loud, ascending *too-weet,* similar to Common Ringed Plover.
Range: Regular spring and fall migrant on outer Aleutians, Pribilofs, and St. Lawrence Island; casual visitor to northern Alaska. Accidental in fall to Washington and California.

Terek Sandpiper *Xenus cinereus L 9" (23 cm)*
Eurasian species. Note long, upturned bill and short orange-yellow legs. In ***breeding adult,*** dark-centered scapulars form two dark lines on back. In flight, shows distinctive wing pattern: dark leading edge, grayer median coverts, dark greater coverts, and white-tipped secondaries.
Voice: Flight call is a series of shrill whistled notes on one pitch, usually in threes.
Range: Rare migrant on outer Aleutians; casual on Pribilofs, on St. Lawrence Island, and in Anchorage area. Accidental in fall to coastal British Columbia and California.

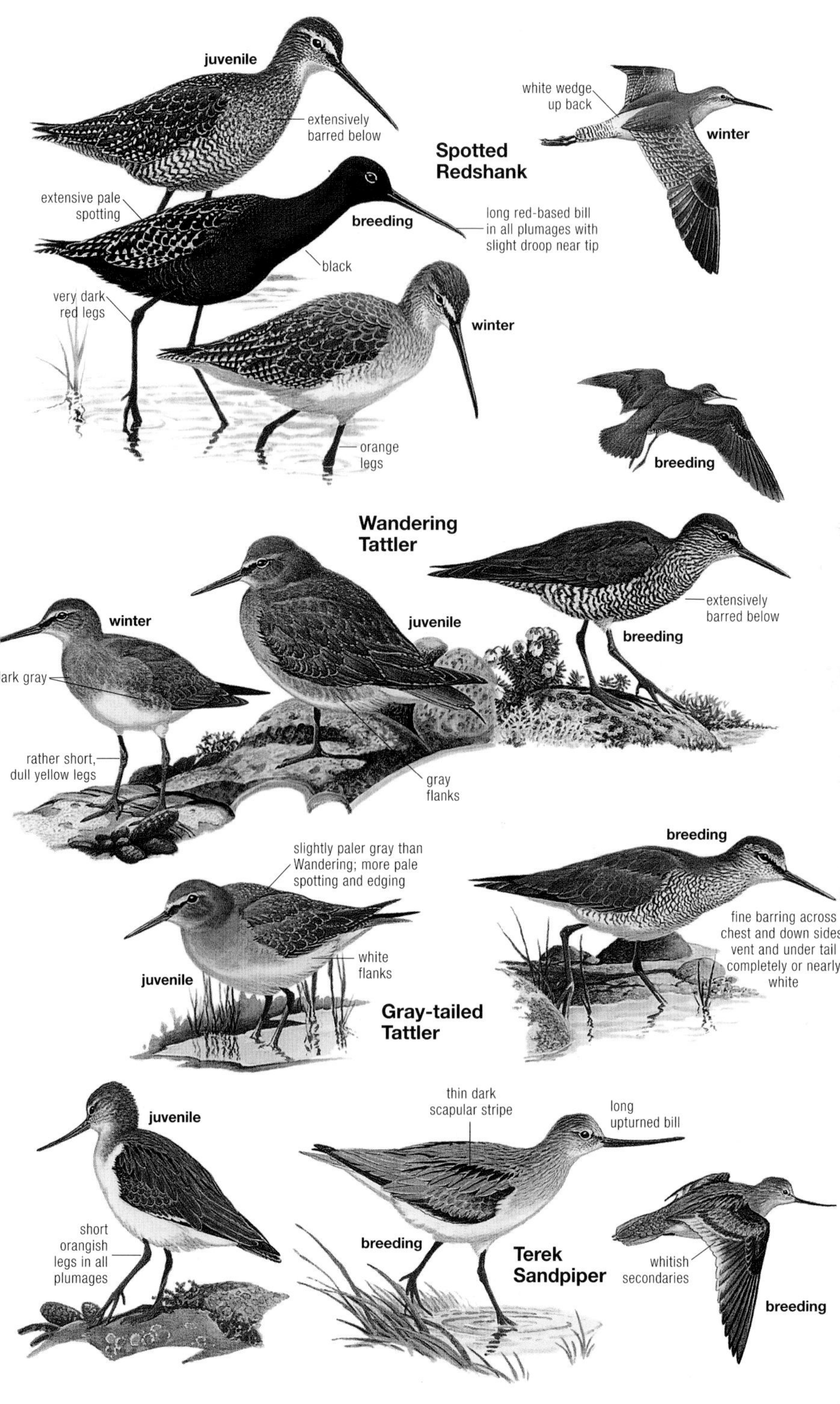

juvenile
extensively barred below
Spotted Redshank
white wedge up back
winter
extensive pale spotting
breeding
long red-based bill in all plumages with slight droop near tip
black
very dark red legs
winter
orange legs
breeding
Wandering Tattler
winter
juvenile
extensively barred below
breeding
ark gray
rather short, dull yellow legs
gray flanks
slightly paler gray than Wandering; more pale spotting and edging
breeding
white flanks
juvenile
Gray-tailed Tattler
fine barring across chest and down sides vent and under tail completely or nearly white
thin dark scapular stripe
long upturned bill
juvenile
short orangish legs in all plumages
breeding
Terek Sandpiper
whitish secondaries
breeding

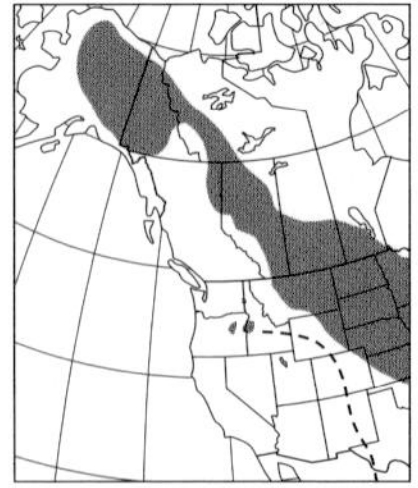

Upland Sandpiper *Bartramia longicauda L 12" (31 cm)*
Small head, with large, dark, prominent eyes; long, thin neck, long tail, long wings. Legs yellow. Prefers fields, where often only its head and neck are visible above the grass. Also perches on posts on breeding grounds. In flight, wings are two-toned.
Voice: Calls are a rolling *pulip pulip* and another like a wolf whistle, heard in flight on breeding grounds.
Range: Overall uncommon and local in western range, where declining. Casual on West Coast and in Southwest in migration.

Whimbrel *Numenius phaeopus L 17½" (45 cm)*
Bold, dark-striped crown; dark eye line extending through lores; long downcurved bill. In flight, North American *hudsonicus* shows dark rump and underwings; Asian *variegatus* has whitish, variably streaked rump and underwings (page 163). Some authorities argue that based on distinct plumage and genetic differences, the Palearctic subspecies should be split from North American Whimbrels; however, all subspecies give similar vocalizations.
Voice: Call is a series of hollow whistles on one pitch.
Range: Fairly common; nests on open tundra; winters on coasts; most winter south of U.S. Rare to casual migrant in interior, except parts of California and southwestern Arizona, where regular. Asian *variegatus* is a rare migrant on islands in western Alaska; casual elsewhere in Pacific region.

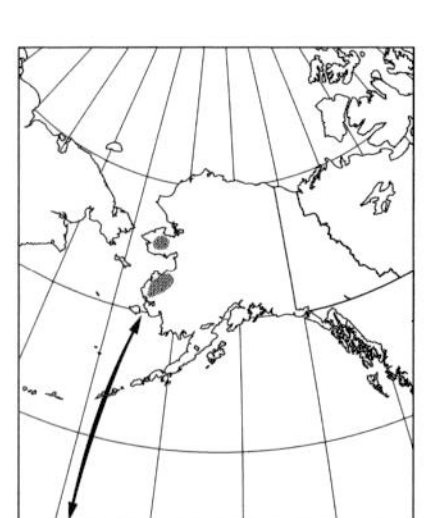

Bristle-thighed Curlew *Numenius tahitiensis L 18" (46 cm)* Bright buff rump and tail (paler when worn) and extensive pattern of large buff spots on upperparts distinguish this species from slightly smaller Whimbrel. Bristle-thighed's bill is also slightly more strongly downcurved near tip. The stiff feathers on the sides and flanks are very hard to see in the field.
Voice: Main call is a loud whistled *chu-a-whit,* and all other vocalizations are completely different from Whimbrel.
Range: Winters South Pacific islands. Migration chiefly over water to western Alaskan breeding grounds. Rare spring migrant on Middleton Island and on Pribilof Islands. Casual in spring and fall on St. Lawrence Island and on the Aleutians. Casual to West Coast in spring, mostly after storms, as in May 1998 when over a dozen were found from coastal Washington to northern California.

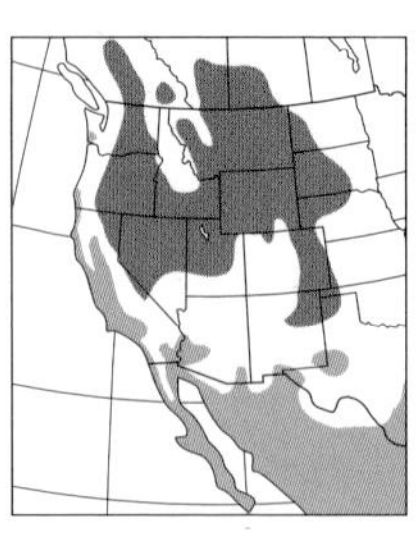

Long-billed Curlew *Numenius americanus L 23" (58 cm)*
Cinnamon brown above, buff below, with very long, strongly downcurved bill. Lacks dark head stripes of Whimbrel. Males and juveniles have shorter bills. Cinnamon-buff wing linings and flight feathers, visible in flight, distinctive in all plumages. At rest closely resembles the smaller Marbled Godwit, if bill is hidden; note paler legs. Two weakly differentiated subspecies; more southerly breeding *americanus* is larger and longer billed than more northerly *parvus,* but differences are clinal. Still, bill length extremes are substantial, and shorter-billed juveniles look more Whimbrel-like.
Voice: Call is a loud musical, ascending *cur-lee.*
Range: Fairly common; nests in wet and dry uplands; in migration and winter found on wetlands and agricultural fields.

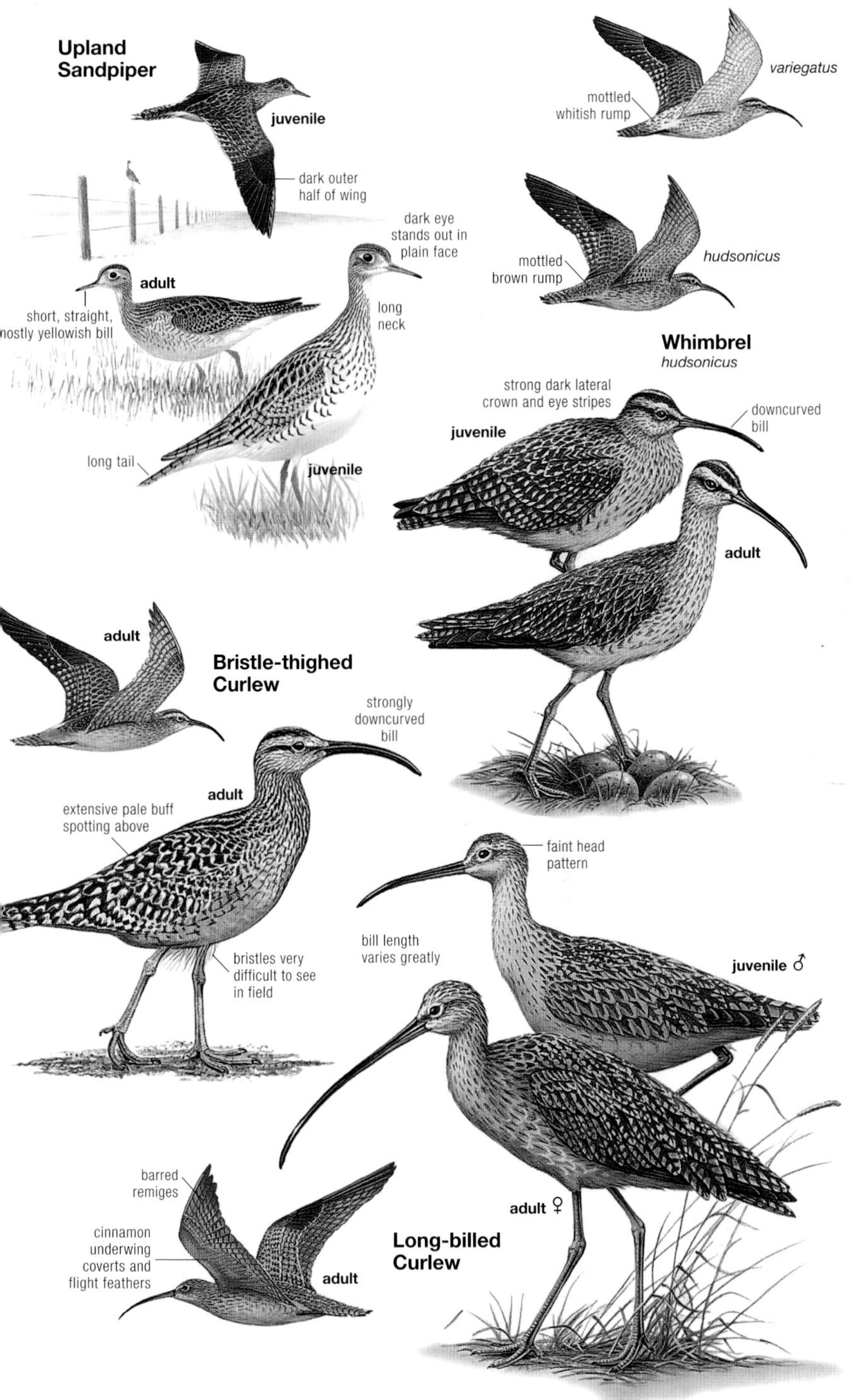
Upland Sandpiper
juvenile
dark outer half of wing
dark eye stands out in plain face
adult
short, straight, mostly yellowish bill
long neck
long tail
juvenile
variegatus
mottled whitish rump
mottled brown rump
hudsonicus
Whimbrel
hudsonicus
strong dark lateral crown and eye stripes
downcurved bill
juvenile
adult
adult
Bristle-thighed Curlew
strongly downcurved bill
adult
extensive pale buff spotting above
bristles very difficult to see in field
faint head pattern
bill length varies greatly
juvenile ♂
barred remiges
cinnamon underwing coverts and flight feathers
adult
adult ♀
Long-billed Curlew

Black-tailed Godwit *Limosa limosa L 16½" (42 cm)*
Eurasian species. Long, bicolored bill is straight or only slightly upcurved. Tail is mostly black, uppertail coverts white. In ***breeding*** plumage, shows chestnut head and neck and heavily barred sides and flanks. ***Winter*** birds (plumage not yet recorded in West) are gray above, whitish below. In all plumages, white wing linings and broad wing stripe are conspicuous in flight.
Voice: Flight call is a rather nasal, mewing, quick *vi-vi-vi.*
Range: Asian *melanuroides* is a rare spring migrant on western Aleutians; casual to Pribilofs and St. Lawrence Island.

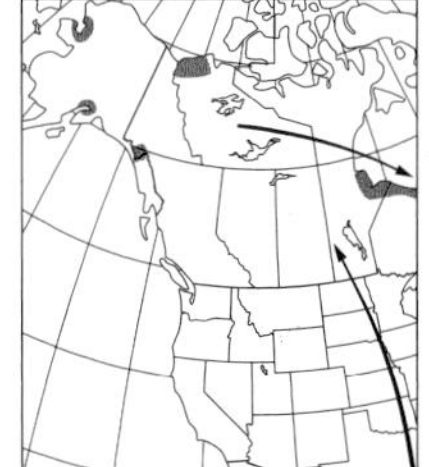

Hudsonian Godwit *Limosa haemastica L 15½" (39 cm)*
Long, bicolored bill, slightly upcurved. Tail is black, uppertail coverts white. ***Breeding male*** is dark chestnut below, finely barred. ***Female*** is larger and much duller. ***Juvenile***'s buff feather edges give upperparts a scaly look. Winter adult resembles Black-tailed Godwit; dark wing linings and narrower white wing stripe are distinctive in flight.
Voice: Generally silent away from breeding grounds; call is a rather high-pitched and rising *pid-wid.*
Range: Breeding range not fully known. Away from breeding grounds, a casual migrant throughout West. Migrates through central Great Plains in spring, well to east in fall. Winters in South America.

Bar-tailed Godwit *Limosa lapponica L 16" (41 cm)*
Long, bicolored bill, slightly upcurved. ***Breeding male*** is reddish brown below; lacks heavy barring of Black-tailed Godwit. ***Female*** is larger and much paler than male. In ***winter*** plumage, Bar-tailed resembles Marbled Godwit but lacks cinnamon tones. Note also Bar-tailed's shorter bill and shorter legs. Black-and-white barred tail distinctive but hard to see at rest. ***Juvenile*** resembles winter adult but is buffier overall. Alaska-breeding *baueri* has barred rump and underwing.
Voice: Calls like Hudsonian, but lower in pitch. Mostly silent away from breeding grounds.
Range: Fairly common on Alaskan breeding grounds. Alaskan subspecies, *baueri,* has been proven to fly nonstop in fall to southwest Pacific wintering grounds. Casual fall migrant on West Coast.

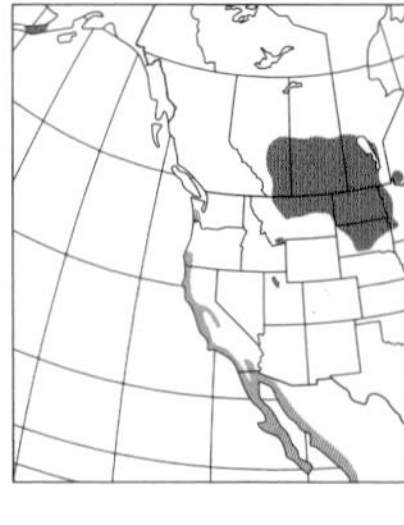

Marbled Godwit *Limosa fedoa L 18" (46 cm)*
Long, bicolored bill, slightly upcurved. Tawny brown; mottled with black above, barred below. Barring is much less extensive on ***winter*** birds and juveniles. The wing coverts are also less patterned on juveniles. Legs are longer than Bar-tailed Godwit. In flight, cinnamon wing linings and cinnamon on primaries and secondaries are distinctive.
Voice: Flight call a slightly nasal *kah-wek.* Also a repeated loud *ga-wi-da, ga-wi-da.*
Range: Common on West Coast in winter. Generally an uncommon migrant in interior West away from breeding grounds. Common at Salton Sea. Nests in grassy meadows, near lakes and ponds.

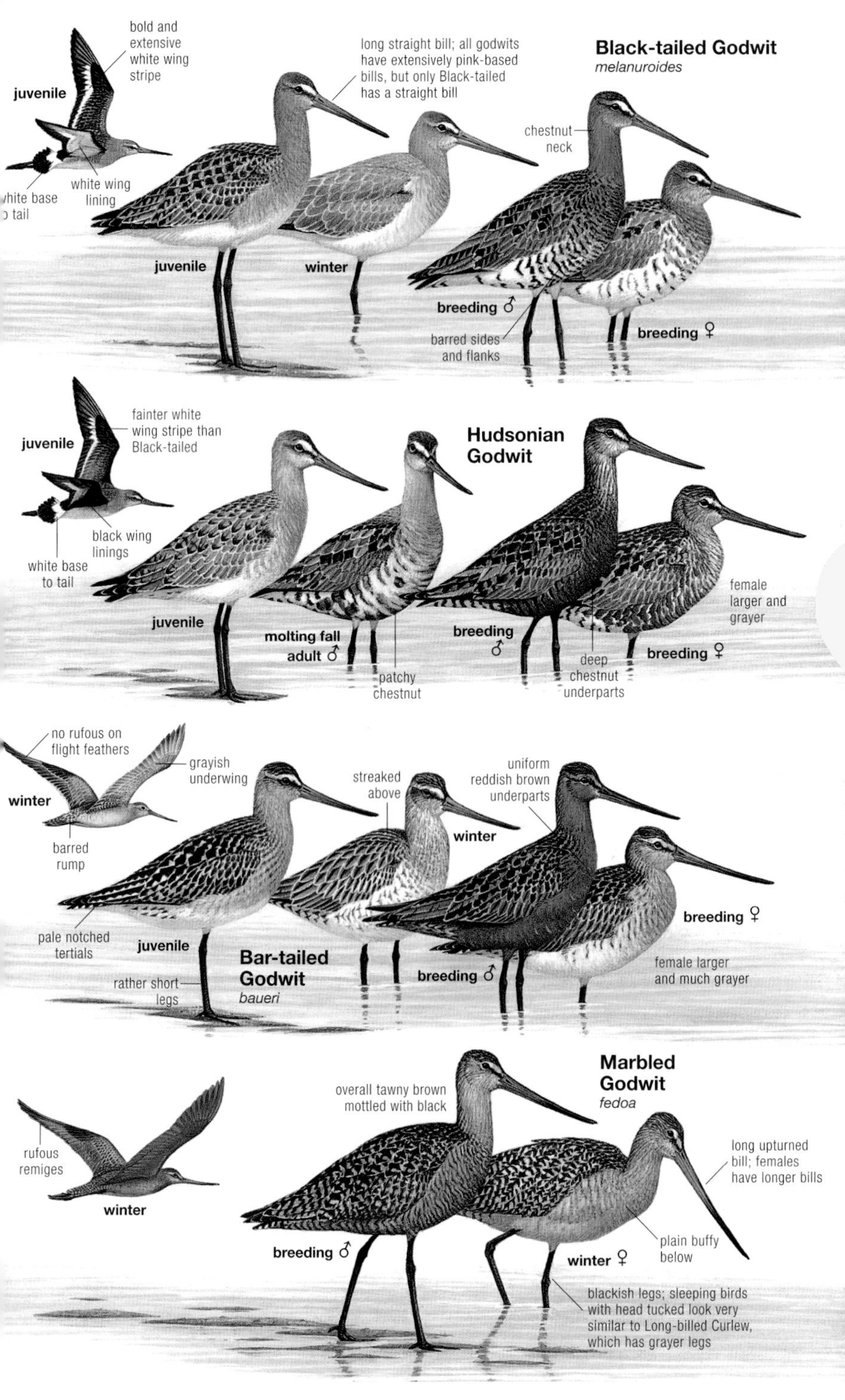
bold and extensive white wing stripe
juvenile
white base to tail
white wing lining
long straight bill; all godwits have extensively pink-based bills, but only Black-tailed has a straight bill
Black-tailed Godwit
melanuroides
chestnut neck
juvenile
winter
breeding ♂
barred sides and flanks
breeding ♀
fainter white wing stripe than Black-tailed
juvenile
black wing linings
white base to tail
Hudsonian Godwit
juvenile
molting fall adult ♂
patchy chestnut
breeding ♂
deep chestnut underparts
breeding ♀
female larger and grayer
no rufous on flight feathers
grayish underwing
winter
barred rump
streaked above
winter
uniform reddish brown underparts
pale notched tertials
juvenile
rather short legs
Bar-tailed Godwit
baueri
breeding ♂
breeding ♀
female larger and much grayer
Marbled Godwit
fedoa
overall tawny brown mottled with black
rufous remiges
winter
long upturned bill; females have longer bills
plain buffy below
breeding ♂
winter ♀
blackish legs; sleeping birds with head tucked look very similar to Long-billed Curlew, which has grayer legs

Ruddy Turnstone *Arenaria interpres L 9½" (24 cm)*

Striking black-and-white head and bib, black-and-chestnut back, and orange legs mark this stout bird in ***breeding*** plumage. Female is duller than ***male.*** Bib pattern and orange leg color are retained in ***winter*** plumage. ***Juvenile*** resembles winter adult but back has a scaly appearance. Turnstones use their slender bills to flip aside shells and pebbles in search of food. In flight, complex pattern on back and wings identifies both Ruddy and Black Turnstones.

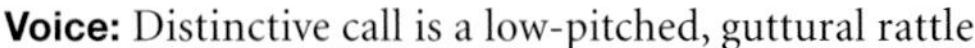

Voice: Distinctive call is a low-pitched, guttural rattle.

Range: Nests on coastal tundra. Winters on mudflats, sandy beaches, rocky shores. Generally a rare to casual inland migrant and more regular in fall; more numerous at the Salton Sea.

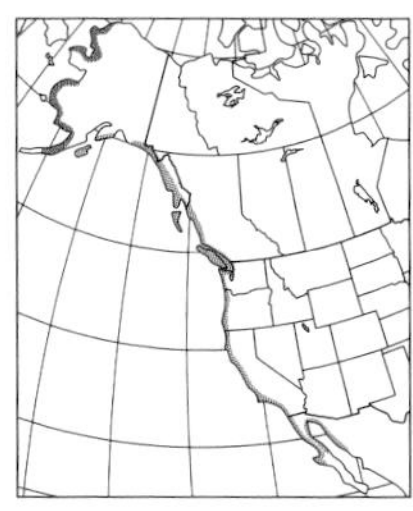

Black Turnstone *Arenaria melanocephala L 9¼" (24 cm)*

Black upperparts. In ***breeding*** plumage head is marked by white eyebrow and lore spot; white spotting visible on sides of neck and breast. Legs dark reddish brown in all plumages. Juvenile (not illustrated) and ***winter adult*** are slate gray and lack lore spot and mottling. Juvenile is somewhat browner (paler), has small round scapulars with thin and even pale edges.

Voice: Calls include a guttural rattle, higher than call of Ruddy Turnstone.

Range: Breeds along immediate coast of western Alaska. Winters on rocky coasts. Nearly annual vary rare migrant to the Salton Sea (mainly in spring); otherwise accidental migrant in the interior. Casual in spring to St. Lawrence Island, Alaska.

Surfbird *Aphriza virgata L 10" (25 cm)*

Base of Surfbird's short, stout bill is yellow; legs are yellowish green. ***Breeding adult***'s head and underparts are heavily streaked and spotted with dusky black; upperparts are edged with white and chestnut; scapulars are mostly rufous. ***Winter adult*** has a solid dark gray head and breast. ***Juvenile***'s head and breast are paler and flecked with white; back appears scaly. In flight, all plumages show a conspicuous black band at end of white tail and rump.

Voice: Usually silent away from breeding grounds apart from soft contact notes; occasionally gives a shrill, whistled *kee-wee-ah.*

Range: Nests on mountain tundra; winters along rocky beaches and reefs, usually in mixed flocks of Black Turnstones and other shorebirds. Surfbird has by far the greatest latitudinal winter range of any shorebird: Some found as far north as southeast Alaska and some travel as far south as Tierra del Fuego. In spring, also found on sandy beaches. Very large numbers stage in fall at Bodega Bay. Casual (mainly spring) migrant at the Salton Sea; several spring records elsewhere from the interior of California.

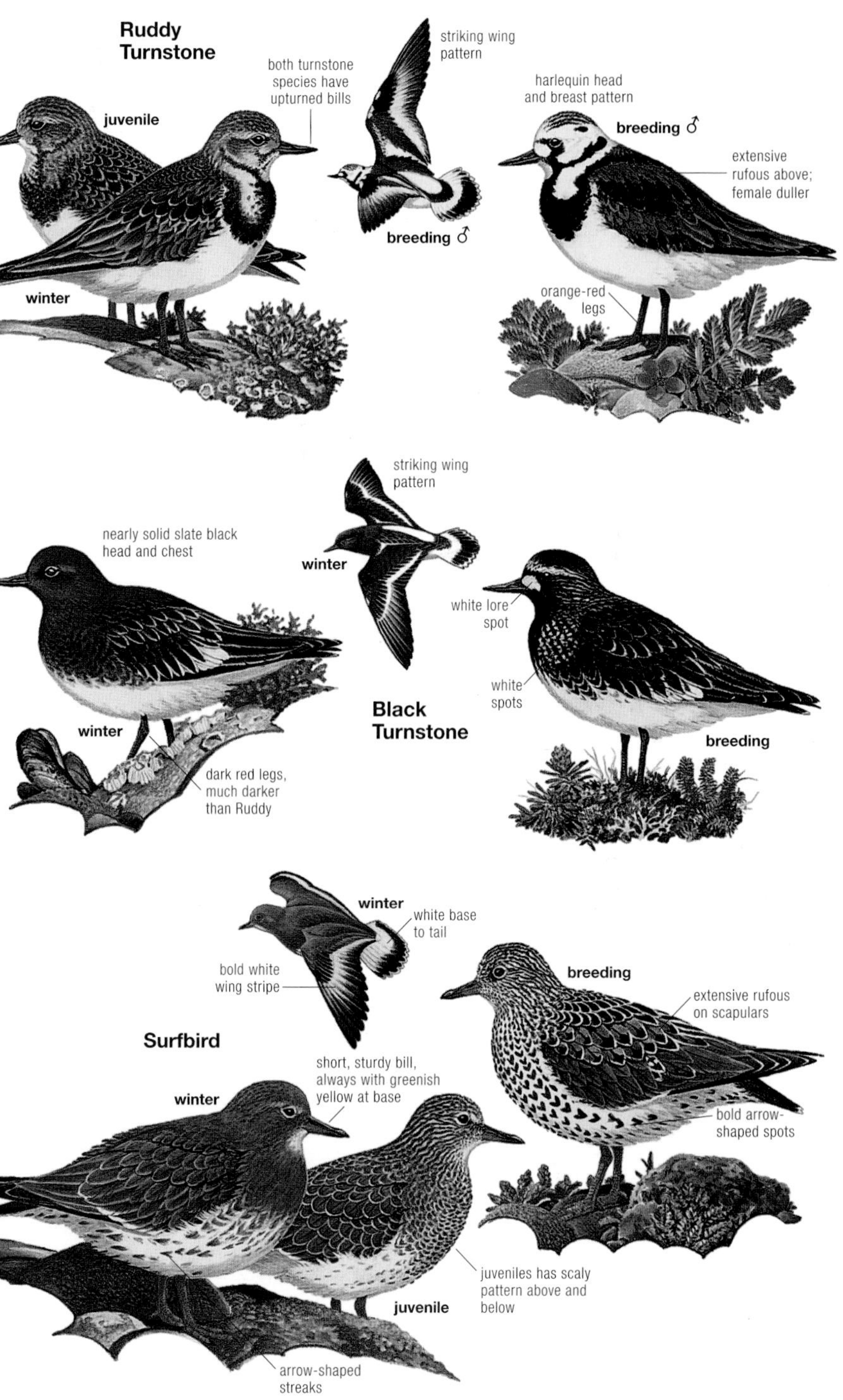

Ruddy Turnstone
both turnstone species have upturned bills
juvenile
winter
striking wing pattern
breeding ♂
harlequin head and breast pattern
breeding ♂
extensive rufous above; female duller
orange-red legs
striking wing pattern
nearly solid slate black head and chest
winter
winter
white lore spot
white spots
Black Turnstone
breeding
dark red legs, much darker than Ruddy
winter
white base to tail
bold white wing stripe
breeding
extensive rufous on scapulars
Surfbird
short, sturdy bill, always with greenish yellow at base
winter
bold arrow-shaped spots
juveniles has scaly pattern above and below
juvenile
arrow-shaped streaks

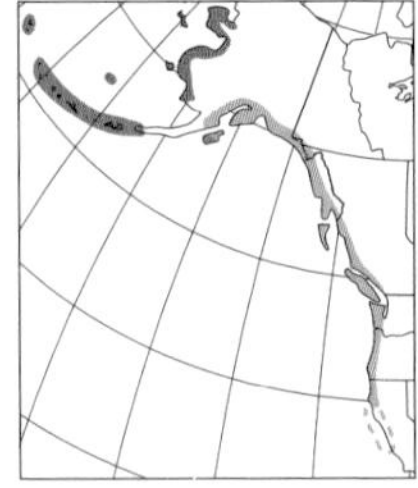

Rock Sandpiper *Calidris ptilocnemis L 9" (23 cm)*
Black patch on lower breast in ***breeding*** plumage; compare with belly patch of Dunlin (page 154). Crown and back are black, edged with chestnut. In flight, shows white wing stripe, and all-dark tail. Nominate breeding on Pribilofs is larger, has paler chestnut above, less black below, bolder white wing stripe. Long, slender bill is slightly downcurved, base greenish yellow. Legs greenish yellow. ***Winter*** bird separated from accidental (in West) Purple Sandpiper by range, duller bill base and legs; from Surfbird (previous page) by longer bill, smaller size, more patterned upperparts and breast.
Voice: Gives a sharp *kwit* and a chattering call.
Range: Nests on tundra. Most winter on rocky shores, often with Black Turnstones and Surfbirds. Migrates late in fall. Casual to southern California. Accidental in interior of British Columbia.

Red Knot *Calidris canutus L 10½" (27 cm)*
Chunky and short legged. ***Breeding adult*** is dappled brown, black, and chestnut above, with buffy chestnut face and breast. In ***winter,*** back is pale gray; underparts white. Distinguished from dowitchers (page 158) by shorter bill, paler crown, and, in flight, by whitish rump finely barred with gray. ***Juvenile*** similar to winter adult but has distinct spotting below, scaly-patterned upperparts, and a light buff wash on breast when fresh.
Voice: Mostly silent; sometimes gives a soft *ka-whit* in flight.
Range: Nests on tundra. In migration and winter, feeds along sandy beaches and on mudflats. Western populations have not suffered dramatic declines as in East; very rare migrant in the interior; more numerous at Salton Sea.

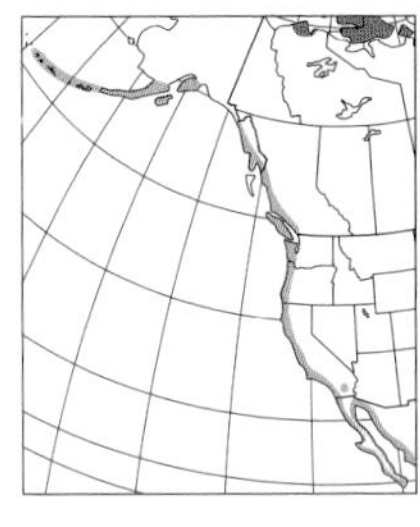

Sanderling *Calidris alba L 8" (20 cm)*
Palest sandpiper in ***winter*** plumage; pale gray above, white below. Bill, legs black. Bold white wing stripe shows in flight. In ***breeding*** plumage (acquired late Apr.), head, mantle, and breast rusty. Feeds on sandy beaches, running to snatch mollusks and crustaceans exposed by retreating waves. ***Juveniles*** blackish above, with pale edges near tips of feathers, resulting in checkered pattern.
Voice: Call a *kip,* often in a series.
Range: A late spring migrant. Generally an uncommon to rare interior migrant, more numerous on northwestern Great Plains.

IDENTIFYING: Rock Sandpiper Subspecies
A close relative of the Atlantic's Purple Sandpiper, Rock has four subspecies, all found in the north Pacific or the Bering Sea regions. Rock is almost strictly coastal. Rock's largest subspecies, *ptilocnemis,* breeds on the Pribilofs and on St. Matthew and Hall Islands, winters mainly on floating ice in Cook Inlet, and is casual south to Washington. It is distinctly paler than the other races, with more white in the wing and a bolder white wing bar. In breeding plumage, it is fringed with yellowish chestnut (rather than chestnut) on the scapulars. In winter plumage, it is paler gray and less streaked ventrally. Of the other races, *tschuktshorum* is the most migratory, breeding in western Alaska (south to Bristol Bay), St. Lawrence Island, and the Chukotski Peninsula, Russian Far East, and wintering from southern Alaska south to the Pacific Northwest (a few to coastal central California). Largely resident on the Aleutians, *couesi* is somewhat darker and smaller. With scapular edges a little paler than *couesi,* Asian *quarta* breeds on the Commander and Kuril Islands and may have occurred casually on the western Aleutians.

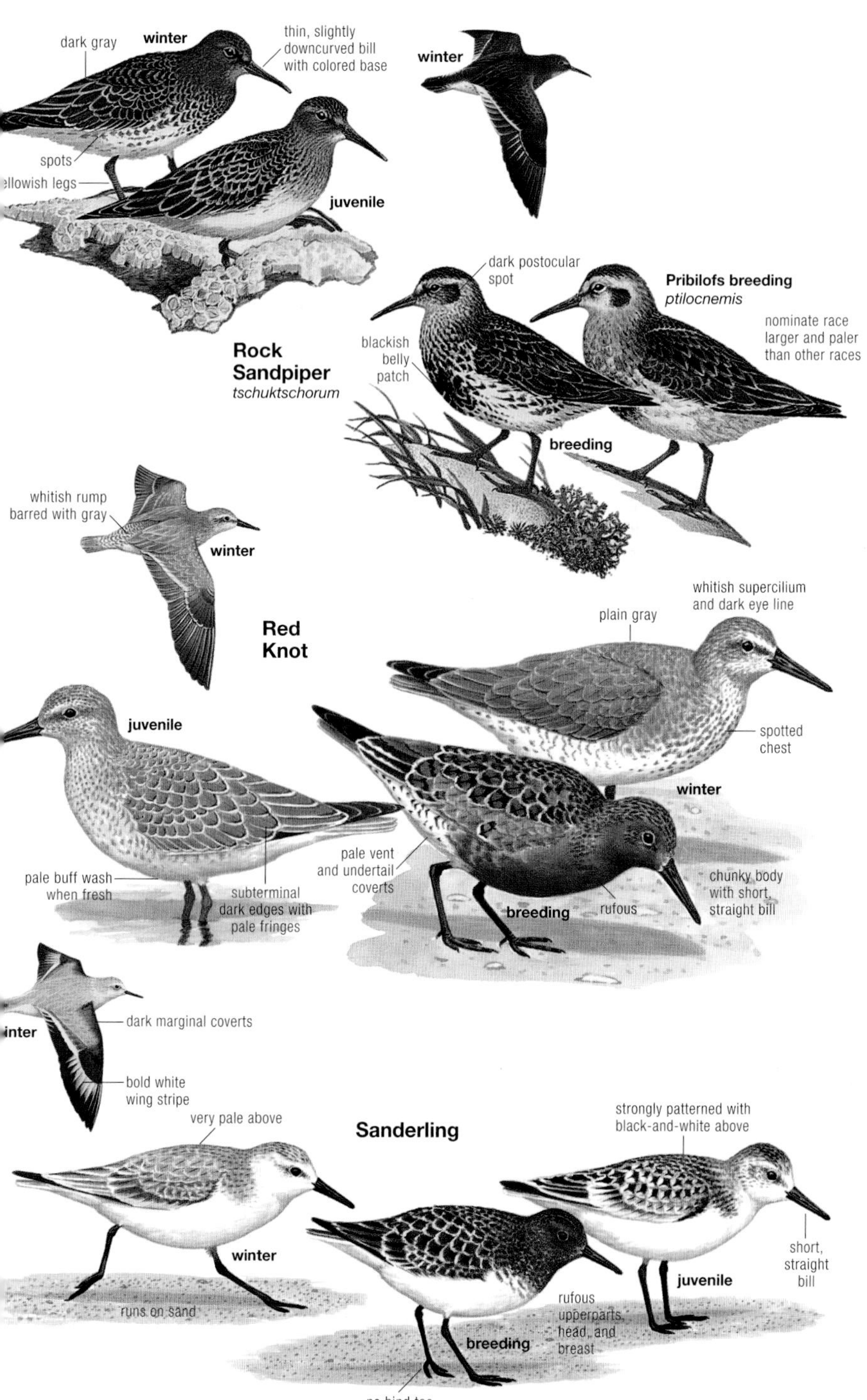
dark gray
winter
thin, slightly
downcurved bill
with colored base
winter
spots
ellowish legs
juvenile
dark postocular
spot
Pribilofs breeding
ptilocnemis
nominate race
larger and paler
than other races
blackish
belly
patch
Rock
Sandpiper
tschuktschorum
breeding
whitish rump
barred with gray
winter
Red
Knot
whitish supercilium
and dark eye line
plain gray
juvenile
spotted
chest
winter
pale vent
and undertail
coverts
chunky body
with short,
straight bill
pale buff wash
when fresh
subterminal
dark edges with
pale fringes
breeding
rufous
dark marginal coverts
inter
bold white
wing stripe
very pale above
Sanderling
strongly patterned with
black-and-white above
winter
short,
straight
bill
juvenile
runs on sand
rufous
upperparts,
head, and
breast
breeding
no hind toe

Peeps

These are seven species of small *Calidris* sandpipers that are difficult to identify. Collectively known as stints by Old World English speakers, they can be roughly divided into four Old World and three New World species. Sometimes the larger Baird's and White-rumped Sandpipers are also included. Keys to identification include learning overall structure and feather topography, behavior, and the distribution patterns of each. It is essential to thoroughly learn our three regular species before attempting to identify one of the Eurasian ones.

Semipalmated Sandpiper *Calidris pusilla L 6¼" (16 cm)*

Black legs; tubular-looking, straight bill, of variable length. Easily confused with Western Sandpiper. In ***breeding*** birds, note that Semipalmated usually lacks spotting on flanks and shows only a tinge of rust on crown, ear patch, and scapulars. ***Juvenile*** is distinguished by stronger supercilium contrasting with darker crown and ear coverts and by more uniform upperparts. Some are brighter above than illustrated. ***Winter*** plumage in Semipalmated —rarely, if ever, seen in West—is very similar to Western, but rounder headed Semipalmated is plumper; note bill shape; face shows slightly more contrast; center of breast never shows the faint streaks visible on some winter Westerns. Semipalmateds tend to pick at the water surface.

Voice: Flight call is a short *churk.*

Range: A tundra breeder. While common in East, a rather rare migrant in West south of Washington and west of Great Plains.

Western Sandpiper *Calidris mauri L 6½" (17 cm)*

Black legs; tapered bill, of variable length (longer in females); distal portion usually slightly drooped. Easily confused with Semipalmated Sandpiper, but blockier headed Western has more attenuated body. ***Breeding*** Western has arrow-shaped spots along sides, rufous at base of scapulars, a bright rufous wash on crown and ear patch. ***Juvenile*** distinguished from juvenile Semipalmated by less prominent supercilium, paler crown and face, brighter rufous edges on back and inner scapulars. ***Winter*** plumage very similar to Semipalmated. Note structure (especially bill shape). In North America, any winter-plumaged individual in fall or winter likely to be Western. Found in similar situations to Semipalmated.

Voice: Flight call is a raspy *jeet.*

Range: Breeds on tundra. A common to abundant migrant.

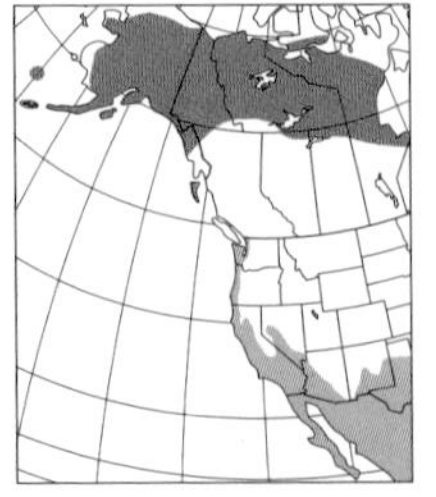

Least Sandpiper *Calidris minutilla L 6" (15 cm)*

Note small size and short, thin bill, slightly downcurved. Always darker above than Western and Semipalmated Sandpipers. Legs are yellowish, but can appear dark in poor light or when smeared with mud. In ***winter*** plumage, has prominent brown breast band. ***Juvenile*** has strong buffy wash across breast. Feeds in a variety of wet habitats, but forages less in the water, often preferring to feed back from the shore's edge.

Voice: Flight call is a high plaintive *kreee.*

Range: A tundra and taiga breeder. A common migrant in West.

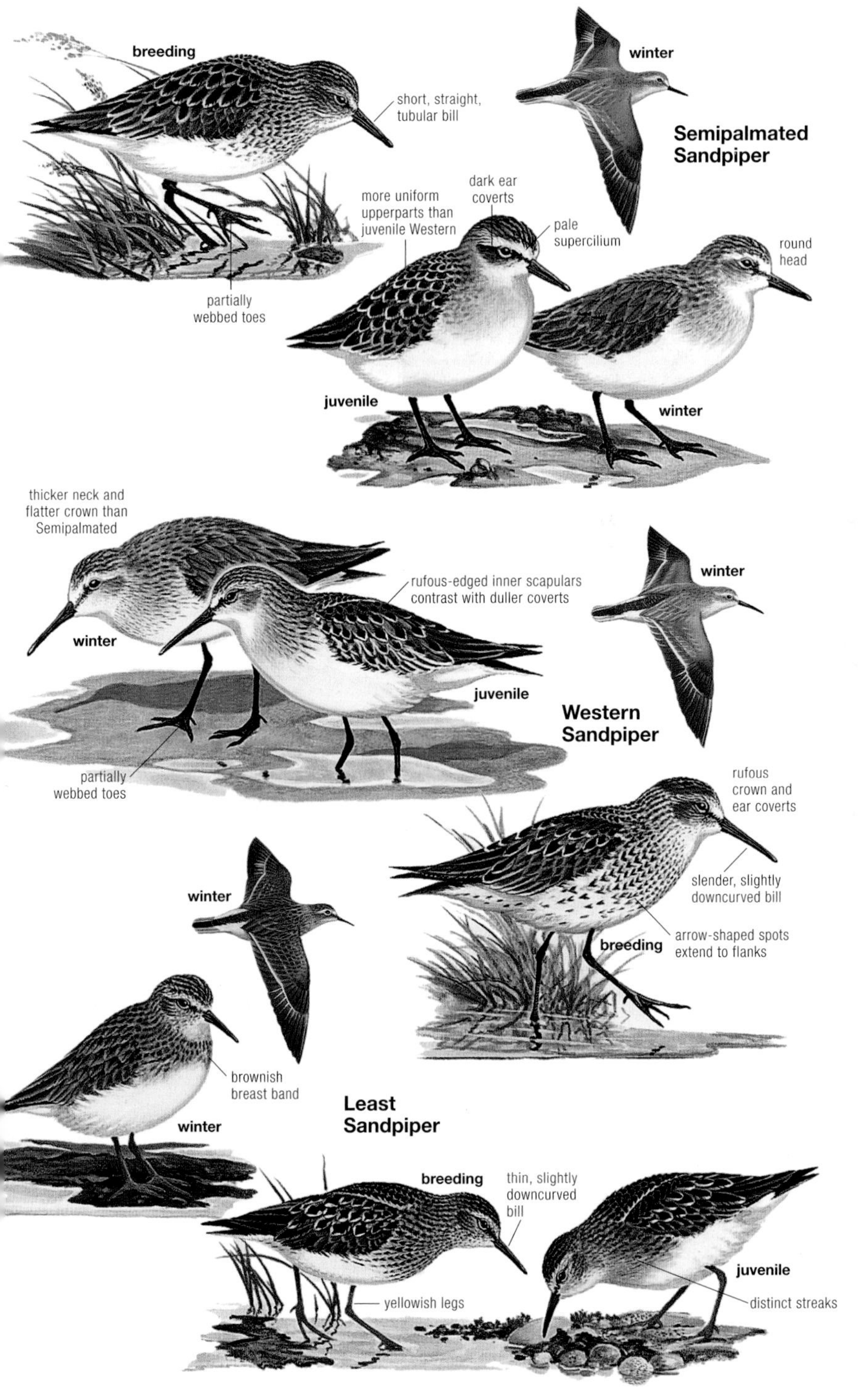
breeding
short, straight, tubular bill
partially webbed toes
winter
Semipalmated Sandpiper
more uniform upperparts than juvenile Western
dark ear coverts
pale supercilium
round head
juvenile
winter
thicker neck and flatter crown than Semipalmated
rufous-edged inner scapulars contrast with duller coverts
winter
winter
juvenile
Western Sandpiper
partially webbed toes
rufous crown and ear coverts
slender, slightly downcurved bill
winter
arrow-shaped spots extend to flanks
breeding
brownish breast band
winter
Least Sandpiper
breeding
thin, slightly downcurved bill
juvenile
yellowish legs
distinct streaks

Rare Stints

These are the four Old World species of peeps that have been found in North America. Of these, Red-necked Stint is the most regular. Of the remaining three, both Temminck's and Long-toed Stints are almost unknown in North America away from Alaska. With any potential find of a rare stint it is essential to get documentation, preferably photographs. Even in migration, shorebirds hold feeding territories, and if flocks are disturbed, they soon return and sort themselves out. If the potential rarity can't be refound, chances are it was a commoner species.

Red-necked Stint *Calidris ruficollis L 6¼" (16 cm)*

Asian species. Rufous on throat and upper breast may be pale and indistinct; look for "necklace" of dark streaks on white lower breast. ***Juvenile*** distinguished from Little Stint by plainer wing coverts and tertials, more uniform crown pattern, and plainer breast sides.
Range: Regular migrant on western Alaska coast and islands. Breeding documented on Seward Peninsula coast; breeding range on map is conjectural. Casual migrant on Pacific coast; accidental in interior.

Little Stint *Calidris minuta L 6" (15 cm)*

Eurasian species. ***Breeding*** adults are brightly fringed with rufous above; throat and underparts white (more suffused with color in later summer adults), with bright buff wash and bold spotting on sides of breast. Redder above than Western and Semipalmated Sandpipers (previous page); compare also with Red-necked Stint. ***Juvenile*** best distinguished from juvenile Red-necked by extensively black-centered wing coverts and tertials, usually edged with rufous; also note split supercilium and streaking on sides of chest.
Range: Very rare on western Alaska islands in spring and fall; casual on West Coasts, accidental (spring) at Salton Sea.

Long-toed Stint *Calidris subminuta L 6" (15 cm)*

Asian species. Distinguished in all plumages from Least Sandpiper by dark forehead, which pinches off prominent white supercilium before it meets the bill (dark forms J-shape on its side); split supercilium. Median coverts are white edged; note also greenish base of lower mandible; yellowish legs.
Voice: Call pitched lower than Least Sandpiper.
Range: Casual in spring on St. Lawrence Island and the Pribilofs; can be fairly common on the outer Aleutians. Accidental in fall from coastal Oregon and California.

Temminck's Stint *Calidris temminckii L 6¼" (16 cm)*

Eurasian species. White outer tail feathers distinctive in all plumages. ***Breeding adult*** resembles larger Baird's Sandpiper (next page) in plumage and shape, but legs greenish yellow; note Baird's dark legs and distinct primary tip projection past tertials. Temminck's ***juvenile*** has dark subterminal edge with buffy fringe.
Voice: Call is a very distinctive, repeated, rapid dry rattle.
Range: Rare migrant on Pribilofs, Aleutians, and St. Lawrence Island. Accidental northern Alaska and coastal Pacific Northwest.

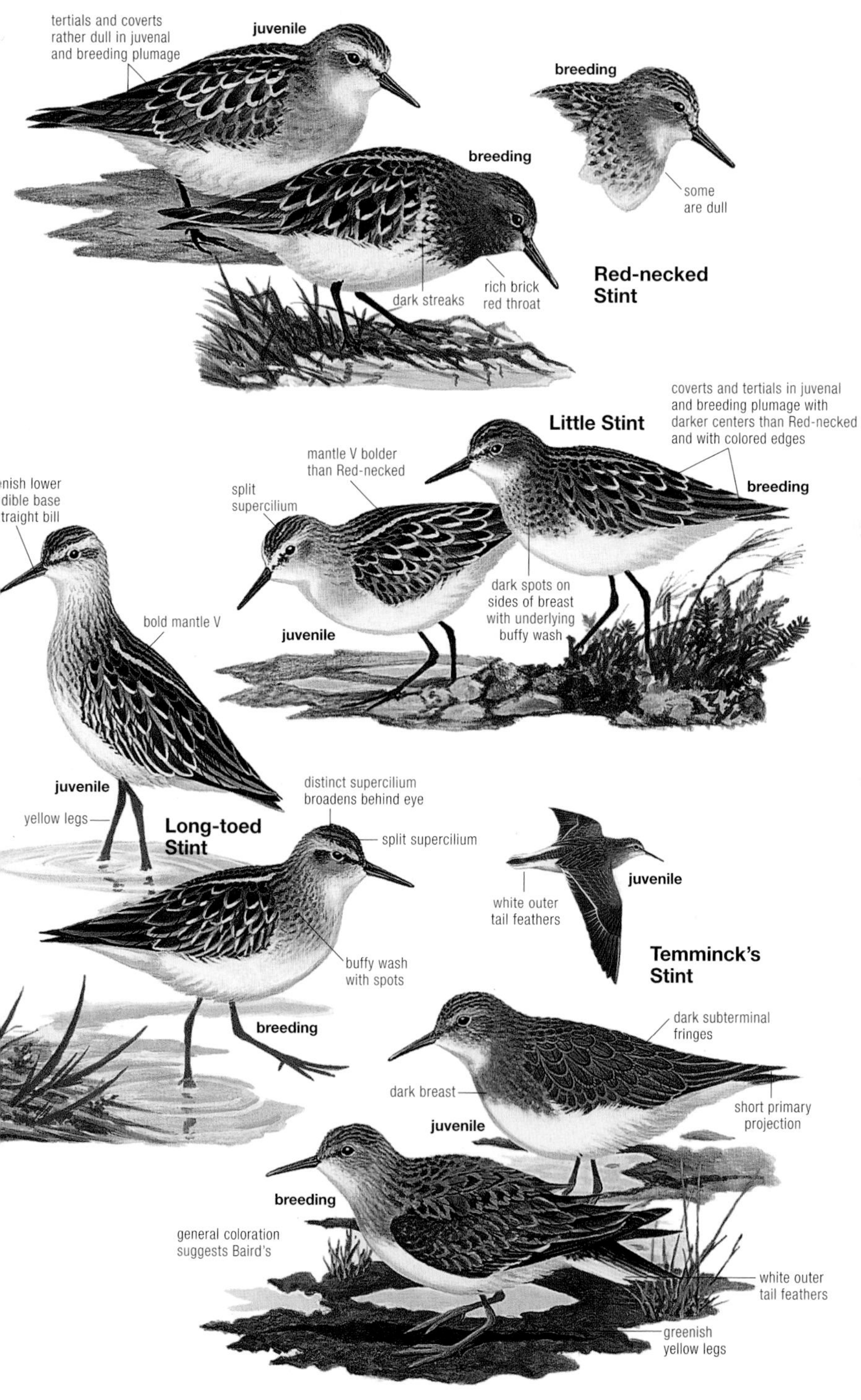
tertials and coverts
rather dull in juvenal
and breeding plumage
juvenile
breeding
breeding
some
are dull
dark streaks
rich brick
red throat
Red-necked
Stint
coverts and tertials in juvenal
and breeding plumage with
darker centers than Red-necked
and with colored edges
Little Stint
mantle V bolder
than Red-necked
breeding
split
supercilium
nish lower
dible base
traight bill
dark spots on
sides of breast
with underlying
buffy wash
bold mantle V
juvenile
juvenile
distinct supercilium
broadens behind eye
yellow legs
Long-toed
Stint
split supercilium
juvenile
white outer
tail feathers
buffy wash
with spots
Temminck's
Stint
dark subterminal
fringes
breeding
dark breast
short primary
projection
juvenile
breeding
general coloration
suggests Baird's
white outer
tail feathers
greenish
yellow legs

White-rumped Sandpiper *Calidris fuscicollis L 7½" (19 cm)* Long primary tip projection beyond tertials and tail on standing bird. Similar to Baird's structurally, but grayer overall, usually has an entirely white rump. In ***breeding*** plumage, streaking extends to flanks. ***Juvenile*** shows rusty edges on crown and back. In winter, head and neck are dark gray, giving a hooded look.
Voice: Flight call note is a very high-pitched insect-like *jeet.*
Range: Regular late spring migrant in small numbers to western Great Plains. Casual spring (mainly) and fall (all records are adults) in West. Winters in southern South America. Feeds on mudflats; nests on tundra.

Baird's Sandpiper *Calidris bairdii L 7½" (19 cm)* Long primary tip projection beyond tertials and tail on standing bird gives the bird a horizontal profile. Buff-brown above and across breast. Pale fringing on ***juvenile***'s back gives a scaly appearance. Distinguished from White-rumped Sandpiper by more buffy brown color and uniform plumage; in flight by dark rump. Distinguished from Least Sandpiper by much larger size, longer and straighter bill, and primary projection.
Voice: Flight call is a low raspy *kreep,* similar to call of Pectoral Sandpiper, but less rich.
Range: Uncommon to common; found on upper beaches and inland on lakeshores, wet fields; nests on tundra. Primary migration is through Great Plains; uncommon (usually juveniles) to West Coast in fall, very rare in spring. Winters in South America; accidental in western North America in midwinter.

Pectoral Sandpiper *Calidris melanotos L 8¾" (22 cm)* Prominent streaking on breast, darker in ***male,*** contrasts sharply with clear white belly. Male is larger than ***female. Juvenile*** has buffy wash on streaked breast. Compare especially with juvenile Sharp-tailed Sandpiper.
Voice: Flight call is a rich, low *churk.*
Range: Feeds in wet meadows, marshes, pond edges; nests on tundra. An uncommon fall migrant (mostly juveniles) and very rare spring migrant in West south of breeding range. Winters in South America.

Sharp-tailed Sandpiper *Calidris acuminata L 8½" (22 cm)* Asian species. Most sightings are ***juveniles,*** distinguished from juvenile Pectoral Sandpiper by white eyebrow that broadens behind the eye; bright buffy breast lightly streaked on upper breast and sides; streaked undertail coverts; and brighter rufous cap and edging on upperparts. ***Breeding adult*** plumage is similar to juvenile, but more spotted below with dark chevrons on flanks; also distinct white eye ring.
Voice: Flight call is a mellow, two-note whistle.
Range: Breeds in Russian Far East; casual spring and fairly common fall migrant (mostly juveniles) in western Alaska; rare fall migrant along entire Pacific coast. Casual in fall and accidental in spring across rest of West. Accidental in winter from coastal California.

White-rumped Sandpiper
no records of a juvenile yet in West
juvenile
fall-molting adult
dull rufous edges
breeding
streaking extends to flanks
white rump normally only visible in flight
juvenile
long wings and primary projection
like White-rumped, long wings extend beyond tail
shaped like White-rumped, but browner
whitish fringe on upperparts
juvenile
breeding
Baird's Sandpiper
juvenile
breeding ♂
breeding ♀
Pectoral Sandpiper
juvenile
darker breast
long wings and primary projection
pectoral band of streaks
yellowish legs
juvenile
juvenile
breeding adult
ruddy crown and bold white eye ring
extensive dark chevrons on sides and flanks
streaks
Sharp-tailed Sandpiper
bold supercilium
juvenile
broader rufous tertial edges than Pectoral
extensive buff on breast below streaking
streaks on sides continue faintly across upper breast
juvenile Sharp-tailed (center) with juvenile Pectorals

Dunlin *Calidris alpina L 8½" (22 cm)*
Medium sized; long bill, curved at tip; in flight shows dark center to rump. ***Breeding*** plumage with reddish upperparts, black belly. Subspecies differ in size, structure, and breeding plumage: *pacifica* in western Alaska and Pacific region; similar *arcticola* (breeds northern Alaska) and *sakhalina* (migrant western Alaska) winter in Asia. Compare to Rock Sandpiper (page 146). In ***winter*** plumage, upperparts and chest brownish gray. ***Juvenile*** rusty above, spotted below.
Voice: Flight call is a harsh, reedy *kree.*
Range: Nests on tundra. Otherwise found on mudflats, marshes, pond edges. Rare on western Great Plains. In North America and northeast Asia, adults and juveniles stay north and molt largely into winter plumage before migrating south.

Curlew Sandpiper *Calidris ferruginea L 8½" (22 cm)*
Range: Eurasian species. Long, downcurved bill has whitish area at base. In ***breeding*** plumage, rich chestnut underparts, mottled chestnut back distinctive. Female slightly paler than male. Many sightings are of birds in patchy spring plumage or molting to winter plumage, showing grayer upperparts and partly white underparts. ***Juvenile*** plumage has scaly pattern above; shows rich buff wash across breast; young birds seen in southern Canada and U.S. are in full juvenal plumage; compare with winter Dunlins and juvenile and transitional Stilt Sandpipers. A few spring records from the Salton Sea have been in a winterlike plumage (probably immatures). White rump is conspicuous in flight.
Voice: Flight call is a soft, rippling *chirrup.*
Range: Has bred in northern Alaska; otherwise casual migrant on islands in western Alaska and elsewhere in West mostly in fall.

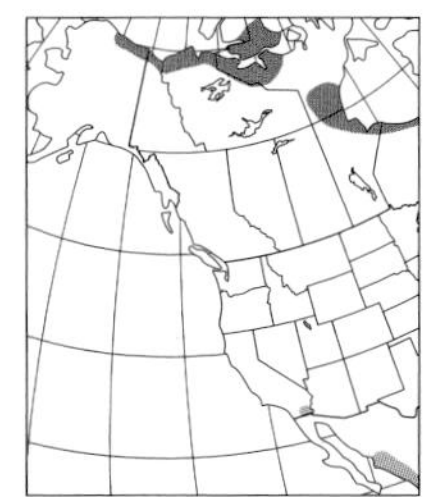

Stilt Sandpiper *Calidris himantopus L 8½" (22 cm)*
Breeding adult has pale eyebrow, chestnut on head, slender, slightly downcurved bill, and heavily barred underparts. ***Winter adult*** is grayer above, whiter below; ***juvenile*** has more sharply patterned upperparts; the two resemble Curlew Sandpiper, but note straighter bill, yellow-green legs, and, in flight, lack of prominent wing stripe, paler tail; early juvenile has a buffy wash on breast. Many juveniles seen in migration are in a transitional plumage, having replaced scapular and other feathers. Feeds like dowitchers, with which it often associates, but note its smaller size and its disproportionately longer legs.
Voice: Flight call is a low, hoarse *querp.*
Range: Uncommon breeder on Alaska's and Yukon's north slope. Common migrant on Great Plains. Generally a rare migrant otherwise in West, except more numerous at the south end of the Salton Sea, where some winter.

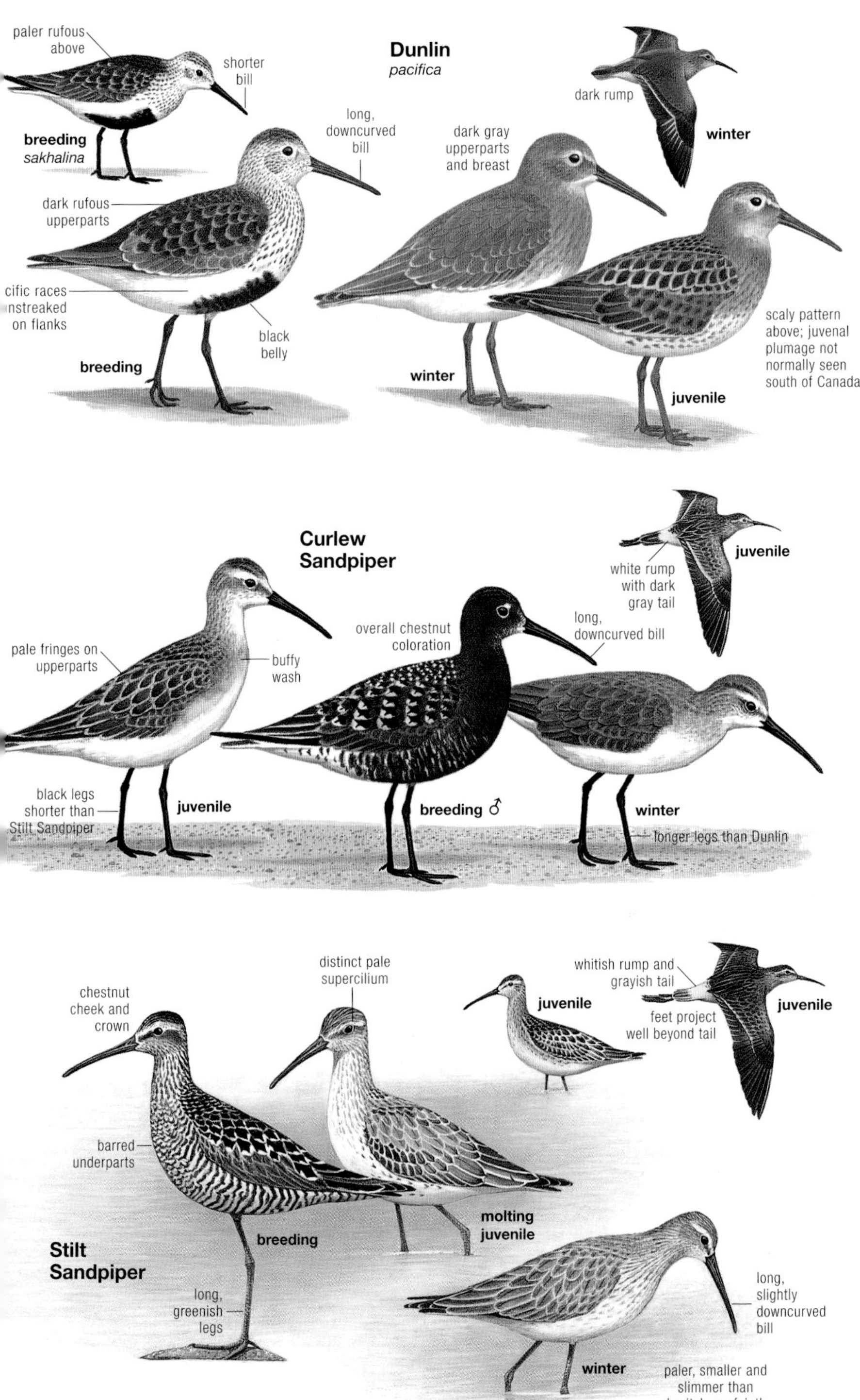
paler rufous
above
shorter
bill
breeding
sakhalina
Dunlin
pacifica
dark rump
winter
long,
downcurved
bill
dark gray
upperparts
and breast
dark rufous
upperparts
cific races
nstreaked
on flanks
black
belly
breeding
winter
scaly pattern
above; juvenal
plumage not
normally seen
south of Canada
juvenile
Curlew
Sandpiper
juvenile
white rump
with dark
gray tail
overall chestnut
coloration
long,
downcurved bill
pale fringes on
upperparts
buffy
wash
black legs
shorter than
Stilt Sandpiper
juvenile
breeding ♂
winter
longer legs than Dunlin
distinct pale
supercilium
whitish rump and
grayish tail
chestnut
cheek and
crown
juvenile
juvenile
feet project
well beyond tail
barred
underparts
molting
juvenile
breeding
Stilt
Sandpiper
long,
greenish
legs
long,
slightly
downcurved
bill
winter
paler, smaller and
slimmer than
dowitchers; faintly
streaked below

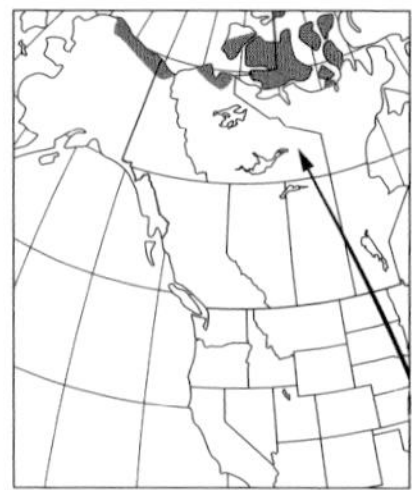

Buff-breasted Sandpiper *Tryngites subruficollis*
L 8¼" (21 cm) Dark eye stands out prominently on buffy face; underparts paler buff; legs orange-yellow. In flight, shows flashy white wing linings. ***Juvenile*** is paler below; white fringes impart a scaly pattern to the upperparts.
Voice: Generally silent.
Range: Nests on tundra. Migrants found in shortgrass habitats, dry mudflats, sometimes upper beaches. Uncommon breeder on Alaska's and Yukon's north slope. Rare to very rare migrant throughout Alaska and very rare fall migrant on West Coast (mostly juveniles). Casual in the interior West. Winters in South America.

Ruff *Philomachus pugnax ♂L 12" (31 cm) ♀L 10" (25 cm)*
Eurasian species. ***Breeding males*** acquire dramatic ruffs in colors that range from black to rufous to white. ***Female*** lacks ruff, is smaller, and has a variable amount of black below. Both sexes have a plump body, small head, and white underwings. Leg color may be yellow, orange, or red. ***Juvenile*** is buffy below, has prominently fringed feathers above. In flight, the U-shaped white band on rump is distinctive in all plumages. Ruff and Buff-breasted Sandpiper are both silent away from breeding grounds.
Voice: Generally silent.
Range: Rare migrant in western Alaska and along West Coast. Casual to northern Alaska where it has once bred (Pt. Lay, 1976), the only breeding record for North America. Casual elsewhere in interior West although annual in California's Central and Imperial Valleys. Very rare in winter in California. Casual in Arizona.

Common Snipe *Gallinago gallinago L 10½" (27 cm)*
Eurasian species. Paler, buffier color overall than Wilson's Snipe; broader white trailing edge to secondaries, fainter flank markings; paler white-striped underwings.
Voice: Flight-display notes of the male are lower pitched than Wilson's; harsh *ski-ape* flight call like Wilson's.
Range: Regular migrant to the western Aleutians where it has bred and been found casually in winter; rarer to the central Aleutians (recorded east to Adak Island), Pribilofs; casual to St. Lawrence Island.

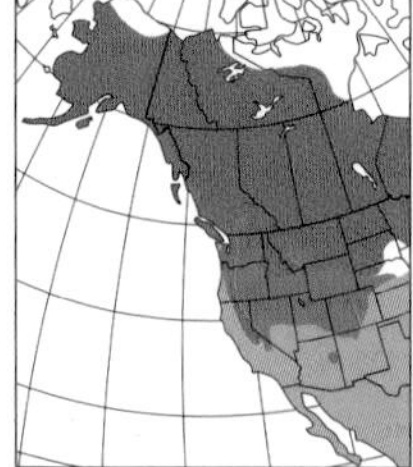

Wilson's Snipe *Gallinago delicata L 10¼" (26 cm)*
Stocky, with very long bill; boldly striped head; and strongly barred flanks.
Voice: Usually seen when fleshed, as it gives a harsh two-syllable *ski-ape* call in rapid, twisting flight. Where breeding, males deliver loud *wheet* notes from perches. In swooping display flight, vibrating outer tail feathers make quavering hoots, like song of Boreal Owl.
Range: Nests in wet meadows, bogs, and swamps; in migration and winter also feeds in marshes, lakeshores, and muddy fields and ditches. Breeds in eastern Aleutians; casual to central Aleutians, Pribilofs, and St. Lawrence Island.

displaying adult
dark crescent
whitish underwing
scaly pattern
dark eye stands out in blank face
spots on sides of breast
juvenile
Buff-breasted Sandpiper
breeding adult
juvenile
yellow legs
buffy underparts
feathering extends out lower mandible
white U-shaped band
juvenile
Ruff
displaying breeding males
♀
summer molting ♂
scaly upperparts
buffy neck and breast
juvenile ♀
back feathers often raised
winter ♂
whitish lores and forehead
leg color variable: greenish to bright orange
small head and plump body
often with colored bill base
summer molting ♀
Wilson's Snipe
underwing
bolder white trailing edge
underwing
dark underwing
faint trailing edge
Common Snipe
gallinago
whitish panel on underwing coverts
displaying
strongly striped head
bold pale stripes on upperparts
flank barring fainter than Wilson's
warmer background color to head, breast, and sides
bold pale stripes on upperparts
heavily barred sides and flanks

Dowitchers

Medium-size, chunky, dark shorebirds, dowitchers have long, straight bills and distinct pale eyebrows. Feeding in mud or shallow water, they probe with a rapid jabbing motion. Dowitchers in flight show a white wedge from barred tail to middle of back. Separating the two species is easiest with juveniles, more difficult with breeding adults, and very difficult in winter except by distinctive calls. Both species give the same song, a rapid *di di da doo,* year-round.

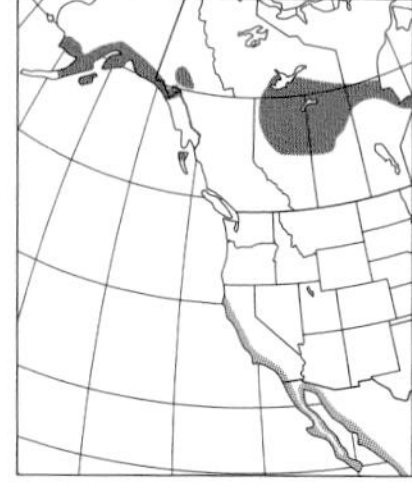

Short-billed Dowitcher *Limnodromus griseus*

L 11" (28 cm) In flight, tail usually looks paler than Long-billed Dowitcher. ***Breeding*** plumage varies among the three subspecies: *griseus* (which breeds in northeast Canada and is not recorded for West), *hendersoni* (central and western Canada), and *caurinus* (Alaska). Unlike Long-billeds, most Short-billeds show some white on the belly, although limited on *hendersoni,* which averages plainer buff underparts than other races and spring Long-billeds. Spots on breast sides (retained in worn breeding plumage in July-Aug.) are always a key feature from Long-billed. In all subspecies, ***juvenile*** is brighter above, buffier and more spotted below than juvenile Long-billed; tertials and visible greater wing coverts have broad reddish buff edges and internal bars, loops, or stripes. ***Winter*** birds are brownish gray above, white below, with gray breast; at close range note fine dark speckling on breast on many birds.

Voice: Call is a mellow *tu tu tu,* repeated in a rapid series as an alarm call.

Range: Feeds at marshes and mudflats. Subspecies *caurinus* is a common migrant along West Coast; small numbers in interior California and western Nevada. Rare farther east, where most birds likely *hendersoni,* a migrant through western Plains. Identity of small breeding population in souther Yukon unknown; tentatively thought to be *caurinus.* Fall migration begins earlier than Long-billed, usually in late June or early July for adults; early Aug. for juveniles. Migrant juveniles are seen through early Oct.

Long-billed Dowitcher *Limnodromus scolopaceus*

L 11½" (29 cm) ***Male***'s bill as long as Short-billed Dowitcher, ***female***'s is longer. In flight, tail usually looks darker than Short-billed. ***Breeding adult*** is entirely reddish below; foreneck spotted and barred (markings below often worn off in worn breeding plumage July–Sept.); sides usually barred. White scapular tips in spring help separate this species from Short-billed. ***Juvenile*** darker above, grayer below than Short-billed; tertials and greater wing coverts are plain, with thin gray edges and rufous tips; some birds show two pale spots near the tips. In ***winter*** birds, breast is unspotted, darker, and more extensively dark than most Short-billed.

Voice: Call is a sharp, high-pitched *keek,* given singly or in a rapid series when alarmed.

Range: Common in migration in West. Fall migration begins later than Short-billed, in mid-July. Juveniles migrate later than adults; rare before Sept. Dowitchers seen inland after mid-Oct. are almost certainly Long-billed.

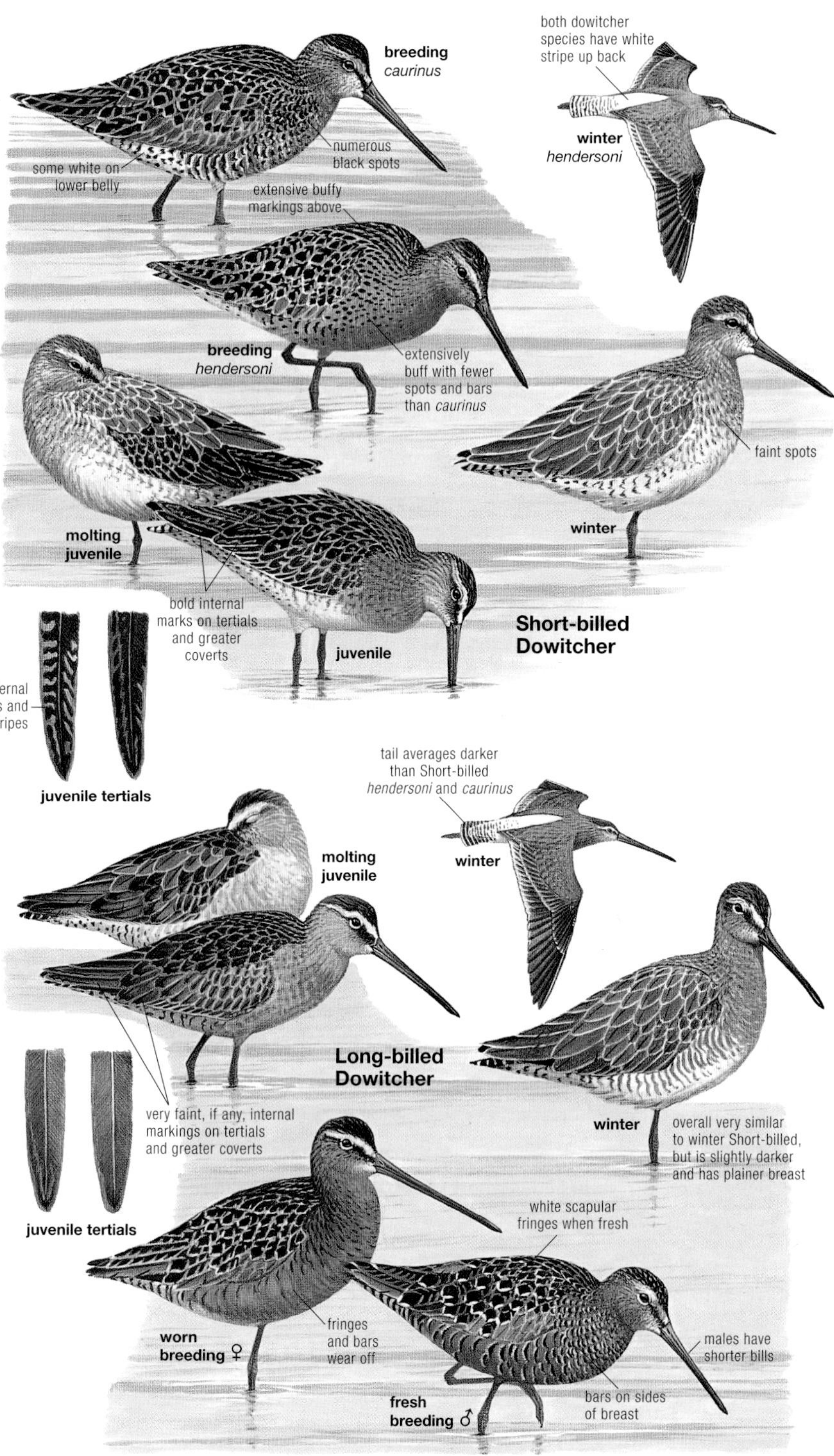

breeding
caurinus
numerous
black spots
some white on
lower belly
both dowitcher
species have white
stripe up back
winter
hendersoni
extensive buffy
markings above
breeding
hendersoni
extensively
buff with fewer
spots and bars
than *caurinus*
faint spots
molting
juvenile
winter
bold internal
marks on tertials
and greater
coverts
juvenile
Short-billed
Dowitcher
nternal
ars and
stripes
juvenile tertials
tail averages darker
than Short-billed
hendersoni and *caurinus*
molting
juvenile
winter
Long-billed
Dowitcher
very faint, if any, internal
markings on tertials
and greater coverts
winter
overall very similar
to winter Short-billed,
but is slightly darker
and has plainer breast
juvenile tertials
white scapular
fringes when fresh
fringes
and bars
wear off
worn
breeding ♀
males have
shorter bills
fresh
breeding ♂
bars on sides
of breast

Phalaropes

These elegant shorebirds have partially lobed feet and dense, soft plumage. Feeding on the water, phalaropes often spin like tops, stirring up larvae, crustaceans, and insects. Females, larger and more brightly colored than the males, do the courting; males incubate the eggs and care for the chicks. In fall, adults and juveniles (particularly Wilson's and Red Phalaropes) rapidly molt to winter plumage; many are seen in transitional plumage farther south.

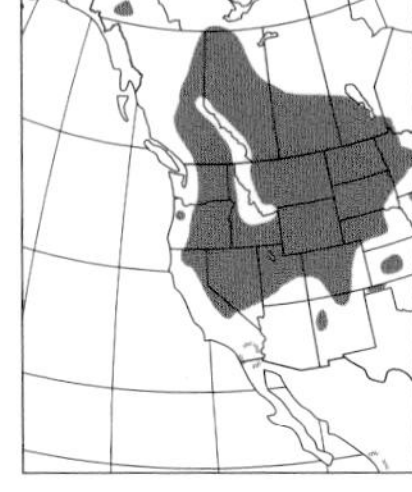

Wilson's Phalarope *Phalaropus tricolor L 9¼" (24 cm)*
Long, thin bill; bold blackish stripe on face and neck. In ***winter*** plumage, upperparts are gray, underparts white; note also lack of distinct dark ear patch; legs yellowish. Briefly held ***juvenal*** plumage resembles winter adult but back is browner with buffy edge to feathers, breast buffy. In flight, white uppertail coverts, whitish tail, and absence of white wing stripe distinguish juvenile and winter birds from other phalaropes.
Voice: Calls include a hoarse *wurk* and other low, croaking notes.
Range: Chiefly an inland phalarope, nesting on grassy borders of shallow lakes, marshes, and reservoirs. Feeds as often on land as on water. Common to abundant in western North America; very rare to Alaska; rare in southern California in winter.

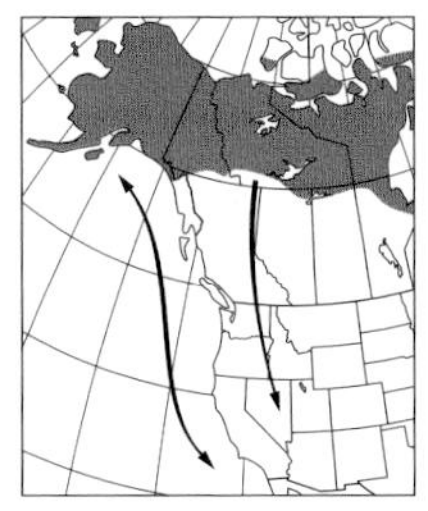

Red-necked Phalarope *Phalaropus lobatus L 7¾" (20 cm)*
Chestnut on front and sides of neck distinctive in ***breeding female,*** less prominent in ***male.*** Both have dark back with bright buff stripes along sides; bill shorter than Wilson's Phalarope, thinner than Red Phalarope. ***Winter*** birds are blue-gray above with whitish stripes; underparts and front of crown white; dark patch extends back from eye. In flight, show white wing stripe, whitish stripes on back, dark central tail coverts. Fresh ***juvenile*** resembles winter adult but is blacker above, with bright buff stripes.
Voice: Call is a high, sharp *kit,* often given in a series.
Range: Breeds on Arctic and subarctic tundra; winters chiefly at sea in Southern Hemisphere; casual in California. Common along and off West Coast and in western portion of the interior West during migration, especially in fall. Generally uncommon farther east.

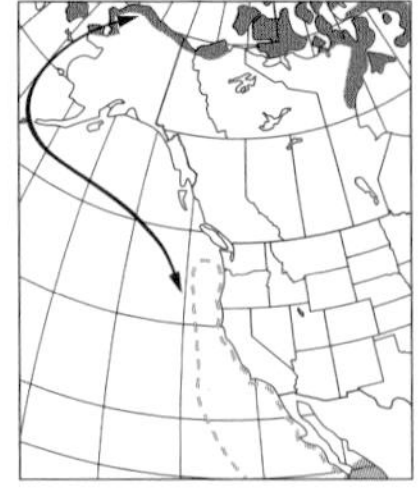

Red Phalarope *Phalaropus fulicarius L 8½" (22 cm)*
Bill shorter and much thicker than other phalaropes; yellow with black tip in breeding adult, usually all-dark in juvenile and winter adult. ***Female*** in breeding plumage has black crown, white face, chestnut red underparts. ***Male*** duller. ***Juvenile*** resembles male but much paler below; juveniles seen in southern Canada and the U.S. are ***molting*** to winter plumage; more closely resemble Red-necked Phalaropes. ***Winter*** bird pale gray above. In flight, shows a bolder white wing stripe than Red-necked and dark central tail coverts.
Voice: Call, a sharp *keip,* is higher-pitched than Red-necked.
Range: Breeds on Arctic shores; winters at sea. Irregularly common off West Coast during migration; rare to very rare inland, chiefly seen in fall.

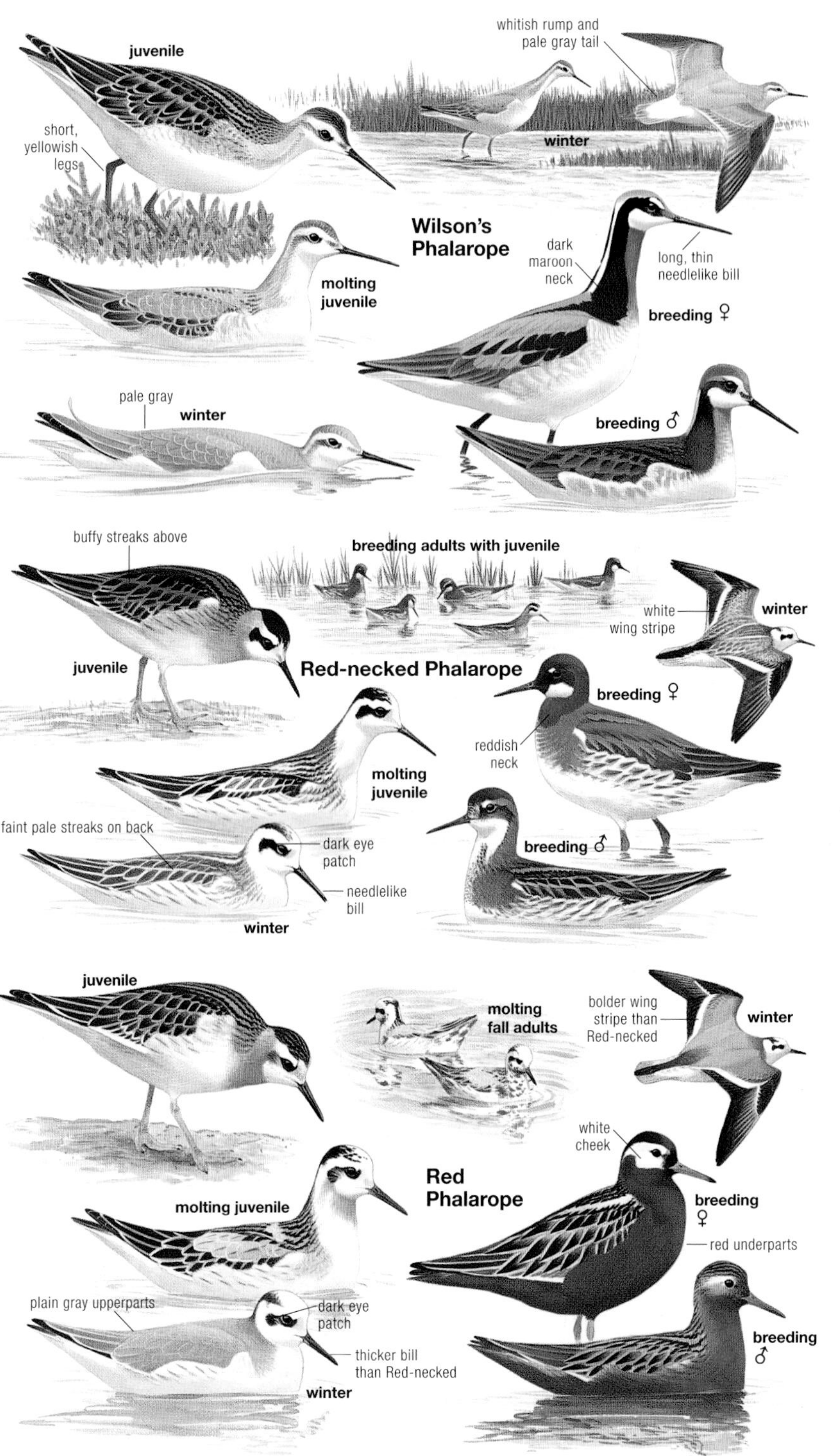
juvenile
whitish rump and pale gray tail
short, yellowish legs
winter
Wilson's Phalarope
dark maroon neck
long, thin needlelike bill
molting juvenile
breeding ♀
pale gray
winter
breeding ♂
buffy streaks above
breeding adults with juvenile
white wing stripe
winter
juvenile
Red-necked Phalarope
breeding ♀
reddish neck
molting juvenile
faint pale streaks on back
dark eye patch
needlelike bill
breeding ♂
winter
juvenile
molting fall adults
bolder wing stripe than Red-necked
winter
white cheek
Red Phalarope
molting juvenile
breeding ♀
red underparts
plain gray upperparts
dark eye patch
thicker bill than Red-necked
winter
breeding ♂

Shorebirds in Flight

Plovers

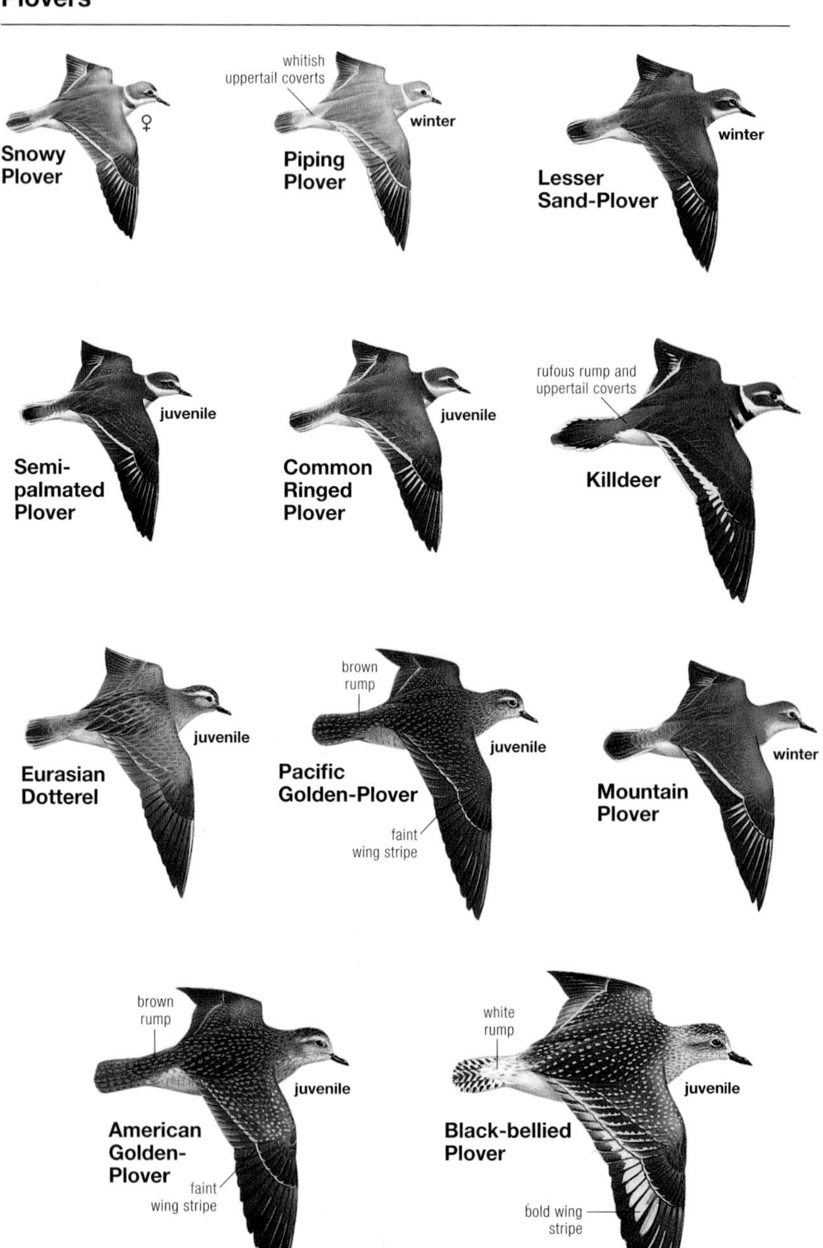

Snowy Plover
♀
whitish uppertail coverts
winter
Piping Plover
winter
Lesser Sand-Plover
juvenile
Semipalmated Plover
juvenile
Common Ringed Plover
rufous rump and uppertail coverts
Killdeer
juvenile
Eurasian Dotterel
brown rump
juvenile
Pacific Golden-Plover
faint wing stripe
winter
Mountain Plover
brown rump
juvenile
American Golden-Plover
faint wing stripe
white rump
juvenile
Black-bellied Plover
bold wing stripe

Godwits and Curlews

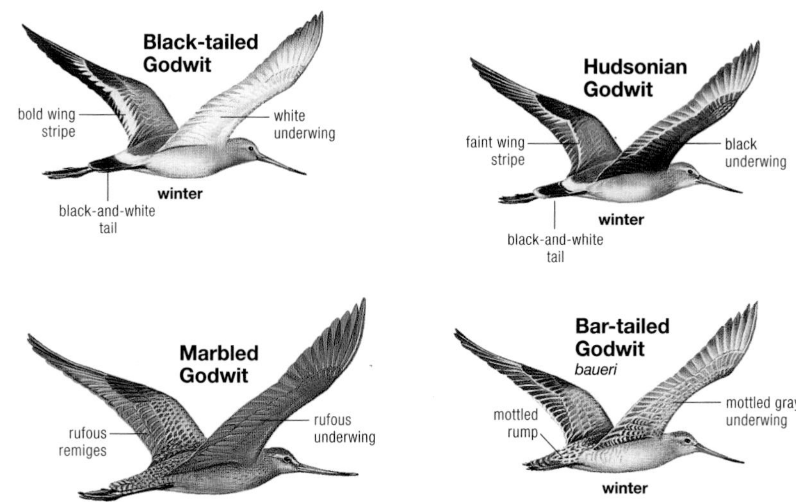

Black-tailed Godwit
bold wing stripe
white underwing
winter
black-and-white tail
Hudsonian Godwit
faint wing stripe
black underwing
winter
black-and-white tail
Marbled Godwit
rufous remiges
rufous underwing
winter
Bar-tailed Godwit
baueri
mottled rump
mottled gray underwing
winter

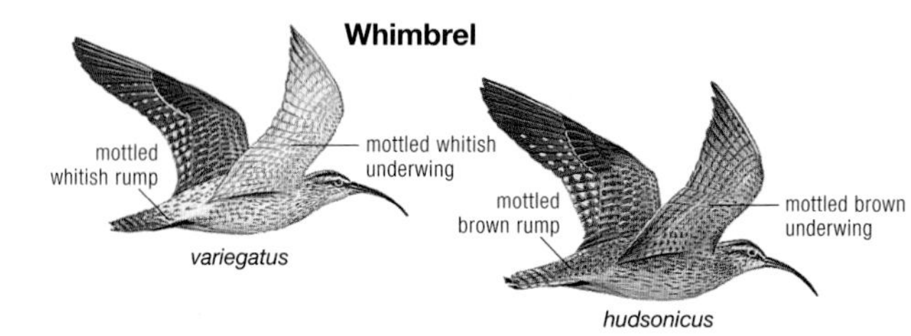

Whimbrel
mottled whitish rump
mottled whitish underwing
variegatus
mottled brown rump
mottled brown underwing
hudsonicus

Bristle-thighed Curlew
pale rufous rump and tail
Long-billed Curlew
rufous remiges
rufous underwing

Shorebirds in Flight

Tringa and Other Sandpipers

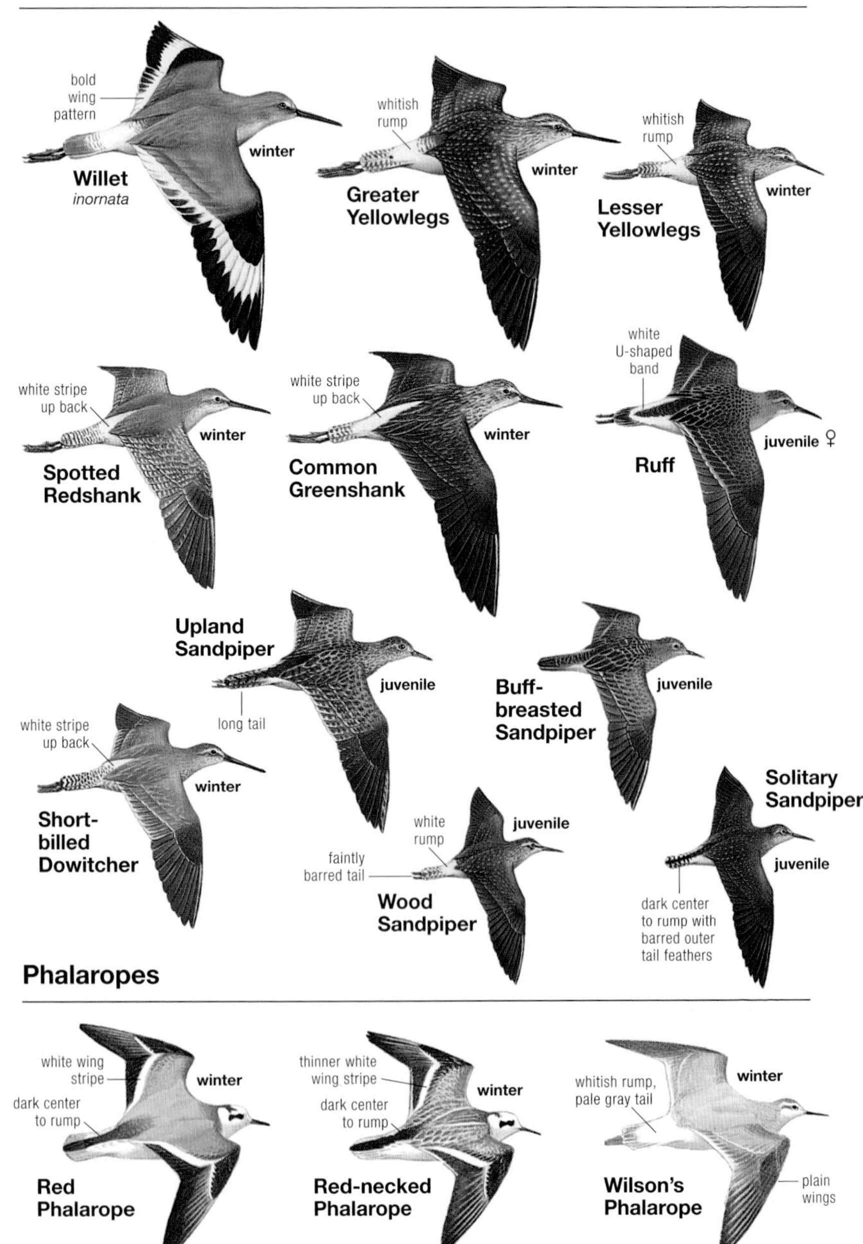
bold wing pattern
winter
Willet
inornata
whitish rump
winter
Greater Yellowlegs
whitish rump
winter
Lesser Yellowlegs
white stripe up back
winter
Spotted Redshank
white stripe up back
winter
Common Greenshank
white U-shaped band
juvenile ♀
Ruff
Upland Sandpiper
long tail
juvenile
Buff-breasted Sandpiper
juvenile
white stripe up back
winter
Short-billed Dowitcher
white rump
faintly barred tail
juvenile
Wood Sandpiper
Solitary Sandpiper
juvenile
dark center to rump with barred outer tail feathers
Phalaropes
white wing stripe
dark center to rump
winter
Red Phalarope
thinner white wing stripe
dark center to rump
winter
Red-necked Phalarope
whitish rump, pale gray tail
winter
Wilson's Phalarope
plain wings

Calidris Sandpipers

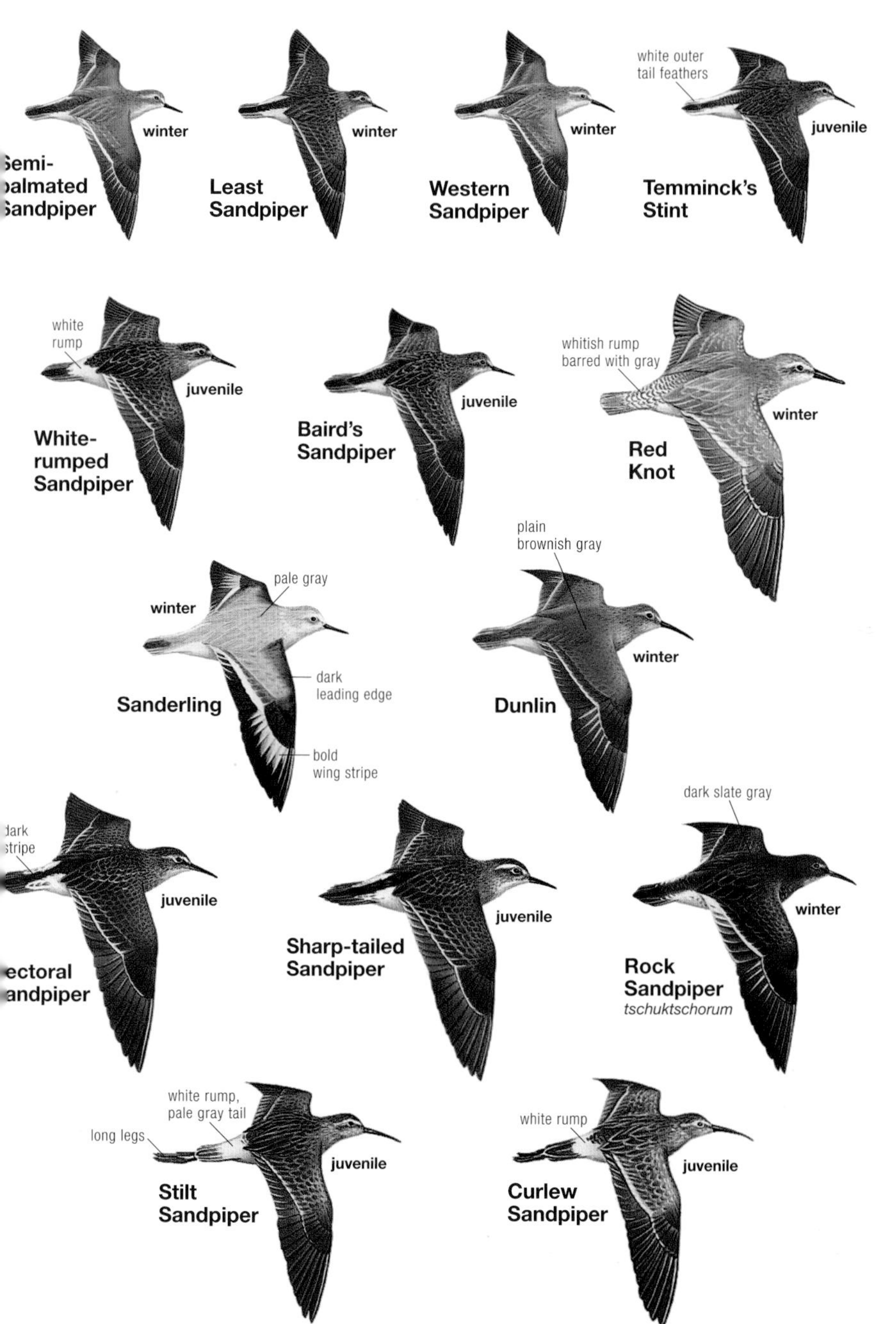

Gulls, Terns, Skimmers (Family Laridae)

A large, diverse family with strong wings and powerful flight. Some species are largely pelagic; others frequent coastal waters or inland lakes and wetlands. Gulls take from about two to four years to reach adult plumage; immatures are often variable and hard to identify. In general, male gulls are larger than females.

Laughing Gull *Leucophaeus atricilla*

L 16½" (42 cm) WS 40" (102 cm) Three-year gull. ***Breeding adult*** has black hood, white underparts, slate gray wings with black outer primaries. In ***winter,*** shows gray wash on nape; compare with the half hood of Franklin's Gull. Second-summer bird has partial hood, some spotting on tip of tail. ***Second-winter*** bird is similar to second-summer bird but has gray wash on sides of breast, lacks hood. ***First-winter*** bird has extensively gray sides, complete tail band, gray wash on nape, slate gray back, dark brown wings; compare with first-winter Franklin's Gull. ***Juvenile*** is like first-winter bird but brown on head and body.

Voice: Calls include a crowing series of *hah* notes; also a single nasal *kow* or *ka-ha.*

Range: In West, regular only at Salton Sea, where fairly common, especially at south end and in adjacent Imperial Valley. Casual elsewhere.

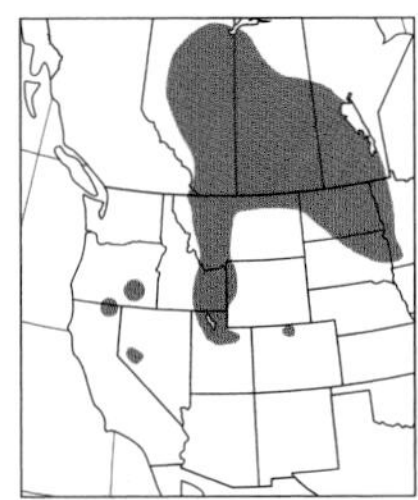

Franklin's Gull *Leucophaeus pipixcan*

L 14½" (37 cm) WS 36" (91 cm) Three-year gull. ***Breeding adult*** has black hood, white underparts variably tinged with pink (some are strongly pinkish), slate gray wings with white bar and black-and-white tips on primaries. Distinguished from Laughing Gull by white bar and large white tips on primaries, pale gray central tail feathers, and broader white eye crescents. All ***winter*** birds have a dark half hood, more extensive than any winter Laughing Gull. Second-summer Franklin's has partial or no bar on primaries. ***First-summer*** bird is like winter adult but lacks white primary bar; bill and legs black. ***First-winter*** bird resembles first-winter Laughing; note white outer tail feathers, half hood, broader eye crescents, white underparts, and, in flight, pale inner primaries. Juvenile is like first-winter bird but back is brown. At all ages, distinguished from Laughing Gull by smaller size, smaller bill with less prominent hook, rounder forehead, less extensive dark on underside of primaries; shorter legs and wings give a stocky look when standing.

Voice: Call like Laughing Gull, but slightly higher and softer.

Range: Common on Great Plains. Otherwise uncommon to rare in West in migration, away from breeding areas. Also rare migrant off West Coast. Very rare in winter in coastal southern California. Very rare to Alaska and northwestern Canada. Winters on west coast of South America.

dark underside
to primaries
has dark "ear muffs,"
but no half hood
like Franklin's
breeding
adult
2nd winter
ong bill with
lightly thicker tip
winter
adult
2nd winter
1st winter
long wings
Laughing
Gull
dark "ear muffs,"
but no hood
gray across breast
and down sides
and flanks
1st winter
overall
brownish
color
broad,
complete
tail band
juvenile
distinctive
black-and-white
wing tip pattern
bill shorter
than
Laughing
thick white
eye crescents in
all plumages
paler underwing
than Laughing
no white band
as in adult
breeding
adult
breeding
adult
winter
adult
old, white
ical spots
1st
summer
white
hind-
neck
bold, dark
half hood
often with pink
tint to underparts
shorter winged
than Laughing
1st
winter
Franklin's
Gull
1st
winter
narrow dark tail
band with white
outer tail feathers
Gulls

Bonaparte's Gull *Chroicocephalus philadelphia*
L 13½" (34 cm) WS 33" (84 cm) Two-year gull. ***Breeding adult*** has slate black hood, black bill, gray mantle with black wing tips that are pale on underside; white underparts, orange-red legs. In flight, shows white wedge on wing. ***Winter*** bird lacks hood. ***First-winter*** bird has a dark brown carpal bar on leading edge of wing, dark band on secondaries, black tail band. First-summer bird may show partial hood; wings and tail are like first-winter. Flight is buoyant, wingbeats rapid.
Voice: Call is a nasal or raspy ternlike *kerrr* or *gerrr.*
Range: Nests in taiga. Uncommon inland migrant in West.

Black-headed Gull *Chroicocephalus ridibundus*
L 16" (41 cm) WS 40" (102 cm) Two-year gull. ***Breeding adult*** has dark brown hood; maroon-red bill and legs; mantle slightly paler gray than Bonaparte's Gull; black wing tips. ***Winter adult*** lacks hood; bill brighter red. ***First-winter*** has orange-red bill. Distinguished from Bonaparte's by larger size and bill color. ***First-summer***'s hood varies from minimal to nearly complete; wings and tail like first-winter. In all plumages, shows dark underside of primaries in flight, darker on adults; compare with Bonaparte's.
Voice: Calls are ternlike; a grating or screeching *ree-ah.*
Range: Rare migrant in western Alaska; casual along West Coast in migration and winter. Accidental in interior West.

Little Gull *Hydrocoloeus minutus*
L 11" (28 cm) WS 24" (61 cm) Two- to three-year gull. ***Breeding adult*** has black hood, black bill, pale gray mantle, white wing tips, white underparts, red legs. ***Winter adult*** has dusky cap, dark spot behind eye. Wings uniformly pale gray above, dark gray to black below, with white trailing edge. Some ***second-winter*** birds are like adult but underwing pattern is incomplete; show some dusky slate in primaries. ***First-winter*** is like Bonaparte's but primaries blackish above, lack white wedge; wings show strong blackish W; crown shows more black. In all plumages, note fluttery wingbeat.
Voice: Occasional nasal and ternlike calls. Gives rapid loud and evenly spaced notes in flight display on breeding grounds.
Range: Western Palearctic species; very rare to casual in West.

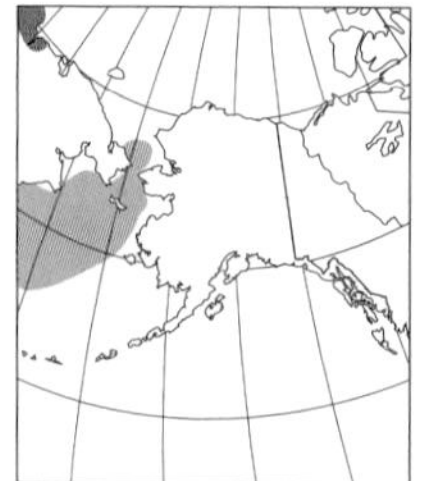

Ross's Gull *Rhodostethia rosea*
L 13½" (34 cm) WS 33" (84 cm) Arctic species. Two-year gull. Variably pink below; upperwing pale gray; underwing pale to dark gray. ***Breeding adult*** has black collar, partial or absent in winter. ***Winter adult*** has partial gray collar that contrasts with white head. ***First-winter*** bird has black at tip of tail, dark spot behind eye; acquires black collar by first summer; in flight, shows M-pattern like Little Gull. In all plumages, note long, pointed wings; long, wedge-shaped tail; and broad, white trailing edge to wings.
Voice: Mostly silent away from Arctic breeding grounds, where it gives ternlike chitters and a mellow yapping.
Range: Mainly a breeder of the Russian Far East. Can be a common fall migrant off Pt. Barrow, Alaska. Rare and irregular in Bering Sea. Casual otherwise in West.

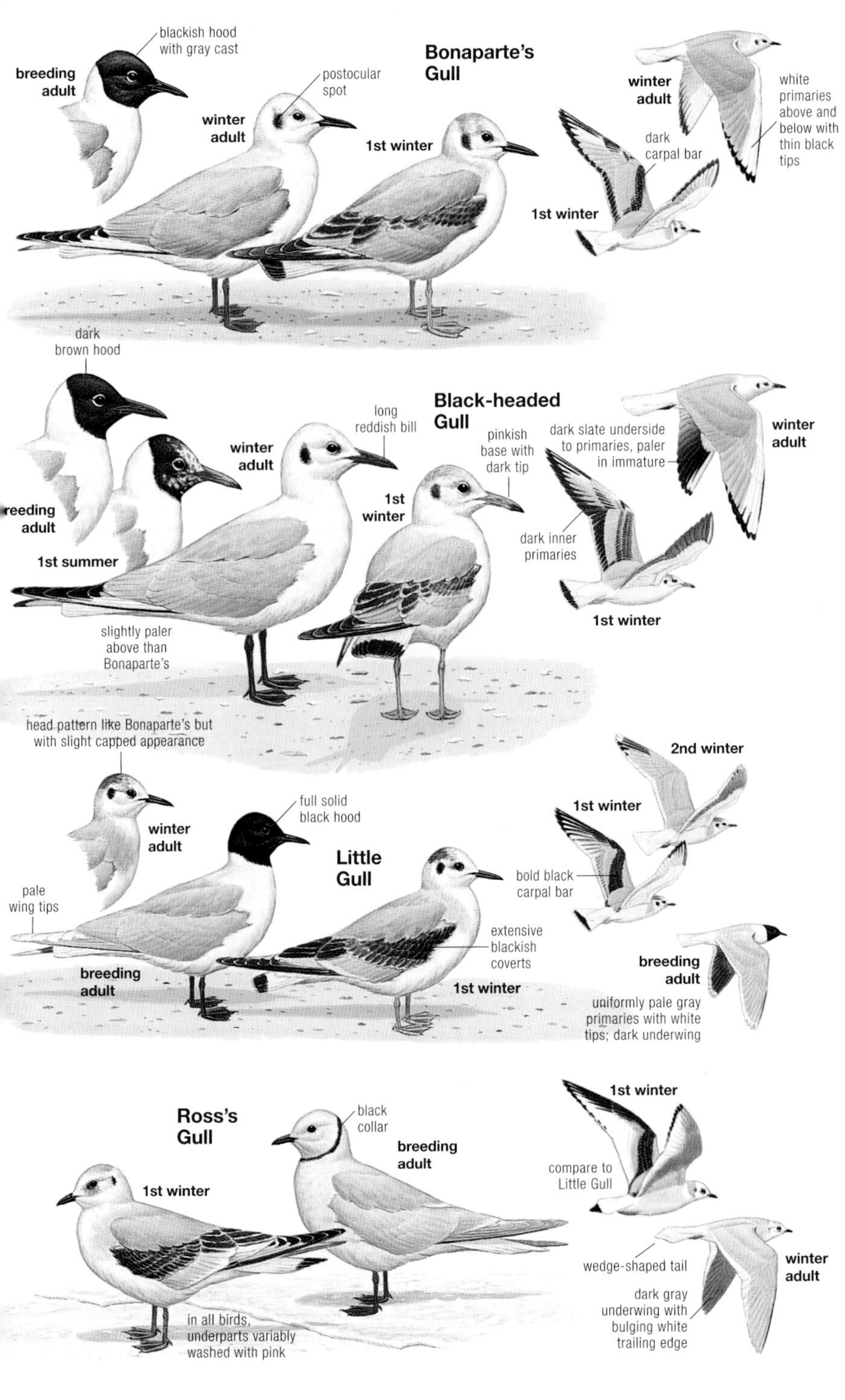
Bonaparte's Gull
breeding adult
blackish hood with gray cast
winter adult
postocular spot
1st winter
winter adult
white primaries above and below with thin black tips
dark carpal bar
1st winter
Black-headed Gull
dark brown hood
reeding adult
1st summer
winter adult
long reddish bill
1st winter
pinkish base with dark tip
dark slate underside to primaries, paler in immature
winter adult
dark inner primaries
1st winter
slightly paler above than Bonaparte's
head pattern like Bonaparte's but with slight capped appearance
winter adult
full solid black hood
Little Gull
pale wing tips
breeding adult
extensive blackish coverts
1st winter
2nd winter
1st winter
bold black carpal bar
breeding adult
uniformly pale gray primaries with white tips; dark underwing
Ross's Gull
black collar
breeding adult
1st winter
in all birds, underparts variably washed with pink
1st winter
compare to Little Gull
wedge-shaped tail
winter adult
dark gray underwing with bulging white trailing edge

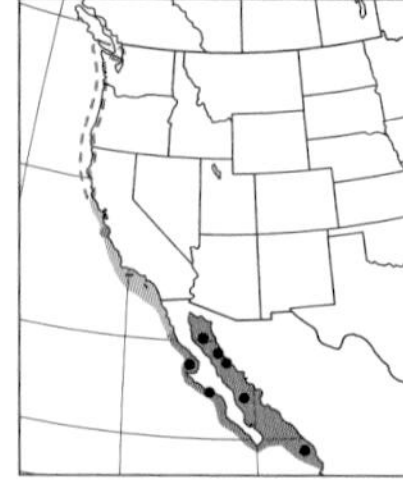

Heermann's Gull *Larus heermanni*

L 19" (48 cm) WS 51" (130 cm) Four-year gull. ***Adult*** distinctive with white head, streaked gray-brown in fall and early winter; red bill; dark gray body; black tail with white terminal band; white trailing edge on wings. Third-winter bird is variably intermediate between adult and second-winter. ***Second-winter*** bird is browner still, with two-toned bill and buff tail band. ***First-winter*** bird has dark brown body, lacks contrasting tail tip and trailing edge on wing. Wings are fairly long, flight buoyant.

Voice: Calls include distinctive low nasal notes.

Range: Common post-breeding visitor from Mexican breeding grounds from early summer to early winter; smaller numbers in late winter and spring along the West Coast; small numbers have irregularly nested on the central California coast. Rare at Salton Sea, where it has recently nested; casual elsewhere inland in California, the Southwest, Nevada, and to southern Alaska. Some of the interior records of adults away from the Salton Sea have been of birds in California Gull colonies but no nesting to date.

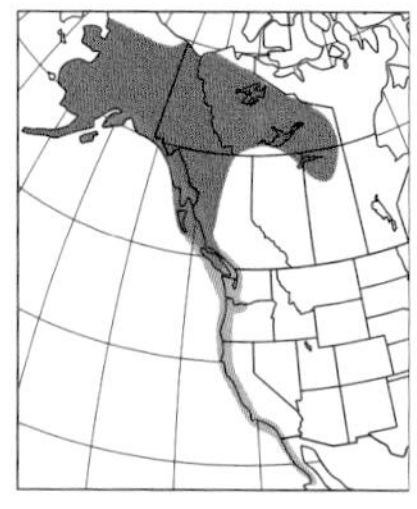

Mew Gull *Larus canus L 16" (41 cm) WS 43" (109 cm)*

Three-year gull. Widespread race in western North America, *brachyrhynchus,* is the smallest of three subspecies found here and has least black on wing tips; in flight, shows much more white on primaries than Ring-billed Gull. European nominate race, *canus* ("Common Gull"), which is unrecorded in western North America, and East Asian *kamtschatschensis* (the largest race) have more extensive black on wing tips. All ***adults*** have white head, washed with brown in ***winter;*** dark gray mantle; thin yellow bill; and most have large, dark eyes. ***Second-winter*** bird is like adult but has two-toned bill; has less white on primaries; variably spotted tail band. ***First-winter*** *brachyrhynchus* is heavily washed with brown below, almost solid brown on belly; spotted with white on breast. Head and nape are washed with soft brown; mantle dark gray; primaries light brown with pale edges. Tail is almost entirely brown, with heavily barred tail coverts; wing linings evenly pale brown. ***Juvenile*** is like first-winter, but brown on the back and head, darker below. Second-winter and adult *kamtschatschensis* have pale eyes; first-winter birds are more like *brachyrhynchus,* but note dark tail band rather than all-dark tail, and paler tail coverts. In flight, first-winter's underwing coverts paler than *brachyrhynchus.* Mew Gulls average smaller than Ring-billed Gulls, especially *brachyrhynchus,* with rounder heads, larger eyes, and thinner bills.

Voice: Calls include a wheezy *kyap* and a mewing *kii-uu.*

Range: Nests in taiga; otherwise in coastal habitats and farm fields. North American race, *brachyrhynchus,* is rare inland in winter in Pacific states, very rare to casual elsewhere in West during migration and winter. Asian race, *kamtschatschensis,* is rare on the Aleutians and islands in the Bering Sea.

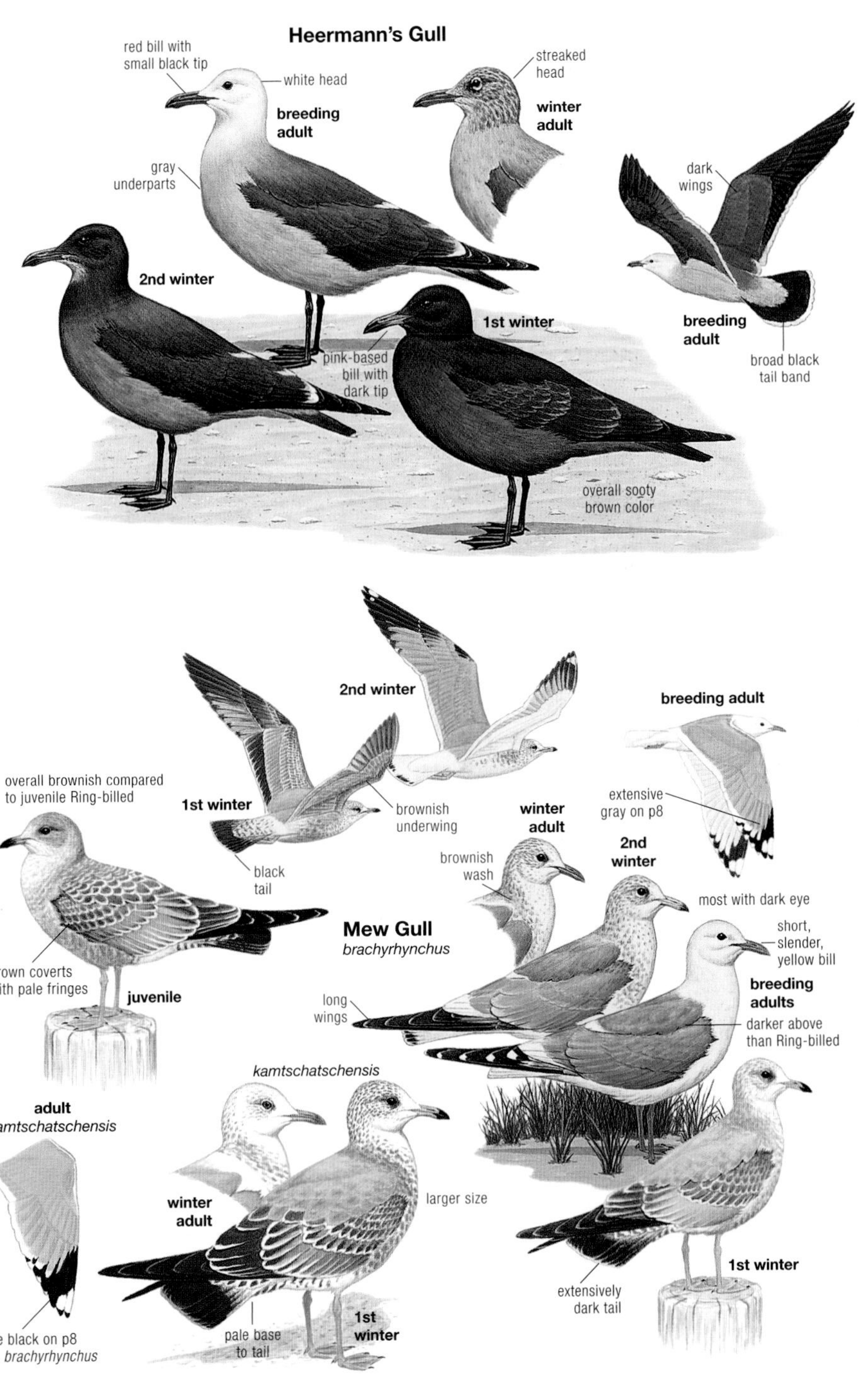
Heermann's Gull
red bill with small black tip
white head
breeding adult
streaked head
winter adult
gray underparts
dark wings
2nd winter
1st winter
pink-based bill with dark tip
breeding adult
broad black tail band
overall sooty brown color
2nd winter
breeding adult
overall brownish compared to juvenile Ring-billed
1st winter
brownish underwing
winter adult
extensive gray on p8
black tail
brownish wash
2nd winter
most with dark eye
Mew Gull
brachyrhynchus
short, slender, yellow bill
breeding adults
juvenile
long wings
darker above than Ring-billed
kamtschatschensis
adult
winter adult
larger size
1st winter
extensively dark tail
pale base to tail
1st winter

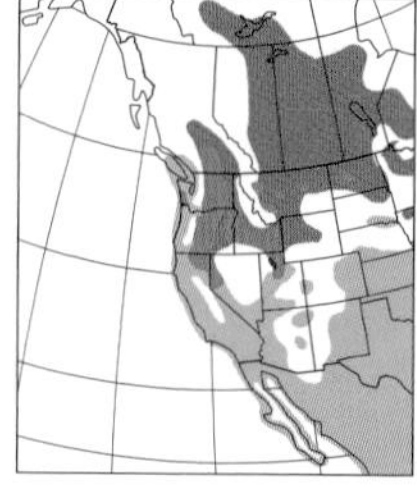

Ring-billed Gull *Larus delawarensis*

L 17½" (45 cm) WS 48" (122 cm) Three-year gull. ***Adult*** has pale gray mantle; yellow bill with black subterminal ring; pale eyes; yellowish legs; head streaked and spotted with brown in ***winter. Second-winter*** bird is like winter adult but bill has broader band, black on primaries is more extensive, tail usually has some blackish terminal spots. ***First-winter*** bird has gray back, brown wings with dark blackish brown primaries, brown-streaked head and nape; underparts white with brown spots and scalloping on breast and throat; tail has medium-wide but variable brown band and extensive mottling above band; uppertail and undertail coverts are lightly barred; secondary coverts medium gray; wing linings mostly white, with some barring. Distinguished from first-winter Mew Gull (*brachyrhynchus*) by white underparts spotted on breast and throat, tail pattern, darker primaries, heavier bill, and paler back. ***Juvenal*** plumage may be largely kept into early winter; resembles first-winter but back brown, spotting below more extensive, and bill more black.

Voice: Calls include a mewing *kee-ew,* a sharper *kyow,* and a whining *sseeaa.* Also an extended "long call."

Range: Locally abundant and widespread; winters uncommonly outside mapped range. Rare to Alaska and Yukon and well offshore in fall. Nonbreeders oversummer south of nesting range.

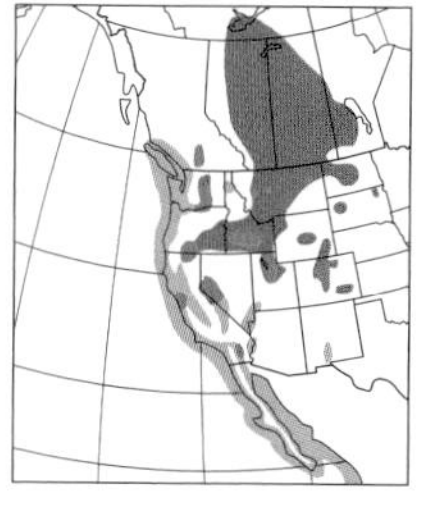

California Gull *Larus californicus*

L 21" (53 cm) WS 54" (137 cm) Four-year gull. ***Adult*** has darker gray mantle than Herring Gull (next page), paler than Lesser Black-backed Gull (page 180), but mantle color and size geographically variable. Prairie Province breeders, *albertensis,* are larger and paler mantled than breeding populations elsewhere (*californicus*). White head, heavily streaked with brown in winter; dark eyes; yellow bill with black and red spots, black spot often smaller in breeding season; gray-green or greenish yellow legs, brighter yellow in breeding season. In flight, shows dusky trailing edge on underwing. Third-winter plumage is like adult but bill is more extensively smudged with black; wings show some brown; tail has some brown spotting. ***Second-winter*** has gray back, brown wings, grayish to blue-green legs, two-toned bill; compare to first-winter Ring-billed Gull. ***First-winter*** is brown overall with veiled gray on scapulars; usually palest on throat, breast, and upper belly; legs pinkish; bill two-toned, the colors sharply defined. In flight, first-winter birds show double dark bar on inner half of wing, caused by darker secondaries and greater secondary covert bases. Distinctly smaller than Western Gull (page 178), with thinner bill. Compare first-winter birds to first- and second-winter Herring and Lesser Black-backed Gulls. ***Juvenile*** is variably pale below, lacks pale bill base.

Voice: Calls include a *kyow,* a higher *kii-ow,* and a slightly nasal, trumpeting "long call"; all lower pitched than Ring-billed.

Range: Nests at lakes; otherwise frequents a wide variety of habitats and in winter common offshore. Uncommon to rare in much of Southwest and southwestern Great Plains and uncommon to southeast Alaska (mainly late summer), rarely farther north. Nonbreeders oversummer south of breeding range.

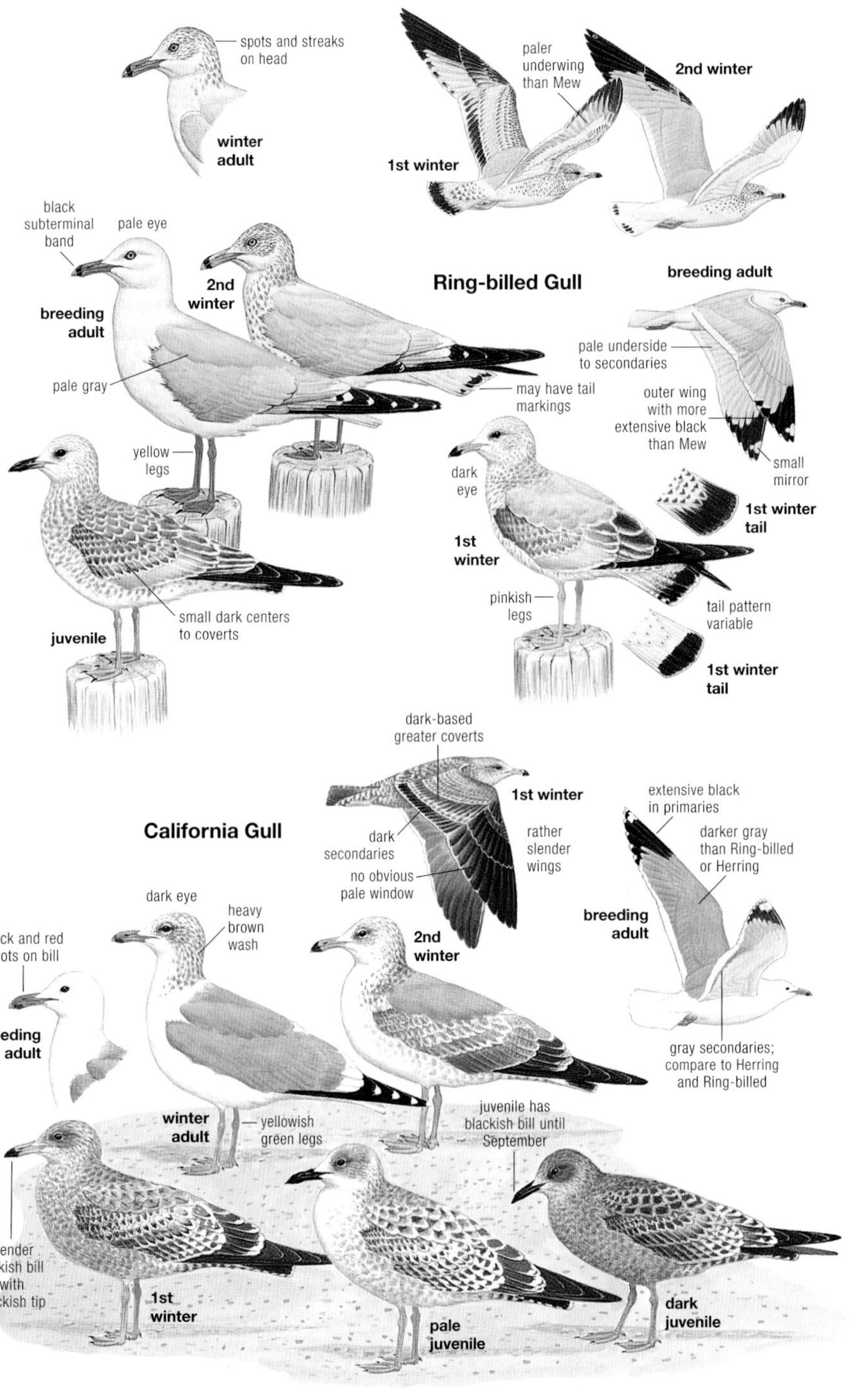
spots and streaks
on head
winter
adult
paler
underwing
than Mew
2nd winter
1st winter
black
subterminal
band
pale eye
2nd
winter
Ring-billed Gull
breeding adult
breeding
adult
pale underside
to secondaries
pale gray
may have tail
markings
outer wing
with more
extensive black
than Mew
yellow
legs
dark
eye
small
mirror
1st winter
tail
1st
winter
pinkish
legs
tail pattern
variable
small dark centers
to coverts
juvenile
1st winter
tail
dark-based
greater coverts
1st winter
extensive black
in primaries
California Gull
dark
secondaries
rather
slender
wings
darker gray
than Ring-billed
or Herring
no obvious
pale window
dark eye
heavy
brown
wash
2nd
winter
breeding
adult
gray secondaries;
compare to Herring
and Ring-billed
winter
adult
yellowish
green legs
juvenile has
blackish bill until
September
1st
winter
pale
juvenile
dark
juvenile

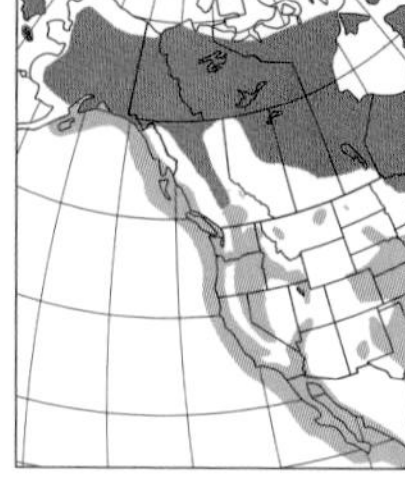

Herring Gull *Larus argentatus*

L 25" (64 cm) WS 58" (147 cm) Highly variable four-year gull. ***Adult*** has pale gray mantle; white head streaked with brown in winter; legs and feet pink; bill yellow with red spot. ***Third-winter*** plumage is like winter adult but with black smudge on bill, some brown on body and wing coverts. ***Second-winter*** bird has pale gray back; brown wings; pale eyes; two-toned bill. ***First-winter*** birds are brown overall, with dark brownish black primaries and tail band, dark eyes, dark bill, with variable pink at base; some may have bill like first-winter California Gull (previous page); but usually distinguished by darker bill, paler face and throat, and, in flight, by pale panel at base of primaries and single dark bar on secondaries. Distinguished from first-winter Western Gull (page 178) by smaller bill, paler and more mottled body plumage, and, in flight, by paler wings with pale panel, and lack of contrast between back and rump. Distinguished from first-winter Lesser Black-backed Gull (page 180) by browner, less contrasting body plumage, usually darker belly, and, in flight, by pale primary and outer secondary coverts and less-contrasting rump pattern. Widespread North American race is *smithsonianus;* Bering Sea region *vegae* has darker mantle in adult plumage; wing-tip pattern to Slaty-backed Gull (page 180); usually has dark eyes; head heavily streaked in winter.

Voice: Series of bugling calls makes up "long call." Also a full *kyow*.

Range: Generally local in the West; common in some regions, uncommon to rare in most. Frequents a wide variety of habitats, from pelagic offshore waters (common to about 100 miles out) to coasts, farm fields, parking lots, and dumps.

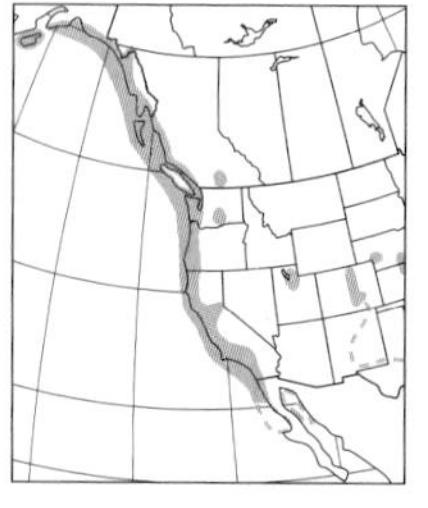

Thayer's Gull *Larus thayeri L 23" (58 cm) WS 55" (140 cm)*

Variable four-year gull. In most ***adults,*** eye is dark brown, mantle slightly darker than Iceland Gull (next page) or Herring Gull; bill yellow with dark red spot; legs darker pink than Herring. Primaries pale gray below, with thin, dark trailing edge; show some black or slaty gray from above. Many have paler eyes. ***Second-winter*** has gray mantle, contrasting gray-brown tail band, many with dark eyes. ***First-winter*** variable but primaries always entirely pale below, darker than mantle above. Distinguished from Herring Gull by smaller size, paler checkered markings in plumage, and paler primaries with whitish edges; from Iceland Gull (very rare in West) by generally darker plumage—primaries darker than mantle, darker secondaries—and usually by unspeckled tail. Some birds are probably best left unidentified, especially when worn in late winter or spring. Compare to bigger billed, larger Glaucous-winged Gull (page 178); immature Glaucous-winged is less mottled and the wing tips are uniform with the mantle. Some consider Thayer's a race of Iceland Gull.

Voice: Calls similar to Herring and Iceland Gull.

Range: Wintering populations localized. Rare to casual in the interior West and to western Alaska.

Herring
Gull
smithsonianus
riking
le eye
extensive
streaking
pale gray
upperparts
juvenile
winter adult
pink legs
obvious pale
window
dark
tail
1st winter
3rd winter
often
more
adultlike
pale eye by late
2nd winter
often
pale headed
1st
winter
2nd
winter
apical spots small
or absent
some dark
in tail
1st
nter
white tail
base
pale underside
to secondaries
breeding
adult
1st winter
vegae
more stippled
upperparts
paler than
smithsonianus
winter
adult
vegae
1st winter
vegae
breeding
adult
vegae
darker mantle
color than
smithsonianus
Thayer's
Gull
eye color
variable
winter adult
2nd
winter
winter
adult
head and
neck washed
with brownish
large white
mirrors
with little
blackish
narrow
dark line
1st winter
breeding
adult
dark
secondary bar
brownish
on outer
webs from
above
dark pink
legs
pale
underwing
1st winter
short
bill
mostly
brownish tertials
me are quite dark
d very similar to
t-winter Herrings
1st winter
brownish
primaries with
pale fringes

Iceland Gull *Larus glaucoides*

L 22" (56 cm) WS 54" (137 cm) Highly variable four-year gull. ***Adults*** have white heads, suffused with brown in winter; most have yellow eyes, a few brown. Late ***second-winter*** birds have pale eyes, gray back, two-toned bill. ***First-winter*** birds are buffy to mostly white; chiefly dark bill is short; eyes dark; wing tips white or irregularly washed with brown. Canadian-breeding adult *kumlieni* have wing tips variably marked with gray; a few are pure white. Greenland-breeding *glaucoides* is slightly smaller and paler overall in all plumages; adults are slightly paler mantled and have pure white wing tips; most migrate southeast to Iceland, a few to Europe; rare or casual to northeast North America. See Thayer's Gull account (previous page) for distinguishing characteristics; told from Glaucous Gull by usually darker bill and structural features (smaller size, rounder head, longer wings that extend beyond tail at rest).

Voice: Calls similar to Herring Gull.

Range: Very rare to casual over much of West. Most, but not all, have shown characteristics of *kumlieni.*

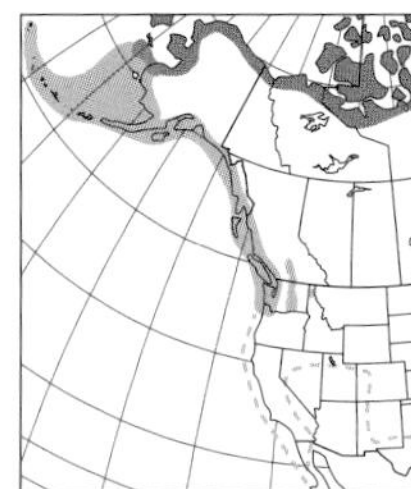

Glaucous Gull *Larus hyperboreus*

L 27" (69 cm) WS 60" (152 cm) Heavy-bodied, four-year gull. All have translucent tips to white primaries. ***Adult*** has very pale gray mantle, yellow eye. Head is streaked with brown in winter. Late ***second-winter*** bird has pale gray back and pale eye. ***First-winter*** birds may be buffy or almost all-white; bill is bicolored. Distinguished from Iceland Gull by size; heavier, longer bill; flatter crown; slightly paler mantle of adults; disproportionately shorter wings, barely extending beyond tail. At all ages, distinguished from Glaucous-winged Gull (next page) by more buffy white color, contrasting pale primaries; in first-winter birds by sharply two-toned bill. Northern Alaskan birds are slightly smaller, and adults have slightly darker mantles, than birds from eastern Canada and Bering Sea. Occasionally hybridizes with Herring Gull.

Voice: Similar to Herring; some calls actually pitched higher.

Range: Rare in winter south to southern California, New Mexico.

IDENTIFYING: Gull Age Classes When identifying many species of gulls, one must *first* properly *age* the bird. It is important to understand the fundamental changes in plumage and bare-part color and pattern that take place in two-year, three-year, and four-year gulls, as well as the effects of abrasion, wear, and bleaching on feathers. It is also crucial to understand the overall timing of molts in gulls, which is complicated by the variation between individuals of the same species that results in varying plumage patterns and bare-part colors among birds of similar age. Some of the larger species may be in almost continuous molt before they reach adulthood.

In this guide, gull ages are linked to a bird's physical age: For instance, a first-winter bird is in its late first and early second calendar year, and a second-winter individual is in its late second and early third calendar year. Some other books use the terms "first cycle," "second cycle," and so on, terms based on molts.

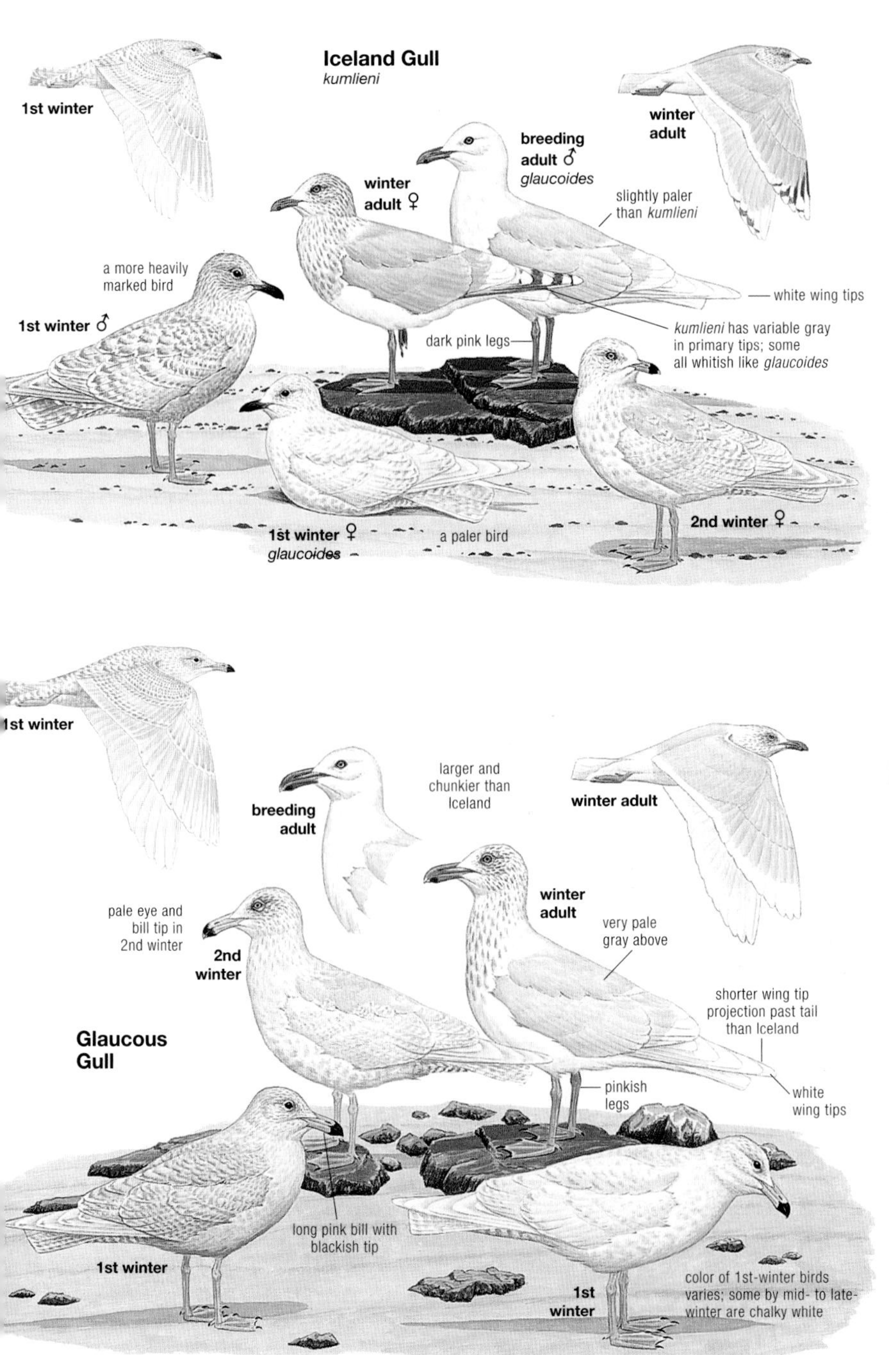
Iceland Gull
kumlieni
1st winter
winter adult
breeding adult ♂
glaucoides
winter adult ♀
slightly paler than kumlieni
a more heavily marked bird
1st winter ♂
white wing tips
dark pink legs
kumlieni has variable gray in primary tips; some all whitish like glaucoides
1st winter ♀
glaucoides
a paler bird
2nd winter ♀
1st winter
larger and chunkier than Iceland
winter adult
breeding adult
winter adult
very pale gray above
pale eye and bill tip in 2nd winter
2nd winter
Glaucous Gull
shorter wing tip projection past tail than Iceland
pinkish legs
white wing tips
long pink bill with blackish tip
1st winter
1st winter
color of 1st-winter birds varies; some by mid- to late-winter are chalky white

Western Gull *Larus occidentalis*

L 25" (64 cm) WS 58" (147 cm) Four-year gull. ***Adults*** north of Monterey, California, have paler backs and darker eyes than southern birds. All adults have white head, dark gray back, pink legs, very large bill. In ***winter,*** head moderately streaked with brown in northern birds, faintly streaked in southern. ***Third-winter*** resembles second-winter Yellow-footed Gull but tail is mostly white. ***Second-winter*** bird has a dark gray back, yellow eyes, two-toned bill, dark brown wings. ***First-winter*** bird is one of the darkest young gulls; bill is black; in flight, distinguished from young Herring Gull by contrast of dark back with paler rump. Note also the often sootier underparts and head; heavier bill. ***Juvenile*** like first-winter but darker. Westerns hybridize extensively with Glaucous-winged Gulls in the Northwest; ***hybrids*** are seen all along the West Coast in winter; two ages shown here. These are easily confused with Thayer's Gull (page 174); note large bill, pattern of wing tips.
Voice: Gives wide variety of calls, many suggestive of Herring Gull, but gives low notes too.
Range: Very rare to casual well inland. Casual to southeast Alaska.

Glaucous-winged Gull *Larus glaucescens*

L 26" (66 cm) WS 58" (147 cm) Four-year gull. ***Adult*** has white head, moderately streaked with brown in winter. Body white, mantle pale gray; primaries the same color as rest of wing above, paler below. Eyes dark; large bill yellow with red spot; legs pink. Third-winter like adult but some buff on body, bill smudged black; some have a partial tail band. ***Second-winter***'s back gray, rest of body and wings pale buff to white with little mottling; tail evenly gray; bill mostly dark. ***First-winter*** uniformly pale gray-brown to whitish with subtle mottling; primaries same color as the mantle; note young Glaucous Gull (previous page) has sharply two-toned bill, pale primaries; young Thayer's (page 174) is smaller, with smaller bill, more speckled body plumage, darker primaries. Glaucous-winged hybridizes with Western; also with Herring (page 174) in south-central Alaska. Hybrids extremely variable.
Voice: Generally like Western Gull; long call thought to be slightly higher pitched.
Range: Rare well inland in Pacific states; casual farther east.

IDENTIFYING: Parts of a Gull

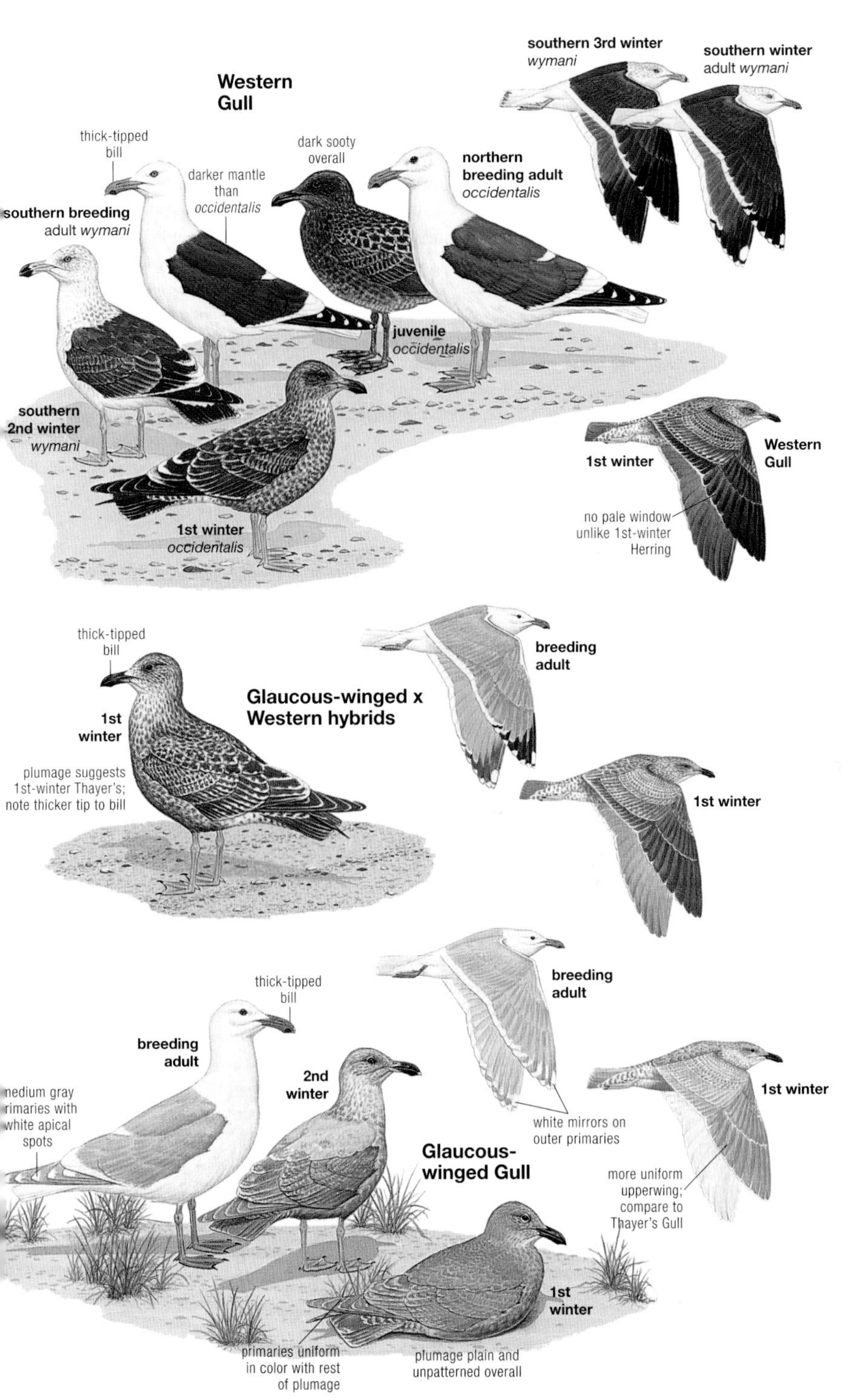

Western Gull
southern 3rd winter wymani
southern winter adult wymani
thick-tipped bill
dark sooty overall
darker mantle than occidentalis
northern breeding adult occidentalis
southern breeding adult wymani
juvenile occidentalis
southern 2nd winter wymani
1st winter
Western Gull
no pale window unlike 1st-winter Herring
1st winter occidentalis
thick-tipped bill
breeding adult
Glaucous-winged x Western hybrids
1st winter
plumage suggests 1st-winter Thayer's; note thicker tip to bill
1st winter
breeding adult
thick-tipped bill
breeding adult
2nd winter
1st winter
medium gray primaries with white apical spots
white mirrors on outer primaries
Glaucous-winged Gull
more uniform upperwing; compare to Thayer's Gull
1st winter
primaries uniform in color with rest of plumage
plumage plain and unpatterned overall

Yellow-footed Gull *Larus livens*

L 27" (69 cm) WS 60" (152 cm) Three-year gull. ***Adult*** is like Western Gull but has yellow legs and feet; note also thicker yellow bill with red spot; dark slate gray wings; yellow eyes. ***Second-winter*** bird is like adult but tail looks entirely black, bill two-toned. In first-winter plumage, head and body are mostly white, back and wings brown, eyes dark, bill mostly dark, legs pinkish. ***Juvenile*** resembles first-winter Western but white belly contrasts sharply with streaked breast; upperparts are more boldly patterned; rump whiter; bill thicker.

Voice: Calls are lower pitched than Western.

Range: Breeds in the Gulf of California. Fairly common post-breeding visitor in summer to Salton Sea; a few usually linger into winter; rarest in spring. Casual to coastal southern California. Accidental eastern California, southern Nevada, Utah, Arizona.

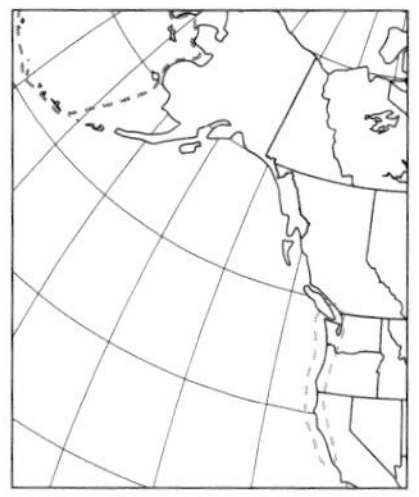

Slaty-backed Gull *Larus schistisagus*

L 25" (64 cm) WS 58" (147 cm) Coastal species of northeast Asia. Four-year gull. ***Adult*** has dark slate gray back and wings, blackish outer primaries separated from mantle by a staggered row of whitish spots. Underside of primaries gray; broad white trailing edge to wings. Legs bright pink; pale eyes. Head heavily mottled in winter. ***Second-summer*** bird has dark back, very pale wings. First-year birds show almost entirely dark tail and wing pattern like Thayer's Gull (page 174); also compare with *vegae* race of Herring Gull (page 174); *vegae* adult has paler upperparts, lacks broad white trailing edge; underside of primaries darker than Slaty-backed.

Voice: Similar to Glaucous-winged Gull.

Range: Uncommon to rare in coastal Alaska, most frequent in the Bering Sea. Very rare in winter south through Pacific states; casual to accidental elsewhere in western North America.

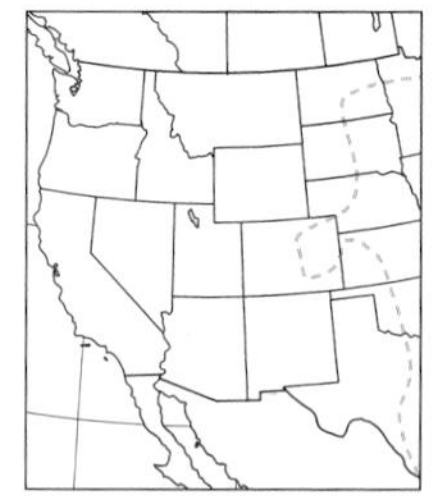

Lesser Black-backed Gull *Larus fuscus*

L 21" (53 cm) WS 54" (137 cm) Western Palearctic species. A four-year gull. ***Adult*** has white head, heavily streaked with brown in winter; white underparts; yellow legs. Third-winter bird has dark smudge on bill; some brown in wings. ***Second-winter*** bird resembles second-winter Herring Gull (page 174) but note dark gray back, much darker underwings. ***First-winter*** bird similar to first-winter Herring Gull but head and belly are paler, upperparts more contrastingly dark and light; bill is always entirely black. Identified in flight by darker primary and secondary coverts, more extensively dark primaries and white outer tail feathers; paler rump contrasts with back. Much smaller than Great Black-backed Gull, found in East. Smaller on average than Herring Gull, with smaller bill, but there is substantial range of overlap; also note longer wings, usually extending well beyond tail at rest. Most birds seen here are of northern European race *graellsii.* A few darker mantled adults of Baltic race, *intermedius,* recorded for East.

Range: Increasing in the West. Rare but annual in fall and winter in eastern Colorado and in California. Casual elsewhere in West, including Alaska.

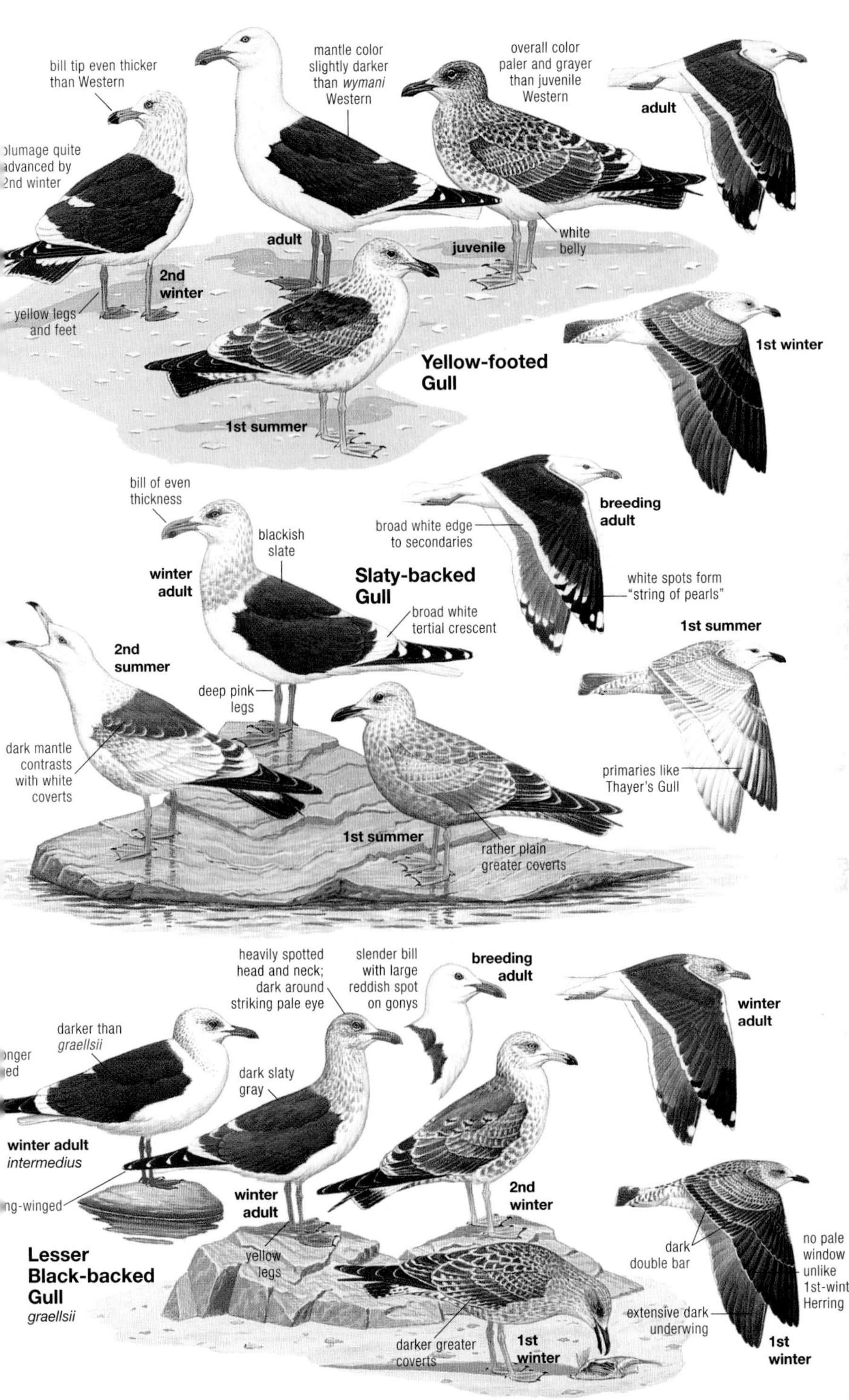

bill tip even thicker than Western
plumage quite advanced by 2nd winter
mantle color slightly darker than *wymani* Western
overall color paler and grayer than juvenile Western
adult
adult
juvenile
white belly
2nd winter
yellow legs and feet
1st winter
Yellow-footed Gull
1st summer
bill of even thickness
breeding adult
broad white edge to secondaries
blackish slate
winter adult
Slaty-backed Gull
white spots form "string of pearls"
broad white tertial crescent
2nd summer
1st summer
deep pink legs
dark mantle contrasts with white coverts
primaries like Thayer's Gull
1st summer
rather plain greater coverts
heavily spotted head and neck; dark around striking pale eye
slender bill with large reddish spot on gonys
breeding adult
winter adult
darker than *graellsii*
dark slaty gray
winter adult *intermedius*
winter adult
2nd winter
Lesser Black-backed Gull *graellsii*
yellow legs
dark double bar
no pale window unlike 1st-wint Herring
extensive dark underwing
darker greater coverts
1st winter
1st winter

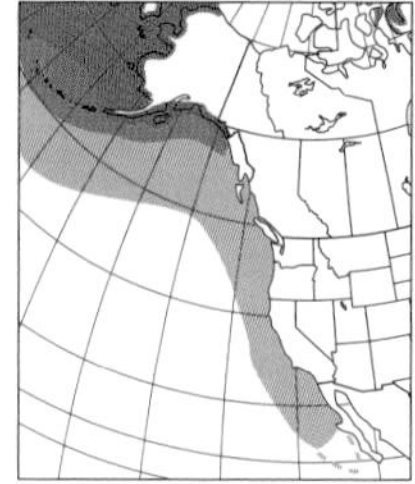

Black-legged Kittiwake *Rissa tridactyla*
L 17" (43 cm) WS 36" (91 cm) Pelagic three-year gull. ***Adult*** has white head, nape smudged with gray in ***winter;*** dark eye; yellow bill; white body with gray mantle. Inner primaries are pale, wing tips inky black; legs black. Second-year bird is like adult but with more black on outermost primary. ***Juvenile*** has dark half collar, retained into early winter; black bill; black spot behind eye; dark tail band; and, in flight, dark W across the wings. Distinguished from young Sabine's Gull by half collar, dark carpal bar. A very few young birds have pinkish legs.
Voice: Call includes a series of *kittiwake*'s.
Range: Nests in large cliff colonies; winters at sea. Seen uncommonly from shore south of breeding range, commonly in some years when a few may summer; casual in interior West.

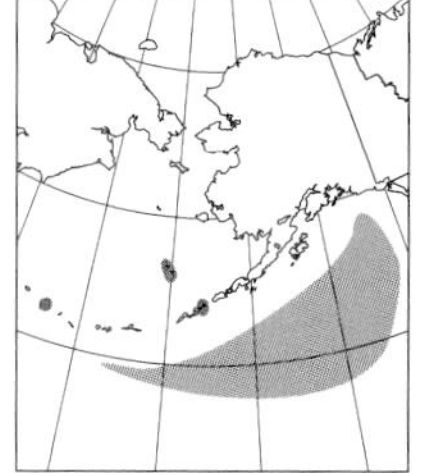

Red-legged Kittiwake *Rissa brevirostris*
L 15" (38 cm) WS 33" (84 cm) Pelagic two-year gull. ***Adult*** distinguished from Black-legged Kittiwake by coral red legs; shorter, thicker bill; darker mantle; wings are not paler on flight feathers as in Black-legged; broader white trailing edge on wings; dusky underside of primaries. In first-year, wing pattern resembles Sabine's Gull, but Red-legged Kittiwake is the only gull to have an all-white tail in first winter. Unlike Black-legged, lacks W on wings.
Voice: Call is higher-pitched and squeakier than Black-legged.
Range: Breeds very locally in cliff colonies, usually close to Black-legged Kittiwake. Very rare away from breeding grounds, even in winter. Casual on and off West Coast.

Sabine's Gull *Xema sabini L 13½" (34 cm) WS 33" (84 cm)*
Two-year gull with striking black-gray-and-white wing pattern in all ages. ***Breeding adult*** has dark gray hood with thin black ring at bottom; black bill with yellow tip; forked tail. First-summer bird is like adult but hood not complete; faint dusky nape. In ***juvenal*** plumage, wing pattern is like adult; crown and nape are soft gray-brown; bill black; tail has dark band.
Voice: Call is a ternlike *kiew,* mainly given on breeding grounds.
Range: Winters at sea mainly in the Southern Hemisphere. Most adults migrate out of North America before acquiring white head, dark nape of winter plumage. Juveniles depart before acquiring more adultlike plumage. Common migrant off West Coast, rarely seen from shore. Rare in fall, casual in spring, in interior.

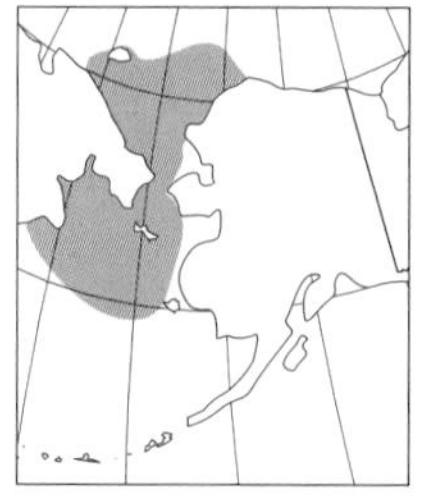

Ivory Gull *Pagophila eburnea L 17" (43 cm) WS 37" (94 cm)*
Two-year arctic gull, ghostly pale. ***Adults*** are strikingly white with a yellow-tipped greenish bill, black eyes, black legs year-round. ***First-winter*** shows a variable amount of speckling on body, heaviest and often patchy on the face forming a smudge; has tail band, and spots on tips of primaries. Short-necked but with long wings.
Voice: Call, heard mostly on breeding grounds, is a ternlike *kew.*
Range: Closely associated with pack ice. Winters primarily in Arctic seas. Uncommon in northern and western Alaska. Casual to British Columbia. Accidental to southern California and Colorado. Global warming imperils species.

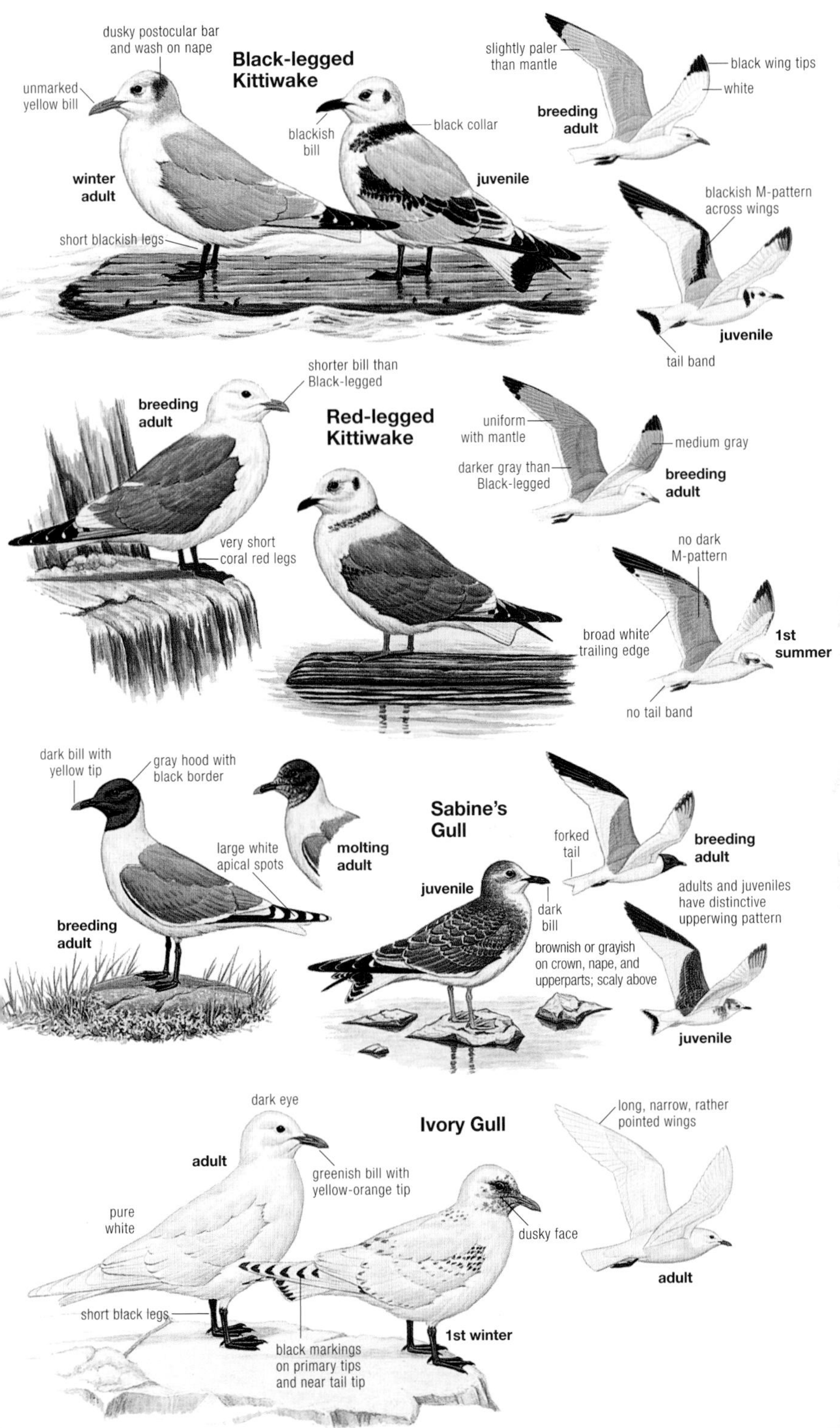

Black-legged Kittiwake
dusky postocular bar and wash on nape
unmarked yellow bill
winter adult
short blackish legs
blackish bill
black collar
juvenile
slightly paler than mantle
black wing tips
white
breeding adult
blackish M-pattern across wings
juvenile
tail band
Red-legged Kittiwake
shorter bill than Black-legged
breeding adult
very short coral red legs
uniform with mantle
medium gray
darker gray than Black-legged
breeding adult
no dark M-pattern
broad white trailing edge
1st summer
no tail band
Sabine's Gull
dark bill with yellow tip
gray hood with black border
molting adult
large white apical spots
breeding adult
juvenile
dark bill
brownish or grayish on crown, nape, and upperparts; scaly above
forked tail
breeding adult
adults and juveniles have distinctive upperwing pattern
juvenile
Ivory Gull
dark eye
adult
greenish bill with yellow-orange tip
pure white
dusky face
short black legs
black markings on primary tips and near tail tip
1st winter
long, narrow, rather pointed wings
adult

Immature Gulls in Flight

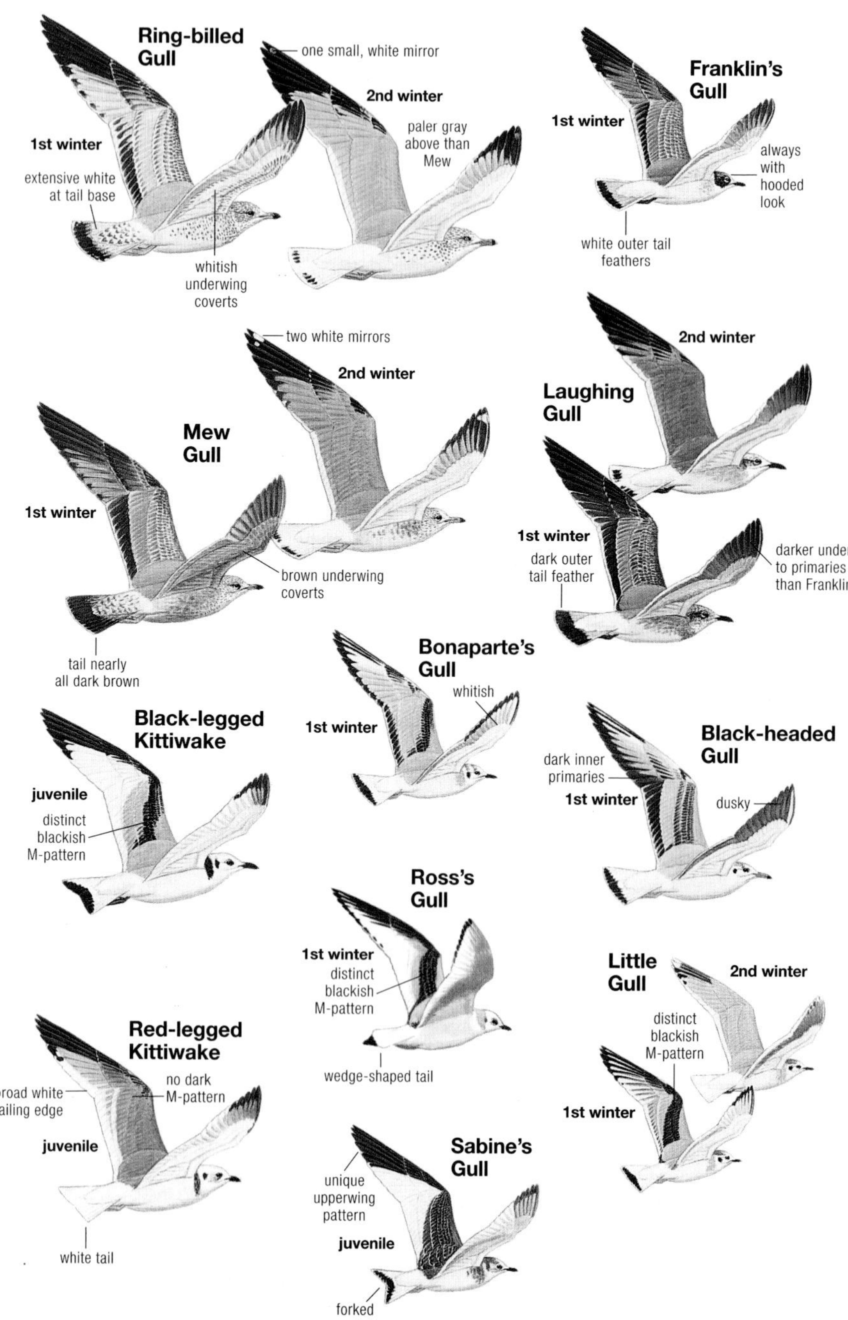
Ring-billed Gull
1st winter
extensive white at tail base
whitish underwing coverts
one small, white mirror
2nd winter
paler gray above than Mew
Franklin's Gull
1st winter
always with hooded look
white outer tail feathers
Mew Gull
1st winter
two white mirrors
2nd winter
brown underwing coverts
tail nearly all dark brown
Laughing Gull
2nd winter
1st winter
dark outer tail feather
darker unders
to primaries
than Franklin
Bonaparte's Gull
1st winter
whitish
Black-legged Kittiwake
juvenile
distinct blackish M-pattern
Black-headed Gull
dark inner primaries
1st winter
dusky
Ross's Gull
1st winter
distinct blackish M-pattern
wedge-shaped tail
Little Gull
2nd winter
distinct blackish M-pattern
1st winter
Red-legged Kittiwake
broad white trailing edge
no dark M-pattern
juvenile
white tail
Sabine's Gull
unique upperwing pattern
juvenile
forked tail

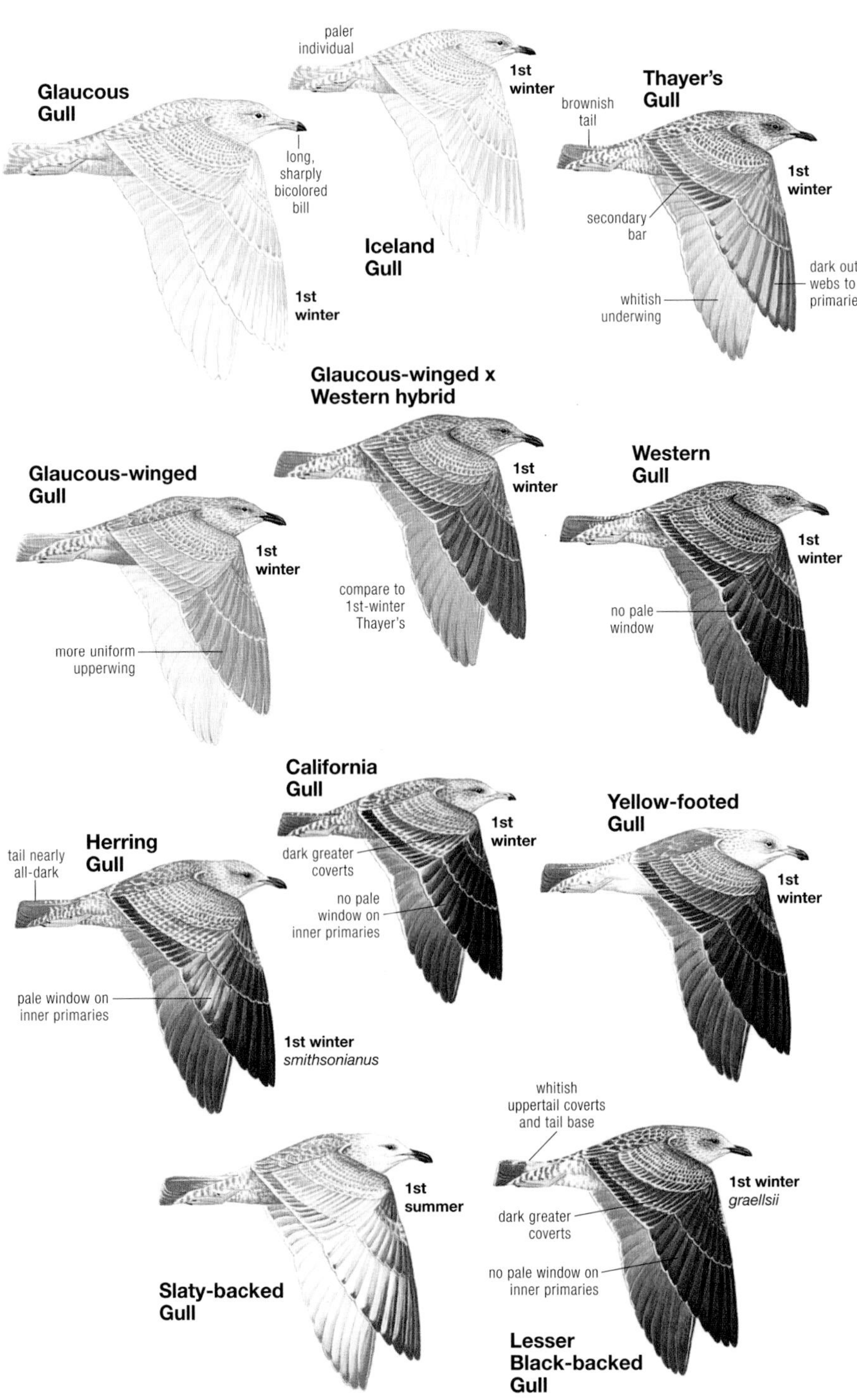

paler
individual
1st
winter
Glaucous
Gull
long,
sharply
bicolored
bill
1st
winter
Iceland
Gull
Thayer's
Gull
brownish
tail
1st
winter
secondary
bar
dark outer
webs to
primaries
whitish
underwing
Glaucous-winged x
Western hybrid
1st
winter
compare to
1st-winter
Thayer's
Glaucous-winged
Gull
1st
winter
more uniform
upperwing
Western
Gull
1st
winter
no pale
window
California
Gull
1st
winter
dark greater
coverts
no pale
window on
inner primaries
Herring
Gull
tail nearly
all-dark
pale window on
inner primaries
1st winter
smithsonianus
Yellow-footed
Gull
1st
winter
Slaty-backed
Gull
1st
summer
whitish
uppertail coverts
and tail base
1st winter
graellsii
dark greater
coverts
no pale window on
inner primaries
Lesser
Black-backed
Gull

Terns

Distinguished from gulls by long, pointed wings and bill and by feeding technique. Most terns plunge-dive into the water after prey. Most species have a forked tail.

Elegant Tern *Thalasseus elegans*

L 17" (43 cm) WS 34" (86 cm) Bill longer, thinner than larger Royal Tern; reddish orange in adults, yellow in some ***juveniles***. In flight, shows mostly pale underside of primaries; compare to Caspian Tern. ***Breeding adult*** is pale gray above with black crown and nape, black crest; white below, often with pinkish tinge. ***Winter adult*** and juvenile have white forehead; black over top of crown extends forward around eye; compare with Royal. Juveniles variably mottled above, may have orange legs; some have less black on crown, like juvenile Royal.

Voice: Sharp *kee-rick* call, very similar to Sandwich Tern.

Range: Breeders arrive in coastal southern California in early Mar. Many postbreeders from western Mexico augment population, and many disperse north up coast, a few to Washington, casually to British Columbia. Lingers late on southern California coast—small numbers into Nov., casually later—but many reports of Elegant Terns in midwinter are blacker faced Royals. Very rare spring and summer at Salton Sea; casual in Southwest.

Royal Tern *Thalasseus maximus*

L 20" (51 cm) WS 41" (104 cm) Orange-red bill, thinner than Caspian. In flight, shows mostly pale underside of primaries; tail more deeply forked than Caspian. ***Adult*** shows white crown most of year; black cap acquired briefly early in ***breeding*** season. In ***winter adult*** and ***juvenile,*** black on nape does not usually extend to encompass eye, but some show more dark that includes the eye; these are best separated by overall size, bill shape, and call. Compare with Elegant Tern.

Voice: Calls include a bleating *kee-rer* and ploverlike whistled *tourreee.*

Range: Nests in dense colonies. Fairly common in winter on southern California coast, where a few breed; casual to central California coast and to the Southwest and western Plains.

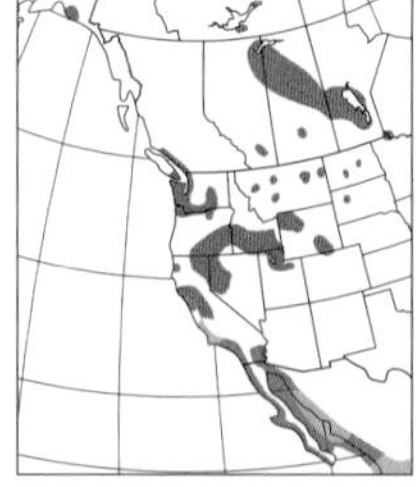

Caspian Tern *Hydroprogne caspia*

L 21" (53 cm) WS 50" (127 cm) Large, stocky; bill orange to coral red with dark near tip, much thicker than Royal Tern. In flight, shows dark underside of primaries; tail less deeply forked than Royal. ***Adult*** acquires black cap in ***breeding*** season; in ***winter adult*** and ***juvenile,*** crown streaked. Never shows fully white forehead of Royal.

Voice: Adult's calls include a harsh, raspy *kowk* and *ca-arr;* immature's call is a distinctive, whistled *whee-you.*

Range: Colonies nest on coasts and in interior wetlands. Expanding breeding range north, with some to Alaska.

eye included
in dark face
long
crest
very long,
slender bill
pale underside
to primaries
Elegant
Tern
breeding
adult
winter
adult
juvenile
pale underside
to base
of primaries
reeding
adult
Royal
Tern
bill
entirely
orange
dark eye usually stands
out in whitish face
short
crest
juvenile
winter
adult
juvenile
broad wings
with "heavy flight"
black under
surface to
primaries
streaked
crown
thick red bill
with dark tip
Caspian
Tern
winter
adult
breeding
adult
juvenile

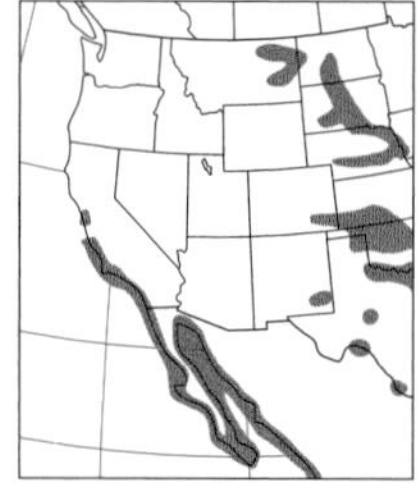

Least Tern *Sternula antillarum* **E**

L 9" (23 cm) WS 20" (51 cm) Smallest North American tern. ***Breeding adult*** is gray above, with black cap and nape, white forehead, yellow bill with dark tip; underparts are white; legs orange-yellow. By late summer, bill base is more greenish. In flight, black wedge on outer primaries is conspicuous; note also the short, deeply forked tail. ***Juvenile*** shows brownish, U-shaped markings; crown is dusky; wings show dark shoulder bar. By first fall, upperparts are gray, crown whiter, but dark shoulder bar is retained. ***First-summer*** birds are more like adults but have dark bill and legs, shoulder bar, black line through eye, dusky primaries. Flight is rapid and buoyant.

Voice: Calls include high-pitched *kip* notes and a shrill *chir-ee-eep.*

Range: Nests in colonies on beaches and sandbars. Declining. Rare migrant on western Plains away from nesting areas and in the Southwest; casual on coast north to Oregon; accidental to Washington and British Columbia. Winters from Central America south.

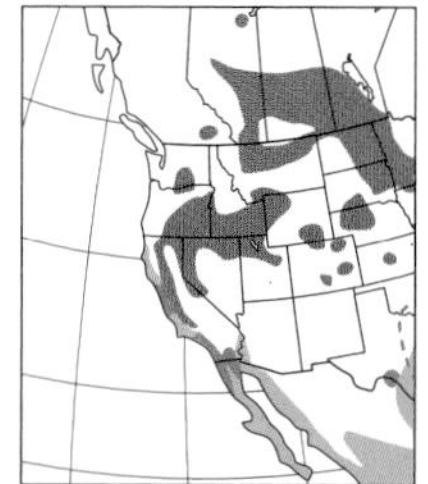

Forster's Tern *Sterna forsteri*

L 14½" (37 cm) WS 31" (79 cm) ***Breeding adult*** is snow white below, pale gray above, with black cap and nape; mostly orange bill, orange legs and feet. Wingbeat much slower than Roseate Tern. Legs and bill longer than Common and Arctic Terns (next page). Long, deeply forked gray tail has white outer edges. In flight, shows pale upperwing area formed by silvery primaries; white rump contrasts with gray back, gray tail. ***Winter*** plumage resembles Common and Arctic but is acquired by mid- to late Aug.—much earlier than those species, which molt chiefly after migration out of U.S. Note also lack of dark shoulder bars; most have dark eye patches not joined at nape as in Common, but many have dark streaks on nape. ***Juveniles*** and ***first-winter*** birds have shorter tails than adults and more dark color in wings. Juvenile has ginger wash on cap and on upperparts.

Voice: Calls include a hoarse *kyarr,* lower and shorter than Common. Also a higher *ket.*

Range: Nests in scattered colonies in marshes.

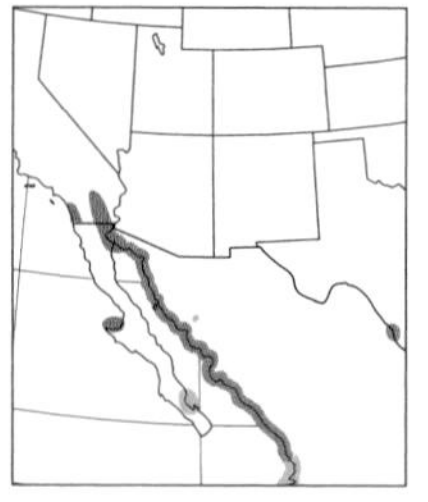

Gull-billed Tern *Gelochelidon nilotica*

L 14" (36 cm) WS 34" (86 cm) ***Breeding adult*** is white below, pale gray above, with black crown and nape, stout black bill, black legs and feet. Stockier and paler than Common Tern (next page); wings broader; tail shorter and only moderately forked. ***Juveniles*** and ***winter*** birds appear largely white headed apart from some fine streaking. Juvenile has pale edgings on upperparts, bill is paler.

Voice: Adult call is a raspy, sharp *kay-wack;* call of juvenile is a faint, high-pitched *peep peep.*

Range: Uncommon nester at south end of Salton Sea (casual in winter) and San Diego Bay. Nests on sandbars and dikes; often seen hunting for insects over fields. Does not hover or dive in water. Casual north on coast in spring to Santa Barbara County; accidental to southern Arizona.

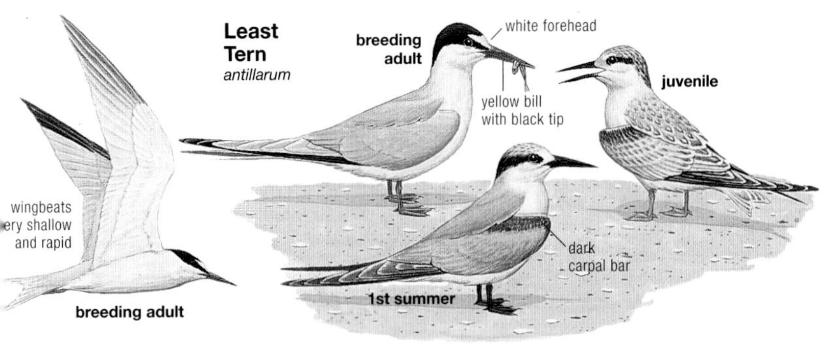
Least
Tern
antillarum
breeding
adult
white forehead
yellow bill
with black tip
juvenile
wingbeats
ery shallow
and rapid
dark
carpal bar
1st summer
breeding adult

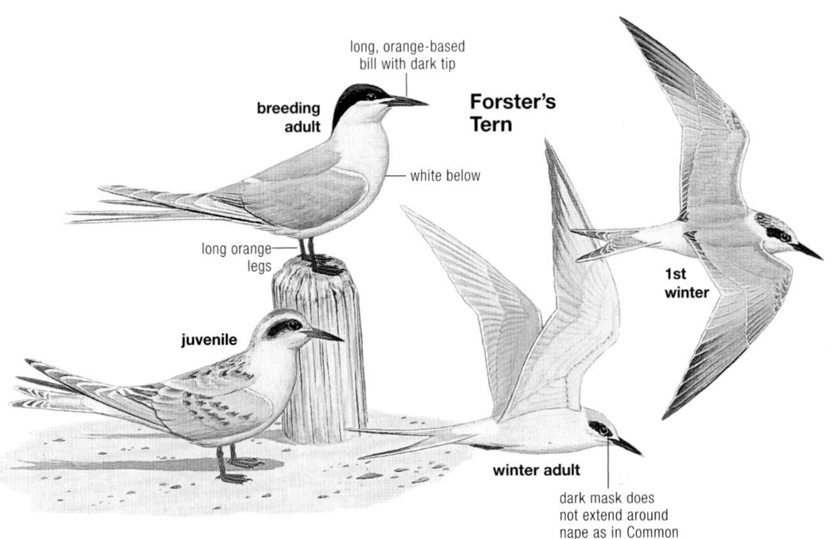
long, orange-based
bill with dark tip
breeding
adult
Forster's
Tern
white below
long orange
legs
1st
winter
juvenile
winter adult
dark mask does
not extend around
nape as in Common

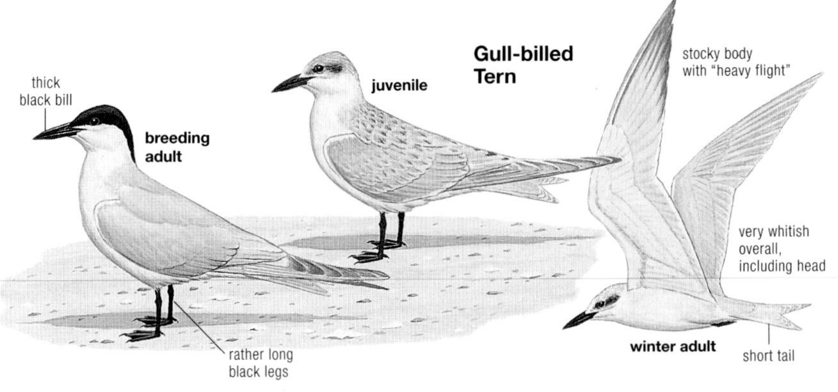
Gull-billed
Tern
stocky body
with "heavy flight"
thick
black bill
juvenile
breeding
adult
very whitish
overall,
including head
rather long
black legs
winter adult
short tail

Common Tern *Sterna hirundo*

L 14½" (37 cm) WS 30" (76 cm) Medium gray above, with black cap, nape; paler below (though grayish in breeding plumage). Bill red, usually tipped with black. Slightly stockier than Arctic, with flatter crown, longer neck and bill. In flight, usually displays a dark wedge, variably shaped, near tip of upperwing; in late summer all outer primaries can appear dark. Note that head projects farther than Arctic. Common's shorter tail gives it a chunkier look. Also compare to Forster's (previous page). Early ***juvenile*** shows some brown above, white below, with mostly dark bill. Juvenile has white forehead; blackish crown, nape; dark gray secondaries; compare juvenile Forster's. All immature and winter plumages have dark shoulder bar. Full ***adult breeding*** plumage acquired by third spring.
Voice: Calls are a sharp *kip* and a distinctive low, piercing, drawn-out *kee-ar-r-r-r.*
Range: Nests in colonies. Fairly common in breeding range. Uncommon and declining migrant on Pacific coast from Washington south; uncommon in fall in western interior; casual in spring. Winters primarily in South America; casual in California. An East Asian subspecies, *longipennis,* rare but regular on the islands of western Alaska in spring, is darker overall; black bill, legs.

Arctic Tern *Sterna paradisaea*

L 15½" (39 cm) WS 31" (79 cm) ***Breeding adult*** medium gray above, with black cap and nape; paler below. Bill deep red. Slightly slimmer than Common Tern, with rounder head, shorter neck and bill. In flight, upperwing appears uniformly gray, lacking dark wedge of Common; underwing shows very narrow black line on trailing edge of primaries; all flight feathers appear translucent. Note also longer tail; head does not project as far as Common. ***Juvenile*** largely lacks brownish wash of early juvenile Common; shoulder bar less distinct; secondaries whitish, a portion of coverts whitish too, creating an effect like Sabine's (page 182). Forehead is white, crown and nape blackish; compare juvenile Forster's (previous page). Full adult breeding plumage is acquired by third spring.
Voice: Calls include a raspy *tr-tee-ar,* higher than Common; also a sharp *keet.*
Range: Migrates well offshore; casual inland during migration, especially in late spring; has nested in Montana. Winters in Antarctic and subantarctic waters.

IDENTIFYING: *Sterna* Terns The three species of western *Sterna* terns—Common, Arctic, and Forster's—present identification challenges. Not only do all three of these species look alike, but within each species there is substantial change in appearance from season to season and between different age categories. Useful field marks for one plumage (such as grayness versus whiteness of the breast, exact color of the primaries) may be of no use in another. Therefore, structural features (including bill size and leg length) are important; they are best appreciated when multiple tern species are found together.

As in the study of gulls, being able to properly age an individual *Sterna* tern and to understand both the basics of tern molt and how wear may affect appearance are important for identification. Fresh juveniles in late summer show variable brownish backs in which the intensity of color (e.g., little brown in juvenile Arctic) and patterning (e.g., Forster's with distinct brownish wash above) are useful characteristics. This

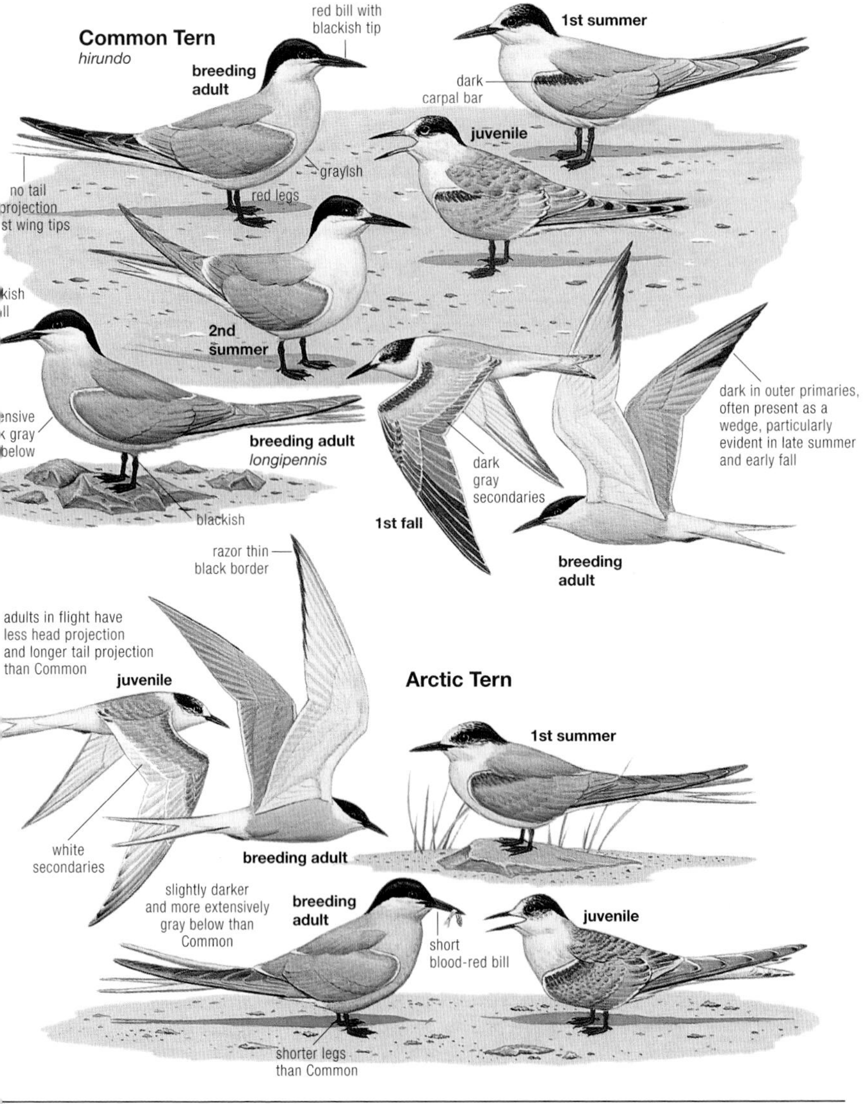

color and patterning largely wear away to gray by autumn.

The presence or absence of a dark carpal (shoulder) bar is another important marker to use in all birds, except breeding adults. First-summer individuals—those that are approximately one year of age—do not breed, so many remain on or close to the wintering grounds, though a few return north to breeding areas. These first-summer terns resemble winter adults but have more worn-looking wings. Second-summer birds (which are in their third calendar year) more closely resemble full adults, although they retain some white flecking on the forehead as well as possibly a trace of the dark carpal bar. Birds of this age may breed.

Other characteristics to emphasize when identifying *Sterna* terns include primary color and pattern of molt, tail length and color, bill and leg color, breast color, and cap pattern. Vocalizations, once learned, can be very useful, too. All give species-specific calls.

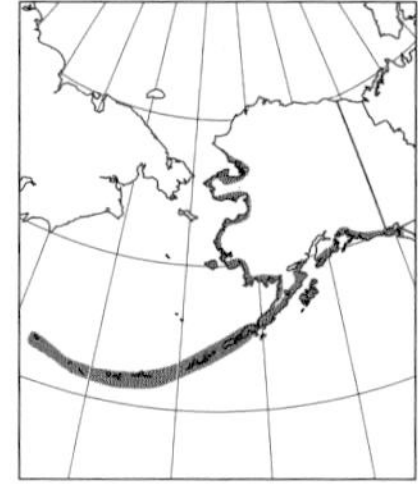

Aleutian Tern *Onychoprion aleutica*

L 13½" (34 cm) WS 29" (74 cm) Dark gray above and below, with white forehead, black cap, black bill, black legs. In flight, distinguished from Common and Arctic Terns by shorter tail, white forehead, and dark, white-edged bar on secondaries, most visible from below. ***Juvenile*** is buff and brown above; legs and lower mandible reddish.

Voice: Call is a squeaky *twee-ee-ee,* vaguely suggestive of House Sparrow and unlike any other tern.

Range: Nests in loose colonies, sometimes with Arctic Terns. Arrives and departs nesting grounds directly from offshore. Casual or accidental in spring off British Columbia. Migration routes uncertain; has been seen in fall and winter off Hong Kong, the Philippines, and Sumatra. Main winter grounds are still unknown, probably southwestern Pacific and Indian Oceans.

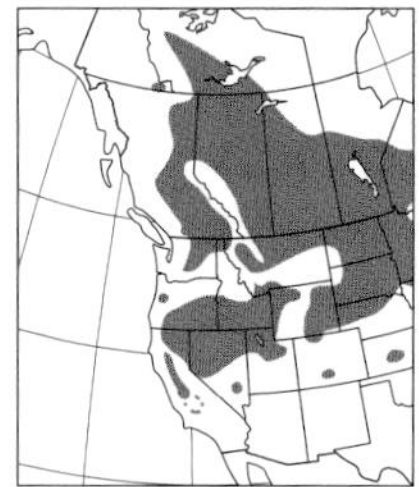

Black Tern *Chlidonias niger L 9¾" (25 cm) WS 24" (61 cm)*

Breeding adult is mostly black, with dark gray back, wings, and tail; white undertail coverts. In flight, shows uniformly pale gray underwing and fairly short tail, slightly forked. Bill is black in all plumages. ***Juvenile*** and winter birds are white below, with dark gray mantle and tail; dark ear patch extends from dark crown; flying birds show dark bar on side of breast. Some juveniles show a contrastingly paler rump. Shoulder bar on upperwing is much darker than juvenile White-winged Tern. First-summer birds can be like winter adults or may have some dark feathers on head and underparts; second-summer birds are like breeding adults, but show some whitish on head; full breeding plumage is acquired by third spring. ***Molting fall adults*** appear patchy black-and-white as they acquire winter plumage in late summer; these birds are easily confused with White-winged.

Voice: Calls include a metallic *kik* and a slurred *k-seek.*

Range: Nests on lakeshores and in marshes; declining over parts of breeding range; generally an uncommon to abundant (Salton Sea) interior migrant; rare migrant on and sometimes off West Coast. Winters in Central and South America.

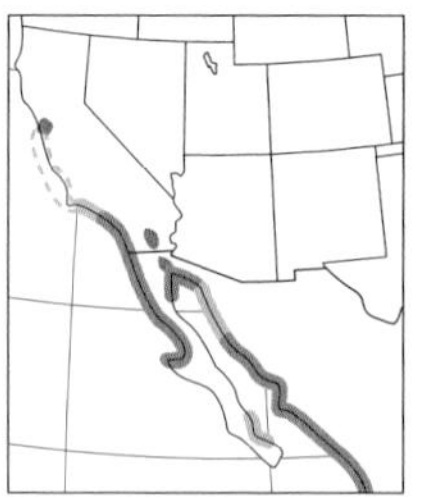

Black Skimmer *Rynchops niger*

L 18" (46 cm) WS 44" (112 cm) No other bird has a lower mandible that is longer than the upper. A long-winged coastal bird, it furrows the shallows with its red, black-tipped bill. Black above and white below; red legs and bill shape are distinctive. Female is distinctly smaller than the male. ***Juvenile*** is mottled dingy brown above. ***Winter adults*** show a white collar.

Voice: Typical call is a nasal *ip* or *yep.*

Range: Nests on sandy beaches, islands, and dikes. Unknown in West prior to 1960s. Nests on coast north to Los Angeles County and at Salton Sea (casual in winter); a few in San Francisco Bay. Winters on coast north to Santa Barbara. Casual inland elsewhere in southern and central California (has nested in Kings County); accidental in northwestern California, the Southwest, and southern Great Plains.

Aleutian Tern
brownish, with scaly pattern above
juvenile
breeding adult
dark secondary bar on underwing
darker upperwing than Arctic
white forehead
extensive gray underparts
shorter tail than Arctic
Black Tern
surinamensis
juvenile
dark bar on sides
gray flanks
dark gray above
pale underwings
breeding adult
dark ear patch extends from crown
molting fall adult
black body
breeding adult
juvenile
white vent and undertail coverts
Black Skimmer
niger
fringed with white
juvenile
very long wings
winter adults
pale collar in winter
striking black-and-white plumage
breeding adult
skimming

Skuas, Jaegers (Family Stercorariidae)

Formerly placed with the Gulls, Terns, and Skimmers, recent molecular evidence indicates that skuas and jaegers are most closely related to Alcidae and belong in their own family. Predatory and piratic seabirds, skuas are broader winged than jaegers. Mostly silent at sea.

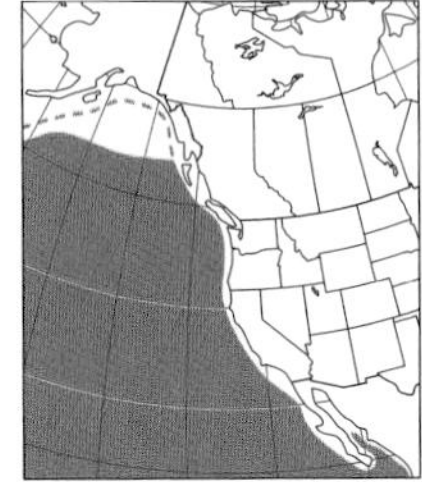

South Polar Skua *Stercorarius maccormicki*

L 21" (53 cm) WS 52" (132 cm) Large, heavy, and barrel-chested; wings broader and more rounded than jaegers; tail shorter and broader. Shows a distinctly hunchbacked appearance in flight, a bold white bar at base of primaries, and a heavier bill than jaegers. In all ages, South Polar Skua shows a uniform mantle coloring. In ***light-morph*** birds, contrastingly pale gray nape is distinctive; light morph also shows grayish head and underparts. ***Dark morph*** is uniformly blackish brown across mantle, with golden hackles on nape; distinguished from subadult Pomarine Jaeger by larger size, broader and more rounded wings, more distinct white wing bar. ***Juveniles*** and immatures of both color morphs are darker than light-morph adults, ranging from dark brown to dark gray. In the field, birds under two years of age are generally indistinguishable from juveniles; birds over two years old are generally indistinguishable from full adults.

Range: Winters (our summer) in the North Pacific, usually from May to early Nov. Most numerous in spring and fall; casual off the southern coast of Alaska. Casually seen from shore. Breeds in Antarctica.

Jaegers

These Arctic breeders have longer, slimmer, and more powerful wings than skuas. Adult plumage and long central tail feathers take three or four years to develop. Complex and variable plumages make identification extremely difficult. Most molts occur after the fall migration.

Pomarine Jaeger *Stercorarius pomarinus*

L 21" (53 cm) WS 48" (122 cm) Body bulkier, bicolored bill longer and thicker, wingbeats slower than Parasitic Jaeger. Most birds show a distinctive second pale underwing patch at base of primaries (fainter or lacking in Parasitic). ***Adult***'s tail streamers, twisted at ends, form dark blobs when seen from side; length is variable, averages longer in male. Note extensive helmet on sides of head, which extends down to "jowls" area. Compare ***dark-morph adults*** and subadults with South Polar Skuas. Some grayish brown ***juveniles*** are dark, some pale, but none shows the foxy red tones of most juvenile Parasitics; central tail feathers barely project past outer tail feathers and have blunt tips.

Range: Nests on Arctic tundra. In most areas, seen less often from shore than Parasitic. Common off West Coast in migration. Uncommon in winter; casual inland; most records from eastern Colorado in late fall. Unlike juveniles of other two jaeger species, juveniles aren't regularly seen well south of breeding grounds until late in fall.

bold white
primary flash
uniform dark
upperparts
intermediate-
morph adult
short,
unded
points
dark-
morph
adult
slight
golden cast
South Polar, like other big skuas, has broad wings and a short tail with a bold white flash at the base of the primaries
juvenile
South Polar
Skua
most look quite dark, except for white wing patches
light-morph
adult
rather thick
bill
light-morph adult
juvenile
dark-morph
breeding adult
double
white wing
flash
light-morph
breeding
adults
thick
two-toned
bill
Pomarine
Jaeger
dark below
gape
long twisted tail feathers, often longer than shown, with thick tip
usually with breast band,
but some adult males lack it
light-morph
juvenile
double white
wing flash
dark
all nonadult jaegers
have checkered
underwing coverts
strong
bars
light-morph
1st summer
very short
and rounded
central tail points
light-morph
juvenile

Parasitic Jaeger *Stercorarius parasiticus*

L 19" (48 cm) WS 42" (107 cm) Smaller size, more slender body, faster wingbeats than Pomarine Jaeger; also smaller head, thinner bill, pointed tail streamers. ***Adult*** lacks helmeted effect of Pomarine; shows small pale area above base of bill. ***Juvenile*** highly variable; shows rufous tips on primaries; distinctive rusty tones particularly evident on ***light morphs;*** tail coverts have fainter, wavier bars than Pomarine. Short central tail feathers are pointed. Also compare with Long-tailed Jaeger.

Range: Nests on Arctic tundra. Fairly common; this is the jaeger species most often seen from shore in migration, often in pursuit of terns. Casual fall migrant inland; more regular on Salton Sea.

Long-tailed Jaeger *Stercorarius longicaudus*

L 22" (56 cm) WS 40" (102 cm) Most lightly built jaeger, with round chest, flat belly, narrow wings, and disproportionately long tail in all ages; bill rather short and thick. Flight is more graceful, ternlike. Note distinctive contrast between grayish mantle and darker flight feathers; usually has only two to three white primary shafts; no pale underwing patch except on ***juvenile. Adult*** has well-defined black cap, no breast band as in most jaegers, and usually very long, pointed central tail streamers. Juvenile's central tail feathers have round, often white-edged tips; stubby bill half dark, half gray; is grayer overall than Parasitic except for dark morph; fringing above whitish, never rusty. ***Light-morph juvenile*** shows distinctive white belly and strong, even, black barring on upper- and undertail coverts; palest birds may have very pale gray heads.

Range: Nests commonly on dry, upland tundra; migrating birds uncommon to fairly common well off West Coast (fall); rare in interior West (mainly in early fall).

IDENTIFYING: Jaegers Separating the three jaeger species is difficult—especially with juveniles and subadults. Key features include overall size and shape, bill size and shape, pattern of white patches and primary shafts on the wing, and shape and length of the central tail feathers.

Pomarine, the largest species, has broad wings and a heavy, bicolored bill. Its prominent pale flash at the base of the primaries and a second smaller flash at the base of the primary coverts are usually diagnostic, although they can also be found on a few juvenile Parasitics. Adult Pomarines have more extensive black on the side of the face, and their long, central tail feathers twist near the end, forming a blob at the tip. Juvenile Pomarines have very short, round-tipped central tail feathers.

Parasitic is smaller and narrower winged than Pomarine and has a rather long but fine bill. Parasitic has a small pale area just above the bill, and the adult's cap is less solidly black than Pomarine's. Parasitic's extended central tail feathers are sharply pointed in all plumages. Some juveniles are light rufous overall; some are blackish with narrow rufous fringes. Juvenile Parasitics have streaked napes and pale rufous-buff fringes on the primaries, unlike Pomarines.

Long-tailed is the smallest jaeger, with buoyant flight. Its short bill appears rather thick. Its wings are long and slender with only two to three white primary shafts; its grayish upperparts contrast with the darker flight feathers. Adults show no white primary patch on the underwing and have a sharply defined black cap. The long central tail feathers are diagnostic, but many migrating adults lack them. Juveniles vary from grayish to dark chocolate overall and are fringed with whitish; paler birds have white bellies, unlike any juvenile Pomarine or Parasitic. Juveniles also lack pale primary tips and have strong, evenly spaced, dark-and-white barring under the tail.

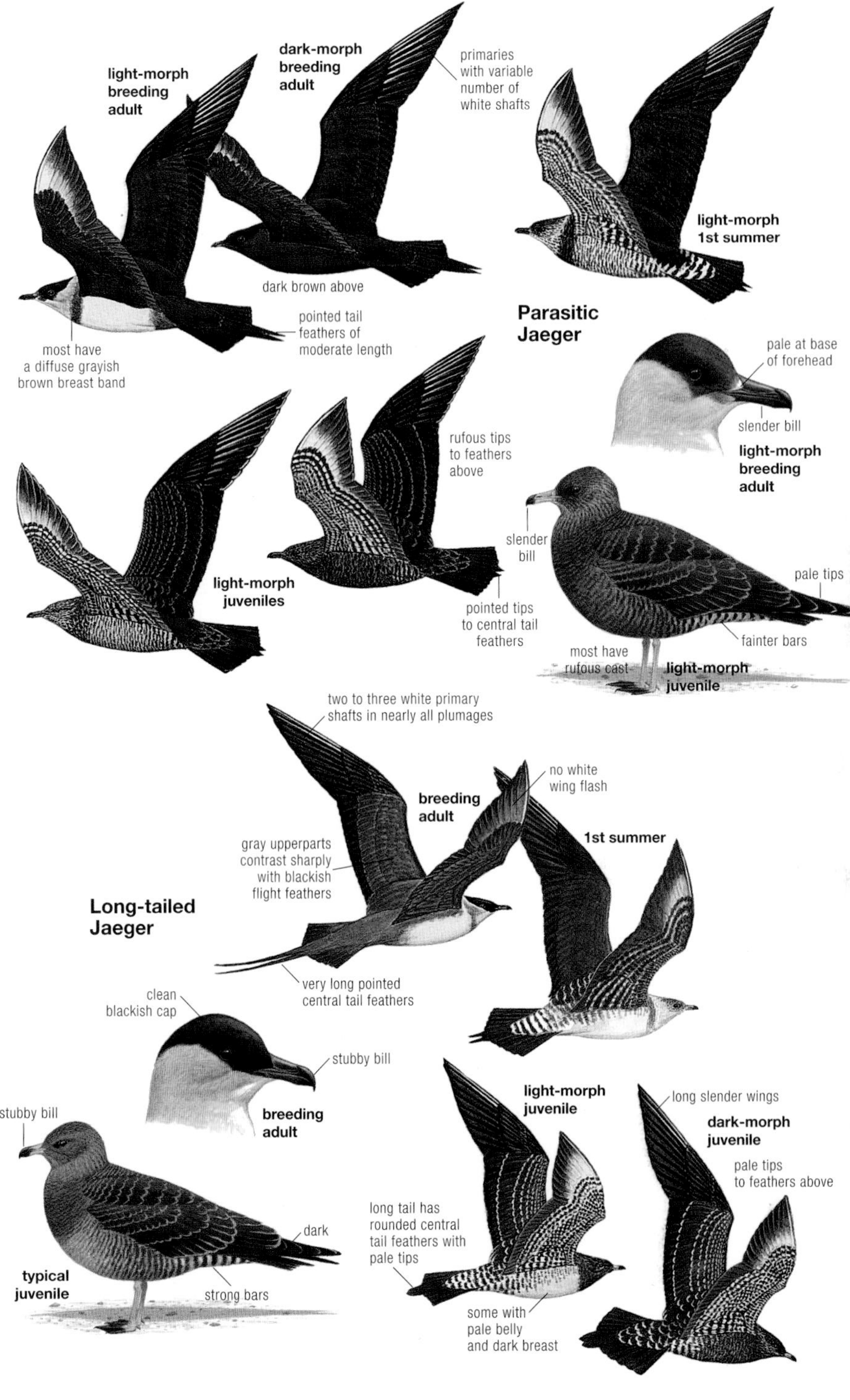
light-morph
breeding
adult
dark-morph
breeding
adult
primaries
with variable
number of
white shafts
light-morph
1st summer
dark brown above
Parasitic
Jaeger
pointed tail
feathers of
moderate length
most have
a diffuse grayish
brown breast band
pale at base
of forehead
slender bill
light-morph
breeding
adult
rufous tips
to feathers
above
slender
bill
pale tips
light-morph
juveniles
pointed tips
to central tail
feathers
fainter bars
most have
rufous cast
light-morph
juvenile
two to three white primary
shafts in nearly all plumages
no white
wing flash
breeding
adult
1st summer
gray upperparts
contrast sharply
with blackish
flight feathers
Long-tailed
Jaeger
very long pointed
central tail feathers
clean
blackish cap
stubby bill
stubby bill
breeding
adult
light-morph
juvenile
long slender wings
dark-morph
juvenile
pale tips
to feathers above
long tail has
rounded central
tail feathers with
pale tips
dark
typical
juvenile
strong bars
some with
pale belly
and dark breast

Auks, Murres, Puffins (Family Alcidae)

These black-and-white "penguins of the north" have set-back legs that give them an upright stance on land. In flight, wingbeats are rapid and shallow. Most species are largely silent at sea.

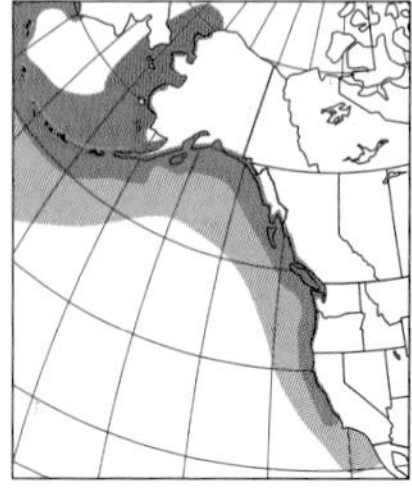

Common Murre *Uria aalge L 17½" (45 cm)*
Large, with a long, slender, pointed bill. Upperparts dark sooty gray, head brownish; underparts white. In ***winter*** plumage, a dark stripe extends from eye across white cheek. ***Juvenile*** has shorter bill; distinguished from Thick-billed Murre by white facial stripe, paler upperparts, mottled flanks, and thinner bill. Chick accompanies adult at sea and can be mistaken for Xantus's Murrelets (page 202).
Range: Numerous off West Coast. Nests in dense colonies on rocky cliffs.

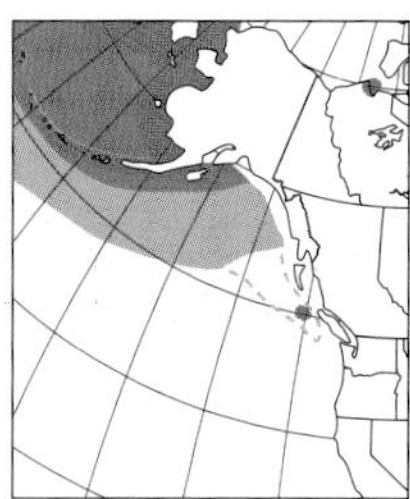

Thick-billed Murre *Uria lomvia L 18" (46 cm)*
Stocky, with a thick, fairly short bill, arched at tip to form a blunt hook. Upperparts and throat of ***adult*** are darker than Common Murre; white of underparts usually rises to a sharp point on the foreneck. Most birds show a distinct white line on cutting edge of upper mandible; in Pacific birds, bill is slightly longer and thinner than in Atlantic birds. In immature and ***winter adult,*** face and neck are more extensively dark than Common. First-summer bird is browner above than adult; otherwise similar to winter bird.
Range: Nests in colonies on rocky cliffs. Common on breeding grounds. Casual on West Coast south of breeding range, where most records are from the Monterey area in California.

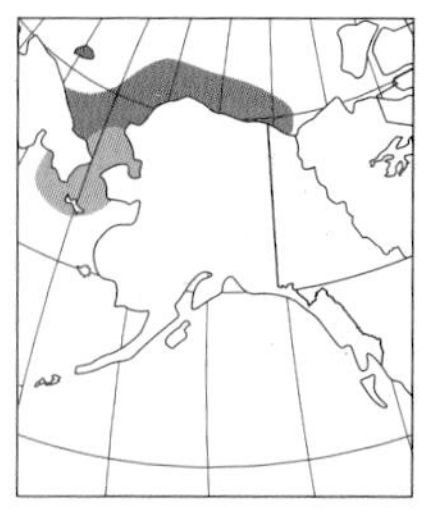

Black Guillemot *Cepphus grylle L 13" (33 cm)*
Breeding adult black overall, with large white patch on upperwing. ***Winter adult*** white; upperparts heavily mottled with black except on nape; wing patch less distinct. Juvenile is sooty above; sides and wing patches mottled. First-summer birds are patchily black-and-white; wing patches mottled. In all plumages, white axillaries and wing linings distinguish Black from Pigeon Guillemot. In high Arctic race, *mandtii,* found in West, juveniles and winter adults are quite pale.
Range: Uncommon and declining within range in West.

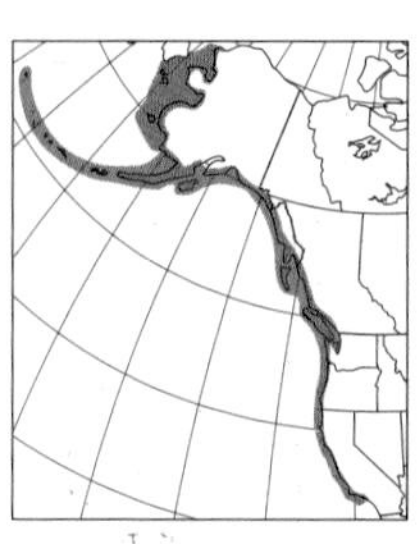

Pigeon Guillemot *Cepphus columba L 13½" (34 cm)*
Breeding and ***winter adults'*** plumage similar to smaller Black Guillemot, but note black bar on white upperwing patch; bar may be obscured in swimming bird. ***Juvenile*** is dusky above; crown and nape darker; wing patch marked with black edgings; breast and sides mottled gray. Compare with juvenile Marbled Murrelet. First-winter Pigeon Guillemot resembles winter adult but is darker. In adults, dusky axillaries and wing linings distinguish Pigeon from Black; immature Pigeons show some pale in center of underwing; also note slightly larger size and stockier shape.
Range: Fairly common; seen near shore in breeding season. Winter range not well-known.

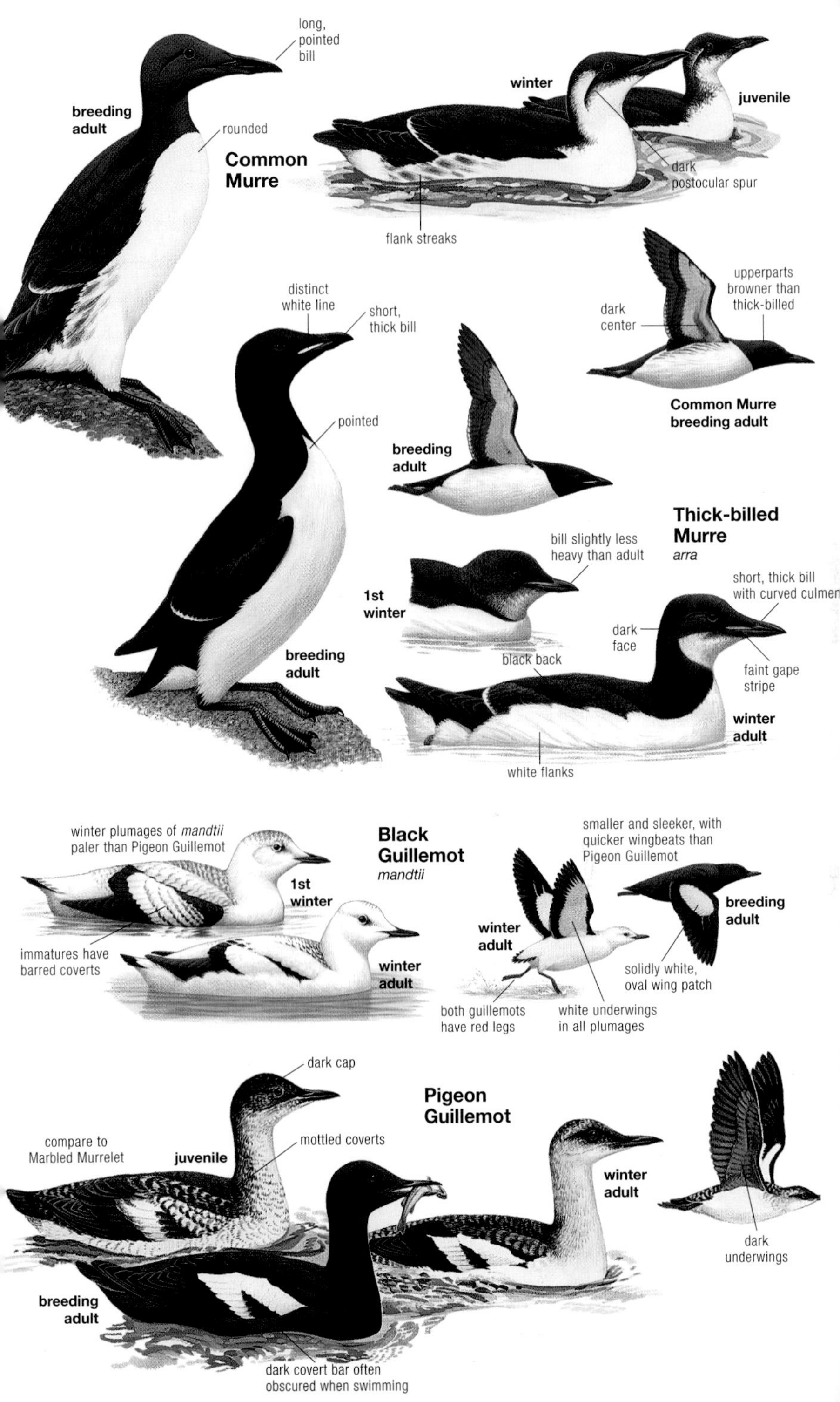

long,
pointed
bill
breeding
adult
rounded
Common
Murre
winter
juvenile
dark
postocular spur
flank streaks
distinct
white line
short,
thick bill
dark
center
upperparts
browner than
thick-billed
Common Murre
breeding adult
pointed
breeding
adult
Thick-billed
Murre
arra
bill slightly less
heavy than adult
1st
winter
short, thick bill
with curved culmen
dark
face
black back
faint gape
stripe
breeding
adult
winter
adult
white flanks
winter plumages of mandtii
paler than Pigeon Guillemot
Black
Guillemot
mandtii
smaller and sleeker, with
quicker wingbeats than
Pigeon Guillemot
1st
winter
breeding
adult
winter
adult
immatures have
barred coverts
winter
adult
solidly white,
oval wing patch
both guillemots
have red legs
white underwings
in all plumages
dark cap
Pigeon
Guillemot
compare to
Marbled Murrelet
juvenile
mottled coverts
winter
adult
dark
underwings
breeding
adult
dark covert bar often
obscured when swimming

Dovekie *Alle alle L 8¼" (21 cm)*
Small and plump with short neck, stubby bill. ***Breeding adult*** is black above, white below; black upper breast contrasts sharply with white underparts; dark wing linings. Usually swims tilted forward in the water. In ***winter*** plumage, throat, chin, and lower face are white, with white curving around behind eye.
Range: Rather rare within very limited breeding range in West in northern Bering Sea (Little Diomede Island, King Island, and St. Lawrence Island). Casual in summer to northern Alaska, the Pribolofs, and the Aleutians. Winter grounds for this isolated population are unknown.

Long-billed Murrelet *Brachyramphus perdix*
L 11½" (29 cm) Native from coastal northeast Asia. In ***winter,*** lacks conspicuous white collar of similar Marbled Murrelet; shows small pale oval patches on sides of nape; in ***breeding*** plumage upperparts are less rufous, throat paler. Formerly considered a race of Marbled.
Range: Casual to both coastal and interior North America; most records are in late summer and fall of winter-plumaged birds.

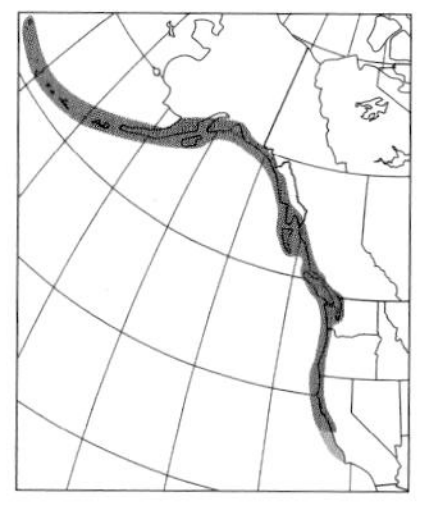

Marbled Murrelet *Brachyramphus marmoratus* **T**
L 10" (25 cm) Bill longer than Kittlitz's Murrelet. Tail all-dark, but white on overlapping uppertail coverts. ***Breeding adult*** dark above, heavily mottled below. In ***winter*** plumage, white on scapulars distinguishes Marbled from other murrelets except Long-billed and Kittlitz's with shorter bill and breast band; white on face of Marbled is variable but less than Kittlitz's. ***Juvenile*** is like winter adult but mottled below; by first winter, underparts are mostly white. All murrelets have more pointed wings and faster flight than auklets.
Voice: Highly vocal; call is a series of loud, high *kree* notes.
Range: Nests slightly inland, usually in trees. Forages usually within a couple of miles of shore. Fairly common in breeding range; very rare in southern California.

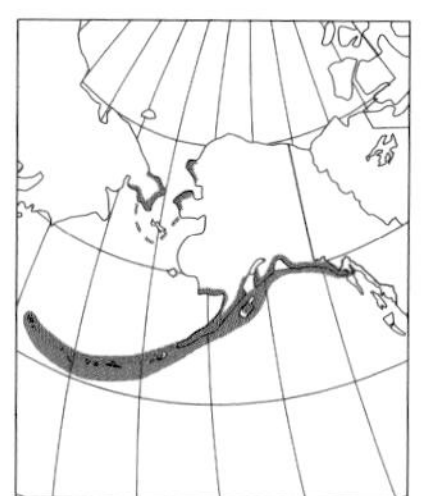

Kittlitz's Murrelet *Brachyramphus brevirostris*
L 9½" (24 cm) Bill shorter than Marbled Murrelet. Outer tail feathers white. ***Breeding adult***'s buffy grayish brown upperparts are heavily patterned; throat, breast, and flanks mottled; belly white. In ***winter,*** note extensive white on face, making eye conspicuous; nearly complete breast band; and white edges on secondaries. ***Juvenile*** distinguished from Marbled by shorter bill, paler face, white outer tail feathers.
Range: Uncommon to fairly common but local and recent evidence of declines. Rare in northern Bering Sea. Accidental to British Columbia and southern California.

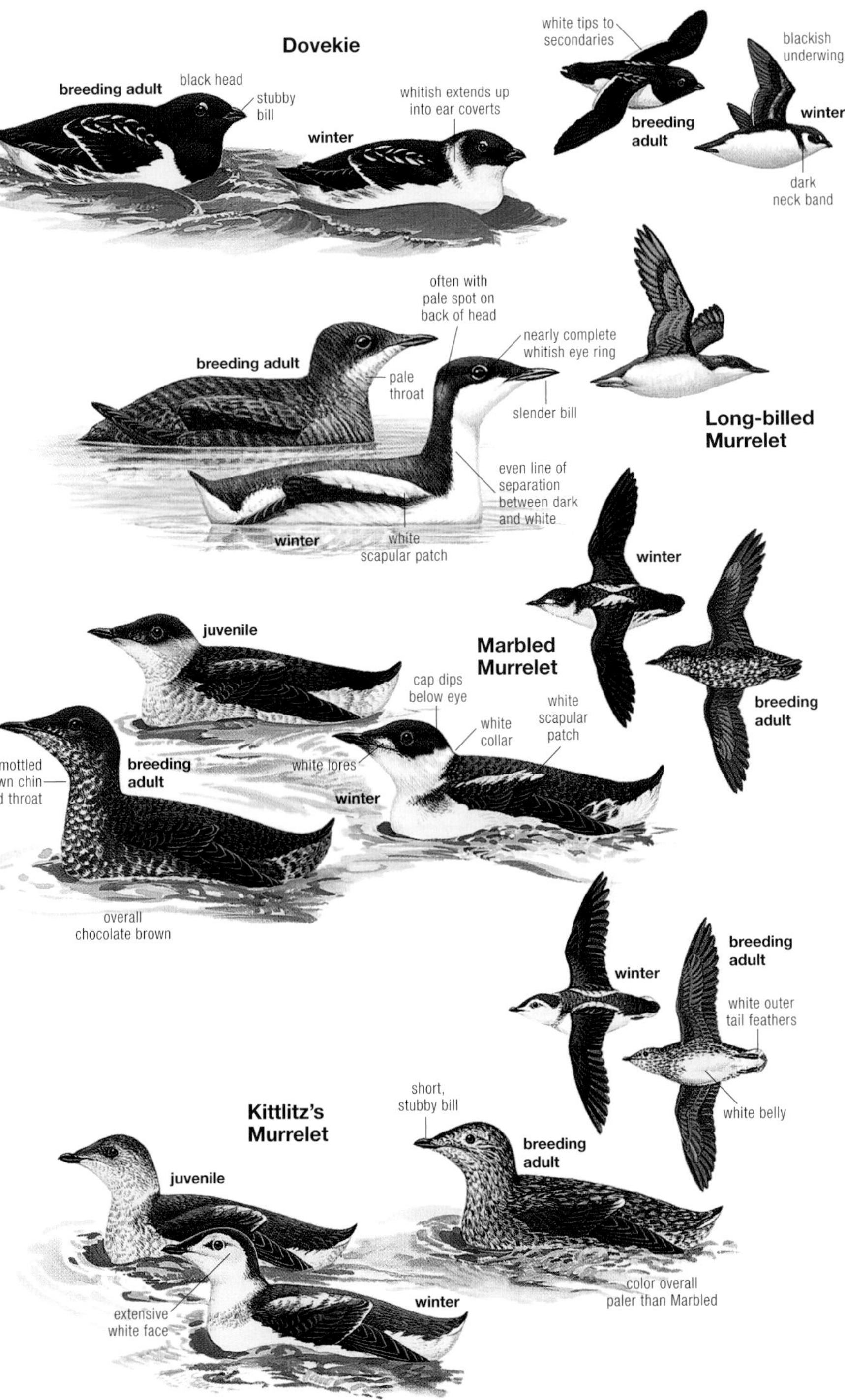
Dovekie
breeding adult
black head
stubby bill
winter
whitish extends up into ear coverts
white tips to secondaries
breeding adult
blackish underwings
winter
dark neck band
often with pale spot on back of head
nearly complete whitish eye ring
breeding adult
pale throat
slender bill
Long-billed Murrelet
even line of separation between dark and white
winter
white scapular patch
winter
juvenile
Marbled Murrelet
cap dips below eye
white scapular patch
white collar
breeding adult
mottled wn chin d throat
breeding adult
white lores
winter
overall chocolate brown
breeding adult
winter
white outer tail feathers
white belly
short, stubby bill
Kittlitz's Murrelet
breeding adult
juvenile
winter
extensive white face
color overall paler than Marbled

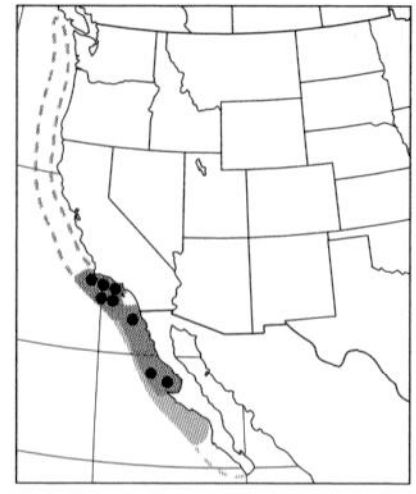

Xantus's Murrelet *Synthliboramphus hypoleucus*

L 9¾" (25 cm) Slate black above, white below. The more southerly breeding race, nominate *hypoleucus*, has much more white in face than southern California-breeding *scrippsi*. Both races distinguished from Craveri's Murrelet by lack of partial dark collar; slightly shorter, stouter bill; lack of black under the bill; and white wing linings, visible when birds rise to flap wings before taking off. Usually seen at least a few miles offshore; nests in colonies on rocky islands, ledges, and sometimes in dense vegetation.

Voice: Call is a piping whistle or series of whistles, heard year-round; calls of nominate race apparently differ.

Range: Uncommon to fairly common; both subspecies move north after breeding as far as Washington, where rare; *scrippsi* casually to southern British Columbia; *hypoleucus* is generally rare in North American waters.

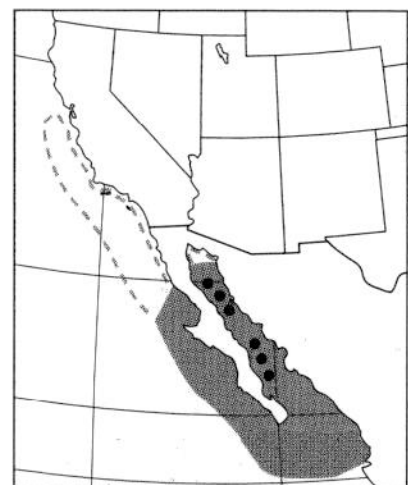

Craveri's Murrelet *Synthliboramphus craveri*

L 8½" (22 cm) Slate black above, white below. Distinguished from Xantus's Murrelet by variably dusky gray wing linings; dark partial collar extending onto breast; slightly slimmer, longer bill; and black color of face extending under the bill. In good light, upperparts have a brownish tinge.

Voice: Call, very different from *scrippsi* Xantus's, is a cicada-like rattle, rising to a reedy trilling when agitated.

Range: Breeds on rocky islands off Baja California. Uncommon and irregular late-summer and fall post-breeding visitor off coast of southern and central California. Pelagic; rarely seen from shore.

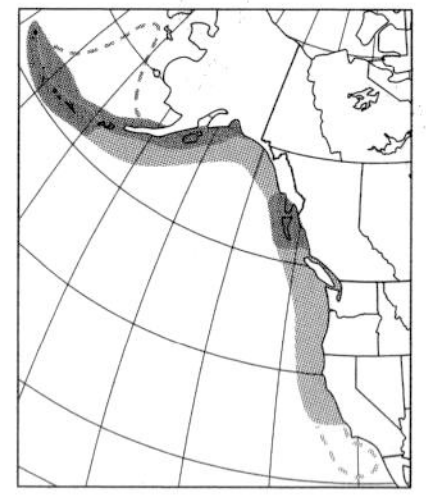

Ancient Murrelet *Synthliboramphus antiquus*

L 10" (25 cm) Black crown and nape contrast with gray back. White streaks on head and nape of ***breeding adult*** give it an "ancient" look. Note also black chin and throat, yellowish bill. ***Winter adult***'s bib is smaller and flecked with white, streaks on head less distinct. ***Immature*** lacks head streaks; throat is mostly white; distinguished from winter Marbled Murrelet (previous page) by heavier, paler bill and by sharp contrast between head and back. In flight, Ancient Murrelet holds its head higher than other murrelets; dark stripe on body at base of wing contrasts with white underparts, white wing linings.

Voice: Call is a short, emphatic *chirrup.*

Range: Uncommon to common; breeds primarily on the Aleutians and other Alaska islands and British Columbia; winters rarely to southern California. Casual inland.

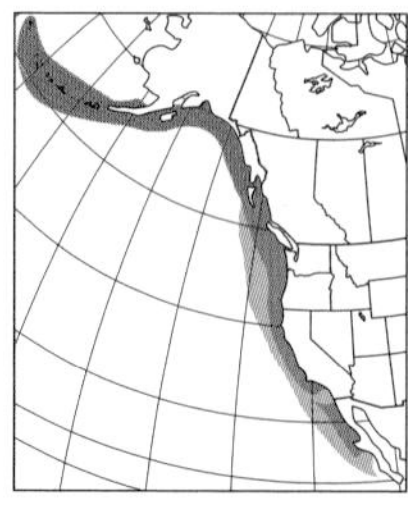

Cassin's Auklet *Ptychoramphus aleuticus* *L 9" (23 cm)*

Small, plump, dark gray bird; wings more rounded than murrelets; bill short and stout, with pale spot at base of lower mandible; pale eyes. Upperparts are dark gray, shading to paler gray below, with whitish belly. Prominent white crescent above eye. Juvenile is paler overall; has darker eye and black bill.

Voice: Call, heard only on breeding grounds, is a weak croaking.

Range: Common; nests in colonies on islands and on isolated coastal cliffs and headlands; pelagic otherwise.

Xantus's Murrelet
slight grayish cast
white underwing coverts
scrippsi
white crescent above eye
hypoleucus
white chin
scrippsi
Craveri's Murrelet
bill longer and thinner than Xantus's
upperparts appear darker than Xantus's
dark under bill
dusky underwing coverts
dark breast spur
breeding adult
Ancient Murrelet
immature
paler
black
black cap
yellowish bill
white eyebrow
winter adult
breeding adult
gray upperparts
ack chin
nd throat
Cassin's Auklet
white crescent above pale eye
adults
wings appear rounder than murrelets
pale
overall gray and chunky

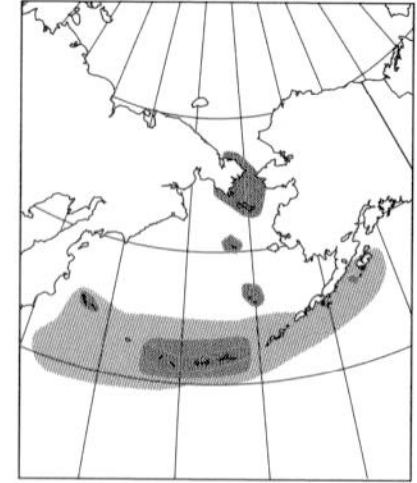

Least Auklet *Aethia pusilla L 6¼" (16 cm)*
Small, chubby, with short neck; dark above, with variably white-tipped scapulars, secondaries and greater coverts; forehead and lores streaked with white bristly feathers. Stubby, knobbed bill is dark red, with pale tip. In ***breeding*** plumage, acquired by Jan., a streak of white plumes extends back from behind eye; underparts heavily mottled with gray to nearly all-white. In ***winter*** plumage, underparts entirely white. ***Juvenile*** resembles winter adult.
Voice: On breeding grounds gives buzzy scratching notes.
Range: Abundant and gregarious; found in immense flocks. Nests on boulder-strewn beaches and islands. Often seen far from shore. Accidental in Northwest Territories and coastal California. Winters throughout Aleutians.

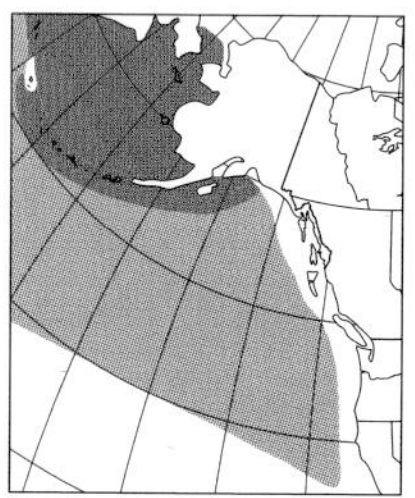

Parakeet Auklet *Aethia psittacula L 10" (25 cm)*
In ***breeding*** plumage, acquired by late Jan., broad upturned bill is orange-red; white plume extends back from behind the eye; dark slate upperparts and throat contrast sharply with white underparts; sides are mottled gray. In ***winter*** plumage, bill duskier; underparts, including throat, entirely white. Compare with larger Rhinoceros Auklet (next page). ***Juvenile*** resembles winter adult. Wings rounded and wingbeats fluttery in comparison to murrelets.
Voice: Silent except on breeding grounds, when call is a musical trill, rising in pitch.
Range: Fairly common on breeding grounds; nests in scattered pairs on rocky shores and sea cliffs. Found in pairs or small flocks in winter, well out to sea. Rare and irregular in winter as far south as California on offshore water of open ocean.

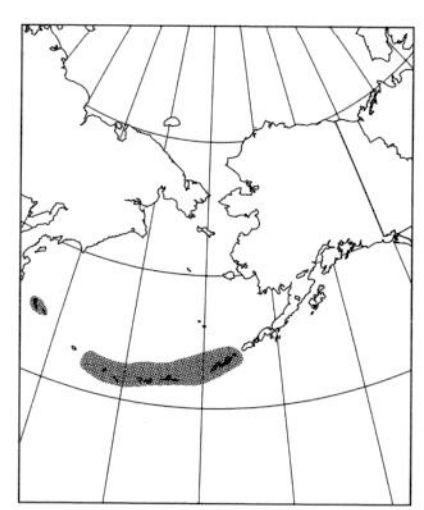

Whiskered Auklet *Aethia pygmaea L 7¾" (20 cm)*
Overall color like Crested Auklet, but note Whiskered is paler on belly and undertail coverts. Three white plumes splay from each side of face; thin crest curls forward. In ***breeding*** plumage, bill is deep red with white tip. In ***winter,*** bill is dusky, plumes and crest less conspicuous. ***Juvenile*** is paler below; bill smaller; lacks crest; less striking head pattern. First-summer bird may lack crest and show reduced plumes. Often seen feeding in riptides.
Voice: On breeding grounds gives mewing notes.
Range: Fairly common but local; nests in Aleutians from Baby Islands off Unalaska Island west to Buldir; and on islands off Russian Far East.

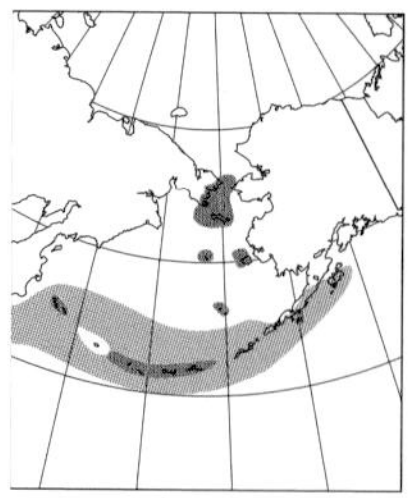

Crested Auklet *Aethia cristatella L 9" (23 cm)*
Sooty black overall; prominent quail-like crest curves forward from forehead; narrow white plume trails from behind yellow eye. ***Breeding adult***'s bill is enlarged by bright orange plates. In ***winter,*** bill is smaller and browner; crest and plume reduced. ***Juvenile*** has short crest, faint plume; bill smaller. Compare with smaller Whiskered Auklet. ***First-summer*** bird has more evident plume back from eye, but bill is still small.
Voice: On breeding grounds gives loud doglike barking calls.
Range: Common and gregarious. Nests in crevices of sea cliffs and rocky shores. Accidental south to Baja California.

Least Auklet
breeding adults
light
white throat
dark
breeding adults
whitish
white underparts
winter adults
juvenile
faint whitish scapular line
Parakeet Auklet
orange-red bill
breeding adults
dark
unique bill shape
juvenile
breeding adult
white belly
dark throat and breast
white underparts
winter adults
bill somewhat darker
white postocular line
Whiskered Auklet
three white head plumes
thin, curled crest
small dark red bill
breeding adult
winter adult
breeding adults
whitish belly
juvenile
winter adult
subdued head pattern in winter adult and especially juvenile
Crested Auklet
thick, curled crest
red-orange bill plates
breeding adult
1st summer
breeding adult
winter adult
uniform dark gray underparts
short crest
juvenile
white line
winter adult
much smaller bill than breeding adult; loses bill plates

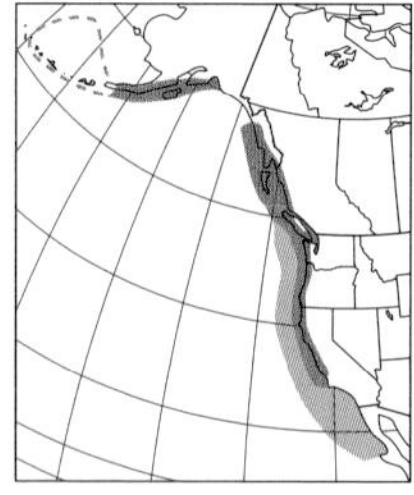

Rhinoceros Auklet *Cerorhinca monocerata L 15" (38 cm)*
Large, heavy-billed auklet with large head and short, thick neck. Blackish brown above; paler on sides, neck, and throat. In flight, whitish on belly blends into dark breast; compare with extensively white underparts of similar Parakeet Auklet (previous page). In ***breeding*** plumage, acquired by Feb., Rhinoceros Auklet has distinct white plumes and a pale yellow "horn" at base of orange bill. ***Winter adult*** lacks horn; plumes are less distinct, bill paler. Juvenile and ***immature*** lack horn and plumes; bill is dusky, eyes darker. Compare with much smaller Cassin's Auklet (page 202).
Voice: On breeding grounds, a series of mooing notes are heard, chiefly at night.
Range: Common along most of the West Coast in fall and winter; often seen in large numbers close to shore.

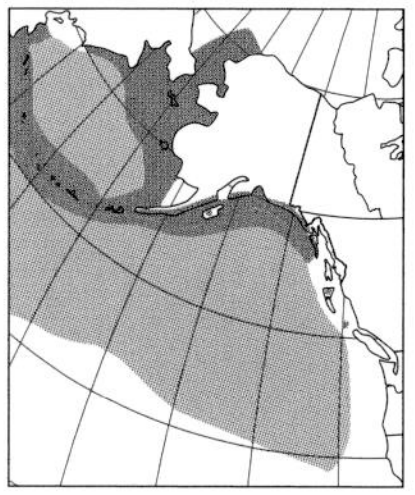

Horned Puffin *Fratercula corniculata L 15" (38 cm)*
A stocky North Pacific species with thick neck, large head, massive bill; underparts are white in all plumages. ***Breeding adult***'s face is white, bill brightly colored. Dark, fleshy "horn" extending up from eye is visible only at close range. ***Winter adult***'s bill is smaller, duller; face is dusky. Bill of ***juvenile*** and first-winter birds smaller and duskier than adult; full adult bill takes several years to develop. In flight, bright orange legs are conspicuous; wings are rounded; wing linings grayish; wings lack white trailing edge.
Voice: On breeding grounds, rising and then falling growling notes suggest Atlantic Puffin.
Range: Locally common; winters well out to sea. Rare and irregular. Irregular straggler off the West Coast to southern California, mainly in late spring and early summer.

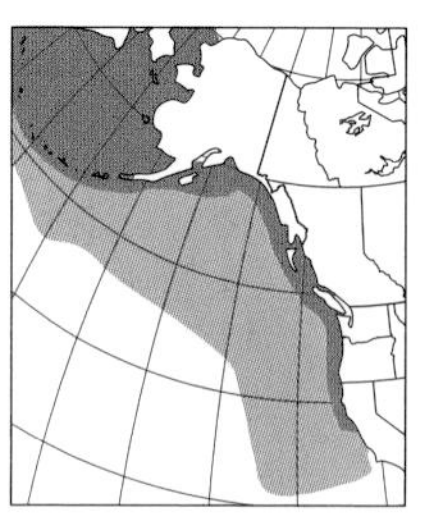

Tufted Puffin *Fratercula cirrhata L 16" (41 cm)*
Stocky, with thick neck, large head, massive bill. Underparts are dark in adults. ***Breeding adult***'s face is white, bill brightly colored; pale yellow head tufts droop over back of neck. ***Winter adult*** has smaller, duller bill; face is gray, tufts shorter or absent. ***Juvenile*** has smaller, dusky bill; dark eye; white or dark underparts. First-winter bird looks like juvenile until spring molt. As in other puffins, full adult bill and plumage take several years to develop. Red-orange feet are conspicuous in flight; wings are rounded; wing linings grayish; wings lack white trailing edge.
Voice: Various low grumbling notes given in breeding colonies.
Range: Common to abundant in northern breeding range; uncommon to rare off northern and central California; very rare or casual off southern California (a few nest in northern California; formerly on northern Channel Islands off southern California). Winters far out at sea.

winter adult
Rhinoceros Auklet
itish belly blends with dark breast
smaller yellowish bill
white plumes
"horn"
plain grayish brown head
immature
winter adult
brighter yellow-orange bill
breeding adult
Horned Puffin
much smaller dark bill
darker bill than breeding
juvenile
juveniles and winter adults darker faced
uniquely shaped and colored bill
"horn"
white face
winter adult
breeding adult
pure white underparts
bill smaller and duller than adult; compare to smaller-billed Rhinoceros Auklet
juvenile
Tufted Puffin
juvenile
dark faced
very thick red bill
some with paler belly
gold "tufts"
winter adult
breeding adult
white face
all-black underparts

Pigeons, Doves (Family Columbidae)

The larger species of these birds usually are called pigeons, the smaller ones doves. All are strong, fast fliers. Juveniles have pale-tipped feathers and lack the neck markings of adults.

Band-tailed Pigeon *Patagioenas fasciata L 14½" (37 cm)*

Purplish head and breast; dark-tipped yellow bill, yellow legs; broad gray tail band; narrow white band on nape, absent on juvenile. Flocks in flight resemble Rock Doves but are uniform, not varied, in plumage and lack contrasting white rump and black band at end of tail.

Voice: Call is a low *whoo-whoo.*

Range: Locally common in low-altitude mixed forests in the Northwest and in oak or oak-conifer woodlands in the Southwest; also increasingly common in suburban gardens and parks. Uncommon in southeast Alaska.

Rock Pigeon *Columba livia L 12½" (32 cm)*

The highly variable city pigeon; multicolored birds were developed over centuries of near domestication. The birds most closely resembling their wild ancestors have head and neck darker than back, black bars on inner wing, white rump, and black band at end of tail. Flocks in flight show a variety of plumage patterns, unlike Band-tailed Pigeon.

Voice: Call is a soft *coo-cuk-cuk-cuk-coooo.*

Range: Introduced from Europe by early settlers; now widespread and common, particularly in urban settings. Nests and roosts chiefly on high window ledges, bridges, silos, and barns. Feeds during the day in parks and fields.

Spotted Dove *Streptopelia chinensis L 12" (31 cm)*

Asian species. Named for spotted collar, distinct in ***adult,*** obscured in ***juvenile.*** Wings and long, white-tipped tail are more rounded than Mourning Dove; wings unmarked.

Voice: Calls include a rather harsh *coo-coo-croooo* and *coo-crrooo-coo,* with emphasis respectively on the last and middle notes.

Range: Introduced in Los Angeles in the early 1900s; formerly well established in southwestern California but sharp declines in recent decades.

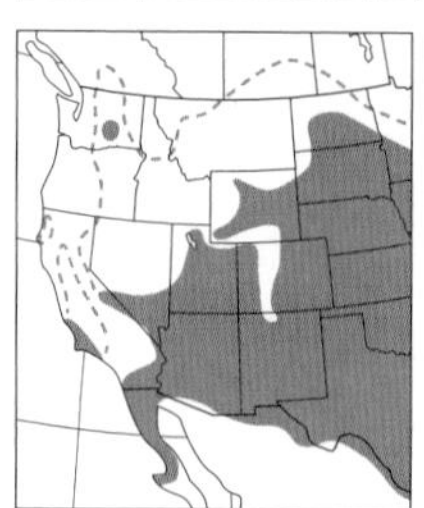

Eurasian Collared-Dove *Streptopelia decaocto*

L 12½" (32 cm) Very pale gray-buff; black collar. Escapes of domesticated "Ringed Turtle-Dove"—formerly named *S. risoria,* derived from African Collared-Dove (*S. roseogrisea*), an Old World species—may form small populations, but do not do well in the wild; they are smaller, paler (but some Eurasian Collared-Doves are pale too), with whitish undertail coverts, gray primaries; shorter tail, less black from below.

Voice: Three-syllable call, *coo-coo-cup.* African Collared-Dove domestics give a two-syllable call.

Range: Eurasian species; introduced to Bahamas, spread to Florida. Common; now nearly widespread across U.S.

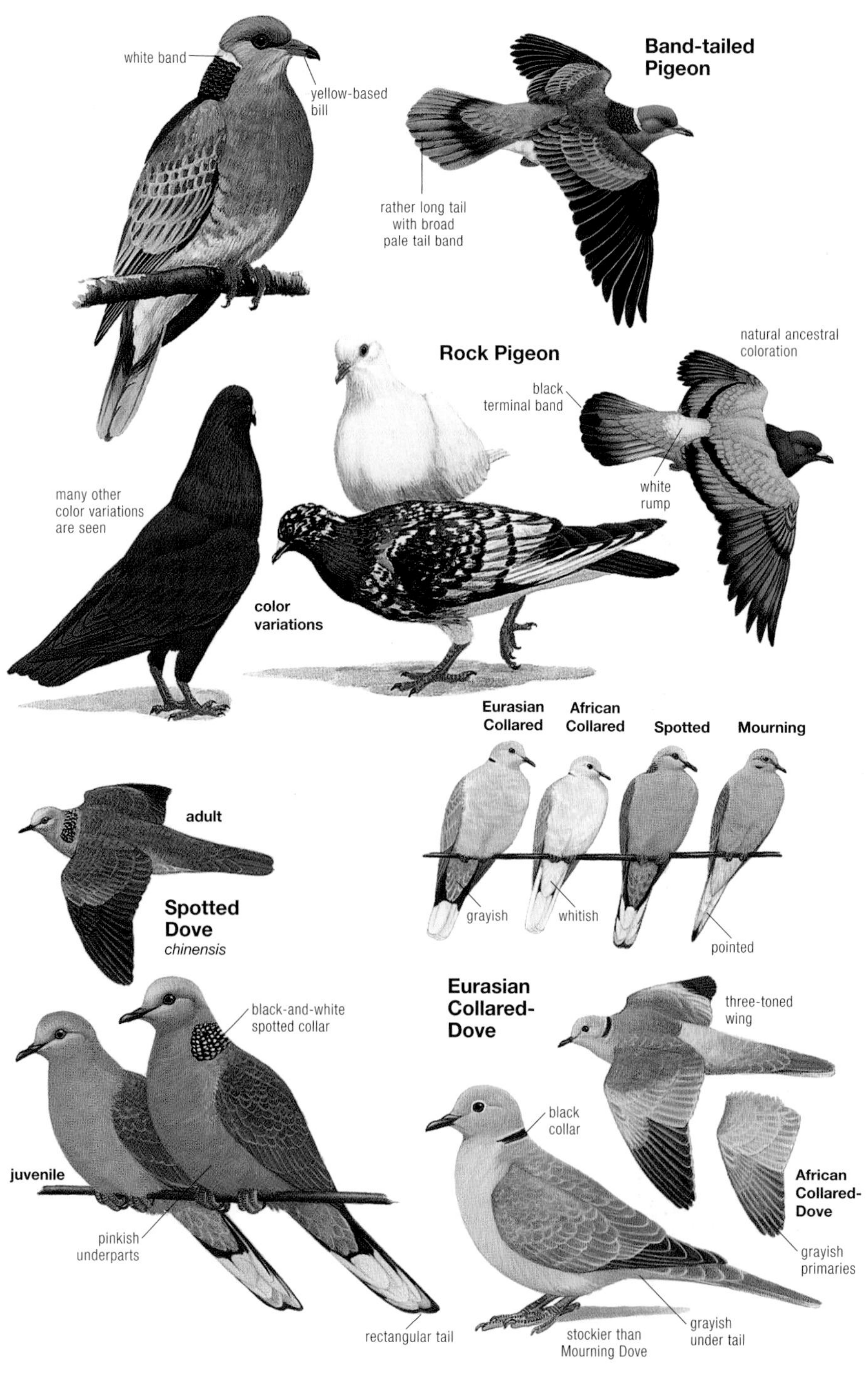

Band-tailed Pigeon
white band
yellow-based bill
rather long tail with broad pale tail band
Rock Pigeon
natural ancestral coloration
black terminal band
white rump
many other color variations are seen
color variations
Eurasian Collared
African Collared
Spotted
Mourning
grayish
whitish
pointed
adult
Spotted Dove
chinensis
black-and-white spotted collar
juvenile
pinkish underparts
rectangular tail
Eurasian Collared-Dove
three-toned wing
black collar
African Collared-Dove
grayish primaries
stockier than Mourning Dove
grayish under tail

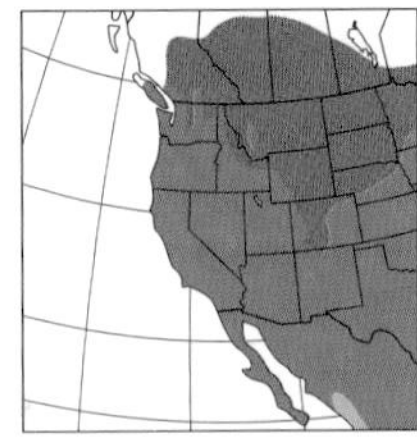

Mourning Dove *Zenaida macroura L 12" (31 cm)*
Trim body; long tail tapers to a point. Black spots on upperwing; pinkish wash below. In flight, shows white tips on outer tail feathers. ***Juvenile*** has heavy spotting; scaled effect on wings.
Voice: Call is a mournful *oowoo-woo-woo-woo.* Wings produce a fluttering whistle as the bird takes flight.
Range: Our most abundant and widespread dove, found in a wide variety of habitats. Rare fall visitor to Alaska, northwestern Canada.

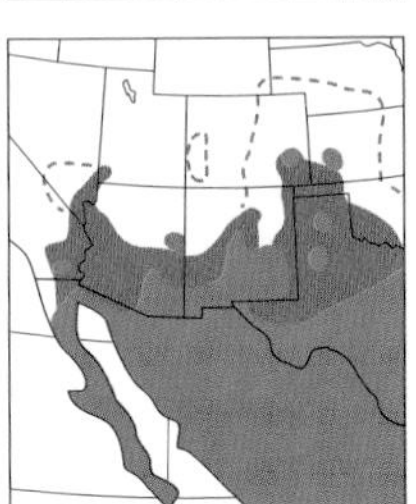

White-winged Dove *Zenaida asiatica L 11½" (29 cm)*
Large white wing patches and shorter, rounded tail distinguish this species from Mourning Dove. Also note slightly larger bill, orange-red eye. On sitting bird, wing patch shows only as a thin white line.
Voice: Drawn-out, loud, cooing call, *who-cooks-for-you,* with many variations, is heard mainly during the breeding season.
Range: Nests singly or in large colonies in dense mesquite, mature citrus groves, riparian woodlands, and saguaro-paloverde deserts; also found in desert towns. Expanding north on Great Plains. Rare to casual visitor to coast and north to Canada; accidental to Alaska (Skagway, Oct. 1981).

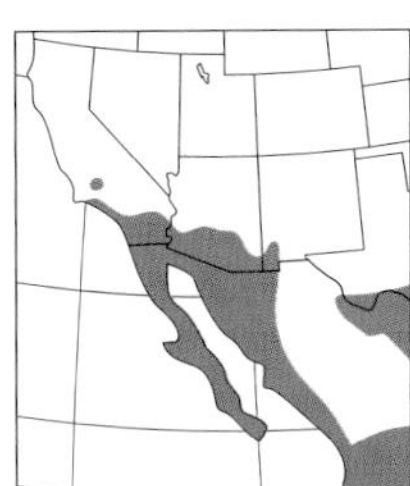

Common Ground-Dove *Columbina passerina*
L 6½" (17 cm) Very small, with pink at base of bill; scaled effect on head and breast; short tail, often raised. Plain scapulars; bright chestnut primaries and wing linings visible in flight. ***Male*** has a slate gray crown, pinkish gray underparts. ***Female*** is grayer, more uniformly colored.
Voice: Call is a repeated soft, ascending *wah-up.*
Range: Forages on open ground in brushy rangeland and agricultural areas (locally in urban areas). Casual north to Oregon in fall and winter.

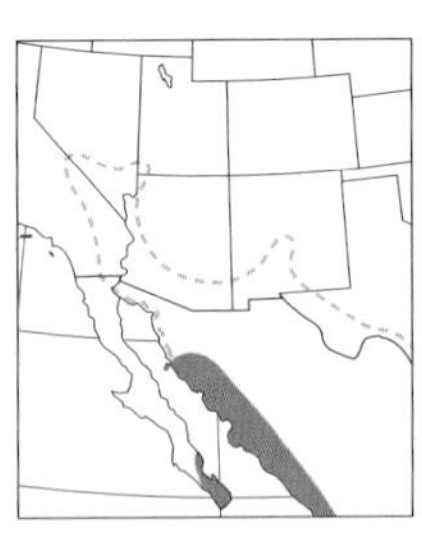

Ruddy Ground-Dove *Columbina talpacoti L 6¾" (17 cm)*
Dark bill; lacks scaling of Common Ground-Dove. All records but one (a male eastern *rufipennis* from Big Bend) in West are western Mexico race *eluta.* ***Male*** *eluta* has a gray crown, rufous on upperparts. ***Female*** mainly gray-brown overall. Both sexes show black on underwing coverts, black linear markings on scapulars.
Voice: Call like Common but a little lower in pitch and faster.
Range: Widespread in Latin America; rare to casual in Southwest, mostly in fall and winter. Has bred in southern Arizona and southeastern California.

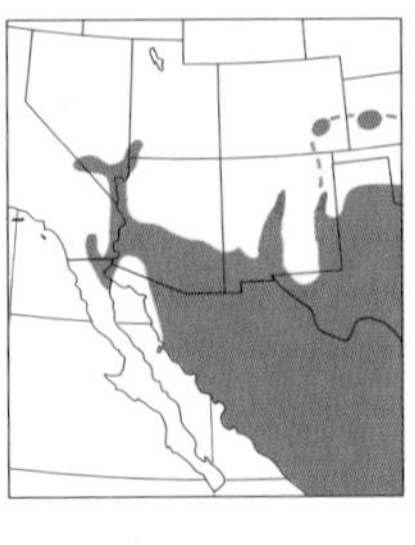

Inca Dove *Columbina inca L 8¼" (21 cm)*
Plumage conspicuously scalloped. In flight, shows chestnut on wings like Common Ground-Dove, but note Inca Dove's longer, white-edged tail.
Voice: Call is a double *cooo-coo.*
Range: Found usually near human habitations, often in parks and gardens. Slowly spreading north and west. Accidental north to Montana.

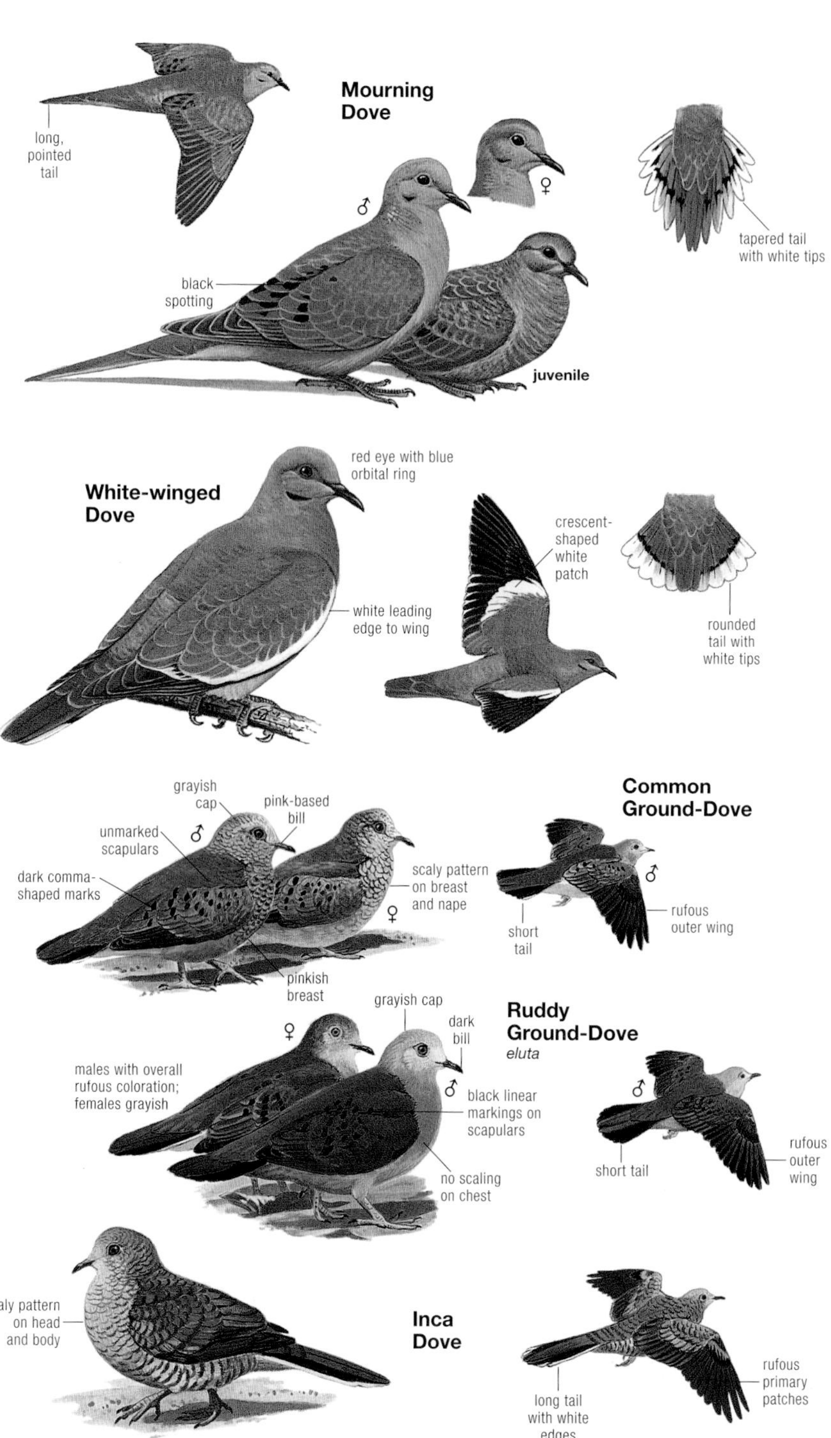

Mourning Dove
long, pointed tail
♂
♀
tapered tail with white tips
black spotting
juvenile
White-winged Dove
red eye with blue orbital ring
crescent-shaped white patch
white leading edge to wing
rounded tail with white tips
Common Ground-Dove
grayish cap
pink-based bill
unmarked scapulars
♂
dark comma-shaped marks
scaly pattern on breast and nape
♀
pinkish breast
♂
short tail
rufous outer wing
Ruddy Ground-Dove
eluta
grayish cap
dark bill
♀
males with overall rufous coloration; females grayish
♂
black linear markings on scapulars
no scaling on chest
♂
short tail
rufous outer wing
Inca Dove
scaly pattern on head and body
long tail with white edges
rufous primary patches

Lories, Parakeets, Macaws, Parrots (Family Psittacidae)

Most parrots in the wild in North America are descendants of escaped cage birds. Shown are those with established populations, mostly from southern parts of California. ABA accepts White-winged, Yellow-chevroned, Monk, and Green Parakeets; Red-crowned Parrot; and Budgerigar; but in West, only Red-crowned Parrot is considered established (California) and has been added to the official California state list.

Yellow-chevroned Parakeet *Brotogeris chiriri*
L 8¾" (22 cm) Native of southern Amazon to northern Argentina. Now outnumbers White-winged in southern California. Lacks white on flight feathers; body is yellow-green; head, including lores, is also yellow-green.
Voice: Gives shrill, metallic *chiri* notes in flight.

White-winged Parakeet *Brotogeris versicolurus*
L 8¾" (22 cm) Native of northern Amazon area and south to east-central Peru. Small numbers established in California by 1960s, but have declined in recent years. Note ***adult***'s white outer secondaries and inner primaries, yellow greater coverts, unfeathered grayish lores; head duller than Yellow-chevroned. Immature similar but reduced or no white on primaries and secondaries.
Voice: Similar to Yellow-chevroned but less shrill, a *te-cle-te* note.

Black-hooded Parakeet *Nandayus nenday*
L 13¾" (35 cm) Also known as Nanday Conure. Native of southwest Brazil to north Argentina. Found, often in flocks, in Los Angeles area. ***Adult*** with black on head, black bill, blue wash on breast, red thighs. Immature similar but has less blue on throat and breast.
Voice: Gives high-pitched screeching notes, a repeated *kree-ah.*

Red-masked Parakeet *Aratinga erythrogenys*
L 13" (33 cm) Native of southwest Ecuador and northwest Peru. In Los Angeles area, often associates with Mitred. ***Adult*** similar to Mitred, but note red on leading edge of wing and underwing coverts, more red on head. Immature is mainly green with only scattered red feathers.
Voice: Gives a variety of calls with a distinct nasal quality, in general less harsh than Mitred Parakeet.

Mitred Parakeet *Aratinga mitrata L 15" (38 cm)*
Native of South America. Numerous in Los Angeles area. ***Adult*** large, green, with white eye ring; red on face, forehead, variable elsewhere on head; underwings are yellow-olive. Immature similar but with less red on head, especially on face, and brown iris.
Voice: Gives a variety of strident and harsh notes including an abrupt *cheeah cheeah* call.

Blue-crowned Parakeet *Aratinga acuticaudata*
L 14" (36 cm) Native of South America. Small numbers established in Los Angeles area. ***Adult*** with blue face; bicolored bill; base of tail reddish below. Immature similar but restricted blue on head.
Voice: Gives a loud, low, hoarse, repeated *cheeah* note.

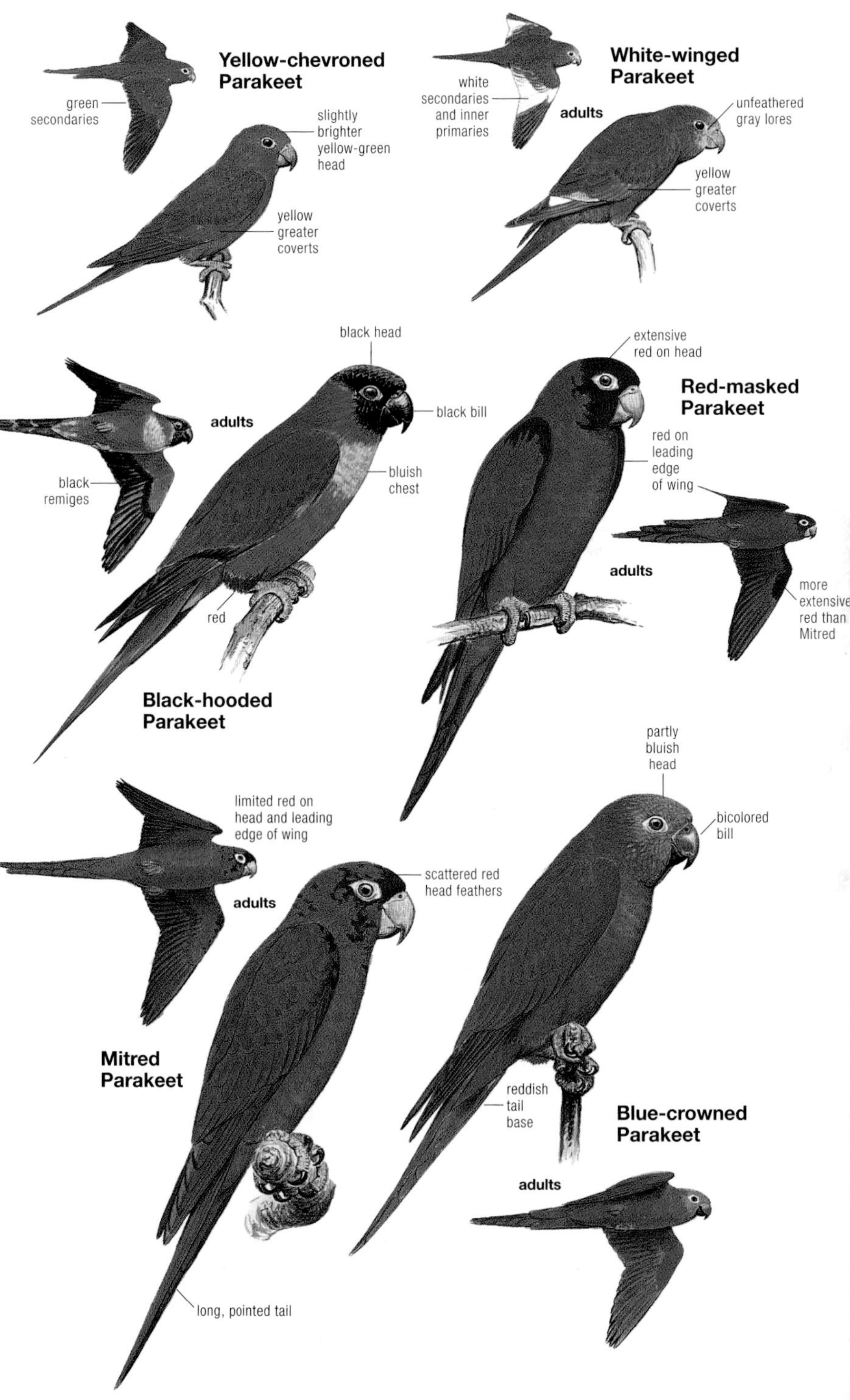
Yellow-chevroned Parakeet
green secondaries
slightly brighter yellow-green head
yellow greater coverts
White-winged Parakeet
white secondaries and inner primaries
adults
unfeathered gray lores
yellow greater coverts
black head
adults
black bill
bluish chest
black remiges
red
Black-hooded Parakeet
extensive red on head
Red-masked Parakeet
red on leading edge of wing
adults
more extensive red than Mitred
partly bluish head
limited red on head and leading edge of wing
adults
scattered red head feathers
bicolored bill
Mitred Parakeet
reddish tail base
Blue-crowned Parakeet
adults
long, pointed tail

Rose-ringed Parakeet *Psittacula krameri L 15¾" (40 cm)*
Small numbers of this Asian and African species established in Los Angeles area and especially Bakersfield area (southern California). Appear to be of Indian race, *manillensis*. Slender tail with very long central feathers; bright red upper mandible. ***Adult male*** shows rose-edged black collar. Female, immature lack head markings.
Voice: Call is a loud, flickerlike *kew.*

Red-crowned Parrot *Amazona viridigenalis L 13" (33 cm)*
Native of northeast Mexico. Established in Los Angeles metro area. Blue on sides of head, yellowish band across tip of tail. ***Adult male*** has red crown; female averages less red; ***immature*** shows even less.
Voice: Calls generally raucous but include a mellow, rolling *rreeoo.*

Lilac-crowned Parrot *Amazona finschi L 13" (33 cm)*
West Mexican species. Small numbers established in Los Angeles area. Like Red-crowned, but has lilac wash on crown and nape; maroon band across forehead; orange eye and a dusky, rather than flesh, cere; longer tail has entirely green central tail feathers. Has likely hybridized with Red-crowned in southern California.
Voice: Calls include a distinctive upslurred whistle.

Yellow-headed Parrot *Amazona oratrix L 14½" (37 cm)*
Drastically declining species from Mexico and Belize. Small but declining numbers established in Los Angeles area. Large, with yellow head; immature shows less yellow. Some escapes are of related Yellow-naped (*A. auropalliata*) and Yellow-crowned (*A. ochrocephala*) Parrots, formerly treated as subspecies of Yellow-headed.
Voice: Calls include a resonant *haa-haa-haa.*

IDENTIFYING: Flight Silhouettes The flight patterns of psittacid genera differ.

Brotogeris. These small parakeets have moderately long, pointed tails. In flight several rapid wingbeats are followed by brief closure of bowed wings. Flight is rapid but seems halting and undulating from wing closures and side-to-side twisting of body.

Psittacula. Rose-ringed Parakeet is of medium size and has a markedly long, slender tail. It appears relatively small headed and thus does not seem "front-heavy." Its wingbeats are deeper and more sweeping than those of other parakeets.

Aratinga, Nandayus, and Myiopsitta. These medium-size parakeets have long, pointed tails. Their bills are moderate to large in size, giving them a more front-heavy look. Flight is rapid and constant; wingbeats are fairly shallow, with wings bowed slightly below the body plane. There is some side-to-side body twisting.

Amazona. These medium- to large-size parrots seem large headed and markedly front-heavy in flight. The tail is squared and moderately short. Wings are bowed down; wingbeats are stiff, continuous, and fast, but flight is slower than in parakeets.

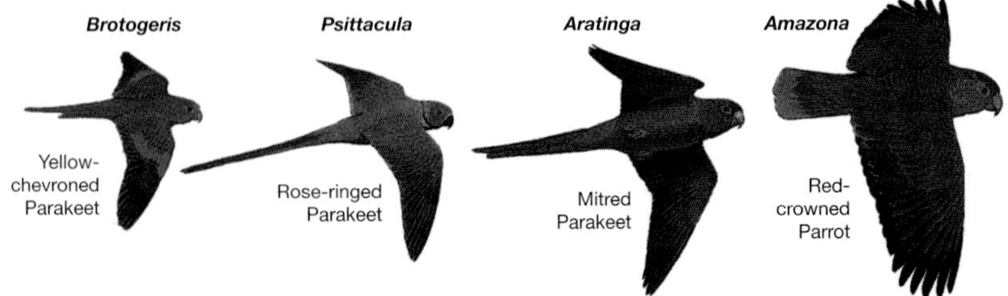

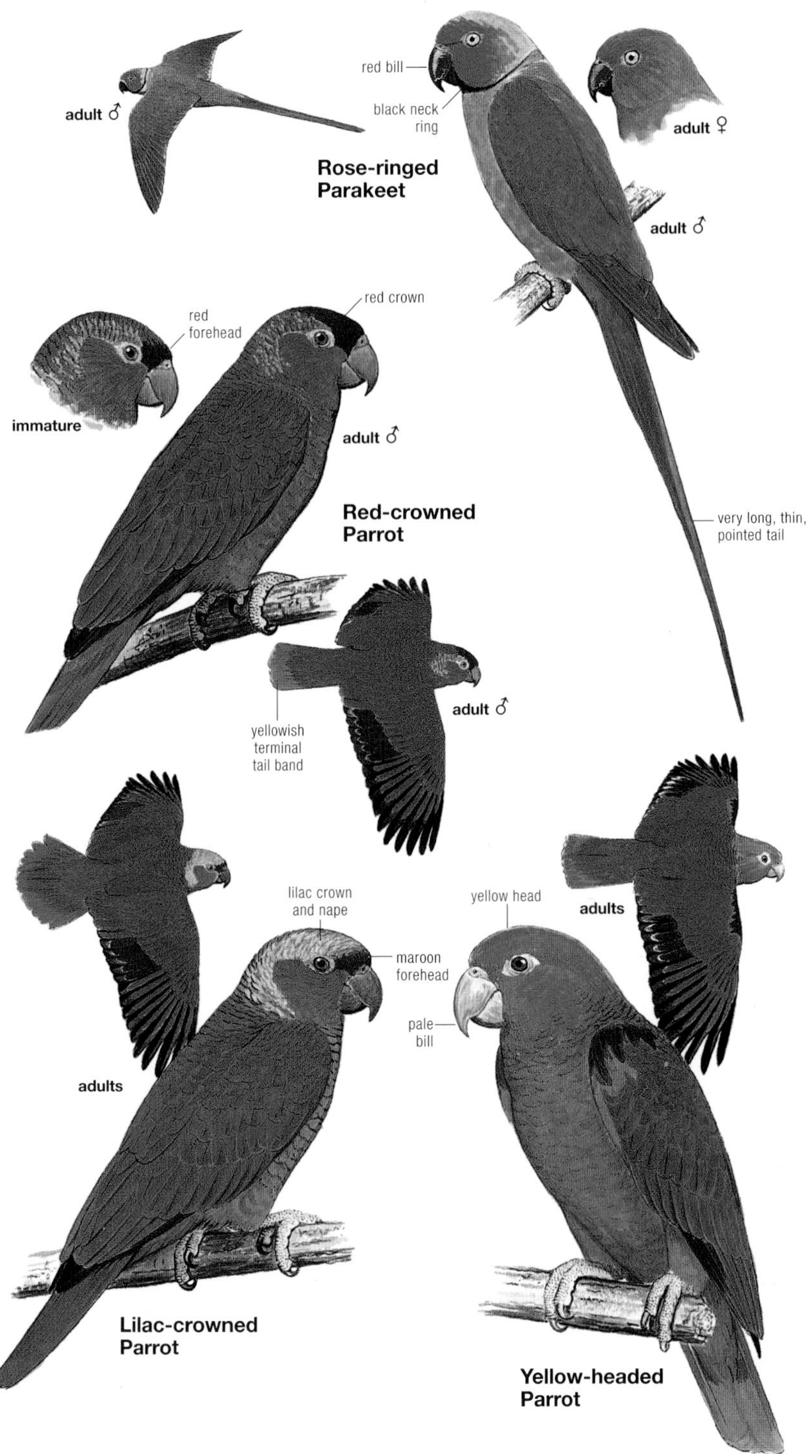
adult ♂
red bill
black neck ring
adult ♀
Rose-ringed Parakeet
adult ♂
red crown
red forehead
immature
adult ♂
Red-crowned Parrot
very long, thin, pointed tail
yellowish terminal tail band
adult ♂
lilac crown and nape
maroon forehead
yellow head
adults
pale bill
adults
Lilac-crowned Parrot
Yellow-headed Parrot

Cuckoos, Roadrunners, Anis (Family Cuculidae)

Of this large family, widespread in the Old World, only a few species are seen in North America. Most are slender with long tails; two toes point forward, two back.

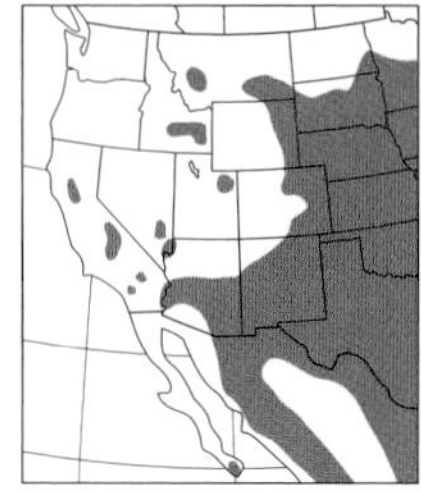

Yellow-billed Cuckoo *Coccyzus americanus L 12" (31 cm)* Grayish brown above, white below; rufous primaries; lower mandible yellow. Under tail patterned in bold black and white. In ***juvenal*** plumage, held well into fall, tail has a much paler pattern and bill may show little or no yellow; may be confused with Black-billed Cuckoo.

Voice: One song sounds hollow and wooden, a rapid staccato *kuk-kuk-kuk* that usually slows and descends to a *kakakowlp-kowlp* ending; also a series of *coo* notes, and a slowly repeated single *koop*.

Range: Breeds in riparian woodland. Formerly a much more widespread breeder in West, including Pacific Northwest. Now extirpated as a breeder there (still a casual visitant) and rare in California. Most breeders now on western Great Plains and the Southwest. Accidental (fall) to southeast Alaska. Winters in South America.

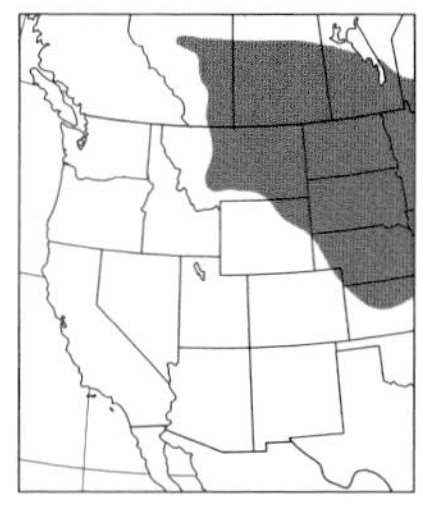

Black-billed Cuckoo *Coccyzus erythropthalmus L 12" (31 cm)* Grayish brown above, pale grayish below. Bill is usually all-dark. Lacks the rufous primaries of Yellow-billed Cuckoo. Note also ***adult***'s reddish orbital ring. Under tail patterned in gray with white tipping; compare juvenile Yellow-billed. ***Juvenile*** Black-billed has a buffy orbital ring; under tail is paler; underparts may have buffy tinge, especially on undertail coverts; primaries may show a little rusty brown.

Voice: Song usually consists of monotonous *cu-cu-cu* or *cu-cu-cu-cu* phrases.

Range: Generally a rare and irregular breeder in riparian and mixed woodland in mapped western range. Very rare breeder in western Idaho; casual to Pacific Northwest (summer) and to California (mainly fall). Accidental in Southwest. Winters in South America.

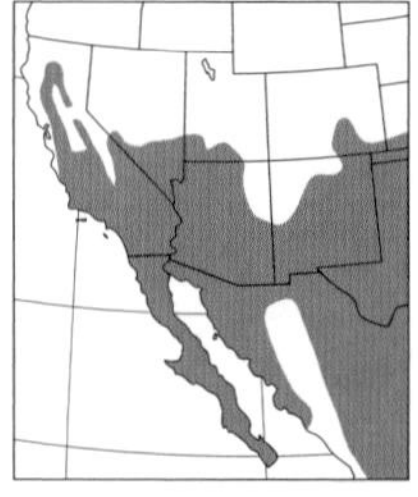

Greater Roadrunner *Geococcyx californianus L 23" (58 cm)* A large, ground-dwelling cuckoo streaked with brown and white. Note the long, heavy bill, conspicuous bushy crest, and long, white-edged tail. Short, rounded wings show a white crescent on the primaries. Eats insects, lizards, snakes, rodents, and small birds.

Voice: Song is a dovelike cooing, descending in pitch.

Range: Fairly common in scrub desert and mesquite groves; generally uncommon in chaparral and open woodland.

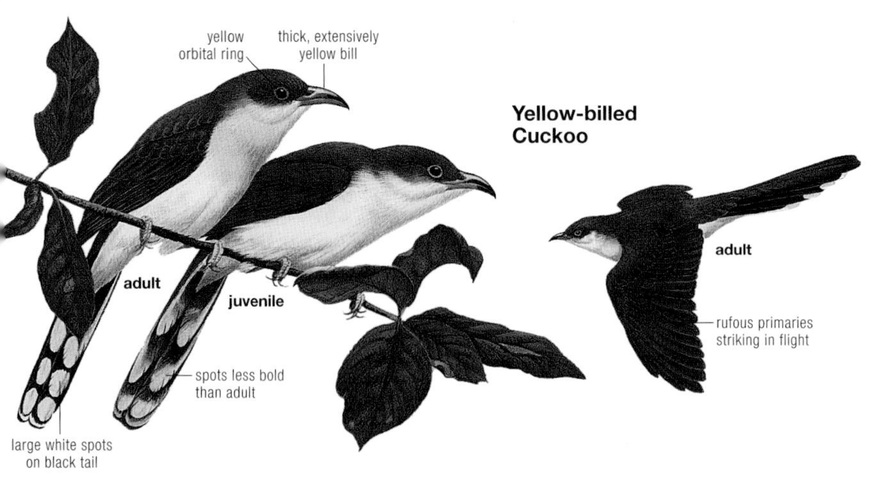

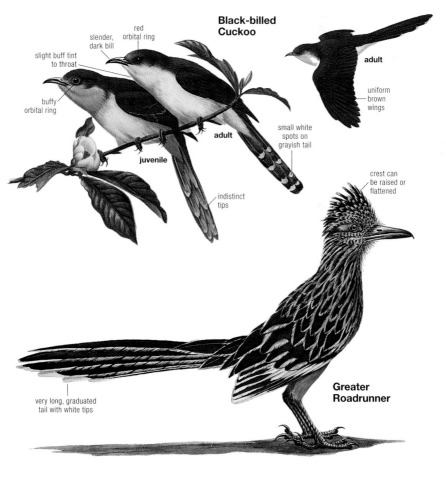

Black-billed Cuckoo

red
orbital ring

slender,
dark bill

slight buff tint
to throat

buffy
orbital ring

adult

uniform
brown
wings

adult

juvenile

small white
spots on
grayish tail

indistinct
tips

crest can
be raised or
flattened

very long, graduated
tail with white tips

Greater Roadrunner

Common Cuckoo *Cuculus canorus L 13" (33 cm)*
Old World species. Closely resembles Oriental Cuckoo. ***Adult male*** and adult gray-morph female are gray above, paler below, with whitish belly narrowly barred with gray. Though variable, birds seen in Alaska are often paler below with narrower barring than Oriental. ***Hepatic morph*** (restricted to females in Common and Oriental Cuckoos) is pale rusty brown above, heavily barred with black on back and tail; rump is paler than hepatic-morph Oriental and either unmarked or only lightly spotted. In flight, both species resemble small falcons.
Voice: Male's song is the familiar *cuc-coo* for which the family is named but call is rarely heard in North America.
Range: Rare spring and summer visitor to central and western Aleutians and Bering Sea islands. One late-June Anchorage record (singing).

Oriental Cuckoo *Cuculus optatus L 12½" (32 cm)*
Eurasian species. ***Adult male*** and adult gray-morph female are darker gray above than Common Cuckoo, paler below, with pale belly barred in dark gray. Barring is often slightly broader, and lower belly and undertail covert region buffier, than Common Cuckoo. In the hand, underwing shows largely unmarked white feathering below the primary coverts (barred in Common Cuckoo); in flight, white on underwing coverts forms more-contrasting bar than Common. ***Hepatic-morph female*** is rusty brown above, heavily barred on back, rump, and tail.
Voice: Song, a variable, hollow note often delivered four times, has not been heard here. Oriental Cuckoo (*C. saturatus*) was formerly considered polytypic, but because of vocal differences it was split into three species: Himalayan Cuckoo (*C. saturatus*), Sunda Cuckoo (*C. lepidus*), and Oriental Cuckoo (*C. optatus*); the latter is described here.
Range: Casual from late spring through fall in western Aleutians, Pribilofs, and St. Lawrence Island and once on mainland.

Barn Owls (Family Tytonidae)

Owls are distinctive birds of prey, divided into structural differences into two families: Barn Owls and Typical Owls. All have immobile eyes in large heads. Fluffy plumage makes their flight soundless. To help locate prey at night, they have a round facial disc and a very acute hearing. Barn Owls are strictly nocturnal. They differ from other owls by their heart-shaped face; short, squared tail; and relatively smaller eyes.

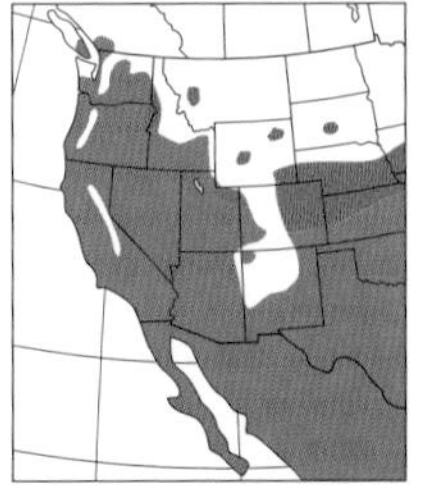

Barn Owl *Tyto alba L 16" (41 cm)*
A pale owl with dark eyes in a heart-shaped face. Rusty brown above; underparts vary from white to cinnamon. Darkest birds are always ***females,*** palest birds ***males.*** Compare with Snowy Owl (page 222).
Voice: Typical call is a raspy, hissing screech.
Range: Roosts and nests in dark cavities in city and farm buildings, cliffs, and trees. Rare to uncommon in many parts of western range, rather common in others.

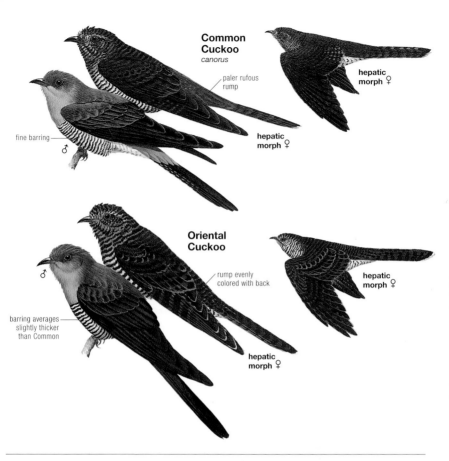

Common Cuckoo
canorus

paler rufous rump

hepatic morph ♀

fine barring

♂

hepatic morph ♀

Oriental Cuckoo

hepatic morph ♀

♂

rump evenly colored with back

barring averages slightly thicker than Common

hepatic morph ♀

Barn Owl
pratincola

dark eyes with whitish heart-shaped face

♂

underparts vary from whitish to cinnamon-buff; males average paler

♀

looks pale in flight with rounded wings and no dark carpal patches as in Short-eared Owl

long legs

Typical Owls (Family Strigidae)

Many species hunt at night and roost during the day. To find owls, search the ground for regurgitated pellets of fur and bone below a nest or roost. Listen for flocks of small songbirds noisily mobbing a roosting owl. Although several species give familiar hooting calls, others make a variety of different sounds, including whistles, chattering, and barking.

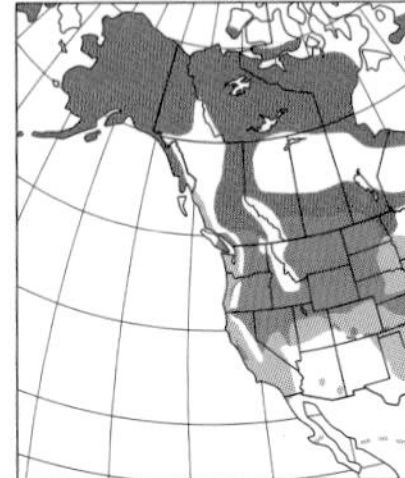

Short-eared Owl *Asio flammeus L 15" (38 cm)*

Tawny; boldly streaked on breast; belly paler, more lightly streaked. Ear tufts are barely visible. In flight, long wings show buffy patch above, black "wrist" mark below; these markings are usually more prominent than Long-eared Owl, which also has less distinct but more individual bars on primaries. Flight is wavering, wingbeats erratic. During the day it roosts on the ground or on open, low perches: short poles, muskrat houses, and duck blinds.

Voice: Typical call, heard in breeding season and sometimes in winter, is a raspy, high barking.

Range: A bird of open country, marshes, tundra, and weedy fields; nests on the ground. Uncommon to fairly common. Somewhat irregular and gregarious in winter; groups may gather where prey is abundant.

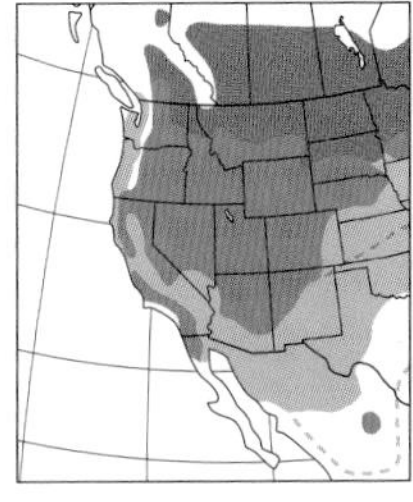

Long-eared Owl *Asio otus L 15" (38 cm)*

A slender owl with long, close-set ear tufts. Boldly streaked and barred on breast and belly. Wings generally have a less prominent buffy patch with more dark barring and a smaller black "wrist" mark than Short-eared Owl; facial disk is rusty. Lives in thick woods; hunts at night over open country and marshes; also locally in desert groves and washes. By day it roosts in a tree, close to the trunk.

Voice: Generally silent except in breeding season. Common call is one or more long *hooo* notes; also various barking notes. Vocal largely during the breeding season. Appears to be largely silent at other seasons—this despite the number of reports (likely mostly erroneous) of briefly calling birds on Christmas Counts.

Range: Uncommon. More gregarious in winter; flocks may roost together. Casual to southeast Alaska. One that came aboard a ship in Bering Sea southwest of St. Lawrence Island on 19 May 2006 was likely nominate *otus* of Old World on range probability.

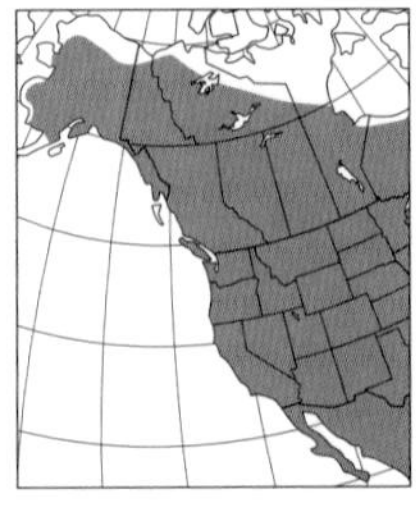

Great Horned Owl *Bubo virginianus L 22" (56 cm)*

Size, bulky shape, and white throat separate this owl from Long-eared Owl; ear tufts distinguish it from other large species. Chiefly nocturnal. Takes prey as large as skunks and grouse.

Voice: Call is a series of three to eight loud, deep hoots; the second and third hoots are often short and rapid. Calls year-round. Juveniles near nest give a loud, raspy begging call.

Range: Nests in trees, caves, or on the ground. Common; habitats vary from forest to city to open desert. Widespread interior race, *subarcticus*, is palest.

Short-eared Owl
flammeus
slow, floppy wingbeats
dark primary covert patch on underwing
buffy and blackish wing patches
very short ear tufts
blackish around eyes
heavily spotted above
streaked below
long ear tufts that are close together
rufous facial disk
blackish around eyes
Long-eared Owl
overall slender body
heavily streaked and barred below
prominent broad ear tufts on either side of head
Great Horned Owl
color of facial disk varies geographically
white
bulky body shape
barred below
overall pale
subarcticus

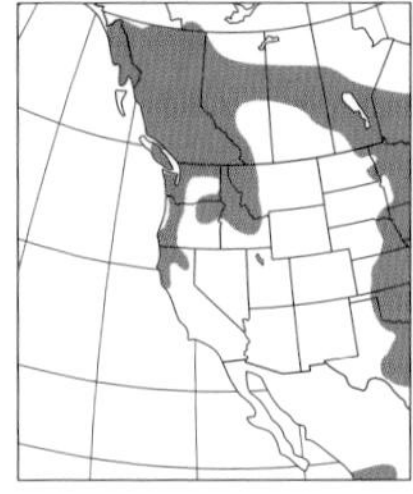

Barred Owl *Strix varia L 21" (53 cm)*
A chunky owl with dark eyes, dark barring on upper breast, dark streaking below. Chiefly nocturnal; daytime roost well hidden. Easily flushed; does not generally tolerate close approach.
Voice: Distinctive call is a rhythmic series of loud hoots: *who-cooks-for-you, who-cooks-for-you-all;* also a drawn-out *hoo-ah,* sometimes preceded by an ascending agitated barking. Much more likely than other owls to be heard in daytime.
Range: Uncommon to fairly common in dense coniferous or mixed woods. Northwestern portion of range is expanding rapidly; now overlaps and has hybridized with similar Spotted Owl. Accidental to Colorado and New Mexico.

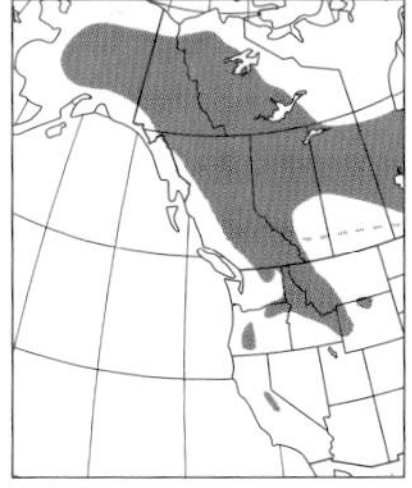

Great Gray Owl *Strix nebulosa L 27" (69 cm)*
Our largest owl. Heavily ringed facial disks make the yellow eyes look small. Lacks ear tufts. Hunts over forest clearings and nearby open country, chiefly by night but also at dawn and dusk; hunts by day during summer in northern part of range.
Voice: Call, heard in breeding season, is a series of deep, resonant *whoo* notes.
Range: Inhabits boreal forests and wooded bogs in the far north, dense coniferous forests with meadows in the mountains farther south. Generally rare to uncommon. Casual to western British Columbia and Washington.

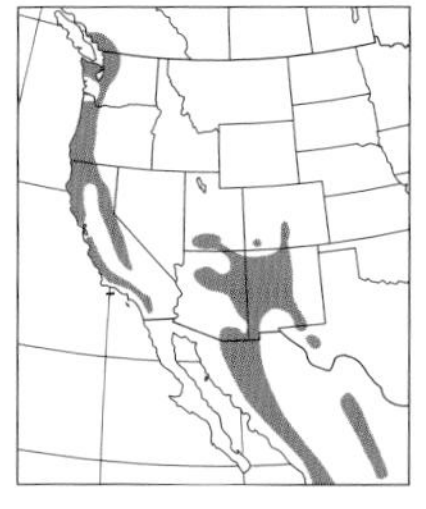

Spotted Owl *Strix occidentalis L 18" (46 cm)*
Large and dark-eyed; white spotting on head, back, and underparts, rather than the barring and streaking of similar Barred Owl. Tamer than Barred, with which it hybridizes. Strictly nocturnal.
Voice: Main call is four doglike barks and cries; contact call, given mainly by females, is a hollow, upslurred whistle, *coooo-weep.*
Range: Inhabits wooded canyons, humid forests. Uncommon; decreasing in number and range due to habitat destruction, especially in the Northwest. The threatened northern race, *caurina* (**T**), is the largest and darkest race, with smaller white spots. The nominate race of central and southern California is paler. Southwestern *lucida* is paler still and more boldly spotted with white.

Snowy Owl *Bubo scandiacus L 23" (58 cm)*
Large white owl, with rounded head and yellow eyes. Dark bars and spots are heavier on females, heaviest on ***immatures;*** old males may be pure white. Preys chiefly on lemmings, hunting by day as well as at night.
Voice: Mostly silent away from breeding site.
Range: An owl of open tundra; nests on the ground. Retreats from northernmost part of range in winter; at least a few are seen annually to limit indicated by dashed line on map. In years when the lemming population plummets, may wander in winter in numbers to southern Canada and norther tier of states; causally as far south as central California and eastern Colorado. These irruptives, usually heavily barred younger birds, often perch conspicuously on the ground or on low stumps, fence posts, and buildings.

Barred Owl
dark eyes
barred breast
vertical streaks
huge size
dark rings on facial disk
black and white at bottom of facial disk gives "bow tie" effect
Great Gray Owl
nebulosa
Spotted Owl
dark eyes
color varies from
kest (Northwest) to
palest (Southwest)
spotted below, including on breast
Snowy Owl
immature
round head
color varies from all-white to heavily barred depending on age and sex

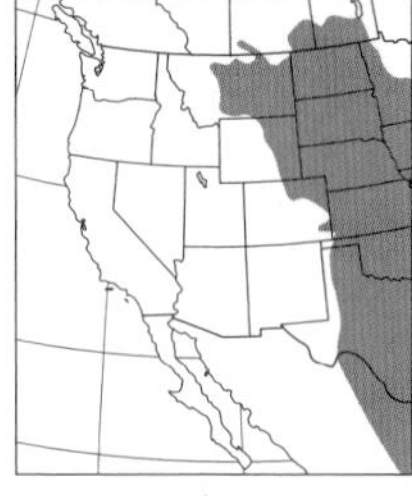

Eastern Screech-Owl *Megascops asio L 8½" (22 cm)*
All three owl species shown on this page are small, with yellow eyes and pale bill tip; bill base is yellow-green on Eastern and Whiskered Screech-Owls and blackish or dark gray on Western. Ear tufts prominent if raised; when flattened, bird has a round-headed look. Underparts on all three are marked by vertical streaks crossed by dark bars: On Eastern, crossbars are spaced well apart and are nearly as wide as vertical streaks; on Western crossbars are closer together and much narrower; Whiskered is like Eastern, but markings have a bolder look. These markings are less distinct on Eastern ***rufous morph;*** the latter predominates in the South; ***gray morph*** on the Great Plains and in the Trans-Pecos, Texas. Lightest and whitest, the *maxwelliae* race is found in the northwestern part of the range; darker *mccallii* is found in eastern and southern portions of Trans-Pecos. Nocturnal; best located and identified by voice.
Voice: Two typical calls: a series of quavering whistles, descending in pitch; and a long single trill, all on one pitch. Sometimes may be heard calling inside roost hole at dawn.
Range: Uncommon in a variety of habitats: woodlots, forests, parks, and suburban gardens. Formerly classified with Western Screech-Owl as one species; range separation is not yet fully known. Both species are found at Big Bend National Park in Texas: Eastern is rare and may not have been recorded recently. Accidental to Alberta and southeastern New Mexico (Roswell).

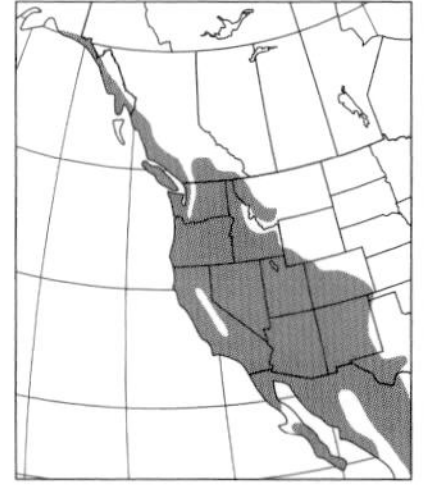

Western Screech-Owl *Megascops kennicottii*
L 8½" (22 cm) Generally gray overall; some birds in the humid coastal Northwest are brownish. Nocturnal; best located and identified by voice. Bill is darker and crossbars are weaker than Eastern Screech-Owl.
Voice: Two common calls: a series of short whistles accelerating in tempo; and a short trill followed immediately by a longer trill, both on the same pitch.
Range: Rare to common in open woodlands, streamside groves, deserts, suburban areas, and parks. Where range overlaps that of Whiskered Screech-Owl, the Western Screech-Owl is generally found at lower elevations.

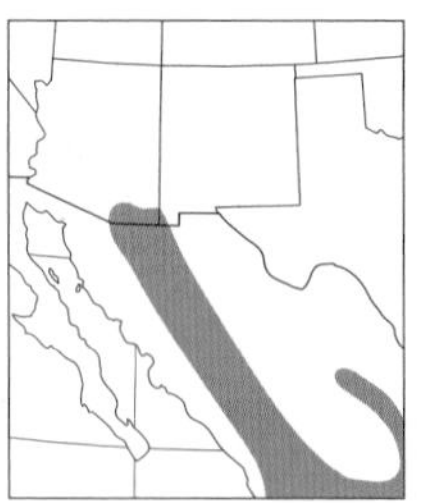

Whiskered Screech-Owl *Megascops trichopsis*
L 7¼" (18 cm) Closely resembles gray Western Screech-Owl but slightly smaller with smaller feet and usually bolder crossbars, similar to Eastern. Nocturnal. Identification best done by voice.
Voice: Two common calls: a series of short whistles on one pitch and at a fairly even tempo; and a series of very irregular hoots, like Morse code.
Range: Inhabits dense oak and oak-conifer woodlands, at elevations from 4,000 to 6,000 feet, but mostly found around 5,000 feet. Generally at higher elevations than Western Screech-Owl.

Eastern Screech-Owl
rufous morph essentially unknown from West
ear tufts
yellow eyes
rufous morph
pale greenish bill
gray morph
strong vertical and horizontal bars on underparts
gray-morph juvenile
overall pale
western Great Plains
maxwelliae
northwest coast
kennicottii
dark bill
weaker crossbars
Whiskered Screech-Owl
aspersus
Western Screech-Owl
dark bill
strong crossbars like Eastern Screech-Owl
small feet

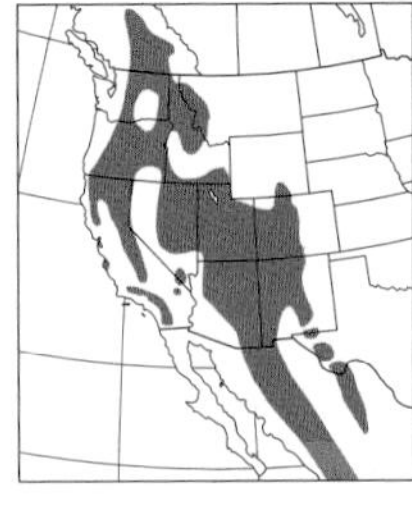

Flammulated Owl *Otus flammeolus* *L 6¾" (17 cm)*
Dark eyes; small ear tufts, often indistinct; variegated red and gray plumage. Birds in the northwestern part of the range are the most finely marked; those in the Great Basin mountains are ***grayish*** and have the coarsest markings; and those breeding in the Southeast are ***reddish.*** Strictly nocturnal.
Voice: Best located at night by its call, heard on the breeding grounds, a series of single or paired low, hoarse, hollow hoots.
Range: Common in oak and pine woodlands, especially ponderosa. Nests and roosts in tree cavities. Highly migratory. Rare in interior lowlands during migration, but likely overlooked.

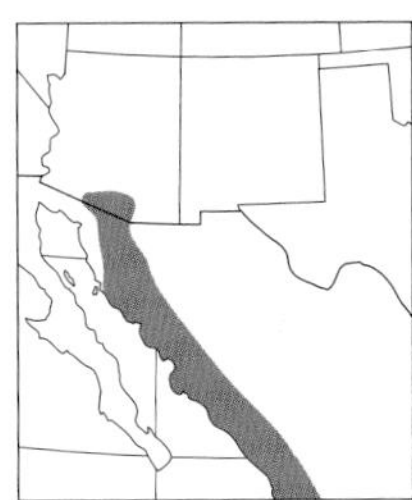

Ferruginous Pygmy-Owl *Glaucidium brasilianum* *L 6¾" (17 cm)* Long tail, reddish with dark or dusky bars. Upperparts gray-brown; crown faintly streaked. Eyes yellow; black nape spots look like eyes on the back of the head. White underparts streaked with reddish brown. Unlike other North American owls, pygmy-owls fly with quick, unmuffled wingbeats. Chiefly diurnal; active any time of day.
Voice: Most common call is a rapid, repeated *took.*
Range: Inhabits saguaro deserts at low elevations in southern Arizona. Roosts in crevices and cavities. Now rare and local, this grayer subspecies (*cactorum*) is considered endangered (**E**).

Elf Owl *Micrathene whitneyi* *L 5¾" (15 cm)*
Our smallest owl. Yellow eyes; very short tail. Lacks ear tufts. Strictly nocturnal; roosts and nests in cavities in saguaros and trees.
Voice: Call, heard on the breeding grounds, is an irregular series of high *churp* notes and chattering notes.
Range: Uncommon to common in desert lowlands and in foothill canyons, especially among oaks and sycamores. Now almost or actually eliminated from California and Nevada; casual in southwest Utah. Accidental in fall to Los Angeles County.

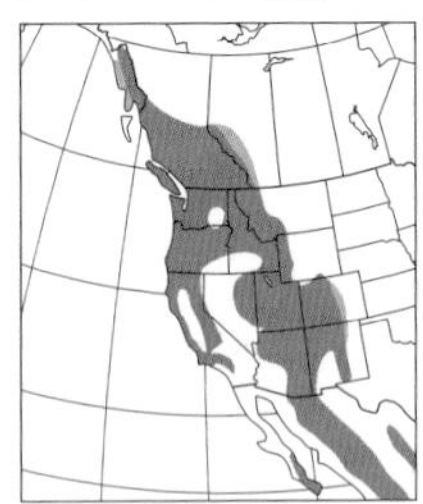

Northern Pygmy-Owl *Glaucidium gnoma* *L 6¾" (17 cm)*
Long tail, dark brown with pale bars. Upperparts are either rusty brown or gray-brown; crown spotted; underparts white with dark streaks. Eyes yellow; black nape spots look like eyes on the back of the head. The grayest birds are to be found in the Rockies; those on the Pacific coast as far north as British Columbia are browner. An aggressive predator, this owl is a favorite target for songbirds. Birders may locate the owl by watching for mobbing songbirds. Chiefly diurnal; most active at dawn and dusk.
Voice: Call is a mellow, whistled, *hoo* or *hoo hoo,* repeated in a well-spaced series; also gives a rapid series of *hoo* or *took* notes followed by a single *took*. Call varies geographically. Nominate race, *gnoma,* seen from southeastern Arizona and extreme southwest New Mexico south through the mountains of Mexico, gives a series of double *took-took* notes with occasional single notes interspersed; considered by some to be a separate species "Mountain Pygmy-Owl," though no marked genetic differences.
Range: Inhabits woodlands in foothills and mountains. Nests in cavities. Casual to Chisos Mountains, Texas.

reddish
type
Southwest
birds often
more reddish
short ears are
often indistinct
dark eyes
grayish
type
Flammulated
Owl
rounded head
with no ear tufts
streaked
crown
Ferruginous
Pygmy-Owl
cactorum
"false eye"
Elf
Owl
whitneyi
yellow eyes
tiny size
very
short
tail
long tail
with rusty bars
spotted
crown
"false eye"
Northern
Pygmy-Owl
Rockies
type
averages grayer
than birds from
Pacific region
Pacific coast
type
long tail
with pale bars

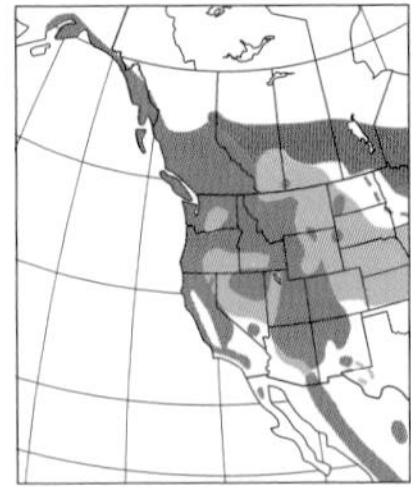

Northern Saw-whet Owl *Aegolius acadicus L 8" (20 cm)*
Reddish brown above; white below with reddish streaks; bill dark; facial disks reddish, without dark border. ***Juvenile*** dark brown above, tawny rust below. Strictly nocturnal. Once found, can be closely approached. A distinctive subspecies, *brooksi*, endemic to Queen Charlotte Islands, British Columbia, much darker and buffier on facial disks and belly.
Voice: Call, heard primarily in breeding season from late winter to late spring, a monotonously repeated single-note whistle; another call sounds raspy, like a saw being sharpened; also gives a rising screech.
Range: Inhabits dense coniferous or mixed forests, wooded swamps, and tamarack bogs. Roosts during day in or near nest hole in breeding season. In winter, preferred roost is in dense evergreens, usually close to end of branch. Large concentrations of regurgitated pellets and "whitewash" build up below favored winter roosts. Very rare over most of winter range; casual in fall and winter in southwestern deserts.

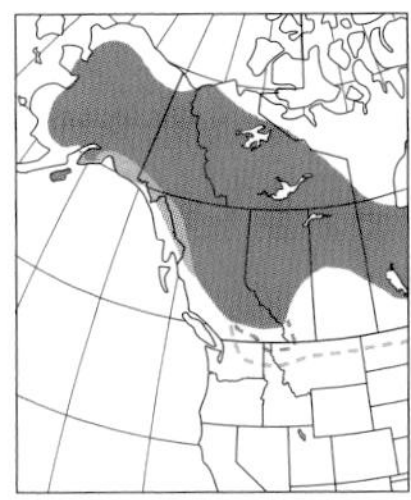

Northern Hawk Owl *Surnia ulula L 16" (41 cm)*
Long tail, falconlike profile, and black-bordered facial disks identify this owl of the northern forests. Underparts are barred with brown. Flight is low and swift; sometimes hunts during daylight as well as at night. Is most often seen, however, perched high in a spruce tree. Usually can be closely approached.
Voice: Mostly silent away from nesting sites.
Range: Mostly nonmigratory, but somewhat irruptive and retreats slightly in winter from northernmost part of range. Casual south to central Oregon.

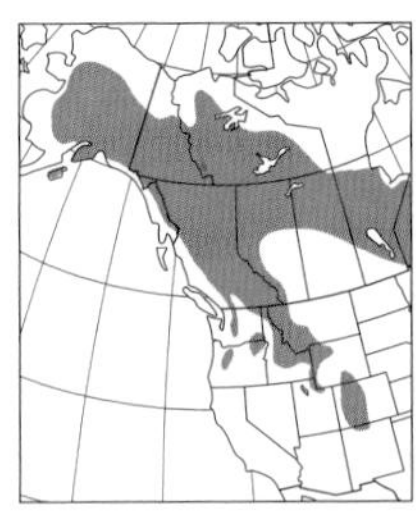

Boreal Owl *Aegolius funereus L 10" (25 cm)*
White underparts streaked with chocolate brown. Whitish facial disk has a distinct black border; bill is pale. Darker above than Northern Saw-whet Owl. ***Juvenile*** is chocolate brown below. Strictly nocturnal.
Voice: Call, heard primarily in breeding season from late winter to midspring, is a short, rapid series of hollow *hoo* notes.
Range: Inhabits dense northern forests, muskeg. Breeds at isolated locations in spruce and fir forests high in the Rockies. Roosts during daylight in dense cover, usually close to tree trunk.

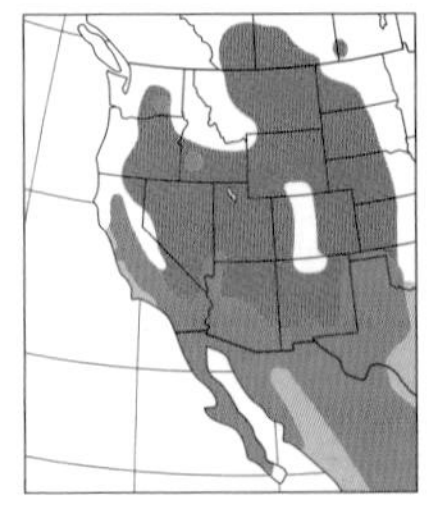

Burrowing Owl *Athene cunicularia L 9½" (24 cm)*
Long legs distinguish this ground dweller from all other small owls. Adult is boldly spotted and barred. ***Juvenile*** is buffy below. Nocturnal; flight low and undulating; often hovers like a kestrel.
Voice: Calls include a soft *coo-coooo* and a chattering series of *chack* notes. Disturbed in its nest, often gives an alarm call that imitates the sound of a rattlesnake.
Range: An owl of open country. Perches conspicuously during daylight at entrance to burrow nest or on low post. Nests in single pairs or small colonies. Declining in much of northern Great Plains; may be partly due to destruction of prairie dog towns, which it frequents. Also declining in many other parts of West.

Northern Saw-whet Owl
acadicus
no dark border to facial disk
dark bill
rufous overall coloration
juvenile
black border to facial disk
Northern Hawk Owl
caparoch
dark barring on underparts
long tail
prominent black border to facial disk
pale bill
Boreal Owl
richardsoni
juvenile
darker body coloration than juvenile Northern Saw-whet
round head
Burrowing Owl
western hypugaea
juvenile
heavily spotted with white above
no dark barring below

Goatsuckers (Family Caprimulgidae)

Wide mouths help these night hunters snare flying insects. Most are located and identified by their distinctive calls.

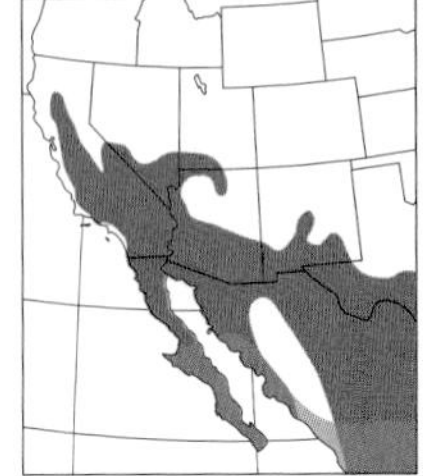

Lesser Nighthawk *Chordeiles acutipennis L 8½" (22 cm)*
Resembles Common Nighthawk but wings shorter and usually more rounded; whitish bar across primaries slightly closer to tip. Upperparts paler and more uniformly mottled; in Common paler wing coverts contrast more with back. Throat is white in ***males,*** usually buffy in ***females*** and juveniles. Underparts buffy, with faint barring. Male has white tail band. Female lacks tail band; note buffy wing bar and markings at base of primaries, often indistinct in juvenile female. Juvenile male's wing bar much smaller. Seen chiefly around dusk. Flies with a fluttery wingbeat.
Voice: Distinctive call, a rapid, tremulous trill, heard only on breeding grounds.
Range: Fairly common; found in dry, open country, scrubland, washes, desert. Rare to casual in winter in southern California. Accidental visitor north to British Columbia, northwest Alaska.

Common Nighthawk *Chordeiles minor L 9½" (24 cm)*
Wings long and pointed; tail slightly forked. Bold white bar across primaries slightly farther from wing tip than Lesser Nighthawk. Subspecies range from dark brown in eastern birds to more grayish in the northern Great Plains race, *sennetti;* color variations are subtle in adults, distinct in juveniles. Throat white in ***male,*** buffy in female; underparts whitish, with bold dusky bars. Female lacks white tail band. ***Juvenile*** shows less white on throat. More active in daylight than other goatsuckers
Voice: Nasal *peent* call distinguishes Common from Lesser. In courtship display, male's wings make a hollow booming sound.
Range: Seen in woodlands, suburbs, and towns. Roosts on the ground, on branches, posts, and roofs. Fairly common over parts of range. Casual migrant nearly throughout Alaska and in southern California away from limited nesting areas.

IDENTIFYING: Common and Lesser Nighthawks In the West, Common and Lesser Nighthawks occur together in many regions, particularly at moderate elevations in the Southwest and lower elevations in the southern Great Basin, and can routinely be seen feeding together. While Common is much more migratory overall, breeding far north into Canada and wintering in South America, it is almost unknown as a migrant in the lowlands of the Southwest or the coastal regions of central and southern California. It arrives very late, not until May or even the first or second week of June over much of the West. Lesser is less migratory but is regular to California's Channel Islands as a stray. (There is even a specimen from northwest Alaska.) It arrives much earlier in southern California and southern Arizona: late Mar. in some areas, by mid-Apr. in most others. While most Lessers winter south of the U.S.-Mexico border, a very few winter in southern California.

Molt timing differs between the two species. Unlike Commons, which only molt on their winter grounds in South America, adult Lessers start molting flight feathers by midsummer on their breeding grounds. Therefore, any nighthawk seen in North America showing such molt is automat-

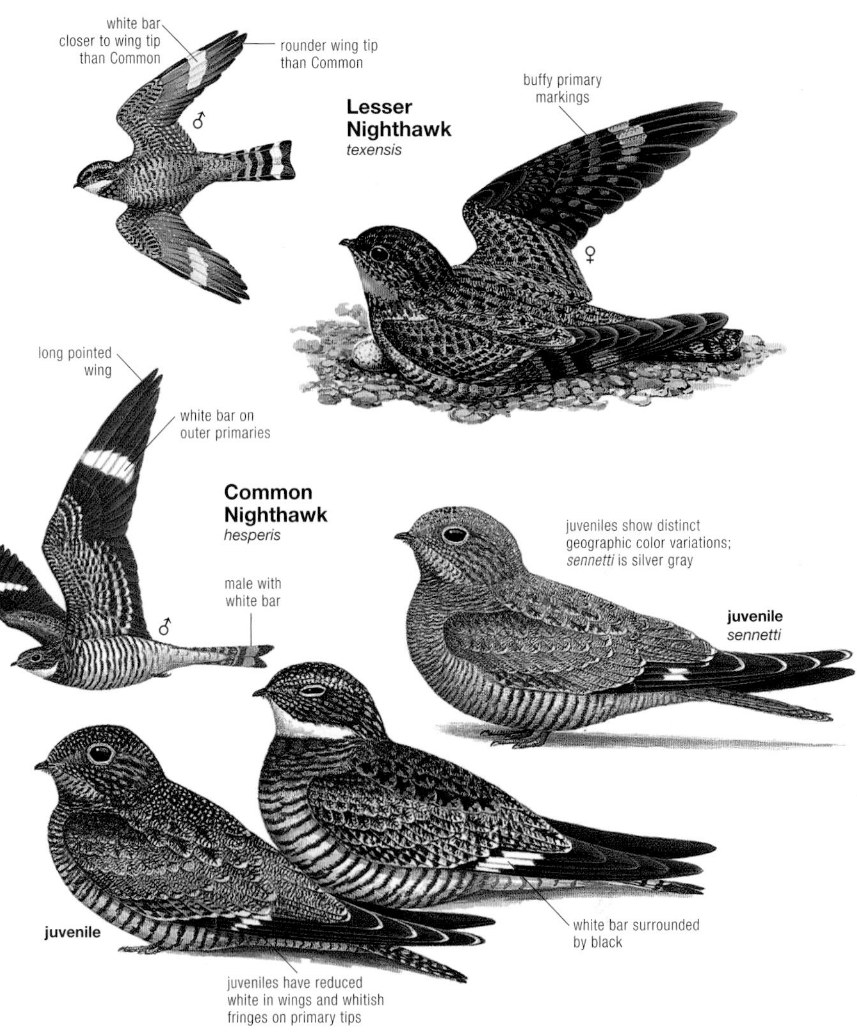

ically a Lesser. Smaller and less contrastingly patterned, Lesser is rounder winged and appears to have a broader "arm" and a shorter, rounder "hand." The pale wing patch is white only on males; it's more buffy on females and seemingly absent on many juveniles. In Lesser, this patch is closer to the wing tip, with many buffy markings just inside of the patch; this area of the wing is dark in Common. Lesser's flight is usually more fluttery and lower to the ground than Common, which often flies quite high and seems to have a stronger and more clipped wingstroke.

Only one subspecies of Lesser occurs north of Mexico, *texensis*. Common shows extensive geographic variation, particularly in the West. These differences are most evident in juveniles (below): Within the West, nominate *minor,* the widespread eastern subspecies, breeds in northwest Canada, possibly eastern Alaska (a fall specimen from California is likely this race); it is the darkest. Somewhat paler is *hesperis* of the Pacific region. The Great Plains subspecies, *sennetti,* is quite pale, almost silver-gray. The Rockies and eastern Great Basin race, *howeli,* is quite buffy. Finally, *henryi,* breeding from the Four Corners region south to western Mexico, is quite richly rufous.

Whip-poor-will *Caprimulgus vociferus* *L* 9¾" (25 cm)
Mottled gray-brown overall; wings rounded; tail long, rounded. Larger and longer tailed than Common Poorwill. Lacks buff collar of Buff-collared Nightjar, which is paler overall. Dark throat contrasts with white or buffy "necklace" and pale underparts. ***Male***'s tail shows extensive white on outer tail feathers; in nominate eastern *vociferus,* white averages more extensive. ***Female***'s tail has buffy tips to outer tail feathers. Southwestern birds, unlike nominate *vociferus,* usually roost on ground and do not allow close approach.

Voice: Song is a loud *whip-poor-will,* rough and burry in southwestern breeding race *arizonae.* This and five other subspecies in the mountains of northern Middle America with like vocalizations probably constitute a different species. Eastern *vociferus* gives a clear-sounding song. Both groups give single *quip* notes when flushed.

Range: Fairly common (*arizonae*) in wooded canyons in mountains of the Southwest. Also breeds rarely and very locally in mountains of southern California and southern Nevada (Sheep Range). Singing *arizonae* recorded in summer north to northwestern California and El Paso County in Colorado. Casual migrant in lowlands. Nominate eastern race (*vociferus*) is a casual migrant to eastern Colorado. Accidental to southern Arizona, southeast Alaska, and possibly San Diego, California.

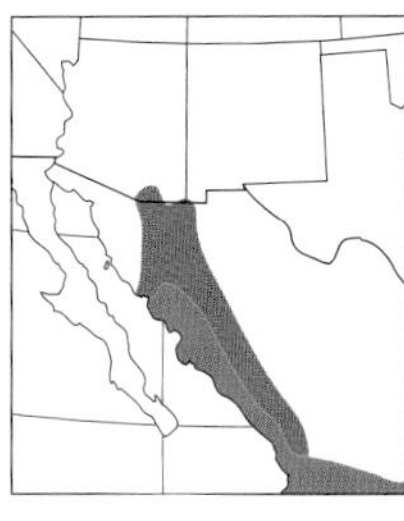

Buff-collared Nightjar *Caprimulgus ridgwayi*
L 8¾" (22 cm) Gray-brown plumage resembles Whip-poor-will, which breeds in higher elevations in wooded mountains, but is lighter and more finely marked. Buff-collared shows distinct buff collar across nape.

Voice: Song is an accelerating series of *cuk* notes ending with *cukacheea.*

Range: Rare, irregular, and local in desert canyons of extreme southwestern New Mexico (Guadalupe Canyon) and especially southeastern Arizona. Accidental in southern California (Ventura County). Usually roosts on the ground by day.

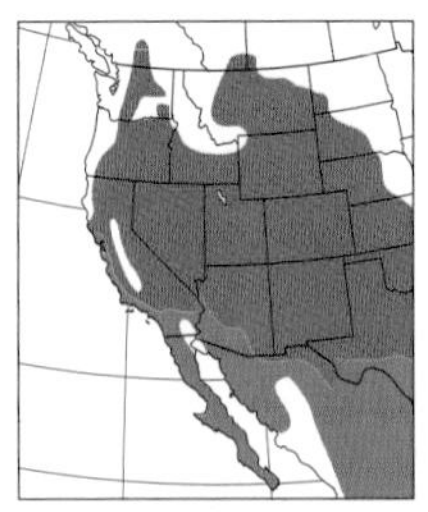

Common Poorwill *Phalaenoptilus nuttallii* *L* 7¾" (20 cm)
Our smallest nightjar, distinguished by short, rounded tail and short, rounded wings. Outer tail feathers are tipped with white, more boldly in ***males*** than females. Plumage is variable; upperparts range from brownish gray to pale gray. Broad white band crosses dark throat and breast. Often seen on roads or roadsides after dusk or before dawn. Flies up a short distance to catch an insect, then returns to the same or a nearby location.

Voice: Song is a whistled *poor-will,* with a final *ip* note audible at close range. Gives soft *cluck* notes year-round.

Range: Fairly common in sagebrush, and on chaparral and rocky slopes. Roosts on the ground. Known to hibernate in cold weather; may winter north into breeding range. Fall migration appears to take place in late Sept. and early Oct., though infrequently recorded.

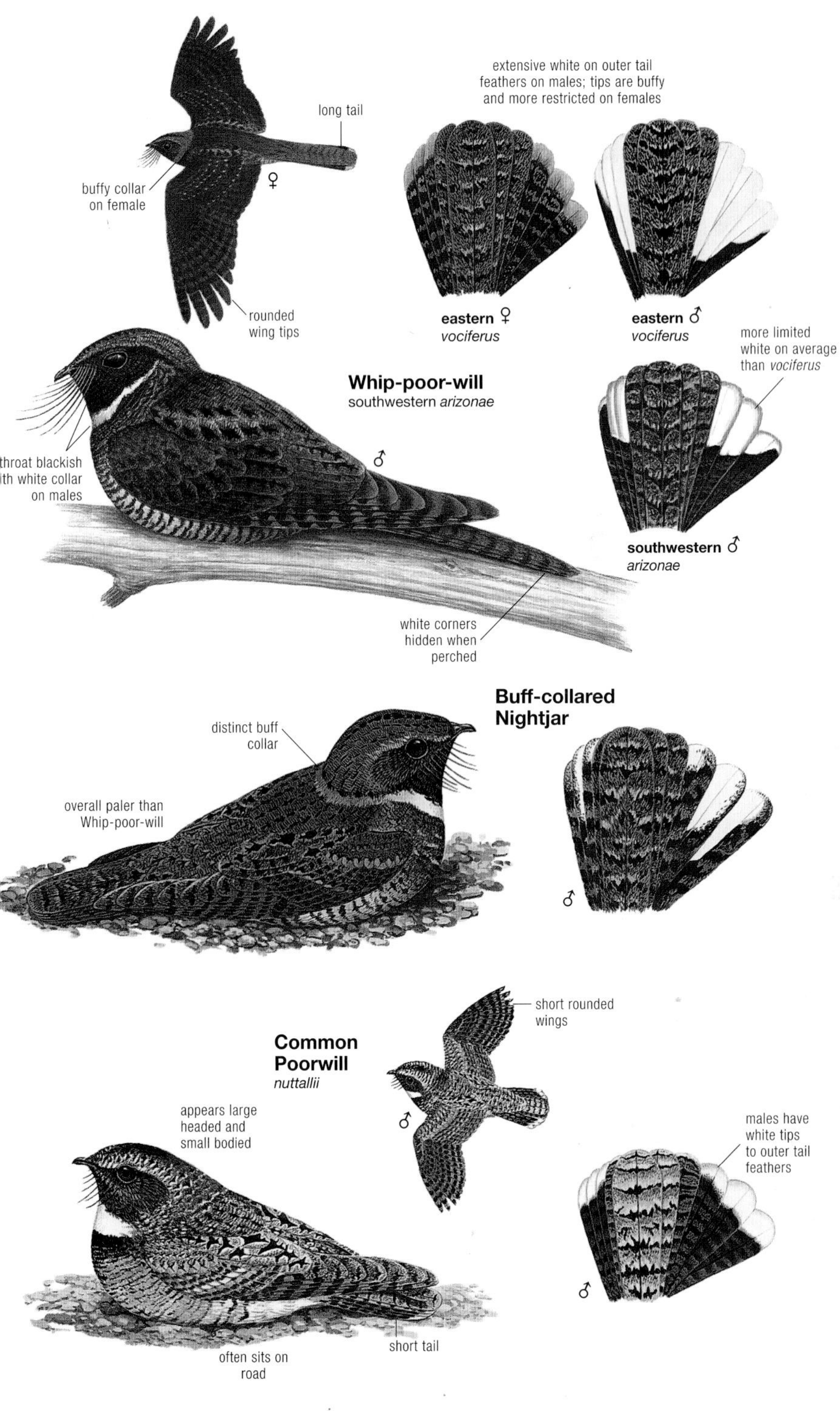
long tail
buffy collar on female
♀
rounded wing tips
extensive white on outer tail feathers on males; tips are buffy and more restricted on females
eastern ♀ vociferus
eastern ♂ vociferus
more limited white on average than vociferus
Whip-poor-will
southwestern arizonae
throat blackish
th white collar
on males
♂
southwestern ♂ arizonae
white corners hidden when perched
Buff-collared Nightjar
distinct buff collar
overall paler than Whip-poor-will
♂
short rounded wings
Common Poorwill
nuttallii
♂
appears large headed and small bodied
males have white tips to outer tail feathers
♂
short tail
often sits on road

Swifts (Family Apodidae)

These fast-flying birds spend the day aloft. Their wings bend closer to their body than swallows.

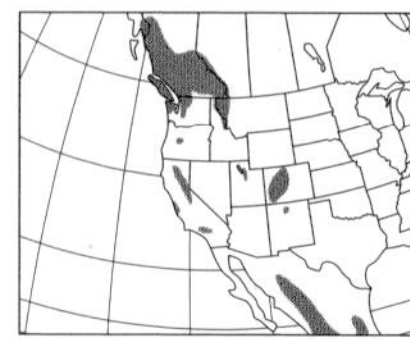

Black Swift *Cypseloides niger L 7¼" (18 cm)*
Blackish overall; long, slightly forked tail, often fanned in flight. Wingbeats rather more leisurely than other swifts; often soars.
Voice: Usually silent, except near nest.
Range: Nests in colonies on cliffs, beneath waterfalls; also wet sea cliffs. Uncommon. Rare in migration. Winters in South America.

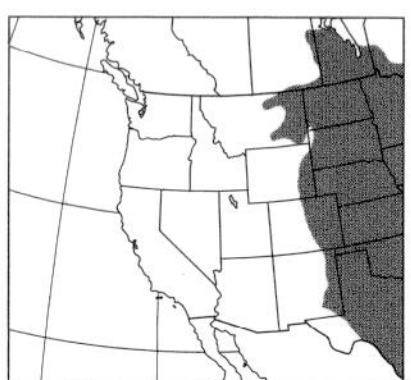

Chimney Swift *Chaetura pelagica L 5¼" (13 cm)*
Cigar-shaped body; short, stubby tail. Larger and usually darker below than similar Vaux's; longer wings, greater tendency to soar.
Voice: Chittering call much louder than Vaux's.
Range: Nests in towns. Uncommon in towns on Plains; very rare west to California; accidental to Northwest Territories and Alaska. Winters in South America.

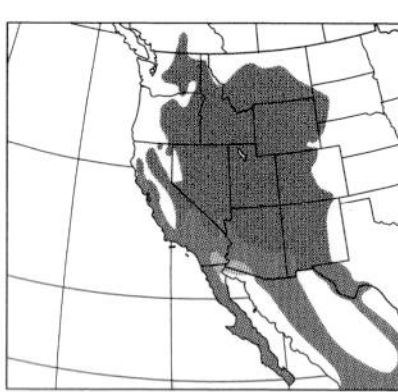

White-throated Swift *Aeronautes saxatalis L 6½" (17 cm)*
Black above, black-and-white below, with long, forked tail. Distinguished from Violet-green Swallow (page 288) by longer, narrower wings, bicolored underparts. In poor light, may be mistaken for Black Swift but is smaller, with faster wingbeats.
Voice: Call is a descending harsh chatter.
Range: Locally common in mountains, canyons, and cliffs.

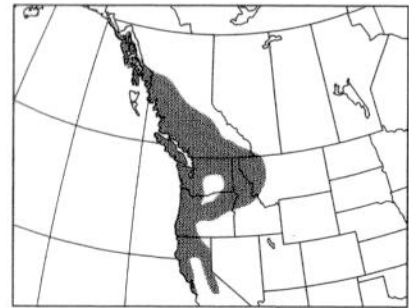

Vaux's Swift *Chaetura vauxi L 4¾" (12 cm)*
Smaller than Chimney Swift; usually paler below and on rump.
Voice: Call softer, higher and more insectlike.
Range: Fairly common in woodlands. Most nest in hollow trees. Rare in winter in southern California. In migration, regular to western Nevada and Arizona.

Hummingbirds (Family Trochilidae)

These birds hover at flowers to sip nectar with needlelike bills. Often identified by twittery calls. Males' throat feathers (gorget) look black in poor light.

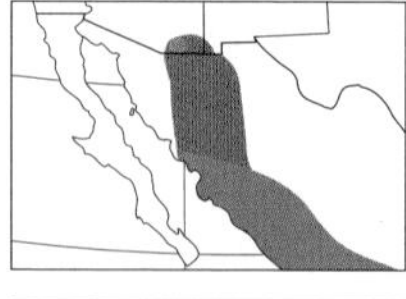

Violet-crowned Hummingbird *Amazilia violiceps L 4½" (11 cm)* Crown violet; underparts entirely white; upperparts bronze green; tail greenish. Long bill is mostly red.
Voice: Call is a loud chattering; song is a series of sibilant *ts* notes.
Range: Uncommon. Casual in California and west Texas.

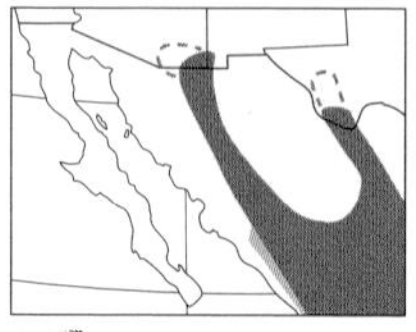

Lucifer Hummingbird *Calothorax lucifer L 3½" (9 cm)*
Bill downcurved. ***Adult male*** has green crown, purple throat, long tail. ***Female*** is rich buff below; broadening pale stripe behind eye; outer tail feathers reddish at base.
Range: Uncommon; rare in southeastern Arizona and southwestern New Mexico and Davis Mountains of west Texas.

soars more than other North American swifts
Black Swift
borealis
white scaling visible at close range; retained through fall migration
juvenile
adult
broader rear and tail than White-throated
soaring
darkish rump, more uniform with upperparts than Vaux's
cigar-shaped body
short tail
Chimney Swift
sooty brown underparts
white flank patches
long pointed tail
white throat, but white here and elsewhere often not visible at a distance, especially in poor light
extensively white below, slender body
White-throated Swift
saxatalis
white secondary tips
Vaux's Swift
vauxi
contrasting rump paler than rest of upperparts
short tail
dark auricular contrasts more with pale underparts than Chimney
smaller and paler below than Chimney; calls are diagnostic
pale postocular gradually broadens to sides of neck
adult ♂
violet crown; duller on juveniles
rich buff
red-based bill
immature ♂
all with long curved bill and purplish throat
adult ♂
striking snowy white underparts
Lucifer Hummingbird
Violet-crowned Hummingbird
ellioti
limited rufous
♀
♀
long tail extends past folded wings
very long pointed tail; fork not usually visible when bird is perched

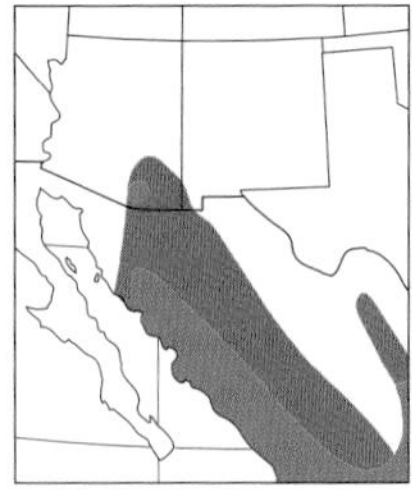

Broad-billed Hummingbird *Cynanthus latirostris*
L 4" (10 cm) ***Adult male*** is dark green above and below, with white undertail coverts, blue gorget, and mostly red bill. Broad, forked tail is blackish blue. ***Adult female*** is duller above, gray below; often shows a narrow white eye stripe; tail more square-tipped. Juvenile resembles female; by late summer, juvenile male begins to show blue and green flecks on throat, green on sides; dark, tail shape helps distinguish it from White-eared Hummingbird.
Voice: Chattering *je-dit* call is similar to Ruby-crowned Kinglet. Male's display call is a whining *zing.*
Range: Common in desert canyons and low mountain woodlands. Very rare in west Texas and to southern California during fall and winter; casual north to Oregon, Idaho, and Colorado.

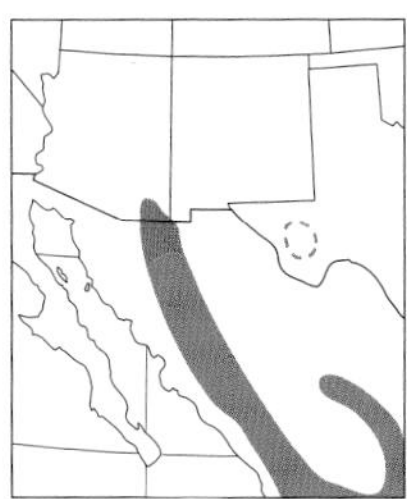

White-eared Hummingbird *Hylocharis leucotis*
L 3¾" (10 cm) Bill shorter than Broad-billed Hummingbird; broad white stripe extends back from eye; has black ear patch, square tail. ***Adult male*** has dark purple crown and chin, emerald green gorget.
Voice: Display call is a repeated, silvery *tink tink tink.* Chattering calls are loud and metallic.
Range: Summer visitor to mountains of Southwest: rare in southeastern Arizona; very rare in southwestern New Mexico and west Texas; accidental to Colorado.

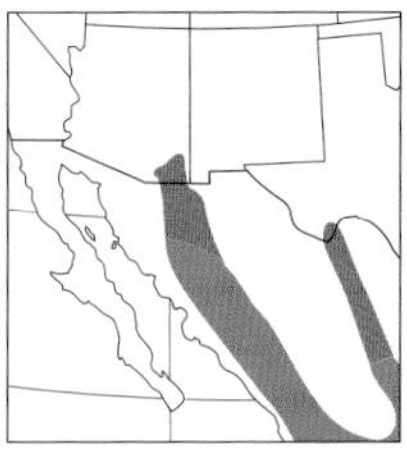

Blue-throated Hummingbird *Lampornis clemenciae*
L 5" (13 cm) ***Adult male***'s throat is blue, ***female***'s gray. Broad white eye stripe and faint white malar stripe border dark ear patch. Outer tail has broad white tips.
Voice: Male's call is a loud, high, repeated *seep.*
Range: Uncommon; found in mountain canyons, especially near streams. Casual north and east of mapped range north to Colorado; accidental to central California.

Berylline Hummingbird *Amazilia beryllina L 4¼" (11 cm)*
Green above and below; chestnut wings, rump, and tail. Base of lower mandible red. ***Male***'s lower belly chestnut, ***female***'s grayish.
Voice: Gives dry, hard buzzy notes. Male's song, lispy, twittering.
Range: Very rare summer visitor from Mexico to mountains of southeastern Arizona; has bred there. Casual to southwestern New Mexico and west Texas.

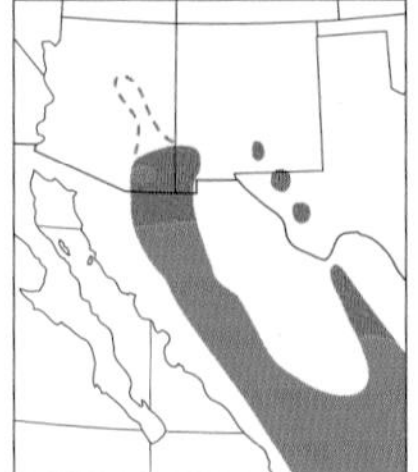

Magnificent Hummingbird *Eugenes fulgens*
L 5¼" (13 cm) ***Adult male*** is green above, with purple crown; metallic green throat; breast and upper belly black and green; lower belly dull brown. Tail is dark green and deeply notched. ***Female*** is duller, lacks purple crown; squarish tail has small, grayish white tips on outer feathers; compare to female Blue-throated Hummingbird, which has stronger eyebrow, much broader white tail tips.
Voice: Main call is a sharp *chip.*
Range: Fairly common in mountains. Casual away from mapped range, north to northern California and Wyoming.

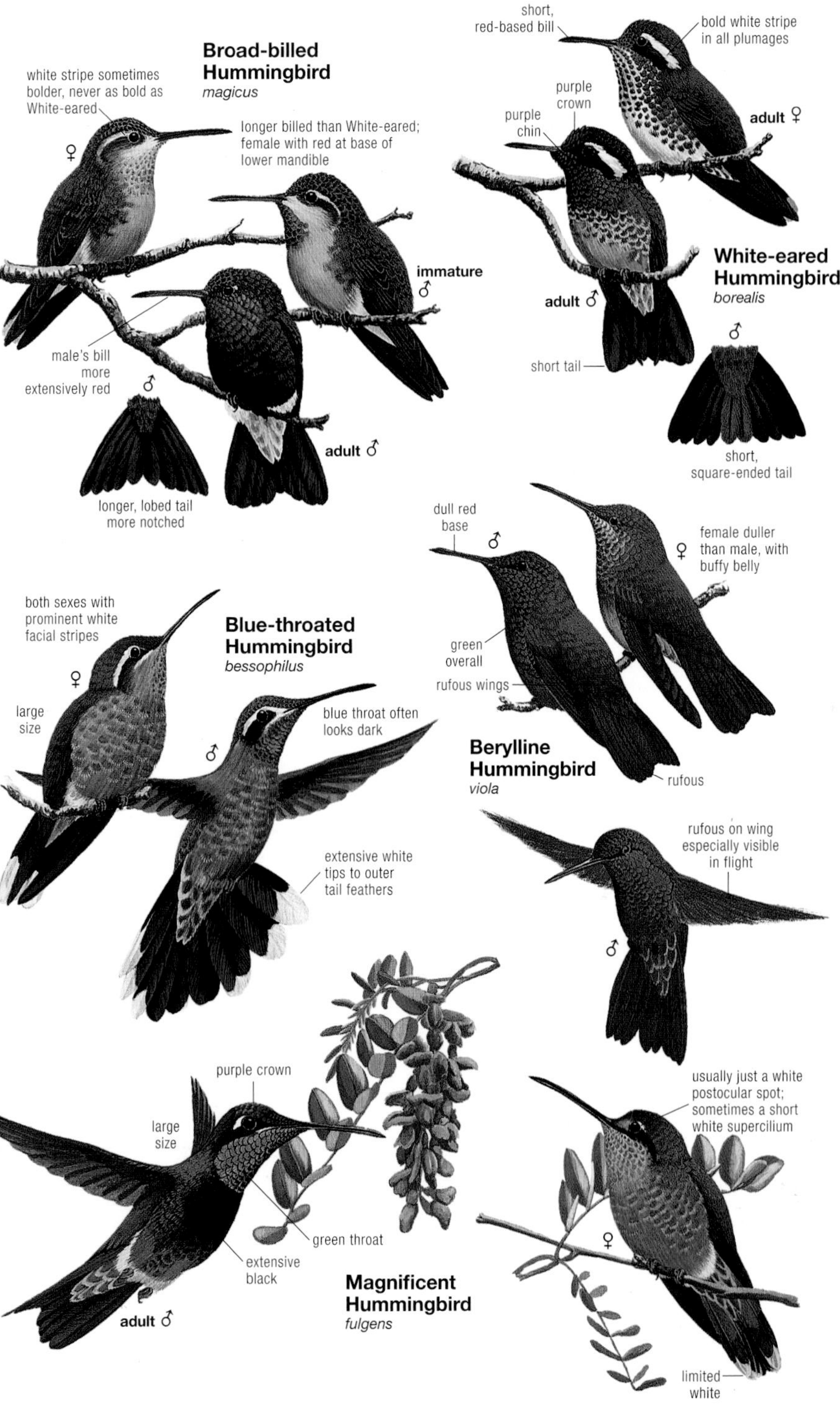
Broad-billed Hummingbird
magicus
white stripe sometimes bolder, never as bold as White-eared
♀
longer billed than White-eared; female with red at base of lower mandible
immature ♂
male's bill more extensively red
♂
adult ♂
longer, lobed tail more notched
short, red-based bill
bold white stripe in all plumages
purple crown
purple chin
adult ♀
White-eared Hummingbird
borealis
adult ♂
short tail
♂
short, square-ended tail
dull red base
♂
♀
female duller than male, with buffy belly
green overall
rufous wings
Berylline Hummingbird
viola
rufous
rufous on wing especially visible in flight
♂
both sexes with prominent white facial stripes
Blue-throated Hummingbird
bessophilus
♀
large size
♂
blue throat often looks dark
extensive white tips to outer tail feathers
purple crown
large size
green throat
extensive black
adult ♂
Magnificent Hummingbird
fulgens
usually just a white postocular spot; sometimes a short white supercilium
♀
limited white

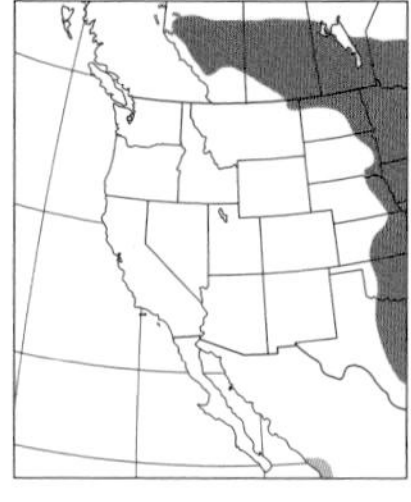

Ruby-throated Hummingbird *Archilochus colubris*
L 3¾" (10 cm) The only hummingbird regularly seen throughout most of the East. Metallic green above. ***Adult male*** has a brilliant red throat (appears black in many lights) and black chin; underparts are whitish; sides and flanks dusky green; tail forked. ***Female***'s throat is whitish; underparts grayish white, with buffy wash on sides; tail is similar to female Black-chinned Hummingbird. Immature resembles adult female. Some ***immature males*** begin to show red spotting on throat by early fall. As with all hummingbirds, adult males migrate earlier than females and immatures. Very difficult to distinguish females and immature males from Black-chinned. Ruby-throated generally has a greener crown, shorter bill; note darker face and more pointed shape of darker primaries, especially the outermost primaries.
Voice: Calls very similar to Black-chinned.
Range: Uncommon migrant on northern Great Plains; casual elsewhere in West, including Alaska.

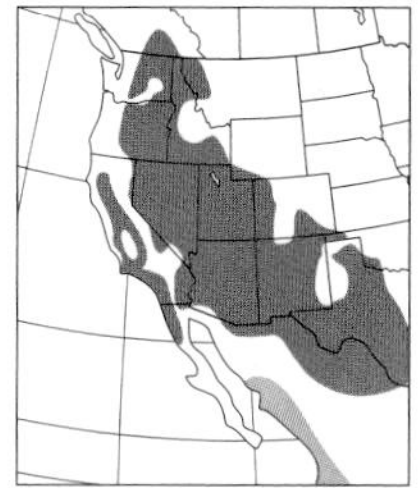

Black-chinned Hummingbird *Archilochus alexandri*
L 3¾" (10 cm) Metallic green above. In good light, ***adult male*** shows violet band at lower border of black throat. Underparts whitish; sides and flanks dusky green. ***Female***'s throat can be all-white or show faint dusky or greenish streaks. Immature resembles adult female; ***immature male*** may begin to show violet on lower throat in the fall. Twitches tail more than Ruby-throated while feeding.
Voice: Call is a soft *tchew;* chase note combines high squeals and *tchew* notes.
Range: Common in lowlands and low mountains.

Costa's Hummingbird *Calypte costae L 3½" (9 cm)*
Adult male has deep violet crown and gorget extending far down sides of neck. ***Female*** is generally grayer above, whiter below, than female Black-chinned Hummingbird; note also tail differences. Best distinguished by voice.
Voice: Call is a high, metallic *tink,* often given in a series. Male's call is a loud *zing.*
Range: Fairly common in desert washes, dry chaparral. Casual north to south coastal Alaska and Montana and east to west Texas.

Anna's Hummingbird *Calypte anna L 4" (10 cm)*
Adult male's head and throat are deep rose red, the color extending a short distance onto sides of neck. ***Female***'s throat usually shows red flecks, often forming a patch of color. In both sexes, underparts are grayish, washed with a varying amount of green. Bill is disproportionately short. Immature resembles female; ***immature male*** usually shows some red on crown. ***Juvenile*** lacks red on throat; compare with smaller female Black-chinned and Costa's Hummingbirds.
Voice: Common call note, a sharp *chick;* chase call is a rapid dry rattling. Male's song is a jumble of high squeaks and raspy notes.
Range: Abundant in coastal lowlands and mountains in California; some in deserts, especially in winter. Rare to New Mexico and west Texas.Casual north to Colorado and to south coastal Alaska.

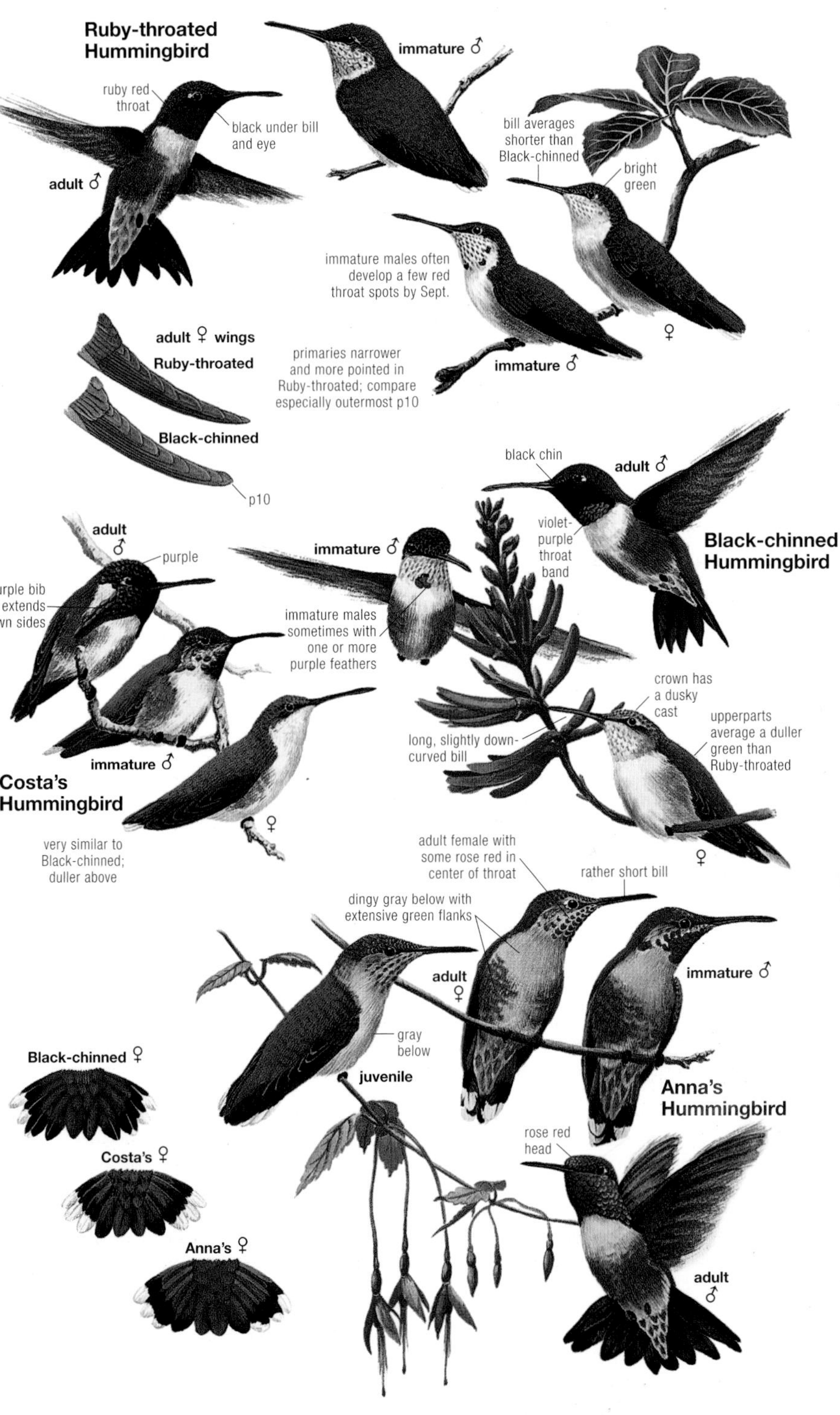
Ruby-throated Hummingbird
ruby red throat
black under bill and eye
adult ♂
immature ♂
bill averages shorter than Black-chinned
bright green
immature males often develop a few red throat spots by Sept.
♀
adult ♀ wings
Ruby-throated
Black-chinned
p10
primaries narrower and more pointed in Ruby-throated; compare especially outermost p10
immature ♂
black chin
adult ♂
violet-purple throat band
Black-chinned Hummingbird
adult ♂
purple
urple bib extends wn sides
immature ♂
immature males sometimes with one or more purple feathers
immature ♂
Costa's Hummingbird
♀
very similar to Black-chinned; duller above
crown has a dusky cast
upperparts average a duller green than Ruby-throated
long, slightly down-curved bill
♀
adult female with some rose red in center of throat
rather short bill
dingy gray below with extensive green flanks
adult ♀
immature ♂
gray below
juvenile
Anna's Hummingbird
Black-chinned ♀
Costa's ♀
Anna's ♀
rose red head
adult ♂

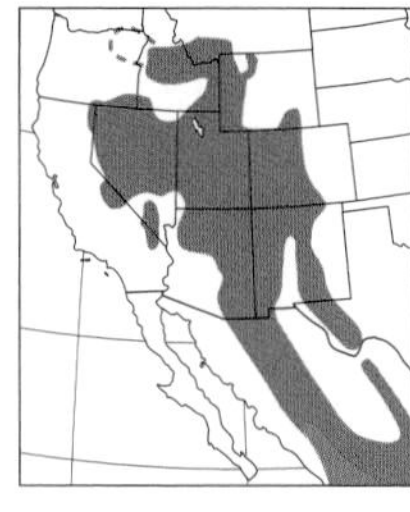

Broad-tailed Hummingbird *Selasphorus platycercus*

L 4" (10 cm) ***Male*** has rose red throat. ***Female*** has blended buff on underparts; similar to smaller, shorter-billed female Calliope, but note tail tip extends well past primaries. Also compare to Rufous and Allen's, which have more rufous in tail.

Voice: Except during winter molt, all *Selasphorus* adult males' wingbeats produce a loud whistle, harsh and trilling in Broad-tailed. Calls include a metallic *chip,* often given in a short series.

Range: Common breeder in Rockies and Great Basin mountain ranges. Casual to coastal southern California and Oregon.

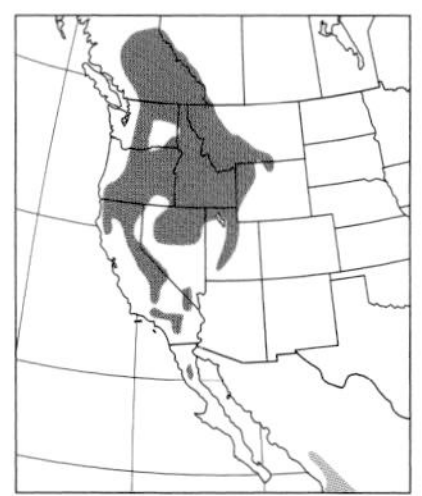

Calliope Hummingbird *Stellula calliope L 3¼" (8 cm)*

Smallest North American bird; very short bill and tail; primary tips extend well past end of tail. Carmine streaks on ***adult male***'s throat form a V-shaped gorget. ***Female***'s underparts similar to female Broad-tailed. Immature male like female but some show some red on throat by late summer.

Voice: Relatively silent. Gives soft high *chip* notes.

Range: Fairly common in summer in mountains. Fall migrant through Rockies region. Rare migrant to coastal California.

Rufous Hummingbird *Selasphorus rufus L 3¾" (10 cm)*

Tail mainly rufous. ***Adult male*** has rufous back, sometimes marked with green, very rarely entirely green; orange-red gorget. ***Immature*** resembles ***adult female;*** immature male may show reddish brown back by winter before acquiring full gorget.

Voice: Buzzy wing whistle and all calls identical to Allen's: Calls include a sibilant *chip,* often given in a series; chase note, *zeee-chup-pity-chup.*

Range: Common fall migrant through Rockies; a few to western Great Plains. Casual in winter in coastal southern California.

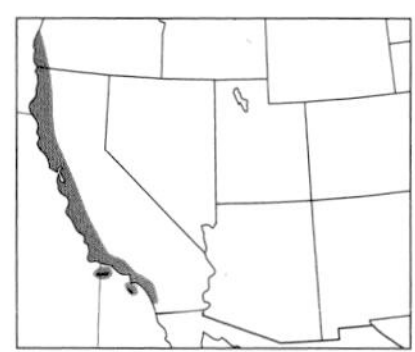

Allen's Hummingbird *Selasphorus sasin L 3¾" (10 cm)*

Adult male has full, orange-red gorget; usually distinguishable from Rufous by solid green back. Adult female and immatures inseparable in the field from female Rufous, though tail feathers are comparatively narrower for each sex and age class.

Voice: Like Rufous Hummingbird.

Range: Allen's migrates earlier in fall and spring than Rufous. Uncommon fall migrant through southeastern Arizona; casual to Nevada, New Mexico, and west Texas. Accidental in Washington.

IDENTIFYING: Calliope and *Selasphorus* Hummingbirds *Selasphorus* hummingbirds (Rufous, Allen's, and Broad-tailed) are similar to Calliope Hummingbirds in female and immature plumages, sharing buffy and greenish upperparts as well as variably rich buff sides and flanks.

Separating Rufous from Allen's is nearly impossible (excepting adult males). Only in-hand measurements of tail feathers of birds of known sex and age are conclusive. (Exceptional photos may also suffice.) One usually just refers to these birds as "Rufous/Allen's," even though Rufous is more likely over most of the West. The "green" standard—a solid green back indicates Allen's—is refuted by a few adult male Rufous specimens with solid green backs. Many others show extensive green flecking or even solid patches of green. Both Rufous and Allen's are compact. Females and immatures have rufous sides and flanks that contrast rather sharply with a white collar; they

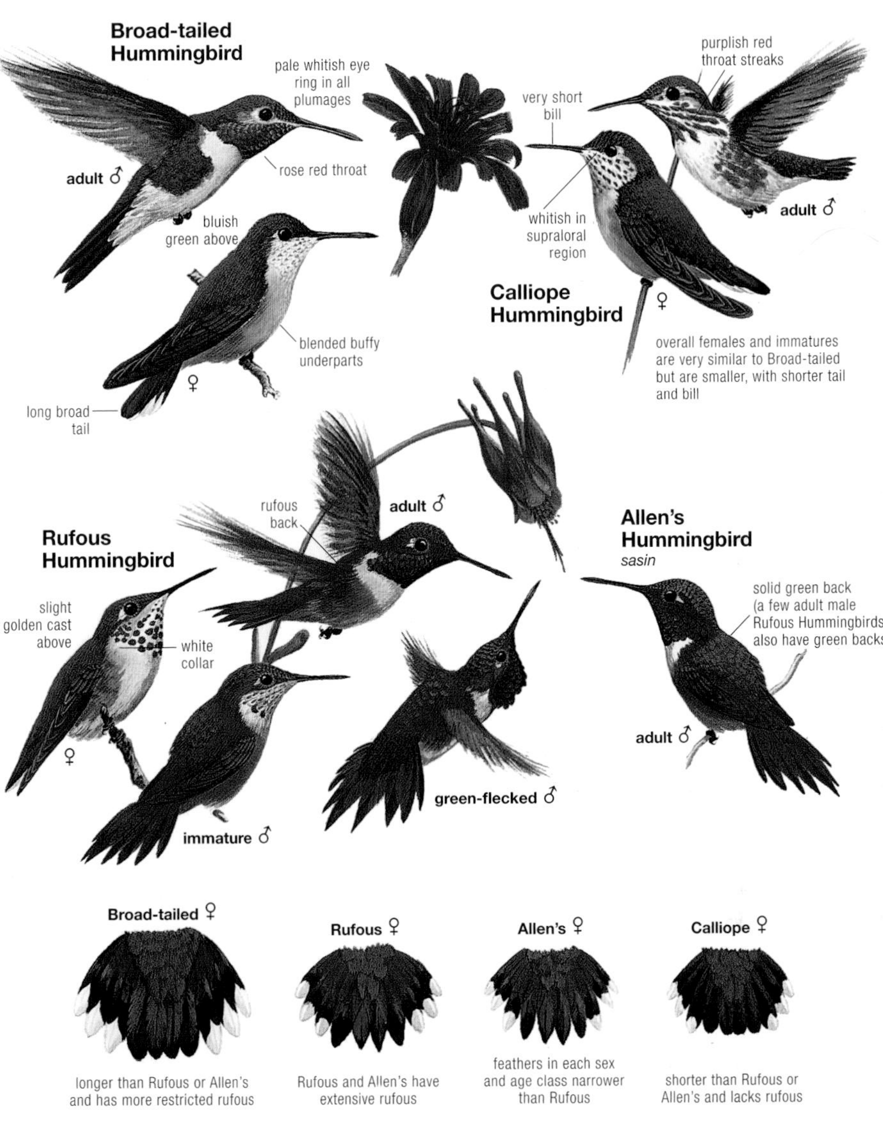

show extensive rufous at the base of the tail. The loud, metallic, and sometimes scratchy *chip* notes of Rufous/Allen's are also very similar.

Broad-tailed, a common breeder in the central and southern Rockies and the Great Basin mountains, is strictly casual to the Pacific region. Though frequent, most reports represent misidentifications with Rufous/Allen's. More elongated and less compact than Rufous/Allen's, Broad-tailed has a longer bill and a larger, longer tail with more restricted rufous. The buff below, duller than Rufous/Allen's, spreads to the sides of the neck, thus there is no collared effect. Broad-tailed's calls are even more strongly metallic than Rufous/Allen's and, once learned, can be diagnositc.

Female and immature Calliopes, which are tiny, closely resemble Broad-tailed in coloration and pattern but have shorter bills and tails and a pale area extending to the supraloral region. Calliope gives a soft *chip* notes. It is not aggressive.

Trogons (Family Trogonidae)

Colorful tropical birds with short, broad bills.

Elegant Trogon *Trogon elegans L 12½" (32 cm)*

Yellow bill, white breast band; under tail delicately barred. ***Male*** is bright green above and has bright red belly. ***Female*** and juvenile are browner and duller.

Voice: Song is a series of croaking *co-ah* notes.

Range: Found in streamside woodlands, mostly at altitudes from 4,000 to 6,000 feet. Very rare in winter in southeastern Arizona. Casual to Big Bend National Park, Texas.

Kingfishers (Family Alcedinidae)

Stocky and short-legged, with a large head, a large bill, and, in two North American species, a ragged crest. Look for kingfishers near woodland streams and ponds and in coastal areas. They hover over water, or watch from low perches, and then plunge headfirst to catch a fish. With their strong bills and feet, they dig nest burrows in stream banks.

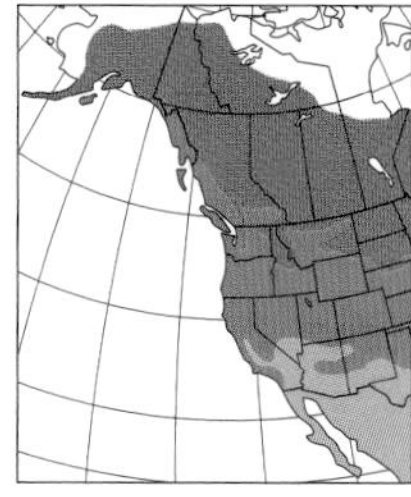

Belted Kingfisher *Ceryle alcyon L 13" (33 cm)*

The only kingfisher in most of North America. Both ***male*** and ***female*** have slate-blue breast band, white belly and undertail coverts. Female has rust belly band and flanks; may be confused with female Ringed Kingfisher, note white belly and smaller size. Juvenile resembles adult but has rust spotting in breast band.

Voice: Call is a loud, dry rattle.

Range: Common and conspicuous along rivers and brooks, ponds and lakes, and estuaries. Much more local in breeding season. Generally solitary. Rare in winter north of mapped range. Casual to western and northern Alaska.

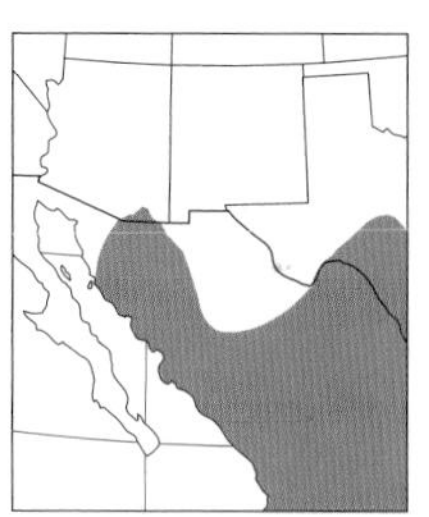

Green Kingfisher *Chloroceryle americana L 8¾" (22 cm)*

Smallest of our kingfishers but with a very long bill; crest inconspicuous. ***Male*** is green above, with white collar; white below, with dark green spotting. ***Female*** has a band of green spots across breast. Juvenile resembles adult female. Often perches on low, sheltered branches. Flight is direct over water and very fast; white outer tail feathers conspicuous in flight. Often hard to see.

Voice: One call, a faint but sharp *tick tick,* often ends in a short rattle; another, a squeaky *cheep,* is given in flight.

Range: Rare resident on clear-flowing streams (including nearby ponds and pools) along San Pedro River; also occasionally along Santa Cruz River and nearby Sonoita Creek near Nogales. Casual elsewhere in southeastern Arizona and along Rio Grande in Big Bend National Park. One was recently found along Gila River in southwestern New Mexico.

white spot on ear coverts
Elegant Trogan
canescens
brownish on head and upperparts
♀
♂
♀
yellow bill
♂
white breast band
delicately barred underside to tail
bright green head and upperparts
bright geranium red belly
blackish terminal tail band
shaggy crest
♂
single bluish band
blue and rufous breast bands
♀
♀
Belted Kingfisher
♂
very long bill
♂
♀
green
green upperparts
rufous chest
Green Kingfisher
extensive white in outer tail feathers visible in flight

Woodpeckers, Allies (Family Picidae)

Strong claws, short legs, and stiff tail feathers enable woodpeckers to climb tree trunks. Sharp bill is used to chisel out insect food and nest holes and to drum a territorial signal.

Red-headed Woodpecker *Melanerpes erythrocephalus* *L 9¼" (24 cm)* Entire head, neck, and throat are bright red in ***adults,*** contrasting with blue-black back and snowy white underparts. ***Juvenile*** is brownish; acquires red head during gradual winter molt. Distinctive white inner wing patches and white rump are visible in all ages in perched and flying birds; wing patches mottled in young birds; on most, spotting remains through first spring.
Voice: In breeding season utters a loud *queark,* similar to Red-bellied Woodpecker (next page) but harsher and sharper; year-round call is a soft, guttural rattle.
Range: Primarily an eastern species. Breeds in clumps of trees and also along rivers on western Great Plains, where overall uncommon. Rare visitor to Alberta; casual vagrant west to Arizona and California; accidental to Oregon and British Columbia.

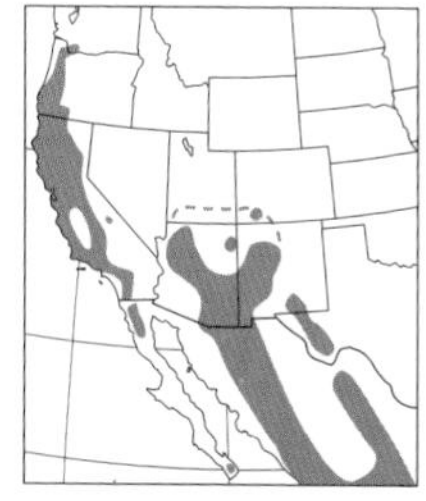

Acorn Woodpecker *Melanerpes formicivorus* *L 9" (23 cm)* Black chin, yellowish throat, white cheeks and forehead, and red cap. ***Female*** has smaller bill than ***male,*** less red on crown. In flight, white rump and small white patches on outer wings are conspicuous. Sociable; generally found in small, noisy colonies. Eats chiefly acorns and other nuts in winter, insects in summer. In the fall, is sometimes seen drilling small holes in a tree trunk or telephone pole and pounding a nut into each hole for a winter food supply. Colonies use the same "granary tree" year after year.
Voice: Most frequent call, a loud *waka,* is usually repeated several times.
Range: Common in oak woods or pine forests where oak trees are abundant. Casual, chiefly in fall, to southwestern deserts and western Great Plains. Accidental to British Columbia.

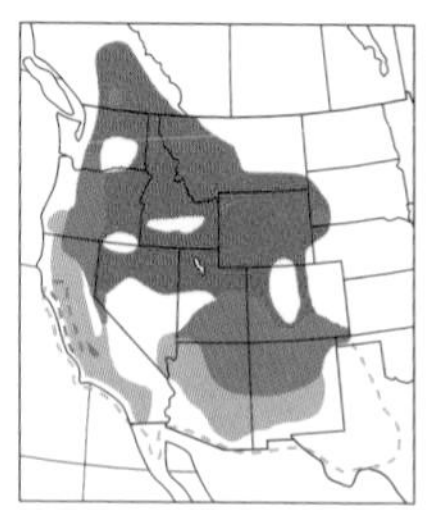

Lewis's Woodpecker *Melanerpes lewis* *L 10¾" (27 cm)* Greenish black head and back; gray collar and breast; dark red face, pinkish belly. In flight, darkness, large size, and slow, steady wingbeats give it a crowlike appearance. ***Juvenile*** lacks collar and red face; belly may be only faintly pink; acquires more adultlike plumage from late fall through winter. Main food, insects, mostly caught in the air; also eats fruit and nuts. Stores acorns, which it first shells, in tree bark crevices. Often perches on telephone poles.
Voice: Often silent. A single squeaky sharp call is given in interactions with other birds; vocalizations more frequent on the nesting grounds.
Range: Uncommon to fairly common in open woodlands of interior; rare on coast. Often gregarious; fall and winter movements unpredictable; uncommon to locally fairly common in some years, almost absent in others. May nest south of mapped range (rarely).

pure white
secondaries
adult
Red-headed
Woodpecker
brownish head
juvenile
red head
barring on
secondaries
adult
white primary
patches
♂
female has black
forecrown bar
♀
clownlike
head pattern
♂
Acorn
Woodpecker
brown head
and no collar
juvenile
dark red
face
gray collar
oily green
upperparts
Lewis's
Woodpecker
pink belly
slow crowlike
wingbeats
adults

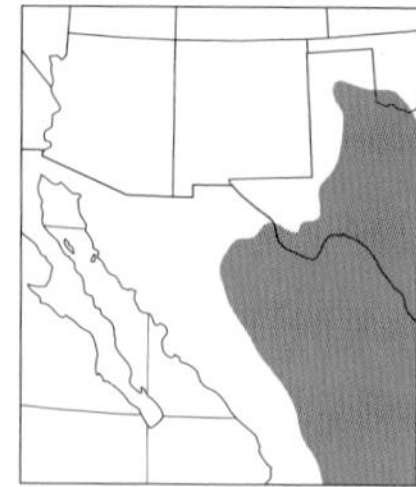

Golden-fronted Woodpecker *Melanerpes aurifrons*
L 9¾" (25 cm) Black-and-white barred back, white rump, usually an all-black tail; golden orange nape, paler in ***females;*** yellow feathering above bill. ***Male*** has a small red cap. Yellow tinge on belly not easily seen. Juvenile has streaked breast, brownish crown. In flight, all plumages show white wing patches, white rump as in Red-bellied and Gila Woodpeckers; unlike them, Golden-fronted shows black, not barred, tail.
Voice: Calls, a rolling *churr-churr* and cackling *kek-kek,* are slightly louder and raspier than Red-bellied.
Range: Fairly common in deciduous woodlands in very limited range in West along and near Rio Grande of west Texas.

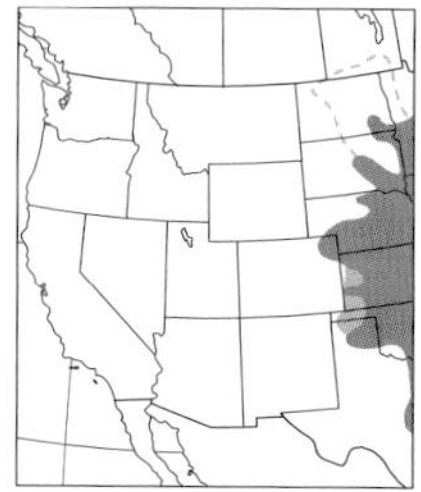

Red-bellied Woodpecker *Melanerpes carolinus*
L 9¼" (24 cm) Black-and-white barred back; white uppertail coverts; barred central tail feathers. Crown and nape are red in ***males. Females*** have red nape only. Small reddish patch or tinge on belly hard to see on both sexes.
Voice: Call, a rolling *churr* or *chiv-chiv,* is slightly softer than that Golden-fronted.
Range: An eastern species, uncommon in deciduous woodlands in northeast Colorado. Casual to New Mexico.

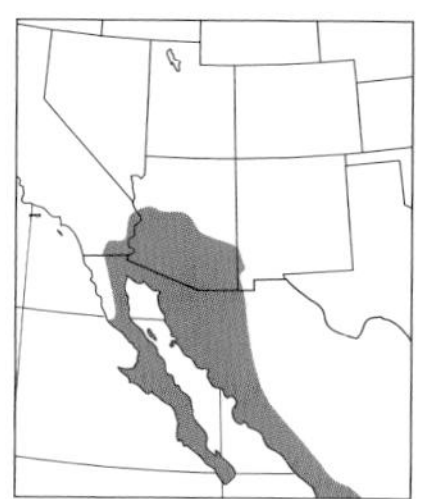

Gila Woodpecker *Melanerpes uropygialis L 9¼" (24 cm)*
Black-and-white barred back and rump; central tail feathers barred. ***Male*** has a small red cap.
Voice: Calls, a rolling *churr* and a loud, sharp, high-pitched *yip,* often given in a series.
Range: Inhabits towns, cactus country, and streamside woods. Accidental to eastern San Diego County, Los Angeles, and the San Francisco Bay Area.

Sapsuckers

These woodpeckers drill evenly spaced rows of holes in trees and then visit these "wells" for sap and the insects it attracts. Red-breasted and Red-naped Sapsuckers were formerly considered subspecies of Yellow-bellied Sapsucker.

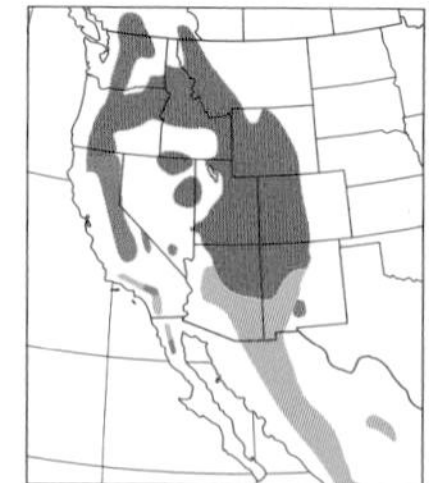

Williamson's Sapsucker *Sphyrapicus thyroideus*
L 9" (23 cm) ***Male*** has black back, white rump, and large white wing patch; black head with narrow white stripes, bright red chin and throat. Breast is black, belly yellow; flanks are barred with black and white. ***Female***'s head is brown; back, wings, and sides barred with dark brown and white; rump white; lacks white wing patch and red chin; breast has large dark patch; belly variably yellow. Juveniles resemble adults but are duller; attain adultlike plumage by Nov. Juvenile male has white throat; juvenile female lacks black breast patch.
Voice: Gives a harsh, shrill raptorlike call.
Range: Fairly common in dry, piney forests of the western mountains; moves south or to lower elevations in winter. Rare to casual in lowlands and to Great Plains, chiefly in fall and winter.

Golden-fronted Woodpecker
aurifrons
red crown
♂
gold feathering above bill
♀
gold nape
white area
central feathers
Red-bellied Woodpecker
solid red crown and nape
♀
♂
red nape
pink on lower belly
speckled white rump
barred central tail feathers
whitish primary patch in both Red-bellied and Golden-fronted
♂
male with red crown
grayish brown forehead
♂
♀
barred central tail feathers
Gila Woodpecker
uropygialis
Williamson's Sapsucker
black breast, yellow belly
brown head
red throat
white head stripes
white wing patch
bright yellow belly
♀
♂
barred back
white rump in both sexes

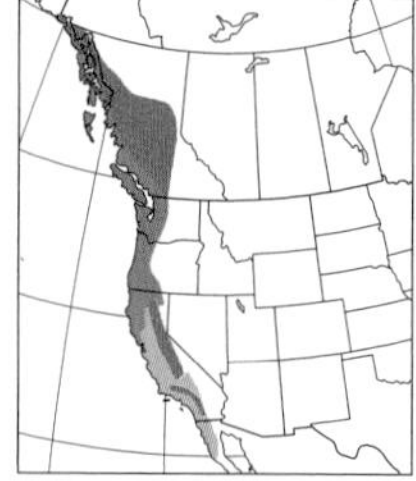

Red-breasted Sapsucker *Sphyrapicus ruber*

L 8½" (22 cm) This and next two species formerly considered one species. All show white wing patches. Red head, nape, and breast; large white wing patch; white rump. Back is black, lightly spotted with yellow in northern subspecies, *ruber;* more heavily marked with white in southern *daggetti.* Belly is yellow in *ruber; daggetti* has paler belly and duller head with longer white moustachial stripe. In both races, briefly held juvenal plumage is brownish, showing little or no red.

Voice: All sapsuckers give a characteristic irregular drumming, slowing toward end. Red-breasted, Yellow-bellied, and Red-naped all give a querulous, descending mewing note year-round.

Range: Common in coniferous or mixed forests in coastal ranges, usually at lower elevations and in moister forests than Williamson's Sapsucker. Most migrate south or move to lower elevations in winter. Red-breasted frequently hybridizes with Red-naped Sapsucker. Hybrids are frequent east through Great Basin and to Arizona. Red-breasteds (mostly *daggetti; ruber* is casual) are uncommon to rare in western Great Basin, casually to Utah and Arizona and west Texas; but every vagrant should be scrutinized carefully to eliminate more numerous hybrids.

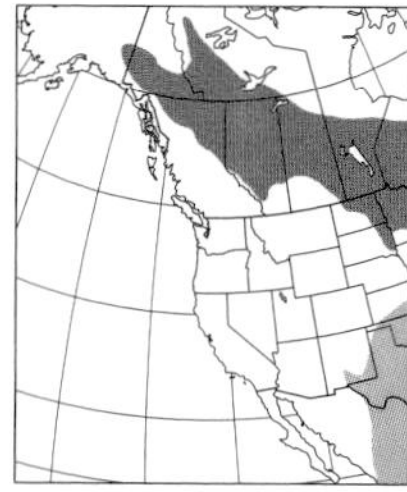

Yellow-bellied Sapsucker *Sphyrapicus varius*

L 8½" (22 cm) Red forecrown on black-and-white head; chin and throat red in ***male,*** white in ***female.*** Back is blackish, with white rump and large white wing patch. Underparts yellowish, paler in female; a few adults show some reddish on nape. ***Juvenile*** retains largely brownish plumage until late in the winter.

Voice: Display drum and calls like Red-breasted Sapsucker.

Range: Fairly common in deciduous and mixed forests. Highly migratory; rare to very rare during fall and winter. Hybridizes with Red-naped in narrow range of overlap.

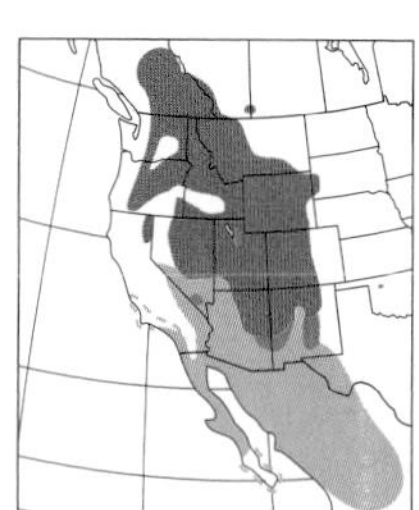

Red-naped Sapsucker *Sphyrapicus nuchalis*

L 8½" (22 cm) Very similar to Yellow-bellied, but has variable red patch on back of head, sometimes lacking; spotting on back more clearly organized into two rows. On ***male,*** extensive red on throat penetrates the surrounding black "frame"; on ***female,*** throat is partly red to almost entirely red on some birds. Juvenile is brownish overall; resembles adult by first fall except for lack of black chest.

Voice: Display drumming and calls like Red-breasted Sapsucker.

Range: Common in deciduous and mixed forests in Rocky Mountains and Great Basin ranges; a very few to the Sierra Nevada. Frequently hybridizes in wide range of overlap with Red-breasted. Rare west of Sierra and deserts north of San Diego County. Very rare in Pacific Northwest west of Cascades. Casual east to western Great Plains.

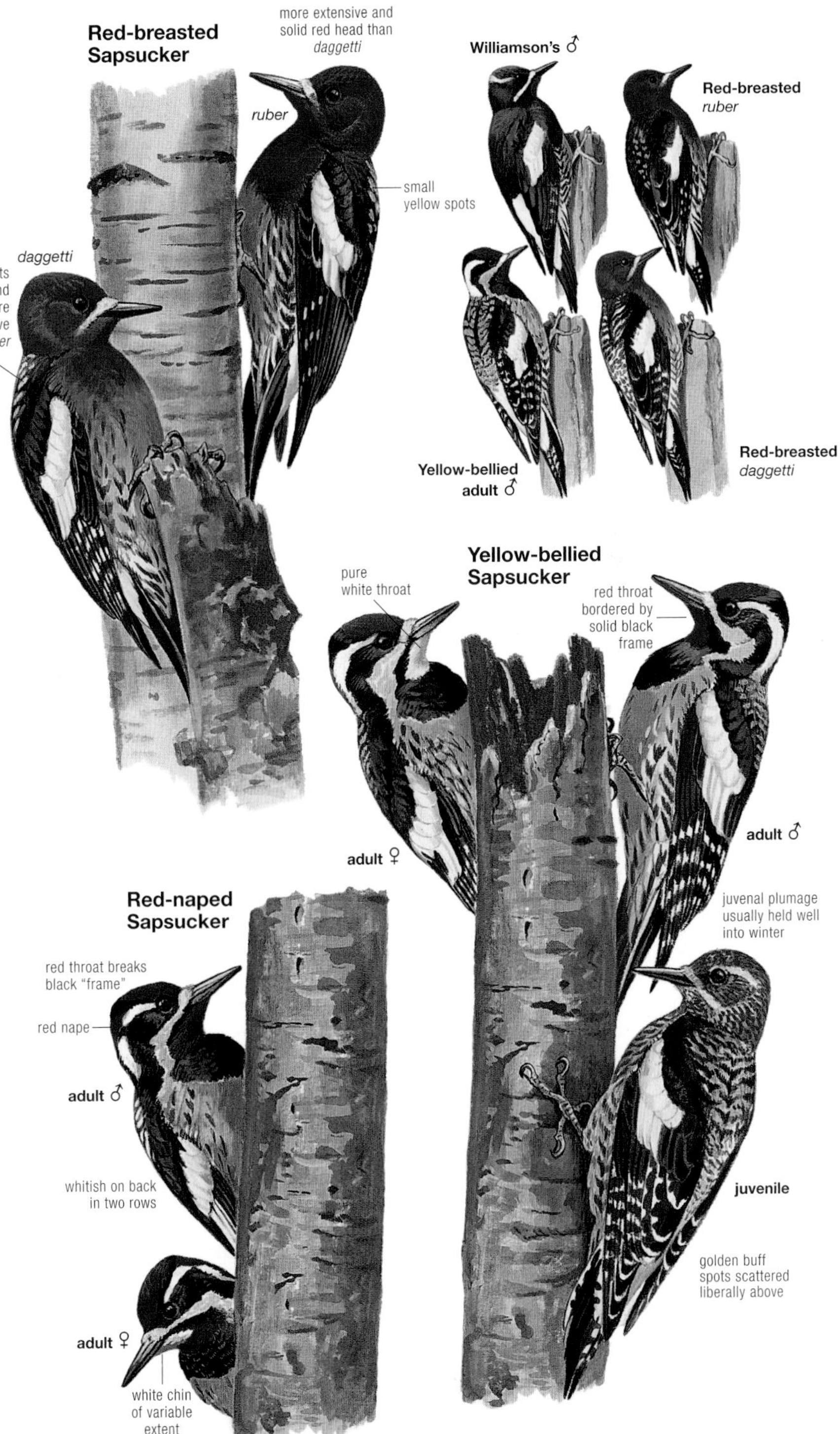
Red-breasted Sapsucker
more extensive and solid red head than daggetti
ruber
small yellow spots
daggetti
ots
and
ore
sive
ber
Williamson's ♂
Red-breasted ruber
Yellow-bellied adult ♂
Red-breasted daggetti
Yellow-bellied Sapsucker
pure white throat
red throat bordered by solid black frame
adult ♂
adult ♀
juvenal plumage usually held well into winter
Red-naped Sapsucker
red throat breaks black "frame"
red nape
adult ♂
whitish on back in two rows
adult ♀
white chin of variable extent
juvenile
golden buff spots scattered liberally above

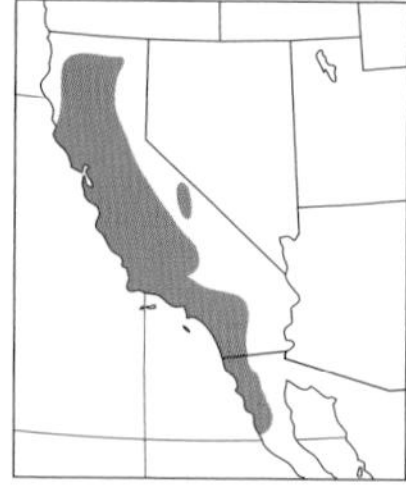

Nuttall's Woodpecker *Picoides nuttallii L 7½" (19 cm)*
Closely resembles Ladder-backed Woodpecker. Nuttall's shows more black on face; white bars on back are narrower, with more extensive solid black just below the nape. White outer tail feathers are sparsely spotted rather than barred; nasal tufts white.
Voice: Call is a low, rattled *prrrt,* much lower than Ladder-backed's *pik;* also gives a series of loud, spaced, descending notes.
Range: Prefers less arid habitat than Ladder-backed; usually seen in chaparral mixed with scrub oak and in wooded canyons and streamside trees. Casual to southern Oregon and western Nevada.

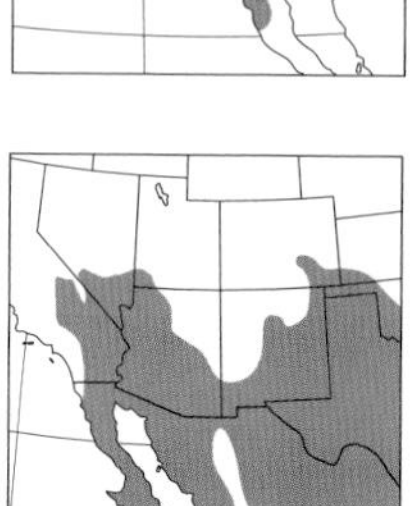

Ladder-backed Woodpecker *Picoides scalaris L 7¼" (18 cm)* Black-and-white barred back, spotted sides; face and underparts slightly buffy or grayish; face marked with black lines. ***Male*** has red crown. In California, Ladder-backed may be confused with Nuttall's Woodpecker. Ladder-backed shows less black on face and is buffy-tinged rather than white below; white barring on back is more pronounced and extends to nape; white outer tail feathers are evenly barred rather than spotted; nasal tufts buffy. Feeds on beetle larvae from small trees; also eats cactus fruits and forages on the ground for insects.
Voice: Call is a crisp *pik,* very similar to Downy and different from Nuttall's rattled *prrrt;* also gives a descending whinny.
Range: Uncommon to common in dry brushlands, mesquite and cactus country; also towns. Accidental to southern coastal San Diego County. Some hybrids with Nuttall's are found in narrow zone of overlap in westernmost deserts of California and the Owens Valley.

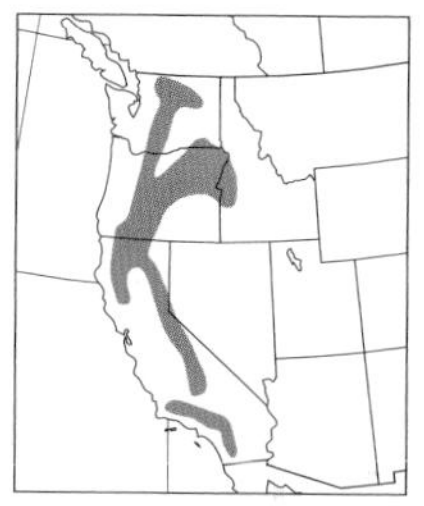

White-headed Woodpecker *Picoides albolarvatus L 9¼" (24 cm)* Head and throat white. ***Male*** has a red patch on back of head. Body is black except for white wing patches. Juvenile has a variable patch of pale red on crown.
Voice: Calls include a sharp, distinctive doubled or tripled *pee-dink* or *pee-dee-dink.*
Range: Nests in coniferous mountain forests, especially ponderosa and sugar pine; feeds primarily on seeds from their cones; also pries away loose bark in search of insects and larvae. Fairly common over most of range; rare and local in the North. Casual at lower altitudes in winter, including coastal lowlands of southern California, the westernmost deserts, the Owens Valley, southern British Columbia, and western Montana.

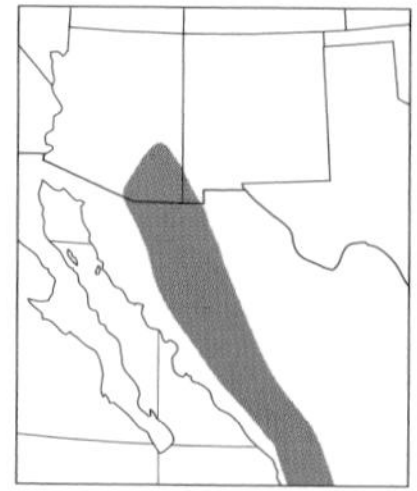

Arizona Woodpecker *Picoides arizonae L 7½" (19 cm)*
Solid brown back distinguishes this species from all other woodpeckers. ***Female*** lacks red patch on back of head.
Voice: Call is a sharp *peek,* similar to Hairy but hoarser.
Range: Uncommon resident in foothills and mountains; generally found in oak, oak-juniper, or pine-oak forests or canyons.

ales, red restricted
) rear crown; more
ensive on juveniles
of both sexes
black face with
white borders
white nasal tufts
white underparts
ower white
ars stop on
ipper back
Nuttall's
Woodpecker
♂
♀
outer tail feathers
with fewer bars than
Ladder-backed
extensive
reddish crown
buffy white face with
narrow black frame
buffy white
nasal tufts
Ladder-backed
Woodpecker
♂
buffy cast
to under-
parts with
spots on
sides and
flanks
white
bars
extend to
nape
black crown
♀
tail more
barred
white head
White-headed
Woodpecker
♂
♂
♀
white wing
patch
long narrow
white patch on
folded wing
♂
brown
upperparts
large spots
♀
Arizona
Woodpecker
Ladder-backed ♂
Nuttall's ♂
Arizona ♂

Downy Woodpecker *Picoides pubescens L 6¾" (17 cm)* White back generally identifies both Downy and similar Hairy Woodpecker. Downy is much smaller, with a smaller bill; outer tail feathers generally have faint dark bars or spots. Birds in the Pacific Northwest have pale gray-brown back and underparts. Rocky Mountain and California birds have less white spotting on wings.

Voice: Downy's call, *pik,* and whinny are softer and higher-pitched than Hairy Woodpecker.

Range: Common; in suburbs, parklands, and orchards, as well as in forests; casual in Southwest south of mapped range.

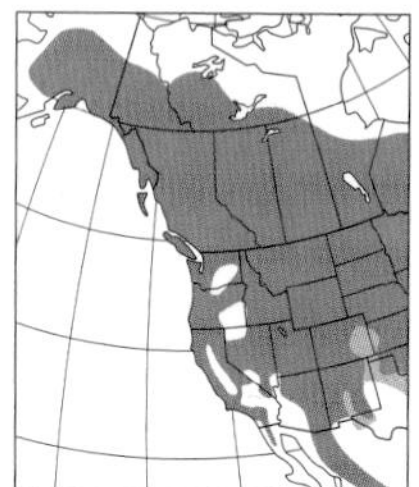

Hairy Woodpecker *Picoides villosus L 9¼" (24 cm)* White back generally identifies both Hairy and similar Downy Woodpecker. Hairy is much larger, with a larger bill; outer tail feathers are entirely white. Birds in the Pacific Northwest have pale gray-brown back and underparts. Rocky Mountain birds have less white spotting on wings. ***Juveniles,*** particularly in the Maritime Provinces, have some barring on back and flanks; sides may be streaked. Juveniles on the Queen Charlotte Islands have heavily barred outer tail feathers. In young males, the forehead is spotted with white; crown streaked with red or orange.

Voice: Calls include a loud, sharp *peek* and a slurred whinny.

Range: Fairly common; inhabits both open and dense forests. Casual visitor to lowlands in Southwest.

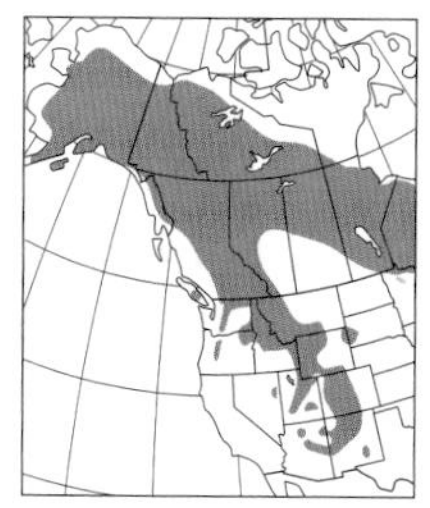

American Three-toed Woodpecker *Picoides dorsalis L 8¾" (22 cm)* Black-and-white barring down center of back distinguishes most races of American Three-toed Woodpecker from similar Black-backed. Both have heavily barred sides. ***Male***'s yellow cap is usually more extensive in Three-toed but less solid. Density of barring on back is intermediate in northwestern race, *fasciatus.* In Rocky Mountain race, nominate *dorsalis,* back is almost entirely white. Back is much darker in eastern race, *bacatus,* unrecorded in West; thinner, white submoustachial stripe helps distinguish it from Black-backed. New English and scientific names reflect a recent split: The eight Old World subspecies are now considered their own species, *P. tridactylus.*

Voice: Call is a soft *pik* or *kimp.* Drumming becomes slightly faster and weaker toward end.

Range: Found in coniferous forests, especially in burned-over and insect-ravaged areas. Accidental (*dorsalis*) northwest Nebraska.

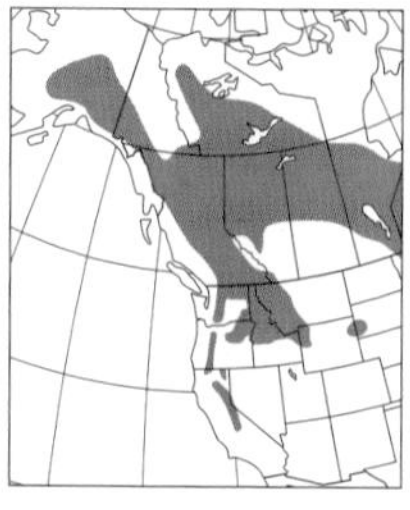

Black-backed Woodpecker *Picoides arcticus L 9½" (24 cm)* Solid black back, heavily barred sides. ***Male*** has a solid yellow cap. Black-backed Woodpecker is larger; has longer, stouter bill; lacks white streak behind the eye, and has a solid black back, which is white (*dorsalis*) or barred (*fasciatus*) in American Three-toed.

Voice: Call note is a single, sharp *pik* or flat *kuk,* lower-pitched than Three-toed.

Range: Inhabits coniferous forests; often found in burned-over areas. Forages on dead conifers, flaking away large patches of loose bark rather than drilling into it, in search of larvae and insects.

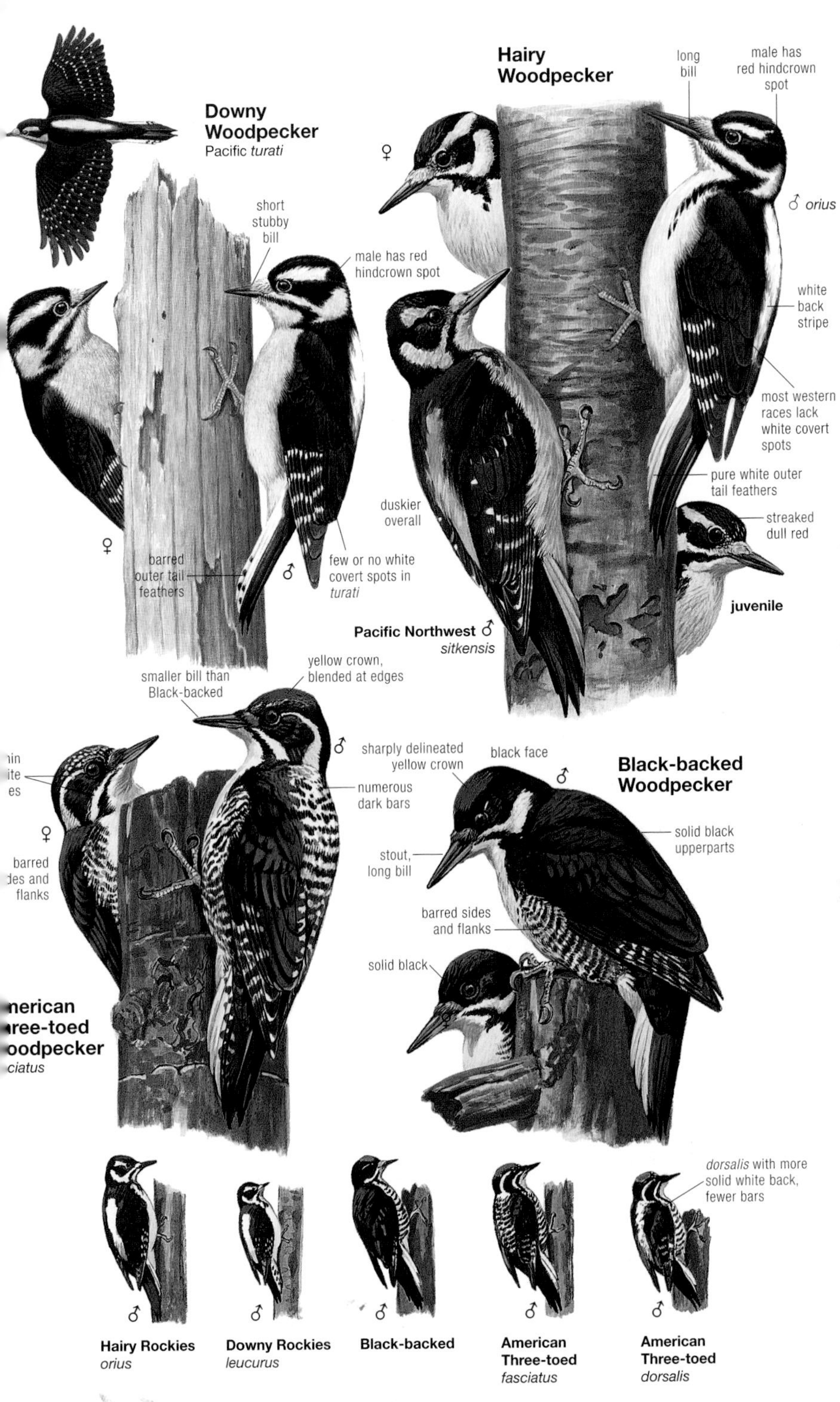

Downy
Woodpecker
Pacific turati
short
stubby
bill
male has red
hindcrown spot
♀
barred
outer tail
feathers
♂
few or no white
covert spots in
turati
Hairy
Woodpecker
long
bill
male has
red hindcrown
spot
♀
♂ orius
white
back
stripe
most western
races lack
white covert
spots
pure white outer
tail feathers
duskier
overall
streaked
dull red
juvenile
Pacific Northwest ♂
sitkensis
smaller bill than
Black-backed
yellow crown,
blended at edges
♂
sharply delineated
yellow crown
black face
♂
Black-backed
Woodpecker
ite
es
numerous
dark bars
♀
solid black
upperparts
barred
des and
flanks
stout,
long bill
barred sides
and flanks
solid black
merican
ree-toed
oodpecker
ciatus
♀
dorsalis with more
solid white back,
fewer bars
♂
♂
♂
♂
♂
Hairy Rockies
orius
Downy Rockies
leucurus
Black-backed
American
Three-toed
fasciatus
American
Three-toed
dorsalis

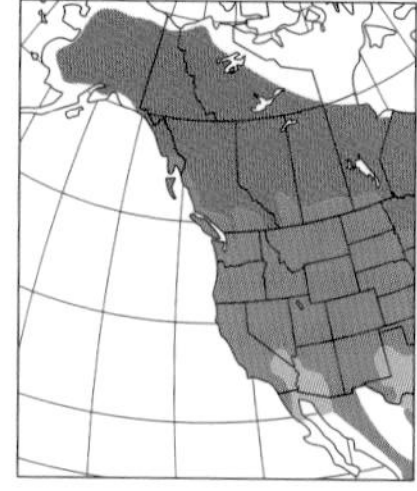

Northern Flicker *Colaptes auratus L 12½" (32 cm)*
Two distinct groups occur: ***"Yellow-shafted Flicker"*** in the East and far north and ***"Red-shafted Flicker"*** in the West. These flickers have a brown, barred back and spotted underparts, with a black crescent-shaped bib. White rump is conspicuous in flight; no white wing patches. Intergrades are regularly seen in the Great Plains. "Yellow-shafted Flicker" has yellow wing lining and undertail color, gray crown, and tan face with red crescent on nape. "Red-shafted Flicker" has brown crown and gray face, with no red crescent. "Yellow-shafted" ***male*** has a black moustachial stripe (red stripe in "Red-shafted" male); ***females*** lack these stripes.
Voice: Call heard on the breeding ground is a long, loud series of *wick-er* notes; a single, loud *klee-yer* is given year-round.
Range: Common in open woodlands and suburban areas. "Yellow-shafted" is rare in fall and winter in the West south and west of breeding range, which extends from Alaska and the Yukon to eastern Colorado.

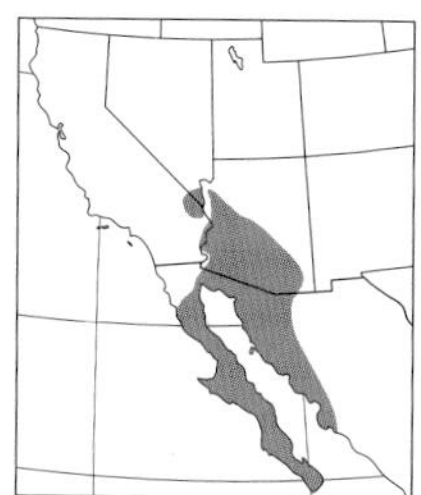

Gilded Flicker *Colaptes chrysoides L 11½" (29 cm)*
Restored to full species status from Northern Flicker. Gilded Flicker's head pattern more like "Red-shafted" Northern, but underwings and base of tail yellow; crown more cinnamon. Note also smaller size; larger black chest patch; paler back with narrower black bars; more crescent-shaped markings below. ***Female*** lacks red moustachial stripe.
Voice: Calls are like Northern Flicker.
Range: Inhabits low desert woodlands; favors saguaro and Joshua trees. Hybrids with "Red-shafted" are noted in cottonwoods at middle elevations in southern Arizona and along the lower Colorado River.

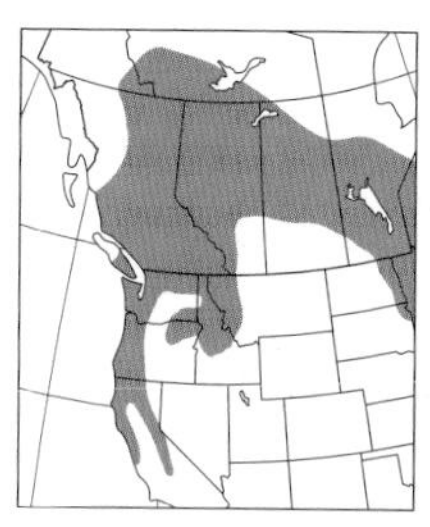

Pileated Woodpecker *Dryocopus pileatus L 16½" (42 cm)*
This is the largest woodpecker now credibly seen in North America. Overall extensively black, including on back and wings; long white stripe on sides of neck. Flies with slow, crowlike wingbeats; note white primary patches and white wing linings. ***Female***'s red cap is less extensive than ***male.*** Juvenal plumage, held briefly, resembles adult but is duller and browner overall. Generally shy.
Voice: Call is a loud *wuck* note or series of notes, given all year, often in flight; similar call of Northern Flicker is given only in the breeding season.
Range: Prefers dense, mature forest. In woodlots and parklands as well as deep woods, listen for its loud, resonant, territorial drumming, given by both sexes but less frequently by females; look for the long rectangular or oval holes it excavates. Carpenter ants in fallen trees and stumps are its major food source. Rather uncommon and local overall. Accidental to southern San Joaquin Valley and coastal Los Angeles County.

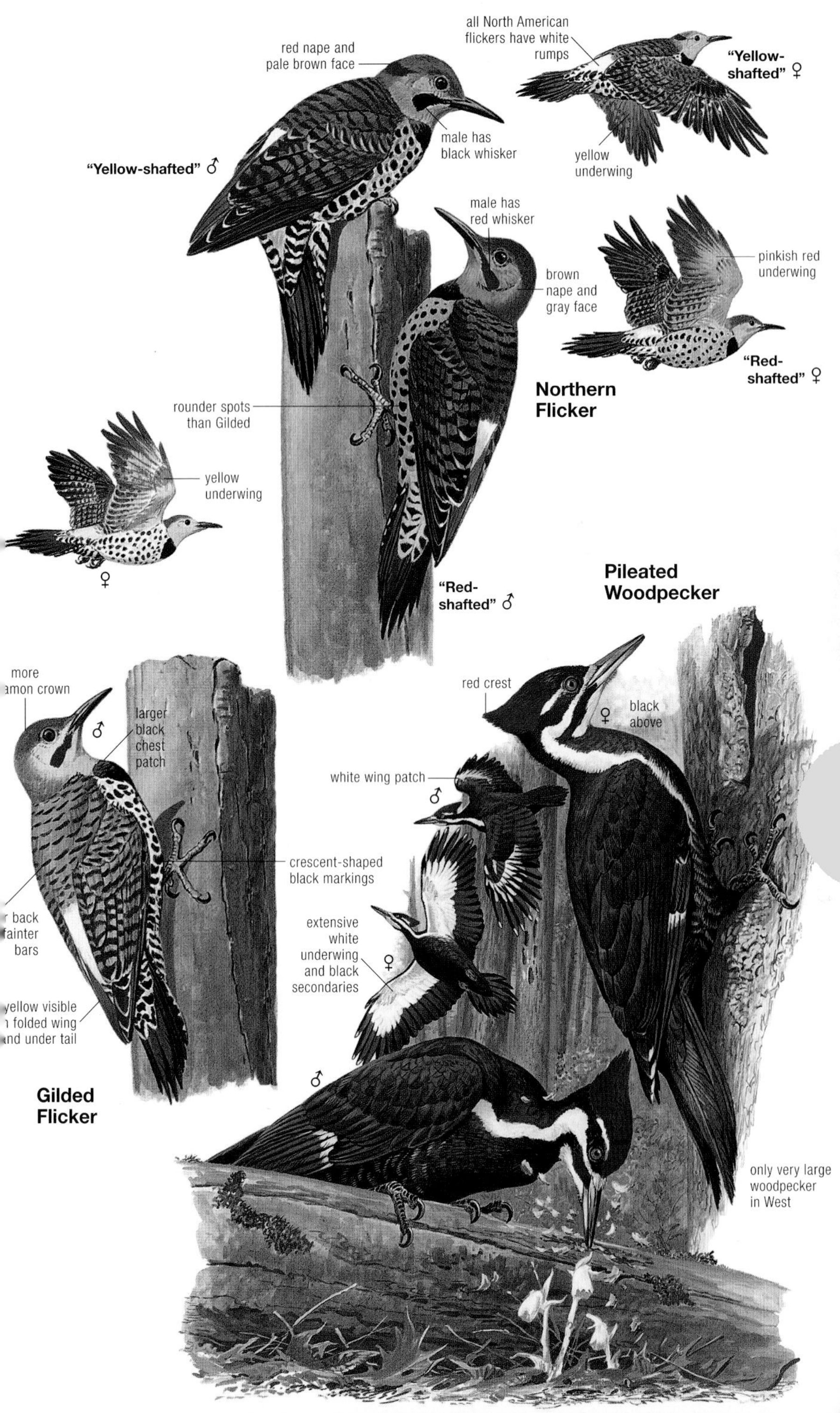
red nape and
pale brown face
male has
black whisker
"Yellow-shafted" ♂
all North American
flickers have white
rumps
"Yellow-
shafted" ♀
yellow
underwing
male has
red whisker
brown
nape and
gray face
pinkish red
underwing
"Red-
shafted" ♀
Northern
Flicker
rounder spots
than Gilded
yellow
underwing
♀
"Red-
shafted" ♂
Pileated
Woodpecker
more
amon crown
♂
larger
black
chest
patch
red crest
♀
black
above
white wing patch
♂
crescent-shaped
black markings
r back
fainter
bars
extensive
white
underwing
and black
secondaries
♀
yellow visible
n folded wing
and under tail
♂
Gilded
Flicker
only very large
woodpecker
in West

Tyrant Flycatchers (Family Tyrannidae)

A typical flycatcher darts out from a fixed perch to catch insects. Most have a large head, bristly "whiskers," and a broad-based, flat bill.

Northern Beardless-Tyrannulet *Camptostoma imberbe* *L 4½" (11 cm)* Grayish olive above and on breast; dull white or pale yellow below. Indistinct whitish eyebrow; small, slightly curved bill. Crown is darker than nape in many birds and often raised in a bushy crest. Distinguished from similar Ruby-crowned Kinglet (page 304) by buffy wing bars and lack of bold eye ring. Difficult to spot; most easily located by voice.
Voice: Song on breeding grounds is a descending series of loud, clear *peer* notes; call, an innocuous, whistled *pee-yerp.*
Range: Rather uncommon in U.S. Often found near streams in sycamore, mesquite, and cottonwood groves.

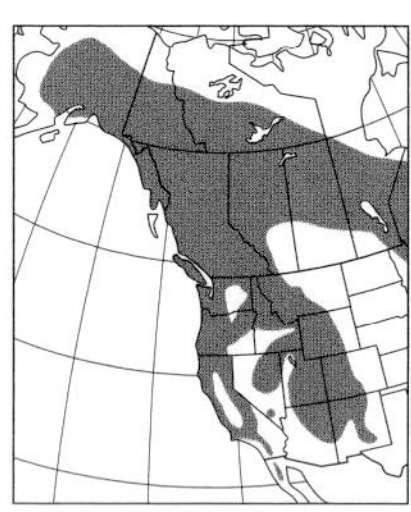

Olive-sided Flycatcher *Contopus cooperi* *L 7½" (19 cm)* Large, with rather short tail. Brownish olive above; white tufts on sides of rump distinctive but often not visible. Throat, center of breast, and belly dull white. Sides and flanks brownish olive and streaked. Bill is mostly dark; center and sometimes base of lower mandible dull orange; often perches on high, dead branches, including in migration.
Voice: Distinctive song is a clear *quick-three-beers,* the second note higher; typical call is a repeated *pip.*
Range: Uncommon to fairly common in coniferous forests and bogs. Casual in winter on coastal slope of southern California.

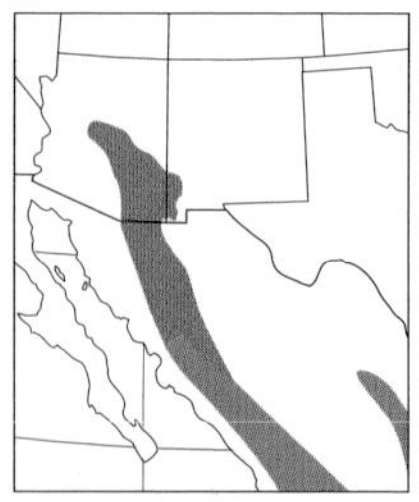

Greater Pewee *Contopus pertinax* *L 8" (20 cm)* Note longer tail, more slender crest (usually visible), and more uniformly colored underparts than Olive-sided; Greater also has all-pale lower mandible. Worn summer birds are overall grayer than freshly molted winter ones. Unlike *Empidonax* flycatchers (next page), most *Contopus* (pewees) do not wag their tails.
Voice: Song is a whistled *ho-say ma-re-ah;* call is a repeated *pip.*
Range: Fairly common in mountain pine-oak woodlands. Very rare in winter in southern Arizona, southern and central California; casual in west Texas.

Western Wood-Pewee *Contopus sordidulus* *L 6¼" (16 cm)* Plumage variable; slightly darker and less greenish than Eastern Wood-Pewee (casual in West); base of lower mandible usually shows some yellow-orange. Identification very difficult; best done by range and voice. Also compare carefully to western races of Willow Flycatcher (next page).
Voice: Calls include a harsh, slightly descending *peeer* and clear whistles suggestive of Eastern's *pee-yer.* Song, heard chiefly on breeding grounds, has three-note *tswee-tee-teet* phrases mixed with the *peeer* note.
Range: Common in open woodlands. No midwinter records in U.S. Winters in South America.

short, pale supercilium

Northern Beardless-Tyrannulet

worn adult

can raise crest

rounded bill tip with orange base

faint wing bars

fresh

white extends up through center

white flank patches show periodically from above

adults

Olive-sided Flycatcher

dark breast sides with diffuse streaking

mostly dark bill

chunky body shape

long wings

short tail

Flycatchers

slender crest

juvenile

spring adult

all-pale lower mandible

blended underparts

Greater Pewee

longer tail than Olive-sided

Western Wood-Pewee

long wings

paler adult

darker adult

variations

occasionally with all-pale lower mandible

Empidonax Flycatchers

All empids are drab, with pale eye rings and wing bars. From spring to summer, plumages grow duller from wear. Some species molt before fall migration, acquiring fresh plumage in late summer. Identification depends on voice, habitat, behavior, and subtle differences in size, bill shape, primary projection, and tail length. Most flip their tails up.

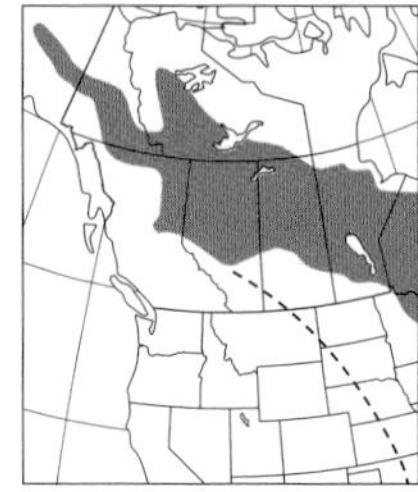

Yellow-bellied Flycatcher *Empidonax flaviventris*
L 5½" (14 cm) Has rather short tail and big head. Olive above, yellow below. Broad yellow eye ring. Lower mandible entirely pale orange. Shows a more extensive olive wash across breast than Acadian Flycatcher; lacks pale area between olive and yellow belly. Also, throat is yellow, rather than whitish; bill smaller. Molts after migration; ***worn fall*** migrants slightly grayer above, duller below.
Voice: Song is a liquid *je-bunk;* also a plaintive, rising *per-wee.* Call, a sharp, whistled *chiu* that sounds somewhat like Acadian.
Range: Nests in bogs and damp coniferous woods. Casual, perhaps very rare fall migrant in West south of breeding range. Potential sightings best confirmed by call. Winters in Central and South America.

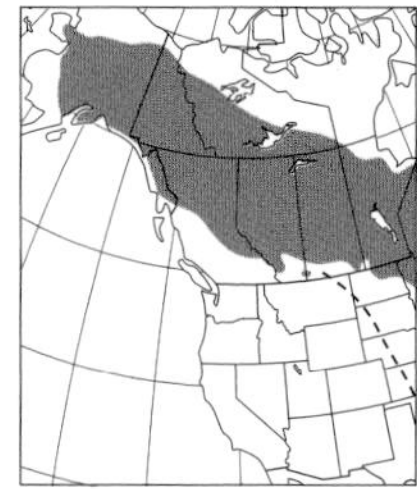

Alder Flycatcher *Empidonax alnorum L 5¾" (15 cm)*
Very similar to Willow Flycatcher, but bill is slightly shorter, eye ring usually more prominent, back greener. Distinguished from eastern race of Willow by darker head; from western races by well defined tertial edges, bolder wing bars, long primary projection. Best identified by voice.
Voice: Call, a loud *pip,* similar to Hammond's but louder. Distinctive song, a falling, wheezy *weeb-ew.* On breeding grounds, also gives a descending *wheer.*
Range: Common in breeding range in brushy habitats near bogs, birch and alder thickets. Likely a regular migrant in eastern Montana. Otherwise a casual, perhaps very rare migrant in West south of breeding range. Exact status clouded by identification problems. Potential sightings best confirmed by call or preferably in spring by song. Winters in South America.

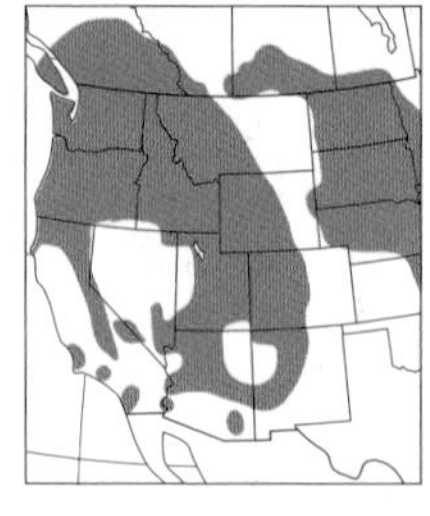

Willow Flycatcher *Empidonax traillii L 5¾" (15 cm)*
Lacks prominent eye ring. Color ranges from pale gray head and greenish back of nominate eastern race, *traillii,* occurring on western Great Plains, to darker headed, browner *brewsteri* in the Northwest. Great Basin race, *adastus* (not illustrated), is paler than *brewsteri;* endangered southwestern *extimus* (**E**) even paler. Western races have duller wing bars, blended tertial edges, and shorter primary projection. Distinguished from pewees (previous page) by shorter wings and upward flicks of tail.
Voice: Call is a liquid *wit.* Songs, a sneezy *fitz-bew;* on breeding grounds, also a rising *brreet;* often sings in spring migration.
Range: Found in brushy habitats in wet areas; also in pastures, mountain meadows. A late spring migrant (usually after mid-May to mid-June). Fall migration protracted. Winters from Mexico to northern South America.

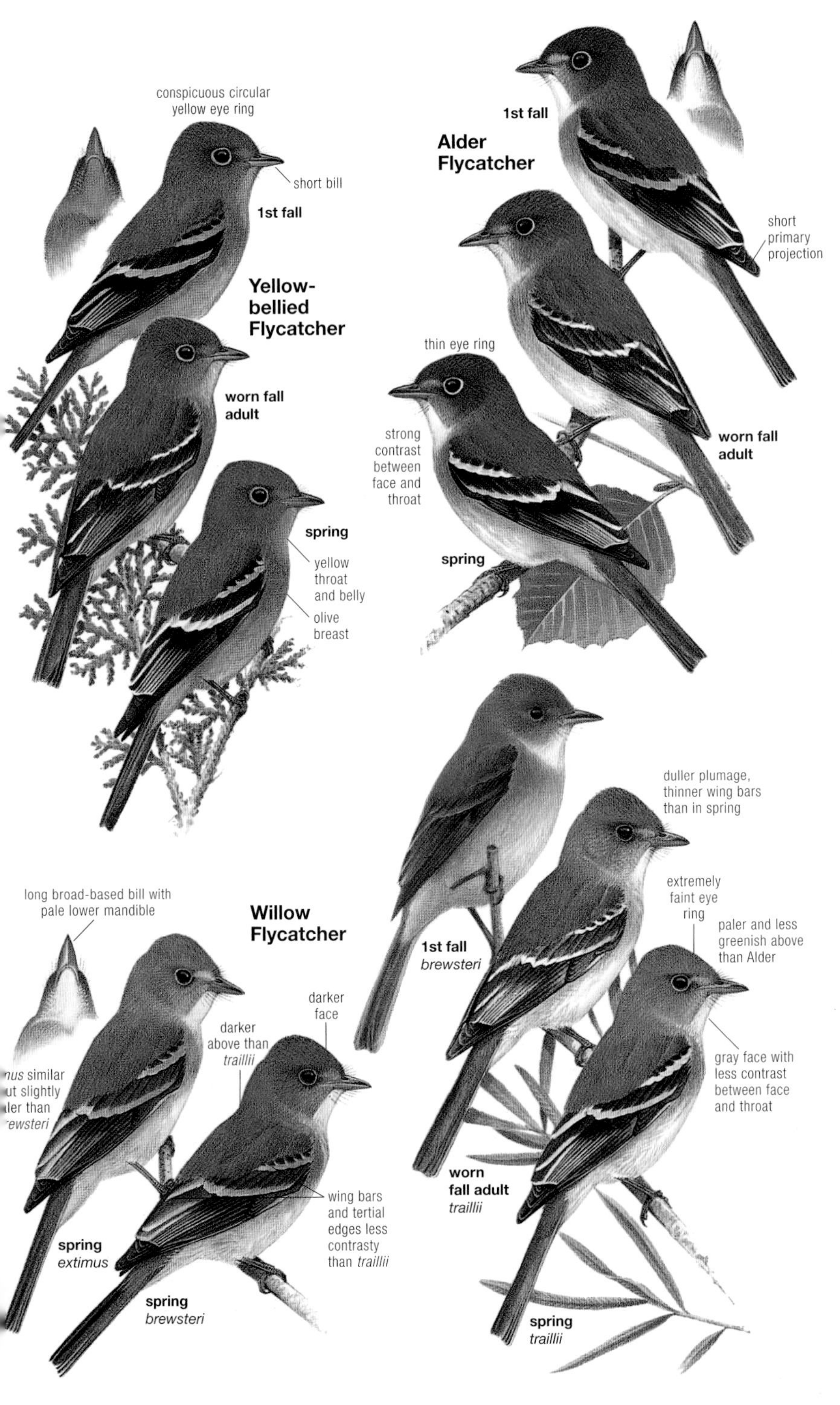
conspicuous circular yellow eye ring
short bill
1st fall
Yellow-bellied Flycatcher
worn fall adult
spring
yellow throat and belly
olive breast
Alder Flycatcher
1st fall
short primary projection
thin eye ring
strong contrast between face and throat
worn fall adult
spring
long broad-based bill with pale lower mandible
Willow Flycatcher
darker face
darker above than traillii
wing bars and tertial edges less contrasty than traillii
spring extimus
spring brewsteri
1st fall brewsteri
duller plumage, thinner wing bars than in spring
extremely faint eye ring
paler and less greenish above than Alder
gray face with less contrast between face and throat
worn fall adult traillii
spring traillii

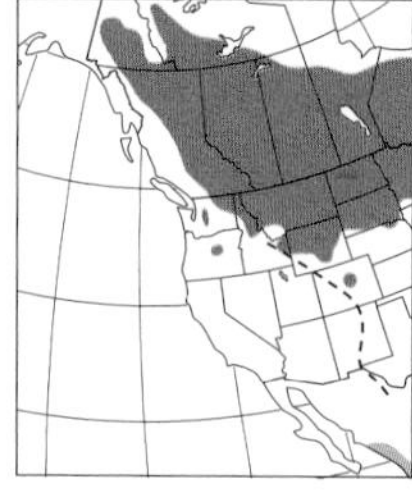

Least Flycatcher *Empidonax minimus L 5¼" (13 cm)*
Smallest eastern empid. Large-headed; bold but variable white eye ring; rather short primary projection. Throat whitish; breast washed with gray; belly and undertail coverts pale yellow. Underparts are usually paler than similar Hammond's Flycatcher. Bill short, triangular; lower mandible mostly pale; wings darker and contrast of wing bars and tertial edges sharper. Molt occurs after fall migration. ***First-fall*** has buffier wing bars.
Voice: Song, a dry *che-bek* accented on the second syllable, is usually delivered in a rapid series; call, a sharp *whit,* is sometimes also given in a series.
Range: Inhabits deciduous woods, orchards, and parks. Regular migrant on western Great Plains; otherwise rare migrant (mostly fall) in West south of breeding range.

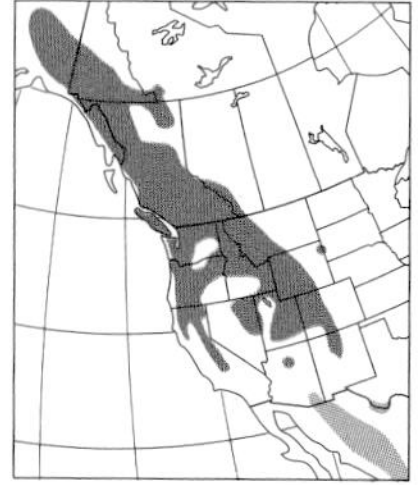

Hammond's Flycatcher *Empidonax hammondii L 5½" (14 cm)* A small empid, with a fairly large head and short tail. White eye ring, usually expanded in a "teardrop" at rear. Grayish head and throat; grayish olive back; gray or olive wash on breast and sides; belly tinged with pale yellow. Molt occurs before migration; ***fall*** birds are much brighter olive above and on sides of breast, yellower below. Bill slightly shorter, thinner, somewhat darker than similar Dusky and Least Flycatchers; primary projection is longer.
Voice: Call note is a sharp *peek.* Song resembles Dusky but is hoarser and lower-pitched, especially on the second note.
Range: Nests chiefly in coniferous forests. Most migrate earlier in spring and later in fall than Dusky.

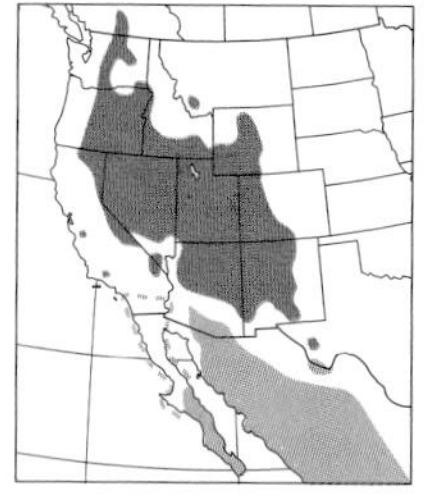

Gray Flycatcher *Empidonax wrightii L 6" (15 cm)*
Gray above, with a slight olive tinge in fresh fall plumage; whitish below, belly washed with pale yellow by late fall. Long bill; on most birds, lower mandible mostly pinkish orange at base, sharply divided from dark tip; on a few, entire lower mandible is pinkish orange. Short primary projection. Long tail, with thin whitish outer edge. Perched bird dips its tail down, like a phoebe.
Voice: Song is a vigorous *chi-wip* or *chi-bit,* followed by a liquid *whilp,* trailing off in a gurgle. Call is a loud *wit.*
Range: Fairly common in dry habitat of Great Basin, in pine or pinyon-juniper. Regular migrant on California coast.

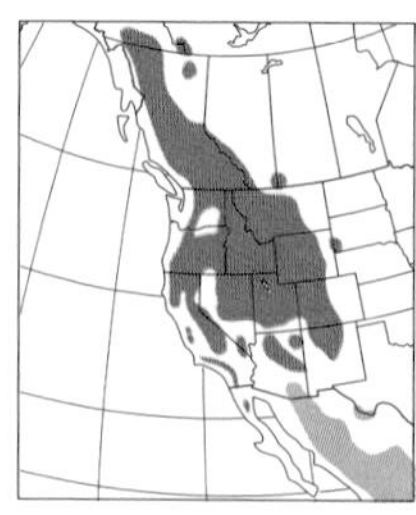

Dusky Flycatcher *Empidonax oberholseri L 5¾" (15 cm)*
Grayish olive above; yellowish below, with whitish throat, pale olive wash on upper breast. White eye ring. Bill partly dark, orange at base of lower mandible blending into dark tip. Bill and tail slightly longer than Hammond's Flycatcher. Short primary projection. Molt occurs after fall migration; fresh late-fall birds are quite yellow below.
Voice: Calls include a *wit* note, softer than Gray Flycatcher; a mournful *deehic,* heard on breeding grounds. Song has several phrases: a clear *sillit;* an upslurred *ggrrreep;* another high *sillit,* often omitted; and a clear, high *pweet.*
Range: Breeds in open woodlands and brush of mountainsides. Very rare on coast and on western Great Plains; casual to Alaska.

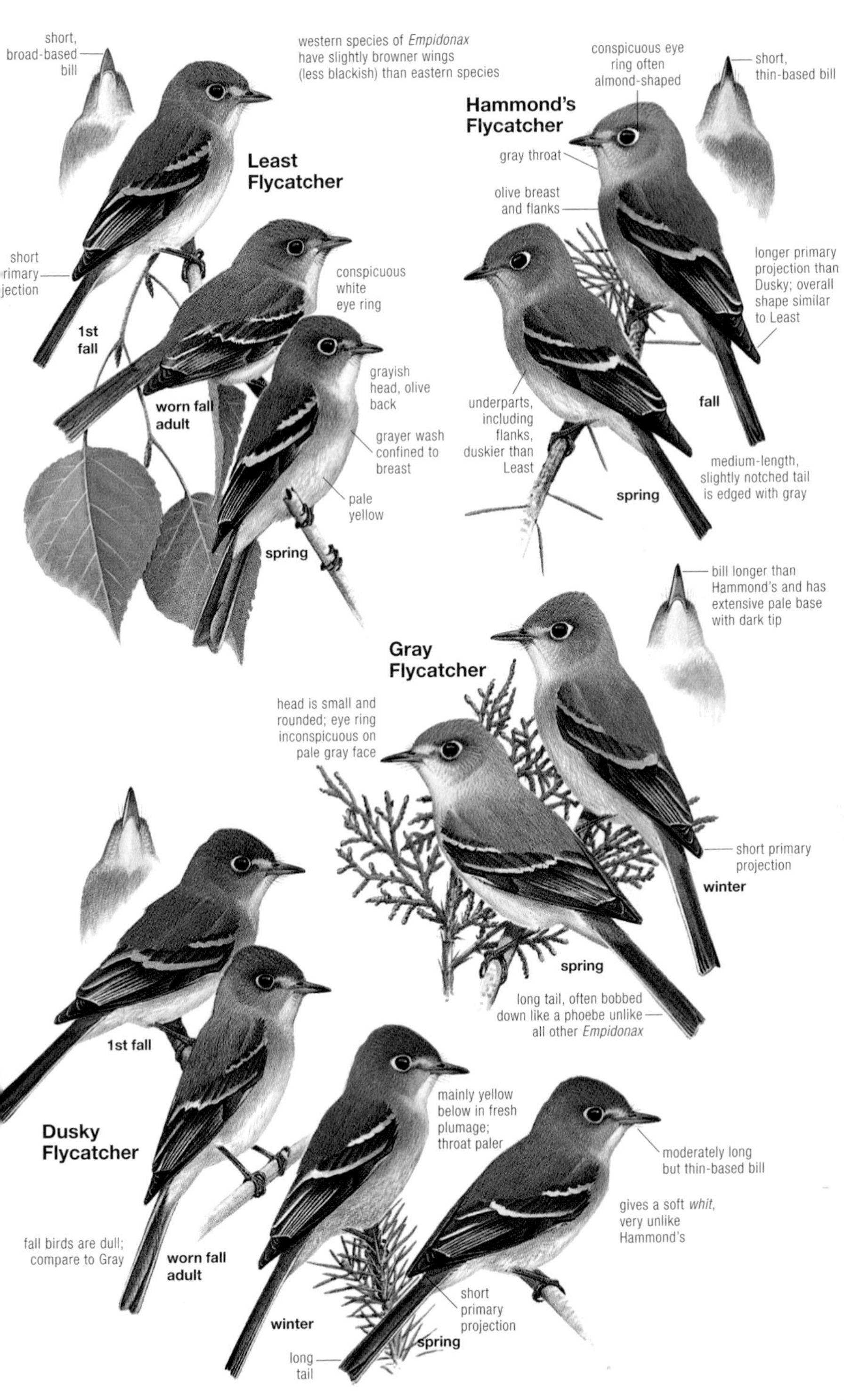
short, broad-based bill
western species of Empidonax have slightly browner wings (less blackish) than eastern species
conspicuous eye ring often almond-shaped
short, thin-based bill
Hammond's Flycatcher
Least Flycatcher
gray throat
olive breast and flanks
short primary projection
conspicuous white eye ring
longer primary projection than Dusky; overall shape similar to Least
1st fall
grayish head, olive back
worn fall adult
grayer wash confined to breast
underparts, including flanks, duskier than Least
fall
medium-length, slightly notched tail is edged with gray
pale yellow
spring
spring
bill longer than Hammond's and has extensive pale base with dark tip
Gray Flycatcher
head is small and rounded; eye ring inconspicuous on pale gray face
short primary projection
winter
spring
long tail, often bobbed down like a phoebe unlike all other Empidonax
1st fall
mainly yellow below in fresh plumage; throat paler
Dusky Flycatcher
moderately long but thin-based bill
gives a soft whit, very unlike Hammond's
fall birds are dull; compare to Gray
worn fall adult
short primary projection
winter
spring
long tail

Pacific-slope Flycatcher *Empidonax difficilis*

L 5½" (14 cm) Formerly considered same species as Cordilleran; known together as Western Flycatcher. Brownish green above; yellowish below with brownish tinge on breast. Broad pale eye ring, often broken above, expanded behind eye; lower mandible entirely orangish. Tail longer, wing tip slightly shorter than Yellow-bellied; wings and back slightly browner; less contrast in wing bars and tertial edges. Pacific-slope molts after arrival on winter grounds, so migrating ***fall adults*** appear more worn than spring birds. ***First-fall*** birds duller; wing bars buffy; variably whitish below, compare with Least Flycatcher (previous page). Channel Islands race, *insulicola,* is slightly duller.

Voice: Call is a sharp *seet;* male gives upslurred *psee-yeet* note. Song is a complex series of notes, including call notes.

Range: Common in moist woodlands, coniferous forests, and shady canyons. Winters mainly in lowlands of western Mexico. Common migrant through Southwest lowlands east to southeastern Arizona. Casual in fall to St. Lawrence Island, Alaska.

Cordilleran Flycatcher *Empidonax occidentalis*

L 5¾" (15 cm) Formerly considered same species as Pacific-slope Flycatcher and together known as Western Flycatcher. Nearly identical but slightly larger, darker, and greener above; more olive and yellow below.

Voice: Separable in field only by male's call, a two-note *pit peet;* some populations in western portion of breeding range give more intermediate notes. *Seet* note perhaps sharper in Cordilleran than Pacific-slope Flycatcher.

Range: Breeds in coniferous forests and canyons in mountains of the West, the northern limit being debatable. Rare in lowlands in migration, even within breeding range. Casual on the Great Plains. Winters in mountains of Mexico.

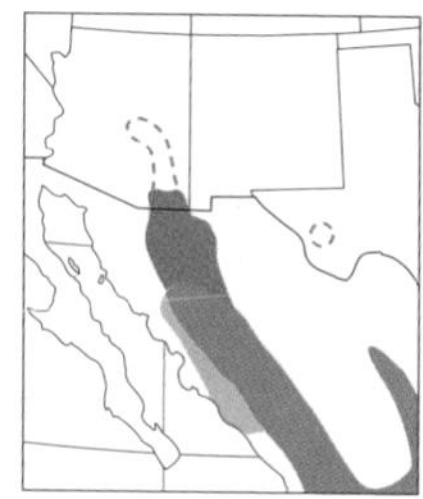

Buff-breasted Flycatcher *Empidonax fulvifrons*

L 5" (13 cm) Smallest *Empidonax* flycatcher. Brownish above; breast cinnamon-buff, paler on worn summer birds. Whitish eye ring; pale wing bars; small bill, with lower mandible entirely pale orange. Molts before migration.

Voice: Call note is a soft *pwit.* Typical song, a quick *chicky-whew* or *chee-lick.*

Range: Small colonies nest in dry woodlands of canyon floors. Very local in Huachuca and Chiricahua Mountains, Arizona (with a few birds farther north); recently in Davis Mountains, Texas; now casual in New Mexico, but recorded recently in Peloncillo and Animas Mountains. Formerly more widespread as a breeder.

IDENTIFYING: Western *Empidonax* Flycatchers Before sorting out the various western species of *Empidonax,* it is first essential to differentiate a *Contopus* pewee from an empid. Western Wood-Pewees, common to abundant at times and conspicuous over much of the West, resemble empids, particularly Willow Flycatcher, which, like pewees, lacks a conspicuous eye ring. Pewees have much longer primary projection than any empid and don't habitually wag their tails (all empids do), except sometimes when singing on territory. Western *Empidonax* species show duller

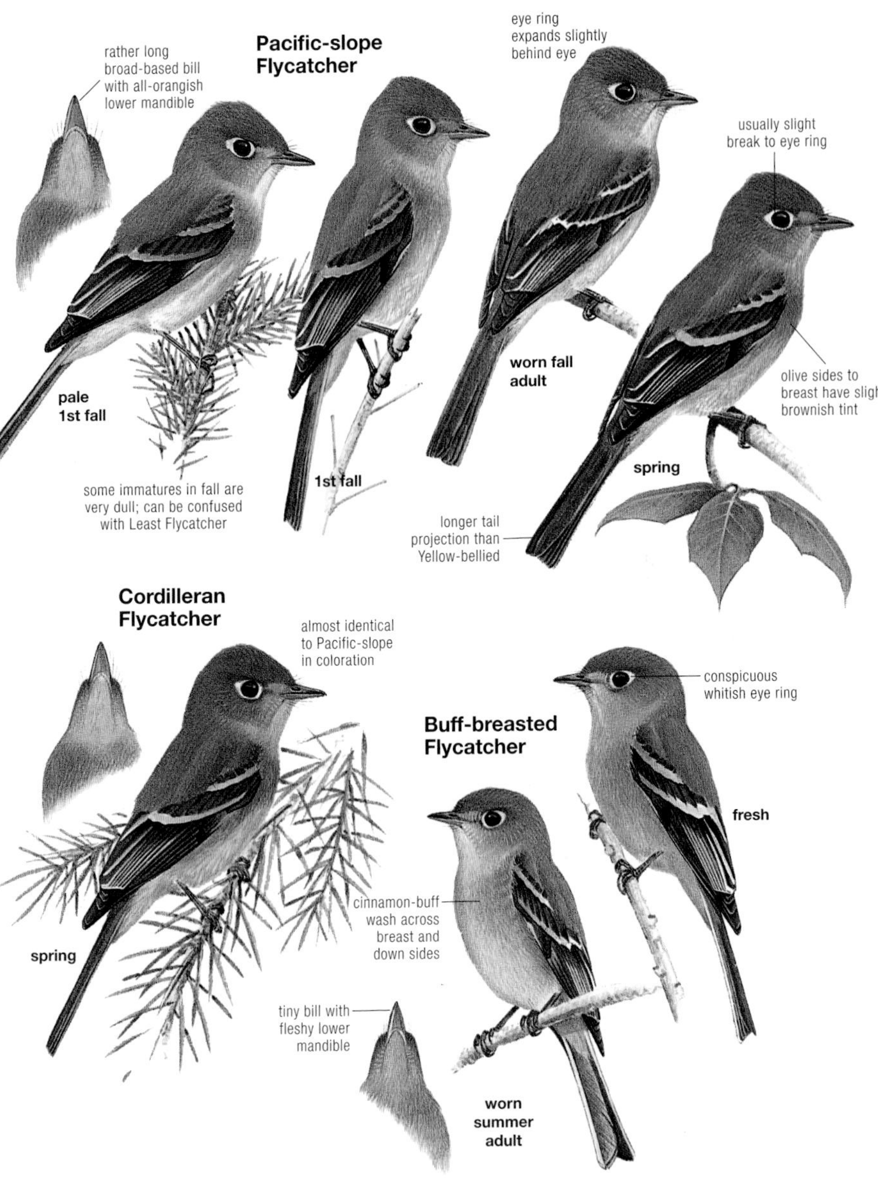

wings and less contrasting tertial edges and wing bars than their eastern congeners. In separating species, consider coloration (shades of grayish, rather than mostly olive or yellowish olive), eye ring strength, primary projection, tail length, and all vocalizations. All empids give contact calls year-round, and it is worth following a silent bird around until it starts calling. Many species give a *whit* call, although the calls differ in character. Some (e.g., Cordilleran and Pacific-slope) and Hammond's give an entirely different call. Finally, the timing of molt can be an important characteristic.

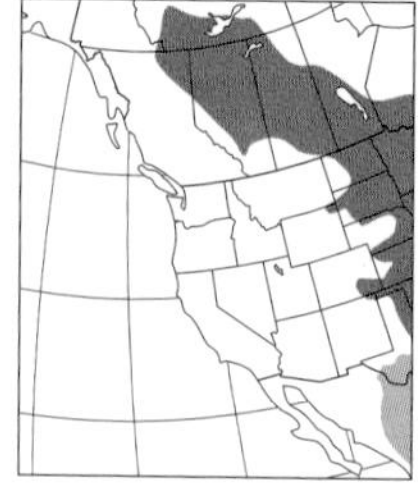

Eastern Phoebe *Sayornis phoebe L 7" (18 cm)*
Brownish gray above, darkest on head, wings, and tail. Underparts mostly white with pale olive wash on sides and breast; ***fresh fall*** bird washed with yellow below. Molts before migration. All phoebes are distinguished from pewees (page 256) by their habit of pumping down and spreading their tails; Eastern Phoebe also by all-dark bill and lack of distinct wing bars. Also compare lack of eye rings and wing bars with *Empidonax* flycatchers (previous pages).
Voice: Distinctive song, a harsh, emphatic *fee-be,* accented on first syllable. Typical call note is a sharp *chip.*
Range: Uncommon to fairly common in woodlands and along streams; often nests under bridges, in eaves and rafters. Casual to rare migrant (chiefly late fall) over much of West. Rare in winter in California and the Southwest.

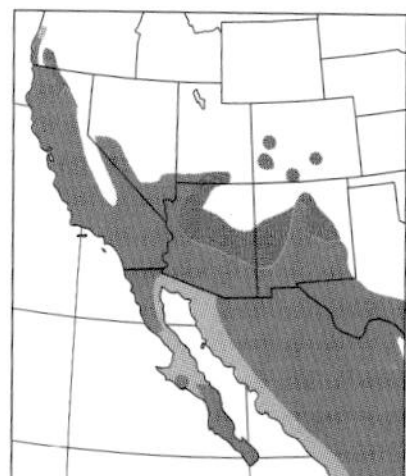

Black Phoebe *Sayornis nigricans L 6¾" (17 cm)*
Black head, upperparts, and breast; white belly and undertail coverts. ***Juvenal*** plumage, held briefly, is browner, with two cinnamon wing bars, cinnamon rump.
Voice: Four-syllable song, a rising *pee-wee* followed by a descending *pee-wee.* Calls include a loud *tseee* and a sharper *tsip,* slightly more plaintive than Eastern Phoebe.
Range: Common near water. Casual to Washington and British Columbia, but range expanding northward.

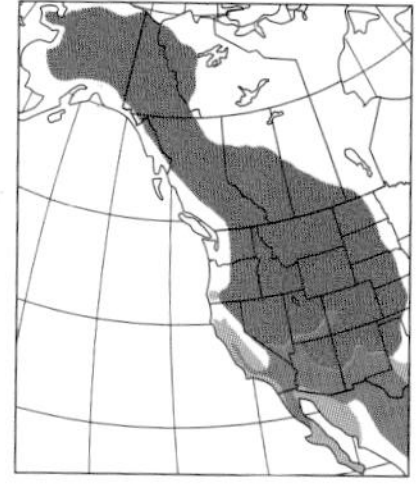

Say's Phoebe *Sayornis saya L 7½" (19 cm)*
Grayish brown above, darkest on head, wings, and tail; breast and throat pale grayish brown; belly and undertail coverts tawny.
Voice: Song is a fast *pit-tse-ar,* often given in fluttering flight. Typical call, a plaintive, whistled *pee-ee,* slightly downslurred.
Range: Fairly common in dry, open areas, canyons, cliffs; perches on bushes, boulders, fences. Highly migratory. An early spring migrant; withdraws from wintering areas in early March. Very rare in coastal Pacific Northwest.

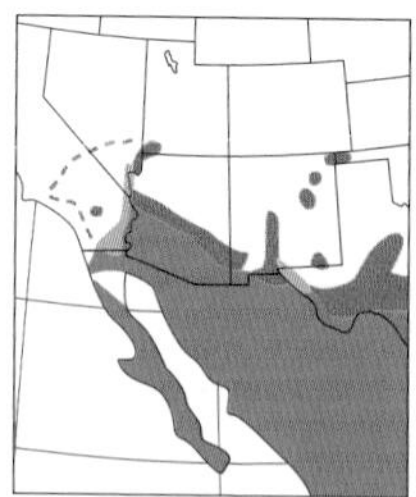

Vermilion Flycatcher *Pyrocephalus rubinus L 6" (15 cm)*
Adult male strikingly red and brown. ***Adult female*** grayish brown above, with blackish tail; throat and breast white, with dusky streaking; belly and undertail coverts are peach; note also whitish eyebrow and forehead. ***Juvenile*** resembles adult female but is spotted rather than streaked below; belly white, often with yellowish tinge. ***Immature male*** begins to resemble adult by midwinter. Frequently pumps and spreads its tail down, like a phoebe.
Voice: Male in breeding season sings during fluttery display flight. Song is a soft, tinkling *pit-a-see pit-a-see;* also sings while perched. Typical call note is a sharp, thin *pseep.*
Range: Uncommon to fairly common and approachable; found along streamsides, near small wooded ponds, and at moist pastures and golf courses. Rare winter visitor to coastal southern California. Casual elsewhere in western North America, primarily in fall and winter.

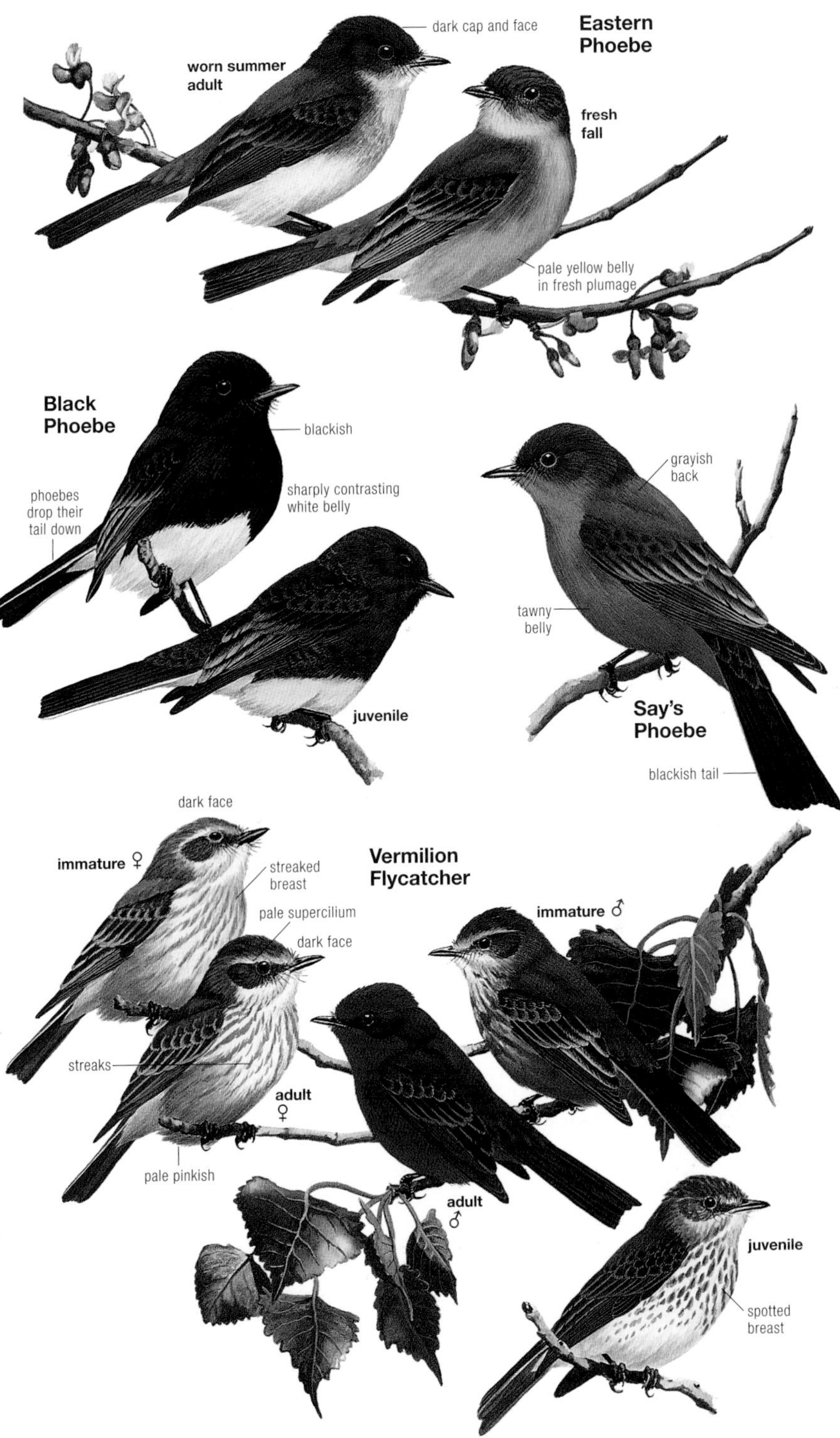
Eastern Phoebe
dark cap and face
worn summer adult
fresh fall
pale yellow belly in fresh plumage
Black Phoebe
blackish
sharply contrasting white belly
phoebes drop their tail down
juvenile
grayish back
tawny belly
Say's Phoebe
blackish tail
dark face
immature ♀
streaked breast
Vermilion Flycatcher
pale supercilium
dark face
immature ♂
streaks
adult ♀
pale pinkish
adult ♂
juvenile
spotted breast

Myiarchus Flycatchers

Myiarchus, with their longer tails and shorter wings, are less visible than kingbirds and tend to work more within the canopy. Bill size, tail pattern (of adults), and brightness of yellow belly are some of the important characteristics to scrutinize in identifying *Myiarchus.*

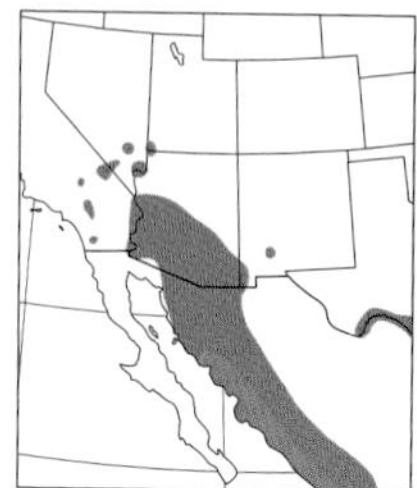

Brown-crested Flycatcher *Myiarchus tyrannulus*
L 8¾" (22 cm) Brownish olive above; as in all *Myiarchus* flycatchers, shows a bushy crest, rufous in primaries; bill longer, thicker, broader than Ash-throated Flycatcher. Throat and breast are pale gray; belly slightly paler yellow than Great Crested Flycatcher. Tail feathers show reddish on outer two-thirds of inner webs. Texas race, *cooperi,* is smaller than southwestern *magister.*
Voice: Song is a clear musical whistle, a rolling *whit-will-do.* Call is a sharp *whit.*
Range: Fairly common in saguaro desert, river groves, lower mountain woodlands. Casual migrant in southern California outside very limited breeding range; and to California coast in fall.

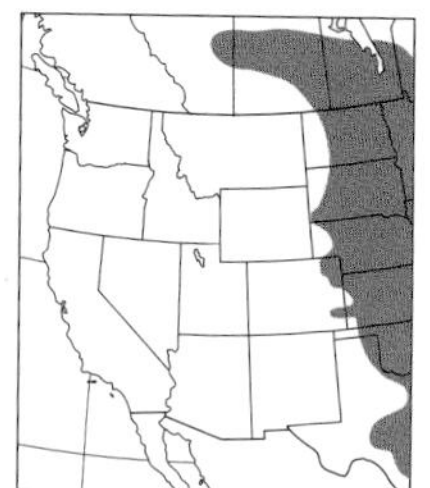

Great Crested Flycatcher *Myiarchus crinitus*
L 8½" (21 cm) Dark olive above. Gray throat and breast; bright lemon yellow belly. Note broad, sharply contrasting edge to inner tertial. Outer tail feathers show entirely reddish inner webs.
Voice: Distinctive call is a loud whistled *wheep*; sometimes given in a quick series. Song is a clear, loud *queeleep, queelur, queeleep.*
Range: Uncommon to rare in limited western breeding range. Rare migrant on Great Plains away from few nesting areas. Very rare on California coast during fall migration (mid-Sept. to mid-Oct.; casual (fall) in Southwest. Accidental to Alaska and northwestern Canada.

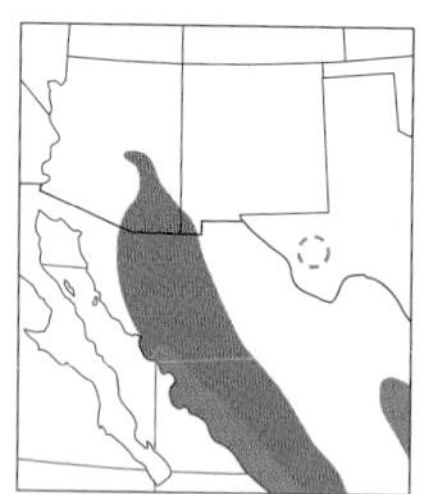

Dusky-capped Flycatcher *Myiarchus tuberculifer*
L 6¾" (17 cm) Smaller, bill larger, belly and undertail coverts usually brighter yellow than Ash-throated Flycatcher; tail shows less rufous. Secondaries have rufous edges, unlike other *Myiarchus.*
Voice: Most common call is a mournful, descending *peeur.*
Range: Fairly common in wooded mountain ranges. Rare in summer in west Texas. Very rare in late fall and winter in southeastern Arizona and southern and central California; casual to Oregon, Nevada, and Colorado.

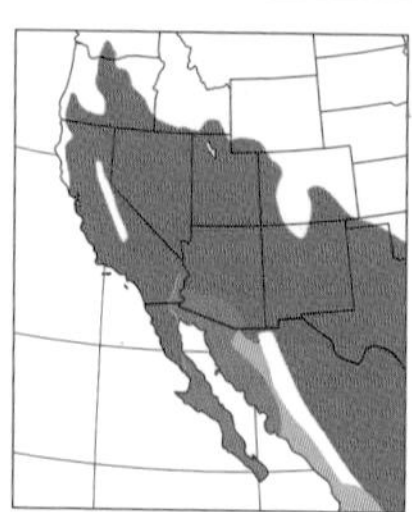

Ash-throated Flycatcher *Myiarchus cinerascens*
L 7¾" (19 cm) Grayish brown above; throat and breast pale gray; underparts paler than Brown-crested. Tail shows rufous on inner webs with dark tips. As in all *Myiarchus* flycatchers, briefly held ***juvenal*** plumage shows mostly reddish tail.
Voice: Distinctive call, heard year-round, is a rough *prrrt.* Song, heard on breeding grounds, is a series of burry *ka-brick* notes.
Range: Common in a wide variety of habitats. Very rare in winter on California coast. Casual north to British Columbia.

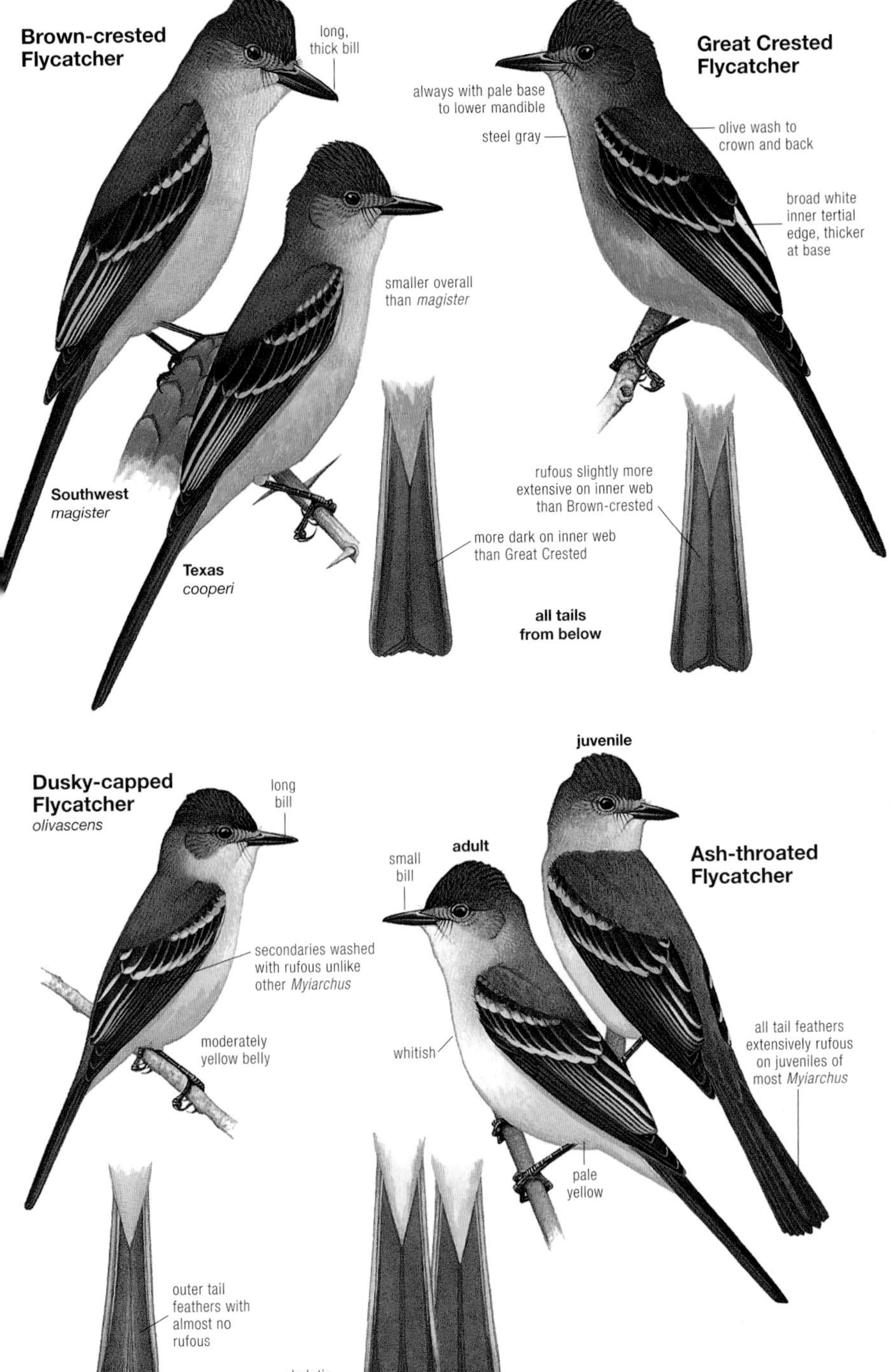

Brown-crested Flycatcher
long, thick bill
Southwest magister
Texas cooperi
smaller overall than magister
more dark on inner web than Great Crested
Great Crested Flycatcher
always with pale base to lower mandible
steel gray
olive wash to crown and back
broad white inner tertial edge, thicker at base
rufous slightly more extensive on inner web than Brown-crested
all tails from below
Dusky-capped Flycatcher
olivascens
long bill
secondaries washed with rufous unlike other Myiarchus
moderately yellow belly
outer tail feathers with almost no rufous
Ash-throated Flycatcher
juvenile
adult
small bill
whitish
pale yellow
all tail feathers extensively rufous on juveniles of most Myiarchus
dark tip
adult
juvenile

Cassin's Kingbird *Tyrannus vociferans* *L 9" (23 cm)*
Dark brown tail; narrow buffy tips and lack of white edges on outer tail feathers help distinguish this species from Western Kingbird. Bill much shorter than Tropical and Couch's Kingbirds. Upperparts darker gray than Western, washed with olive on back; paler wings contrast with darker back. White chin contrasts with dark gray head and breast. Belly dull yellow. ***Juvenile*** is duller, slightly browner above, with bold buffy edges on wing coverts; paler below.
Voice: Most common call, given year-round, is a short, loud *chi-bew,* accented on second syllable.
Range: Fairly common in varied habitats; usually prefers denser foliage and hillier country than Western Kingbird. Scarce migrant away from breeding areas. Accidental to Oregon and Idaho.

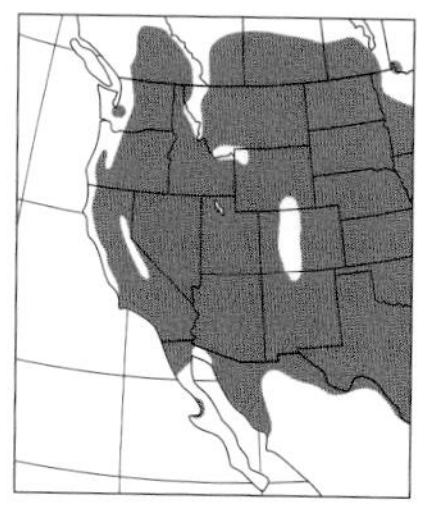

Western Kingbird *Tyrannus verticalis* *L 8¾" (22 cm)*
Black tail, with white edges on outer feathers. Bill much shorter than Tropical and Couch's Kingbirds. Upperparts ashy gray, paler than Cassin's Kingbird, tinged with olive on back; dark wings contrast with paler back. Throat and breast pale gray; belly bright lemon yellow. ***Juvenile*** has slightly more olive on back and buffy edges on wing coverts, brownish tinge on breast, paler yellow belly.
Voice: Common call is a sharp *whit.*
Range: Common in dry, open country; perches on fences and telephone lines. A scarce migrant to coastal Pacific Northwest; casual north to Alaska and northwest Canada. Casual in winter in California.

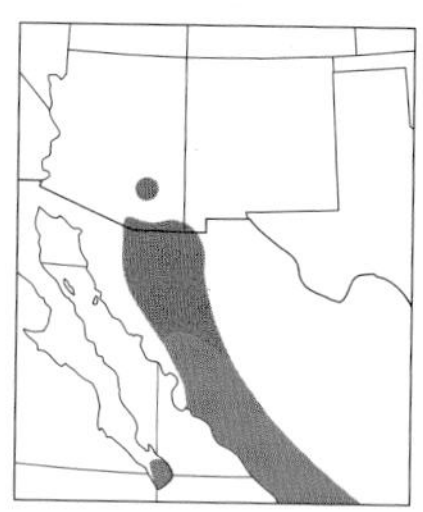

Thick-billed Kingbird *Tyrannus crassirostris*
L 9½" (24 cm) Large, with very large bill. ***Adult*** is dusky brown above, with a slightly darker head and seldom-seen yellow crown patch; whitish underparts washed with pale gray on breast, pale yellow on belly and undertail coverts. Yellow is brighter and more extensive in fresh fall adult and in ***first-fall*** birds, which have buffy edgings on wing coverts. Fall birds resemble Tropical Kingbird, but have heavier bill and darker head.
Voice: Common call is a loud, high, whistled *pureet.*
Range: Perches high in sycamores of lowland streamsides. Breeds in Guadalupe Canyon and around Patagonia; rare elsewhere in southeastern Arizona. Casual during fall and winter west to southern California and in summer to west Texas (Big Bend). Accidental to British Columbia and Colorado.

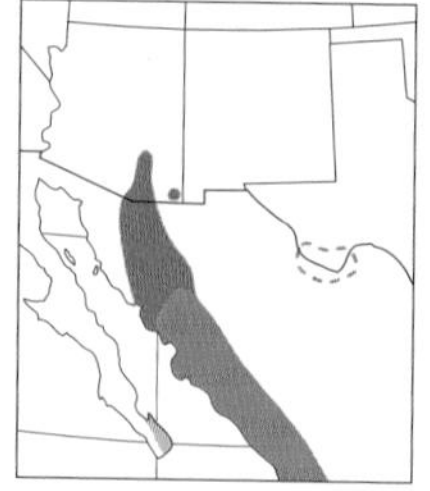

Tropical Kingbird *Tyrannus melancholicus* *L 9¼" (24 cm)*
Almost identical to Couch's Kingbird (casual in West). Bill is thinner and longer; back slightly grayer, less green; at close range, tips of individual primaries are unevenly staggered on adults. Distinguished from Western and Cassin's Kingbirds by larger bill, darker ear patch, brighter underparts, and slightly notched brown tail.
Voice: Distinctive call is a rapid, twittering *pip-pip-pip-pip.*
Range: Uncommon and local in southeastern Arizona; rare along Rio Grande in Big Bend National Park; found in lowlands near water. Rare but regular during fall and winter along the West Coast to British Columbia, casually to southeast Alaska.

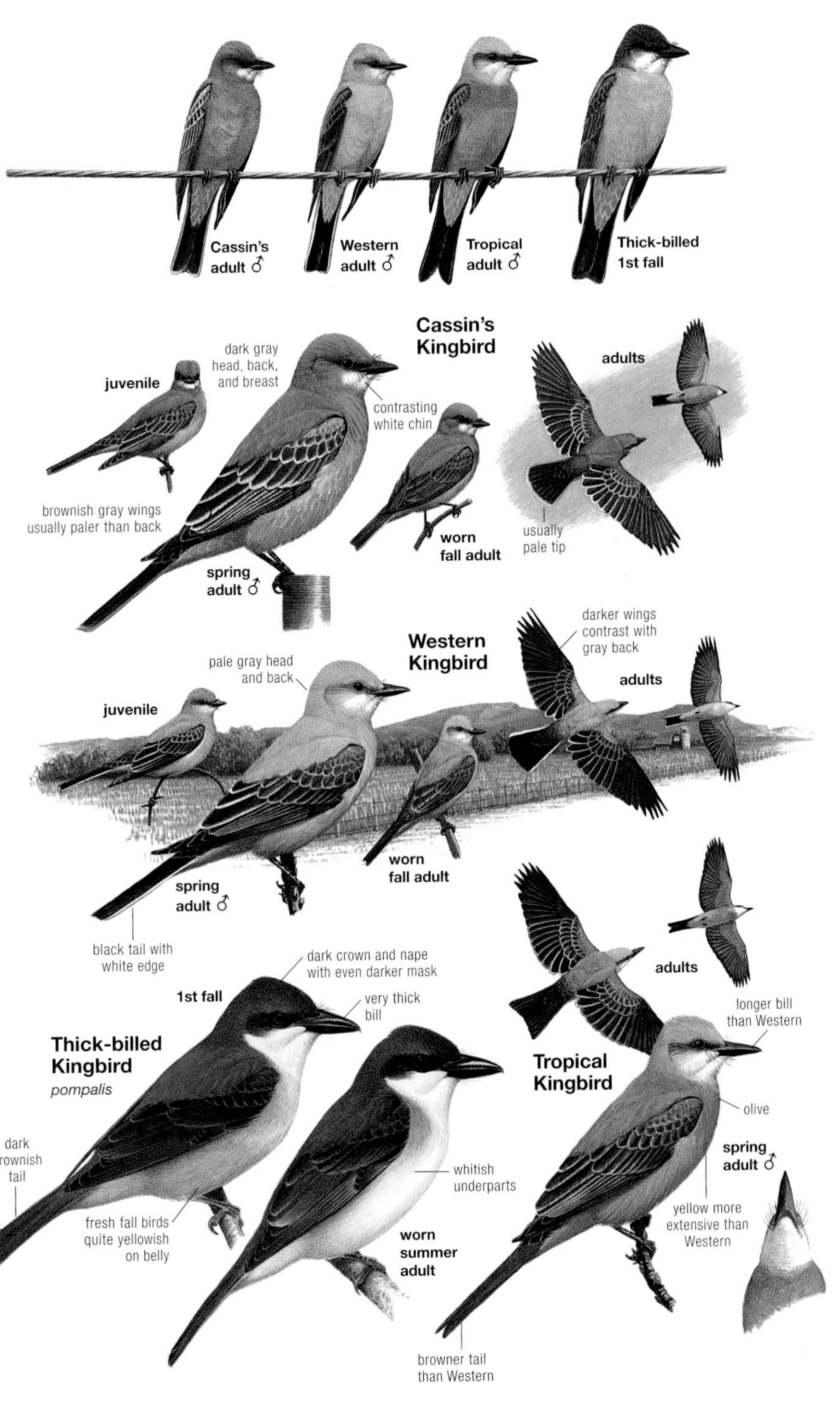

Cassin's adult ♂
Western adult ♂
Tropical adult ♂
Thick-billed 1st fall
Cassin's Kingbird
dark gray head, back, and breast
juvenile
contrasting white chin
adults
brownish gray wings usually paler than back
worn fall adult
usually pale tip
spring adult ♂
Western Kingbird
darker wings contrast with gray back
pale gray head and back
adults
juvenile
worn fall adult
spring adult ♂
black tail with white edge
dark crown and nape with even darker mask
adults
1st fall
very thick bill
longer bill than Western
Thick-billed Kingbird
pompalis
Tropical Kingbird
olive
dark
rownish
tail
whitish underparts
spring adult ♂
fresh fall birds quite yellowish on belly
worn summer adult
yellow more extensive than Western
browner tail than Western

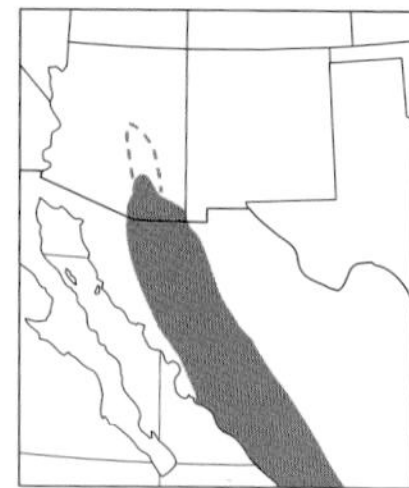
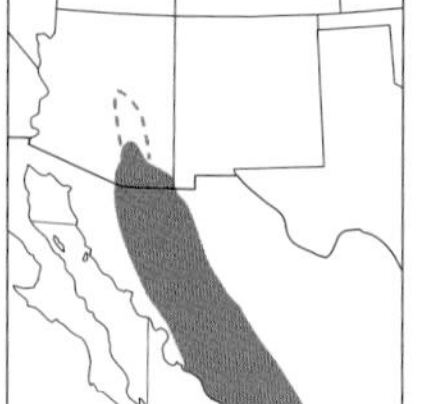

Sulphur-bellied Flycatcher *Myiodynastes luteiventris*
L $8\frac{1}{2}$" (22 cm) Boldly streaked above and below. Upperparts often show an olive tinge; rump and tail rusty red; underparts pale yellow.
Voice: Loud call is an excited chatter, like the squeaking of a rubber duck. Song is a soft *tre-le-re-re.*
Range: Fairly common in woodlands of mountain canyons, usually at elevations between 5,000 and 6,000 feet. Inconspicuous; often perches high in the canopy. Casual to New Mexico in summer; casual to and coastal California (fall). Accidental to west Texas and Colorado.

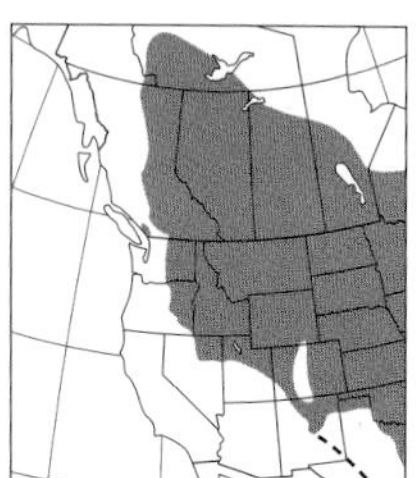
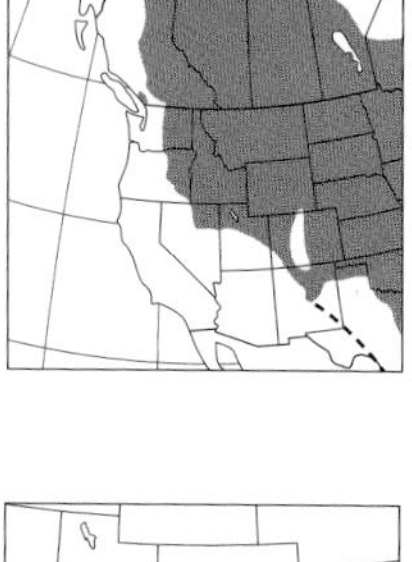

Eastern Kingbird *Tyrannus tyrannus L $8\frac{1}{2}$" (22 cm)*
Black head, slate gray back; tail has a broad white terminal band. Underparts are white, with a pale gray wash across the breast. Orange-red crown patch is seldom visible. ***Juvenile*** brownish gray above, darker on breast.
Voice: Call is a harsh *dzeet* note, also given in a series.
Range: Uncommon to fairly common and conspicuous in woodland clearings, farms, and orchards; often seen near water. Rare migrant to Southwest, the West Coast, and Alaska, where recorded north and west to Nome and Point Barrow. Winters in South America.

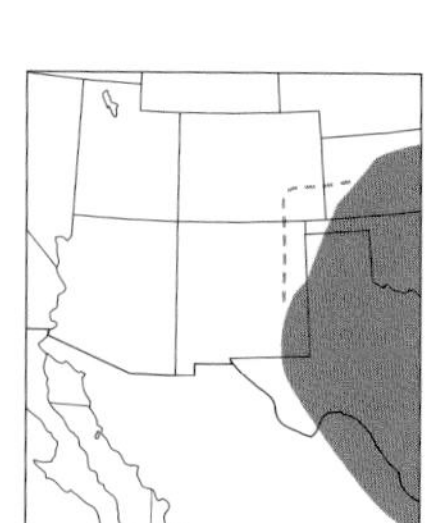
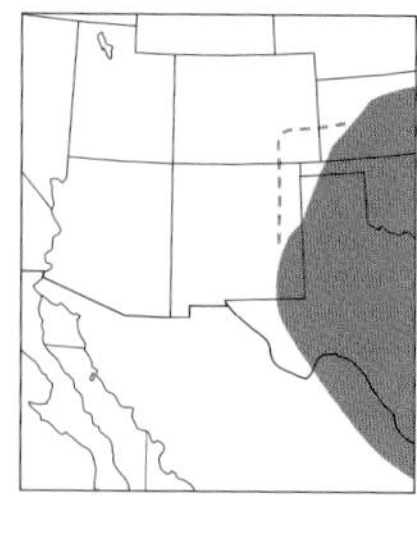

Scissor-tailed Flycatcher *Tyrannus forficatus*
L 13" (33 cm) Pearl gray above; whitish below with orange-buff flanks and salmon pink underwing, which is best viewed in flight. Has very long outer tail feathers, white with black tips; also salmon pink wing linings with reddish axillaries. ***Male***'s tail is longer than female's; ***juvenile*** is paler overall, with shorter tail.
Voice: Song and calls similar to Western Kingbird.
Range: Uncommon to fairly common in limited western breeding range; found in semi-open country. This species in an early spring and late fall migrant. Very rare to casual wanderer in much of western North America; recorded north to Alaska.

Becards

Becards are possibly related to the tyrannid flycatchers. Tropical in distribution, just one species barely reaches the southern U.S.

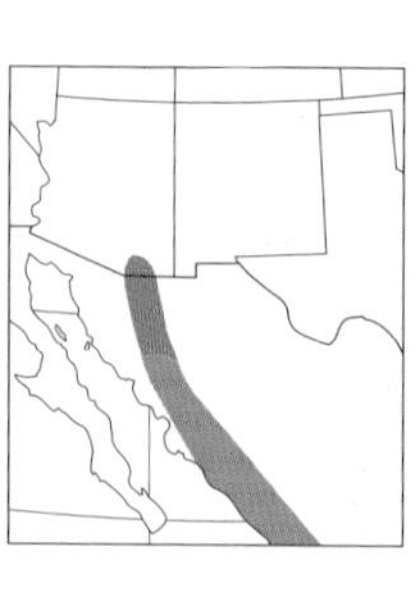

Rose-throated Becard *Pachyramphus aglaiae*
L $7\frac{1}{4}$" (18 cm) Rosy throat distinctive in male; west Mexico ***adult male,*** *albiventris*, has blackish cap, pale gray underparts. ***Female*** has slate gray crown, browner back. ***First-fall male*** shows partially pink throat; acquires full adult plumage after second summer. Foot-long nest is suspended from a tree limb.
Voice: Call, a thin, mournful *seeoo,* is sometimes preceded by chatter.
Range: Range extends north from west Mexico to southeastern Arizona, where it is very local. Casual in winter. Accidental to west Texas.

dark mask
bordered by
whitish lines
rk streaks
yellowish
nderparts
Sulphur-bellied
Flycatcher
rufous
tail
blackish
small bill
Eastern
Kingbird
juvenile
white
belly
white
tail tip
juvenile
reddish pink
adult ♂
Scissor-tailed
Flycatcher
pale gray head
and back
juvenile
ult
♂
orange
buff
long forked tail with extensive white;
female and juvenile have shorter tails
blackish
cap
thick,
stubby bill
1st fall ♂
♀
pale buff
underparts
dark
cap
rose
throat
Rose-
throated
Becard
albiventris
adult
♂

Shrikes (Family Laniidae)

These masked hunters scan the countryside from lookout perches, then swoop down on insects, rodents, snakes, and small birds. Known as "butcher-birds," they often impale their prey on thorns. Recent research indicates that this is to mark territory and attract mates.

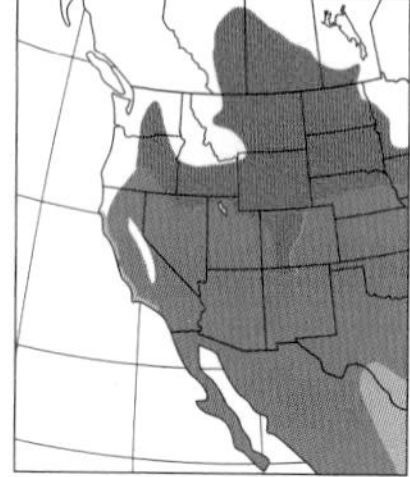

Loggerhead Shrike *Lanius ludovicianus L 9" (23 cm)*
Slightly smaller and darker than Northern Shrike. Head and back medium gray; underparts white, clean or very faintly barred. Broad black mask extends above eye and thinly across top of bill. All-dark bill, shorter than Northern Shrike, with smaller hook. Rump varies from gray to whitish. ***Juvenile*** is paler and barred overall, with brownish gray upperparts; acquires ***adult*** plumage by first fall. Seen in flight, wings and tail are darker and white wing patches smaller than Northern Mockingbird (page 316).
Voice: Song is a medley of low warbles and harsh, squeaky notes; calls include a harsh *shack-shack.*
Range: Hunts in open or brushy areas, diving from a low perch and then rising swiftly to the next lookout. Fairly common but overall declining over parts of range. The endangered race *mearnsi* (**E**) is endemic to San Clemente Island off southern California. Rare visitor to Pacific Northwest.

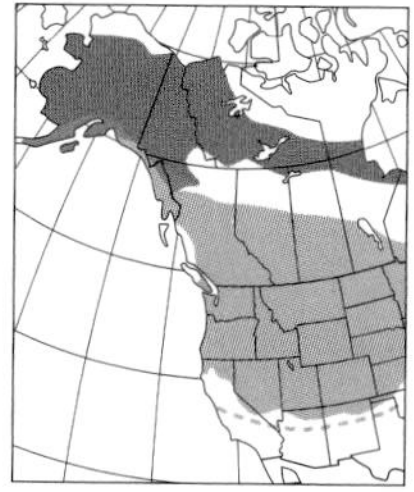

Northern Shrike *Lanius excubitor L 10" (25 cm)*
Larger than Loggerhead Shrike, with paler head and back, lightly barred underparts; rump whitish. Mask narrower than Loggerhead, does not extend above eye; feathering above bill is white. Bill longer, with a more distinct hook. Often bobs its tail. ***Juvenile*** brownish above and more heavily barred below than adult. ***Immature*** grayer; retains barring on underparts until first spring.
Voice: Song and calls similar to Loggerhead.
Range: Uncommon; often perches high in tall trees.

Vireos (Family Vireonidae)

Short, sturdy bills slightly hooked at the tip characterize these small songbirds. Vireos are closely related to shrikes. Some have "spectacles" and wing bars. Others have eyebrow stripes and no wing bars. They are generally chunkier and less active than warblers.

Hutton's Vireo *Vireo huttoni L 5" (13 cm)*
Grayish olive above, with pale area in lores; white eye ring broken above eye. Subspecies vary from paler, grayer southwestern *stephensi* to greener coastal races such as *huttoni.* Separated from Ruby-crowned Kinglet by larger size, thicker bill, lack of dark area below lower wing bar, and voice.
Voice: Song is a repeated or mixed rising *zu-wee* and descending *zoe zoo;* also a flat *chew.* Calls include a low *chit* and whining chatter; birds from interior Southwest give a harsher *tchurr-ree.*
Range: Fairly common in woodlands; casual to western Nevada, southeastern California, and southwestern Arizona.

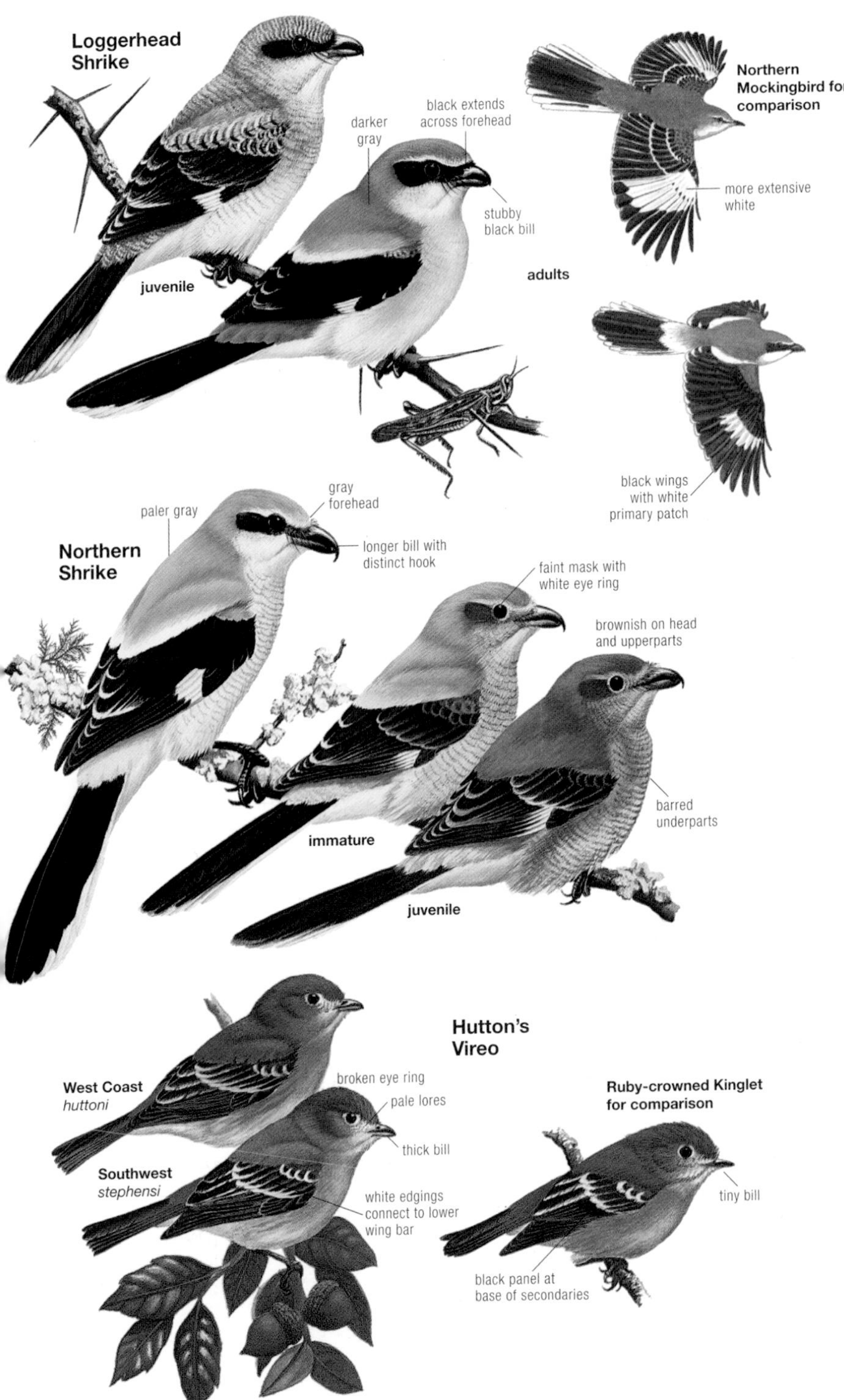

Loggerhead Shrike
juvenile
darker gray
black extends across forehead
stubby black bill
adults
Northern Mockingbird for comparison
more extensive white
black wings with white primary patch
Northern Shrike
paler gray
gray forehead
longer bill with distinct hook
faint mask with white eye ring
brownish on head and upperparts
barred underparts
immature
juvenile
Hutton's Vireo
West Coast
huttoni
broken eye ring
pale lores
thick bill
Southwest
stephensi
white edgings connect to lower wing bar
Ruby-crowned Kinglet for comparison
tiny bill
black panel at base of secondaries

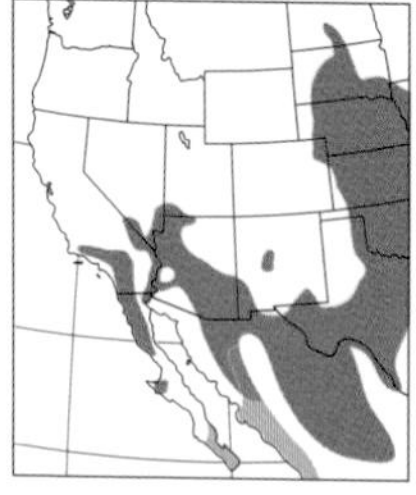

Bell's Vireo *Vireo bellii* *L 4¾" (12 cm)*
Plumage variable. Endangered West Coast race, *pusillus* (**E**), is gray above, whitish below, with indistinct white spectacles; one or two whitish wing bars. More easterly nominate race, casual in West, is greenish above, yellowish below; often bobs tail. Southwestern *medius* and *arizonae* are intermediate. Active, rather secretive.
Voice: Song, a series of harsh, scolding notes. Calls are wrenlike.
Range: Uncommon to fairly common in moist woodlands, bottomlands, and mesquite. Rarely seen during migration.

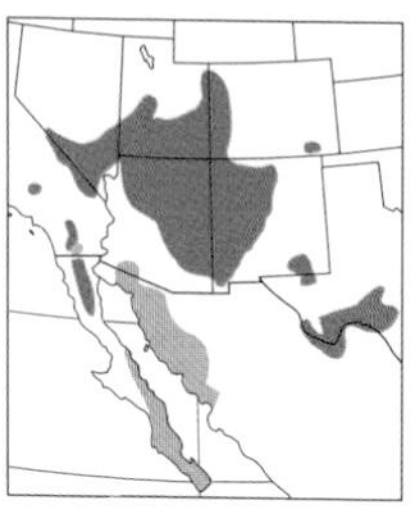

Gray Vireo *Vireo vicinior* *L 5½" (14 cm)*
White eye ring; wings brownish, with faint wing bars, the lower more prominent; short primary projection; long tail. Compare with smaller West Coast race, *pusillus*, of Bell's Vireo. Sticks to undergrowth; flicks tail as it forages.
Voice: Song is a series of musical *chu-wee chu-weet* notes, faster and sweeter than Plumbeous. Calls include shrill, descending musical notes.
Range: Breeds in semiarid habitat. Almost unknown as a migrant; accidental on southern California coast and offshore islands and in Wyoming and western Great Plains.

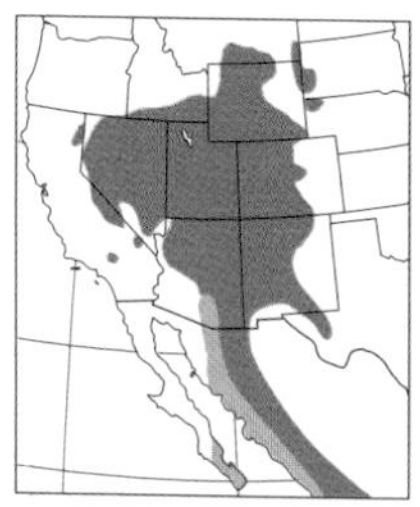

Plumbeous Vireo *Vireo plumbeus* *L 5¼" (13 cm)*
Larger, with bigger bill than Cassin's Vireo; also has sharper contrast between head and throat; gray upperparts. Pattern of tail feathers similar to Blue-headed Vireo. White wing bars and flight feather edges; pale yellow, if present, only on flanks. Sides of breast gray, sometimes tinged olive. Compare worn summer birds to shorter winged Gray Vireo.
Voice: Song is hoarser than Blue-headed; call a harsh chatter.
Range: Fairly common in varied woodland habitats; rare to California coast in fall and winter. Casual to Oregon.

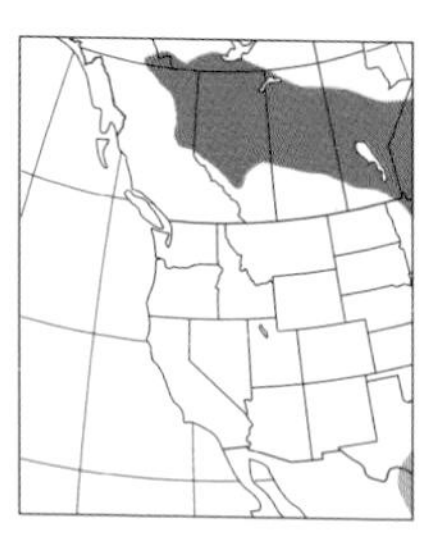

Blue-headed Vireo *Vireo solitarius* *L 5" (13 cm)*
Adult male's solid blue-gray hood contrasts with white spectacles and throat; hood of female and immatures partly gray. All ages have bright olive back; yellow-tinged wing bars and tertials; greenish yellow edges to dark secondaries. Distinct white on outer tail; bright yellow sides and flanks, sometimes mixed with green.
Voice: Song is similar to Red-eyed Vireo, but slower; call like Plumbeous.
Range: Fairly common in mixed woodlands; very rare migrant (chiefly fall) in West, but separation from Cassin's is difficult. Uncommon migrant on western Great Plains.

Cassin's Vireo *Vireo cassinii* *L 5" (13 cm)*
Similar to Blue-headed, but slightly smaller and duller. Less contrast between head and throat; duller, whitish wing bars and tertial edges; less white in tail. Immature female can have entirely green head; compare to Hutton's Vireo.
Voice: Song is hoarser than Blue-headed Vireo, like Plumbeous; call similar.
Range: Uncommon migrant from Colorado to west Texas.

Bell's Vireo

overall grayish color
one rather faint wing bar
rather long tail
subdued head pattern
West Coast
pusillus

bellii
bellii, casual in West, much more olive and yellow than *pusillus; medius* and *arizonae* are intermediate

Gray Vireo

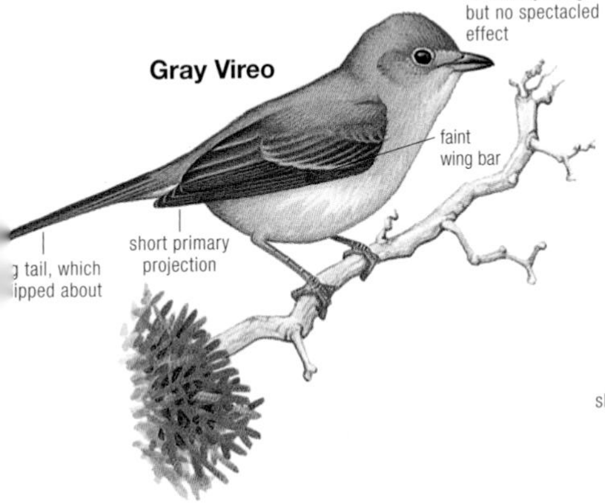
whitish eye ring but no spectacled effect
faint wing bar
short primary projection
tail, which
ipped about

Plumbeous Vireo

plumbeus

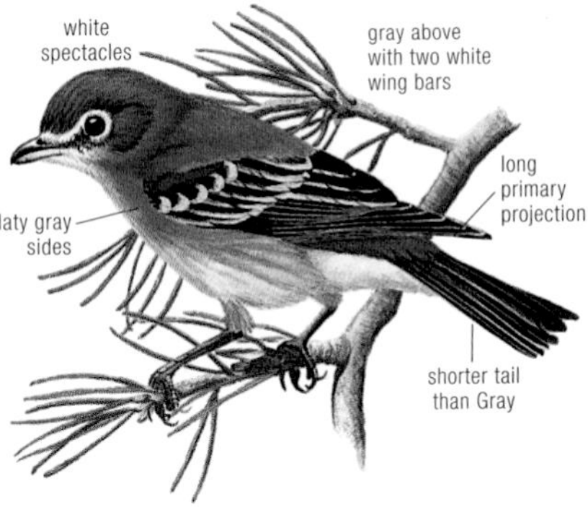
white spectacles
gray above with two white wing bars
long primary projection
slaty gray sides
shorter tail than Gray

Blue-headed Vireo

solitarius

white spectacles, bluish gray head
sharp contrast between auricular and throat
yellow sides with some olive
♂

Cassin's Vireo

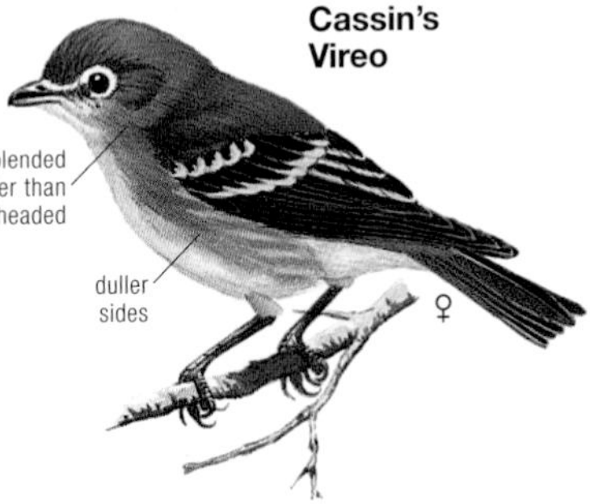
more blended border than Blue-headed
duller sides
♀

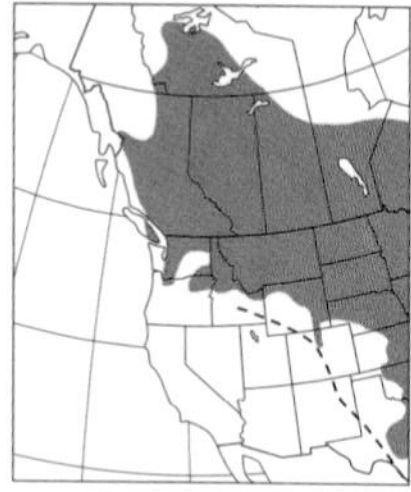

Red-eyed Vireo *Vireo olivaceus L 6" (15 cm)*
Blue-gray crown; white eyebrow bordered above and below with black. Olive back, darker wings and tail; white underparts. Lacks wing bars. Ruby red iris visible at close range. ***First-fall*** bird has brown iris. Immatures and some fall adults have pale yellow on flanks and undertail coverts.
Voice: Persistent song, sung all day, a variable series of deliberate, short phrases. Calls include a nasal, whining *quee.*
Range: Uncommon to fairly common in western breeding range; rare migrant south of breeding range. Winters in South America.

Yellow-green Vireo *Vireo flavoviridis L 6" (15 cm)*
Similar to Red-eyed Vireo, but bill longer; head pattern more blended. Strong yellow-green wash above extends onto sides of face; extensive yellow on sides, flanks, and under tail; brightest in fall.
Voice: Song is a rapid but hesitant series of notes, suggesting House Sparrow.
Range: Very rare in fall to coastal California; to southern Arizona in summer. Casual to New Mexico and Nevada.

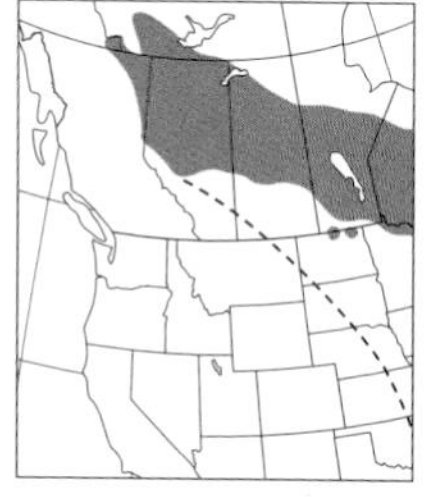

Philadelphia Vireo *Vireo philadelphicus L 5¼" (13 cm)*
Adult variably yellow below, palest on belly. Greenish above, with contrasting grayish cap, dull grayish olive wing bar, dull white eyebrow, and dark eye line. First-fall birds and most ***fall*** adults are often brighter yellow below. Distinguished from Warbling Vireo by dark eye line extending through lores, darker cap, dark primary coverts, and yellow at center of throat and breast. Similar Tennessee Warbler (page 328) has a thinner bill, white undertail coverts.
Voice: Song very closely resembles Red-eyed Vireo but is generally slightly slower, thinner, and higher-pitched.
Range: Uncommon; found in open woodlands, streamside willows and alders. Casual to very rare in West south and west of breeding range; chiefly occurs in fall. Winters in Central America.

Warbling Vireo *Vireo gilvus L 5½" (14 cm)*
Gray or olive-gray above; western birds, especially Pacific race *swainsoni,* are smaller than nominate (breeds in Canada west to Alberta), with slighter bill. Underparts white. Dusky postocular stripe; white eyebrow, without dark upper border; brown eye. Lacks wing bars. Smaller and paler than Red-eyed Vireo; crown does not contrast strongly with back. Birds in fresh ***fall*** plumage tend to be greener above, pale yellow on sides of flanks.
Voice: Song of *gilvus* is delivered in long, melodious, warbling phrases; song of *swainsoni* less musical, with higher tones and break near beginning. Calls include a peevish rising *cheee* and low *chut* notes.
Range: Breeds in deciduous woods; most common vireo in West. Larger eastern nominate race breeds west to southwestern Alberta. Casual in winter to southern California. Winters in Mexico and Central America. Casual fall migrant to western Alaska.

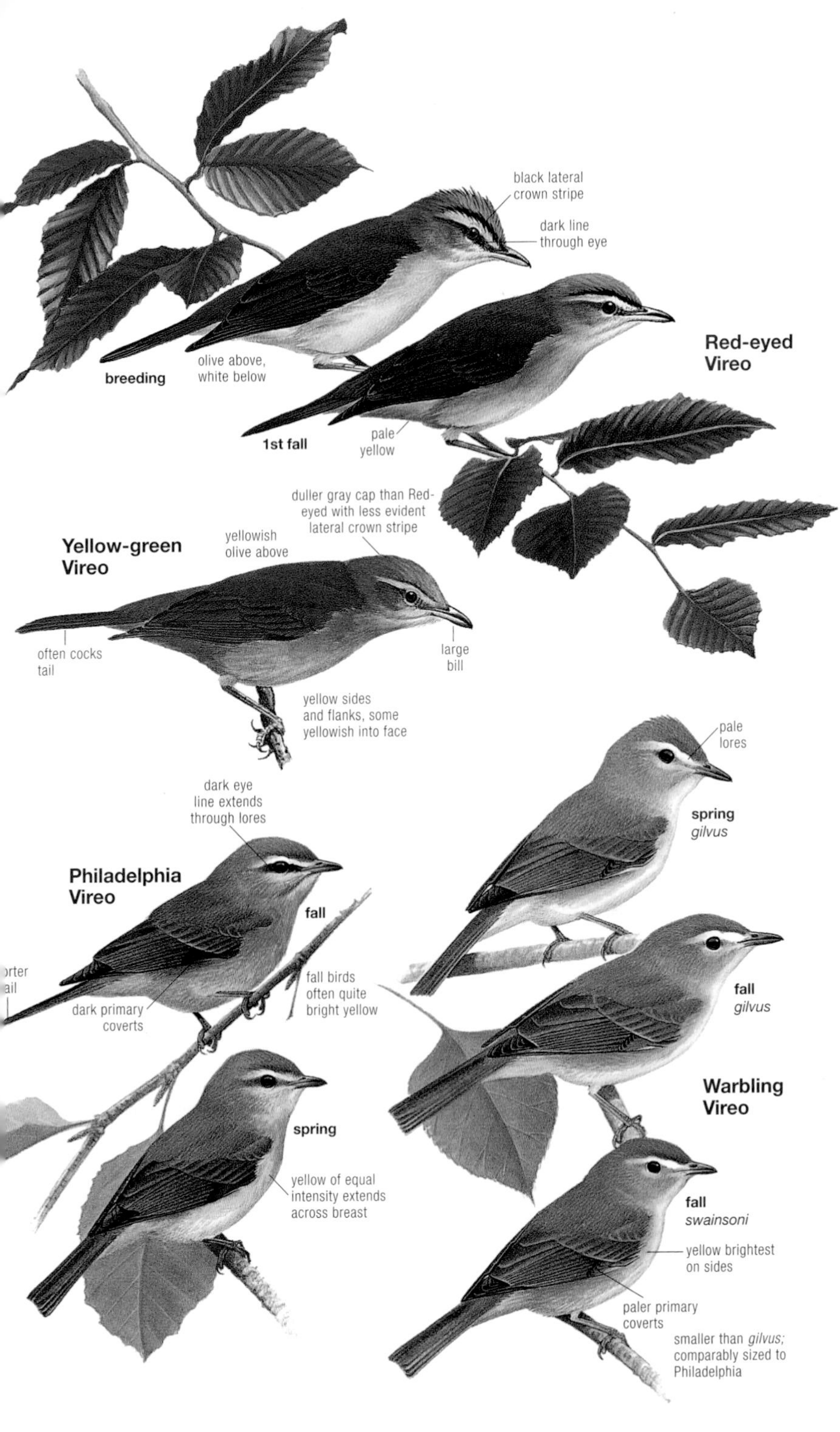
black lateral
crown stripe
dark line
through eye
Red-eyed
Vireo
breeding
olive above,
white below
1st fall
pale
yellow
duller gray cap than Red-
eyed with less evident
lateral crown stripe
yellowish
olive above
Yellow-green
Vireo
often cocks
tail
large
bill
yellow sides
and flanks, some
yellowish into face
pale
lores
spring
gilvus
dark eye
line extends
through lores
Philadelphia
Vireo
fall
fall birds
often quite
bright yellow
dark primary
coverts
fall
gilvus
Warbling
Vireo
spring
yellow of equal
intensity extends
across breast
fall
swainsoni
yellow brightest
on sides
paler primary
coverts
smaller than gilvus;
comparably sized to
Philadelphia

Crows, Jays (Family Corvidae)

Harsh voice and aggressive manner draw attention to these large, often gregarious birds. In most species, bristles cover nostrils. Powerful, all-purpose bill efficiently handles a varied diet.

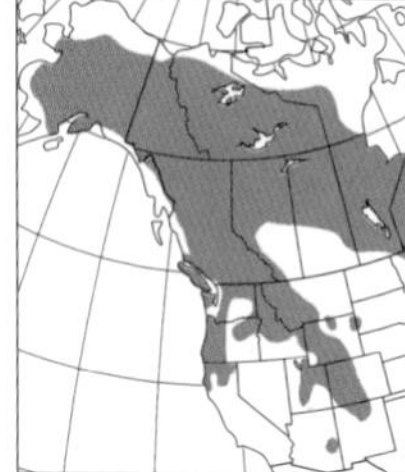

Gray Jay *Perisoreus canadensis L 11½" (29 cm)*
A fluffy, long-tailed jay with small bill and no crest. The three subspecies groups are shown here: Nominate *canadensis,* one of several races common in northern boreal forests, has a white collar and forehead, with dark gray crown and nape; *capitalis,* in the southern Rockies, has a paler crown, head appears mostly white; *obscurus,* coastal resident in the Northwest from Washington to northwestern California, has a larger, darker cap extending to the crown, with underparts paler than in other races. ***Juveniles*** of all races are sooty gray overall, with a faint white moustachial streak. Familiar camp and cabin visitors.
Voice: Call notes include a whistled *wheeoo* and a low *chuck.*
Range: Casual (*obscurus*) south on California coast to Sonoma County.

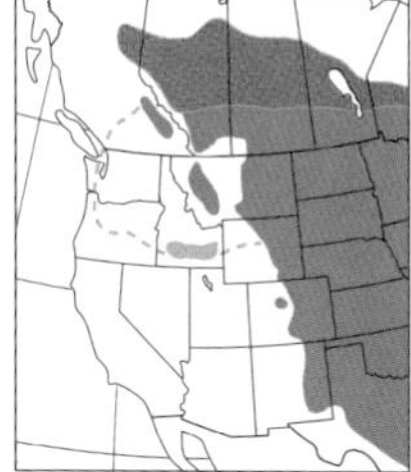

Blue Jay *Cyanocitta cristata L 11" (28 cm)*
Crested jay with black barring and white patches on blue wings and tail, black "necklace" on whitish underparts.
Voice: Most common of varied calls is a piercing *jay jay jay;* also gives a musical *weedle-eedle* and mimics the call of Red-shouldered Hawk. Generally very noisy and bold.
Range: Uncommon to fairly common on western Great Plains in suburbs, parks, and woodlands. Rare and irregular to the Northwest in fall and winter. Casual (mostly winter) to California, Arizona, and west Texas.

Steller's Jay *Cyanocitta stelleri L 11½" (29 cm)*
Crested; dark blue and black overall. Some races, including nominate from coast to northern Rockies, have darker backs and bluish streaks on forehead. Central and southern Rockies race, *macrolopha,* has long crest, paler back, white streaks on forehead, white mark over eye; largest race, *carlottae* (not shown), resident on the Queen Charlotte Islands off British Columbia, is almost entirely black above. Where ranges overlap in the eastern Rockies, Steller's Jay occasionally hybridizes with Blue Jay.
Voice: Calls include a series of *shack* or *shooka* notes and other calls suggestive of Red-shouldered and Red-tailed Hawks.
Range: Common in pine-oak woodlands and coniferous forests. Bold and aggressive; often scavenges at campgrounds and picnic areas. Rare and irregular fall and winter visitor to lower elevations of the Great Basin, west Texas, and southern California, to the southwestern deserts, and to the western Great Plains.

Gray
Jay
sooty
overall
dark rear
to head
whitish
forehead
small bill
pale gray underparts
paler and whiter
headed than
nominate race
darker above with
more extensive
dark nape
juvenile
pale tail
tips
pale
tail tips
boreal
adult
canadensis
southern
Rockies
adult
capitalis
Northwest
adult
obscurus
Blue
Jay
bluish
crest
blackish
throat band
extensive
white
in wings
white
tail tips
Steller's
Jay
black
crest
bluish
lines
longer
crest
grayer
back
white forehead
streaks and
white above eye
stelleri
southern
Rockies
macrolopha

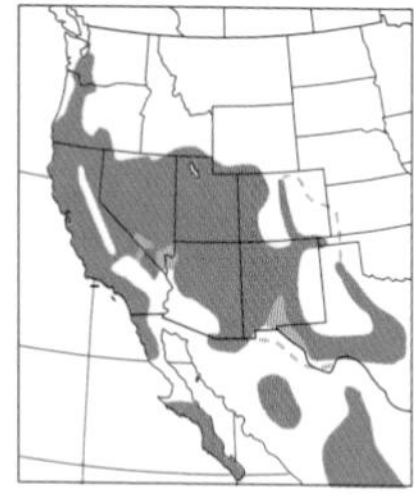

Western Scrub-Jay *Aphelocoma californica*
L 11" (28 cm) Long tail; blue above; variable bluish band on chest. Coastal races, including nominate *californica,* deeper blue above; contrasting brown patch; distinct white eyebrow and blue breast band; undertail coverts geographically variable; may or may not be bluish. Tame and widespread; found in urban areas. Interior races in West (possibly a separate species) are duller than coastal birds with browner flanks, less of a breast band, and less back contrast; *nevadae* from Great Basin is thinner billed than *woodhouseii* farther east. The only reported hybridization between coastal and interior groups is from the Pine Nut Mountains on the California-Nevada border south of Carson City. Western, Island, and Florida were formerly considered one species, Scrub Jay.
Voice: Calls include raspy *shreep,* often in a short series; slightly higher, more upslurred, and not as harsh in interior subspecies.
Range: Fairly common (interior races) to common (coastal races). Rare and irregular (mostly interior races) to southwestern lowland deserts and western Great Plains in fall and winter. Casual (coastal races) to southwest British Columbia.

Island Scrub-Jay *Aphelocoma insularis L 12" (30 cm)*
Recent declines may reflect presence of West Nile virus, which has caused declines in other members of the family. Larger and with much larger bill than Western; darker blue above; always shows rich blue undertail coverts. Birds hold individual territory; takes several years for young birds to acquire territory and breed.
Voice: Calls similar to Western, but slightly lower and deeper.
Range: Restricted to Santa Cruz Island, California, where it is the only scrub-jay.

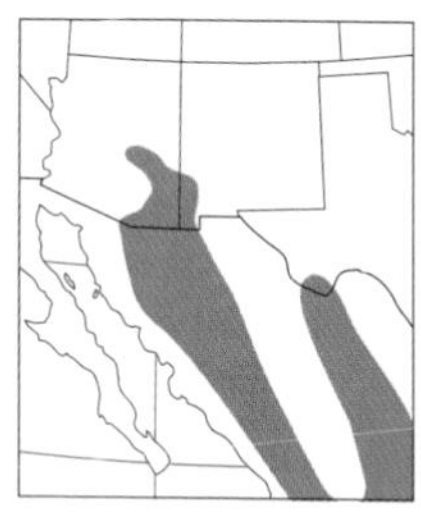

Mexican Jay *Aphelocoma ultramarina L 11½" (29 cm)*
Blue above, with slight grayish cast on back, brownish patch on center of back. Lacks crest. Distinguished from scrub-jays by absence of white throat and white eyebrow and by chunkier shape; flight is more direct. Texas race, *couchii,* has richer blue head. Arizona ***juvenile*** *arizonae* retains pale bill past post-juvenal molt. Has cooperative breeding system similar to Florida Scrub-Jay.
Voice: Calls include a loud, ringing *week,* given singly or in a series are very similar in both subspecies groups.
Range: Common in pine-oak canyons of the Southwest, where it greatly outnumbers scrub-jays. Accidental (*arizonae*) to El Paso and to near Alpine, Texas (*couchii*).

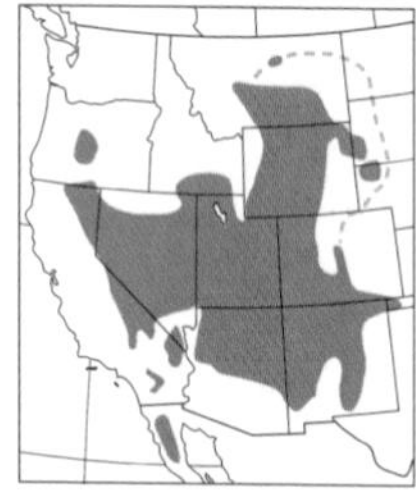

Pinyon Jay *Gymnorhinus cyanocephalus L 10½" (27 cm)*
Blue overall; blue throat streaked with white; bill long and spiky; tail short. Immature is duller. Flight is direct, with rapid wingbeats, unlike scrub-jays' undulating flight.
Voice: Typical flight call is a high-pitched, piercing *mew,* audible over long distances. Also gives a rolling series of *queh* notes.
Range: Generally seen in large flocks, often numbering in the hundreds; nests in loose colonies. Common in pinyon-juniper woodlands of interior mountains, high plateaus; also yellow pine woodlands. Casual to Great Plains, west Texas, coastal California.

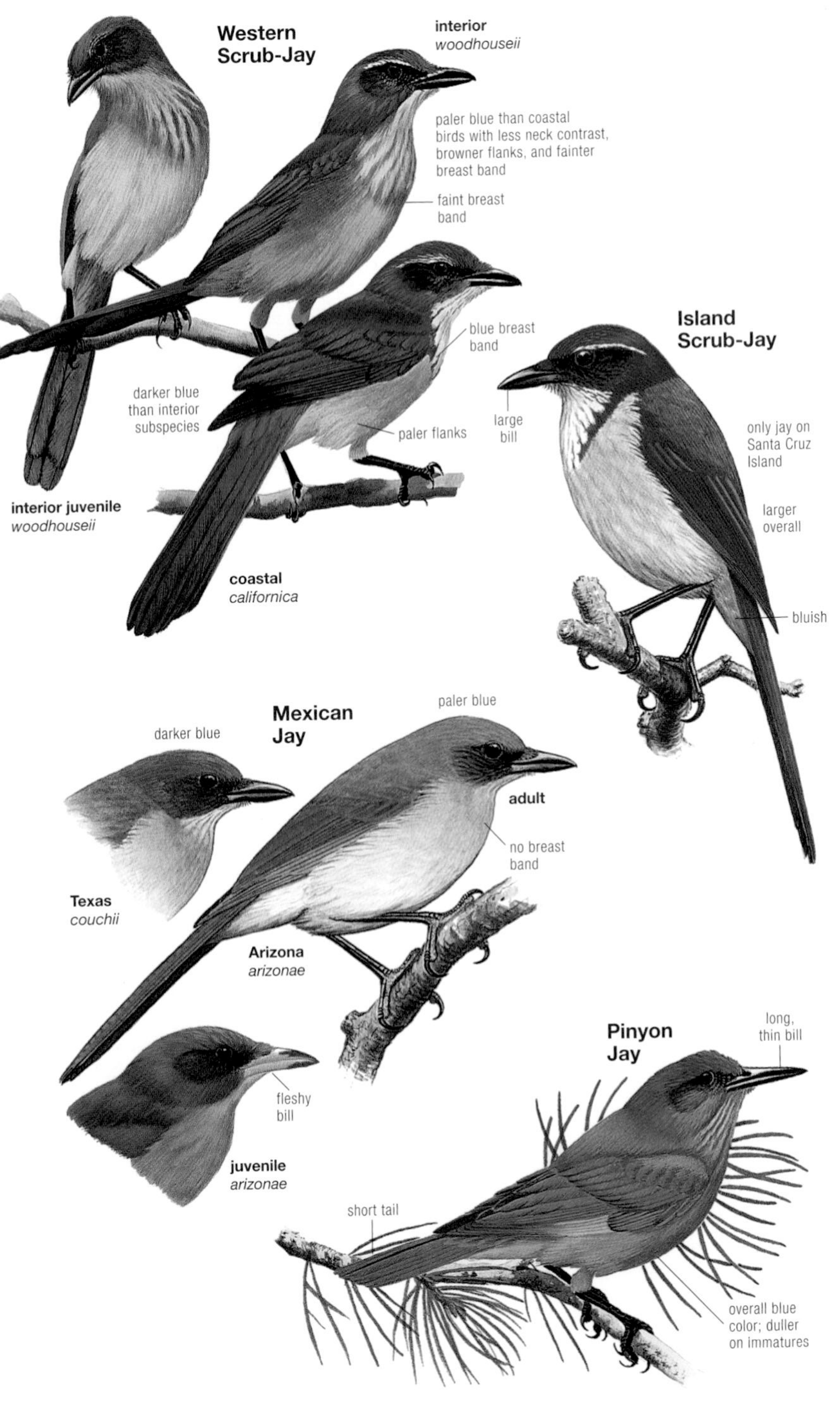

Western Scrub-Jay
interior
woodhouseii
paler blue than coastal birds with less neck contrast, browner flanks, and fainter breast band
faint breast band
blue breast band
darker blue than interior subspecies
paler flanks
interior juvenile
woodhouseii
coastal
californica
Island Scrub-Jay
large bill
only jay on Santa Cruz Island
larger overall
bluish
Mexican Jay
paler blue
darker blue
adult
no breast band
Texas
couchii
Arizona
arizonae
fleshy bill
juvenile
arizonae
Pinyon Jay
long, thin bill
short tail
overall blue color; duller on immatures

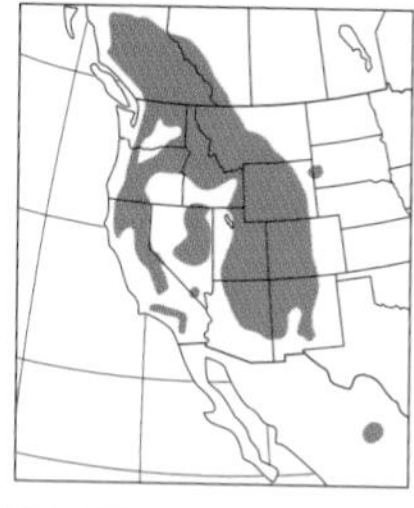

Clark's Nutcracker *Nucifraga columbiana L 12" (31 cm)*
Chunky gray bird with black wings and black central tail feathers. White wing patches and white outer tail feathers are conspicuous in flight. Wingbeats are deep, slow, crowlike. Locally common in high coniferous forests at timberline.
Voice: Calls include a very nasal, grating, drawn-out *kra-a-a.*
Range: Every 10 to 20 years, Nutcrackers irrupt out of core range into desert and coastal lowland areas of the West and to west Texas; also north to Alaska and the Yukon.

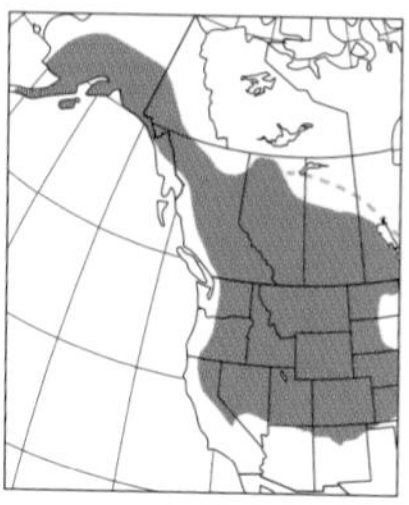

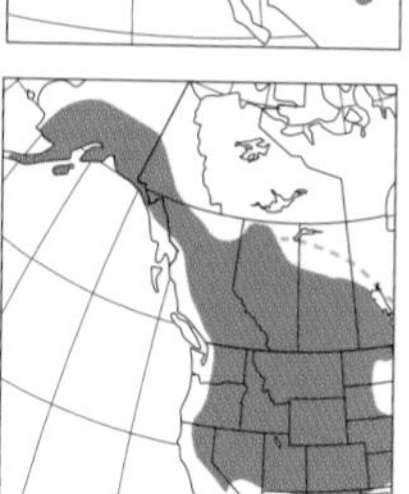

Black-billed Magpie *Pica hudsonia L 19" (48 cm)*
Readily identified as a magpie by black and white markings and unusually long tail with iridescent green highlights. White wing patches flash in flight. Black bill and range distinguish this species from look-alike Yellow-billed Magpie. Ranges almost overlap.
Voice: Gregarious and noisy; typical calls include a whining *mag* and a series of loud, harsh *chuck* notes. Calls and many behavioral traits resulted in North American Black-billed Magpie being split from Old World populations of magpie, whose calls are faster and lower-pitched.
Range: Uncommon to common inhabitant of open woodlands and thickets in rangelands and foothills, especially along watercourses. Black-billed Magpies casually stray south and east of normal range in winter, although some out-of-range birds are probably escapes.

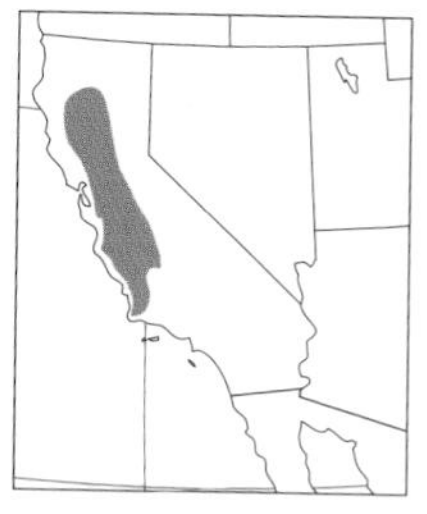

Yellow-billed Magpie *Pica nuttalli L 16½" (42 cm)*
Similar to Black-billed Magpie, but never occurs in Black-billed's normal range. Distinguished by yellow bill and by a yellow patch of bare skin around the eye; extent of yellow variable, sometimes fully encircles eye; may be related to state of molt rather than individual variation, or may be a combination of both. Both species roost and feed in flocks, usually nest in loose colonies, but Yellow-billed Magpie's behavior is more colonial than Black-billed.
Voice: Calls are similar to Black-billed.
Range: Prefers oaks, especially more open oak savanna, also orchards and parks. Common resident of rangelands and foothills of central and northern Central Valley, California, and coastal valleys south to Santa Barbara County. Not prone to wandering, but casual north almost to Oregon; most out-of-range individuals presumed to be escapes. Formerly occurred south to Conejo Valley in western Los Angeles County and eastern Ventura County in 19th century. Recent sharp declines in core range reflect losses from West Nile virus. Some authorities believe that Yellow-billed Magpie is more closely related to the North American Black-billed than either is to the Old World races of the Magpie.

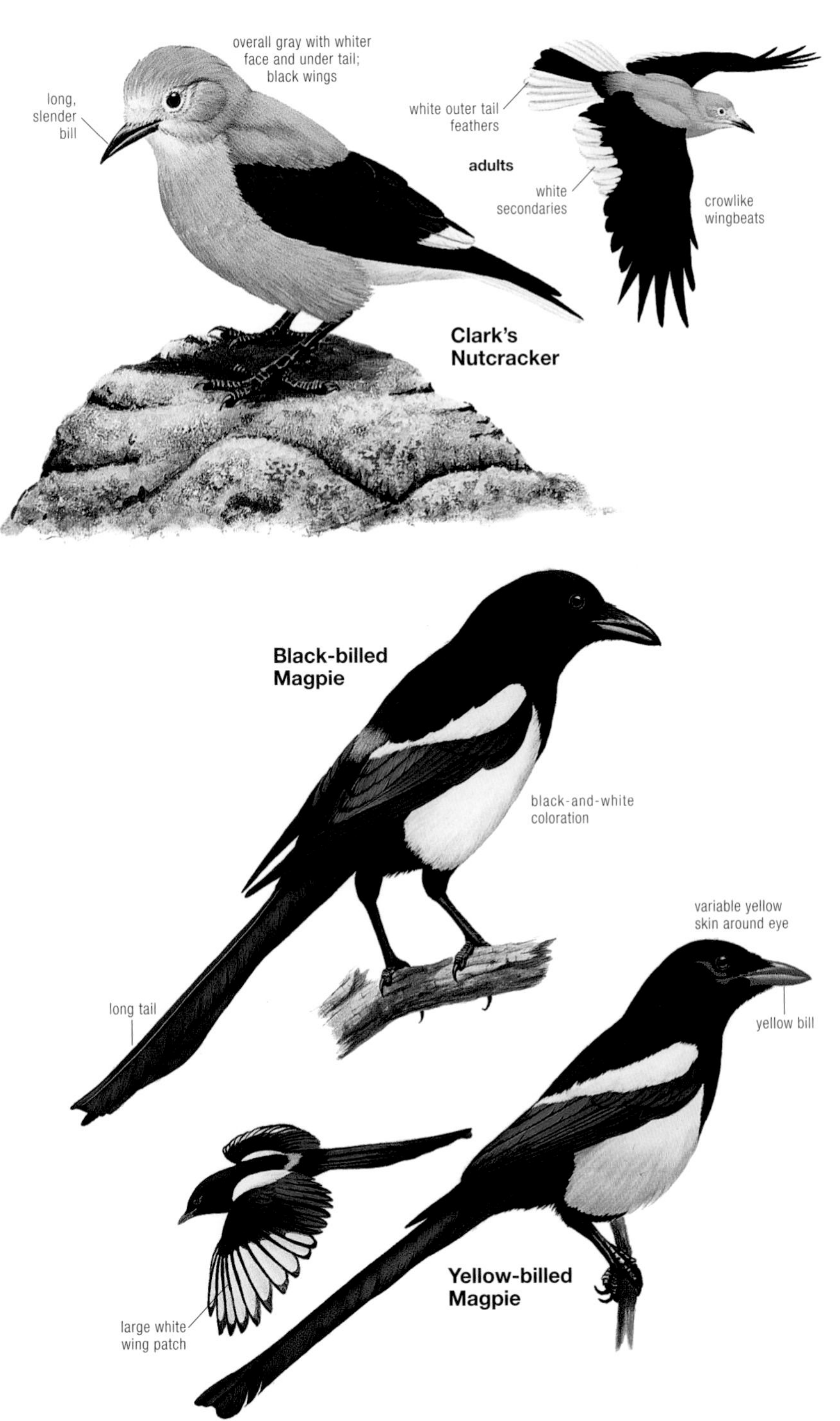
overall gray with whiter face and under tail; black wings
long, slender bill
white outer tail feathers
adults
white secondaries
crowlike wingbeats
Clark's Nutcracker
Black-billed Magpie
black-and-white coloration
variable yellow skin around eye
yellow bill
long tail
Yellow-billed Magpie
large white wing patch

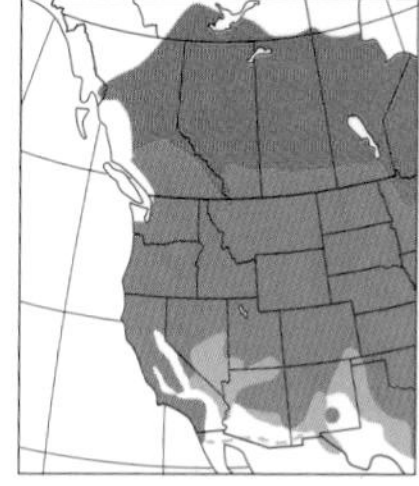

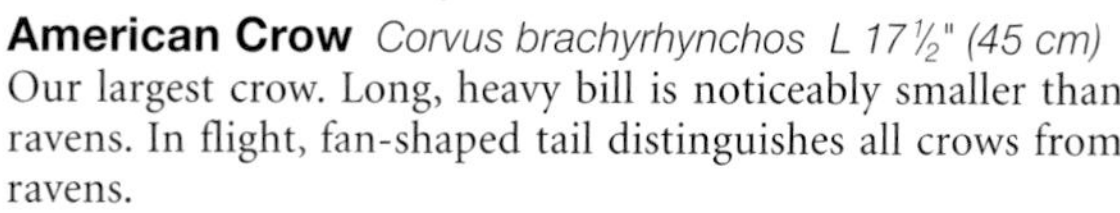

American Crow *Corvus brachyrhynchos L 17½" (45 cm)*
Our largest crow. Long, heavy bill is noticeably smaller than ravens. In flight, fan-shaped tail distinguishes all crows from ravens.
Voice: Adult is readily identified by familiar *caw* call. Juvenile gives a higher-pitched, nasal *cah* begging call.
Range: Generally common throughout most of its range in a wide variety of habitats. May form large foraging flocks and nighttime roosts in fall and winter. Some populations are migratory and migrants are seen—often in flocks late in fall, and early in spring—in northern desert areas. Rare and irregular in winter in southeastern California and southern Arizona.

Northwestern Crow *Corvus caurinus L 16" (41 cm)*
Not shown. Nearly identical to American Crow but slightly smaller. Best clue is range. In areas of presumed overlap with American (e.g., Puget Sound), crows are best not identified to species. Northwestern is considered by some to be a subspecies of American Crow.
Voice: Call is somewhat hoarser and lower than that of American but beware of similarly sounding juvenile American Crow.
Range: Inhabits northwestern coastal areas and islands, where a common scavenger along the shore. Southern and inland limits of the range are uncertain.

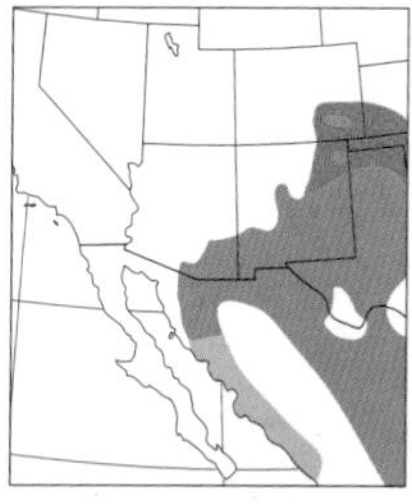

Chihuahuan Raven *Corvus cryptoleucus L 19½" (50 cm)*
Heavier bill and wedge-shaped tail distinguish both raven species from crows. Distinguished from Common Raven by shorter wings and shorter, less wedge-shaped tail; bristles extend farther out on shorter, thicker appearing bill. Neck feathers white rather than grayish at base, but usually obscured.
Voice: Frequent call, a drawn-out croak, usually slightly higher pitched than Common Raven.
Range: Fairly common in desert areas and scrubby grasslands.

Common Raven *Corvus corax L 24" (61 cm)*
Large, with long, heavy bill and long, wedge-shaped tail. Larger than Chihuahuan Raven; note thicker, shaggier throat feathers and nasal bristles that do not extend as far out on larger bill. Genetic affinities of some populations from California suggest a closer relationship to Chihuahuan Raven than to those from other regions.
Voice: Most common call is a low, drawn-out croak but many other calls.
Range: Found in a variety of habitats, including mountains, deserts, and coastal areas. Common and increasing in West. Casual on the western Great Plains.

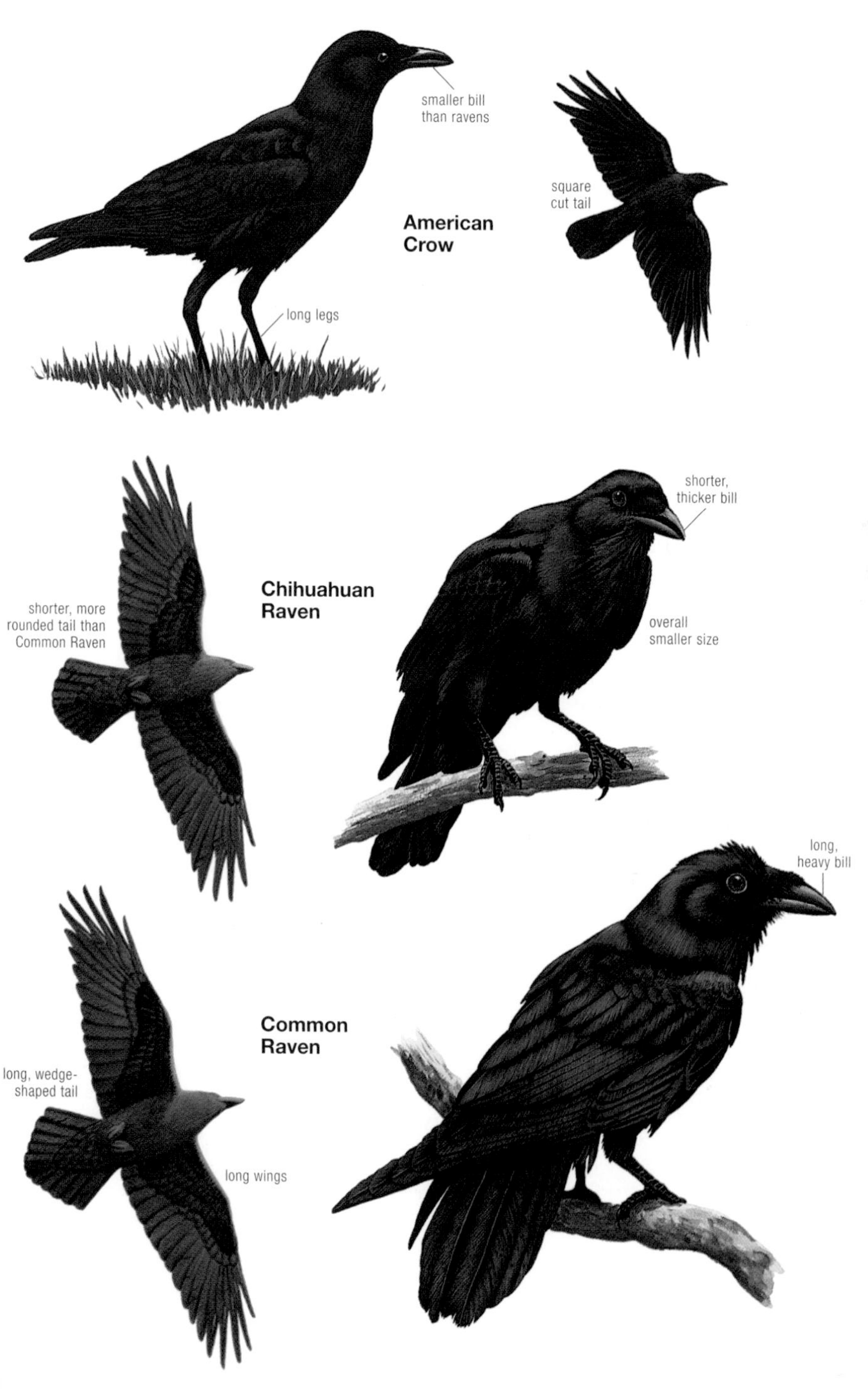
smaller bill
than ravens
square
cut tail
American
Crow
long legs
shorter,
thicker bill
Chihuahuan
Raven
shorter, more
rounded tail than
Common Raven
overall
smaller size
long,
heavy bill
Common
Raven
long, wedge-
shaped tail
long wings

Larks (Family Alaudidae)

Ground dwellers of open fields, larks are slender-billed seed- and insect-eaters. They seldom alight on trees or bushes. On the ground, they walk rather than hop.

Sky Lark *Alauda arvensis L 7¼" (18 cm)*
Old World species. A plain brown bird with slender bill; slight crest is raised when bird is agitated. Upperparts heavily streaked; buffy white underparts streaked on breast and throat. Dark eye prominent. Asian *pekinensis* is darker and more heavily streaked above. All juveniles have a scaly brown mantle. In flight, shows a conspicuous white trailing edge on the inner wing and white edges on tail.
Voice: Song is a continuous outpouring of trills and warblings, delivered in high hovering or circling song flight. Call is a liquid *chirrup* with buzzy overtones.
Range: Nominate *arvensis,* a widespread European race introduced to southern Vancouver Island, British Columbia, in the early 1900s, is resident there on open slopes and fields. The population on the nearby San Juan Islands in Washington is now extirpated. Highly migratory *pekinensis,* rare on western Aleutians and Pribilofs and casual on central Aleutians and St. Lawrence Island; accidental in winter in Washington and northern California.

Horned Lark *Eremophila alpestris L 6¾-7¾" (17-20 cm)*
Head pattern distinctive in all subspecies: black "horns"; white or yellowish face and throat with broad black stripe under eye; black bib. ***Female*** duller overall than ***male,*** horns less prominent. Conspicuous in flight is the mostly black tail with white outer feathers, brown central feathers. Brief juvenal plumage has whitish markings above, streaks below; can be confused with Sprague's Pipit (page 324). Western subspecies vary widely in overall color; selected extremes are shown here: *enthymia* (Plains, not illustrated), *ammophila* (deserts of the Southwest), large *arcticola* (northwestern Canada, Alaska), and *hoyti* (central Arctic coast) are very pale; *sierrae* (northeastern California) and *strigata* (coastal Northwest) are yellower on head and chest, *strigata* is also more streaked underneath; *rubea* (Central Valley, California) is redder dorsally; *insularis* (Channel Islands, California) is streaked below; *flava* (from Palearctic; casual fall vagrant to Alaska) has a yellow throat and supercilium. Some subspecies are highly migratory, others are largely resident. Winter flocks of hundreds may comprise several subspecies.
Voice: Calls include a high *tsee-ee* or *tsee-titi.* Song is a weak twittering, delivered from the ground or in flight.
Range: Widespread and common. Prefers dirt fields, gravel ridges, and shores.

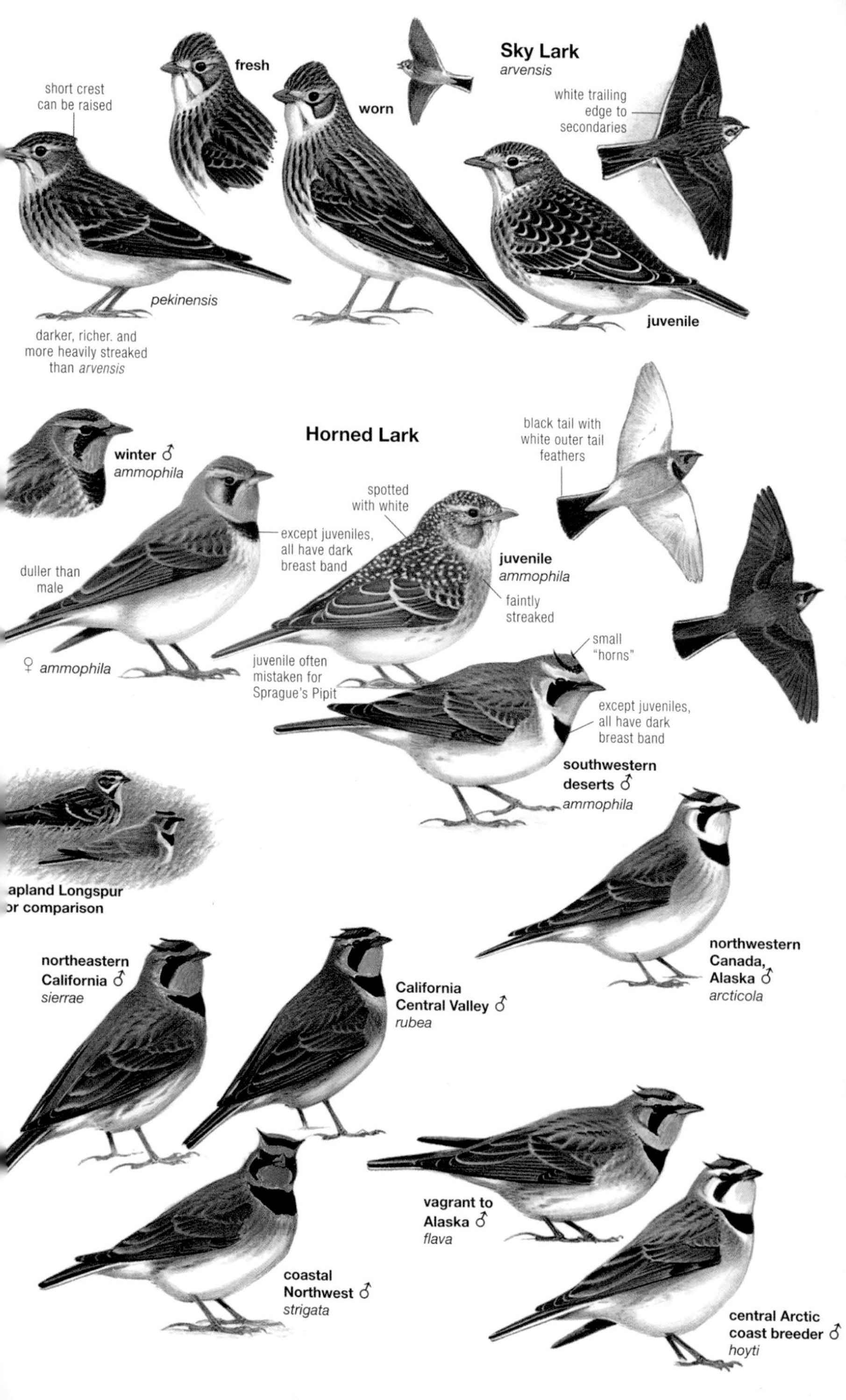

Sky Lark
arvensis
short crest
can be raised
fresh
worn
white trailing
edge to
secondaries
pekinensis
juvenile
darker, richer. and
more heavily streaked
than arvensis
Horned Lark
winter ♂
ammophila
black tail with
white outer tail
feathers
spotted
with white
except juveniles,
all have dark
breast band
duller than
male
juvenile
ammophila
faintly
streaked
♀ ammophila
juvenile often
mistaken for
Sprague's Pipit
small
"horns"
except juveniles,
all have dark
breast band
southwestern
deserts ♂
ammophila
apland Longspur
or comparison
northwestern
Canada,
Alaska ♂
arcticola
northeastern
California ♂
sierrae
California
Central Valley ♂
rubea
vagrant to
Alaska ♂
flava
coastal
Northwest ♂
strigata
central Arctic
coast breeder ♂
hoyti

Swallows (Family Hirundinidae)

With their slender bodies and long, pointed wings, swallows resemble swifts, but their "wrist" angle is sharper and farther from the body; flight is more fluid. Adept aerialists, swallows dart to catch flying insects. Flocks perch in long rows on branches and wires.

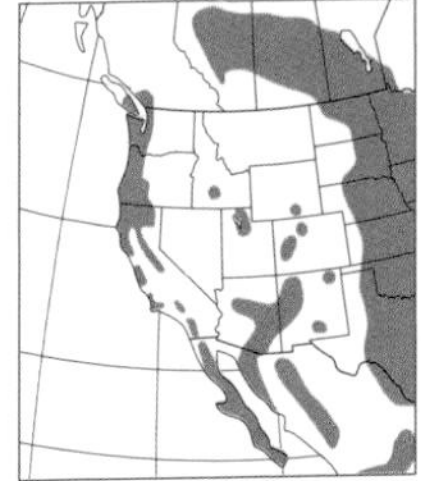

Purple Martin *Progne subis L 8" (20 cm)*

Male is dark, glossy purplish blue. ***Female*** and juvenile are gray below. ***First-spring males*** have some purple below. In flight, male especially resembles European Starling (page 320), but note forked tail, longer wings, and typical swallow flight, short glides alternating with rapid flapping.

Voice: Loud, rich, liquid gurgling and whistles; also a low *chirr.*

Range: Uncommon to fairly common where suitable nest sites available. Declining over parts of West. Casual to Alaska and the Yukon, including to Bering Sea region; winters in South America.

Violet-green Swallow *Tachycineta thalassina*

L 5¼" (13 cm) White on cheek extends above eye; white flank patches extend onto sides of rump; compare with larger Tree Swallow. May also be confused with White-throated Swift (page 234). Female is duller above than ***male. Juvenile*** is gray-brown above; white except on rump may be mottled or grayish.

Voice: Gives rapid and high-pitched twittering notes.

Range: Common in a variety of woodland habitats. Nests in hollow trees or rock crevices, often forming loose colonies. A rather late fall migrant. Casual to western Alaska.

Tree Swallow *Tachycineta bicolor L 5¾" (15 cm)*

Dark, glossy greenish blue above, slightly duller in female, greener in fall plumage; white below. White cheek patch does not extend above eye as in Violet-green Swallow. ***Juvenile*** is gray-brown above; usually has more diffuse breast band than Bank Swallow. ***First-spring female*** shows varying amount of adult color on crown and back.

Voice: Calls and song include whistles and liquid gurgles or chirps.

Range: Common in wooded habitat near water and where dead trees provide nest holes; also in fence posts and in nest boxes.

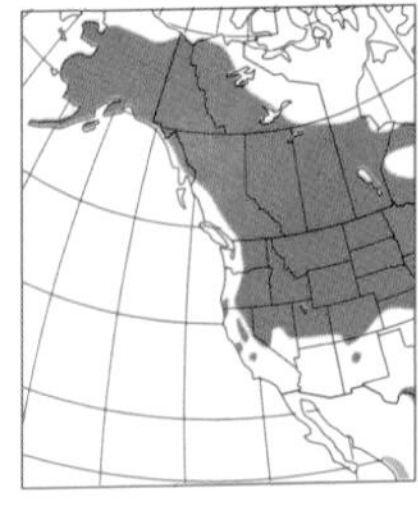

Bank Swallow *Riparia riparia L 4¾" (12 cm)*

Our smallest swallow. Distinct brownish gray breast band, often extending in a line down center of breast. Throat is white; white curves around rear border of ear patch. ***Juvenile*** has thin buffy wing bars; compare with juvenile Northern Rough-winged Swallow and juvenile Tree Swallow. Locally common throughout most of range. Unlike Northern Rough-winged, wingbeats are shallow and rapid; also paler rump and back contrasts with darker wings.

Voice: Call a buzzy, short *dzrrt*, often delivered in rapid series like high-tension powerlines.

Range: Nests in large colonies, excavating nest burrows in steep riverbank cliffs, gravel pits, and highway cuts. Winters chiefly in South America; often migrates in large flocks; scarce on coast.

eastern ♀
subis
darker overall
than western
races
dark purple
overall
adult ♂
Purple
Martin
1st spring ♂
eastern ♀
subis
often soars;
wingbeats are
slow and deep
adult ♂
broad
wings
paler below
than nominate
eastern race
western ♀
arboricola
adult
1st spring ♀
adult
Tree
Swallow
dark
brownish
above
white tertial
tips
juvenile
fall adult
spring adult
dark blue
upperparts
adults
♂
small size
with fluttery
wingbeats
Violet-green
Swallow
♂
juvenile
up
of
np
white
above eye
adult ♂
mainly green upperparts
and snowy white underparts
flies with
shallow
flaps
Bank
Swallow
riparia
small size
juvenile
pale coloring
wraps around
back of ear
coverts
dark
breast band

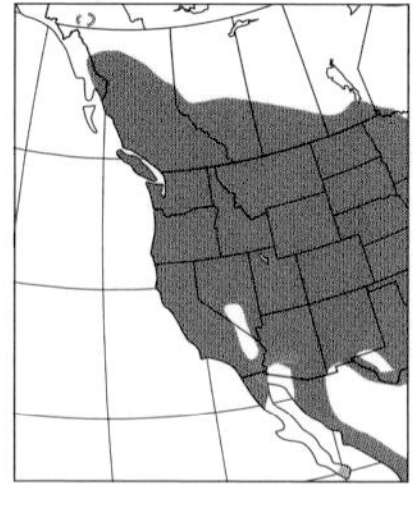
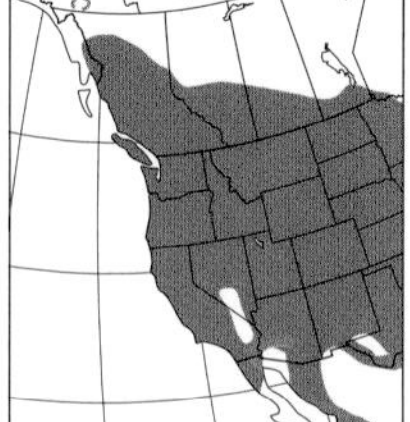

Northern Rough-winged Swallow

Stelgidopteryx serripennis L 5" (13 cm) Brown above, whitish below, with gray-brown wash on chin, throat, and upper breast. Lacks Bank Swallow's distinct breast band; wings are longer, wingbeats deeper and slower. ***Juvenile*** has cinnamon wing bars.
Voice: Call a distinct low buzzy *zzrt.*
Range: Nests in single pairs in riverbanks, cliffs, culverts, and under bridges. Migrates singly or in small flocks. A few winter to coastal California; very rare to rare to southeast Alaska and the Yukon.

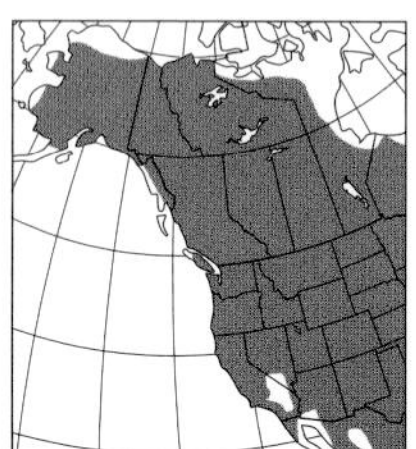

Cliff Swallow *Petrochelidon pyrrhonota L 5½" (14 cm)*

Squarish tail and buffy rump distinguish this swallow from all others except Cave Swallow. Most Cliff Swallows have dark chestnut and blackish throat, pale forehead. A primarily southwestern race, *melanogaster,* has cinnamon forehead like Cave Swallow, but throat is dark chestnut. All ***juveniles*** are much duller and grayer than adults; throat is paler, forehead darker.
Voice: Calls include a rough squeaky *chri,* a nasal *trrr,* a rattle.
Range: Locally common around bridges, rural settlements, and in open country on cliffs. Nests in colonies, building gourd-shaped mud nests. An early spring and early fall migrant. Winters in South America.

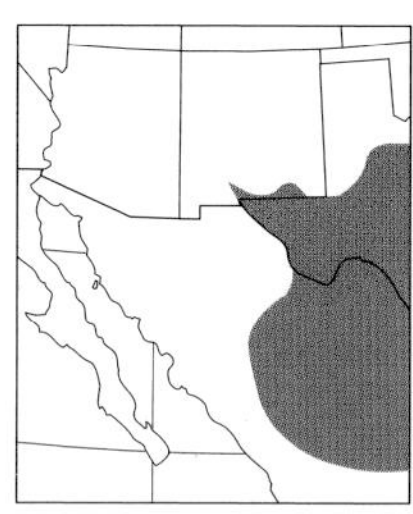

Cave Swallow *Petrochelidon fulva L 5½" (14 cm)*

Squarish tail; distinguished from Cliff by buffy throat color extending through auriculars and around nape setting off dark cap; rump averages a richer color; cinnamon forehead; ***juvenile*** much paler; compare with southwestern subspecies of Cliff also with cinnamon forehead.
Voice: Call a rising *pweih,* much sweeter than Cliff Swallow.
Range: Southwestern subspecies is *pelodoma* from Mexico; larger and paler than *fulva* from West Indies (unrecorded in West). Nests in colonies in limestone caves, sinkholes, culverts, and under bridges, sometimes with Barn and Cliff Swallows. Casual to southern Arizona, southeastern California.

Barn Swallow *Hirundo rustica L 6¾" (17 cm)*

Long, deeply forked tail. Throat is reddish brown; upperparts blue-black; underparts usually cinnamon or buffy. Two Eurasian, white-bellied races have occurred casually in western and northern Alaska: *rustica,* which has a solid dark breast band, and *gutturalis,* with incomplete breast band, which also has been found on Queen Charlotte Islands, British Columbia. In all ***juveniles,*** tail is shorter but still noticeably forked; underparts pale.
Voice: Call a short, sweet, single or double *vit* or *veet*; song a series of squeaky notes.
Range: Common; generally nests on or inside farm buildings, under eaves, bridges, and docks and inside culverts, in pairs or small colonies. Rare and somewhat irregular, but increasing, in winter in Southwest and Pacific states; winters primarily in Central and South America. North American *erythrogaster* is casual to central and western Alaska.

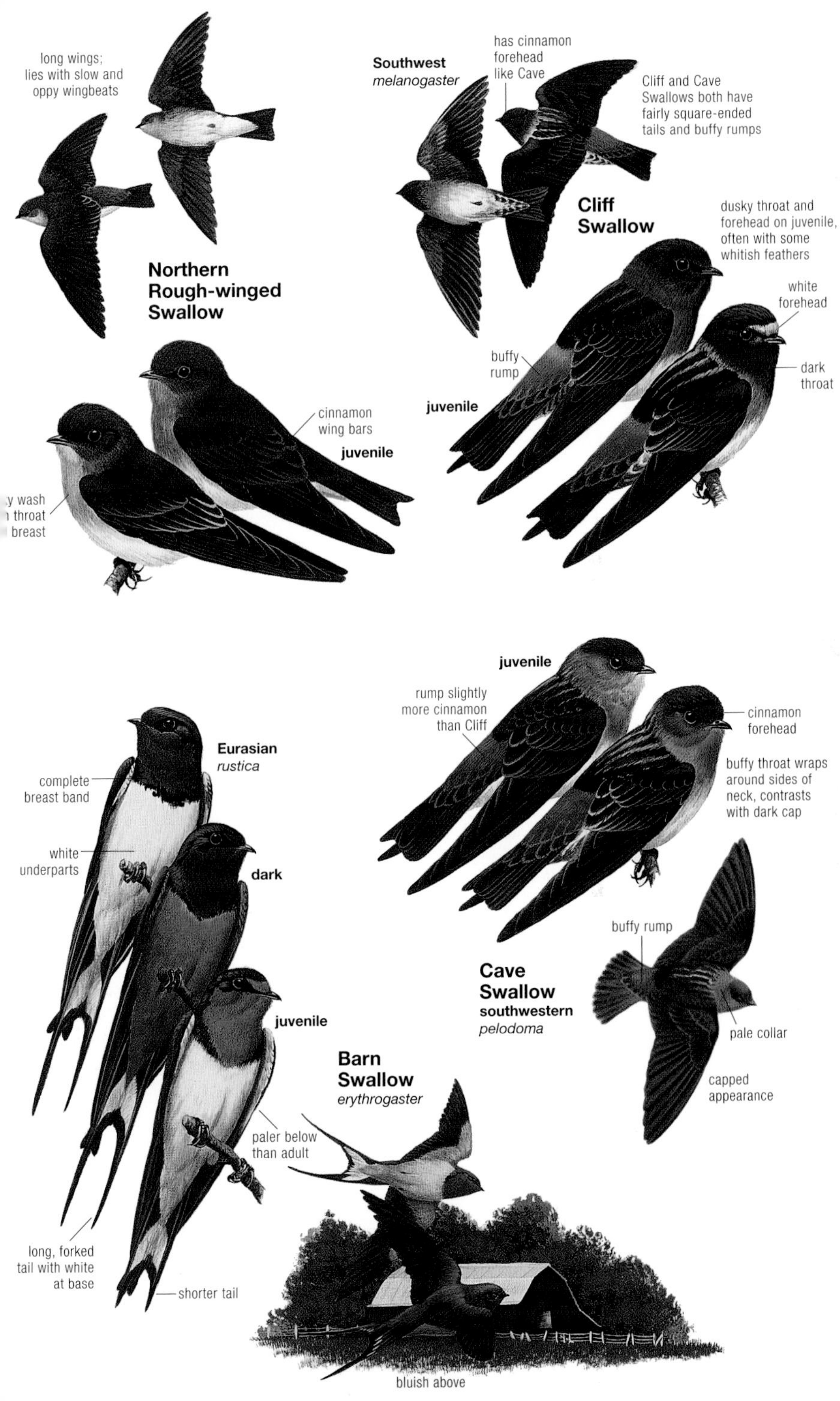
long wings;
lies with slow and
oppy wingbeats
Northern
Rough-winged
Swallow
cinnamon
wing bars
juvenile
y wash
 throat
 breast
Southwest
melanogaster
has cinnamon
forehead
like Cave
Cliff and Cave
Swallows both have
fairly square-ended
tails and buffy rumps
Cliff
Swallow
dusky throat and
forehead on juvenile,
often with some
whitish feathers
white
forehead
buffy
rump
dark
throat
juvenile
Eurasian
rustica
complete
breast band
white
underparts
dark
juvenile
paler below
than adult
long, forked
tail with white
at base
shorter tail
Barn
Swallow
erythrogaster
bluish above
juvenile
rump slightly
more cinnamon
than Cliff
cinnamon
forehead
buffy throat wraps
around sides of
neck, contrasts
with dark cap
buffy rump
Cave
Swallow
southwestern
pelodoma
pale collar
capped
appearance

Babblers (Family Timaliidae)

Wrentit *Chamaea fasciata L 6½" (17 cm)*
Color varies from warm buffy brown in northern populations to grayer in southern birds. Note distinct cream-colored eye and lightly streaked buffy breast; long, rounded tail usually cocked. Usually heard before they are seen.
Voice: Male's loud song, sung year-round, begins with a series of accelerating notes and runs into a descending trill: *pit-pit-pit-tr-r-r-r.* Female's song lacks trill. Both sexes give soft, low *prr* note, often in a series.
Range: Common resident in chaparral and evergreen brushland.

Chickadees, Titmice (Family Paridae)

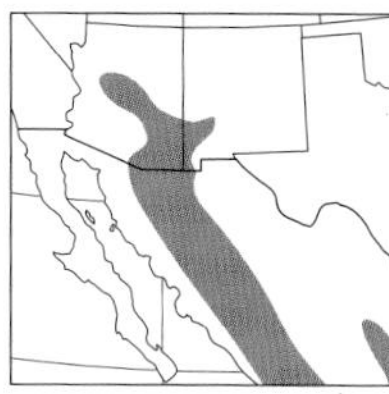

Bridled Titmouse *Baeolophus wollweberi L 5¼" (13 cm)*
Note distinct crest, black-and-white facial pattern, black throat.
Voice: Most common call is a rapid, high-pitched variation of *chick-a-dee-dee,* similar to Juniper Titmouse. Song is a rapid and clipped series of whistled notes.
Range: Resident in stands of oak, juniper, and sycamore in Southwest range. Accidental to westernmost Arizona.

Oak Titmouse *Baeolophus inornatus L 5" (13 cm)*
Grayish brown with a short crest. Northern race, *inornatus,* is slightly smaller, paler, and smaller billed than *affabilis* (shown here) from southwestern California and northern Baja; birds from Little San Bernadino Mountains are paler, grayer than *affabilis.*
Voice: Song is variable, a repeated series of syllables made up of whistled, alternating, high and low notes. Call is a hoarse *tschick-a-dee.*
Range: Common in warm, dry oak and mixed woodlands.

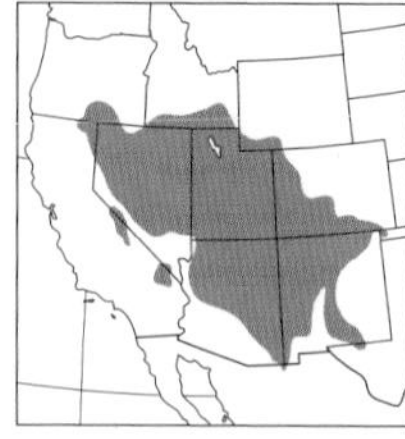

Juniper Titmouse *Baeolophus ridgwayi L 5¼" (13 cm)*
Like Oak Titmouse; range overlaps on northern California Modoc plateau. Larger, paler, grayer than Oak.
Voice: Song, a rolling series of syllables, rapid, with uniform pitch. Call, a hoarse *tschick-a-dee* similar to Bridled. Overall, chattering call notes more clipped, delivered much more rapidly than Oak.
Range: Uncommon to fairly common in juniper or pinyon-juniper woodland. Casual to western Great Plains.

Black-crested Titmouse *Baeolophus atricristatus L 5¾" (15 cm)* Resplit from Tufted. ***Adult*** has black crest, pale forehead. ***Juvenile*** crown darker than upperparts; forehead dirty white.
Voice: Calls louder, sharper than Tufted. Song is also like Tufted, but notes are slightly higher and are delivered more rapidly.
Range: Resident in wooded areas of Chisos and Davis mountains of west Texas.

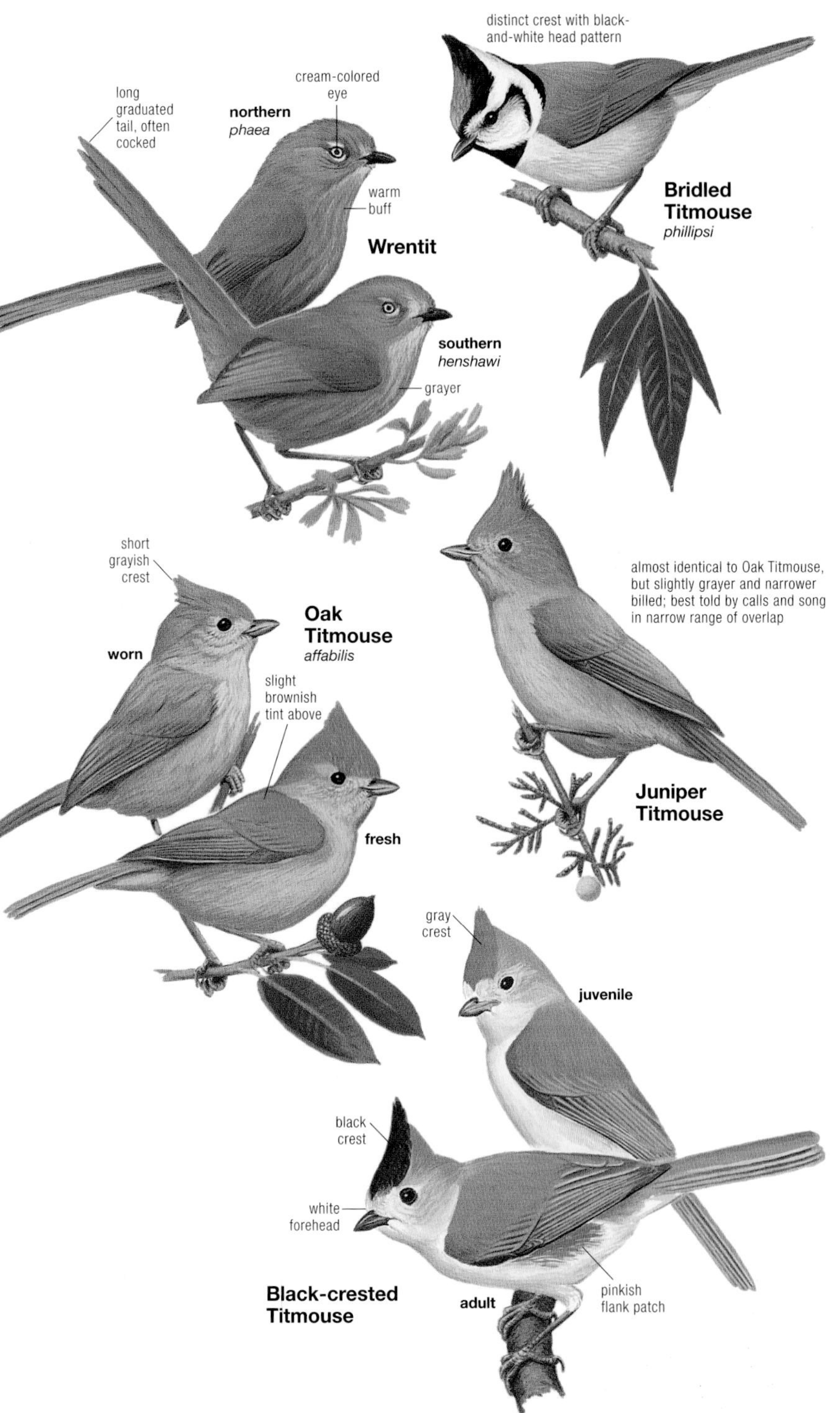
distinct crest with black-and-white head pattern
Bridled Titmouse
phillipsi
long graduated tail, often cocked
cream-colored eye
northern
phaea
warm buff
Wrentit
southern
henshawi
grayer
short grayish crest
Oak Titmouse
affabilis
worn
slight brownish tint above
fresh
almost identical to Oak Titmouse, but slightly grayer and narrower billed; best told by calls and song in narrow range of overlap
Juniper Titmouse
gray crest
juvenile
black crest
white forehead
Black-crested Titmouse
adult
pinkish flank patch

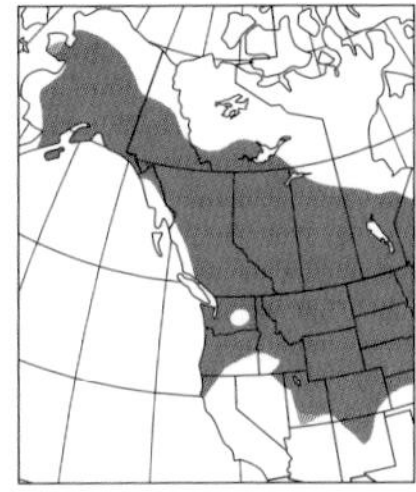

Black-capped Chickadee *Poecile atricapillus*
L 5¼" (13 cm) Black cap and bib; cheeks more extensively and purer white than similar Carolina Chickadee, which has not occurred in West. Easily told from Mountain Chickadee by lack of white eyebrow and more colored flanks. Plumage is geographically variable: *occidentalis* from Pacific Northwest is darker; *nevadensis* from Great Basin is palest subspecies. Best distinction is voice.
Voice: Call is a lower, slower *chick-a-dee-dee-dee* than Carolina; typical song, a clear, whistled *fee-bee* or *fee-bee-ee,* the first note higher in pitch; vocalizations show some geographic variation.
Range: Uncommon to common in open woodlands, clearings, and suburbs. Usually forages in thickets and low branches of trees. Partial to riparian woodland along streams and rivers, especially in drier areas. Casual to northernmost Arizona.

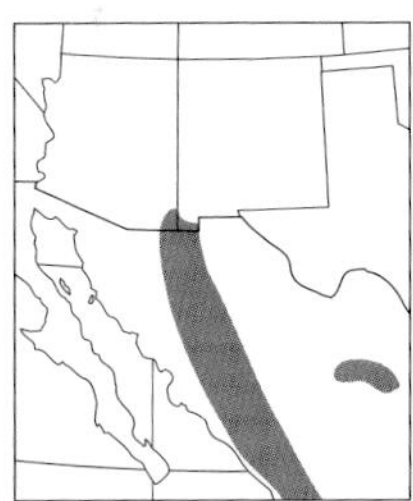

Mexican Chickadee *Poecile sclateri L 5" (13 cm)*
A Mexican species. The only breeding chickadee in its range. Extensive black bib is distinctive, along with dark gray flanks. Lacks white eyebrow of Mountain Chickadee.
Voice: Song is a warbled whistle; call note, a husky buzz.
Range: Fairly common resident in coniferous and pine-oak forests; found in U.S. only in Chiricahua Mountains of southeastern Arizona; fewer in Animas and especially Peloncillo Mountains of southwestern New Mexico. Occasionally moves to lower elevations in winter.

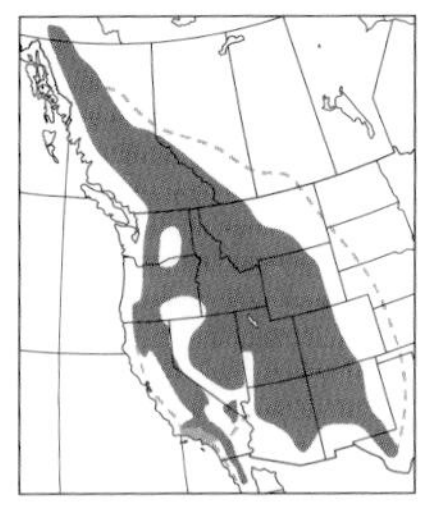

Mountain Chickadee *Poecile gambeli L 5¼" (13 cm)*
White eyebrow and pale gray sides distinguish this species from other chickadees; lack of crest separates it from Bridled Titmouse (previous page). Birds of Rocky Mountain nominate race *gambeli* are tinged with buff on back, sides, flanks, and have broader white eyebrow than *baileyae.*
Voice: Call is a hoarse *chick-adee-adee-adee;* typical song, a three- or four-note descending whistle, *fee-bee-bay* or *fee-bee fee-bee.*
Range: Common resident in coniferous and mixed woodlands. Some descend irregularly to lower elevations in fall and winter, very rarely to western Great Plains.

Chestnut-backed Chickadee *Poecile rufescens*
L 4¾" (12 cm) Sooty brown cap, white cheeks, black bib; back and rump chestnut. Over most of its range, this species has bright chestnut sides and flanks; *neglectus* (not shown) on coast of northern California (Marin County) has pale chestnut wash on back and flanks; *barlowi,* south of Golden Gate Bridge to northern Santa Barbara County, shows almost no chestnut below.
Voice: Call is a hoarse, rapid *tseek-a-dee-dee.*
Range: Found in coniferous forests, deciduous woodlands. Usually feeds high in trees. Casual south to southern Santa Barbara and Ventura counties in California and east to western Alberta.

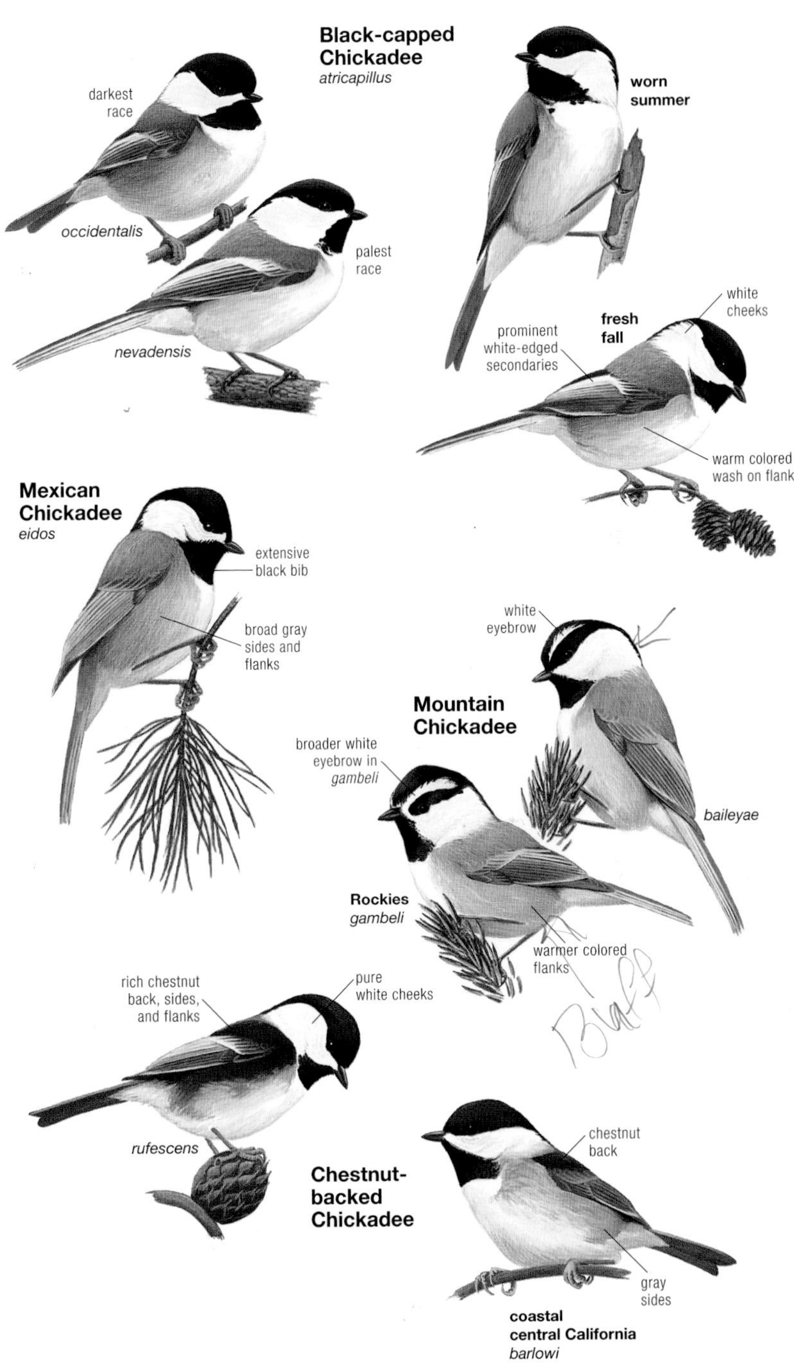
Black-capped Chickadee
atricapillus
darkest race
occidentalis
palest race
nevadensis
worn summer
fresh fall
white cheeks
prominent white-edged secondaries
warm colored wash on flanks
Mexican Chickadee
eidos
extensive black bib
broad gray sides and flanks
white eyebrow
Mountain Chickadee
broader white eyebrow in gambeli
baileyae
Rockies
gambeli
warmer colored flanks
rich chestnut back, sides, and flanks
pure white cheeks
rufescens
Chestnut-backed Chickadee
chestnut back
gray sides
coastal central California
barlowi

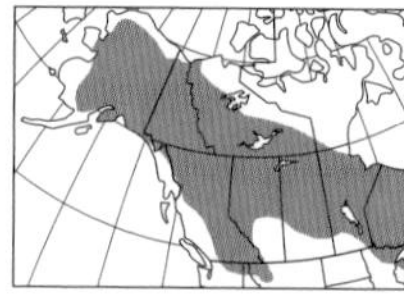
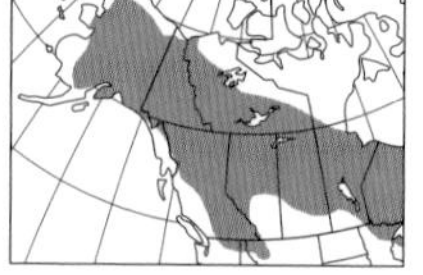

Boreal Chickadee *Poecile hudsonicus* *L 5½" (14 cm)*
Grayish brown on crown and back, with pinkish brown flanks. Note that rear portion of cheeks is heavily washed with gray.
Voice: Call is a nasal *tseek-a-day-day.*
Range: Uncommon to fairly common in coniferous forests.

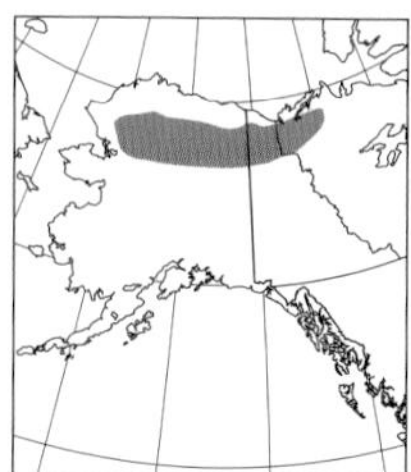

Gray-headed Chickadee *Poecile cinctus* *L 5½" (14 cm)*
Gray-brown above, whitish below, with white cheek patch, black bib, buffy sides and flanks. Distinguished from Boreal Chickadee by more extensively white cheeks, longer tail, paler flanks, and pale edges on wing coverts.
Voice: Distinctive call, a series of peevish *dee deer* notes.
Range: Rare; found in willows and spruces edging tundra. Still known as the Siberian Tit in the Old World. Casual to central Alaska (Fairbanks).

Penduline Tits, Verdins (Family Remizidae)

Small, spritely birds with finely pointed bills. They inhabit arid scrub country, feed in brush chickadee-style, and build spherical nests.

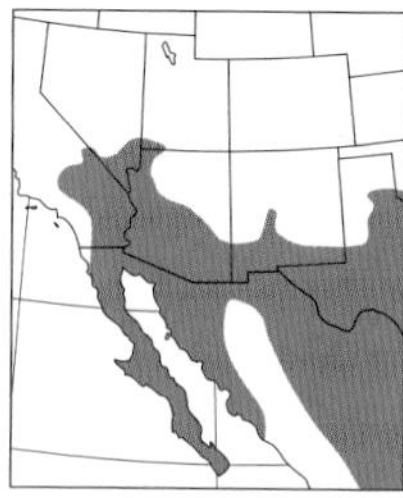

Verdin *Auriparus flaviceps* *L 4½" (11 cm)*
Adult has dull gray plumage, chestnut shoulder patches, yellow head and throat. ***Juvenile*** is brown-gray overall; shorter tail helps separate it from Bushtit. Compare also with Lucy's Warbler (page 330).
Voice: Song is a plaintive three-note whistle, the second note higher. Calls include hard, rapid *chip* notes.
Range: Common in mesquite, other dense thorny shrubs of the southwestern deserts. Accidental to coastal southern California north to Santa Barbara County; former resident in the Tijuana River Valley south of San Diego.

Long-tailed Tits, Bushtits (Family Aegithalidae)

A longer tail distinguishes these tiny birds from other chickadee-like species. Except during nesting, usually feeds in large, busy, twittering flocks. Nest is an elaborate hanging structure.

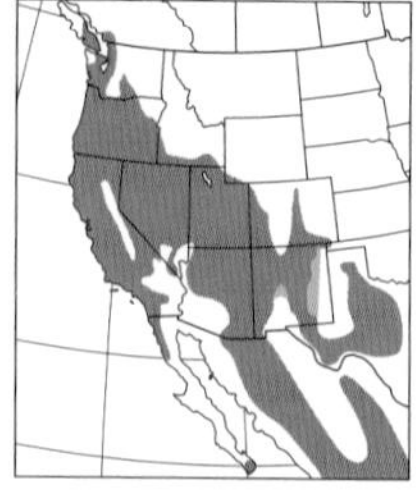

Bushtit *Psaltriparus minimus* *L 4½" (11 cm)*
Gray above, paler below; females have pale eyes, males' eyes are dark. Coastal birds have brown crown; interior birds show brown ear patch and gray cap. ***Juvenile male*** and some adult males in the Southwest have a black mask, formerly considered a separate species, the ***"Black-eared Bushtit."*** Found in flocks, often with other species, except during breeding season.
Voice: Calls are soft twittering notes given in louder excited chatter when a raptor appears; interior subspecies notes are sharper and delivered more slowly.
Range: Fairly common to common in a wide variety of woodlands. Irregular fall and winter movements in some interior populations.

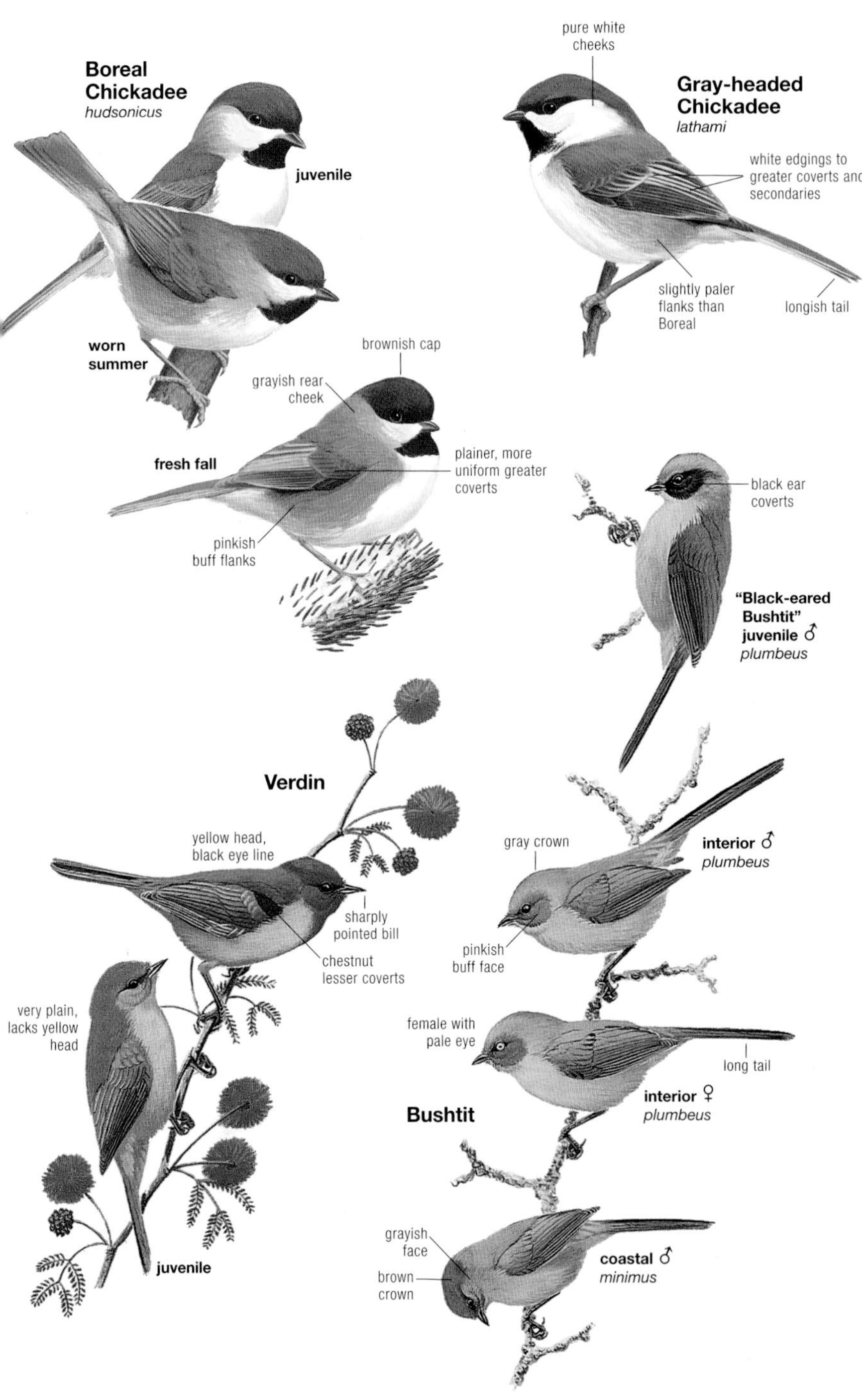
Boreal Chickadee
hudsonicus
juvenile
worn summer
fresh fall
brownish cap
grayish rear cheek
plainer, more uniform greater coverts
pinkish buff flanks
pure white cheeks
Gray-headed Chickadee
lathami
white edgings to greater coverts and secondaries
slightly paler flanks than Boreal
longish tail
black ear coverts
"Black-eared Bushtit" juvenile ♂
plumbeus
Verdin
yellow head, black eye line
sharply pointed bill
chestnut lesser coverts
very plain, lacks yellow head
juvenile
gray crown
interior ♂
plumbeus
pinkish buff face
female with pale eye
long tail
interior ♀
plumbeus
Bushtit
grayish face
brown crown
coastal ♂
minimus

Creepers (Family Certhiidae)

With curved bills, these little tree-climbers dig insects and larvae from bark. Stiff tail feathers serve as props.

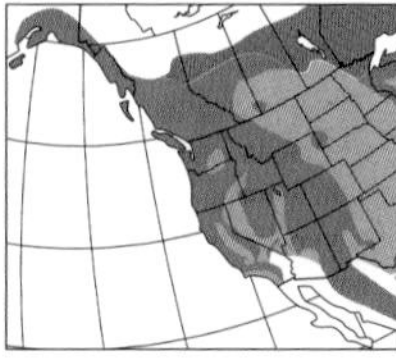

Brown Creeper *Certhia americana* *L 5¼" (13 cm)*
Camouflaged by streaked brown plumage, creepers spiral upward from base of a tree, then fly to a lower place on another tree.
Voice: Call is a soft, sibilant *see;* song, a high-pitched, variable *see see see titi see.* Fairly common but hard to spot.
Range: Nests in coniferous and mixed woodlands. Generally solitary; sometimes seen in winter flocks of titmice and nuthatches.

Nuthatches (Family Sittidae)

These short-tailed acrobats climb up, down, and around tree trunks and branches.

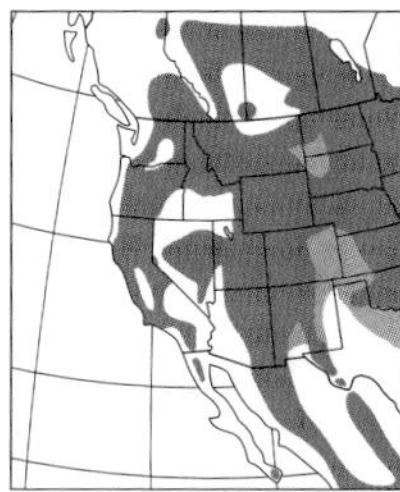

White-breasted Nuthatch *Sitta carolinensis*
L 5¾" (15 cm) Black cap tops all-white face and breast; extent of rust below is variable. Western birds have longer, thinner bills, more blended tertial centers.
Voice: Typical song is a rapid series of nasal whistles on one pitch in *carolinensis* and *aculeata*. Call is usually a low-pitched, repeated, nasal *yank* in eastern nominate race; high-pitched in West Coast *aculeata;* higher-pitched and given in a rapid series by Great Basin *tenuissima* and Rockies *nelsoni.*
Range: Fairly common. Eastern bids found west to northeastern British Columbia in deciduous forest; to eastern Montana and Colorado along major rivers; western races found in oaks and conifers.

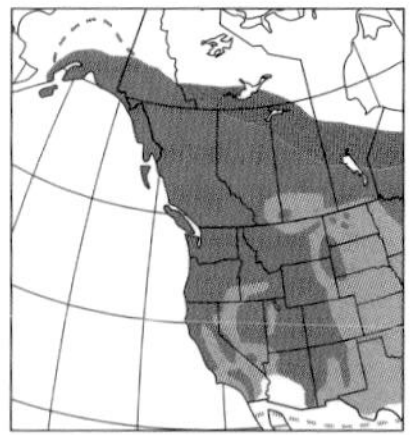

Red-breasted Nuthatch *Sitta canadensis* *L 4½" (11 cm)*
Black cap and eye line, white eyebrow, rust underparts; ***female*** and juvenile have duller head, paler underparts.
Voice: High-pitched, nasal call sounds like a toy tin horn.
Range: Resident in northern and subalpine conifers; gleans small branches and outer twigs. Irruptive migrant; numbers and winter range vary yearly. Casual in fall to western Alaska, including Bering Sea islands.

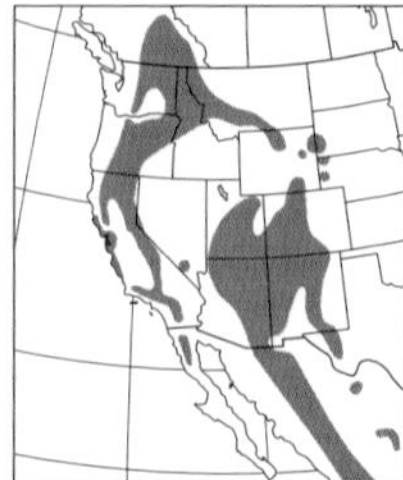

Pygmy Nuthatch *Sitta pygmaea* *L 4¼" (11 cm)*
Gray-brown cap; creamy buff underparts. Pale nape spot visible at close range. Dark eye line bordering cap, most distinct in interior populations.
Voice: Typical calls, a high, rapid *peep peep* and a piping *wee-bee;* grouped in three or more notes in coastal nominate race, *pygmaea.*
Range: Favors yellow-pine forest, except for birds in coastal California pines. Roams in loose flocks. Very rare and irregular fall and winter visitor to lowlands and east to Great Plains.

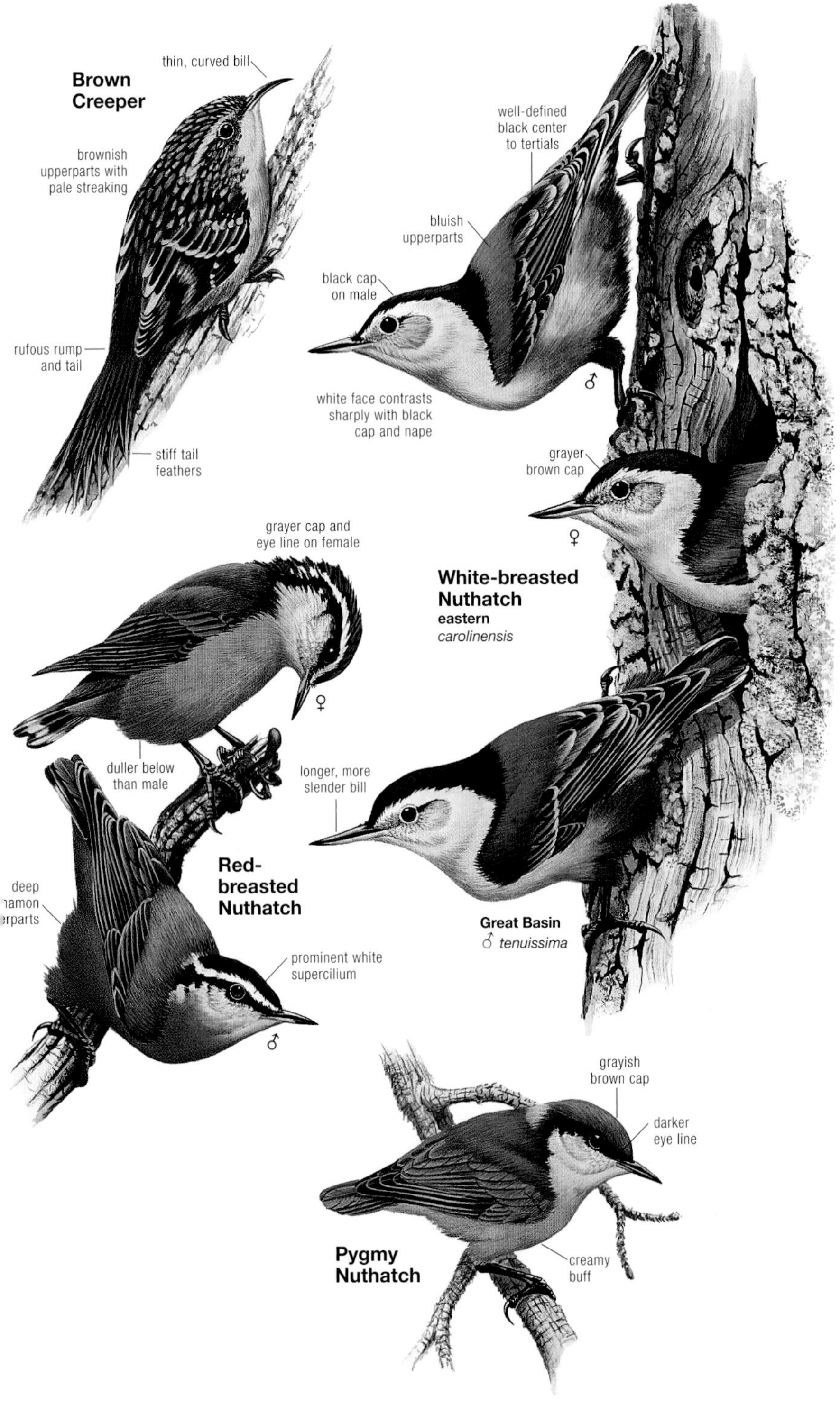
Brown Creeper
thin, curved bill
brownish upperparts with pale streaking
rufous rump and tail
stiff tail feathers
White-breasted Nuthatch
eastern
carolinensis
well-defined black center to tertials
bluish upperparts
black cap on male
white face contrasts sharply with black cap and nape
♂
grayer brown cap
♀
longer, more slender bill
Great Basin
♂ tenuissima
Red-breasted Nuthatch
grayer cap and eye line on female
♀
duller below than male
deep
ıamon
ːrparts
prominent white supercilium
♂
Pygmy Nuthatch
grayish brown cap
darker eye line
creamy buff

Dippers (Family Cinclidae)

Aquatic birds that wade and even swim underwater in clear, rushing mountain streams to feed.

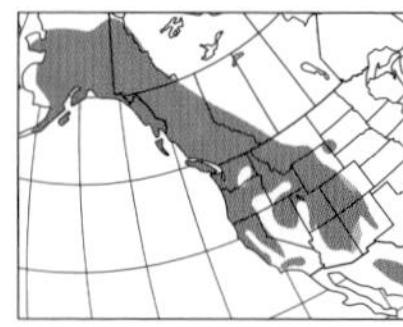

American Dipper *Cinclus mexicanus L 7½" (19 cm)*
Adult sooty gray; dark bill; tail and wings short. ***Juvenile*** has paler, mottled underparts and pale bill.
Voice: Song is loud, musical, and wrenlike.
Range: Found along mountain and foothill streams. Some descend in winter. Casual vagrant well outside mapped range.

Wrens (Family Troglodytidae)

Found in most of North America, wrens are chunky with slender, slightly curved bills; tails are often uptilted. Loud song and vigorous territorial defense belie the small size of most species.

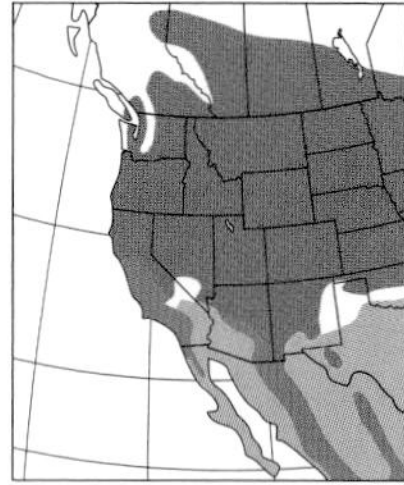

House Wren *Troglodytes aedon L 4¾" (12 cm)*
Brown above, with faint eyebrow. Separated from Winter Wren by longer tail, less prominent barring on belly, and larger overall size. ***Juvenile*** shows a bright rufous rump; darker buff below. Birds from mountains of southeastern Arizona, formerly known as ***"Brown-throated Wren,"*** have a barely buffier throat and breast, bolder eyebrow. Populations farther south in Mexico more distinct.
Voice: Exuberant song is a cascade of bubbling whistled notes. Calls include a soft *chek* and a harsh scald.
Range: Common in shrubs, farms, gardens, and parks.

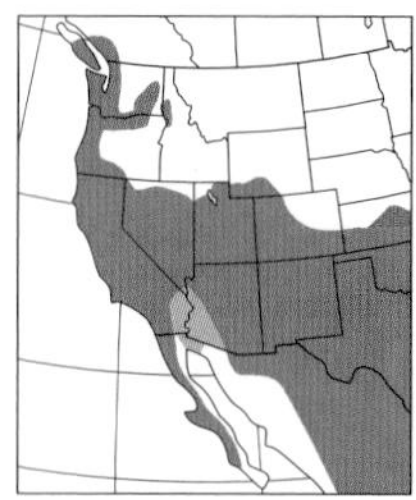

Bewick's Wren *Thryomanes bewickii L 5¼" (13 cm)*
Long, sideways-flitting tail, edged with white spots; long white eyebrow. Subspecies differ mainly in dorsal color. Widespread *eremophilus* of the western interior is the grayest; western coastal races grow browner and darker as one travels north. Northwest *calaphonus* (not shown) is dark, richly colored, with a rufous cast.
Voice: Song variable, a high, thin buzz and warble, similar to Song Sparrow. Calls include a flat, hollow *jip*.
Range: Found in brushland, hedgerows, stream edges, and open woods. Casual to western Montana.

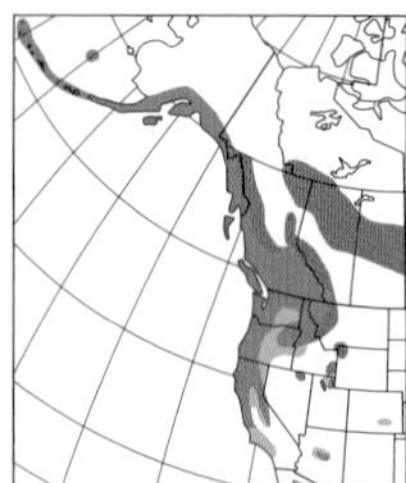

Winter Wren *Troglodytes troglodytes L 4" (10 cm)*
Very small size; stubby tail; dark barring on belly. Widespread eastern subspecies, *hiemalis,* from the north, breeds west to northeastern British Columbia. Western subspecies, *pacificus,* is richer buff on throat and breast, darker on back. Races from Bering Sea islands and Aleutians are larger, paler, and longer billed.
Voice: Song is a long, rapid series of melodious trills, slower and richer in eastern birds. Call is a *timp-timp* like Wilson's Warbler in western races; a *kelp-kelp* call like Song Sparrow in eastern *hiemalis.*
Range: Rather secretive; nests in dense brush, ferns, and tree-falls, especially along stream banks, in moist coniferous woods; in winter may be found in any type of dense woodland understory. Eastern *hiemalis* casual in winter to Southwest and California.

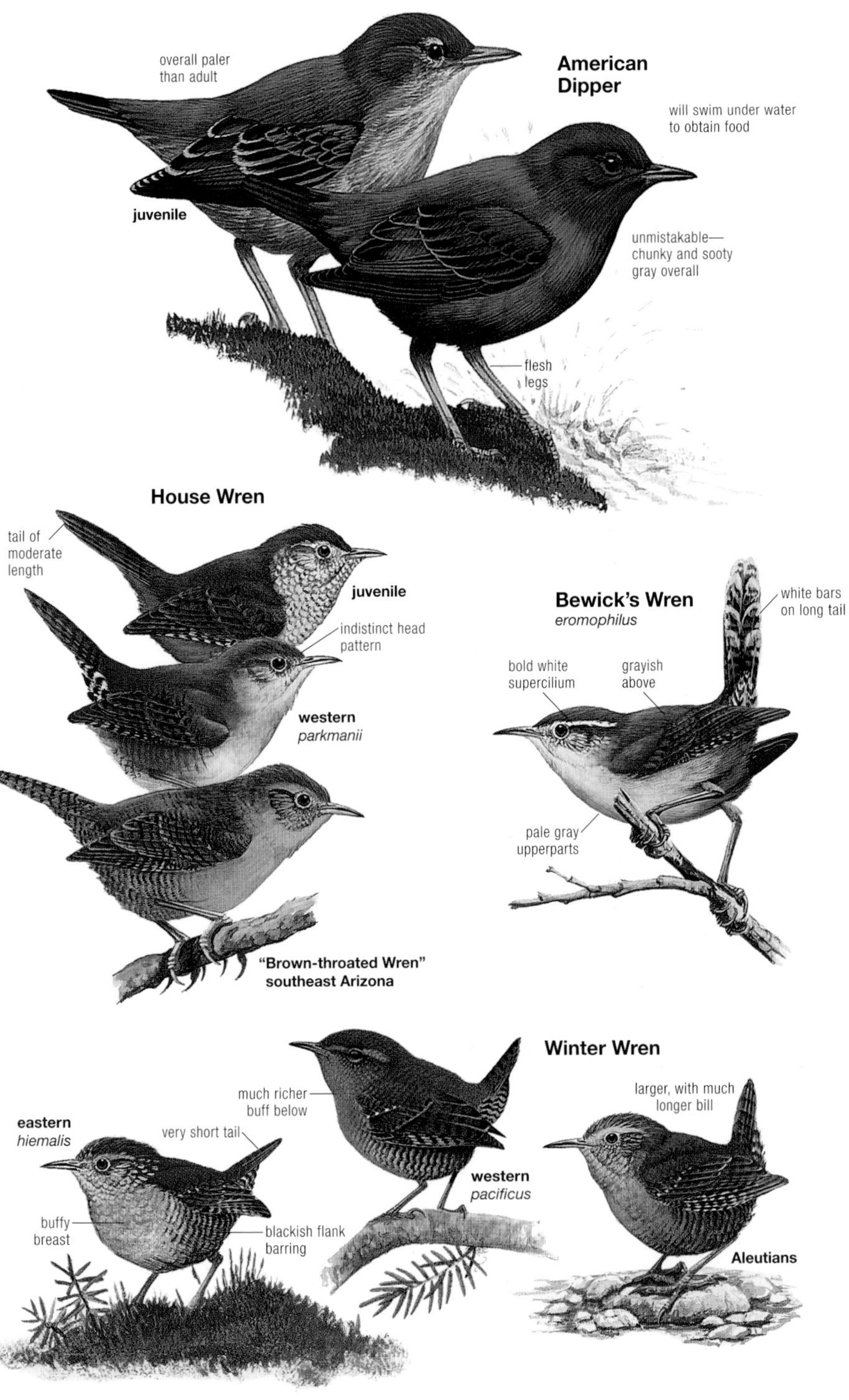
American Dipper
overall paler than adult
will swim under water to obtain food
juvenile
unmistakable—chunky and sooty gray overall
flesh legs
House Wren
tail of moderate length
juvenile
indistinct head pattern
western
parkmanii
"Brown-throated Wren" southeast Arizona
Bewick's Wren
eromophilus
white bars on long tail
bold white supercilium
grayish above
pale gray upperparts
Winter Wren
much richer buff below
larger, with much longer bill
eastern
hiemalis
very short tail
buffy breast
blackish flank barring
western
pacificus
Aleutians

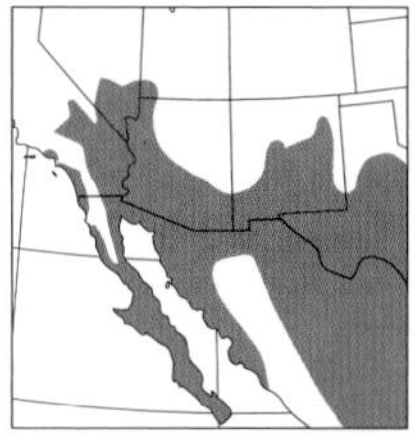

Cactus Wren *Campylorhynchus brunneicapillus*
L 8½" (22 cm) Large; dark crown; streaked back, heavily barred wings and tail, broad white eyebrow. Breast densely spotted with black; threatened California *sandiegense* less densely spotted.
Voice: Song, heard all year, is a low-pitched, harsh, rapid *cha cha cha cha cha.* Call is a variety of low, croaking notes.
Range: Uncommon to common in cactus country. Bulky nests are tucked into the protective spines of a bush or cactus.

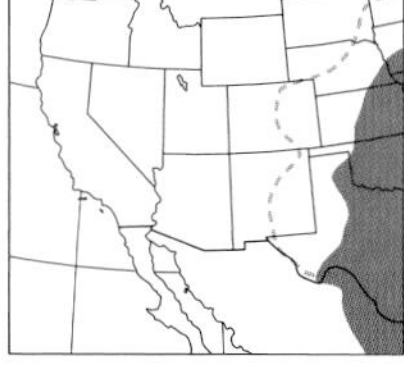

Rock Wren *Salpinctes obsoletus L 6" (15 cm)*
Dull gray-brown above with contrasting cinnamon rump, buffy flanks and tail tips, broad blackish tail band. Breast finely streaked. Frequently bobs its body, especially when alarmed.
Voice: Song, a variable mix of buzzes and trills; call, a buzzy *dzeeee.*
Range: Fairly common in arid, sunny talus slopes, scrublands, and dry washes. Accidental to Northwest Territories.

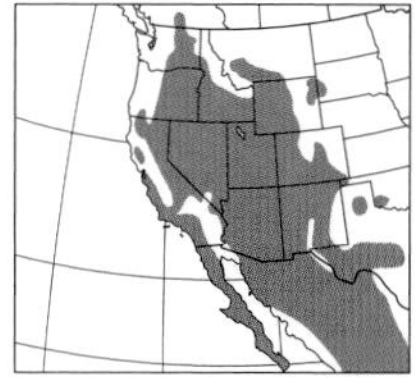

Carolina Wren *Thryothorus ludovicianus L 5½" (14 cm)*
Deep rusty brown above, variably warm buff below; white throat and prominent white eye stripe.
Voice: Vivacious, melodious song is a loud, clear *teakettle tea-kettle teakettle;* sings year-round.
Range: Rather rare in woodland along Rio Grande to Big Bend region. Casual to Colorado, New Mexico, and Arizona.

Canyon Wren *Catherpes mexicanus L 5¾" (15 cm)*
White throat and breast, chestnut belly. Long bill aids in extracting insects from deep crevices.
Voice: Loud, silvery song, a decelerating, descending series of liquid *tee* and *tew* notes. Typical call is a sharp, buzzy *jeet.*
Range: Fairly common in canyons and cliffs, often near water; may also build its cuplike nest in stone buildings and chimneys.

Sedge Wren *Cistothorus platensis L 4½" (11 cm)*
Often difficult to see. Crown and back streaked; eyebrow whitish or buffy and indistinct; underparts largely buff.
Voice: Song begins with a few single notes followed by a weak staccato trill or chatter; call note is a rich *chip,* often doubled.
Range: Nests in wet meadows and sedge marshes. Uncommon and local; limited in western breeding range on western Great Plains. Casual elsewhere in West.

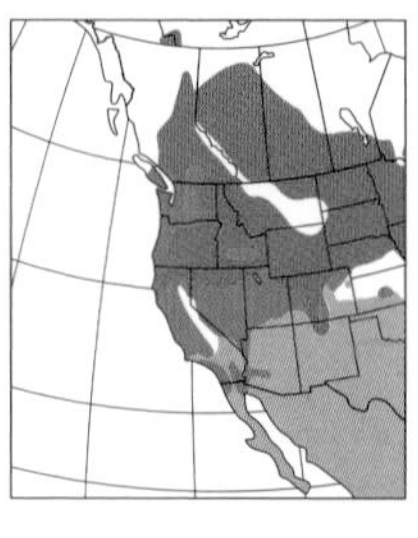

Marsh Wren *Cistothorus palustris L 5" (13 cm)*
Somewhat secretive. Much plumage variation in eastern and western races. Where ranges overlap on central Great Plains just to east of western region, eastern birds darker, more richly colored, with black-and-white speckled neck; western birds duller, with brownish smudges on neck.
Voice: Songs are a mechanical-sounding mix of bubbling and trilling notes; more liquid in the East; harsher and much more variable in the West. Alarm call, a sharp *tsuk,* is often doubled.
Range: Common in reedy marshes, cattail swamps. Nest attached to reeds above water. Casual to northwestern Canada.

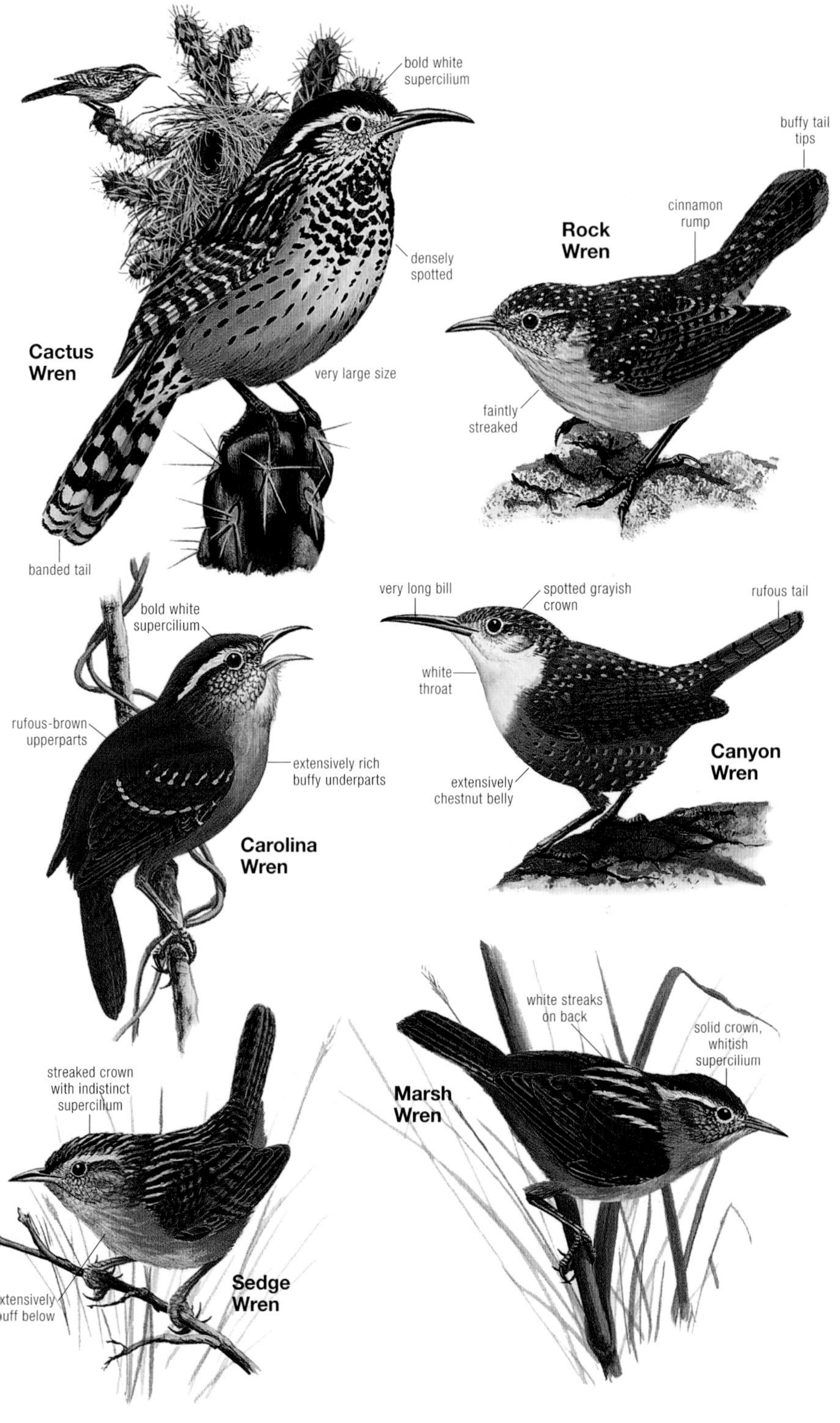
bold white supercilium
buffy tail tips
cinnamon rump
Rock Wren
densely spotted
Cactus Wren
very large size
faintly streaked
banded tail
very long bill
spotted grayish crown
rufous tail
bold white supercilium
white throat
rufous-brown upperparts
extensively rich buffy underparts
Canyon Wren
extensively chestnut belly
Carolina Wren
white streaks on back
solid crown, whitish supercilium
streaked crown with indistinct supercilium
Marsh Wren
Sedge Wren
xtensively
uff below

Kinglets (Family Regulidae)

These small, active birds often hover to feed and join mixed-species flocks in fall and winter.

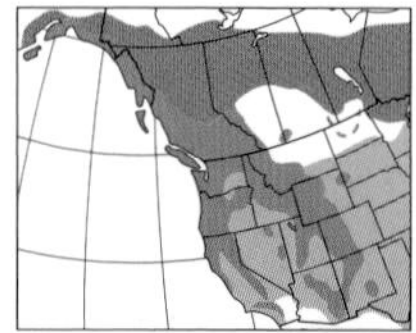

Golden-crowned Kinglet *Regulus satrapa L 4" (10 cm)*
Distinct head pattern. Crown stripe orange in ***male,*** yellow in ***female.***
Voice: Call is a series of high, thin *tsee* notes. Song, almost inaudibly high, is a series of *tsee* notes accelerating into a trill.
Range: Rare to fairly common breeder in coniferous woodlands.

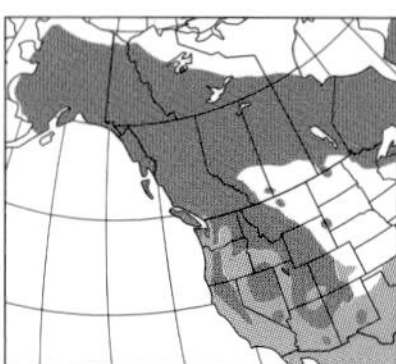

Ruby-crowned Kinglet *Regulus calendula L 4¼" (11 cm)*
Male's red crown patch seldom visible; dusky underparts. Compare carefully with Golden-crowned. Active; flicks wings rapidly.
Voice: Calls include a *je-ditt.* Song is several high, thin *tsee* notes, then *tew* notes, ending with warbled three-note phrases.
Range: Common. Breeds in coniferous woodlands; otherwise found in a a variety of habitats in migration and winter.

Old World Warblers, Gnatcatchers (Family Sylviidae)

Old World Warblers are a large, diverse group. Gnatcatchers are found only in the New World.

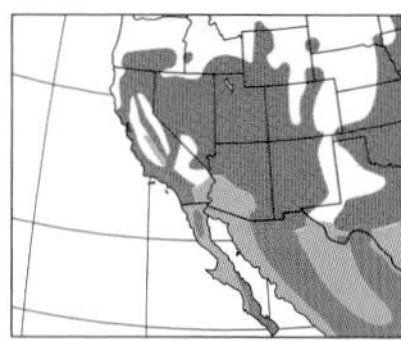

Blue-gray Gnatcatcher *Polioptila caerulea L 4¼" (11 cm)*
Active. Long tail with white outer tail feathers is not graduated. ***Male*** bluish above; in ***breeding*** plumage has black line on sides of crown. ***Female*** grayer.
Voice: Call is a querulous *pwee.*
Range: Favors woodlands, thickets, and chaparral.

Black-capped Gnatcatcher *Polioptila nigriceps*
L 4¼" (11 cm) West Mexican species. ***Female*** and winter birds separated from Blue-grays by more graduated outer tail feathers; from Black-taileds by longer bills and white outer tail feathers; ***breeding male***'s black cap extends below eye.
Voice: Calls like California Gnatcatcher or Bewick's Wren.
Range: Very rare in southeastern Arizona.

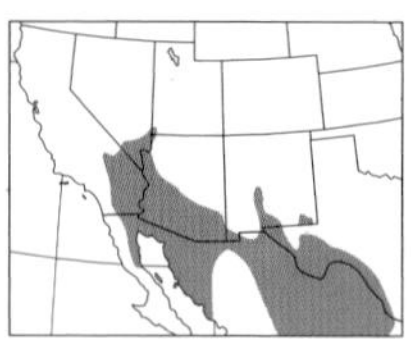

Black-tailed Gnatcatcher *Polioptila melanura L 4" (10 cm)*
White terminal spots on graduated tail feathers; short bill. ***Breeding male*** has glossy black cap, white eye ring; ***female*** browner.
Voice: Calls include rasping *cheeh* and hissing *ssheh;* call harsher than Blue-gray. Song is a rapid series of *jee* notes.
Range: Desert resident; partial to washes.

California Gnatcatcher *Polioptila californica* **T**
L 4¼" (11 cm) Similar to Black-tailed, but darker with less white in outer tail feathers, less distinct eye ring.
Voice: Call, a rising and falling, kitten-like *zeeer.*
Range: Local resident in sage scrub of southwestern California.

broad yellow median crown stripe bordered by black lateral crown stripe
Golden-crowned Kinglet
satrapa
orange median crown stripe
bold whitish supercilium
whitish underparts
slightly broken whitish eye ring
tiny bill
male's red crown usually concealed
pale olive underparts
Ruby-crowned Kinglet
calendula
tail less
duated than
Black-tailed
pure white outer tail feathers
thin black line over eye
breeding ♂
Blue-gray Gnatcatcher
caerulea
graduated tail with white outer tail feathers
long bill
black cap dips under eye
breeding ♂
Black-capped Gnatcatcher
strongly graduated tail with white tips to outer tail feathers
Black-tailed Gnatcatcher
breeding ♂
k cap comes to eye;
vinter, male has gray
with short black line
above eye
more restricted white
black cap like Black-tailed
overall darker above and below than Black-tailed
breeding ♂
California Gnatcatcher
californica

Dusky Warbler *Phylloscopus fuscatus L 5½" (14 cm)*
Asian species. Underparts creamy white, with buffy brown wash on flanks and undertail coverts. Dusky brown, not greenish, upperparts and lack of wing bar distinguish Dusky from Arctic Warbler.
Voice: Calls include a hard *tschick,* like Lincoln's Sparrow.
Range: Casual on islands off western Alaska, and in fall off south coastal Alaska and in California.

Arctic Warbler *Phylloscopus borealis L 5" (13 cm)*
Long, yellowish white eyebrow; straw-colored legs and feet. Broad, dark eye line, mottled ear patches. Has olive upperparts, and pale wing bar on tips of greater coverts; faint second wing bar. Olive wash on sides and flanks; long primary projection. Stout bill is thicker, straighter than Orange-crowned Warbler (page 328); lacks streaking below. Compare also to accidental Willow and Wood Warblers (page 425) and Yellow-browed Warblers (page 426). Larger specimens taken in the western Aleutians with larger bills are either of nominate race, *borealis,* with paler underparts, or of yellower *xanthrodyas* (not shown). Alaskan race, *kennicotti,* is smaller, with smaller bill than either of the Asian races.
Voice: Song is a long, loud series of toneless buzzy notes. Calls include a buzzy *dzik.*
Range: Fairly common in western and central Alaska; casual in fall to California; nests in willow and alder thickets.

Old World Flycatchers (Family Muscicapidae)

Short-legged birds that perch upright and obtain insects primarily through fly-catching. May flick wings or tail. Species of genus *Ficedula* nest in cavities, whereas those of the genus *Muscicapa* build exposed nests. They are not related to New World flycatchers.

Gray-streaked Flycatcher *Muscicapa griseisticta*
L 6" (15 cm) East Asian species. Larger and with smaller head than Dark-sided (page 426); primary projection longer. Note distinctive, but variable, streaking below; paler supraloral spot; more distinct submoustachial stripe usually shows some markings; undertail coverts white.
Range: Casual to western Aleutians mainly in late spring; also several Pribilof records in spring and fall.

Taiga Flycatcher *Ficedula albicilla L 5¼" (13 cm)*
Asian species. Distinct white oval patches at base of outer tail feathers visible in flight, barely visible on folded tail from below; prominent eye ring. ***Breeding male*** with reddish throat. ***Females*** and winter males have whitish throats; grayish wash on breast. All show extensive patch of black on uppertail coverts. Perches low; often drops to ground to catch prey, then returns to perch.
Voice: Frequently flicks tail up while giving rattled *trrt* call; also a metallic *tic* and harsh *ze-it.*
Range: Casual in late spring to western Aleutians; one spring and one fall record on St. Lawrence Island, and one spring record for Pribilofs. Accidental (fall) in California.

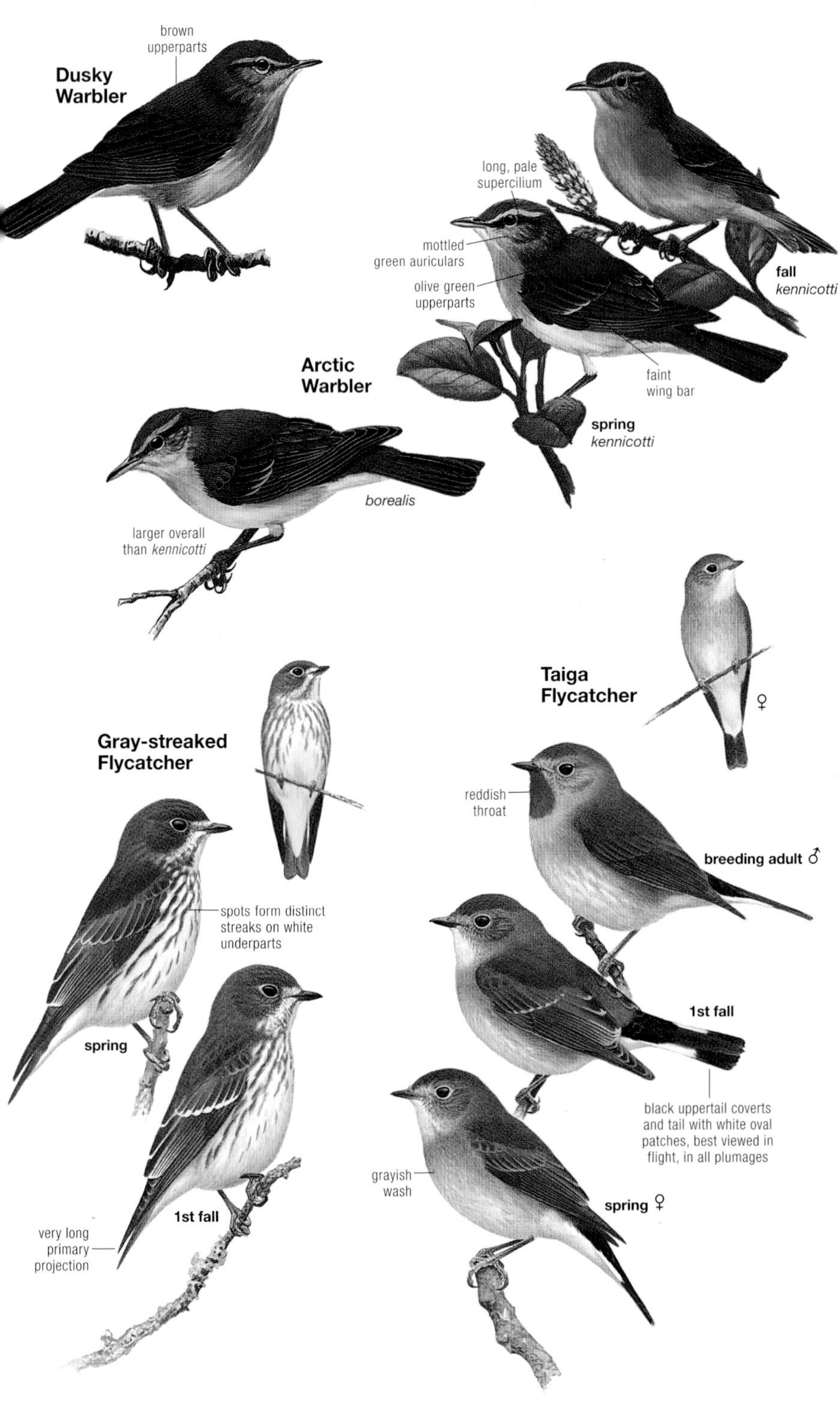
Dusky Warbler
brown upperparts
Arctic Warbler
long, pale supercilium
mottled green auriculars
olive green upperparts
fall
kennicotti
faint wing bar
spring
kennicotti
borealis
larger overall than kennicotti
Taiga Flycatcher
♀
Gray-streaked Flycatcher
reddish throat
breeding adult ♂
spots form distinct streaks on white underparts
1st fall
spring
black uppertail coverts and tail with white oval patches, best viewed in flight, in all plumages
grayish wash
spring ♀
1st fall
very long primary projection

Thrushes (Family Turdidae)

With narrow, notched bills, these eloquent songsters of many habitats feed on insects and fruit.

Siberian Rubythroat *Luscinia calliope L 6" (15 cm)*

Asian species. ***Male*** has a ruby red throat and a broad, white submoustachial stripe. ***Females*** have white throats, often with some pink on adults and buffy on immatures; compare with smaller Bluethroat, which has rufous tail patches, dark breast band, and paler underparts.

Voice: Calls include a whistled *quee-ah* and a deep, low *shack* note, sometimes in a series when agitated. Song is long and varied with various warbled and lisping notes.

Range: Rare spring and fall migrant on western Aleutians, very rare on Pribilofs, casual on St. Lawrence Island.

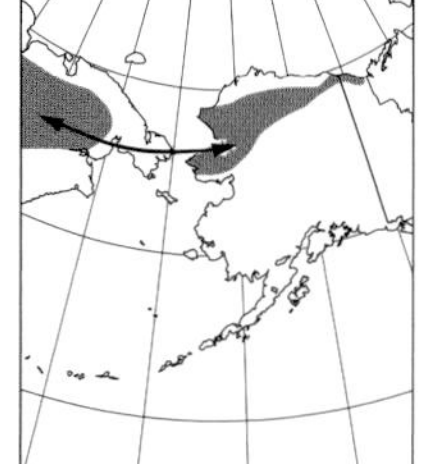

Bluethroat *Luscinia svecica L 5½" (14 cm)*

Colorful throat pattern distinguishes ***breeding male*** from all other birds. In all plumages, rufous patches at base of tail are conspicuous in flight, which is low off the ground. In ***female*** and immature, note dark breast band. Runs on ground, usually with tail cocked. Generally furtive, but in courtship, males sing from high perches and in elaborate display flight.

Voice: Varied, melodious song often begins with a crisp, metallic *ting ting ting;* call, *tchak,* is often given in a series.

Range: Uncommon; nests in tundra thickets near water. Regular migrant on St. Lawrence Island; casual on Pribilofs and western Aleutians.

Northern Wheatear *Oenanthe oenanthe L 5¾" (15 cm)*

Tail pattern distinctive: white rump, tail with dark central and terminal band. Western Arctic-breeding birds, the nominate race, are whitish, with a buff tinge. ***Males*** in fall and winter resemble females. Active; bob their tails.

Voice: Calls include *chak* and whistled *wheet,* often combined. Song, a scratchy warbling mixed with call notes, is often given in flight with tail spread.

Range: Uncommon. For breeding, prefers open, stony habitats. Rare migrant to Pribilofs and Aleutians (mainly fall); casual (mainly fall) to California; accidental elsewhere.

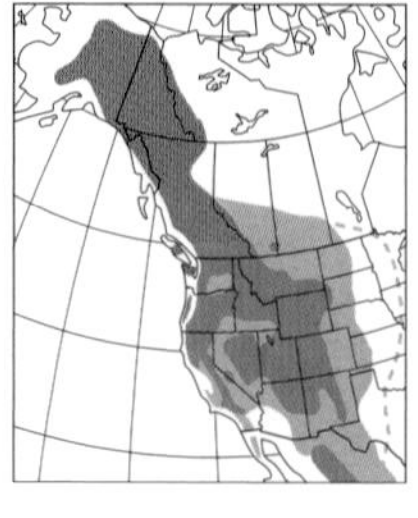

Townsend's Solitaire *Myadestes townsendi*

L 8½" (22 cm) Large and slender; gray overall, with bold white eye ring. Buff wing patches and white outer tail feathers are most conspicuous in flight. Often seen on a high perch, from which it sometimes fly-catches.

Voice: Call note is a high-pitched *eek;* song, heard all year, a loud, complex, melodious warbling.

Range: Nests on the ground. Fairly common in coniferous forests on mountain slopes; in winter, also in wooded valleys, canyons, and shelterbelts where juniper berries are available. Highly migratory. Very rare along coast.

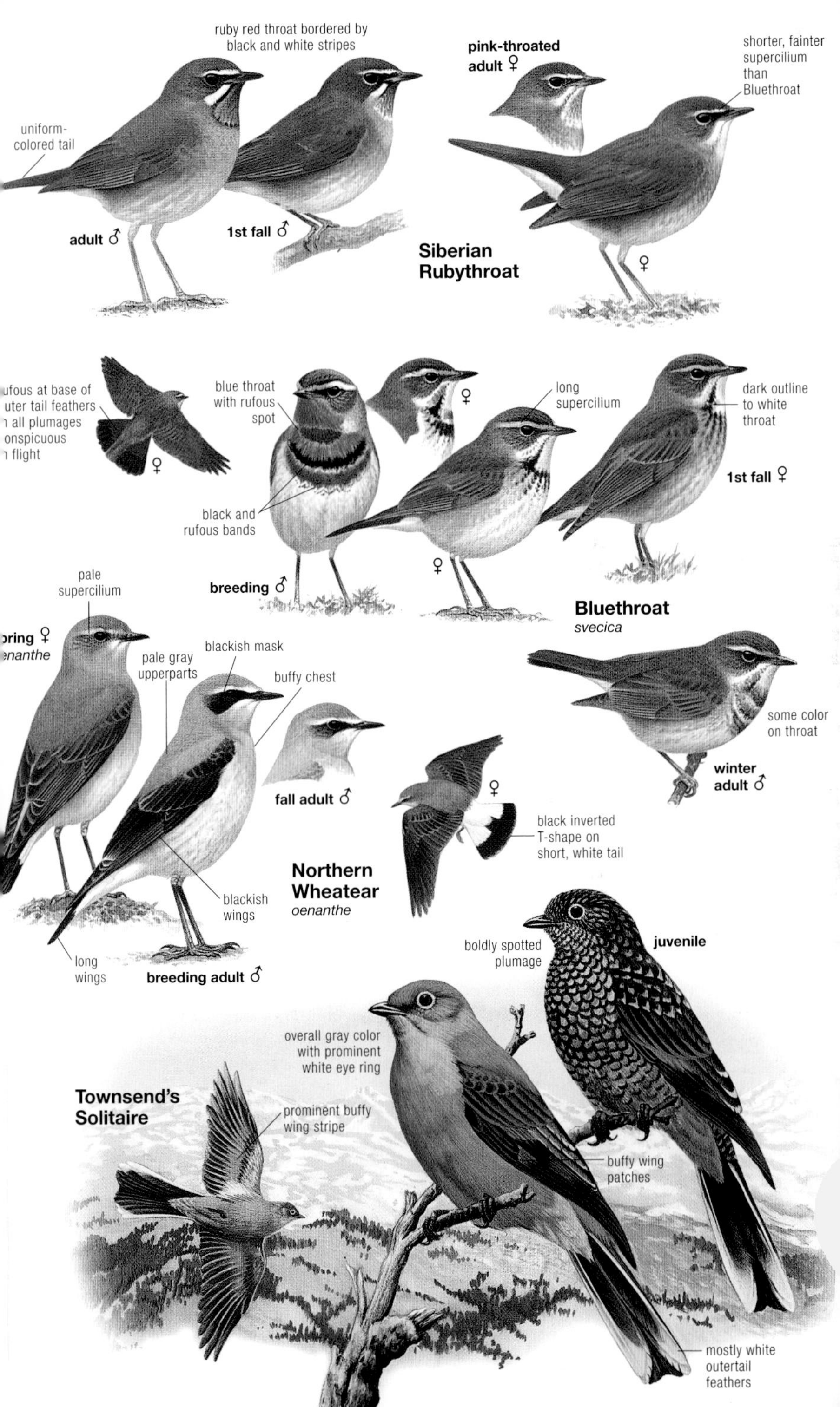
ruby red throat bordered by black and white stripes
uniform-colored tail
adult ♂
1st fall ♂
pink-throated adult ♀
shorter, fainter supercilium than Bluethroat
Siberian Rubythroat
♀
ufous at base of uter tail feathers n all plumages onspicuous n flight
♀
blue throat with rufous spot
♀
long supercilium
dark outline to white throat
1st fall ♀
black and rufous bands
breeding ♂
♀
Bluethroat
svecica
pale supercilium
pring ♀
enanthe
blackish mask
pale gray upperparts
buffy chest
some color on throat
winter adult ♂
fall adult ♂
♀
black inverted T-shape on short, white tail
Northern Wheatear
oenanthe
blackish wings
long wings
breeding adult ♂
boldly spotted plumage
juvenile
overall gray color with prominent white eye ring
Townsend's Solitaire
prominent buffy wing stripe
buffy wing patches
mostly white outertail feathers

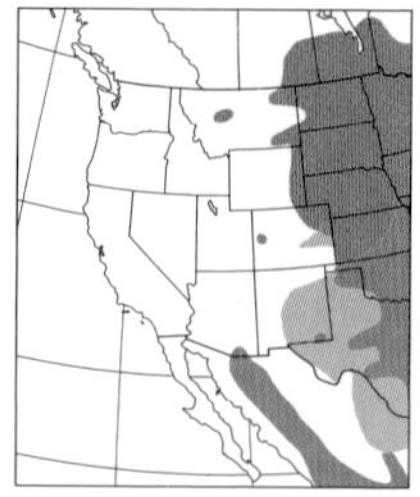

Eastern Bluebird *Sialia sialis* L 7" (18 cm)
Chestnut throat, sides of neck, breast, sides, and flanks; contrasting white belly, white undertail coverts. ***Male*** is uniformly deep blue above; ***female*** grayer. The subspecies resident in the mountains of southeastern Arizona, *fulva,* is paler overall. All subspecies distinguished from Western Bluebird by chestnut on throat and sides of neck and by white, not grayish, belly and under tail.
Voice: Call note is a musical, rising *chur-lee,* extended in song to *chur chur-lee chur-lee.*
Range: Uncommon in West. Nominate has been recorded west to Alberta and in southeastern Arizona (winter). Found in open woodlands, farmlands, and orchards. Nests in holes in trees and posts; also in nest boxes.

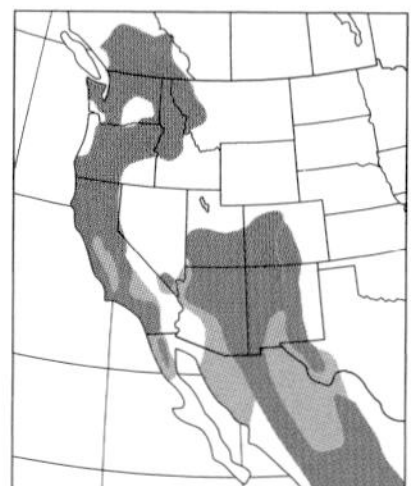

Western Bluebird *Sialia mexicana* L 7" (18 cm)
Male's upperparts and throat are deep purple-blue; breast, sides, and flanks chestnut; belly and undertail coverts grayish. Most birds show some chestnut on shoulders and upper back. ***Female*** duller, brownish gray above; breast and flanks tinged with chestnut, throat pale gray.
Voice: Call note is a mellow *few,* extended in brief song to *few few fawee.*
Range: Nests in holes in trees and posts; also in nest boxes. Common in woodlands, farmlands, orchards; in desert areas during winter, found in mesquite-mistletoe groves. Casual on western Great Plains.

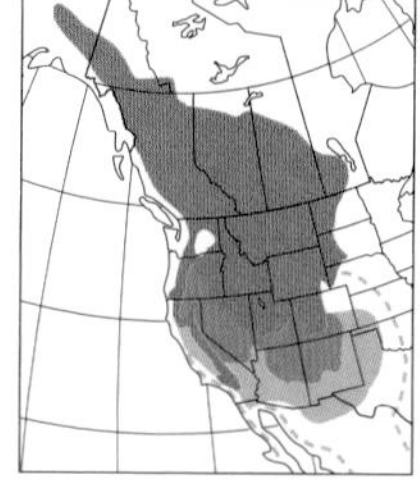

Mountain Bluebird *Sialia currucoides* L 7¼" (18 cm)
Male is sky blue above, paler below, with whitish belly and undertail coverts. ***Female*** is brownish gray overall, with white belly and undertail coverts; white edges on coverts give folded wing a scalloped look. In fresh fall plumage, female's throat and breast are tinged with red-orange; brownish rear flank contrasting with white undertail coverts distinguishes her from female Eastern Bluebird, which has reddish flank. Note also longer, thinner bill and longer primary tip projection of Mountain Bluebird.
Voice: Call is a thin *few;* song, a low, warbled *tru-lee.* More often than other bluebirds, hovers above prey, chiefly insects, before dropping to catch them; also catches insects in flight.
Range: Nests in tree cavities, buildings, and nest boxes. Inhabits open rangelands, meadows, generally at elevations above 5,000 feet; in winter, found primarily in open lowlands and desert. Highly migratory, but winter movements unpredictable; in some years many to southwestern deserts, in other winters almost absent.

IDENTIFYING: Female Bluebirds All three species of bluebirds occur in the West, although, amazingly, Eastern Bluebird has yet to occur in the Pacific region. A paler resident race, *fulva,* is found in the mountains of southeastern Arizona and perhaps eastern New Mexico.

With its paler collar, Eastern is distinctive in all plumages. Both Mountain and Western Bluebirds lack this collar. Unlike Eastern and Western, Mountain lacks rufous on the underparts, but in fresh fall plumage, its warm brown tones below can look slightly reddish in some lights.

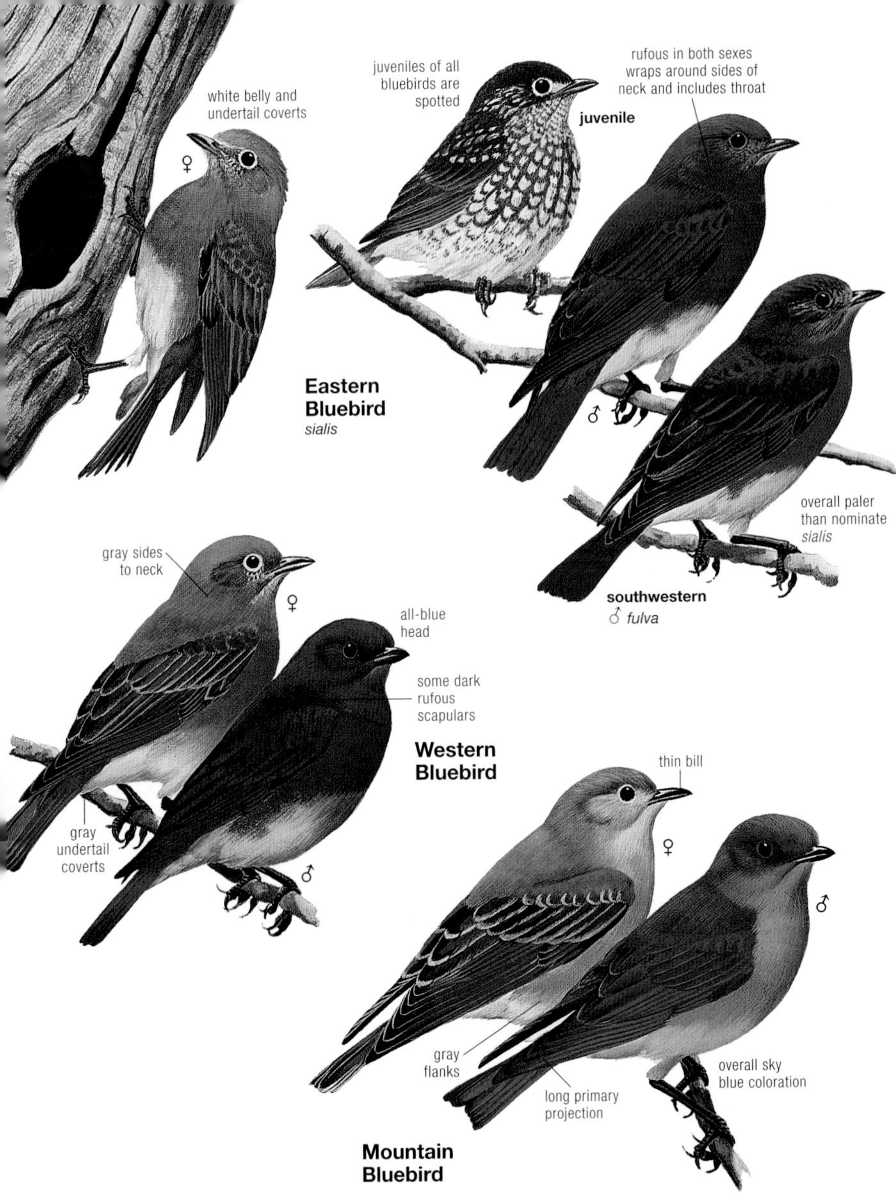

Both Mountain and Eastern have pure white undertail coverts, whereas Western is grayish there. Mountain is slender billed and long winged; both Eastern and Western appear thicker billed and have shorter wings. The color of blue in the wing and tail differs between the three species, as do the vocalizations.

Mountain interbreeds occasionally with Eastern on the western Great Plains. Hybridization has occurred between Western and Eastern too, so any bird well out of range should be looked at carefully with that in mind.

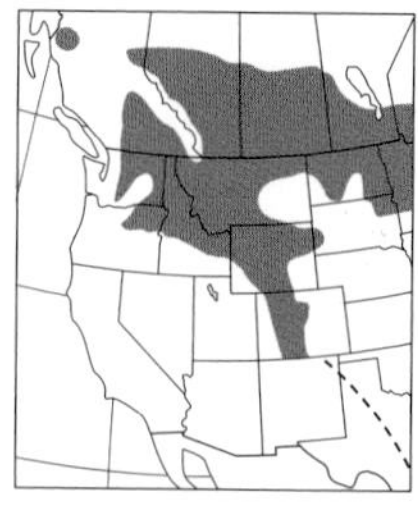

Veery *Catharus fuscescens L 7" (18 cm)*
Reddish brown above, white below, with gray flanks, grayish face, incomplete and indistinct gray eye ring. Upperparts duller, breast more spotted in more westerly *salicicola* than in eastern *fuscescens,* but geographical boundaries ambiguous between subspecies and in part reflect individual variation and trends.
Voice: Song is a descending series of *veer* notes; call is a sharp, descending, whistled *veer.*
Range: Uncommon; found in dense, moist woodlands and streamside thickets. Casual migrant to California and southwest; most reports likely pertain to *ustulatus* Swainson's Thrush.

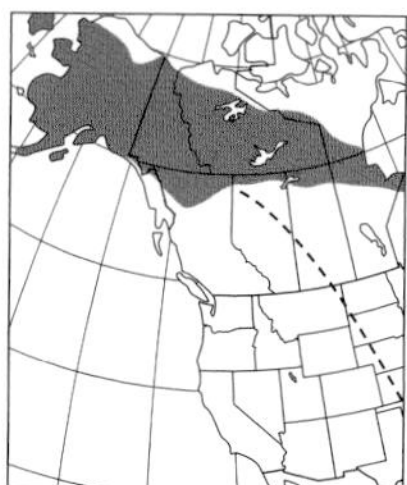

Gray-cheeked Thrush *Catharus minimus L 7¼" (18 cm)*
Gray-brown above, faint, incomplete eye ring. Dark spots on breast, which is usually less buffy than Swainson's; flanks brownish gray.
Voice: Thin, nasal song is somewhat like Veery's, but first and last phrases drop, middle one rises; call, a sharp *pheu* similar to Veery's, but higher-pitched, not descending.
Range: Favors woodlands. Rare migrant on Great Plains; casual elsewhere (fall) in West south of breeding range.

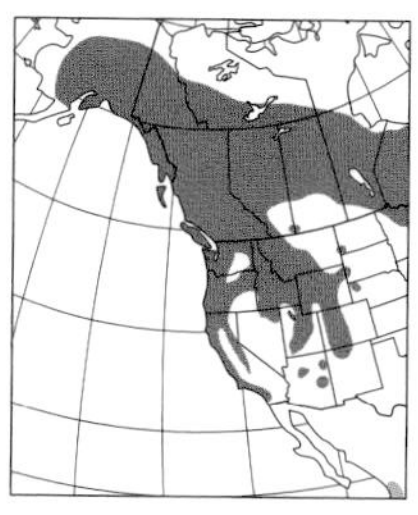

Swainson's Thrush *Catharus ustulatus L 7" (18 cm)*
Brownish above, with buffy lores and bold buffy eye ring; bright buffy breast with dark spots; brownish gray sides and flanks. Pacific coast race, *ustulatus,* and similar *oedicus* are reddish brown above, less distinctly spotted below and have buffier flanks; distinguished from *salicicola* race of Veery by face pattern, buffy brown sides and flanks, and voice.
Voice: Song is an ascending spiral of varied whistles; common call is a liquid *whit* in Pacific coast races, a sharper *quirk* in others; at night a peeping *queep* is heard.
Range: Fairly common; found in moist woods, swamps. Pacific subspecies common migrants in the deserts of southeastern California in spring (rare in fall); a few migrate through southern Arizona. More easterly *swainsoni* and Alaskan *incanus* breed well west but are trans-Gulf migrants; winter in South America. Pacific races winter from western Mexico to western slope of Central America.

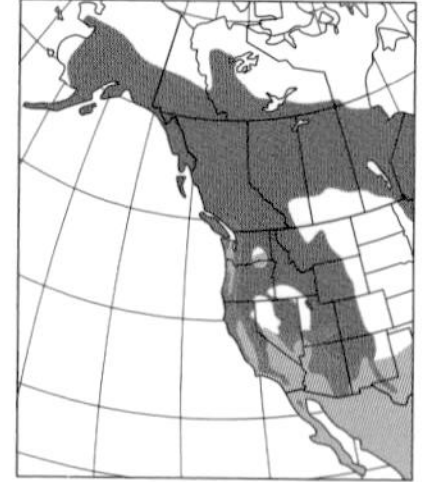

Hermit Thrush *Catharus guttatus L 6¾" (17 cm)*
Complete, often whitish eye ring; reddish tail. Upperparts vary from rich brown to gray-brown. Eastern races, such as widespread *faxoni,* have buff-brown flanks and are casual in West. Western mountain races, such as *auduboni,* are larger and grayish with a pale rufous tail; smaller and darker Alaska-breeding *guttatus,* with a darker rufous tail, winters commonly over most of California. Often flicks wings and slowly raises tail.
Voice: Song is a serene series of clear, flutelike notes, with an introductory note followed by several quavering notes; similar phrases are repeated at different pitches. Calls include a deeper *chuck,* often doubled, and a whiny, upslurred *wee.*
Range: Fairly common; found in coniferous or mixed woodlands, thickets, and gardens.

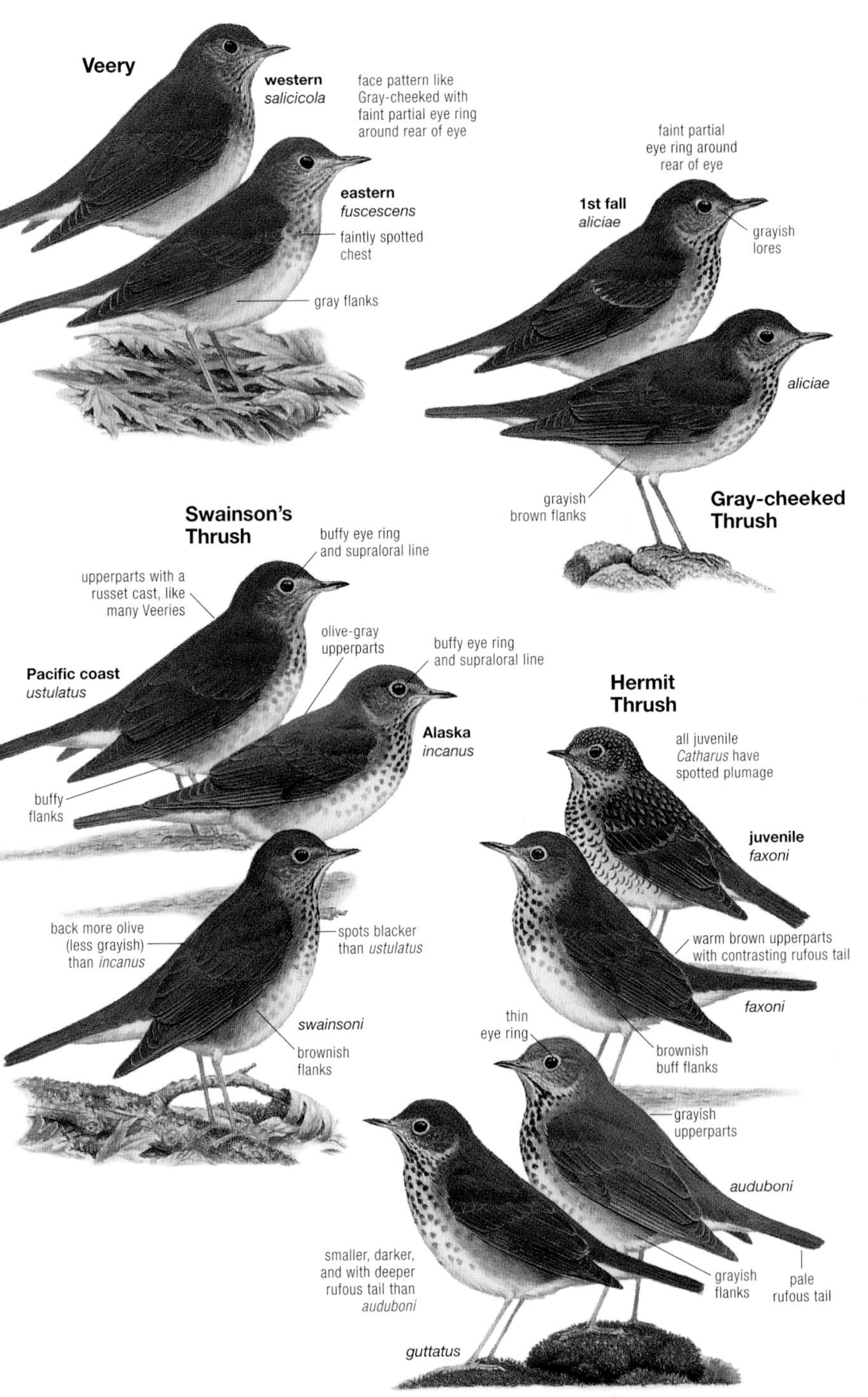
Veery
western
salicicola
face pattern like
Gray-cheeked with
faint partial eye ring
around rear of eye
eastern
fuscescens
faintly spotted
chest
gray flanks
faint partial
eye ring around
rear of eye
1st fall
aliciae
grayish
lores
aliciae
grayish
brown flanks
Gray-cheeked
Thrush
Swainson's
Thrush
buffy eye ring
and supraloral line
upperparts with a
russet cast, like
many Veeries
olive-gray
upperparts
buffy eye ring
and supraloral line
Pacific coast
ustulatus
Alaska
incanus
buffy
flanks
Hermit
Thrush
all juvenile
Catharus have
spotted plumage
juvenile
faxoni
back more olive
(less grayish)
than incanus
spots blacker
than ustulatus
warm brown upperparts
with contrasting rufous tail
faxoni
swainsoni
brownish
flanks
thin
eye ring
brownish
buff flanks
grayish
upperparts
audubon
smaller, darker,
and with deeper
rufous tail than
auduboni
grayish
flanks
pale
rufous tail
guttatus

American Robin *Turdus migratorius L 10" (25 cm)*
Gray-brown above, with darker head and tail; bill yellow; underparts brick red; lower belly white. Most western birds paler and duller overall than eastern nominate *migratorius* (shown here), which breeds to western Alaska; in most, tail has white corners, visible in flight. Northwestern race, *caurinus*, is equally dark but lacks white tail spots; breeds north to southeast Alaska. ***Juvenile***'s underparts are tinged with cinnamon, heavily spotted with brown.
Voice: Loud, liquid song is a variable *cheerily cheer-up cheerio.* Calls include a single *tup* and a rapid *tut tut tut;* a high, thin *ssip* in flight.
Range: Common, widespread. Often seen on lawns, head cocked as it searches for earthworms; also eats insects and berries. Nests in shrubs, in trees, on sheltered windowsills and eaves. In winter, found in moist woodlands, swamps, suburbs, and parks. Numbers vary greatly from winter to winter. Breeding range has expanded south.

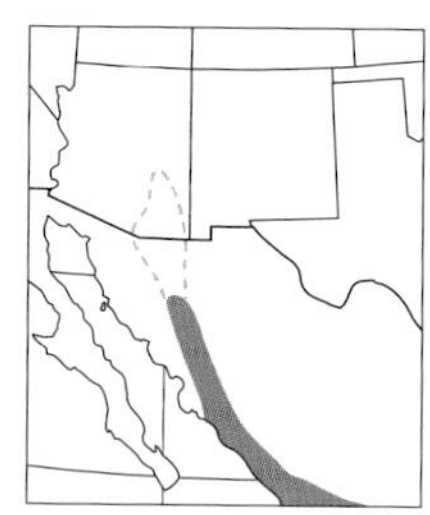

Rufous-backed Robin *Turdus rufopalliatus L 9¼" (24 cm)*
West Mexican species. Distinguished from American Robin by reddish brown back and wing coverts, uniformly gray head with no white around eye, and more extensively streaked throat. Somewhat secretive; found in treetops and dense shrubbery.
Voice: Calls include a plaintive, drawn-out, whistled *teeeuu,* a clucking series of *chuk* notes and, in flight, a high, thin *ssi.*
Range: Very rare winter visitor to southern Arizona, casual to western Texas, southern New Mexico, and southern California.

Eyebrowed Thrush *Turdus obscurus L 8½" (22 cm)*
Asian species. Brownish olive above, distinct white eyebrow. Belly is white, sides pale buffy orange. ***Male*** has dark gray throat and breast; ***female***'s throat is white and streaked; browner head shows little contrast with rest of upperparts. Wing linings pale gray.
Voice: Flight call is a high, piercing, drawn-out *dzee.*
Range: Regular spring migrant on the Aleutians, casual in fall; very rare on St. Lawrence Island, Pribilofs, and casual in northern Alaska; accidental in California (late spring).

Dusky Thrush *Turdus naumanni L 9½" (24 cm)*
Asian species. White eyebrow conspicuous on blackish head. Wings mostly rusty rufous, underwing almost entirely rufous. Below, white edgings give a scaly look to dark breast and sides. Note also distinctive white crescent across breast. Female and immature average duller overall. Several sight records of redder nominate race for western Alaska's islands, however intergrades between these two races are numerous in Asia.
Voice: Call is a series of *shack* notes; also a shrill, wheezy *shrree* similar to European Starling.
Range: Casual spring and fall migrant on western Aleutians; accidental on St. Lawrence Island, Point Barrow, and in winter south to coastal Washington.

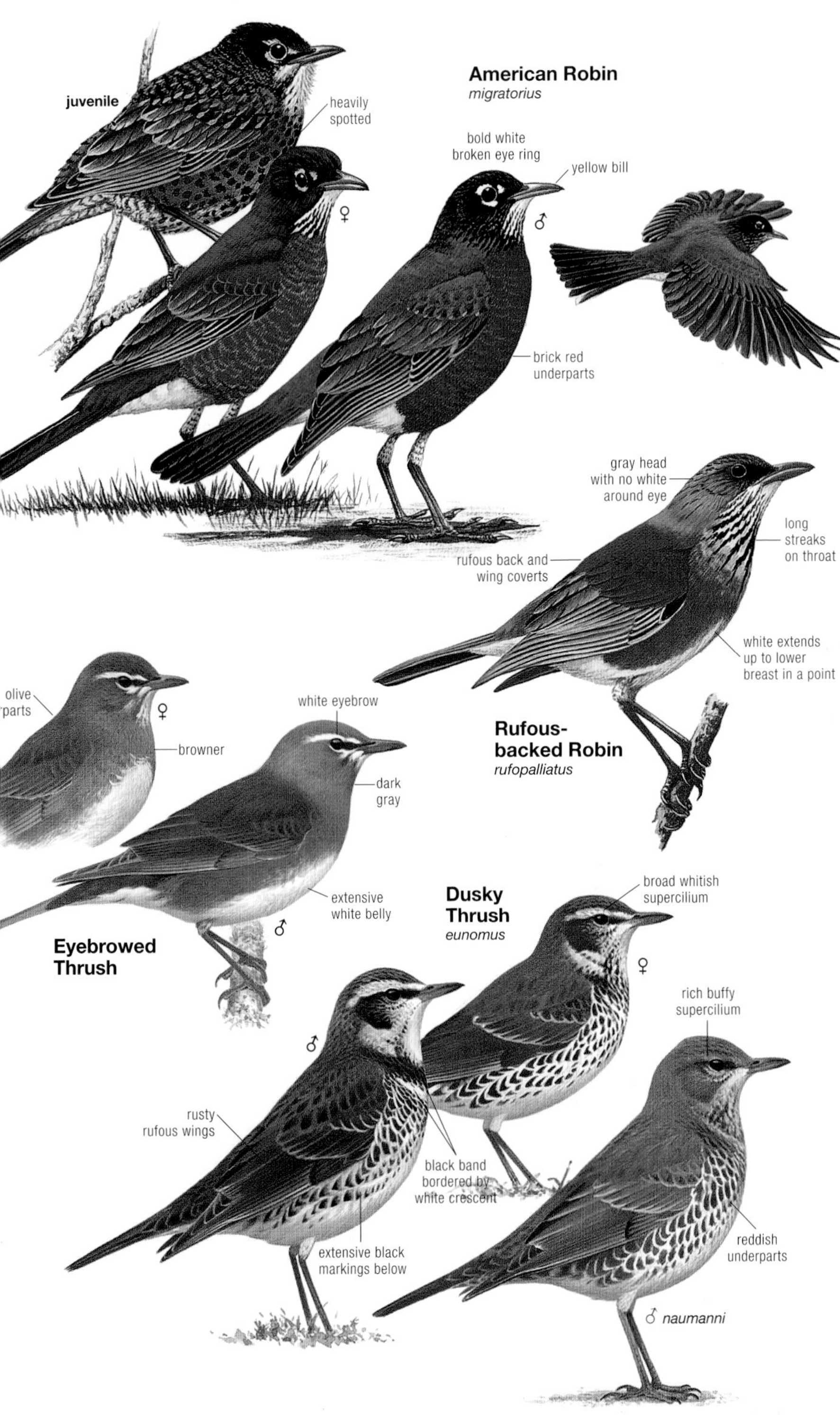
American Robin
migratorius
juvenile
heavily spotted
bold white broken eye ring
yellow bill
♀
♂
brick red underparts
gray head with no white around eye
long streaks on throat
rufous back and wing coverts
white extends up to lower breast in a point
Rufous-backed Robin
rufopalliatus
olive parts
♀
browner
white eyebrow
dark gray
extensive white belly
♂
Eyebrowed Thrush
Dusky Thrush
eunomus
broad whitish supercilium
♀
rich buffy supercilium
♂
rusty rufous wings
black band bordered by white crescent
extensive black markings below
reddish underparts
♂ naumanni

Varied Thrush *Ixoreus naevius* *L 9½" (24 cm)*
Male has grayish blue nape and back, orange eyebrow; underparts orange with black breast band; buffy orange bar on underwing prominent in flight. ***Female*** distinguished from American Robin (previous page) by orange eyebrow and wing bar, dusky breast band, and unmarked throat. ***Juvenile*** resembles female but has white belly, scalier-looking throat and breast. In a very rare variant morph, all orange color is replaced by white.
Voice: Call is a soft, low *tschook;* song is a slow series of variously pitched notes, rapidly trilled.
Range: Common in dense, moist woodlands, especially coniferous forests. Generally feeds in trees but also on ground. Rare to casual east of Pacific states. Numbers vary from year to year in southern part of mapped winter range. Typically does not associate with American Robins.

Aztec Thrush *Ridgwayia pinicola* *L 9¼" (24 cm)*
Mexican species. ***Male*** is blackish brown above, with white patches on wings, white uppertail coverts; tail broadly tipped with white; contrasty underparts. ***Female*** is browner, more streaked on throat and breast. ***Juvenile*** is heavily streaked above with creamy white; underparts whitish and heavily scaled with brown.
Voice: Calls are a quavering *wheeerr,* a metallic *wheer,* and a clear *sweee-uh.*
Range: Rare and irregular to southeastern Arizona, mainly in late summer; casual to west Texas.

Mockingbirds, Thrashers (Family Mimidae)

These notable singers are unequaled in North America for the rich variety and volume of their song. Some mimic the songs of other species.

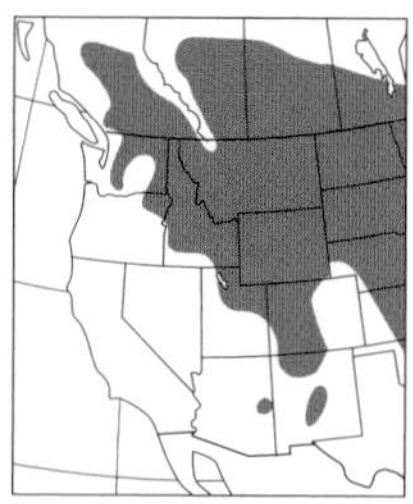

Gray Catbird *Dumetella carolinensis* *L 8½" (22 cm)*
Plain dark gray with a black cap and a long, black tail, often cocked; undertail coverts chestnut.
Voice: Song is a mixture of melodious, nasal, and squeaky notes interspersed with catlike *mew* notes; some are good mimics. Most readily identified by harsh, downslurred *mew* call; also gives a low *quirt* and a clucking noise.
Range: Uncommon to fairly common in western breeding range, but rather secretive in thickets; generally rare away from mapped range. Accidental to Alaska.

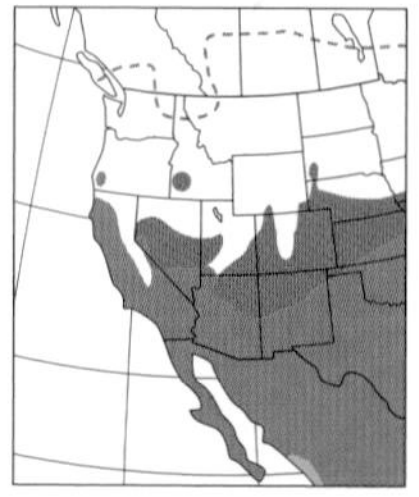

Northern Mockingbird *Mimus polyglottos* *L 10" (25 cm)*
White outer tail feathers and white wing patches flash in flight and in territorial and displays.
Voice: Song is a mixture of original and imitative phrases, each repeated several times. Often sings at night. Imitates other species' songs and calls. Both sexes sing in fall, claiming feeding territories. Call is a loud, sharp *check.*
Range: Found in a variety of habitats, including towns. Casual well north of mapped range, as far as Alaska.

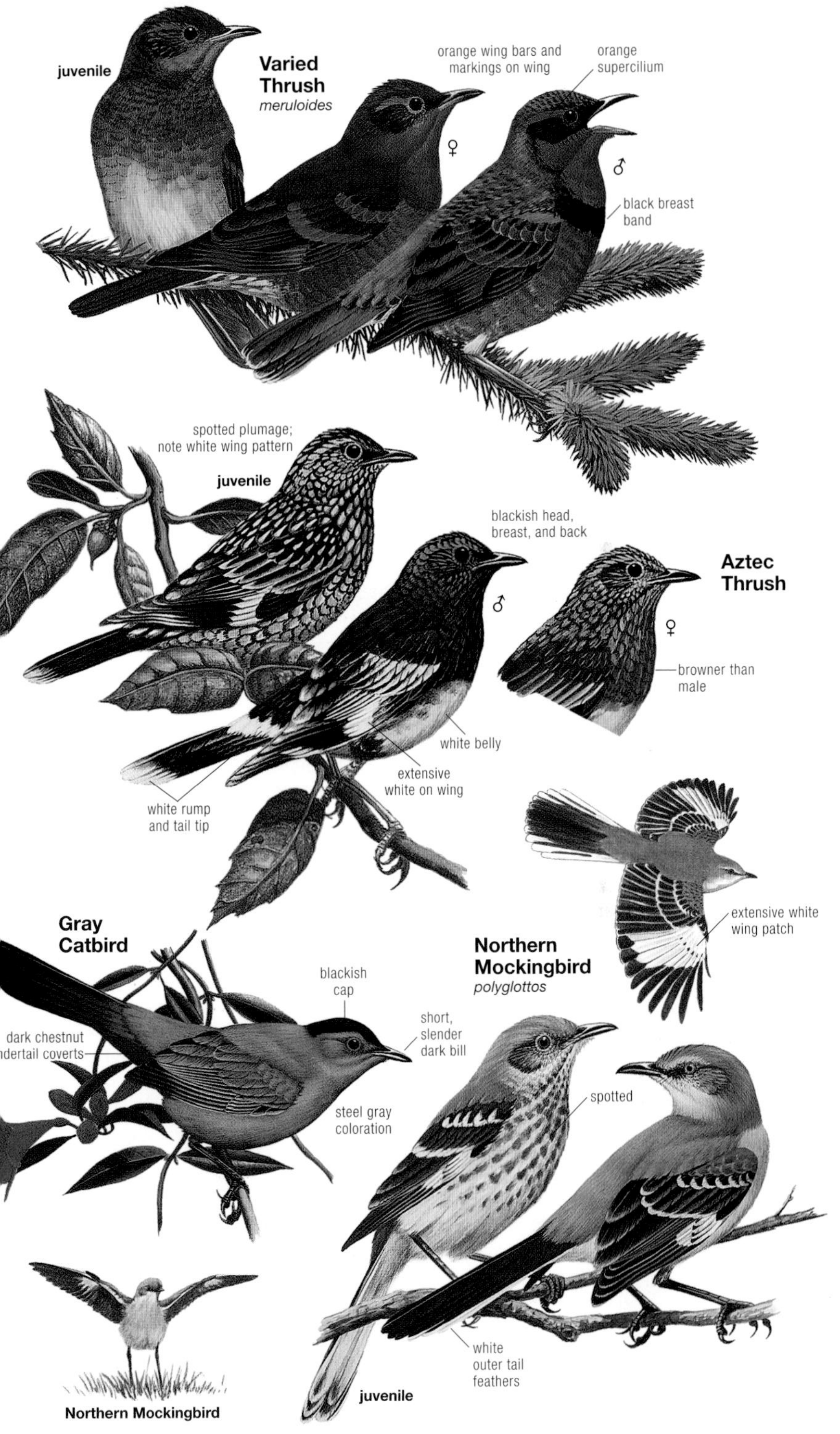
juvenile
Varied Thrush
meruloides
orange wing bars and markings on wing
orange supercilium
♀
♂
black breast band
spotted plumage; note white wing pattern
juvenile
blackish head, breast, and back
Aztec Thrush
♂
♀
browner than male
white belly
extensive white on wing
white rump and tail tip
extensive white wing patch
Gray Catbird
Northern Mockingbird
polyglottos
blackish cap
short, slender dark bill
dark chestnut
ndertail coverts
steel gray coloration
spotted
white outer tail feathers
juvenile
Northern Mockingbird

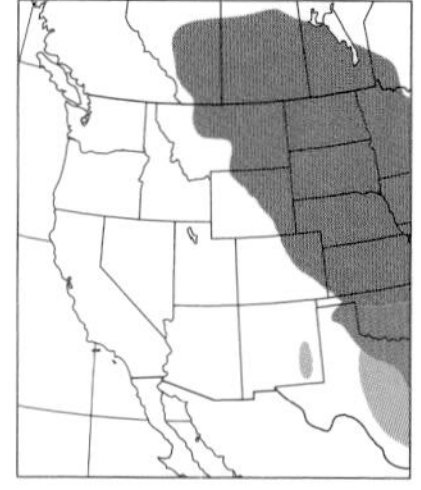

Brown Thrasher *Toxostoma rufum* *L 11½" (29 cm)*
Reddish brown above and heavily streaked below. Immature's eyes are darker.
Voice: Sings a series of varied melodious phrases, each phrase usually given only two or three times. Seldom imitates other birds. Calls include a sharp *spuck* and a low *churr.*
Range: Uncommon in western breeding range and on western Great Plains. Otherwise rare to very rare in the West. Accidental to northern Alaska and Northwest Territories.

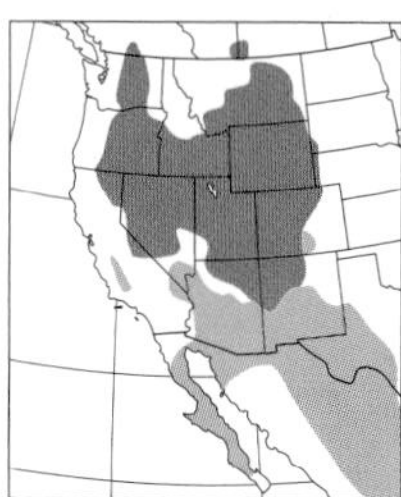

Sage Thrasher *Oreoscoptes montanus* *L 8½" (22 cm)*
Yellow eye, white wing bars, white-cornered tail. Grayish above, boldly streaked below. ***Worn*** late-summer birds show much less streaking, can resemble Bendire's Thrasher. Juvenile has streaked head and back.
Voice: Song is a long series of warbled phrases. Calls include a *chuck* and a high *churr.*
Range: Nests in sagebrush plains. Rarely winters north into breeding range. Very rare to Pacific coast, mainly in migration.

Bendire's Thrasher *Toxostoma bendirei* *L 9¾" (25 cm)*
Breast mottled; bill shorter and usually less curved than Curve-billed Thrasher; base of lower mandible pale. White tail tips are similar to *oberholseri* race of Curve-billed Thrasher. Distinctive arrowhead-shaped spots on breast are not present in ***worn*** summer plumage.
Voice: Song is a sustained, melodic warbling, each phrase repeated one to three times. Low *chuck* call note is seldom heard.
Range: Uncommon and local; found in open farmlands, Joshua trees, and brushy desert. Casual to southern California coast in late summer, fall, and winter.

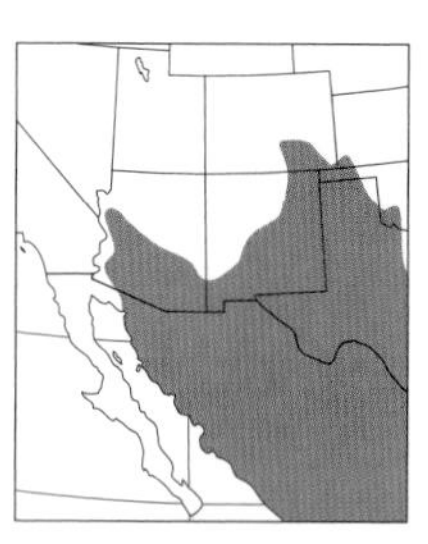

Curve-billed Thrasher *Toxostoma curvirostre*
L 11" (28 cm) Breast mottled; bill all-dark, longer, heavier, and usually more strongly curved than Bendire's Thrasher. Breast spots indistinct in the westernmost race, *palmeri*, found in southern Arizona. Race from extreme southeastern Arizona to southern Texas, *oberholseri*, shows clearer spotting below, has pale wing bars and conspicuous white tips on tail. ***Juveniles*** have shorter bills. Genetic sampling indicates that the *curvirostre* group, of which *oberholseri* is a subspecies, and the *palmeri* group may represent separate species, but studies did not include samples from the region of overlap immediately to the west of Chiricahua Mountains, Arizona.
Voice: Distinctive call, a sharp upslurred *whit-wheet,* sometimes three-noted (*palmeri*) or even-pitched *whit-whit* (*oberholseri*). Elaborate and melodic song includes low trills and warbles.
Range: Common in canyons, semiarid brushlands. Some seasonal movement in Great Plains population. Casual (*palmeri*) in southeastern California; accidental west to coastal southern California and north to Montana. Additional records to the east of region on northern Great Plains.

rufous upperparts
long
rufous tail
Brown
Thrasher
rufum
Sage
Thrasher
short bill
small size
streaked
underparts
worn
sh
ps
shorter bill with pale
base to lower mandible
spots on breast
are triangular
when fresh
fresh
worn
Bendire's
Thrasher
overall color a
warmer brown
than Curve-billed
juvenile
palmeri
thick,
curved bill
striking
orange iris
spots less obvious below than
oberholseri with smaller and
less contrasty tail tips and less
contrasty wing bars
palmeri
whitish wing bars
Bendire's
Curve-billed
palmeri
oberholseri
round spots
below
oberholseri
Curve-billed
Thrasher
white tail
tips
like palmeri
Curve-billed

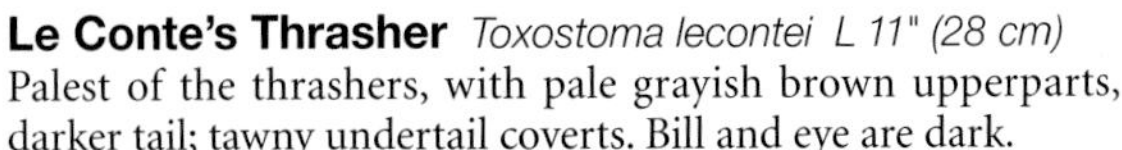

Le Conte's Thrasher *Toxostoma lecontei* L 11" (28 cm)
Palest of the thrashers, with pale grayish brown upperparts, darker tail; tawny undertail coverts. Bill and eye are dark.
Voice: Song, heard chiefly at dawn and dusk, is loud, melodious. Calls include an ascending, whistled *tweeep.*
Range: Prefers arid, sparsely vegetated habitats. Uncommon resident over most of range.

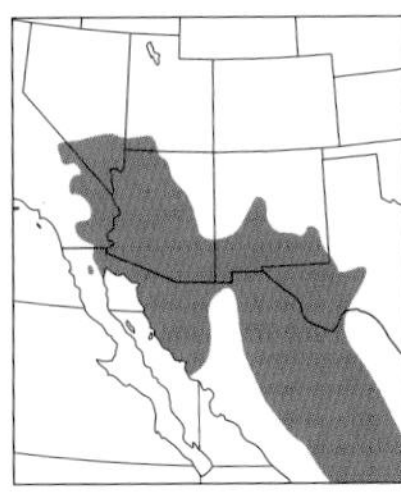

Crissal Thrasher *Toxostoma crissale* L 11½" (29 cm)
Large and slender, with a distinctive chestnut undertail patch and a dark malar streak.
Voice: Song is varied and musical, its cadence more leisurely than Curve-billed Thrasher. Calls include a repeated *chideery* and a whistled *toit-toit-toit.*
Range: Rare to fairly common resident. Very secretive, hiding in underbrush. Found mainly in dense mesquite and willows along streams and washes; locally on lower mountain slopes.

California Thrasher *Toxostoma redivivum* L 12" (31 cm)
Dark above, with pale eyebrow, dark eye, dark cheeks. Pale throat contrasts with dark breast; belly and undertail coverts tawny buff. Darker overall than Crissal Thrasher.
Voice: Calls are a low, flat *chuck* and *chur-erp.* Song is loud and sustained, with mostly guttural phrases, often repeated once or twice. Imitates other species and sounds.
Range: Fairly common to common resident in chaparral and other dense brushy habitats; casual to southern Oregon.

Starlings (Family Sturnidae)

Widespread Old World family. Chunky and glossy birds; most species are gregarious and bold.

European Starling *Sturnus vulgaris* L 8½" (22 cm)
Eurasian species. Adult in ***breeding*** plumage is iridescent black, with a yellow bill with blue base in male, pink in female. In fresh ***fall*** plumage, feathers are tipped with white and buff, giving a speckled appearance; bill brownish. In flight, note short, square tail, stocky body, and short, broad-based, pointed wings that appear pale gray from below. ***Juvenile*** is gray-brown, with brown bill.
Voice: Song notes include squeaks, gurgles, warbles, chirps, and twittering; also imitates songs of other species. Otherwise, often silent, though gives various harsh calls in interactions with others and has a soft, breezy flight call.
Range: Introduced in New York in 1890-91, it soon spread across the continent and is found in a wide variety of human-altered habitats. Abundant in many areas, bold, aggressive, it often competes successfully with native species for nest holes. Outside nesting season, usually seen in large flocks, sometimes mixed with blackbirds. Casual to central Alaska and the Yukon. One collected on Shemya Island in the western Aleutians likely originated from North America.

paler overall
than Crissal
thin, long,
strongly
downcurved bill
Le Conte's
Thrasher
very long
tail
tawny undertail
coverts
thin, long, strongly
downcurved bill
grayish
overall
thin, dark malar
stripe bordered
by thin, whitish
submoustachial
California
Thrasher
ong, strongly
wncurved bill
very long
tail
white
throat
chestnut
undertail coverts
Crissal
Thrasher
overall
brown
coloration
very long
tail
tawny undertail
coverts
fall
plumage
eavily spotted
with whitish
Brown-headed Cowbird
for comparison
triangular
wings
winter
slender
dark bill
European
Starling
vulgaris
short
tail
yellow bill
glossy
plumage
overall
grayish
brown
dull, blurred
streaks
breeding ♂
juvenile

Accentors (Family Prunellidae)

Most species in this small Eurasian family are found in mountainous country. One species strays to North America.

Siberian Accentor *Prunella montanella L 5½" (14 cm)*
Bright tawny buff below. Dark crown, with broad gray median stripe. Note buffy eyebrow that broadens behind head; dark cheek patch with buff spots below; gray patch on side of neck.
Voice: Call is a high, thin series of *see* notes.
Range: Rare fall migrant to Bering Sea islands; two fall records from western Aleutians (Shemya Island). Otherwise casual in fall and winter to mainland Alaska, Pacific Northwest; records for British Columbia, Washington, Idaho, southwestern Montana.

Wagtails, Pipits (Family Motacillidae)

Slender-billed birds. Most species pump tails as they walk. Wagtail flight strongly undulating.

Eastern Yellow Wagtail *Motacilla tschutschensis L 6½" (17 cm)* Olive above, yellow below; shorter tail than other wagtails. In ***breeding*** plumage, Alaskan nesting *tschutschensis* has a speckled breast band. Asian *simillima,* recognized by some, seen in migration on Aleutians and Pribilofs, averages greener above, yellower below. ***Females*** duller, ***immatures*** whitish below.
Voice: Call is a loud *tsweep,* similar to Eastern Kingbird's. Song is a rapid series of buzzy notes on one pitch, sometimes delivered in flight display.
Range: Generally fairly common to common on Alaska and northern Yukon breeding grounds; casual fall (late Aug. to Sept.) migrant on coast from British Columbia to California.

White Wagtail *Motacilla alba L 7¼" (18 cm)*
Breeding adult *ocularis* has black nape, gray back; black eye line, throat, bib, and usually chin. In flight, shows mostly dark wings. In breeding adult male *lugens* upperparts black, wings mostly white; chin usually white. ***Breeding adult female*** *lugens* similar, but duller above; ***winter adults*** retain distinct wing pattern. In nominate *alba* face is white in all plumages. Juveniles of all races are brownish above with two faint wing bars. ***Immature*** closer to adult but retains most of juvenile wing; immature *ocularis* has darker bases to median coverts than *lugens,* but separation is problematic.
Voice: Calls include a two-note *chizzik* given in flight and a whistled *chee-wee* from a perch. Song is a series of high, short phrases.
Range: Northeast Asian *ocularis* breeds sparingly in western Alaska; *lugens* breeds coastal East Asia (south of *ocularis*), has nested and hybridized with *ocularis* in western Alaska, was formerly treated as a separate species, the Black-backed Wagtail. Both races are casual down the West Coast, mainly in fall and winter. There are a few interior records.

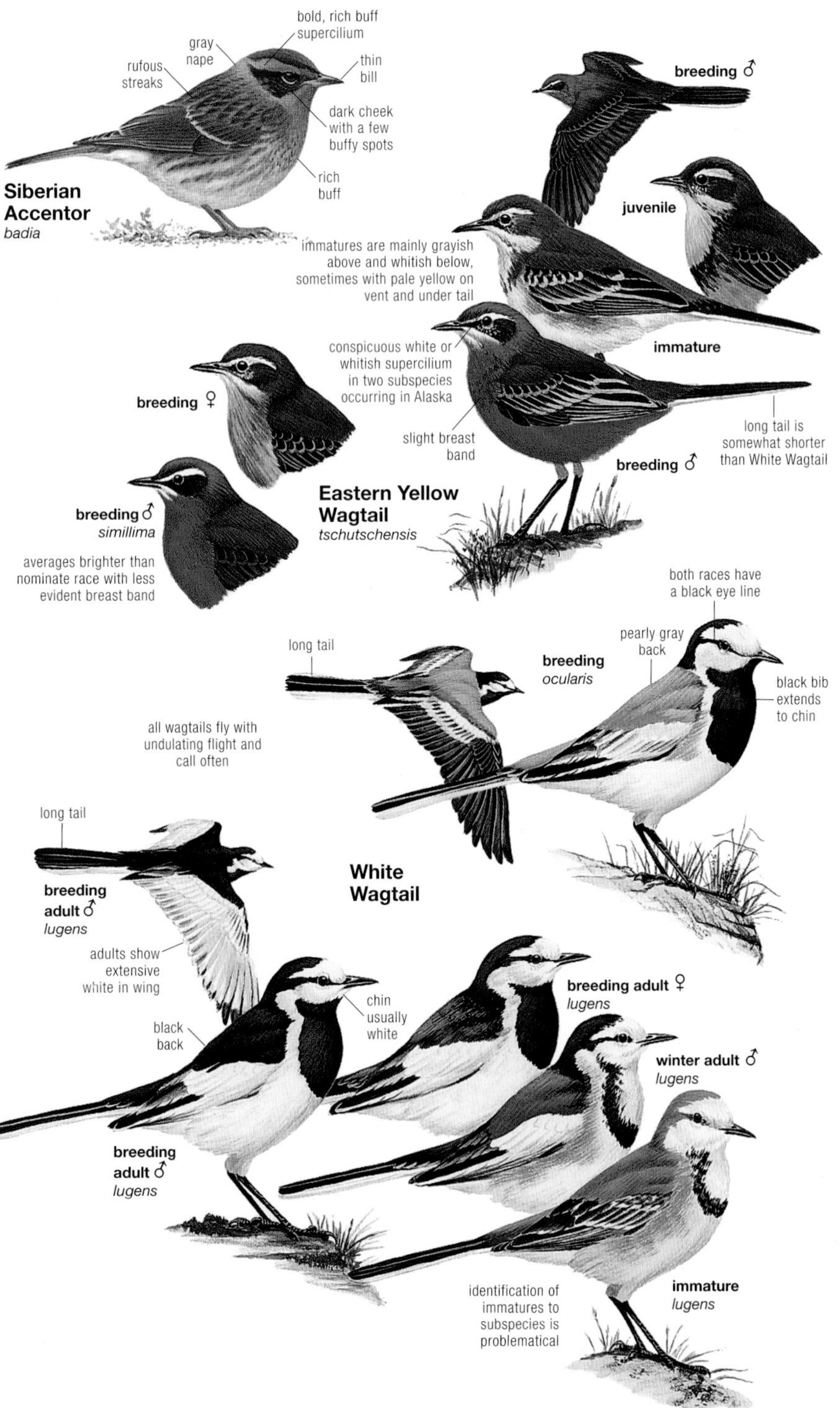

Siberian Accentor
badia
bold, rich buff supercilium
gray nape
rufous streaks
thin bill
dark cheek with a few buffy spots
rich buff
breeding ♂
juvenile
immatures are mainly grayish above and whitish below, sometimes with pale yellow on vent and under tail
immature
conspicuous white or whitish supercilium in two subspecies occurring in Alaska
breeding ♀
slight breast band
long tail is somewhat shorter than White Wagtail
breeding ♂
breeding ♂
simillima
Eastern Yellow Wagtail
tschutschensis
averages brighter than nominate race with less evident breast band
both races have a black eye line
long tail
pearly gray back
breeding
ocularis
black bib extends to chin
all wagtails fly with undulating flight and call often
long tail
White Wagtail
breeding adult ♂
lugens
adults show extensive white in wing
chin usually white
black back
breeding adult ♀
lugens
winter adult ♂
lugens
breeding adult ♂
lugens
immature
lugens
identification of immatures to subspecies is problematical

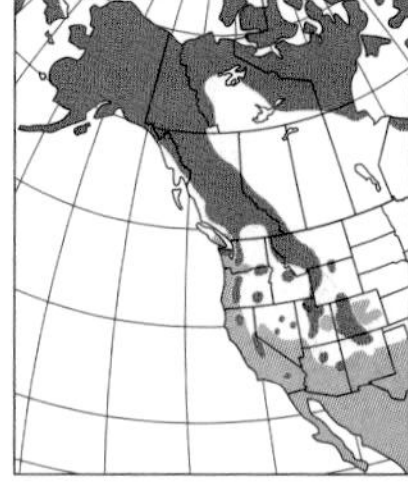

American Pipit *Anthus rubescens* *L 6½" (17 cm)*
Breeding birds are grayish above and faintly streaked below, except for the *alticola* race, from the Rockies and California's high mountains, which has richly colored underparts with fewer or no streaks. In ***winter*** American Pipit becomes browner above and more streaked below. Bill mostly dark; legs dark or tinged with pink. Tail has white outer feathers. An Asian subspecies, *japonicus,* more boldly streaked below, with pink legs, white wing bars.
Voice: Call, given in flight, is a sharp *pip-pit;* song, a rapid series of *chee* or *cheedle* notes, is usually delivered in flight on breeding grounds.
Range: Common and widespread; nests on tundra in the far north, mountaintops farther south. Winter flocks are found in fields, in other shortgrass environments, and on upper beaches. Subspecies *japonicus* is rare in western Alaska and casual in fall in coastal California.

Olive-backed Pipit *Anthus hodgsoni* *L 6" (15 cm)*
Asian species. Grayish olive back, faintly streaked. Eyebrow orange-buff in front of eye, white behind. Broken white stripe borders dark ear spot. Throat and breast rich buff, with rather large black spots on breast. Belly pure white; legs pink.
Voice: Call is a buzzy *tsee.* Song is a rapidly delivered series of high-pitched warbles and trills and even higher thin notes.
Range: Rare migrant on western Aleutians; casual to Pribilofs and St. Lawrence Island; accidental to California and Nevada.

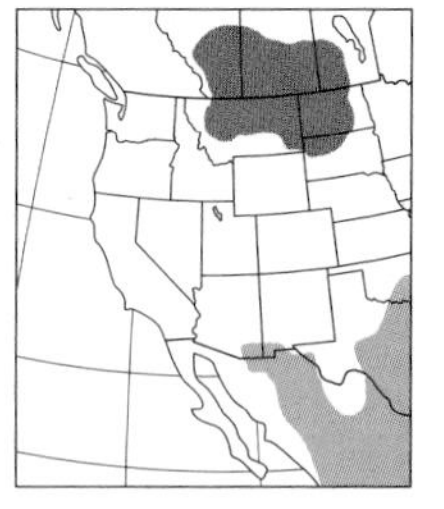

Sprague's Pipit *Anthus spragueii* *L 6½" (17 cm)*
Dark eye prominent in pale buff face. Pale edges on rounded back feathers give a scaly look; rump is streaked. Underparts whitish, with a buffy wash and short, dark streaks on the breast. Legs pinkish. Outer tail feathers are more extensively white than American Pipit. Compare also with juvenile Horned Lark (page 286). Secretive and somewhat solitary. Does not pump tail.
Voice: Call is a loud, squeaky *squeet,* usually given two or more times. Song, given continuously in high flight, is a descending series of musical *tzee* and *tzee-a* notes.
Range: Nests in prairies; winters in grassy fields. Uncommon. Rather rarely noted in migration. Rare in winter to southeastern California; casual in migration elsewhere in California and in Oregon and eastern British Columbia.

Red-throated Pipit *Anthus cervinus* *L 6" (15 cm)*
Note unpatterned nape. Pinkish red head and breast are distinctive in ***breeding male,*** less extensive in ***breeding female*** and fall adult. Fall ***immatures*** and some breeding females show no red.
Voice: Call, given in flight, is a high, piercing *tseee,* dropping in pitch at the end. Loud, varied song is delivered from the ground or in song flight.
Range: Regular migrant on islands in Bering Sea; rare fall migrant along California coast; casual inland and in Northwest. A few spring records in West (coastal and interior).

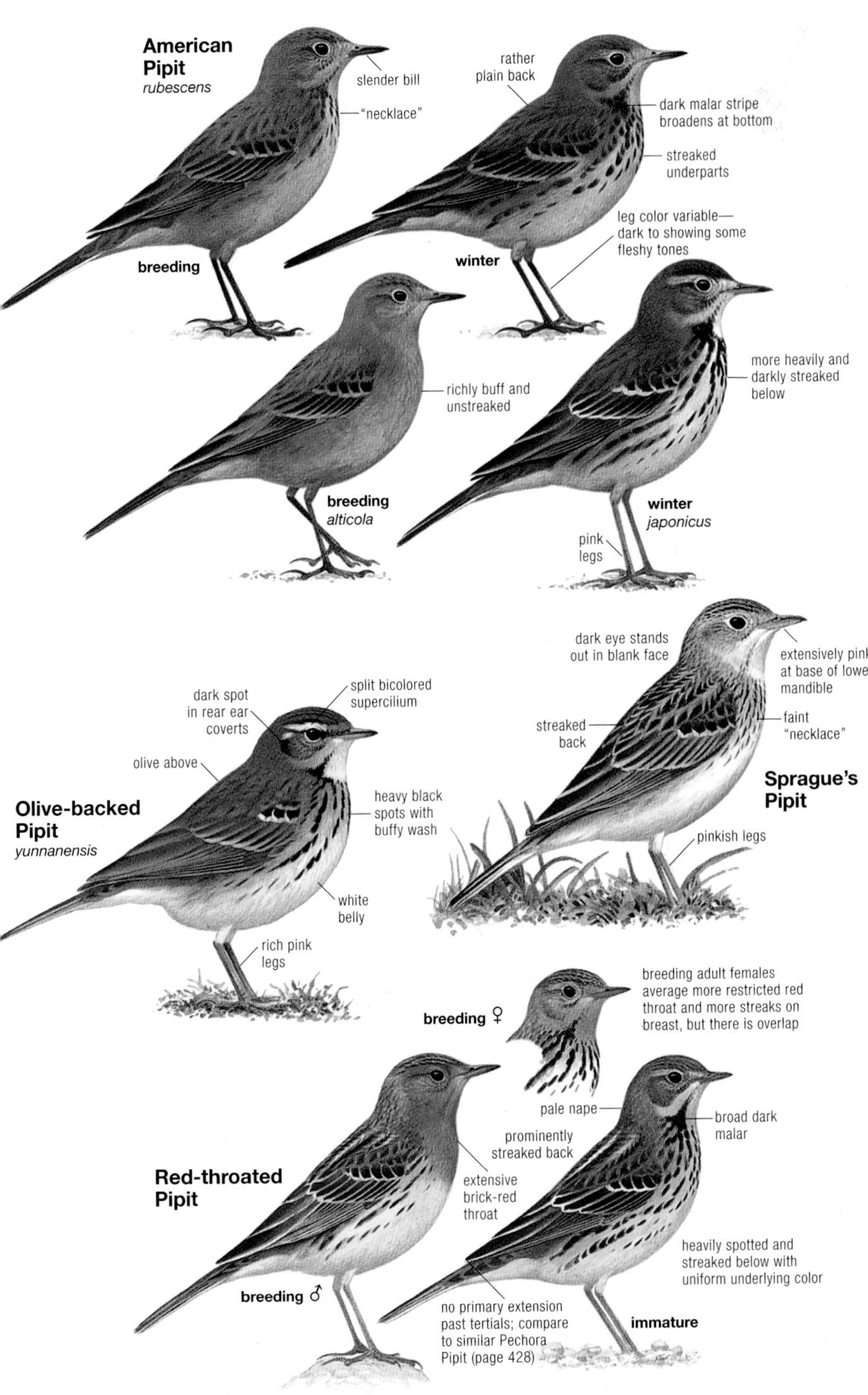

American Pipit
rubescens
slender bill
"necklace"
breeding
rather plain back
dark malar stripe broadens at bottom
streaked underparts
leg color variable—dark to showing some fleshy tones
winter
richly buff and unstreaked
breeding
alticola
more heavily and darkly streaked below
winter
japonicus
pink legs
dark eye stands out in blank face
extensively pink at base of lower mandible
faint "necklace"
streaked back
Sprague's Pipit
pinkish legs
dark spot in rear ear coverts
split bicolored supercilium
olive above
Olive-backed Pipit
yunnanensis
heavy black spots with buffy wash
white belly
rich pink legs
breeding ♀
breeding adult females average more restricted red throat and more streaks on breast, but there is overlap
pale nape
broad dark malar
prominently streaked back
Red-throated Pipit
extensive brick-red throat
heavily spotted and streaked below with uniform underlying color
breeding ♂
no primary extension past tertials; compare to similar Pechora Pipit (page 428)
immature

Waxwings (Family Bombycillidae)

Red, waxy tips on secondary wing feathers are often indistinct, and sometimes they are absent altogether. All waxwings have sleek crests, silky plumage, and yellow-tipped tails. Where berries are ripening, waxwings come to feast in amiable, noisy flocks.

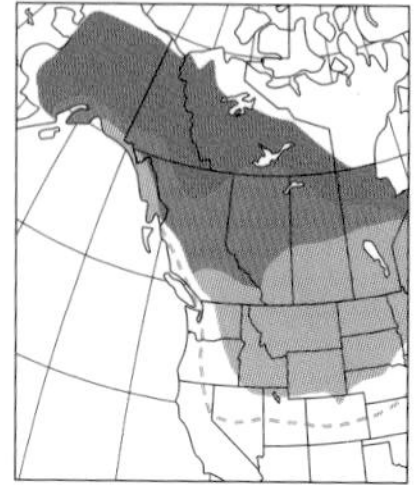

Bohemian Waxwing *Bombycilla garrulus L 8¼" (21 cm)*

Larger and grayer than Cedar Waxwing; undertail coverts cinnamon. White and yellow spots on wings. In flight, white wing patch at tips of primary coverts is conspicuous in flight. ***Juvenile*** browner above, streaked below, with pale throat. Feeds on berries and small fruits. Also eats insects, flower petals, and sap.

Voice: Distinctive call, a buzzy twittering, lower and harsher than Cedar Waxwing.

Range: Nests in open coniferous or mixed woodlands; often seen perched on top of a black spruce. Winter range varies widely and unpredictably; large flocks visit scattered locations. Casual to southern California, northern Arizona, and northern New Mexico. Individuals are sometimes seen in flocks of Cedar Waxwings.

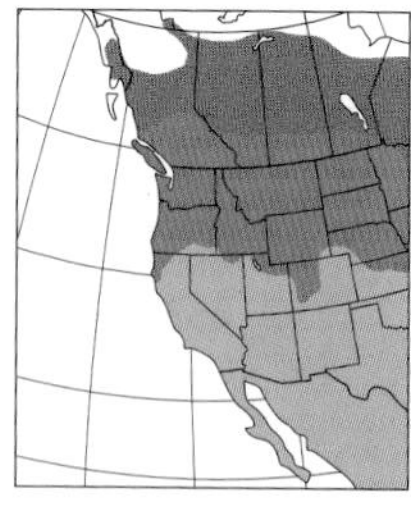

Cedar Waxwing *Bombycilla cedrorum L 7¼" (18 cm)*

Smaller and browner than Bohemian Waxwing; belly pale yellow; undertail coverts white. Lacks yellow spots on wings. ***Juvenile*** is streaked; lacks white wing patches of juvenile Bohemian. Since this species usually nests late in summer, juvenal plumage is seen well into fall.

Voice: Call is a soft, high-pitched, trilled whistle.

Range: Found in open habitats where berries are available; also eats insects, flower petals, and sap. Highly gregarious in migration and winter. Very rare to central Alaska.

Silky-flycatchers (Family Ptilogonatidae)

This New World tropical family of slender, crested birds is closely related to the waxwings. The family's common name describes their soft, sleek plumage and agility in catching insects on the wing.

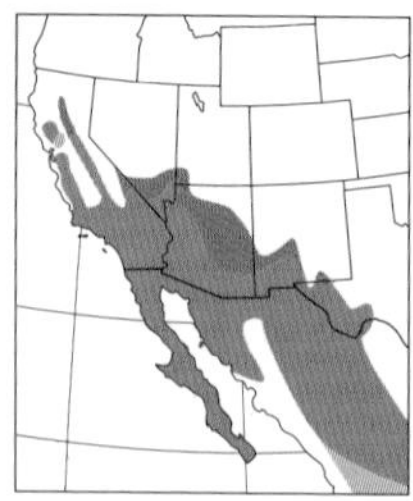

Phainopepla *Phainopepla nitens L 7¾" (20 cm)*

Male is shiny black; white wing patch conspicuous in flight. In both sexes, note distinct crest, long tail, red eyes. Juvenile resembles ***adult female,*** but has browner eyes; both have gray wing patches. Young males acquire patchy black in fall.

Voice: Distinctive call note is a low-pitched, whistled, querulous *wurp?* Song is a brief warble, seldom heard. Flight is fluttery but direct, and often very high.

Range: Nests in early spring in mesquite brushlands, feeding chiefly on insects and mistletoe berries. In late spring they move into cooler, wetter habitat and raise a second brood. In fall some wander to California coast and offshore islands. Casual north to Oregon, Washington, southern British Columbia, and Colorado.

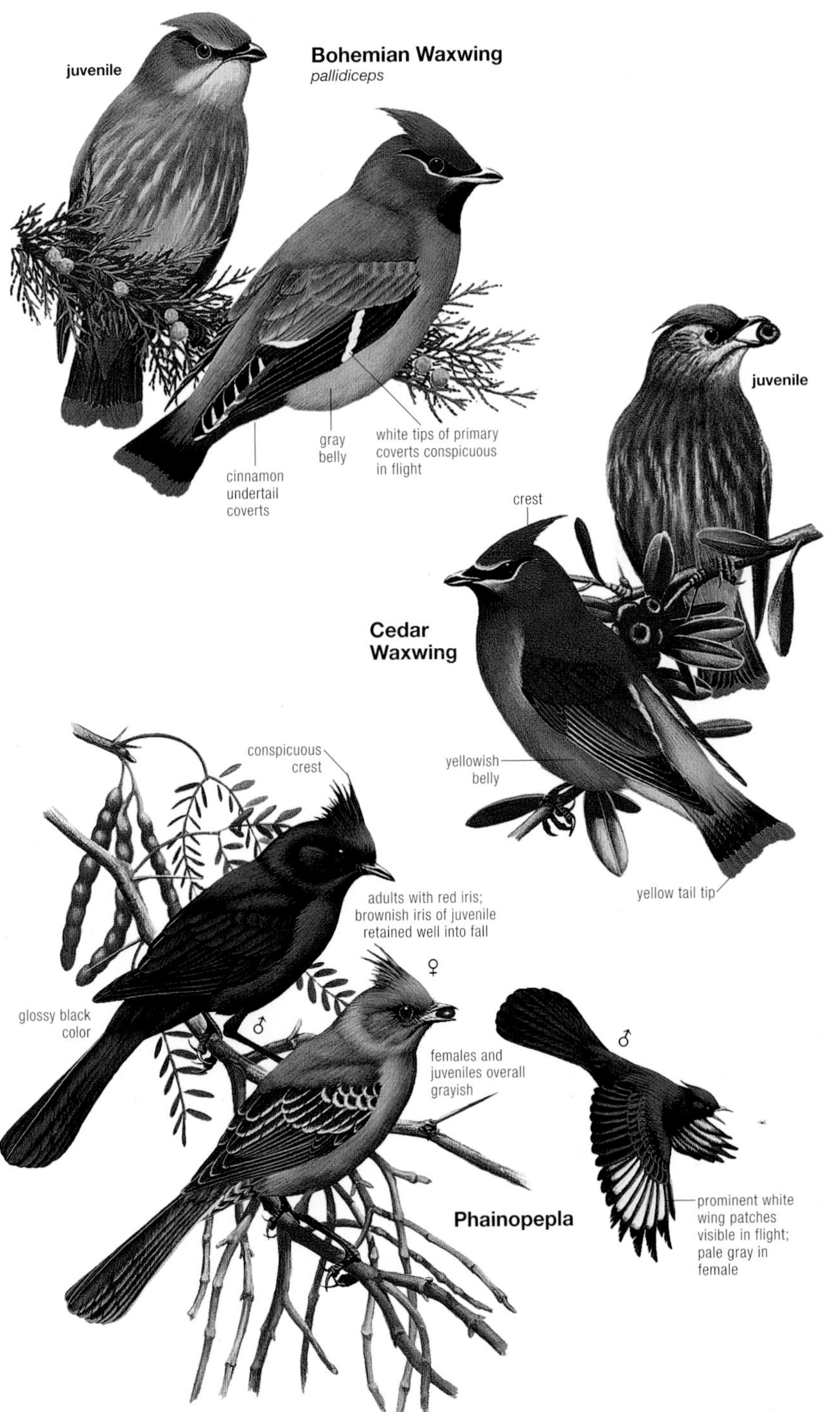

Bohemian Waxwing
pallidiceps
juvenile
gray belly
white tips of primary coverts conspicuous in flight
cinnamon undertail coverts
juvenile
crest
Cedar Waxwing
yellowish belly
yellow tail tip
conspicuous crest
adults with red iris; brownish iris of juvenile retained well into fall
♀
glossy black color
♂
♂
females and juveniles overall grayish
Phainopepla
prominent white wing patches visible in flight; pale gray in female

Wood-Warblers (Family Parulidae)

About half of the numerous species in this New World family occur in North America.

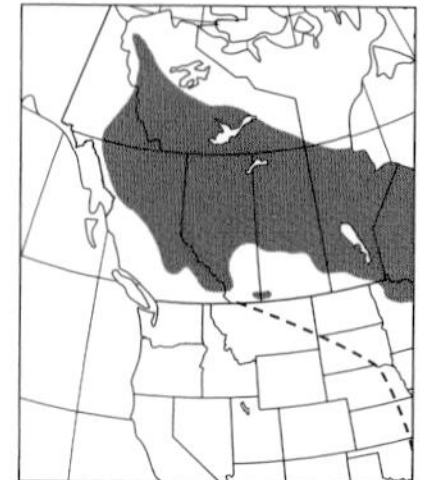

Tennessee Warbler *Vermivora peregrina L 4¾" (12 cm)*
Plump, with short tail and long, straight bill. ***Breeding male*** in spring is green above with gray crown, bold white eyebrow; white below. ***Female*** is tinged with yellow or olive overall, especially in fresh fall plumage. Adult male in fall resembles spring adult female but shows more yellow below. Immature also yellowish below; resembles young Orange-crowned, but is greener above and has a shorter tail and usually white undertail coverts. Spring male may be confused with Warbling and Red-eyed Vireos (page 276); note especially Tennessee Warbler's slimmer bill, greener back.
Voice: Distinctive full song consists of three-parts: Several rapid two-syllable notes are followed by a few higher single notes, ending with a staccato trill. Call is a sharp *chip;* flight call a thin *seet.*
Range: Found in coniferous and mixed woodlands in summer. Nests on the ground. Rare to fairly common. Probable rare breeder in Alaska. Rare migrant in West south of breeding grounds. Casual to western Alaska. Very rare in winter in coastal California.

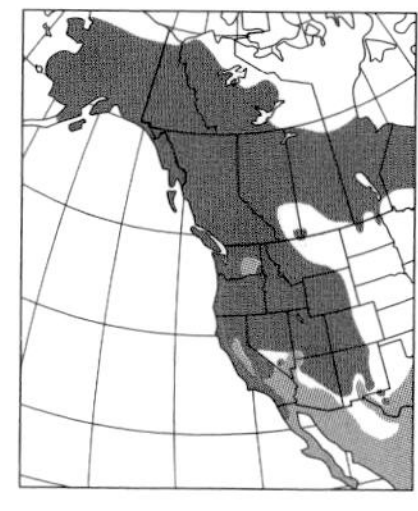

Orange-crowned Warbler *Vermivora celata L 5" (13 cm)*
Olive above, paler below. Yellow undertail coverts and faint, blurred streaks on sides of breast distinguish this species from similar Tennessee Warbler. Note also that Orange-crowned's bill is thinner and slightly downcurved; tail is longer. Plumage varies among subspecies from the smaller, brighter, yellower birds of western U.S., such as Pacific *lutescens,* to the duller *orestera* (not shown) of the Great Basin and Rockies, to the dullest, *celata,* which breeds across Alaska and Canada and winters primarily in southeastern U.S.; *celata* is one of the latest fall migrant warblers. Tawny orange crown, absent in some females and ***immatures,*** is seldom discernible in the field. Immature *celata* can be particularly drab. Young birds are similar to immature Tennessees but show yellow undertail coverts and grayer upperparts.
Voice: Song is a high-pitched staccato trill, faster in *lutescens;* call note, a sharp, somewhat metallic *chip;* also a thin *seet.*
Range: Common. Inhabits open, brushy woodlands, forest edges, and thickets. Nests on the ground; generally feeds in low branches, often in dead leaf clumps. Rare in fall on Bering Sea islands.

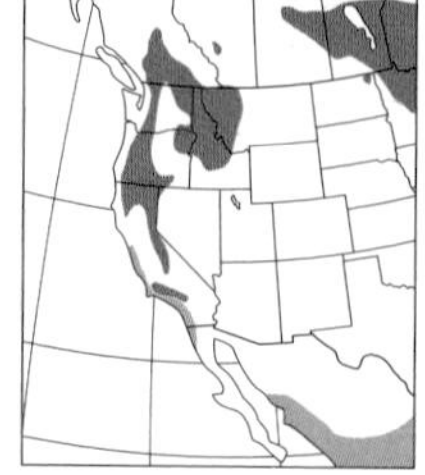

Nashville Warbler *Vermivora ruficapilla L 4¾" (12 cm)*
Bold white eye ring, gray head, olive upperparts, and white area below legs. Rump brighter on longer-tailed western race *ridgwayi,* which more often wags its tail. Female is duller than ***male.***
Voice: Song of *ridgwayi* is a series of sweet phrases followed by a trill; sweeter and more varied than eastern *ruficapilla.* Call is a sharp, metallic *chink,* sharper in *ridgwayi.*
Range: Fairly common; found in montane mixed woodlands. Rare migrant on western Great Plains, some likely of eastern *ruficapilla.* Accidental on St. Lawrence Island, Alaska.

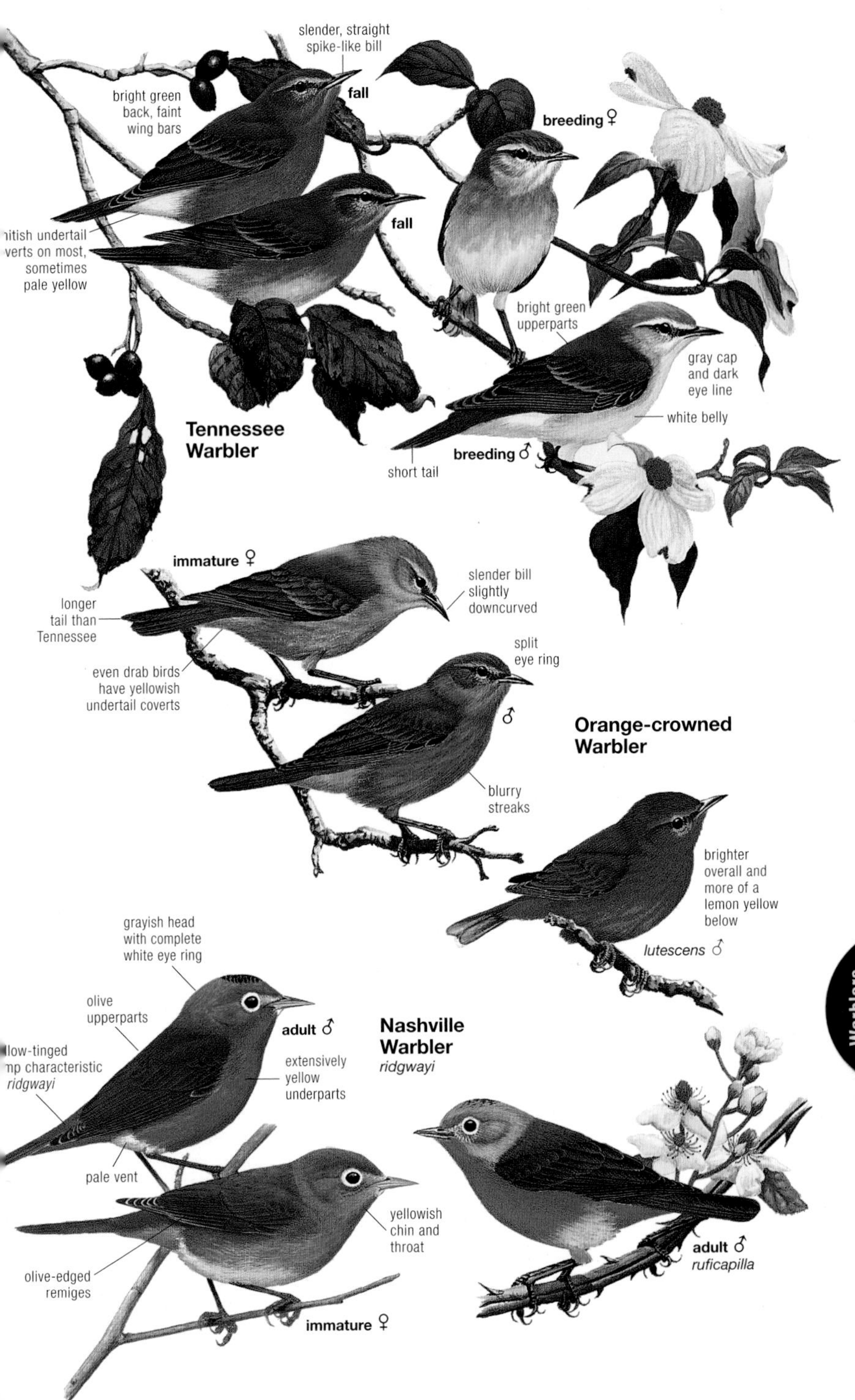
slender, straight
spike-like bill
bright green
back, faint
wing bars
fall
breeding ♀
itish undertail
verts on most,
sometimes
pale yellow
fall
bright green
upperparts
gray cap
and dark
eye line
white belly
Tennessee
Warbler
breeding ♂
short tail
immature ♀
slender bill
slightly
downcurved
longer
tail than
Tennessee
even drab birds
have yellowish
undertail coverts
split
eye ring
♂
Orange-crowned
Warbler
blurry
streaks
brighter
overall and
more of a
lemon yellow
below
lutescens ♂
Warblers
grayish head
with complete
white eye ring
olive
upperparts
adult ♂
Nashville
Warbler
ridgwayi
llow-tinged
mp characteristic
ridgwayi
extensively
yellow
underparts
pale vent
yellowish
chin and
throat
olive-edged
remiges
immature ♀
adult ♂
ruficapilla

Colima Warbler *Vermivora crissalis* *L 5¾" (15 cm)*
Mexican species. Larger and browner than Virginia's Warbler; rufous crown patch usually visible.
Voice: Song is a trill similar to Orange-crowned Warbler. Call is a loud note similar to Virginia's but not quite as sharp.
Range: Range extends to oak woodlands of Chisos Mountains, Big Bend National Park, Texas. Casual to Davis Mountains farther north, and a small population of presumed hybrids with Virginia's exists there at high elevations.

Virginia's Warbler *Vermivora virginiae* *L 4¾" (12 cm)*
Bold white eye ring on gray head; upperparts gray. Yellow patch on breast, yellow undertail coverts. Female is duller overall. Fall ***immature*** is browner; little or no yellow on breast. Often wags its long tail.
Voice: Song is a rapid series of thin notes, often ending with lower notes; call is a sharp *chink.*
Range: Common in mountain brushlands and stunted oaks. Rare to coastal California in fall; casual in winter. Casual to Oregon, where it may breed rarely in mountains of southeast.

Lucy's Warbler *Vermivora luciae* *L 4¼" (11 cm)*
Pale gray above, whitish below, with a short tail. ***Male***'s chestnut-red crown, patch, and rump distinctive. Female and ***immatures*** duller.
Voice: Lively song is a musical trill. Call is a sharp *chink.*
Range: Fairly common to common in mesquite and cottonwoods along watercourses; nests in tree cavities. Rare in fall, casual in winter to coastal California; casual north to Oregon and Idaho.

Northern Parula *Parula americana* *L 4½" (11 cm)*
Short-tailed warbler, gray-blue above with yellowish green upper back, two bold white wing bars. Throat and breast bright yellow, belly white. In ***adult male,*** reddish and black bands cross breast. In female and immature male, bands are fainter or absent.
Voice: One song is a rising buzzy trill, ending with an abrupt *zip* in eastern birds; no clear final note in more westerly birds.
Range: An eastern species. In West a rare migrant (more in spring) and very rare summer resident throughout. It has nested in coastal California. Casual in winter in California and the Southwest.

Chestnut-sided Warbler *Dendroica pensylvanica* *L 5" (13 cm)* ***Breeding male*** has yellow crown, black eye line, black whisker stripe; extensive chestnut on sides; ***female*** has greenish crown, less chestnut. Fall adults and ***immatures*** lime green above, with white eye ring, whitish underparts, yellowish wing bars. Often cocks its tail.
Voice: Song is a whistled *please please pleased to meetcha;* call, a *chip* note like Yellow Warbler.
Range: An eastern species. In West a rare breeder in Alberta; otherwise a rare migrant in West. Scattered summer records; it has nested along Colorado's Front Range. Casual (almost annual) in winter in California and southern Arizona. Casual to Alaska.

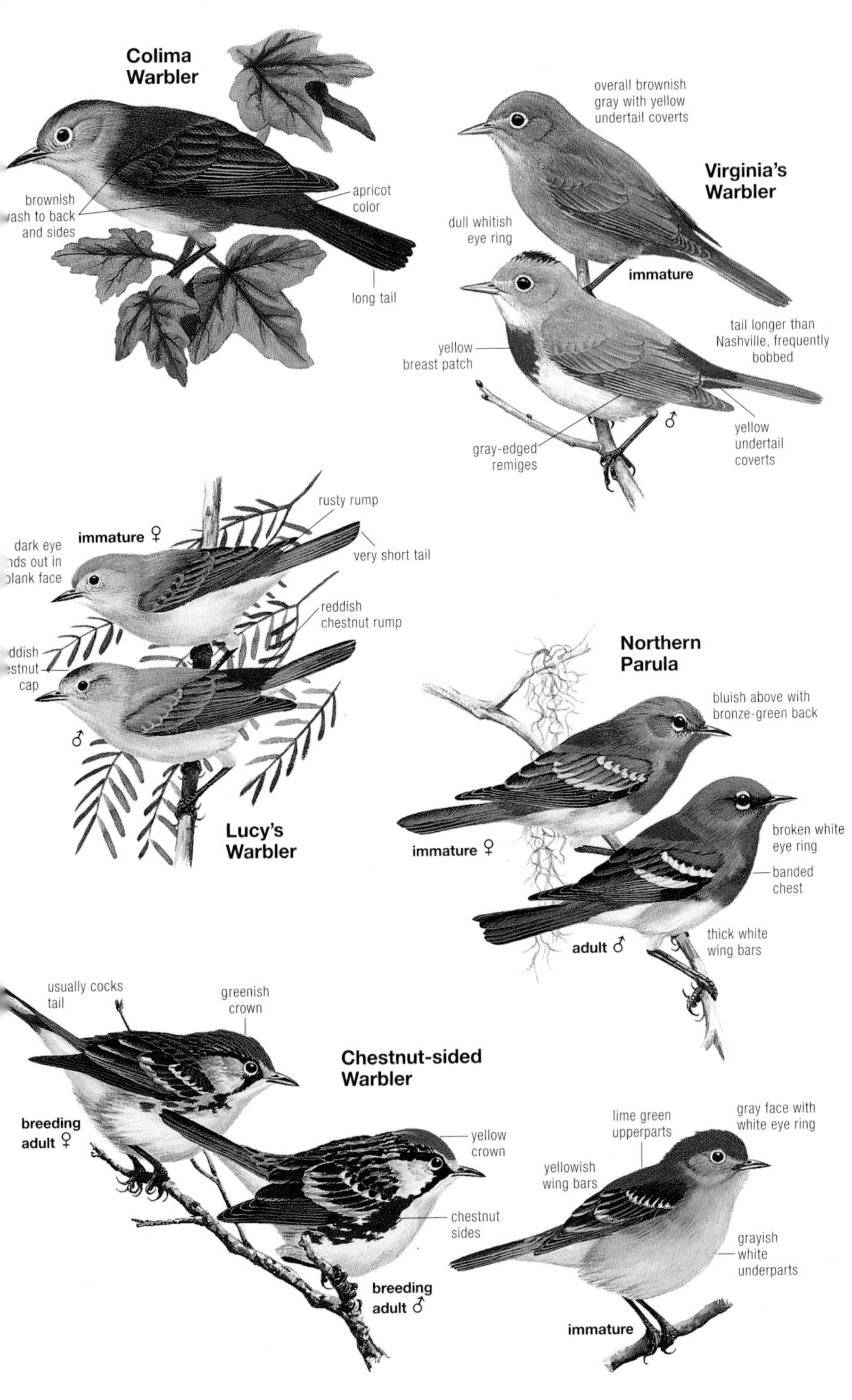

Colima Warbler
brownish
wash to back
and sides
apricot
color
long tail
overall brownish
gray with yellow
undertail coverts
Virginia's Warbler
dull whitish
eye ring
immature
tail longer than
Nashville, frequently
bobbed
yellow
breast patch
♂
yellow
undertail
coverts
gray-edged
remiges
rusty rump
immature ♀
very short tail
dark eye
stands out in
blank face
reddish
chestnut rump
reddish
chestnut
cap
♂
Lucy's Warbler
Northern Parula
bluish above with
bronze-green back
broken white
eye ring
banded
chest
immature ♀
thick white
wing bars
adult ♂
usually cocks
tail
greenish
crown
Chestnut-sided Warbler
breeding
adult ♀
yellow
crown
chestnut
sides
breeding
adult ♂
lime green
upperparts
gray face with
white eye ring
yellowish
wing bars
grayish
white
underparts
immature

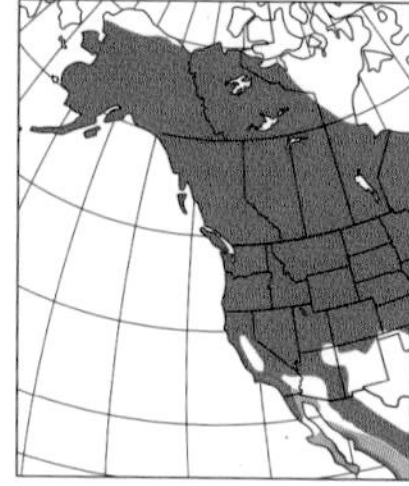

Yellow Warbler *Dendroica petechia L 5" (13 cm)*
Plump, yellow overall, with short tail; dark eye prominent in uniformly yellow face; reddish streaks below are distinct in ***male,*** faint or absent in ***female; immatures*** are duller. Much geographic variation: Northern races are greener above; southwest *sonorana* is pale with faint red streaks below. Resident subspecies in mangroves from Mexico south are known as "Mangrove Warbler"; adult males of most subspecies have chestnut heads; immatures of this subspecies are dull.
Voice: Rapid, variable song is sometimes written *sweet sweet sweet I'm so sweet.* Call is a sweet, rich *chip,* often delivered rapidly.
Range: Favors wet habitats, especially willows and alders, open woodlands, orchards. A common and widespread migrant in West; small numbers winter from coastal California to southern Arizona. A summer record of an immature male "Mangrove Warbler" from east of Phoenix.

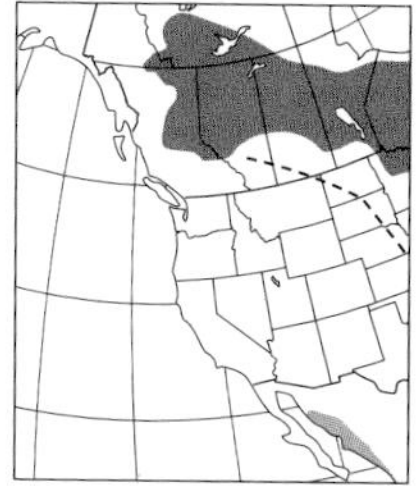

Magnolia Warbler *Dendroica magnolia L 5" (13 cm)*
Male is blackish above, with white eyebrow, white wing patch, yellow rump; broad white tail patches. Underparts yellow, streaked on breast and sides; undertail coverts white; under tail white except for black band at tip. Female has two wing bars; some ***first-spring females*** have dull white eye ring. ***Fall adults*** and ***immatures*** are drabber, with grayish olive upperparts; white eye ring; faint gray band across breast. Compare immature Prairie Warbler (page 340). Magnolia Warbler does not bob tail.
Voice: Song is a short, whistled *weety-weety-weeteo.* Call is a unique, weak, downslurred, nasal *tchif* or *wenk.*
Range: Fairly common in moist coniferous forests in western breeding range. Rare throughout the West in migration. Casual in winter in California and Arizona, and in migration to Alaska (probably nearly annual).

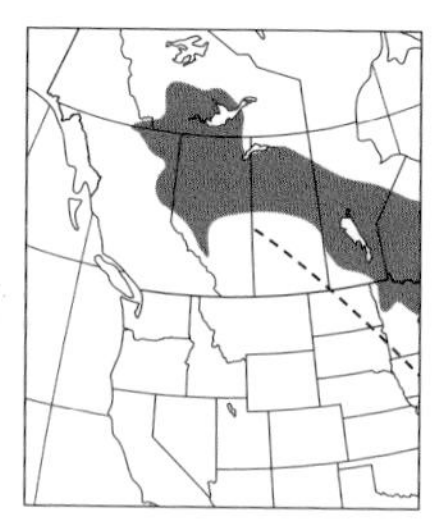

Cape May Warbler *Dendroica tigrina L 5" (13 cm)*
Most plumages have yellow on face, the color usually extending to sides of neck. Note also short tail; yellow or greenish rump; thin bill, slightly downcurved. ***Breeding male***'s chestnut ear patch and striped underparts distinctive; wing patch white. ***Female*** drabber, grayer, with two narrow white wing bars. ***Immature male***'s ear patch is less distinct. ***Immature female*** can be extremely drab, with gray face and only a tinge of yellow below and on rump; always has greenish edges on flight feathers. Often shows aggressive behavior.
Voice: One song is a high, thin *seet seet seet seet;* call, a very high, thin *sip.*
Range: Uncommon in limited western breeding range in western Canada. Otherwise very rare to casual vagrant in West. Casual in winter from California and Arizona and in migration from Alaska. Fewer records in recent years, perhaps reflecting overall population decline.

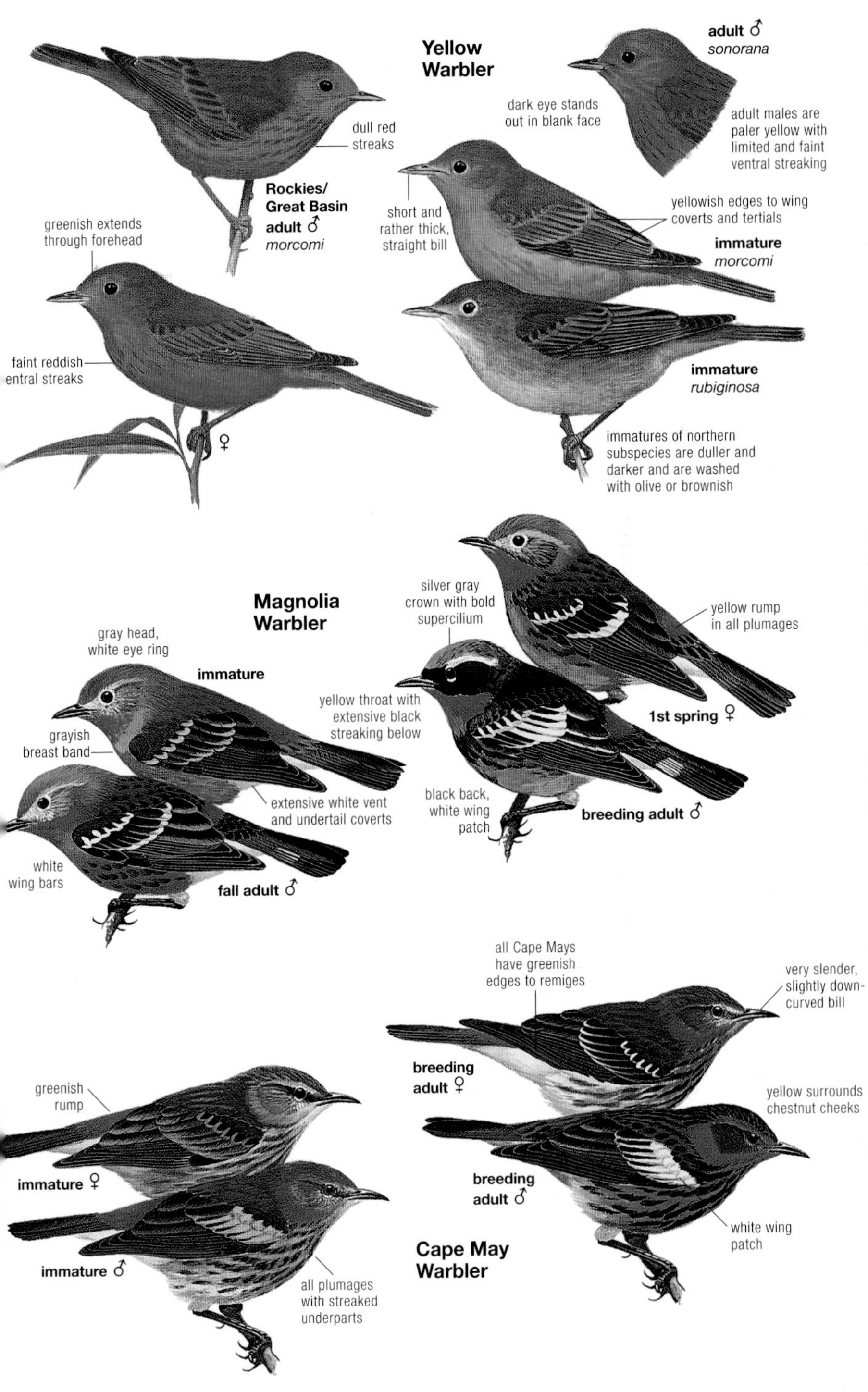
Yellow
Warbler
adult ♂
sonorana
dull red
streaks
dark eye stands
out in blank face
adult males are
paler yellow with
limited and faint
ventral streaking
Rockies/
Great Basin
adult ♂
morcomi
short and
rather thick,
straight bill
yellowish edges to wing
coverts and tertials
greenish extends
through forehead
immature
morcomi
faint reddish
entral streaks
immature
rubiginosa
♀
immatures of northern
subspecies are duller and
darker and are washed
with olive or brownish
Magnolia
Warbler
silver gray
crown with bold
supercilium
yellow rump
in all plumages
gray head,
white eye ring
immature
yellow throat with
extensive black
streaking below
1st spring ♀
grayish
breast band
extensive white vent
and undertail coverts
black back,
white wing
patch
breeding adult ♂
white
wing bars
fall adult ♂
all Cape Mays
have greenish
edges to remiges
very slender,
slightly down-
curved bill
breeding
adult ♀
greenish
rump
yellow surrounds
chestnut cheeks
immature ♀
breeding
adult ♂
white wing
patch
immature ♂
all plumages
with streaked
underparts
Cape May
Warbler

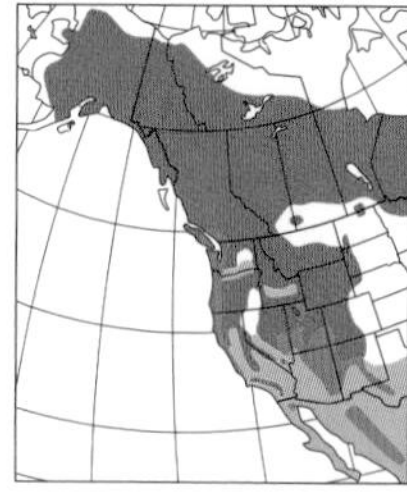

Yellow-rumped Warbler *Dendroica coronata*
L 5½" (14 cm) Yellow rump, yellow patch on side, yellow crown patch, white tail patches. In northern and eastern birds, ***"Myrtle Warbler,"*** note white eyebrow, white throat and sides of neck, contrasting cheek patch. Western birds, ***"Audubon's Warbler,"*** have yellow throat, except for a few immature females. Some males in the mountains of the Southwest show more black and are probably intergrades of the larger, darker *nigrifrons,* breeding in the mountains of northwest Mexico. All ***females*** and fall males are duller than ***breeding males*** but show same basic pattern.
Voice: Song, a slow warble, usually rising or falling at the end in "Audubon's"; a musical trill in one song of "Myrtle." Call note of "Myrtle" is lower, flatter.
Range: Common to abundant in coniferous or mixed woodlands. "Myrtle" is fairly common in winter on West Coast; scarce in the Southwest. "Myrtle" and "Audubon's" hybridize frequently from southeast Alaska through the Canadian Rockies of British Columbia.

Black-throated Blue Warbler *Dendroica caerulescens*
L 5¼" (13 cm) ***Male***'s black throat, cheeks, and sides separate blue upperparts, white underparts. Bold white patch at base of primaries. ***Female***'s pale eyebrow is distinct on dark face; upperparts brownish olive; underparts buffy; wing patch smaller, occasionally absent on immature females.
Voice: Typical song is a slow series of four or five wheezy notes, the last note higher: *zwee zwee zwee zweeee* or a slower *zur zurr zreee.* Call is a single sharp *dit,* like Dark-eyed Junco.
Range: An eastern species that winters in the West Indies. Rare fall (mostly Oct.) vagrant to the West. Casual in winter and in spring. Accidental to southeast Alaska.

Blackburnian Warbler *Dendroica fusca L 5" (13 cm)*
Fiery orange throat, broad white wing patch, triangular ear patch, conspicuous in ***adult male. Female*** and immature male have paler throat, ***immature female*** paler still; note also the two white wing bars, streaked back, and bold yellow or buffy eyebrow, broader behind the eye, that curls around onto side of neck. Orange or yellow forehead stripe and white in outer tail feathers are distinct in all males, less so in females. Compare carefully to Townsend's Warbler (next page).
Voice: One song, a short series of high notes followed by a squeaky, ascending trill, ends on a very high note. Calls include a sharp *tchik;* flight call a buzzy *zeet.*
Range: Rather rare breeder in coniferous or mixed forests of east-central Alberta. Otherwise, vagrants are seen rarely in coastal California in fall migration; casual in winter and spring; casual elsewhere in West.

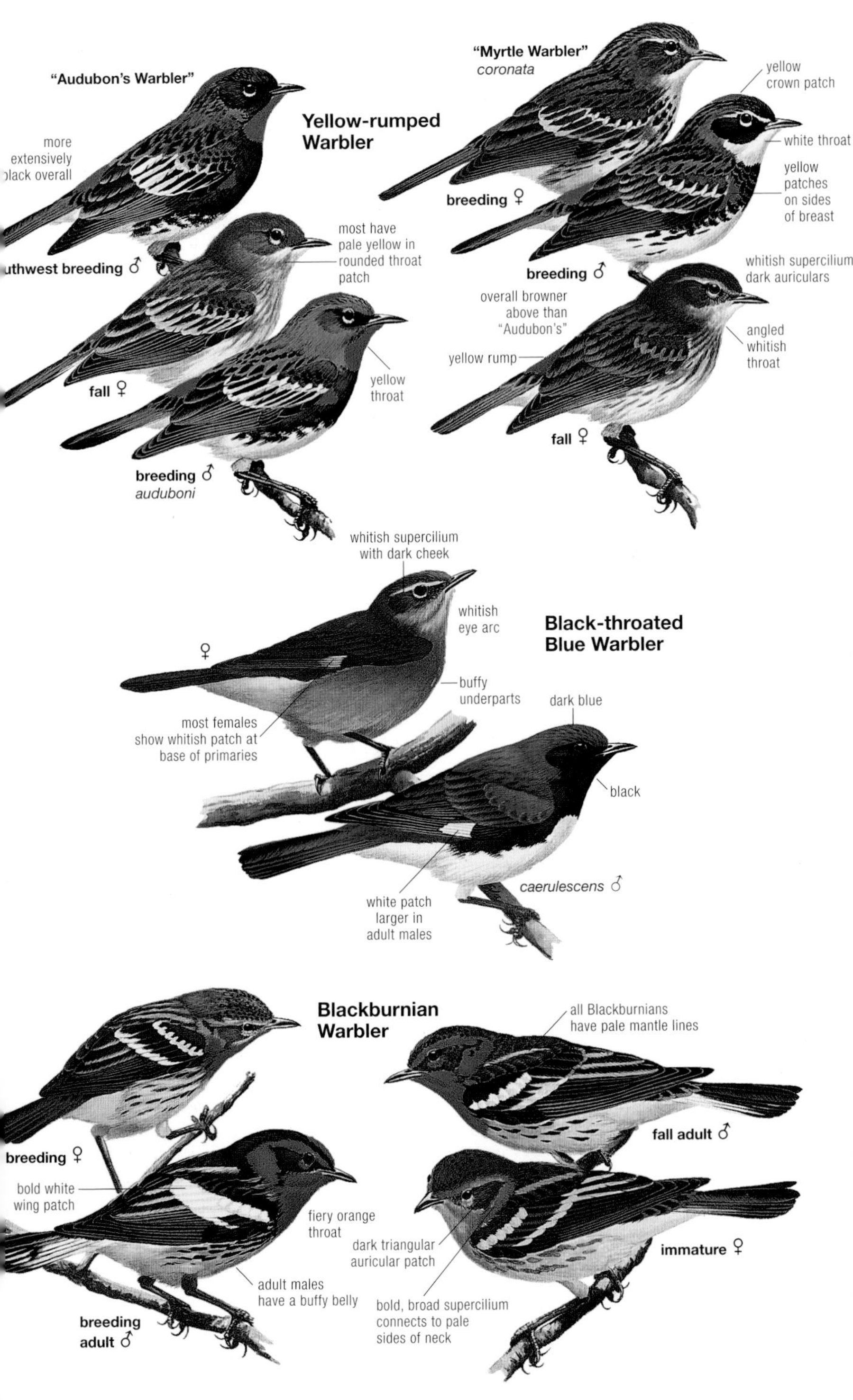

"Audubon's Warbler"
Yellow-rumped Warbler
more extensively black overall
uthwest breeding ♂
most have pale yellow in rounded throat patch
fall ♀
yellow throat
breeding ♂
auduboni
"Myrtle Warbler"
coronata
yellow crown patch
white throat
yellow patches on sides of breast
breeding ♀
breeding ♂
whitish supercilium, dark auriculars
overall browner above than "Audubon's"
angled whitish throat
yellow rump
fall ♀
whitish supercilium with dark cheek
whitish eye arc
Black-throated Blue Warbler
♀
buffy underparts
dark blue
most females show whitish patch at base of primaries
black
caerulescens ♂
white patch larger in adult males
Blackburnian Warbler
all Blackburnians have pale mantle lines
fall adult ♂
breeding ♀
bold white wing patch
fiery orange throat
dark triangular auricular patch
immature ♀
adult males have a buffy belly
bold, broad supercilium connects to pale sides of neck
breeding adult ♂

Black-throated Gray Warbler *Dendroica nigrescens*
L 5" (13 cm) ***Adult*** plumage is basically the same year-round: black-and-white head; gray back streaked with black; white underparts, sides streaked with black; small yellow spot between eye and bill. Lacks central crown stripe of Black-and-white Warbler (page 340); undertail coverts are white. Immature male resembles ***adult male;*** immature ***female*** is brownish gray above, throat white.
Voice: Varied songs include a buzzy *weezy weezy weezy weezy-weet.* Call is flat *tchip,* slightly duller than Townsend's. Flight call, like the other related species on this page, is a thin, nonbuzzy *see.*
Range: Inhabits woodlands, brushlands, chaparral. Very rare migrant on western Great Plains.

Townsend's Warbler *Dendroica townsendi L 5" (13 cm)*
Dark crown, dark ear patch bordered in yellow. Olive above, streaked with black; yellow breast, white belly, yellowish black-streaked sides. ***Adult male***'s throat and upper breast are black; ***female*** and immature male have streaked lower throat. ***Immature female*** is duller. Frequently hybridizes with Hermit Warbler; ***hybrids*** usually have the yellowish, streaked underparts of Townsend's, yellow head of Hermit.
Voice: Variable song is a series of hoarse *zee* notes; *tchip* call similar to Black-throated Gray but sharper.
Range: Breeds in coniferous forests. In migration and winter also deciduous and mixed woodlands. Regular fall migrant on western Great Plains; casual to western Alaska.

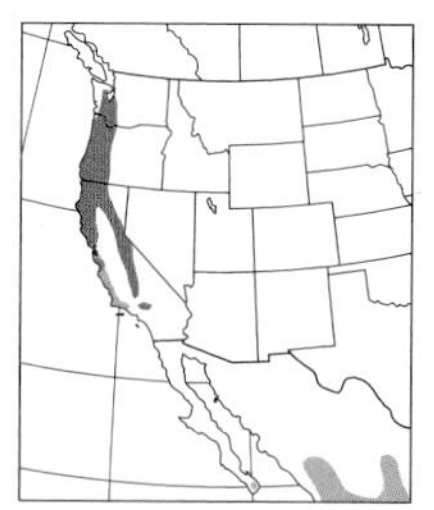

Hermit Warbler *Dendroica occidentalis L 5½" (14 cm)*
Yellow head, with dark markings extending from nape onto crown. ***Male*** has black chin and throat; in ***female*** and ***immature,*** chin is yellowish, throat shows less or no dark color. Immature female is more olive above.
Voice: Song is a high *seezle seezle seezle seezle zeet-zeet.* Call notes like Townsend's.
Range: Fairly common in forests; nests in tall conifers. Regular migrant through mountains of Southwest. Uncommon to rare in California winter range. Casual in spring to southwest British Columbia.

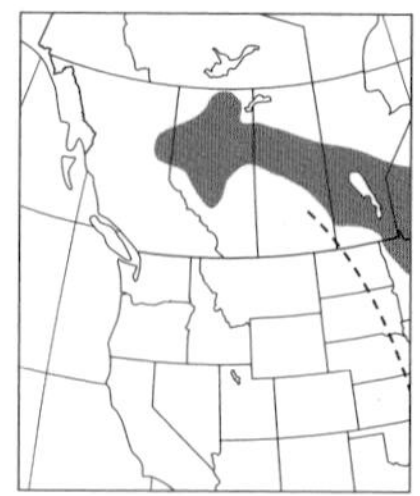

Black-throated Green Warbler *Dendroica virens*
L 5" (13 cm) Bright olive green upperparts; yellow face with greenish ear patch. Underparts are white, tinged with yellow on sides of vent and often on breast. ***Male*** has black throat and upper breast and black-streaked sides. ***Female*** and ***immatures*** show much less black below; immature female generally has dark streaking only on sides.
Voice: One song is a hoarse *zeee zeee zee-zo-zee;* the other, often written as *trees, trees, whispering trees.* Call notes are like Townsend's and Hermit.
Range: Uncommon to fairly common in coniferous or mixed forests in summer in western Canada; otherwise a very rare migrant in West, mostly in late fall. Casual in winter in coastal California. Accidental to southeast Alaska.

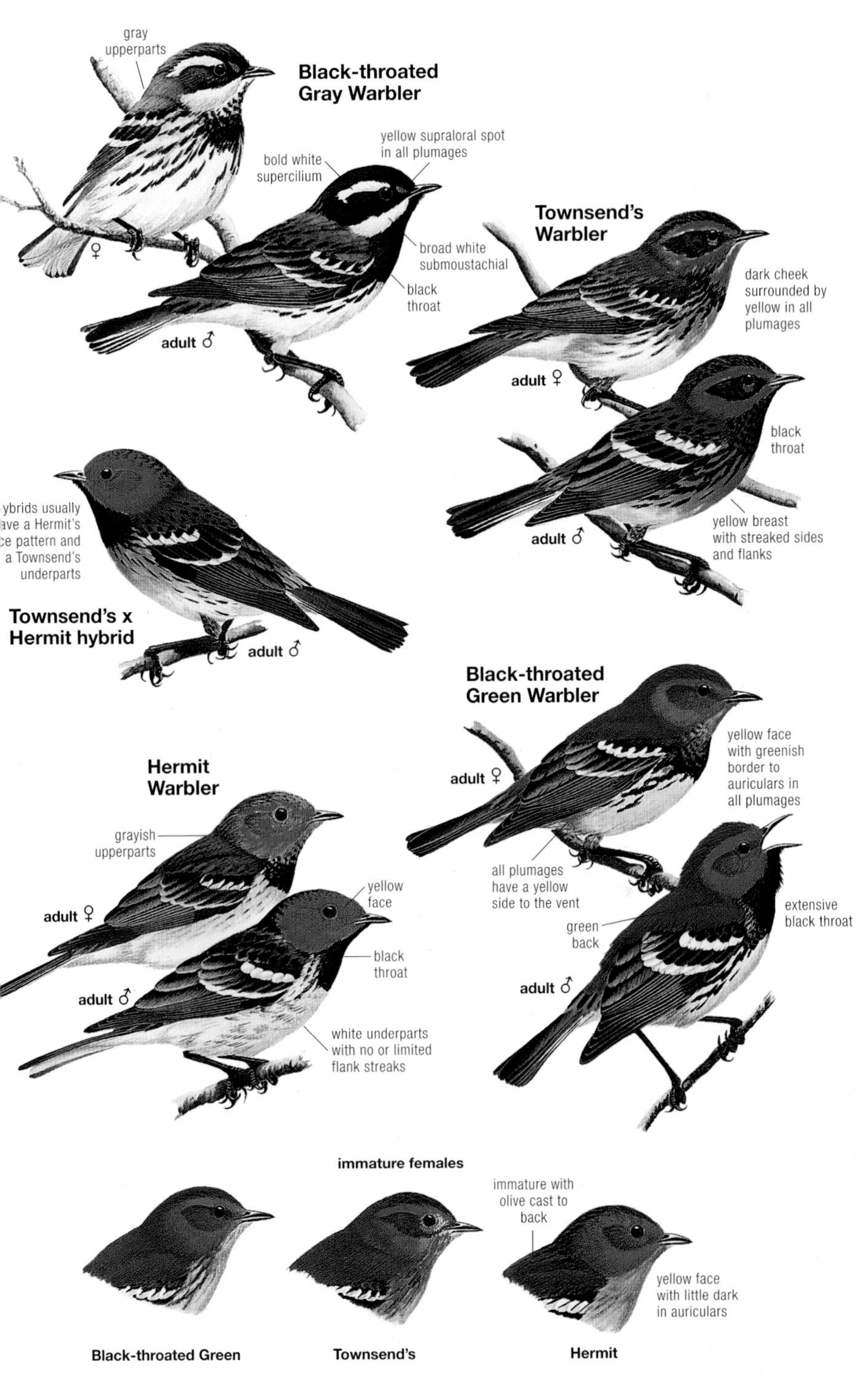

gray
upperparts
Black-throated
Gray Warbler
bold white
supercilium
yellow supraloral spot
in all plumages
broad white
submoustachial
black
throat
♀
adult ♂
Townsend's
Warbler
dark cheek
surrounded by
yellow in all
plumages
adult ♀
black
throat
adult ♂
yellow breast
with streaked sides
and flanks
ybrids usually
ave a Hermit's
ce pattern and
a Townsend's
underparts
Townsend's x
Hermit hybrid
adult ♂
Black-throated
Green Warbler
yellow face
with greenish
border to
auriculars in
all plumages
adult ♀
all plumages
have a yellow
side to the vent
extensive
black throat
green
back
adult ♂
Hermit
Warbler
grayish
upperparts
adult ♀
yellow
face
black
throat
adult ♂
white underparts
with no or limited
flank streaks
immature females
immature with
olive cast to
back
yellow face
with little dark
in auriculars
Black-throated Green
Townsend's
Hermit

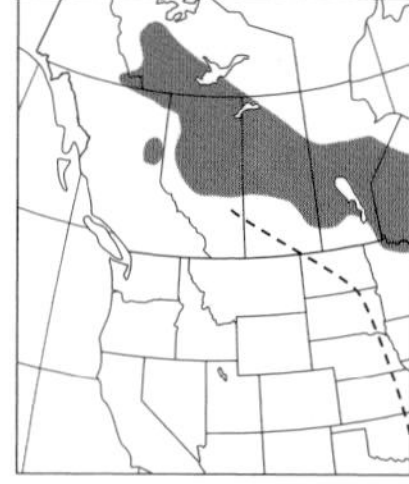

Bay-breasted Warbler *Dendroica castanea*

L 5½" (14 cm) ***Breeding male*** has chestnut crown, throat, and sides; black face; creamy patch at each side of neck; two white wing bars. ***Female*** is duller. ***Fall adults*** and ***immatures*** resemble Blackpoll and Pine Warblers. Bay-breasted is brighter green above, wing bars are thicker; underparts show little or no streaking and little yellow; flanks usually show some buff or bay color; legs usually entirely dark; undertail coverts are buffy or whitish. Short tail projection past undertail coverts for both Bay-breasted and Blackpoll.

Voice: Song consists of high-pitched double notes. Calls include a sharp *chip*.

Range: Nests in coniferous forests. Uncommon in western Canadian breeding range.Otherwise, very rare to casual in West. A few winter records from southern California.

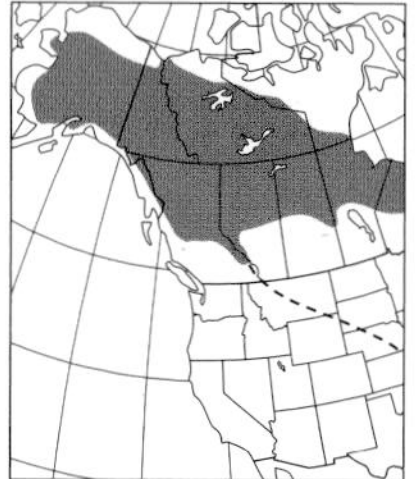

Blackpoll Warbler *Dendroica striata L 5½" (14 cm)*

Solid black cap, white cheeks, and white underparts identify ***breeding male;*** back and sides boldly streaked with black. Compare with Black-and-white Warbler (page 340). ***Female*** is duller overall, variably greenish above and pale yellow below; some are gray; note streaking. ***Fall adults*** and immatures resemble Bay-breasted and Pine Warblers. Blackpoll is mostly pale greenish yellow below, with dusky streaking on sides; legs pale on front and back, dark on sides; undertail coverts long and usually white.

Voice: Song, a series of high *tseet* notes. Calls include a sharp *chip*.

Range: Nests in varied habitats. Uncommon to common in northern breeding range; otherwise, a rare migrant (uncommon in spring on western Great Plains from Colorado north), chiefly in fall on California coast.

Pine Warbler *Dendroica pinus L 5½" (14 cm)*

Relatively large bill; long tail projection past undertail coverts; throat color extends onto sides of neck, setting off dark cheek patch. ***Male*** is greenish olive above, without streaking; throat and breast yellow, with dark streaks on sides of breast; belly and undertail coverts white. ***Female*** is duller. ***Immatures*** are brownish or brownish olive above, with whitish wing bars and brownish tertial edges; male is dull yellow below, female largely white; both have brown wash on flanks.

Voice: Song is a twittering musical trill, varying in speed. Calls include a flat, sweet *chip*.

Range: An eastern species, very rare in late fall and winter to California, chiefly southern California. Casual elsewhere in West.

IDENTIFYING: Bay-breasted, Blackpoll, and Pine Warblers These three species are not characteristic of the West, although Blackpoll breeds west through Alaska; some migrate down the Pacific coast and are regular, especially in spring on the western Great Plains. Bay-breasted has a limited western breeding range in Canada and is a very rare to casual migrant elsewhere. Pine is very rare to casual anywhere in the West.

Blackpolls and Bay-breasteds are structured alike in that they are short tailed (with long undertail coverts) and chunky, whereas Pines have long tail projection past the undertail coverts. Pine always shows sharply contrasting auriculars with the throat; in Bay-breasted and Black-

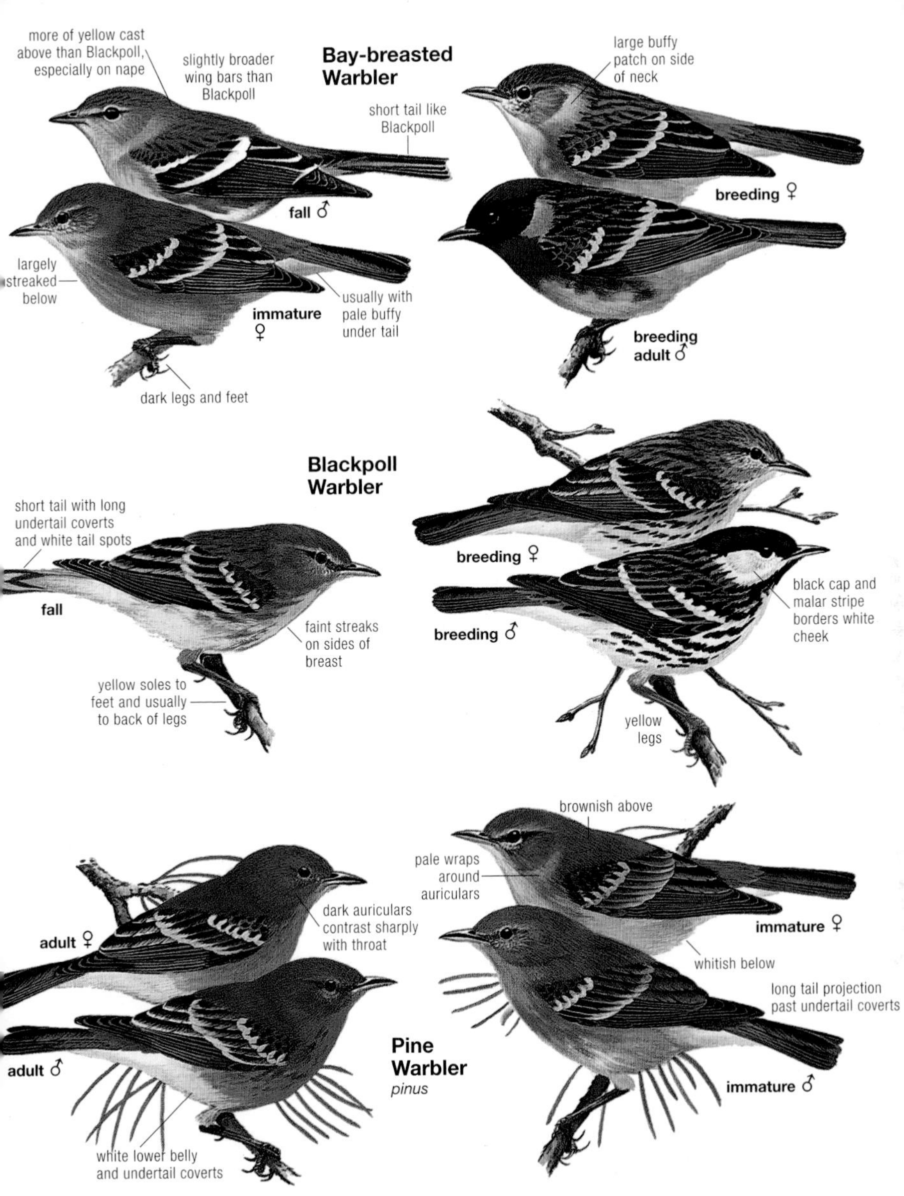

poll, this area is blended. Fall Bay-breasteds and Blackpolls are quite similar in overall coloration (yellow-olive with white wing bars). Most Bay-breasteds show some hint of chestnut color, at least, on the lower flank. They have broader wing-bars, and they are clearer breasted (compare Blackpoll's faintly streaked sides) and brighter above, especially on the crown and nape. Pines are variable: Males are olive to olive brown above and extensively yellow below; females are duller, and immature females are mainly brownish above and whitish below, with little or no yellow. Pines also have duller and less contrasty wingbars as well as duller tertial edges; their primaries lack whitish tips. Pines and Bay-breasteds have darker legs and feet than Blackpolls.

Prairie Warbler *Dendroica discolor L 4¾" (12 cm)*
Adult male olive above, with faint chestnut streaks on back; bright yellow eyebrow, yellow patch below eye; bright yellow below, streaked with black on sides of neck and body. Two indistinct wing bars. ***Female*** and immature male are slightly duller. ***Immature female*** is duller still, grayish olive above; distinguished from fall Magnolia Warbler (page 332) by lack of complete eye ring or gray breast band. Prairie usually forages in lower branches and brush; wags or flicks tail.
Voice: Distinctive song is a rising series of buzzy *zee* notes. Call is a flat *tsuk*.
Range: An eastern species. Casual in the West, except in coastal California, where it is rare in fall.

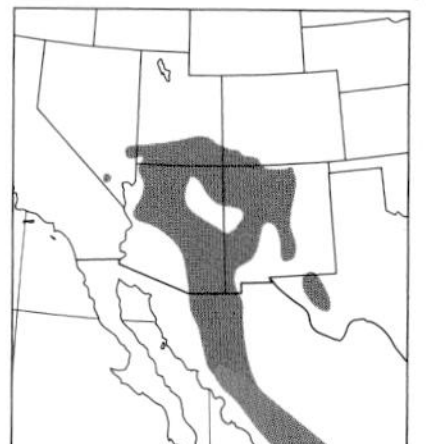

Grace's Warbler *Dendroica graciae L 5" (13 cm)*
Black-streaked gray back; throat and upper breast bright yellow; rest of underparts white, with black streaks on sides; short bill; yellow eyebrow becomes white behind eye. ***Female*** slightly duller and browner above.
Voice: Song is a rapid, accelerating trill. Call is a sweet *chip*.
Range: Inhabits coniferous or mixed forests of southwestern mountains, especially yellow pines. Usually forages high in the trees. Very rare to southern California.

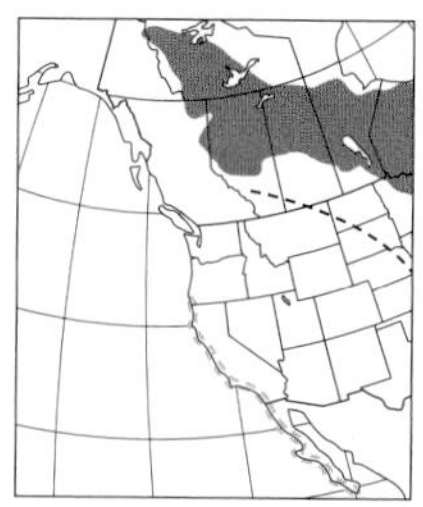

Palm Warbler *Dendroica palmarum L 5½" (14 cm)*
Upperparts olive. ***Breeding adult*** of eastern race (breeds east of Hudson Bay), *hypochrysea*, has chestnut cap, yellow eyebrow, and entirely yellow underparts, with chestnut streaking on sides of breast. Fall adults and immatures lack chestnut cap and streaking; yellow is duller. Western nominate race, *palmarum*, has whitish belly and darker streaks on sides of breast; less chestnut. ***Fall adults*** and immatures are drab. Habitually wags its tail.
Voice: Song is a rapid, buzzy trill. Call is a sharp *tsik*.
Range: Uncommon in western breeding range; nests in brush at edge of spruce bogs. During migration and winter, found in woodland borders, open brushy areas, and marshes. Regular on West Coast in fall and winter, very rare inland (*palmarum*); *hypochrysea* casual to California.

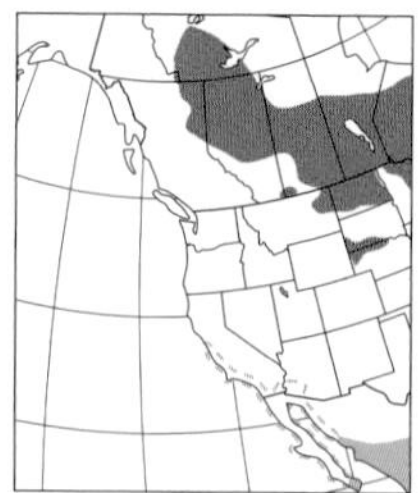

Black-and-white Warbler *Mniotilta varia L 5¼" (13 cm)*
The only warbler that regularly creeps along branches and up and down tree trunks like a nuthatch. Boldly striped on head, most of body, and undertail coverts. ***Male***'s throat and cheeks are black in breeding plumage; in winter, chin is white. ***Female*** and ***immatures*** have pale cheeks; female diffusely streaked on buffy flanks; buffy wash particularly bright on immatures.
Voice: Song is a long series of high, thin *wee-see* notes. Calls include a sharp *chip* and high *seep-seep*.
Range: Frequents mixed woodlands. Uncommon in western Canadian breeding range. Rare otherwise in West, most frequent in migration.

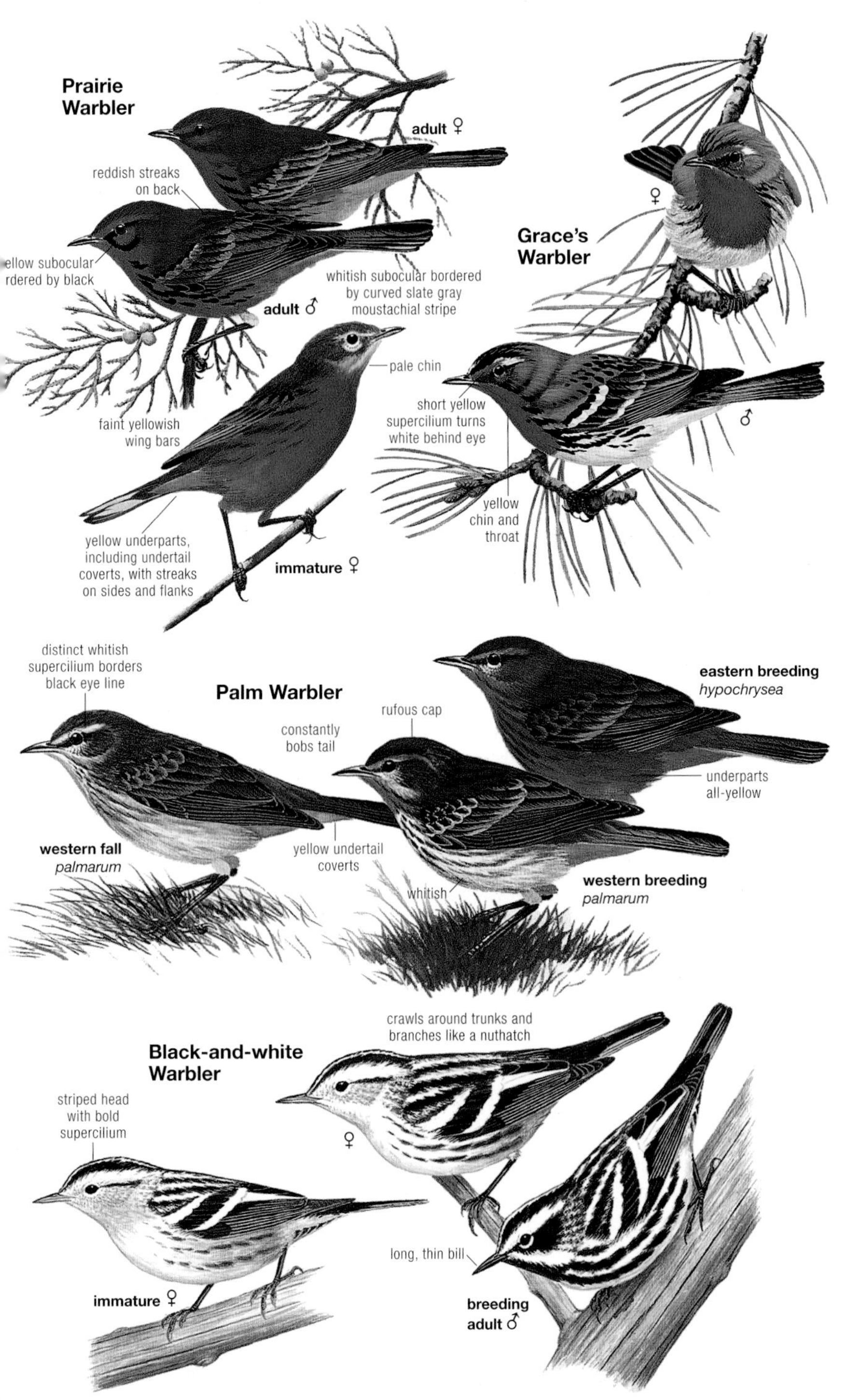
Prairie Warbler
adult ♀
reddish streaks on back
ellow subocular rdered by black
adult ♂
whitish subocular bordered by curved slate gray moustachial stripe
pale chin
faint yellowish wing bars
yellow underparts, including undertail coverts, with streaks on sides and flanks
immature ♀
Grace's Warbler
♀
short yellow supercilium turns white behind eye
♂
yellow chin and throat
distinct whitish supercilium borders black eye line
Palm Warbler
eastern breeding
hypochrysea
rufous cap
constantly bobs tail
underparts all-yellow
western fall
palmarum
yellow undertail coverts
whitish
western breeding
palmarum
Black-and-white Warbler
crawls around trunks and branches like a nuthatch
striped head with bold supercilium
♀
long, thin bill
immature ♀
breeding adult ♂

Prothonotary Warbler *Protonotaria citrea L 5½" (14 cm)*
Large, plump, short tailed, and very long billed. Eyes are large, dark, and prominent. ***Male***'s head and underparts golden yellow, fading to white undertail coverts; wings blue-gray, without wing bars; blue-gray tail has large white patches. ***Female*** duller, head less golden.
Voice: Song is a series of loud, ringing *zweet* notes; gives a dry *chip* note and buzzy flight call.
Range: An eastern species. Casual to rare vagrant in West, especially in fall.

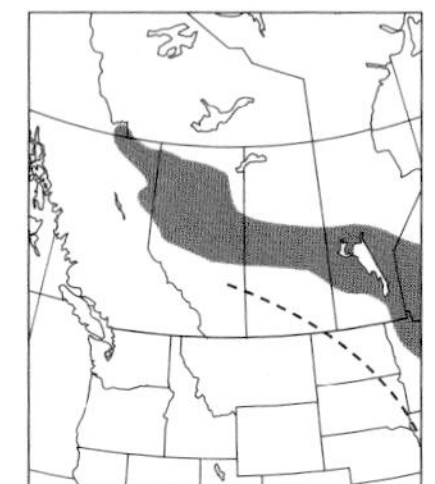

Canada Warbler *Wilsonia canadensis L 5¼" (13 cm)*
Black "necklace" on bright yellow breast identifies ***male;*** note also "spectacles" composed of bold yellow supraloral. In ***females,*** necklace is dusky and indistinct. Male is blue-gray above, females duller. All birds have white undertail coverts. Usually forages in undergrowth or low branches, but also seen fly-catching.
Voice: Song begins with one or more short, sharp *chip* notes and continues as a rich and highly variable warble. Call, a sharp *tick.*
Range: Uncommon in western breeding range in dense woodlands and brush. Winters in South America. Casual vagrant over much of the West; very rare in fall along California coast.

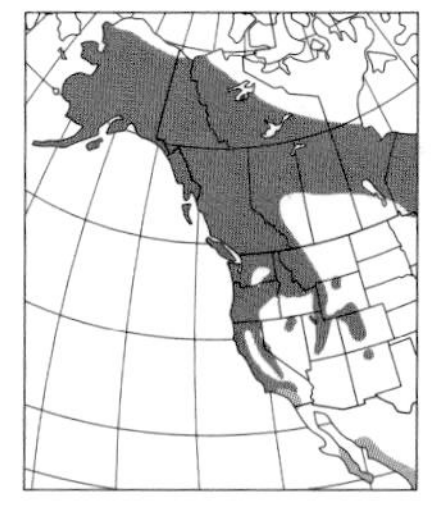

Wilson's Warbler *Wilsonia pusilla L 4¾" (12 cm)*
Olive above; yellow below, with yellow lores. Long tail is all-dark above and below, and often cocked. ***Male*** has black cap; in ***females,*** cap is blackish or absent, forehead yellowish. Yellow lores and lack of white in tail help distinguish female Wilson's from female Hooded Warbler. Coloration varies geographically from bright *chryseola* of Pacific states to duller and olive-faced nominate, *pusilla,* of the East, breeding west to the Northwest Territories; *pileolata* (shown) from Alaska and Rockies is intermediate. Females average more black on cap in western races.
Voice: Song is a rapid, variable series of *chee* notes; common call is a sharp *chimp*; also a *tsip,* the frequent flight call.
Range: Common to abundant in West; nests in dense, moist woodlands, bogs, willow and alder thickets, and streamside tangles. Small numbers winter regularly in coastal California and southern Arizona.

Hooded Warbler *Wilsonia citrina L 5¼" (13 cm)*
All ages have dark lores, unlike Wilson's Warbler; also bigger bill and larger eye. Extensive black hood identifies ***male. Adult female*** shows blackish or olive crown and sides of neck; sometimes has black throat or black spots on breast; ***immature female*** lacks black. Note that in both sexes tail is white below; seen from above, white outer tail feathers are conspicuous as the bird flicks its tail open. Generally stays hidden in dense undergrowth.
Voice: Song is loud, musical, whistled variations of *ta-wit ta-wit ta-wit tee-yo.* Call is a flat, metallic chink.
Range: An eastern species. Rare migrant in the Southwest and California, where it has nested; has also nested in Colorado; casual in other western states.

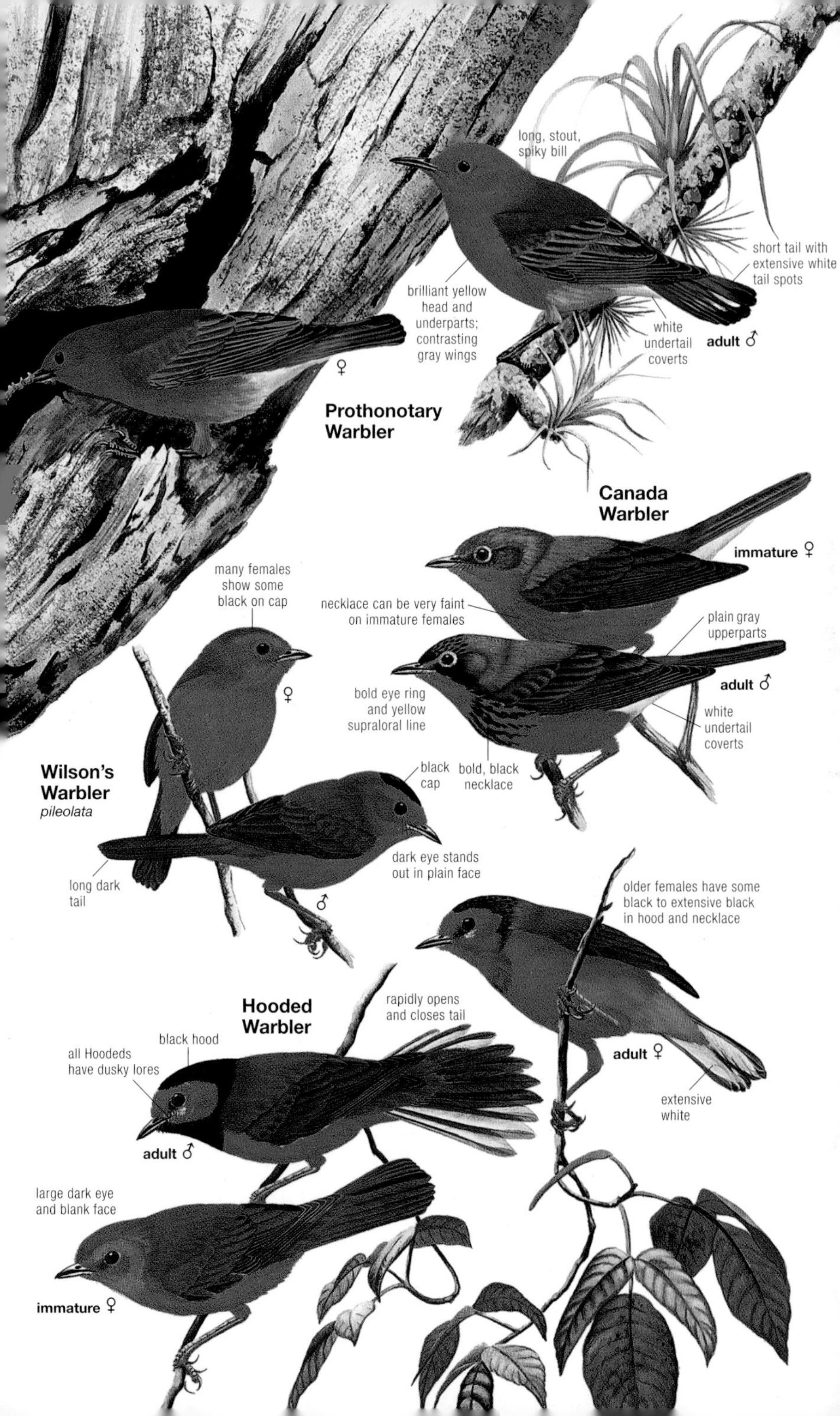
long, stout, spiky bill
short tail with extensive white tail spots
brilliant yellow head and underparts; contrasting gray wings
white undertail coverts
adult ♂
♀
Prothonotary Warbler
Canada Warbler
immature ♀
many females show some black on cap
necklace can be very faint on immature females
plain gray upperparts
adult ♂
♀
bold eye ring and yellow supraloral line
white undertail coverts
Wilson's Warbler
pileolata
black cap
bold, black necklace
dark eye stands out in plain face
long dark tail
♂
older females have some black to extensive black in hood and necklace
rapidly opens and closes tail
Hooded Warbler
black hood
all Hoodeds have dusky lores
adult ♀
extensive white
adult ♂
large dark eye and blank face
immature ♀

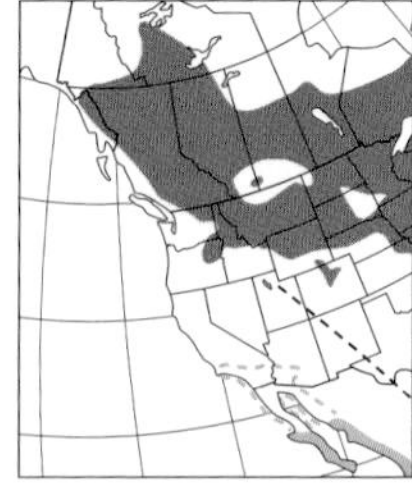

American Redstart *Setophaga ruticilla L 5¼" (13 cm)*
Male glossy black, with bright orange patches on sides, wings, and tail; belly and undertail coverts white. ***Female*** is gray-olive above, white below with yellow patches. Immature male resembles female; in ***first-spring*** plumage, lores are usually black, breast has some black spotting; adult male plumage is acquired by second fall. Like redstarts of the genus *Myioborus,* often fans its tail and spreads its wings when perched.
Voice: Variable song is a series of high, thin notes usually followed by a wheezy, downslurred note. Call is a rich, sweet *chip.*
Range: Uncommon to common in second-growth woodlands. Rare migrant in California and the Southwest. Has declined in the West; casual to western Alaska.

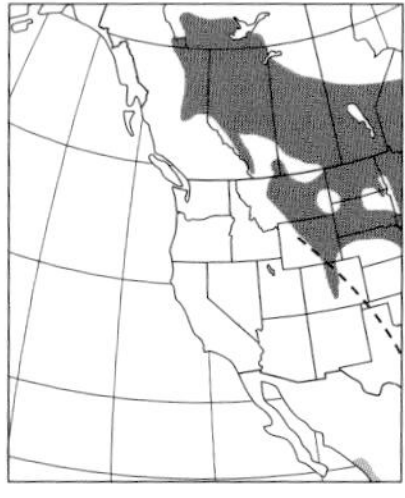

Ovenbird *Seiurus aurocapilla L 6" (15 cm)*
Russet crown bordered by dark stripes; bold white eye ring. Olive above; white below, with bold streaks of dark spots; pinkish legs. Generally seen on the ground; walks, with tail cocked, rather than hops.
Voice: Typical song is a loud *teacher teacher teacher,* rising in volume. Calls include a sharp, dry *chip.*
Range: Rare to fairly common breeder in mature forests in western breeding range. Otherwise, overall a rare migrant in West.

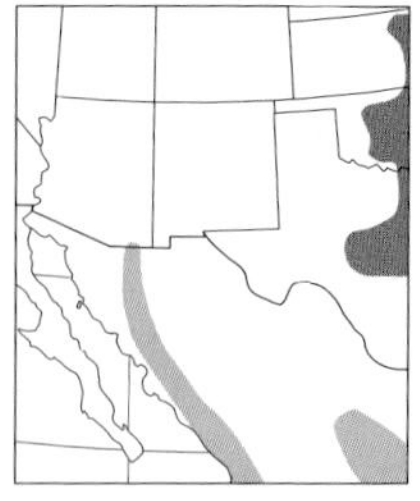

Louisiana Waterthrush *Seiurus motacilla L 6" (15 cm)*
Distinguished from Northern Waterthrush by contrast between white underparts and salmon-buff flanks; bicolored eyebrow, pale buff in front of eye, white and much broader behind eye; larger bill; bubblegum pink legs. A ground dweller; walks, rather than hops, bobbing its tail constantly but usually slowly.
Voice: Call note, a sharp *chick,* is slightly flatter than Northern Waterthrush. Song begins with three or four shrill, slurred notes followed by a brief, rapid jumble.
Range: Rare migrant and winter visitor in southeastern Arizona. Casual elsewhere; most records from California.

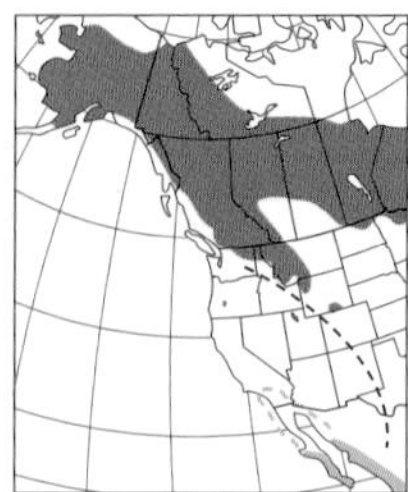

Northern Waterthrush *Seiurus noveboracensis*
L 5¾" (15 cm) Distinguished from Louisiana Waterthrush by lack of contrast in color between flanks and rest of underparts; buffy eyebrow is of even width throughout or slightly narrowing behind eye; smaller bill; drabber leg color. Some birds are whiter below, with whiter eyebrow. A ground dweller; walks, rather than hops, bobbing its tail constantly and usually rapidly.
Voice: Call note, a metallic *chink,* is slightly sharper than Louisiana Waterthrush. Song begins with loud, emphatic notes and ends in lower notes, delivered more rapidly.
Range: Found chiefly in woodland bogs, swamps, streams, puddles, and thickets. Uncommon to common in western breeding range. Rare to uncommon migrant in California and the Southwest, where a few also winter.

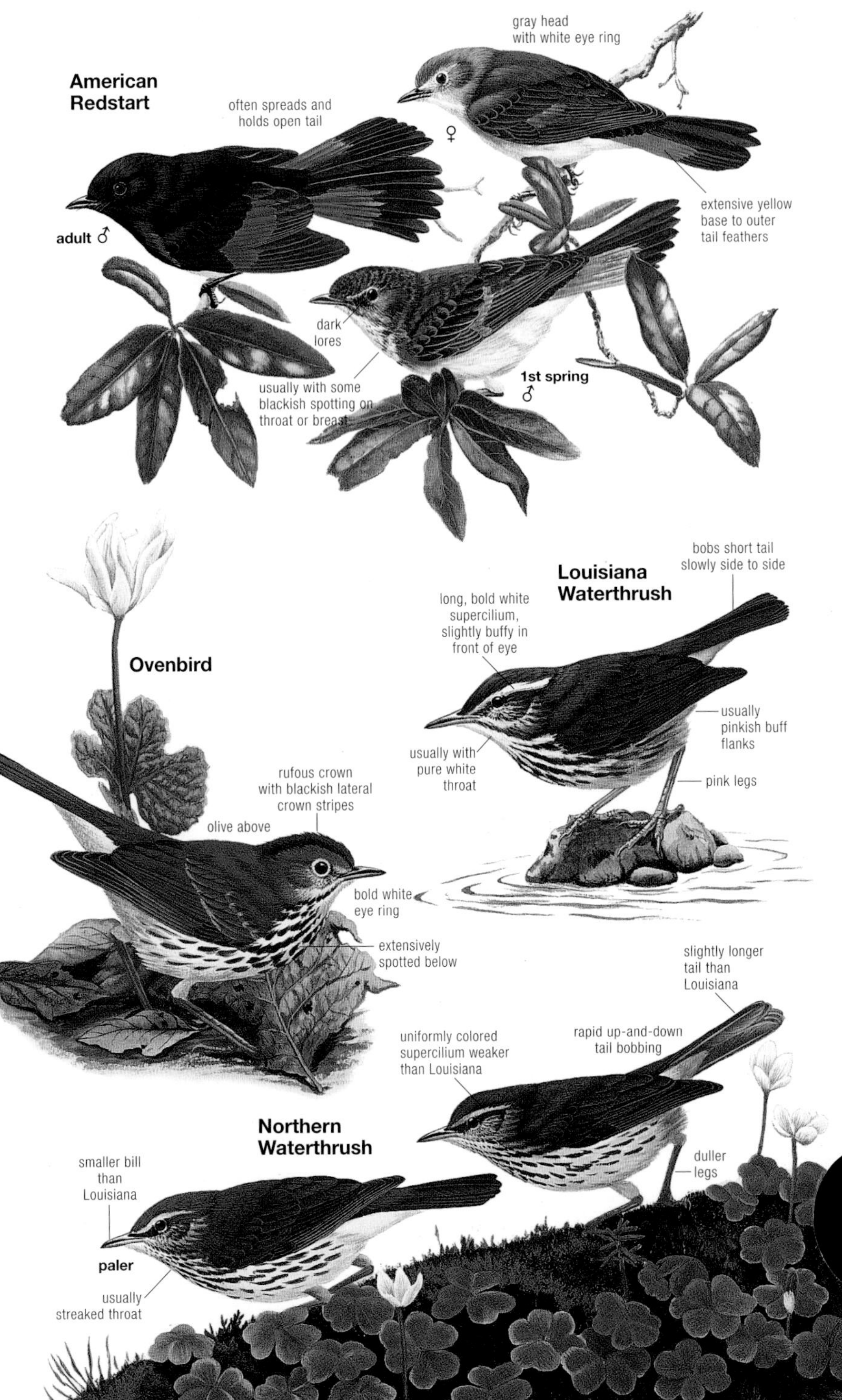

American Redstart
often spreads and holds open tail
gray head with white eye ring
♀
adult ♂
extensive yellow base to outer tail feathers
dark lores
usually with some blackish spotting on throat or breast
1st spring ♂
Louisiana Waterthrush
bobs short tail slowly side to side
long, bold white supercilium, slightly buffy in front of eye
Ovenbird
usually pinkish buff flanks
usually with pure white throat
pink legs
rufous crown with blackish lateral crown stripes
olive above
bold white eye ring
extensively spotted below
slightly longer tail than Louisiana
uniformly colored supercilium weaker than Louisiana
rapid up-and-down tail bobbing
Northern Waterthrush
smaller bill than Louisiana
duller legs
paler
usually streaked throat

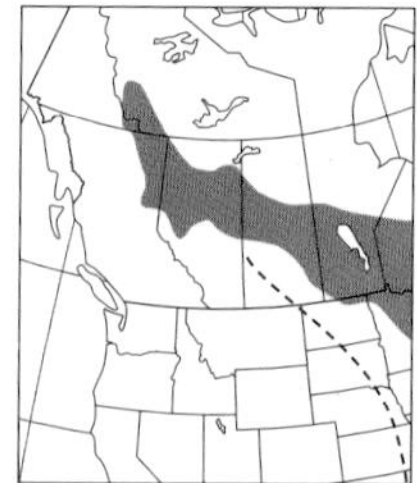

Mourning Warbler *Oporornis philadelphia L 5¼" (13 cm)*
Lack of bold white eye ring distinguishes ***adult male*** from Connecticut Warbler. ***Adult female*** and especially ***immatures*** may show a thin, nearly complete eye ring, but compare with Connecticut. Immature generally has more yellow on throat than MacGillivray's; compare also with female Common Yellowthroat (page 348). Immature males often show a little black on breast. Hops rather than walks.
Voice: Call is a flat, hollow *chip.* Song is a series of slurred two-note phrases followed by two or more lower phrases.
Range: Fairly common in limited western breeding range in dense undergrowth, thickets, moist woods; nests on ground like all *Oporornis.* Otherwise very rare to casual migrant in West; accidental in California in winter.

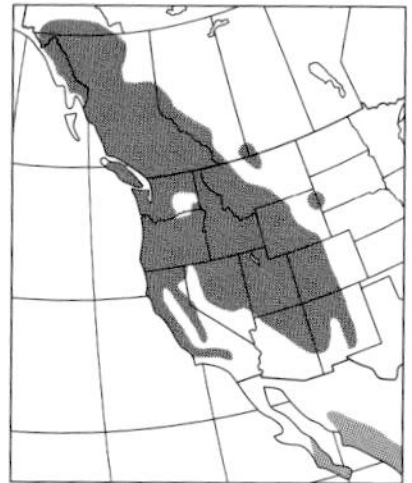

MacGillivray's Warbler *Oporornis tolmiei L 5¼" (13 cm)*
Bold white crescents above and below eye distinguish all plumages from male Mourning and all Connecticut Warblers. Crescents may be very hard to distinguish from the thin, nearly complete eye ring found on female and immature Mourning Warblers. ***Immature*** MacGillivray's generally has grayer throat than immature Mourning with a fairly distinct breast band above yellow belly. Field identification often difficult. Hops rather than walks.
Voice: Call is a sharp, harsh *tsik.* Two-part song is a buzzy trill ending in a downslur.
Range: Fairly common; found in dense undergrowth. Casual to western Alaska and in winter in coastal California.

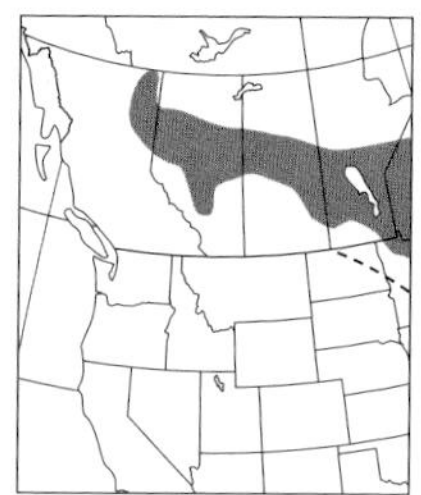

Connecticut Warbler *Oporornis agilis L 5¾" (15 cm)*
Large eye with bold white eye ring conspicuous on ***male***'s gray hood and ***female***'s brown or gray-brown hood. Eye ring is sometimes slightly broken on one side only. ***Immature*** has a brownish hood and brownish breast band. A large, stocky warbler, noticeably larger than Mourning and MacGillivray's Warblers. Like Mourning, long undertail coverts give Connecticut a short-tailed, plump appearance. Walks rather than hops.
Voice: Loud, accelerating song repeats a brief series of explosive *beech-er* or *whip-ity* notes. *Chip* note rarely heard.
Range: Uncommon in limited western breeding range, where it is partial to pure and mixed stands of trembling aspen. Otherwise in the West, casual to accidental migrant except from coastal California where very rare but annual in fall. Winters in central South America.

IDENTIFYING: *Oporornis* Warblers Only one species of *Oporornis* is widespread in the West—MacGillivray's. Mourning and Connecticut have limited breeding ranges in western Canada, and both are very rare to casual in migration through the remainder of the West. Connecticut is basically known only as a very rare migrant on the northern portion of the Great Plains and as fall vagrant to California, mostly along the coast or the offshore islands.

MacGillivray's and Mourning are obviously more closely related to each other, and some birds can be very difficult to separate. But Mourning is similarly shaped to Connecticut (chunky and short tailed) whereas MacGillivray's appears longer tailed. Connecticut's behavior is very different: It

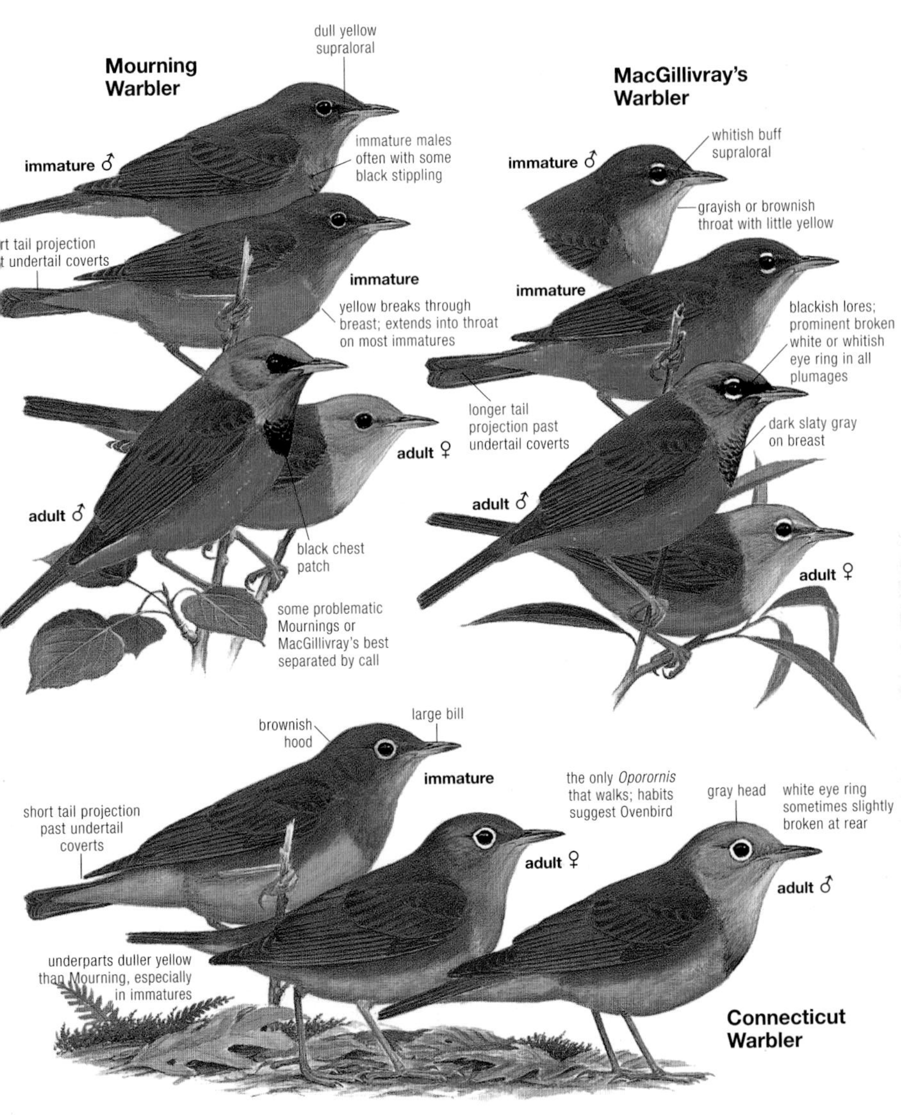

is the one *Oporornis* that actually walks along the ground or on branches. (The others hop.) Connecticut is duller yellow below and has a conspicuous full to slightly broken eye ring. Fall immature Mournings usually have yellow throats; the males often have some black stippling on the chest, which is diagnostic. A few immature MacGillivray's are also washed with yellow on the throat.

Perhaps for a few, calls are the only trustworthy distinguishing characteristic: Mourning's hollow call is quite suggestive of Bewick's Wren. The call of MacGillivray's is sharper. Connecticut rarely chips, and usually only a buzzy Yellow Warbler–like *zeet* flight call is heard. The flight calls of both MacGillivray's and Mourning are thinner and not buzzy.

Common Yellowthroat *Geothlypis trichas L 5" (13 cm)*
Adult male's broad black mask is bordered above by white in western subspecies, below by bright yellow throat and breast; undertail coverts yellow. ***Female*** lacks black mask; has whitish eye ring. Races vary geographically in color of upperparts and extent of yellow below. Southwestern race, *chryseola,* is brightest below and shows the most yellow. ***Immature*** is duller and browner overall. Often cocks tail.
Voice: Variable song; one version is a loud, rolling *wichity wichity wichity wich.* Calls include a raspy *chuck.*
Range: Common; stays low in grassy fields, shrubs, and marshes.

Rufous-capped Warbler *Basileuterus rufifrons L 5¼" (13 cm)* Rufous crown, bold white eyebrow, throat extensively bright yellow. Long tail, often cocked. Generally stays low in the undergrowth.
Voice: Song begins with musical *chip* notes and accelerates into a series of dry, whistled warbles; call, a *tik,* is often doubled or in a rapid series.
Range: Mexican species, casual to Big Bend, Texas; and southeastern Arizona (has nested). Inhabits brush and woodlands of foothills or low mountains.

Painted Redstart *Myioborus pictus L 5¾" (15 cm)*
Bright red lower breast and belly; black head and upperparts; bold white wing patch. White outer tail feathers conspicuous as the bird fans its tail. ***Juvenile*** acquires full adult plumage by end of summer.
Voice: Song is a series of rich, liquid warbles; call is a clear, whistled *chee.*
Range: Found in pine-oak canyons. Very rare visitor to southern California; a scattering of records elsewhere north to southern British Columbia.

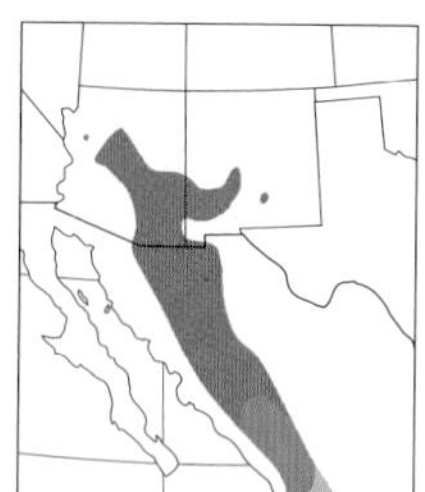

Red-faced Warbler *Cardellina rubrifrons L 5½" (14 cm)*
Adult's red-and-black face pattern distinctive; back and tail gray, rump and underparts white. Immature is duller, face pinkish.
Voice: Song is a series of varied, ringing *zweet* notes.
Range: A warbler of high mountains, generally found above 6,000 feet. Fairly common, especially in fir and spruce mixed with oaks. Nests on the ground. Rare to west Texas; casual to southern California. Accidental to northern California, Nevada, Wyoming, and Colorado.

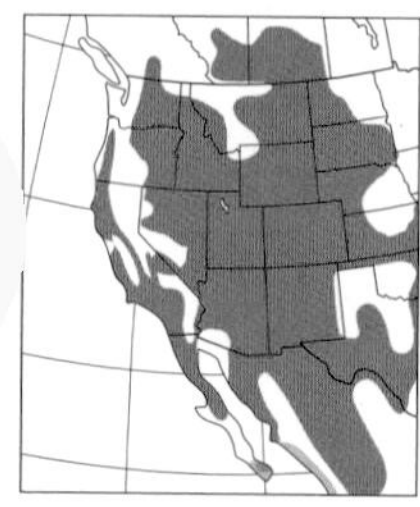

Yellow-breasted Chat *Icteria virens L 7½" (19 cm)*
Our largest warbler, with long tail, thick bill, and white spectacles. Lores black in ***male,*** gray in ***female.***
Voice: Unmusical song is a jumble of harsh, chattering clucks, rattles, clear whistles, and squawks, sometimes given in hovering display flight.
Range: Inhabits dense thickets and brush. Rather shy. Casual on West Coast in winter.

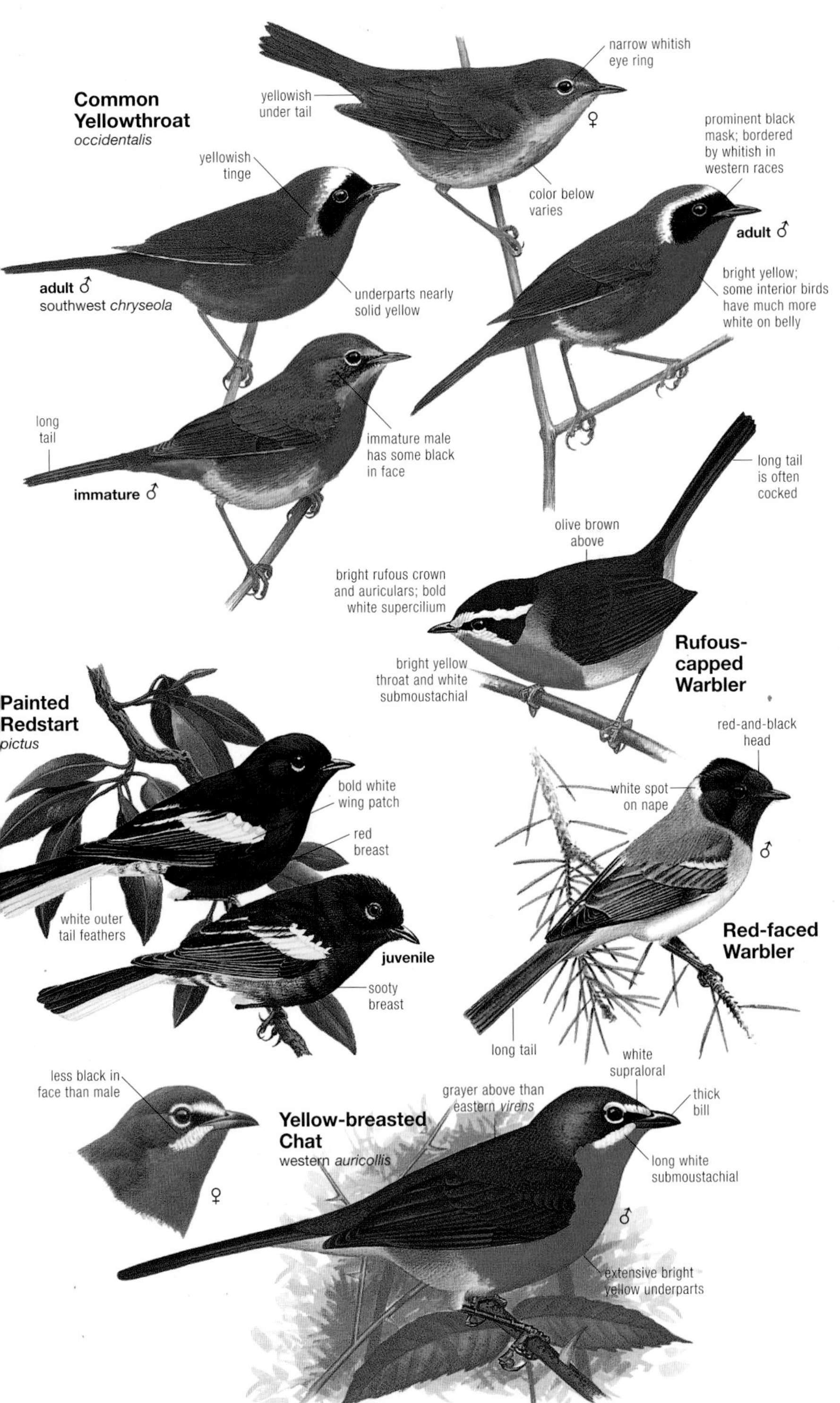
Common Yellowthroat
occidentalis
narrow whitish eye ring
yellowish under tail
♀
prominent black mask; bordered by whitish in western races
yellowish tinge
color below varies
adult ♂
bright yellow; some interior birds have much more white on belly
adult ♂
southwest chryseola
underparts nearly solid yellow
long tail
immature male has some black in face
immature ♂
long tail is often cocked
olive brown above
bright rufous crown and auriculars; bold white supercilium
Rufous-capped Warbler
bright yellow throat and white submoustachial
Painted Redstart
pictus
red-and-black head
white spot on nape
bold white wing patch
red breast
♂
white outer tail feathers
Red-faced Warbler
juvenile
sooty breast
long tail
white supraloral
less black in face than male
grayer above than eastern virens
thick bill
Yellow-breasted Chat
western auricollis
long white submoustachial
♀
♂
extensive bright yellow underparts

Olive Warbler (Family Peucedramidae)

This species was recently placed in its own family because relationships are uncertain.

Olive Warbler *Peucedramus taeniatus* L 5¼" (13 cm)
Dark face patch broadens behind eye. Long, thin bill; two broad white wing bars; outer tail feathers extensively white. ***Adult male***'s head, throat, and nape tawny brown. ***Female*** has olive crown, yellow face; pale yellow throat and breast. Juveniles and ***first-fall*** birds resemble female but are paler or whitish below; crown is gray. Young male acquires adult plumage by second fall.
Voice: Typical song is a loud *peeta peeta peeta,* similar to Tufted Titmouse; distinctive call is a soft, whistled *phew.*
Range: Favors open coniferous forests at elevations above 7,000 feet. Nests and forages high in trees. A few remain on breeding grounds in winter. Casual to west Texas.

Tanagers (Family Thraupidae)

These brightly colored, mostly fruit-eating, tropical birds are related to warblers.

Flame-colored Tanager *Piranga bidentata* L 7¼" (18 cm)
Has gray bill with visible "teeth"; blackish rear border to ear patch; streaked back; white wing bars and tertial tips; whitish tail corners. Hybrids with Western Tanager are regularly noted in southeastern Arizona. ***Male*** of nominate west Mexican race, *bidentata,* is flaming orange; eastern *sanguinolenta* male slightly redder. ***Female*** and immature are colored like female Western Tanager. ***First-spring males*** have brighter yellow head; some spotting.
Voice: Song similar to Western and Scarlet Tanagers; call is also similar, but huskier, low-pitched *prreck.*
Range: Resident from northern Mexico to western Panama; very rare to mountains of southeastern Arizona in spring and summer; casual to west Texas.

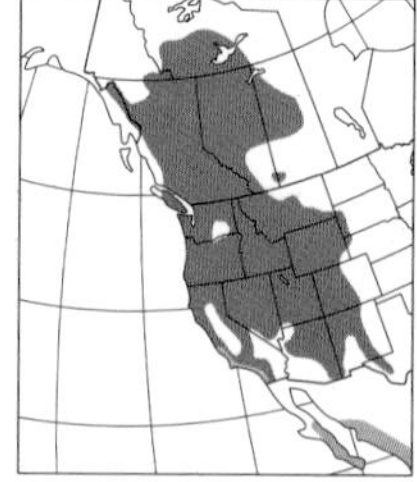

Western Tanager *Piranga ludoviciana* L 7¼" (18 cm)
Conspicuous wing bars, often paler and thinner in ***female,*** upper bar yellow in ***male.*** Male's red head becomes more yellowish and finely streaked in ***winter*** with some orange restricted to face. Female's grayish back contrasts with greenish yellow nape and rump. Some females are duller below, grayer above. Compare to female orioles (pages 396 and 398).
Voice: Song is like Scarlet Tanager; call is a *pit-er-ick*; also a whistled flight call.
Range: Breeds in coniferous and mixed forests. Rare in winter north along coastal slope to central California. Uncommon migrant in western Great Plains.

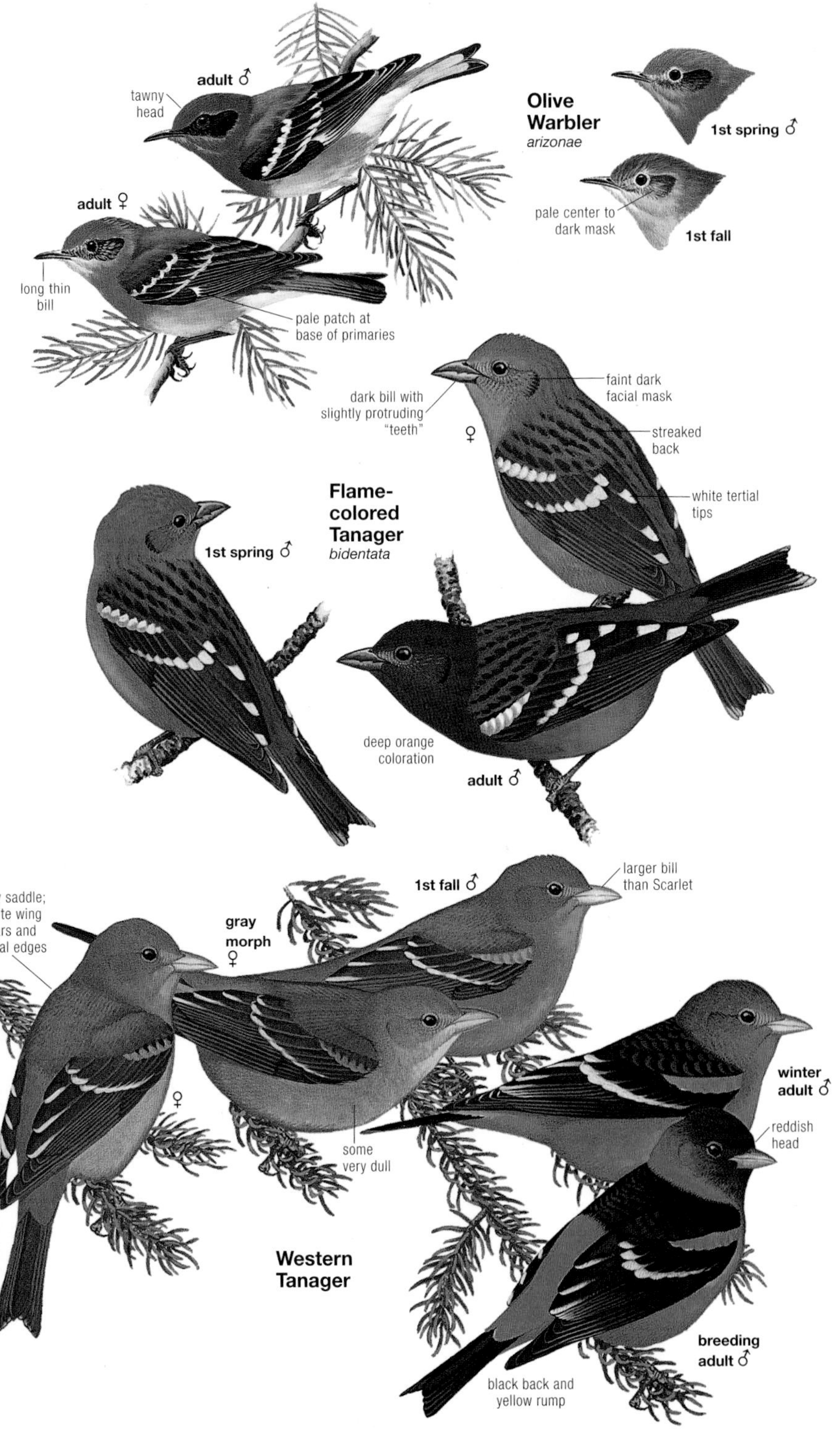
adult ♂
tawny head
Olive Warbler
arizonae
1st spring ♂
adult ♀
pale center to dark mask
1st fall
long thin bill
pale patch at base of primaries
faint dark facial mask
dark bill with slightly protruding "teeth"
♀
streaked back
Flame-colored Tanager
bidentata
white tertial tips
1st spring ♂
deep orange coloration
adult ♂
1st fall ♂
larger bill than Scarlet
ıy saddle; ıite wing ars and tial edges
gray morph ♀
♀
winter adult ♂
reddish head
some very dull
Western Tanager
breeding adult ♂
black back and yellow rump

Hepatic Tanager *Piranga flava* L 8" (20 cm)
Large grayish cheek patch and gray wash on flanks set off brighter throat, breast, and cap in both sexes; dark bill with gray base. ***Adult male*** plumage is acquired by second fall; dull red plumage retained year-round. Juvenile resembles yellow-and-gray ***female*** but is heavily streaked overall; immature male resembles female.
Voice: Song is robinlike. Call is a single low *chuck*.
Range: Breeds on mountains of Southwest; rare to eastern California and Colorado. Very rare migrant in lowlands and in winter in southeastern Arizona and southern California; casual to southern Nevada; accidental Wyoming.

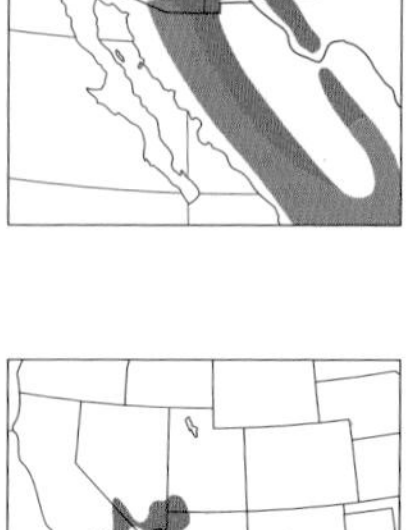

Summer Tanager *Piranga rubra* L 7¾" (20 cm)
Adult male is rosy red year-round. ***First-spring male*** usually has red head. Some ***females*** show overall reddish wash; most have a mustard tone, lack olive of female Scarlet Tanager; bill larger. Western birds (*cooperi*) are larger and paler; females generally grayer above.
Voice: Song is robinlike; call is a staccato *ki-ti-tuck*.
Range: Uncommon to fairly common in cottonwood groves. Rarely winter in California. Eastern *rubra* occurs rarely but regularly in West.

Scarlet Tanager *Piranga olivacea* L 7" (18 cm)
Breeding male bright red and black. In late summer, becomes splotchy green-and-red as he molts to yellow-green winter plumage. ***Female*** has uniformly olive head, back, and rump; whitish wing linings; bill smaller than Summer Tanager. Immature ***male*** resembles adult male, but note brownish primaries and secondaries. Some immatures show faint wing bars.
Voice: Robinlike song (hoarser than Summer Tanager) of raspy notes, *querit queer query querit queer,* is heard in deciduous forests. Call is a hoarse *chip-burr.*
Range: An eastern species. Very rare vagrant in the West, most in late fall.

IDENTIFYING: Female-plumaged Tanagers Separating female tanagers can indeed be challenging in the West. The widespread and common species in the West is Western Tanager. Summer and Hepatic Tanagers are pretty much restricted as breeders to the Southwest, the latter generally being found at lower elevations. Scarlet is a rare vagrant to the West. In California, the great majority of the records are for late fall, but on the Great Plains it is more regular in the spring.

Western and Scarlet are similarly colored in yellowish and olive hues. Western is larger and larger billed, and it has a gray (rather than olive) back saddle. Scarlet in particular appears quite stubby billed and shorter tailed. Western has distinctive wing bars (the upper one is often strongly yellow), but in worn plumage, Western can appear to almost lack wing bars. Summer is a more ochre color overall, but the color is variable; some females have a dull reddish cast to some of feather groups. Hepatic appears brightest on the crown, throat, and breast, with cheeks that appear grayer; it also appears darker billed. Another species that is closely related to Western, Flame-colored Tanager, has started appearing with regularity in recent years (casual to west Texas) to southeastern Arizona. Among other features, Flame-colored's streaked back is distinctive on both sexes.

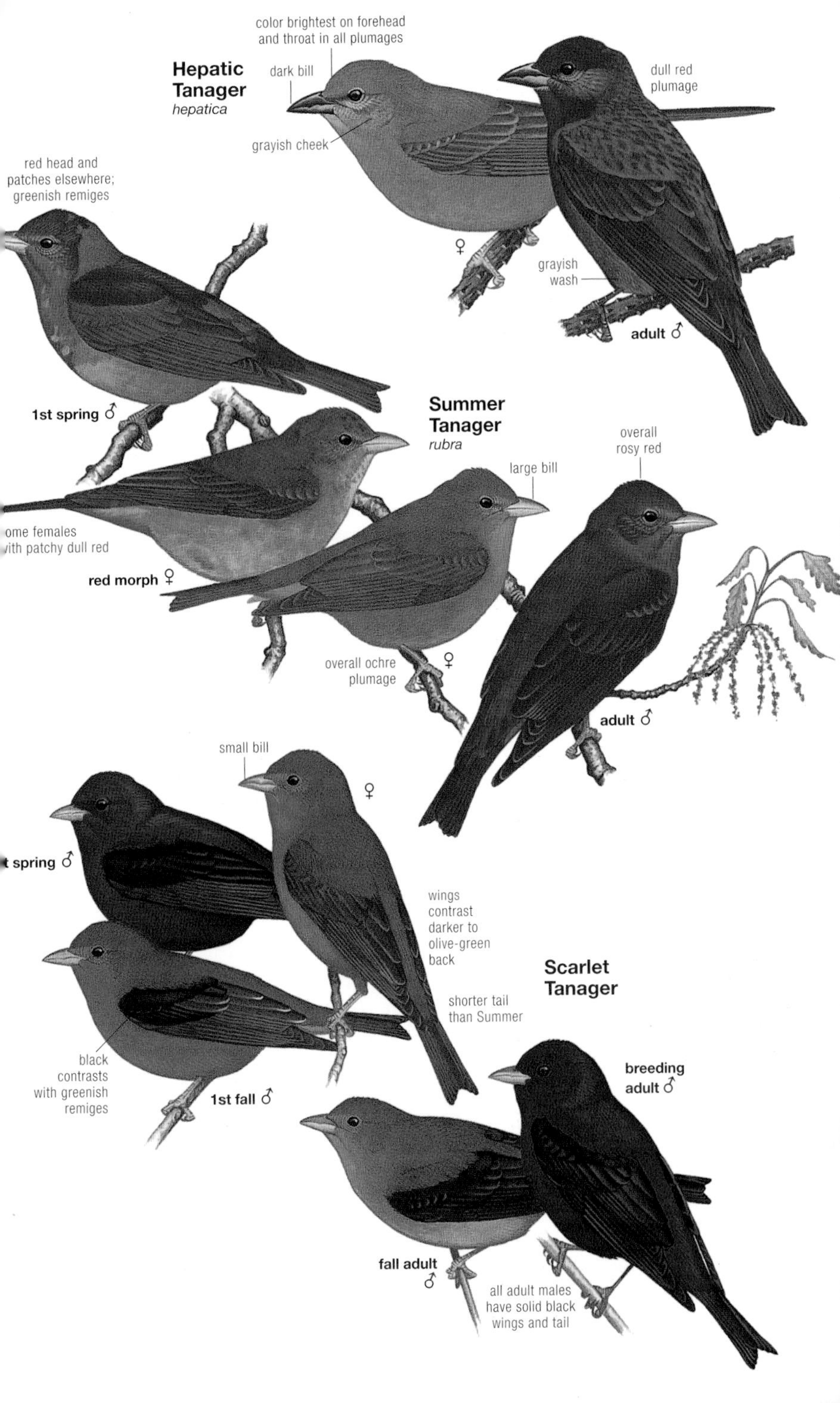
Hepatic
Tanager
hepatica
color brightest on forehead
and throat in all plumages
dark bill
grayish cheek
dull red
plumage
♀
grayish
wash
adult ♂
red head and
patches elsewhere;
greenish remiges
1st spring ♂
Summer
Tanager
rubra
overall
rosy red
large bill
ome females
vith patchy dull red
red morph ♀
overall ochre
plumage
♀
adult ♂
small bill
♀
t spring ♂
wings
contrast
darker to
olive-green
back
Scarlet
Tanager
shorter tail
than Summer
black
contrasts
with greenish
remiges
1st fall ♂
breeding
adult ♂
fall adult
♂
all adult males
have solid black
wings and tail

Emberizids (Family Emberizidae)

All Emberizids have conical bills. This large family includes towhees, sparrows, longspurs, and *Emberiza* buntings.

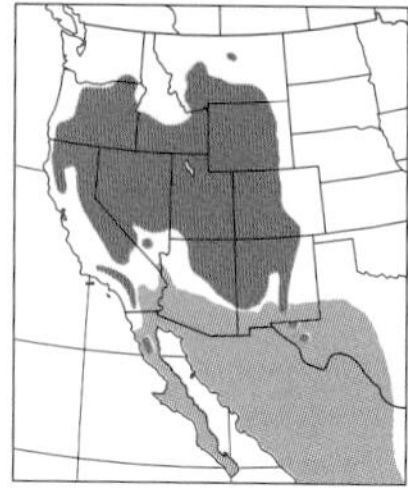

Green-tailed Towhee *Pipilo chlorurus L 7¼" (18 cm)*

Olive above with reddish crown, distinct white throat bordered by dark stripe and white stripe. ***Juvenile*** has two faint olive wing bars; plumage is streaked overall; upperparts tinged with olive; lacks reddish crown.

Voice: Calls include a catlike *mew.* Clear, whistled song begins with *weet-chur,* ends in raspy trill.

Range: Fairly common in dense brush and chaparral and on mountainsides and high plateaus. Rare on West Coast, western Great Plains.

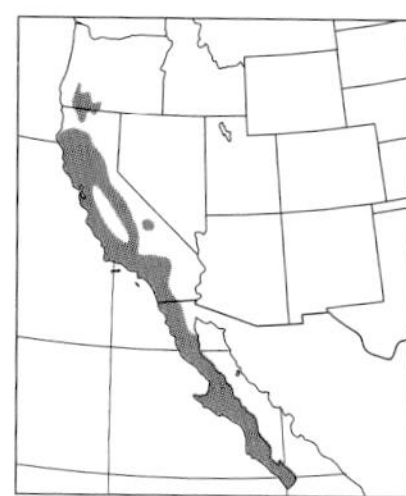

California Towhee *Pipilo crissalis L 9" (23 cm)*

Brownish overall; crown slightly warmer brown than rest of upperparts. Buff throat is bordered by a distinct broken ring of dark brown spots; no dark spot on breast as in Canyon Towhee. Lores are same color as throat and contrast with cheek; undertail coverts warm cinnamon. ***Juvenile*** shows faint wing bars.

Voice: Call is a sharp, metallic *chink* note; also gives some thin, lispy notes and an excited, squealing series of notes, often delivered as a duet by a pair. Song, accelerating *chink* notes with stutters in the middle, is heard mostly in late afternoon.

Range: Common resident in chaparral, parks, and gardens. The race*eremophilus* (**T**) of Inyo County, California, is threatened. With Canyon Towhee, California was formerly considered one species, Brown Towhee.

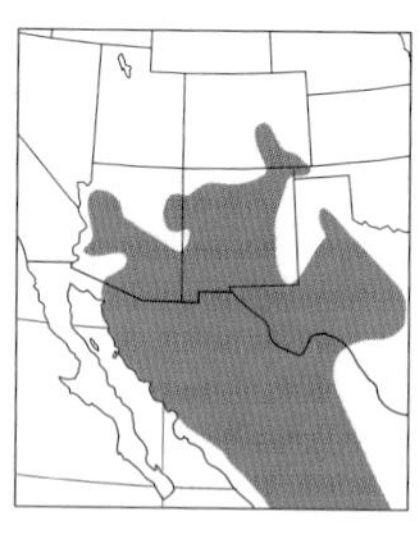

Canyon Towhee *Pipilo fuscus L 8" (20 cm)*

Similar to California Towhee. Canyon is paler, grayish rather than brown, with shorter tail; more contrast in reddish crown, which gives a capped appearance; crown is sometimes raised as short crest. Larger whitish belly patch with diffuse dark spot at junction with breast; paler throat bordered by finer streaks; lores the same color as cheek; distinct buffy eye ring. Juveniles are streaked below.

Voice: Call is a shrill *chee-yep* or *chedep.* Song is more musical and less metallic than California; opens with a call note, followed by sweet slurred notes. Also gives a duet of lisping and squealing notes, like California.

Range: Favors arid, hilly country; desert canyons. Largely resident within range; no range overlap with California.

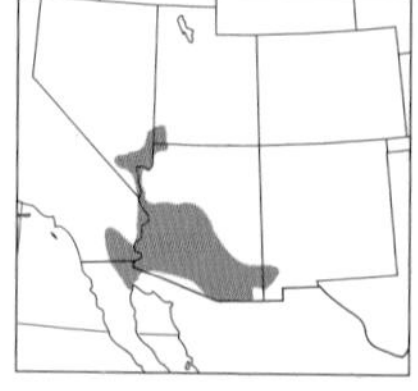

Abert's Towhee *Pipilo aberti L 9½" (24 cm)*

Black face; upperparts cinnamon brown, underparts paler, with cinnamon undertail coverts.

Voice: Call is a sharp *peek;* song is, a series of *peek* notes.

Range: Common within its range, but somewhat secretive. Inhabits desert woodlands and thickets, at lower altitudes than similar Canyon Towhee. Also found in suburban yards and orchards.

Green-tailed Towhee

olive wings and tail

dull rufous crown

white throat, submoustachial, and supraloral

fall

spring

gray

juvenile

extensively streaked

California Towhee

juvenile

crown fairly uniform with rest of head

blurry streaks

no breast spot

Canyon Towhee

pale rufous crown

buffy throat

itish belly with inconspicuous breast spot

Abert's Towhee

pale bill

blackish around bill

overall warm brown coloration

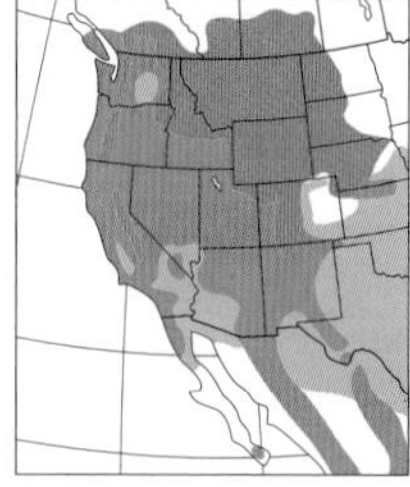

Spotted Towhee *Pipilo maculatus L 7½" (19 cm)*
Distinguished from similar Eastern Towhee (casual in West) by white spotting on back and scapulars; also white on tips of median and greater coverts, which forms white wing bars. In general, ***females*** differ less from ***males*** than in Eastern; *arcticus* from Great Plains shows the greatest difference. In both sexes the amount of white spotting above and white in tail shows marked geographical variation, with *arcticus* displaying most white. Races, principally *montanus*, from the Great Basin and Rockies show less white. Northwest coast's *oregonus* is darkest and shows least white of all the races. White increases southward to *megalonyx* of southern California and *falcinellus* (not shown) of the Central Valley region.
Voice: Song and calls also show great geographical variation. Interior races give introductory notes, then a trill. Pacific coast birds sing a simple trill of variable speed. Call of *montanus* is a descending and raspy mewing. Great Plains *arcticus* and all coastal races give an upslurred, questioning *queee.*
Range: Some populations are largely resident whereas others are migratory; *arcticus* is the most migratory. Casual to Alaska.

Genus *Aimophila*

These are rather large sparrows with long, rounded tails and large bills. They are not gregarious, and most are highly secretive outside of the breeding season.

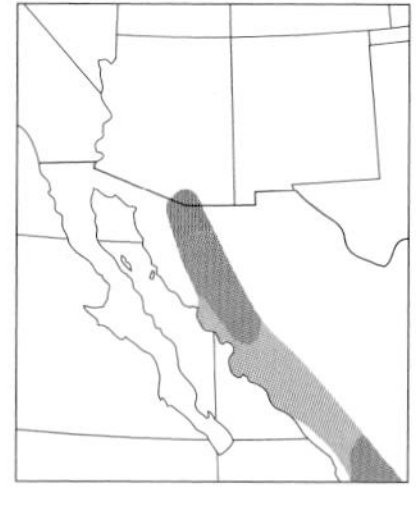

Five-striped Sparrow *Aimophila quinquestriata*
L 6" (15 cm) Dark brown above; gray breast and sides; white throat bordered by black and white stripes. Dark central spot at base of breast. Juvenile lacks the streaks found on juveniles of other sparrow species.
Voice: Song is a series of phrases, each preceded by a few introductory notes. Call is a loud, hollow *tchep.*
Range: West Mexican species; range barely reaches southeastern Arizona. Highly specialized habitat: tall, dense shrubs on rocky, steep hillsides, and canyon slopes. Very local; most often seen in breeding season, when vocalizing more; few winter records, but likely overlooked.

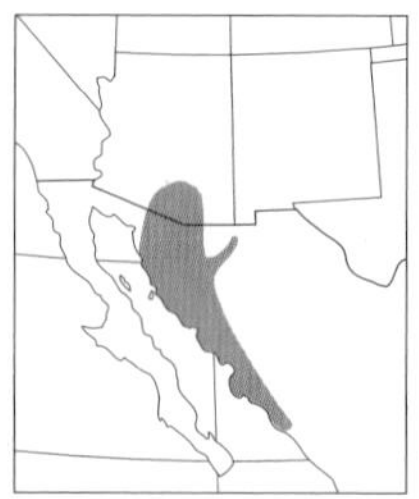

Rufous-winged Sparrow *Aimophila carpalis L 5¾" (15 cm)*
Pale gray head marked with reddish eye line and black moustachial and malar stripe on side of face; two-toned bill, with pale lower mandible; sides of crown streaked with reddish brown. Back is gray-brown, streaked with black; two whitish wing bars. Reddish lesser wing coverts distinctive but difficult to see. Underparts grayish white, without streaking. Tail long, rounded. ***Juvenile***'s facial stripes are less distinct; wing bars buffier; bill dark; breast, sides lightly streaked; plumage can be seen as late as Nov.
Voice: Distinctive call note is a sharp, high *seep.* Variable song comprises several *chip* notes followed by an accelerating trill of *chip* or *sweet* notes.
Range: Fairly common but local; found in flat areas of desert grass mixed with brush and cactus.

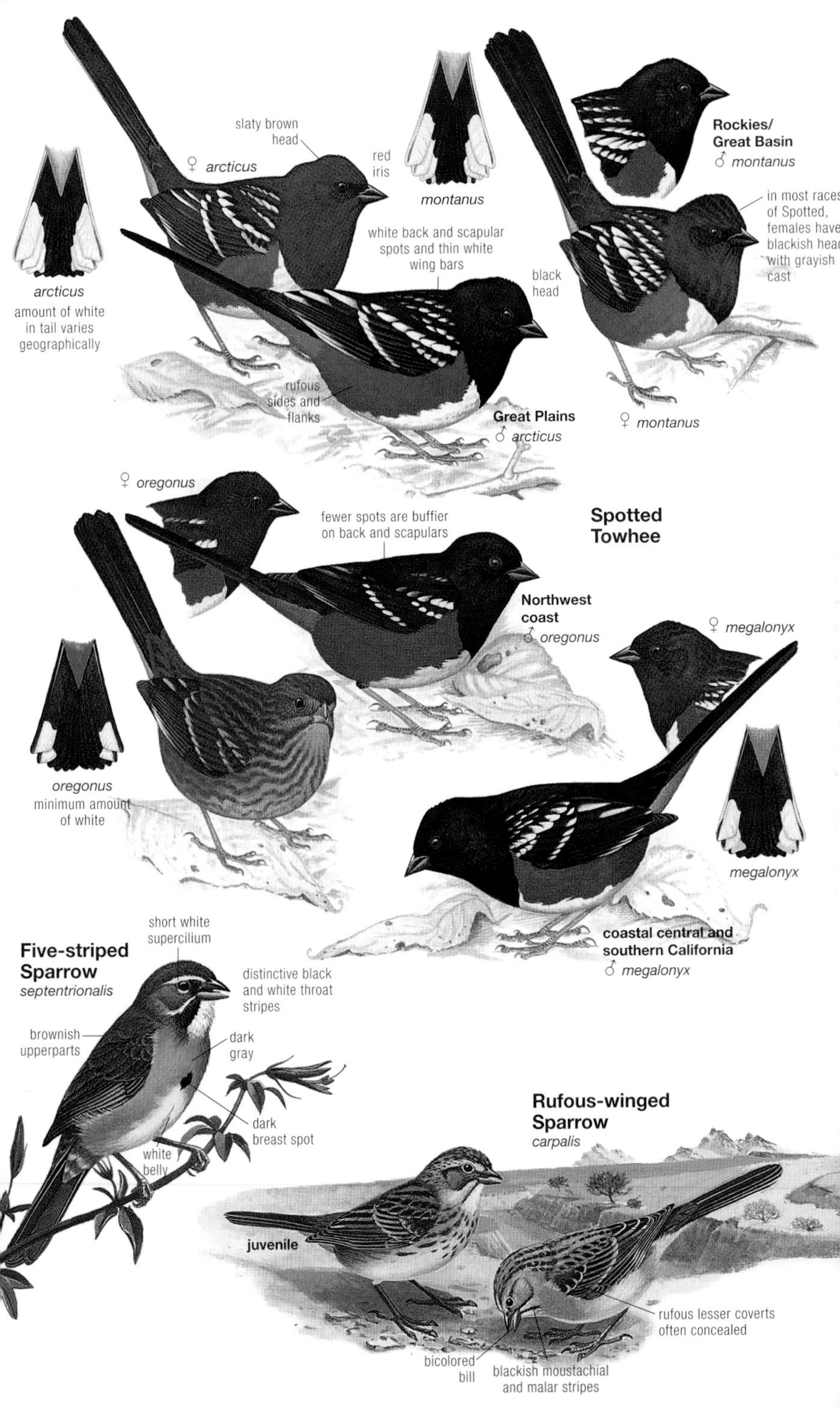
arcticus
amount of white in tail varies geographically
slaty brown head
red iris
♀ arcticus
montanus
Rockies/ Great Basin
♂ montanus
in most races of Spotted, females have blackish head with grayish cast
white back and scapular spots and thin white wing bars
black head
rufous sides and flanks
Great Plains
♂ arcticus
♀ montanus
♀ oregonus
fewer spots are buffier on back and scapulars
Spotted Towhee
Northwest coast
♂ oregonus
♀ megalonyx
oregonus
minimum amount of white
megalonyx
coastal central and southern California
♂ megalonyx
Five-striped Sparrow
septentrionalis
short white supercilium
distinctive black and white throat stripes
brownish upperparts
dark gray
dark breast spot
white belly
Rufous-winged Sparrow
carpalis
juvenile
rufous lesser coverts often concealed
bicolored bill
blackish moustachial and malar stripes

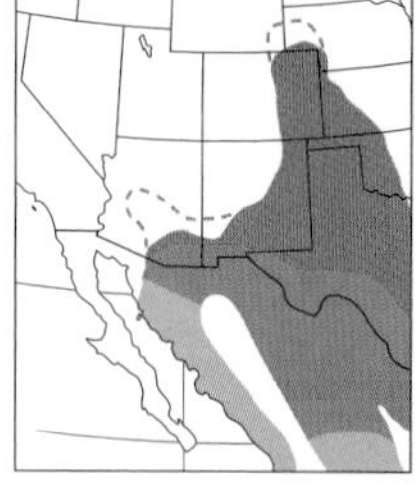

Cassin's Sparrow *Aimophila cassinii L 6" (15 cm)*
A large, drab sparrow, with large bill, fairly flat forehead. Long, rounded tail is dark gray-brown; distinctive white tips on outer feathers are most conspicuous in flight. Gray upperparts are streaked with dull black, brown, and variable amount of rust; blackish marks form anchor marks; underparts are grayish white, usually with a few short streaks on the flanks. ***Juvenile*** is streaked below; paler overall than juvenile Botteri's Sparrow. In fresh fall plumage, shows bolder white wing bars than similar Botteri's as well as black-centered, white-fringed tertials.
Voice: Best located and identified by song, often given in brief, fluttery song flight: typically a soft double whistle, then a loud, sweet trill, followed by a low whistle, and a final, slightly higher note; or a series of *chip* notes ending in a trill or warbles. Also gives a trill of *pit* notes.
Range: Secretive; inhabits arid grasslands with scattered shrubs, cactus, and mesquite. Irregular at northern edge of breeding range, probably due to variation in rainfall. Casual to California and southern Nevada in spring and fall.

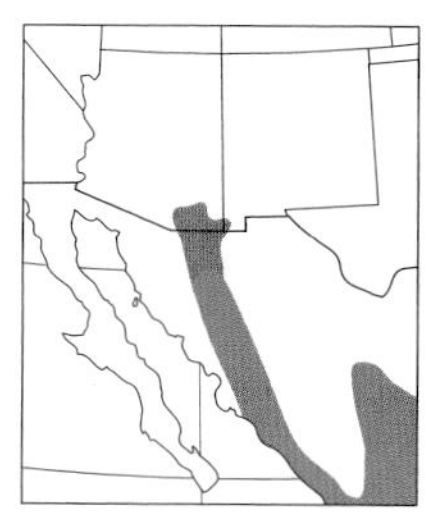

Botteri's Sparrow *Aimophila botterii L 6" (15 cm)*
A large, plain sparrow with large bill, fairly flat forehead; tail long, rounded, dusky brown, lacking white tips and central barring of very similar Cassin's Sparrow. Upperparts streaked with dull black, rust or brown, and gray; underparts unstreaked; throat and belly whitish, breast and sides buff. The southwestern subspecies *arizonae*, which breeds in southeastern Arizona and extreme southwestern New Mexico, is quite reddish above. ***Juvenile***'s belly is buffy; breast is broadly streaked, sides are narrowly streaked.
Voice: Best located and identified by song: several high sharp *tsip* or *che-lik* notes, often followed by a short, accelerating, rattly trill.
Range: Generally secretive; inhabits grasslands (particularly sacaton grass) dotted with mesquite, cactus, and brush. A pair present in June 1997 in Presidio County, west Texas, was not identified to subspecies.

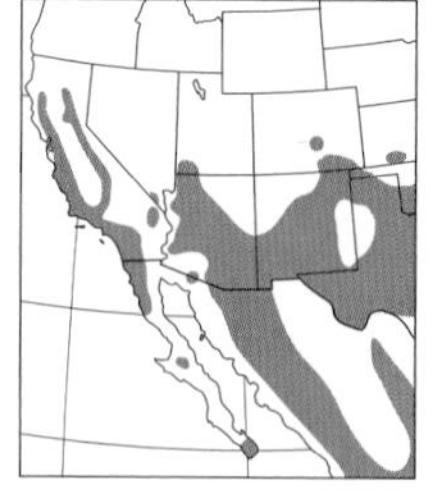

Rufous-crowned Sparrow *Aimophila ruficeps L 6" (15 cm)*
Gray head with dark reddish crown, distinct whitish eye ring, rufous line extending back from eye, single black malar stripe on each side of face. Gray-brown above, with reddish streaks; gray below; long, rounded tail. Subspecies range in overall color from paler, grayer *eremoeca,* found over most of eastern interior range, to widespread southwestern race, *scottii,* which is paler and reddish. Pacific coastal races are slightly smaller and darker and show variable amounts of reddish above. ***Juvenile*** is buffier above; breast and crown streaked; may show two pale wing bars.
Voice: Distinctive call is a sharp *dear,* usually given in a series; song is a rapid, bubbling series of *chip* notes.
Range: Uncommon to locally common resident on rocky hillsides and steep brushy or grassy slopes.

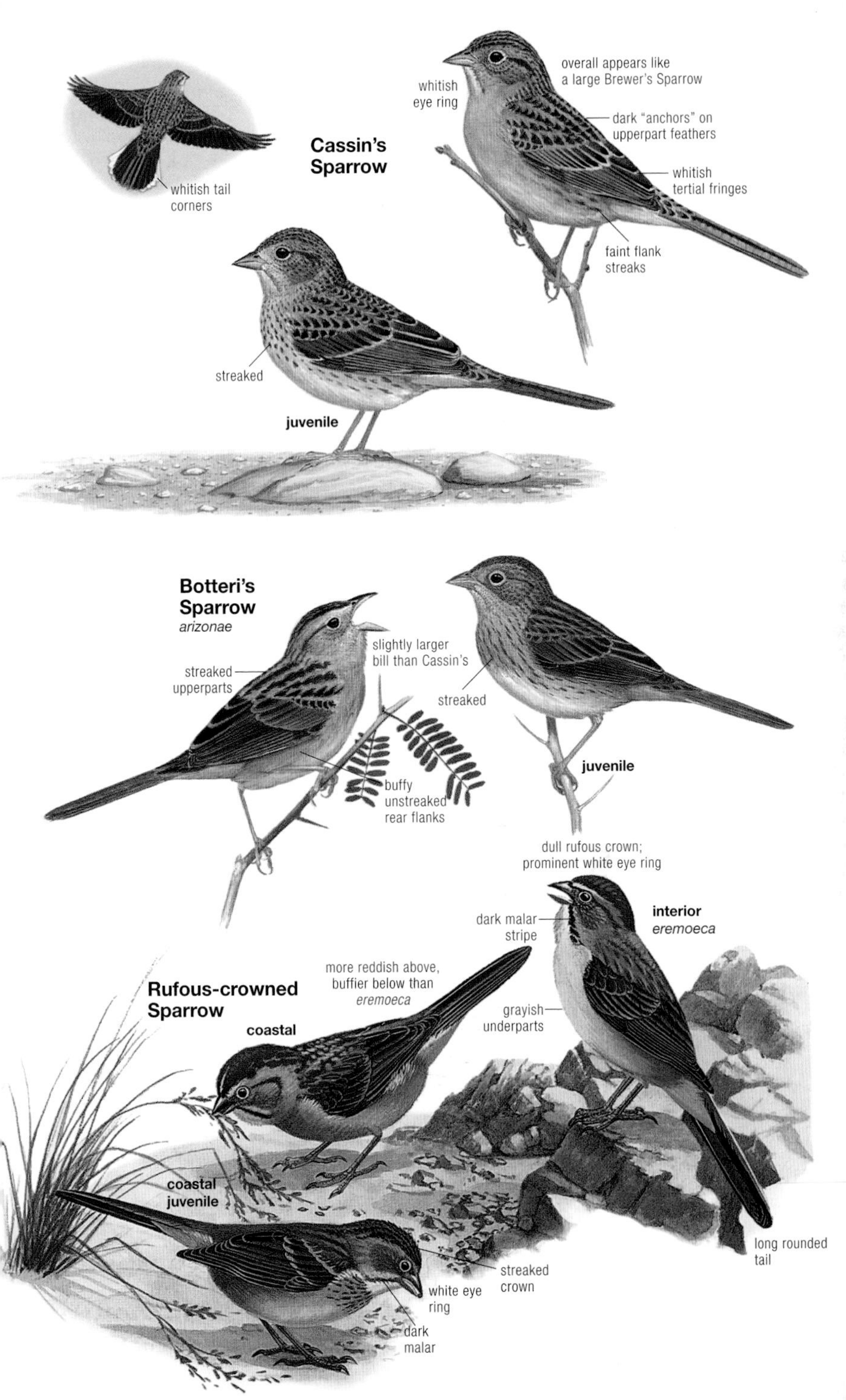
Cassin's Sparrow
whitish tail corners
whitish eye ring
overall appears like a large Brewer's Sparrow
dark "anchors" on upperpart feathers
whitish tertial fringes
faint flank streaks
streaked
juvenile
Botteri's Sparrow
arizonae
slightly larger bill than Cassin's
streaked upperparts
streaked
buffy unstreaked rear flanks
juvenile
dull rufous crown; prominent white eye ring
dark malar stripe
interior
eremoeca
Rufous-crowned Sparrow
more reddish above, buffier below than eremoeca
coastal
grayish underparts
coastal juvenile
long rounded tail
streaked crown
white eye ring
dark malar

Genus *Spizella*

Spizella sparrows are small and slim, and they have long, notched tails. They are gregarious, except during breeding season. Immatures and winter birds of special species may be difficult to separate.

Chipping Sparrow *Spizella passerina L 5½" (14 cm)*
Breeding adult identified by chestnut crown, white eyebrow, black line extending from bill through eye to ear; note also gray nape and cheek with no dark moustachial stripe; gray unstreaked rump. ***Winter adult*** has streaked crown showing some rufous color. ***First-winter*** bird averages little or no rufous on the crown; breast and sides tinged with buff. ***Juvenal*** plumage, often held into Oct., especially in the West, underparts prominently streaked; crown usually lacks rufous; rump may show streaks.
Voice: Song, rapid trill of dry *chip* notes, is all on one pitch. Flight call, also given perched, is a high, hard *seep* or *tsik.*
Range: Widespread and common, found on lawns and in fields, woodland edges, and pine-oak forests. Casual to western Alaska. Very rare in winter north of mapped range.

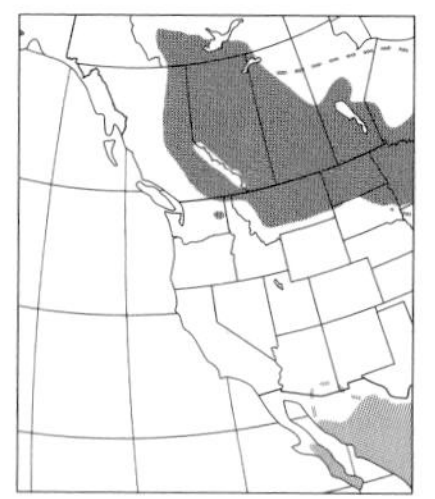

Clay-colored Sparrow *Spizella pallida L 5½" (14 cm)*
Brown crown with black streaks and a distinct buffy white or whitish median crown stripe. Broad, whitish eyebrow; pale lores; brown cheek outlined by dark postocular and moustachial stripes; conspicuous pale submoustachial stripe. Nape gray; back and scapulars are buffy brown, with dark streaks; rump is not streaked but color does not contrast with back as in Chipping Sparrow. Adult in fall and winter is buffier overall. ***Juvenile*** and ***immature*** birds are much buffier; gray nape and pale stripe on sides of throat stand out more; in juvenile, breast and sides are streaked.
Voice: Song is a brief series of insectlike buzzes. Flight call is a thin *sip.*
Range: Fairly common to common in western breeding range and fairly common migrant on western Great Plains. Rare but regular in fall, very rare in winter and spring to remainder of West; casual to the Yukon and Alaska.

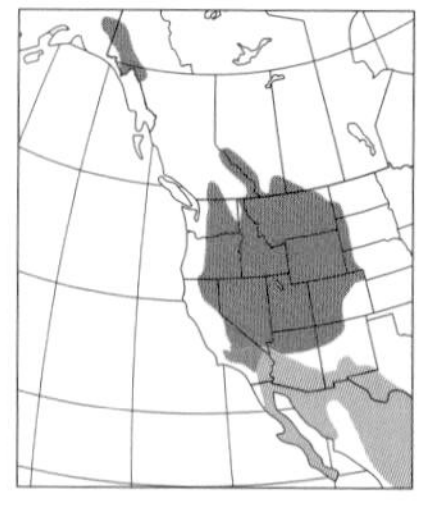

Brewer's Sparrow *Spizella breweri L 5½" (14 cm)*
Brown crown with fine black streaks; unlike Clay-colored, no clearly defined, pale median crown stripe or strong contrast. Distinct whitish eye ring; grayish white eyebrow; ear patch pale brown with darker borders; pale lores; dark malar stripe. Upperparts buffy brown, streaked; rump buffy brown, may be lightly streaked. ***Juvenile*** buffier overall, lightly streaked breast, sides. Immatures and fall and winter adults somewhat buffy below. Another subspecies, *taverni* (not shown) of the alpine zone of the Canadian Rockies to east-central Alaska, has a slightly different song, slightly larger bill, some streaking on flanks; juveniles heavily streaked.
Voice: Song is a series of varied bubbling notes and buzzy trills at different pitches. Call is a thin *sip,* like Clay-colored.
Range: Breeds in sagebrush flats. Scarce migrant along western Great Plains and Pacific coast.

rufous crown
white supercilium
dark eye line in all plumages
breeding
no dark moustachial stripe
Chipping Sparrow
passerina
contrasty gray rump, but often hidden by folded wings
winter adult
juvenile
streaky juvenal plumage seen into October
buffy breast
1st winter
all have pale lores unlike Chipping
bold head pattern, including strong median crown stripe and buffy cast to plumage
contrasty grayish nape
dark moustachial and broad, pale submoustachial stripes
breeding
brownish rump
immature
juvenile
Clay-colored Sparrow
head pattern like Clay-colored, but more muted and without contrastingly pale median crown stripe
white eye ring
brownish rump
juvenile
Brewer's Sparrow
breweri

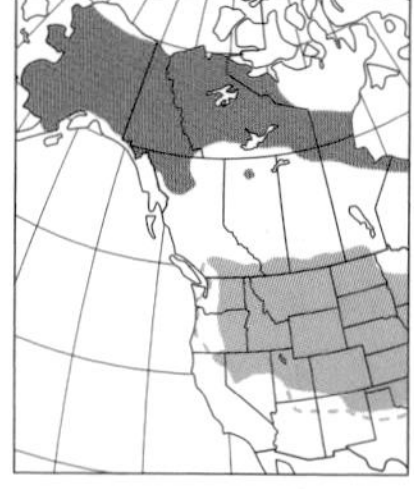

American Tree Sparrow *Spizella arborea L 6¼" (16 cm)*
Large *Spizella* with rufous patches on sides of breast; buffy sides; dark central breast spot; outer tail feathers thinly edged with white. ***Winter*** birds buffier; crown also less solidly rufous. ***Juvenile*** streaked on head and underparts. Western *ochracea* paler overall.
Voice: Calls are a musical *teedle-eet* and a thin *seet.* Song begins with several clear notes followed by a variable, rapid warble.
Range: Fairly common on western Great Plains. Breeds along edge of tundra, in open areas with scattered trees and brush. Winters in weedy fields, marshes, groves of small trees. Uncommon to rare west of Rockies, casual south to southern California, Arizona.

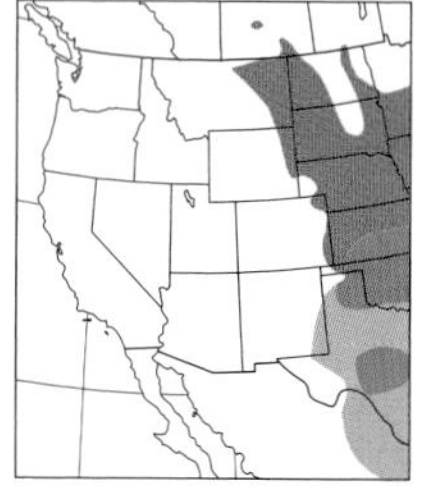

Field Sparrow *Spizella pusilla L 5¾" (15 cm)*
Gray face with reddish crown, distinct whitish eye ring, bright pink bill. Back is streaked except on gray-brown rump. Breast and sides are buffy red; belly grayish white; legs pink. ***Juvenile*** streaked below; wing bars buffy. Birds in westernmost part of range, *arenacea* (only subspecies recorded in West so far), are paler and grayer; extremes are shown here.
Voice: Song is a series of clear, plaintive whistles accelerating into a trill; *chip* note is similar to Orange-crowned Warbler.
Range: Uncommon in limited western mapped range in open, brushy swales and fields. Casual west of mapped range.

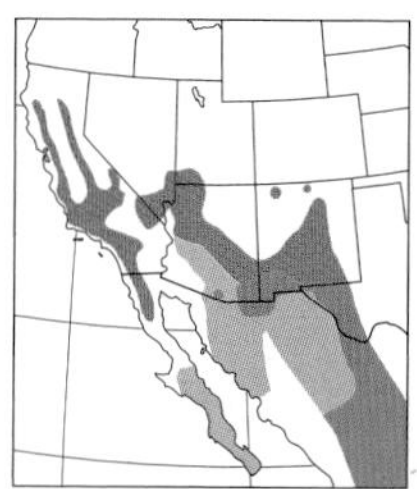

Black-chinned Sparrow *Spizella atrogularis L 5¾" (15 cm)*
Medium gray overall; back and scapulars rusty, with black streaks; bill bright pink; long tail. ***Male*** has black lores and chin; long tail is all-dark. ***Female*** has less or no black. ***Juvenile*** and winter birds lack any black on face; juvenile is faintly streaked.
Voice: Plaintive song begins with slow *sweet sweet sweet* and continues in a rapid trill. Call is a high, thin *seep.*
Range: Inhabits brushy arid slopes in foothills and mountains. Rarely seen in migration. Casual north to Oregon.

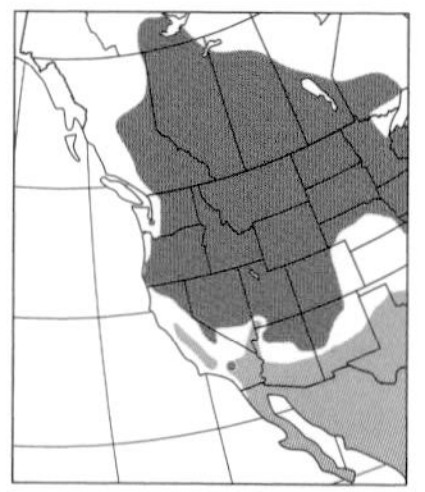

Vesper Sparrow *Pooecetes gramineus L 6¼" (16 cm)*
White eye ring; dark ear patch bordered in white along lower and rear edges; white outer tail feathers. Lacks bold eyebrow of Savannah (next page). Distinctive chestnut lesser coverts not easily seen.
Voice: Song is rich and melodious: two long, slurred notes followed by two higher notes, then a series of short, descending trills. Call is a sharp tip; also a *Spizella*-like flight call.
Range: Uncommon to fairly common in dry grasslands, farmlands, clearings, and sagebrush. Rare along most of Pacific coast.

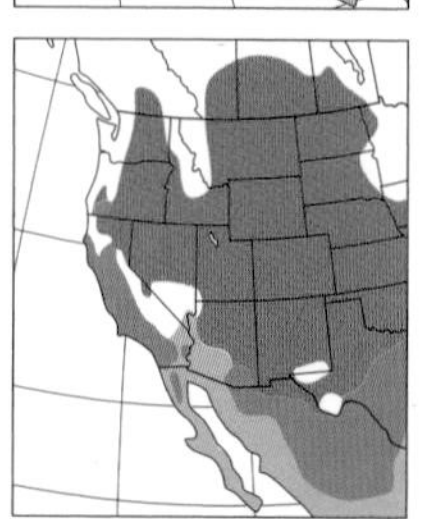

Lark Sparrow *Chondestes grammacus L 6½" (17 cm)*
Head pattern distinctive in adults; note dark central breast spot. ***Juvenile***'s colors are duller; breast, sides, and crown streaked. In all ages, white-cornered tail is conspicuous in flight.
Voice: Song begins with two loud, clear notes, followed by a series of rich, melodious notes and trills and unmusical buzzes. Call is a sharp *tsip,* often a rapid series.
Range: Gregarious, found in various types of open country, often along roads. Accidental to the Yukon and Alaska.

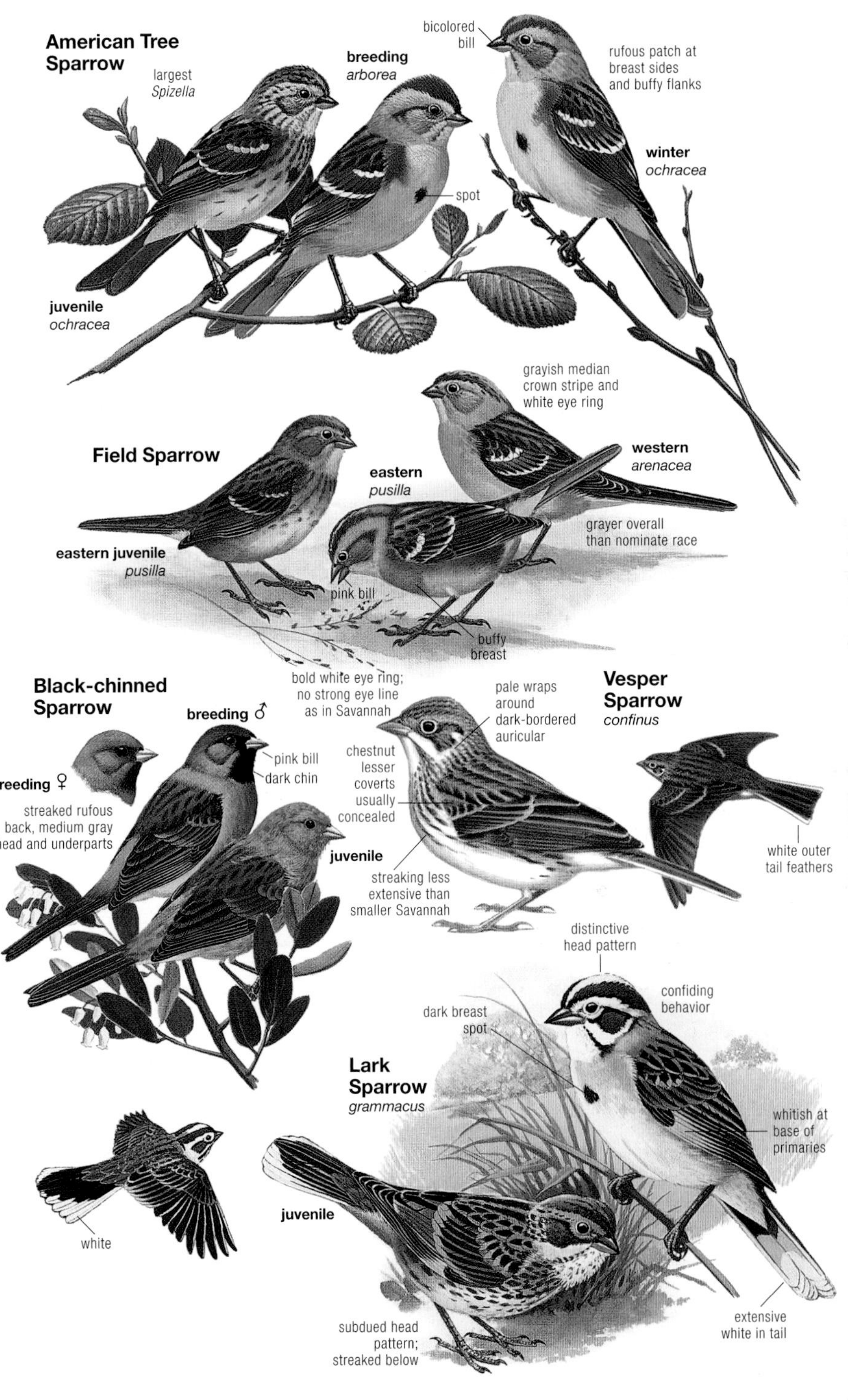
American Tree Sparrow
largest Spizella
breeding arborea
bicolored bill
rufous patch at breast sides and buffy flanks
winter ochracea
spot
juvenile ochracea
Field Sparrow
grayish median crown stripe and white eye ring
western arenacea
eastern pusilla
grayer overall than nominate race
eastern juvenile pusilla
pink bill
buffy breast
Black-chinned Sparrow
breeding ♂
pink bill
dark chin
reeding ♀
streaked rufous back, medium gray head and underparts
juvenile
bold white eye ring; no strong eye line as in Savannah
pale wraps around dark-bordered auricular
Vesper Sparrow confinus
chestnut lesser coverts usually concealed
streaking less extensive than smaller Savannah
white outer tail feathers
distinctive head pattern
confiding behavior
dark breast spot
Lark Sparrow grammacus
whitish at base of primaries
white
juvenile
subdued head pattern; streaked below
extensive white in tail

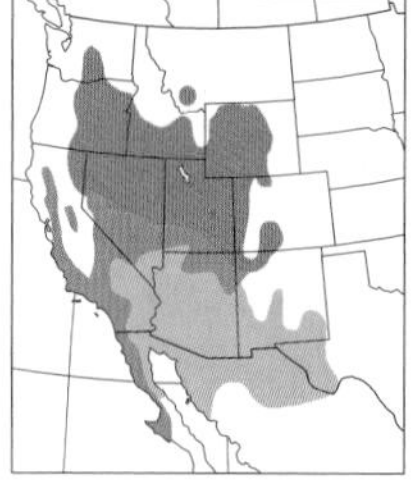

Sage Sparrow *Amphispiza belli L 6¼" (16 cm)*
White eye ring, white supraloral, broad white submoustachial stripe bordered by variable dark malar stripe. Back buffy brown with dusky streaks on interior (largest and palest) race, *nevadensis*. Dark central breast spot, dusky streaking on sides. ***Juvenile*** is duller overall but more streaked. Smaller California coastal race, *belli*, is much darker, lacks streaks on back, has stronger malar stripe, as does intermediate *canescens*. Runs on ground, tail cocked.
Voice: From a low perch, male sings a geographically variable jumbled series of rising and falling phrases. Twittering call consists of thin, juncolike notes.
Range: Interior *nevadensis* and *canescens* favor alkaline flats in sagebrush, saltbush. Coastal *belli* found in montane chaparral. Casual (*nevadensis*) to southern British Columbia and western Great Plains. Ongoing studies may reveal that this complex represents two or three species.

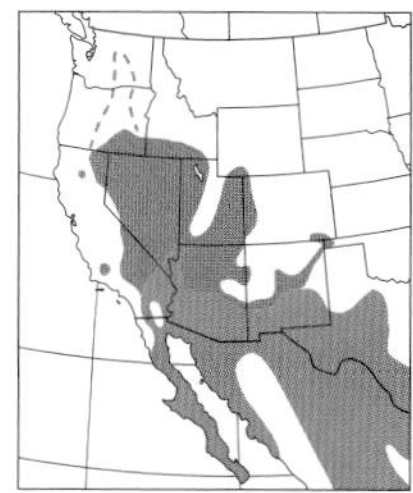

Black-throated Sparrow *Amphispiza bilineata*
L 5½" (14 cm) Triangular black throat patch with bold white border; bold supercilium; unstreaked above. ***Juvenal*** plumage, often held well into fall, lacks black on throat; note bold white eyebrow; breast, back finely streaked. In all ages, extent of white on tail greater than Sage.
Voice: Song is rapid and pitched high: two clear notes followed by a trill; calls are faint, tinkling notes.
Range: Fairly common in desert, especially on rocky slopes. Irregular interior Pacific Northwest; casual to British Columbia, Alberta.

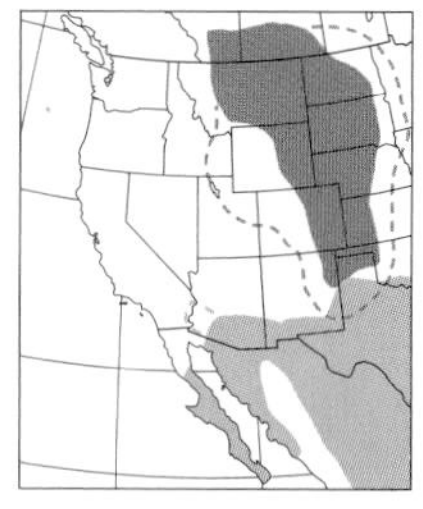

Lark Bunting *Calamospiza melanocorys L 7" (18 cm)*
Stocky, with short tail and whitish wing patches; bill bluish gray. ***Breeding male*** is mostly black. ***Female*** streaked below with brown primaries. ***Winter male*** similar, but has black primaries and throat. In flight, looks short and round winged, with shallow wingbeats. Gregarious in migration and winter.
Voice: Distinctive call is a soft *hoo-ee*. Song is a varied series of rich whistles and trills.
Range: Common; nests in dry plains, especially in sagebrush. Rare in fall and winter to West Coast; casual to Pacific Northwest.

Savannah Sparrow *Passerculus sandwichensis*
L 5½" (14 cm) Highly variable. Eyebrow yellow or whitish; pale median crown stripe; strong postocular stripe. The numerous subspecies vary geographically; extremes are shown here. West Coast races show increasingly darker color from north to south: Alaskan and interior races paler, widespread *nevadensis* palest; *beldingi* of southern California coastal marshes darkest. ***"Large-billed Sparrow,"*** *rostratus* (breeds north of Colorado region, winters on the edge of Salton Sea, rarely in coastal California) dull with large bill.
Voice: Song begins with two or three *chip* notes, followed by two buzzy trills. Distinctive flight call, a thin *seep*. Song of *rostratus*, markedly different from other races, has short, high notes, followed by about three buzzy *dzeeee* notes; call, a soft, metallic *zink*.
Range: Common in a variety of open habitats, marshes.

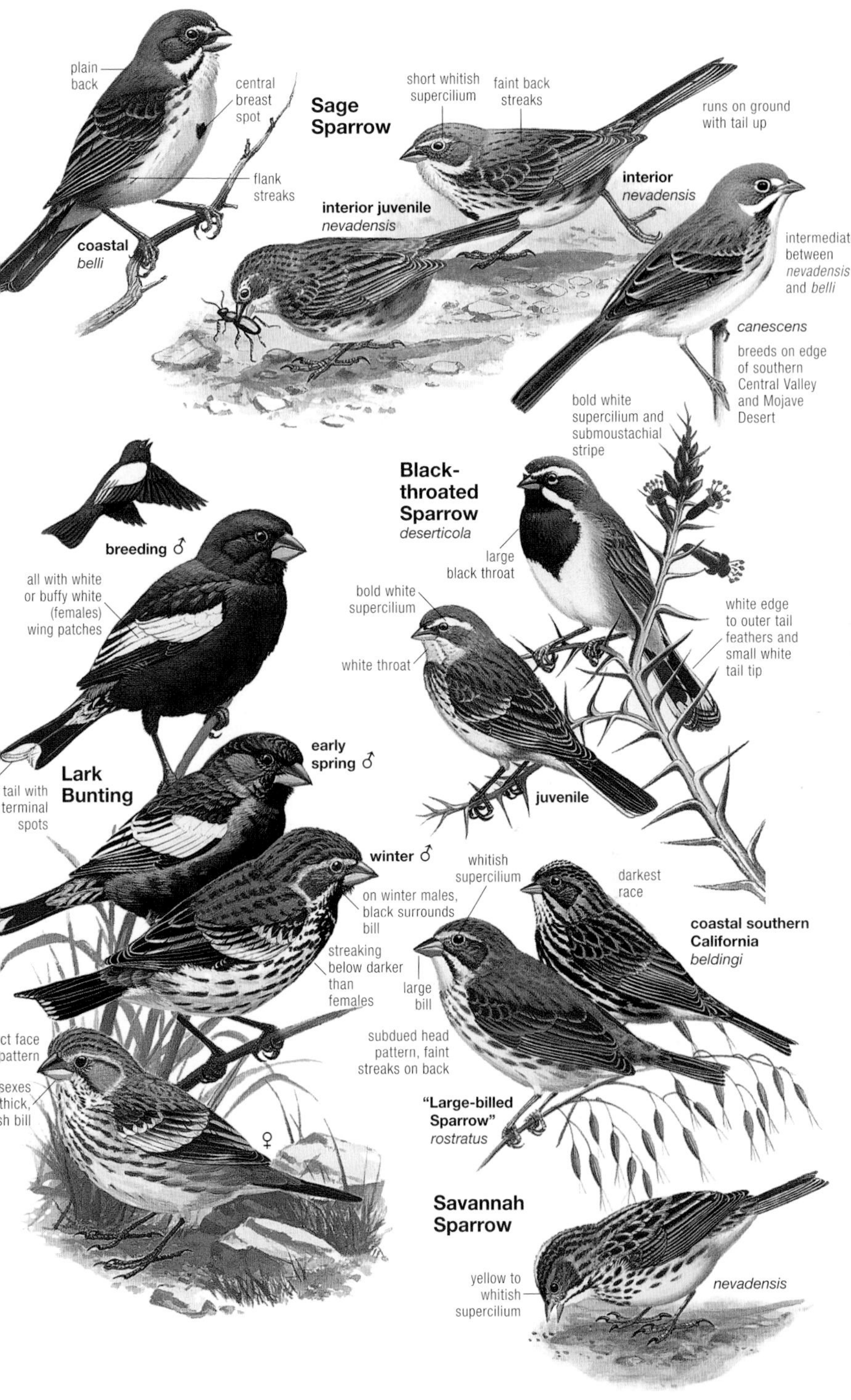

Sage Sparrow
plain back
central breast spot
flank streaks
coastal belli
short whitish supercilium
faint back streaks
runs on ground with tail up
interior nevadensis
interior juvenile nevadensis
intermediate between nevadensis and belli
canescens
breeds on edge of southern Central Valley and Mojave Desert
bold white supercilium and submoustachial stripe
Black-throated Sparrow deserticola
large black throat
bold white supercilium
white throat
white edge to outer tail feathers and small white tail tip
juvenile
breeding ♂
all with white or buffy white (females) wing patches
Lark Bunting
tail with terminal spots
early spring ♂
winter ♂
on winter males, black surrounds bill
streaking below darker than females
ct face pattern
sexes thick, sh bill
♀
whitish supercilium
darkest race
coastal southern California beldingi
large bill
subdued head pattern, faint streaks on back
"Large-billed Sparrow" rostratus
Savannah Sparrow
yellow to whitish supercilium
nevadensis

Genus *Ammodramus*

Sparrows of the genus *Ammodramus* tend to be large headed and large billed; they are usually secretive.

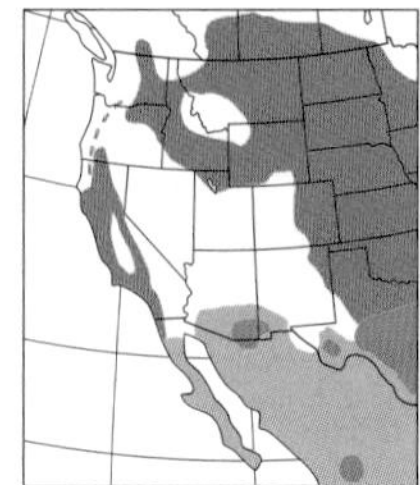

Grasshopper Sparrow *Ammodramus savannarum*
L 5" (13 cm) Small, chunky; short tail, flat head. Buffy breast. Dark crown has a pale central stripe; note also white eye ring, yellow-orange spot in front of eye. Lacks broad buffy orange eyebrow of Le Conte's. Compare also with female Orange Bishop (page 410). ***Juvenile***'s breast and sides streaked with brown. ***Fall*** birds are buffier below but never as bright as Le Conte's. Widespread race is rather pale *perpallidus; ammolegus* of southeastern Arizona is more reddish.
Voice: Main song, one or two high *chip* notes followed by grasshopperlike *buzz;* also a series of varied squeaky and buzzy notes.
Range: Found in pastures, grasslands, and old fields. Somewhat secretive; feeds and nests on the ground; rarely seen in migration.

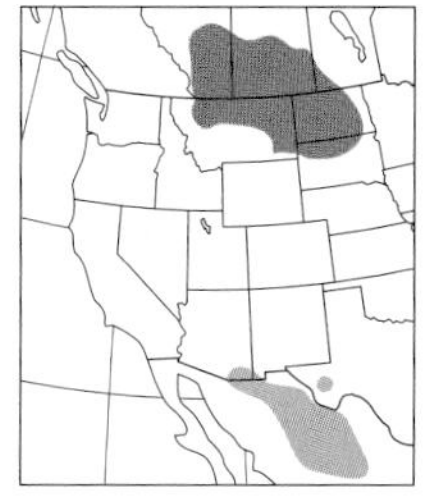

Baird's Sparrow *Ammodramus bairdii L 5½" (14 cm)*
Orange tinge to head (duller on worn summer birds), usually with less distinct median crown stripe than Savannah (previous page); note two isolated dark spots behind ear patch, lack of postocular line. Short, dark, widely spaced streaks on breast form distinct necklace. ***Juvenile***'s white fringes impart a scaly pattern to the upperparts. Very secretive, especially away from breeding grounds.
Voice: Song consists of two or three high, thin notes, followed by a single warbled note and a low trill.
Range: Uncommon, local, declining. Found in grasslands, weedy fields. Rarely seen in migration. Casual (fall) to coastal California.

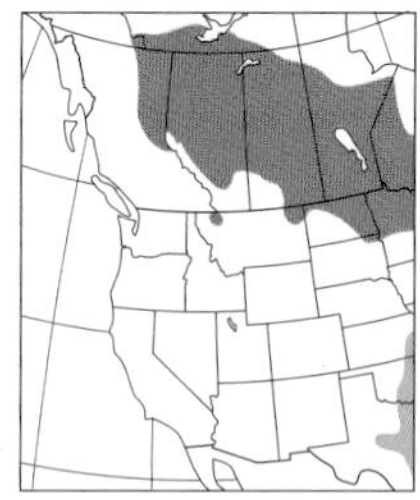

Le Conte's Sparrow *Ammodramus leconteii L 5" (13 cm)*
White central crown stripe, becoming orange on forehead, chestnut streaks on nape, and straw-colored back streaks distinguish Le Conte's from sharp-tailed sparrows. Bright, broad, buffy orange eyebrow, thinner bill, and orange-buff breast and streaked sides separate it from Grasshopper. ***Juvenal*** plumage, seen on breeding grounds and in fall migration, is buffy; crown stripe tawny; breast heavily streaked. Secretive.
Voice: Song is a short, high, insectlike buzz.
Range: A bird of wet grassy fields, marsh edges. Fairly common in western breeding range; casual otherwise in West.

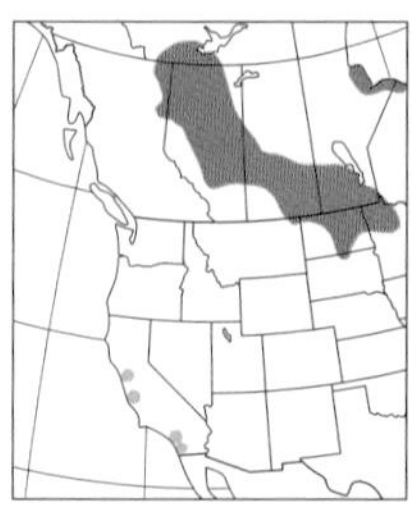

Nelson's Sharp-tailed Sparrow *Ammodramus nelsoni*
4¾" (12 cm) Told from Le Conte's by gray median crown stripe; whitish or gray streaks on scapulars; gray, streakless nape. ***Juvenile*** has fainter median crown stripe; duller nape; variably thicker eye line; less contrast above; largely lacks streaking across breast.
Voice: Song, a wheezy *p-tssssshh-uk,* ends on a lower note.
Range: Uncommon and local in western breeding range. Very rare in winter on California coast. Casual migrant otherwise. A very late spring migrant. Western breeders and all others recorded are of bright prairie race, *nelsoni;* a few perhaps of similar *alterus.*

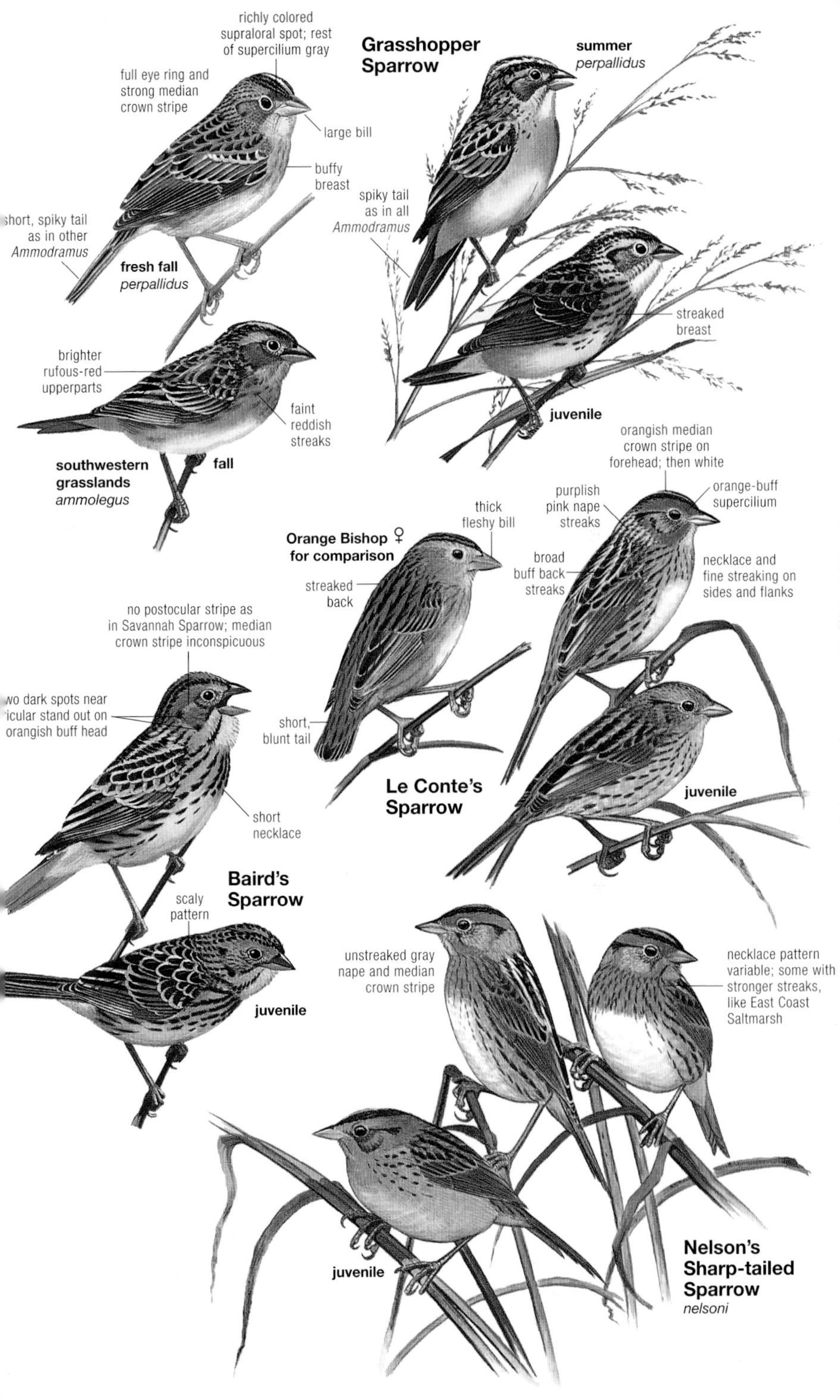
richly colored
supraloral spot; rest
of supercilium gray
Grasshopper
Sparrow
summer
perpallidus
full eye ring and
strong median
crown stripe
large bill
buffy
breast
spiky tail
as in all
Ammodramus
short, spiky tail
as in other
Ammodramus
fresh fall
perpallidus
streaked
breast
brighter
rufous-red
upperparts
faint
reddish
streaks
juvenile
southwestern
grasslands
ammolegus
fall
orangish median
crown stripe on
forehead; then white
purplish
pink nape
streaks
orange-buff
supercilium
thick
fleshy bill
Orange Bishop ♀
for comparison
broad
buff back
streaks
necklace and
fine streaking on
sides and flanks
streaked
back
no postocular stripe as
in Savannah Sparrow; median
crown stripe inconspicuous
wo dark spots near
icular stand out on
orangish buff head
short,
blunt tail
Le Conte's
Sparrow
juvenile
short
necklace
Baird's
Sparrow
scaly
pattern
juvenile
unstreaked gray
nape and median
crown stripe
necklace pattern
variable; some with
stronger streaks,
like East Coast
Saltmarsh
juvenile
Nelson's
Sharp-tailed
Sparrow
nelsoni

Genus *Melospiza*

Members of the genus *Melospiza* have relatively long, rounded tails and are found in brushy habitats.

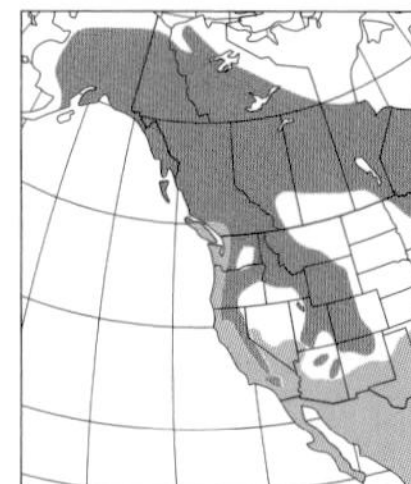

Lincoln's Sparrow *Melospiza lincolnii L 5¾" (15 cm)*
Buffy wash and fine streaks on breast and sides, contrasting with whitish, unstreaked belly. Note broad gray eyebrow, whitish chin and eye ring. Briefly held ***juvenal*** plumage is paler overall than juvenile Swamp Sparrow. Distinguished from juvenile Song Sparrow by shorter tail, slimmer bill, and thinner malar stripe, often broken. Often raises slight crest when disturbed.
Voice: Two call notes: a flat *tschup,* repeated in a series as an alarm call; and a sharp, buzzy *zeee.* Rich, loud song, a rapid, bubbling trill.
Range: Found in brushy bogs and mountain meadows; in winter prefers thickets.

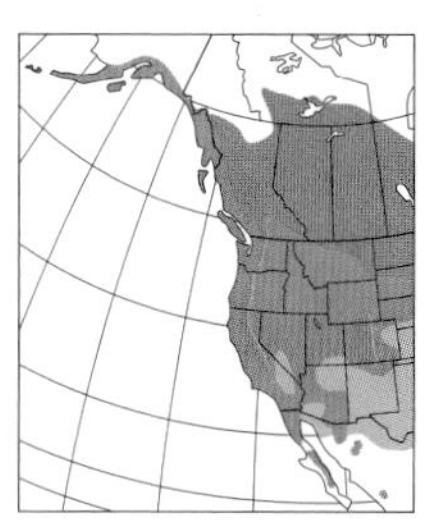

Song Sparrow *Melospiza melodia L 4¾-6¾" (13-17 cm)*
All subspecies have long, rounded tail, pumped in flight. All show broad grayish eyebrow and broad, dark malar stripe bordering whitish throat. Highly variable. Upperparts are usually streaked. Underparts whitish; streaking on sides and breast often converges in a central spot. Legs and feet are pinkish. ***Juvenile*** is buffier overall, with finer streaking. The numerous subspecies vary geographically in size, bill shape, overall coloration, and streaking. Eastern birds, now generally treated as one race, nominate *melodia,* breed west to northeastern British Columbia; winter west to west Texas. Large Alaskan races, the largest resident on the Aleutians, reach an extreme in the gray-brown *maxima;* paler races such as *fallax* inhabit southwestern deserts; *morphna* represents the darker, redder races of the Pacific Northwest; *heermanni* is one of the blackish-streaked California races.
Voice: Typical song has three or four short clear notes followed by a buzzy *tow-wee,* then a trill. Distinctive call note is a nasal, hollow *chimp.*
Range: Generally common; found in brushy areas and marshes, especially dense streamside thickets.

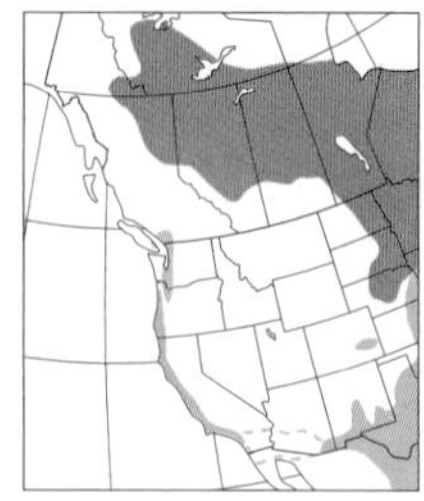

Swamp Sparrow *Melospiza georgiana L 5¾" (15 cm)*
Gray face; rich rufous upperparts and wings; variable black streaks on back; white throat. ***Breeding adult*** has reddish crown, gray breast, and whitish belly. ***Winter adult*** is buffier overall; crown is streaked, shows gray central stripe; sides are rich buff. Briefly held ***juvenal*** plumage is usually even buffier; darker overall than juvenile Lincoln's or Song Sparrows; wings and tail redder. ***Immature*** resembles winter adult.
Voice: Typical song is a slow, musical trill, all on one pitch. Two call notes: a prolonged *zeee,* softer than Lincoln's Sparrow, and an Eastern Phoebe–like *chip.*
Range: Nests in dense, vegetation in marshes and bogs. Winters in marshes and brushy fields. Generally rare in the West south of breeding range where fairly common.

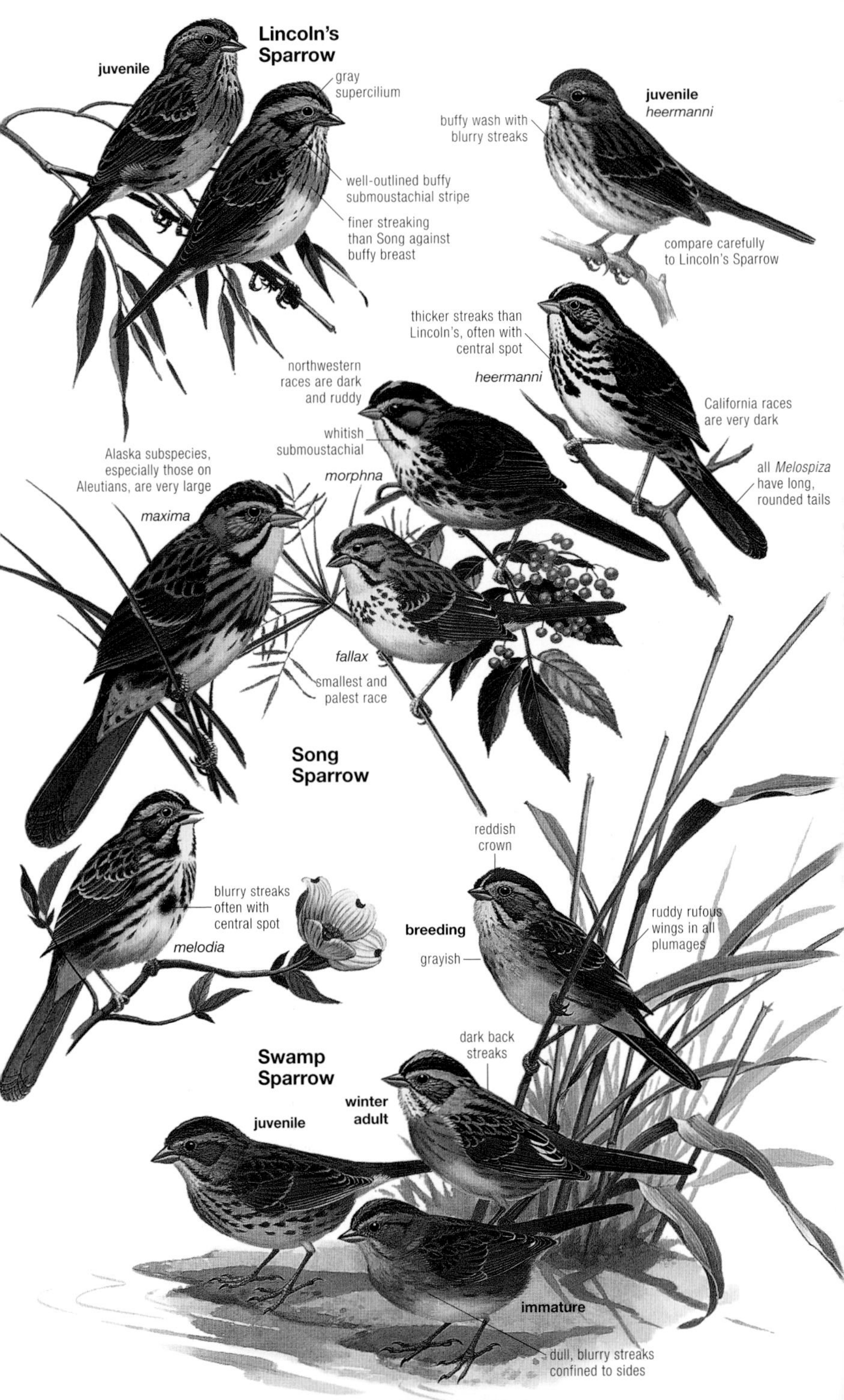

Lincoln's Sparrow
juvenile
gray supercilium
well-outlined buffy submoustachial stripe
finer streaking than Song against buffy breast
juvenile heermanni
buffy wash with blurry streaks
compare carefully to Lincoln's Sparrow
thicker streaks than Lincoln's, often with central spot
heermanni
California races are very dark
all Melospiza have long, rounded tails
northwestern races are dark and ruddy
whitish submoustachial
morphna
Alaska subspecies, especially those on Aleutians, are very large
maxima
fallax
smallest and palest race
Song Sparrow
blurry streaks often with central spot
melodia
reddish crown
breeding
grayish
ruddy rufous wings in all plumages
Swamp Sparrow
dark back streaks
winter adult
juvenile
immature
dull, blurry streaks confined to sides

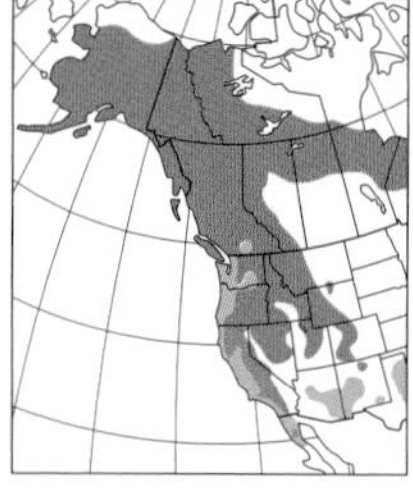

Fox Sparrow *Passerella iliaca L 7" (18 cm)*
Large and highly variable species. Most subspecies have reddish rump and tail; reddish in wings; underparts heavily marked with triangular spots merging into a larger spot on central breast. The many named subspecies are divided into four subspecies groups; may represent distinct species. The brightest, *iliaca,* and the slightly duller *zaboria* (***"Red"*** group) breed in the far north, from Seward Peninsula, Alaska, to Newfoundland; winter mostly in southeastern U.S. Western mountain races have gray head and back, grayish olive base to bill; range from small-billed Rockies *schistacea* (***"Slate-colored"*** group) to large-billed California *stephensi* (***"Thick-billed"*** group). Dark coastal races (***"Sooty"*** group), with browner rumps and tails, vary from sooty *fuliginosa* of the Pacific Northwest to paler *unalaschcensis* of southwest Alaska.
Voice: Songs are sweet, melodic in northern, "Red" group; include harsher trills in other races. Large-billed Pacific races give a sharp *chink* call, like California Towhee; others give a hard *thk* note, like Lincoln's Sparrow but louder, though in "Slate-colored," call is slightly downslurred, more of a *tewk.*
Range: Uncommon to common; found in undergrowth in coniferous or deciduous woodlands and montane chaparral. Within "Sooty" group, paler northernmost races migrate the farthest south; it is casual east to Arizona. The "Slate-colored" group migrates primarily southwest to California. The "Red" group very rare south of breeding range in West.

Genus *Zonotrichia*

This genus, the "crowned" sparrows, includes some of the largest sparrows in North America. They have striking crown patterns and generally plain underparts as adults. In the nonbreeding season they form flocks in brushy areas. Their whistled songs, often quavering, may be given year-round.

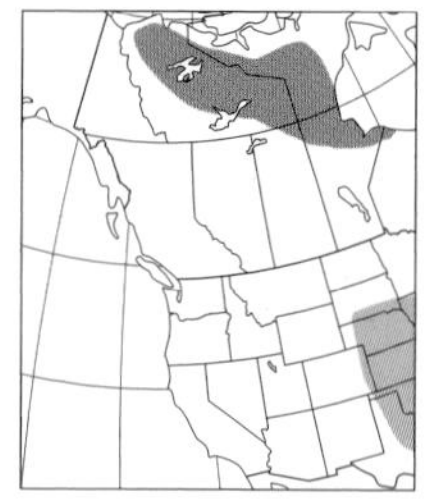

Harris's Sparrow *Zonotrichia querula L 7½" (19 cm)*
Large sparrow with black crown and bib; pink bill. ***Winter adult***'s crown is blackish; cheeks buffy; throat may be all-black or show partial white band. In ***breeding*** plumage the crown and face are extensively black and the sides of the head are silvery gray with a prominent black postocular mark. ***Immature*** resembles winter adult but shows less black; white throat is bordered by dark malar stripe.
Voice: Song is a series of long, clear, quavering whistles, often beginning with two notes on one pitch followed by two notes on another pitch. Calls include a loud *wink* and a drawn-out *tseep.*
Range: Nests in stunted boreal forest; winters in open woodlands, brushlands, and hedgerows. Rare migrant and winter visitor over much of West.

small bill
"Slate-colored"
schistacea
gray back
large bill
in both groups, rufous tail contrasts with gray rump and back
Fox Sparrow
fous tail
"Thick-billed"
stephensi
rufous streaking on gray back
rufous in cheek
"Red"
iliaca
"Sooty"
unalaschcensis
rufous streaking below
thick, dark streaks coalescing on breast
"Sooty" races overall dark brown with little contrast between tail and back; more southerly breeding races darker than those from south-coastal and southwestern Alaska
"Sooty"
fuliginosa
black crown and bib
large pink bill
breeding
winter adults
dark postocular spot in all plumages
Harris's Sparrow
dark chest patch
immature
brownish flank streaking

Golden-crowned Sparrow *Zonotrichia atricapilla*
L 7" (18 cm) Yellow patch tops black crown; back brownish, streaked with dark brown; breast, sides and flanks grayish brown. Bill is dusky above, pale below. Yellow is less distinct on ***immature***'s brown crown. Briefly held ***juvenal*** plumage has dark streaks on breast and sides. ***Winter adults*** are duller overall; amount of black on crown varies.
Voice: Song is a series of three or more plaintive, whistled notes: *oh dear me.* Calls include a soft *tseep* and a flat *tsick.*
Range: Fairly common in stunted boreal bogs and in open areas near tree line, especially in willows. Winters in dense woodlands, tangles, and brush. Rare well east of coastal region in migration and winter.

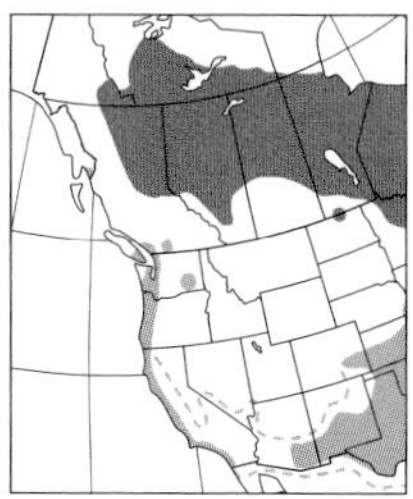

White-throated Sparrow *Zonotrichia albicollis*
L 6¾" (17 cm) Conspicuous and strongly outlined white throat; mostly dark bill; dark crown stripes and eye line. Broad eyebrow is yellow in front of eye; remainder is either white or tan. Upperparts rusty brown; underparts grayish, sometimes with diffuse streaking. ***Juvenile***'s eyebrow and throat are grayish, breast and sides heavily streaked.
Voice: Song is a thin whistle, generally two single notes followed by three triple notes: *pure sweet Canada Canada Canada,* often heard in winter. Calls include a sharp *pink* and a drawn-out, lisping *tseep.*
Range: Nests in mixed woodlands; winters in woodland undergrowth, brush, and gardens. Generally rare in the West south of breeding range; usually found with Golden-crowned or White-crowned Sparrow.

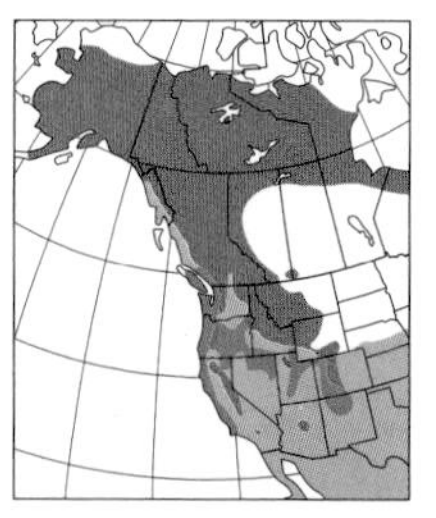

White-crowned Sparrow *Zonotrichia leucophrys*
L 7" (18 cm) Black-and-white striped crown; pink, orange, or yellowish bill; whitish throat; underparts mostly gray. ***Juvenile***'s head brown and buff, underparts streaked. ***Immature*** has tan and brownish head stripes, clean grayish white below; compare with immature Golden-crowned. Both *leucophrys,* mainly found in the east Canadian tundra (probably casual in West), and very similar, slightly paler *oriantha* (not shown), mainly of the High Sierra, southern Cascades, and Rockies and Great Basin ranges, have a black supraloral area and large, dark pink bill; *gambelii,* breeding from Alaska to Hudson Bay, has whitish supraloral and a smaller, orange-yellow bill; in coastal *nuttalli* and *pugetensis* (not shown), breast and back are browner, bill dull yellow, supraloral pale.
Voice: Song, often heard in winter, is usually one or more thin, whistled notes followed by a twittering trill; *leucophrys* and *gambelii* give a more mournful song with no trill at the end. Calls include a loud *pink* (sharper in *oriantha*) and sharp *tseep.*
Range: Common in various habitats. Montane *oriantha* winters primarily in western Mexico; small numbers irregularly to southeastern Arizona; late spring (primarily May) and early fall migrant (Sept.) in relation to *gambelii.* With Pacific races, *nuttalli* is resident, wing shorter than *pugetensis* (not shown). A few *pugetensis* winter inland in the Pacific states; casual to western Nevada.

yellow supraloral
spot; dark bill

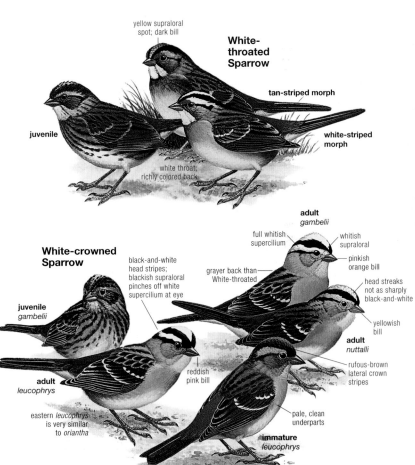

White-throated Sparrow

tan-striped morph

juvenile

white-striped
morph

white throat;
richly colored back

adult
gambelii

full whitish
supercilium

whitish
supraloral

pinkish
orange bill

White-crowned Sparrow

black-and-white
head stripes;
blackish supraloral
pinches off white
supercilium at eye

grayer back than
White-throated

head streaks
not as sharply
black-and-white

juvenile
gambelii

yellowish
bill

adult
nuttalli

reddish
pink bill

rufous-brown
lateral crown
stripes

adult
leucophrys

eastern *leucophrys*
is very similar
to *oriantha*

pale, clean
underparts

immature
leucophrys

Genus *Junco*

Familiar birds at feeders in winter, juncos are quite gregarious except during breeding season. All have white outer tail feathers.

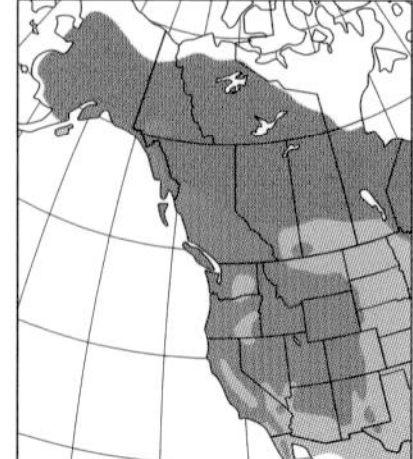

Dark-eyed Junco *Junco hyemalis L 6¼" (16 cm)*
Variable; most races have a gray or brown head and breast sharply set off from white belly. White outer tail feathers are conspicuous in flight. ***Male*** of the ***"Slate-colored Junco"*** group of subspecies has a dark gray hood; upperparts are entirely or mostly gray. ***Female*** is browner overall. ***Juveniles*** of all races are streaked. Northern "Slate-colored" breeds west to Alaska and winters mostly in eastern North America; uncommon to rare in the West. Male ***"Oregon Junco"*** of the West has slaty to blackish hood, rufous-brown to buffy brown back and sides; females have duller hood color. Of the eight subspecies in the "Oregon" group (two are resident in northern Baja California), the more southerly races are paler. ***"Pink-sided Junco,"*** *mearnsi* (considered within "Oregon" group)—breeding in the central Rockies and wintering from western Great Plains to the foothills of the Southwest and northern Mexico, rarely to southern California—has broad, pinkish cinnamon sides that sometimes meet across the breast, blue-gray hood, and blackish lores. ***"White-winged Junco,"*** *aikeni*—breeding in the Black Hills area and wintering largely in the Front Range south to north-central New Mexico, rarely on Great Plains and casually to Southwest and California—is mostly pale gray above, usually with two thin, white wing bars; also larger, with a bigger bill and more white on tail. In ***"Gray-headed Junco"*** of the southern Rockies, the pale gray hood is barely darker than the underparts; back is rufous. It winters on the western Great Plains and in the foothills of the Southwest and northern Mexico, rarely to California. In much of Arizona and New Mexico, largely resident "Gray-headed," *dorsalis,* has an even paler throat and a large, bicolored bill, black above and bluish below. Intergrades between some races frequent.
Voice: Song is a musical trill on one pitch, often heard in winter. Varied calls include a sharp *dit* and, in flight, a rapid twittering. Some songs and calls of "Gray-headed" *dorsalis* are more suggestive of Yellow-eyed Junco.
Range: Breeds in coniferous or mixed woodlands. In migration and winter, found in a variety of habitats, usually in flocks, which in Southwest and western Great Plains contain multiple subspecies.

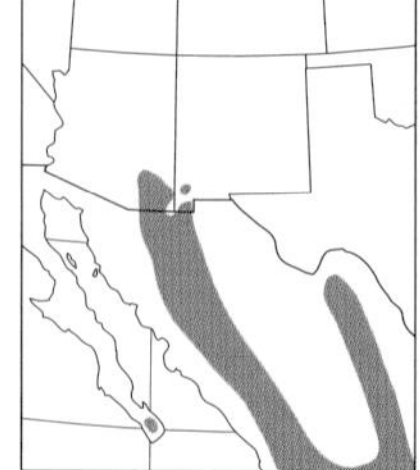

Yellow-eyed Junco *Junco phaeonotus L 6¼" (16 cm)*
Bright yellow eyes, set off by black lores. Pale gray above, with a bright rufous back and rufous-edged greater wing coverts and tertials; underparts paler gray. ***Juveniles*** are similar to juveniles of gray-headed races of Dark-eyed Junco; eye is brown, becoming pale before changing to yellow of adult; look for rufous on wings.
Voice: Song is a variable series of clear, thin whistles and trills. Calls include a high, thin *seep,* similar to Chipping Sparrow.
Range: Resident in coniferous and pine-oak mountains, generally above 6,000 feet. Some move to lower altitude in winter. Casual to west Texas.

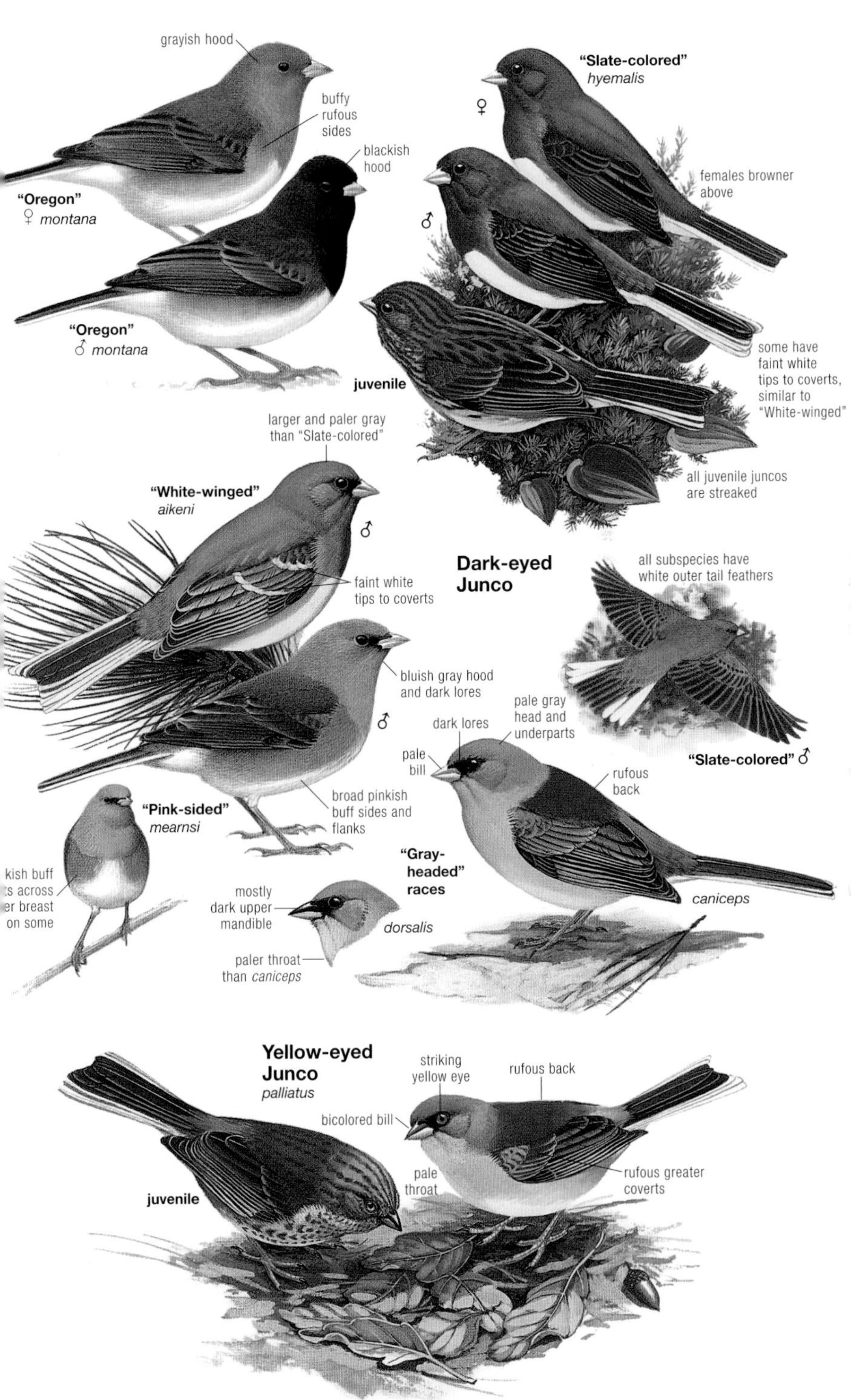

grayish hood
buffy
rufous
sides
blackish
hood
"Oregon"
♀ montana
"Oregon"
♂ montana
"Slate-colored"
hyemalis
♀
females browner
above
♂
juvenile
some have
faint white
tips to coverts,
similar to
"White-winged"
larger and paler gray
than "Slate-colored"
all juvenile juncos
are streaked
"White-winged"
aikeni
♂
faint white
tips to coverts
Dark-eyed
Junco
all subspecies have
white outer tail feathers
bluish gray hood
and dark lores
♂
pale gray
head and
underparts
dark lores
pale
bill
"Slate-colored" ♂
rufous
back
"Pink-sided"
mearnsi
broad pinkish
buff sides and
flanks
"Gray-
headed"
races
caniceps
mostly
dark upper
mandible
dorsalis
paler throat
than caniceps
Yellow-eyed
Junco
palliatus
striking
yellow eye
rufous back
bicolored bill
pale
throat
rufous greater
coverts
juvenile

Genus *Calcarius*

Longspurs are open-country, ground-loving birds. Plumages may vary greatly between male and female, breeding versus nonbreeding.

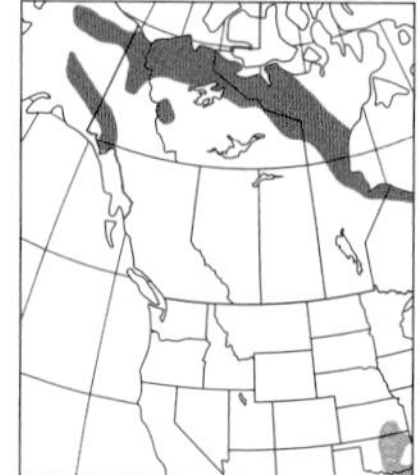

Smith's Longspur *Calcarius pictus L 6¼" (16 cm)*

Outer two feathers on each side of tail are almost entirely white. Bill is thinner than in other longspurs. Note long primary projection, a bit shorter than Lapland, but much longer than Chestnut-collared or McCown's (next page); shows rusty edges to greater coverts and tertials. ***Breeding adult male*** has black-and-white head, rich buff nape and underparts; white patch on shoulder, often obscured. ***Breeding adult female*** and all ***winter*** plumages are duller, crown streaked, chin paler. Dusky ear patch bordered by pale buff eyebrow; pale area on side of neck often breaks through dark rear edge of ear patch. Underparts are pale buff with thin reddish brown streaks on breast and sides. Females have much less white on lesser coverts than males.

Voice: Typical call is a dry, ticking rattle, harder and sharper than Lapland and McCown's Longspurs. Song, heard in spring migration and on the breeding grounds, is delivered only from the ground or a perch. It consists of rapid, melodious warbles, ending with a vigorous *wee-chew.*

Range: Generally uncommon and secretive, especially in migration and winter. Nests on open tundra and damp, tussocky meadows. Winters to east of our region on southeastern Great Plains in open, grassy areas; sometimes seen with Lapland Longspurs. Casual in West south of breeding range.

Lapland Longspur *Calcarius lapponicus L 6¼" (16 cm)*

Outer two feathers on each side of tail are partly white, partly dark. Note also, especially in winter plumages, the reddish edges on the greater coverts and on the tertials. The reddish edges of the tertials form an indented, or notched, shape. ***Breeding adult male***'s head and breast are black and well outlined: a broad white or buffy stripe extends back from eye and down to sides of breast; nape is reddish brown. ***Breeding adult female*** and all ***winter*** plumages are duller; note bold dark triangle outlining plain buffy ear patch; dark streaks (female) or patch (male) on upper breast; dark streaks on side. On all winter birds, note broad buffy eyebrow and buffier underparts; belly and under tail are white, unlike Smith's Longspur; also compare head and wing patterns. ***Juvenile*** is yellowish and heavily streaked above and on breast and sides. Often found amid flocks of Horned Larks and Snow Buntings; look for Lapland's darker overall coloring and smaller size.

Voice: Song, heard only on the breeding grounds, is a rapid warbling, frequently given in short flights. Calls include a musical *tee-lee-oo* or *tee-dle* and, in flight, a dry rattle distinctively mixed with whistled *tew* notes.

Range: Common. Breeds on Arctic tundra; winters in grassy fields, grain stubble, and on shores. May be common on western Great Plains; otherwise uncommon to rare over much of West.

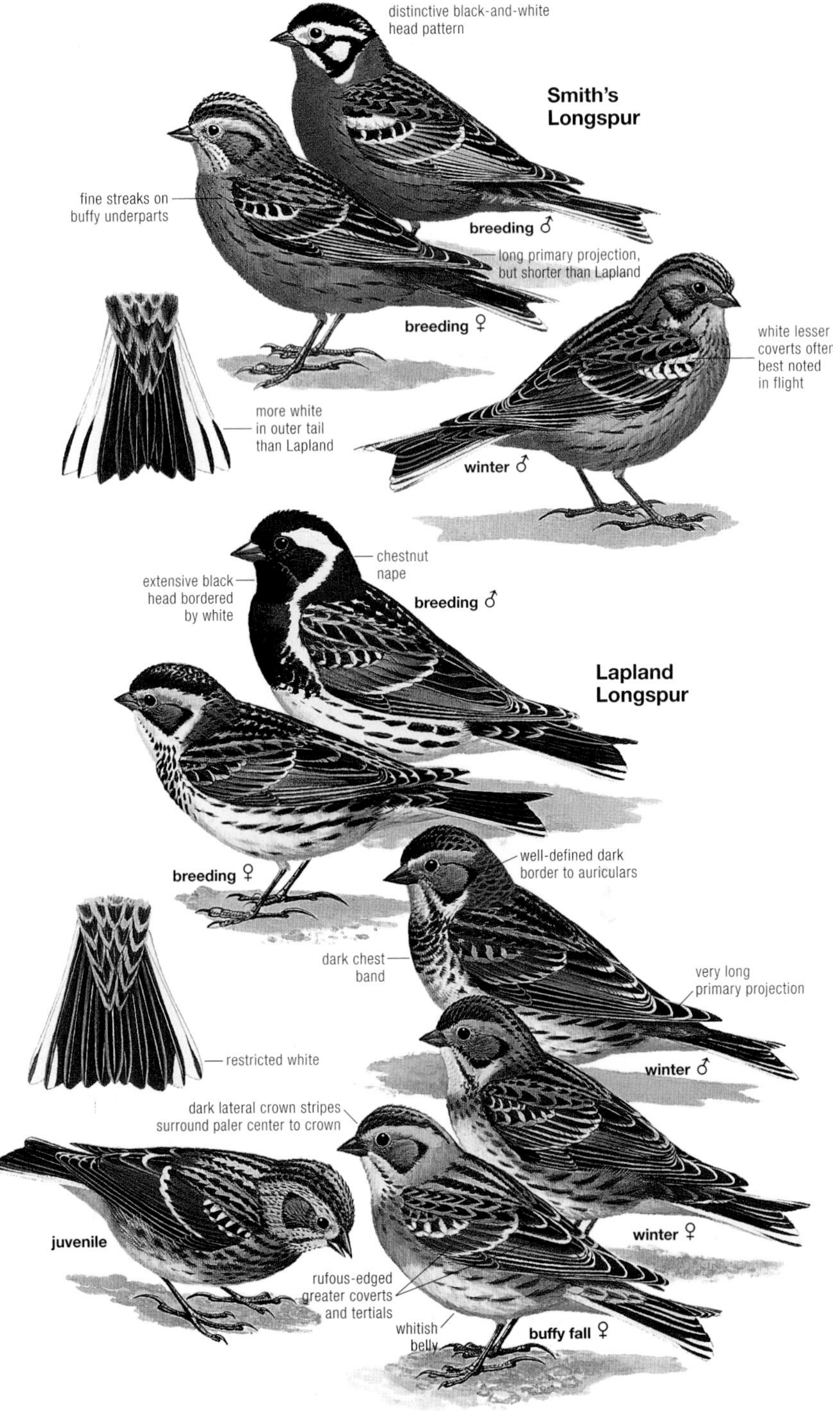

distinctive black-and-white head pattern
Smith's Longspur
fine streaks on buffy underparts
breeding ♂
long primary projection, but shorter than Lapland
breeding ♀
white lesser coverts often best noted in flight
more white in outer tail than Lapland
winter ♂
chestnut nape
extensive black head bordered by white
breeding ♂
Lapland Longspur
breeding ♀
well-defined dark border to auriculars
dark chest band
very long primary projection
restricted white
winter ♂
dark lateral crown stripes surround paler center to crown
juvenile
winter ♀
rufous-edged greater coverts and tertials
whitish belly
buffy fall ♀

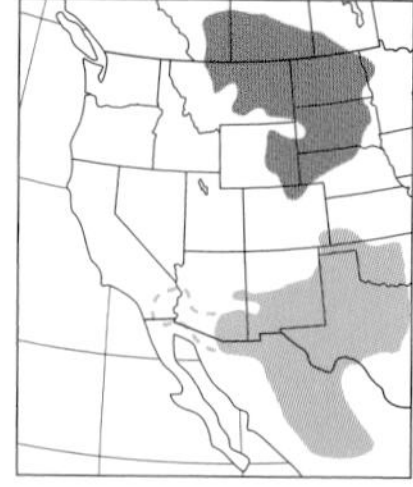

Chestnut-collared Longspur *Calcarius ornatus*

L 6" (15 cm) White tail marked with blackish triangle. Short primary projection; primary tips barely extend to base of tail. ***Breeding adult male***'s black-and-white head, buffy face, and black underparts are distinctive; a few have chestnut on underparts. Lower belly and undertail coverts whitish. Upperparts black, buff, and brown; chestnut collar, whitish wing bars. ***Winter male*** paler; feathers edged in buff and brown, obscuring black underparts. Male has small white patch on shoulder, often hidden; compare with Smith's (previous page). Breeding adult female resembles ***winter female*** but is darker, usually shows some chestnut on nape. Juvenile's pale feather fringes give upperparts a scaled look; tail pattern and bill shape distinguish juvenile from juvenile McCown's. Fall and winter birds have smaller, grayer bills than McCown's.

Voice: Song, heard only on breeding grounds, is a pleasant rapid warble, given in song flight or from a low perch. Distinctive call, a two-syllable *kittle*, repeated one or more times. Also gives a soft, high-pitched rattle and a short *buzz* call.

Range: Fairly common; nests in moist upland prairies. Somewhat shy; generally found in dense grass; gregarious in fall and winter. Casual during migration to Pacific Northwest; more regularly to California.

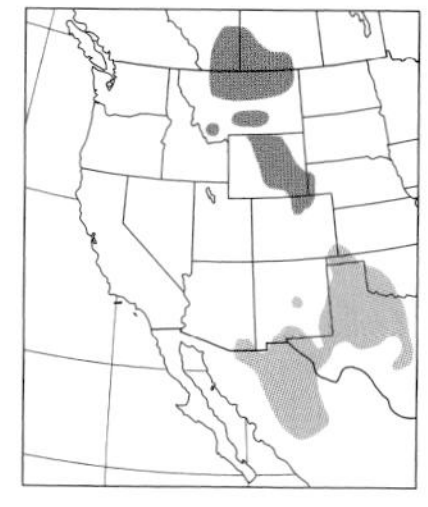

McCown's Longspur *Calcarius mccownii L 6" (15 cm)*

White tail marked by dark inverted-T shape. Note also stouter, thicker-based bill than bills of other longspurs. Primary projection slightly longer than Chestnut-collared Longspur; in perched bird, wings extend almost to tip of short tail. ***Breeding adult male*** has black crown, black malar stripe, black crescent on breast; gray sides. Upperparts streaked with buff and brown, with gray nape, gray rump; chestnut median coverts form contrasting crescent. ***Breeding adult female*** has streaked crown; may lack black on breast and show less chestnut on wing. In ***winter adults,*** bill is pinkish with dark tip; feathers are edged with buff and brown. Winter adult female is paler than female Chestnut-collared, with fewer streaks on underparts and a broader buffy eyebrow. Plain appearance suggestive of female House Sparrow. Some winter males have gray on rump; variable blackish on breast; retain chestnut median coverts. ***Juvenile*** is streaked below; pale fringes on feathers give upperparts a scaled look; paler overall than juvenile Chestnut-collared. In winter, often amid flocks of Horned Larks; look for McCown's chunkier, shorter tailed shape, slightly darker plumage, mostly white tail, thicker bill, and undulating flight.

Voice: Song, heard only on breeding grounds, is a series of exuberant warbles and twitters, generally given in song flight. Calls include a dry rattle, a little softer and more abrupt than Lapland Longspur, interspersed with occasional *pink* notes; also gives single finchlike notes.

Range: Locally fairly common but range has shrunk substantially since the 19th century. Nests in dry shortgrass plains; in winter, also found in plowed fields and dry lake beds. Very rare visitor to interior California, Nevada. Casual to coastal California, southern Oregon, and British Columbia.

Chestnut-collared Longspur

chestnut collar

breeding males

short primary projection

black breast and belly

winter ♂

small darkish bill

veiled black breast and belly

winter ♀

faint streaks

dark triangle on white tail

McCown's Longspur

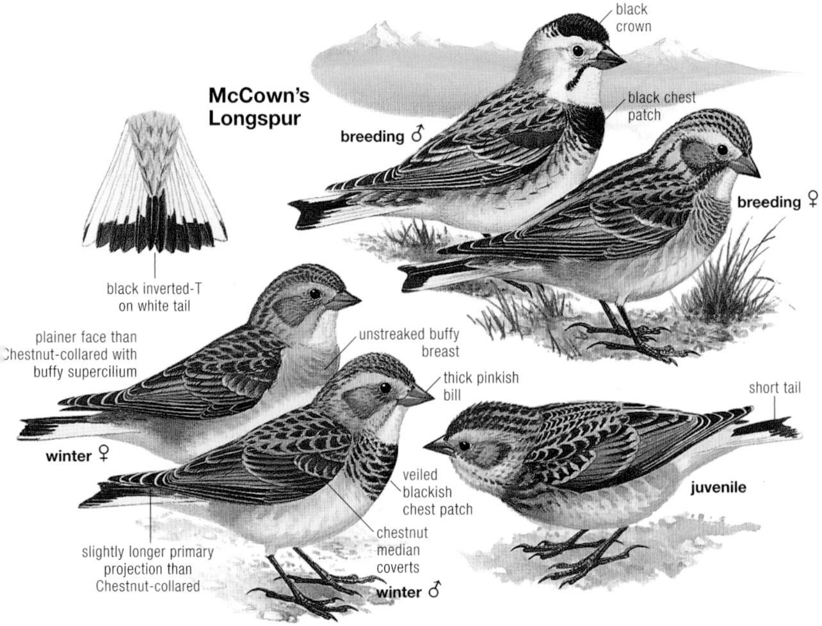

black crown

black chest patch

breeding ♂

breeding ♀

black inverted-T on white tail

plainer face than Chestnut-collared with buffy supercilium

unstreaked buffy breast

thick pinkish bill

short tail

winter ♀

veiled blackish chest patch

juvenile

chestnut median coverts

slightly longer primary projection than Chestnut-collared

winter ♂

Genus *Plectrophenax*

These two species—Snow Bunting and closely related McKay's Bunting—share many affinities with longspurs.

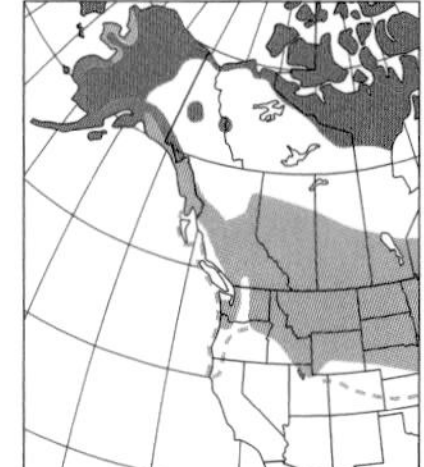

Snow Bunting *Plectrophenax nivalis L 6¾" (17 cm)*
Black-and-white breeding plumage acquired by end of spring by wear. Bill is black in summer, orange-yellow in winter. In all seasons, note long black-and-white wings. ***Males*** usually show more white overall than ***females,*** especially in the wings. ***Juvenile*** is grayish and streaked, with buffy eye ring; very similar to juvenile McKay's Bunting. ***First-winter*** plumage, acquired before migration, is darker overall than adult.
Voice: Calls include a sharp, whistled *tew;* a short buzz; and a musical rattle or twitter. Song, heard only on the breeding grounds, is a loud, high-pitched musical warbling.
Range: Fairly common; breeds on tundra, rocky shores, and talus slopes. During migration and winter, found on shores, especially sand dunes, beaches, and fields and along roadsides, often in large flocks that may include Lapland Longspurs and Horned Larks. Accidental to southern California and Arizona.

McKay's Bunting *Plectrophenax hyperboreus*
L 6¾" (17 cm) ***Adult breeding*** plumage mostly white, with less black on wings and tail than Snow Bunting; ***female*** shows a white panel on greater coverts. ***Winter*** plumage is edged with rust or tawny brown, but male is whiter overall than Snow Bunting; female very similar to male Snow Bunting. Juvenile is buffy gray and streaked, with gray head, prominent buffy eye ring; very similar to juvenile Snow Bunting.
Voice: Calls and song similar to Snow Bunting.
Range: Known to breed only on Hall and St. Matthew Islands in the Bering Sea. A few sometimes present in late spring on St. Lawrence Island; summer rarely on Pribilofs. Rare to uncommon in winter along west coast of Alaska; casual in winter south on coast to Oregon, in interior of Alaska and on Aleutians. Some authorities think McKay's may be a subspecies of Snow Bunting.

Rustic Bunting *Emberiza rustica L 5¾" (15 cm)*
Eurasian species. Has a slight crest, whitish nape spot, and prominent pale line extending back from eye. ***Male*** has black head; upperparts bright chestnut with buff and blackish streaks on back; outer tail feathers white. Underparts are white, with chestnut breast band and streaks on sides. ***Female*** and fall and winter males have brownish head pattern, with pale spot at rear of ear patch. Female may be confused with Little Bunting; note Rustic's larger size, heavier bill with pink lower mandible, diffuse rusty streaking below, and lack of eye ring.
Voice: Call note is a hard, sharp *jit* or *tsip.* Song is a soft, bubbling warble.
Range: Uncommon spring migrant on western and central Aleutians, rare in fall; very rare on other islands in Bering Sea; casual elsewhere from West Coast region.

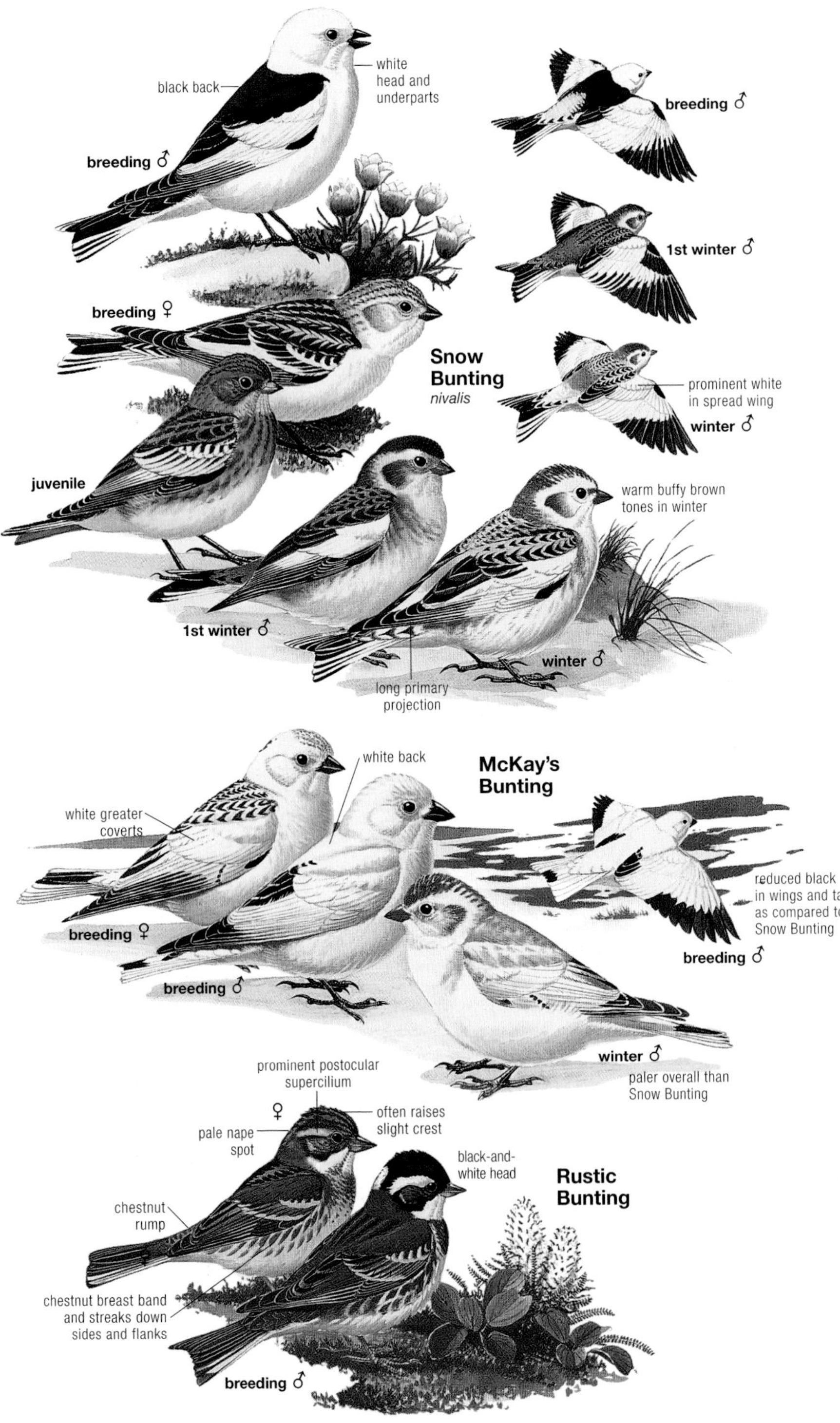

black back
white
head and
underparts
breeding ♂
breeding ♂
1st winter ♂
breeding ♀
Snow
Bunting
nivalis
prominent white
in spread wing
winter ♂
juvenile
warm buffy brown
tones in winter
1st winter ♂
winter ♂
long primary
projection
white back
McKay's
Bunting
white greater
coverts
reduced black
in wings and tail
as compared to
Snow Bunting
breeding ♀
breeding ♂
breeding ♂
winter ♂
paler overall than
Snow Bunting
prominent postocular
supercilium
♀
pale nape
spot
often raises
slight crest
black-and-
white head
Rustic
Bunting
chestnut
rump
chestnut breast band
and streaks down
sides and flanks
breeding ♂

Cardinals, Saltators, Allies (Family Cardinalidae)

In North America, these seedeaters include Northern Cardinal, certain grosbeaks, the *Passerina* and other buntings, and Dickcissel.

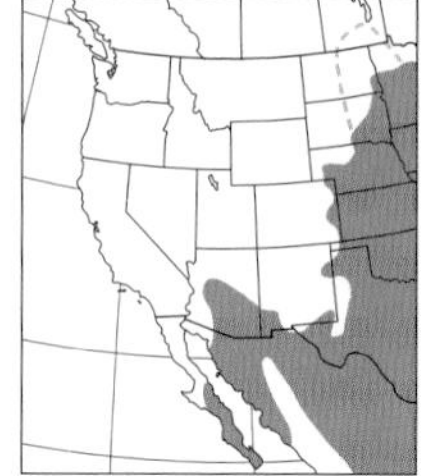

Northern Cardinal *Cardinalis cardinalis L 8¾" (22 cm)*

Conspicuous crest and cone-shaped reddish orange bill. ***Male*** is red overall, with black face. ***Female*** is buffy brown or buffy olive, tinged with red on wings, crest, and tail. ***Juvenile*** is browner overall, with a dusky bill; juvenile female lacks red tones. Bill shape and color help distinguish female and juvenile from similar Pyrrhuloxia.

Voice: Song is a loud, liquid whistling with many variations, including *cue cue cue* and *cheer cheer cheer* and *purty purty purty.* Both sexes sing almost year-round. Common call is a sharp *chip.*

Range: Very small numbers of eastern birds occur west to eastern Colorado. Southeastern *superbus* is fairly common in southern Arizona to very rare in southeastern California; small population possibly now extirpated; casual to Inyo County, California, and southern Nevada (Las Vegas); brighter red with reduced black on forehead. A small introduced population exists in the Los Angeles area; local escapes seen elsewhere. Inhabits woodland edges, streamside thickets, and suburban gardens.

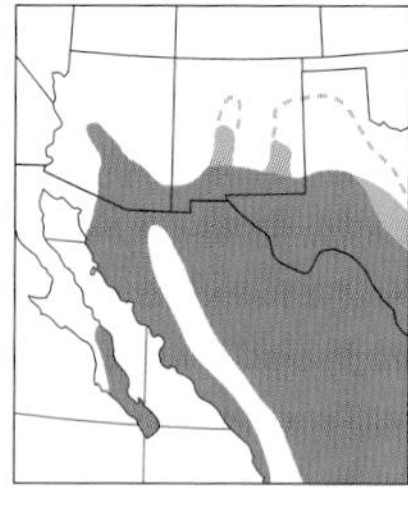

Pyrrhuloxia *Cardinalis sinuatus L 8¾" (22 cm)*

Thick, strongly curved, pale bill helps distinguish this species from female and juvenile Northern Cardinal. ***Male*** is gray overall, with red on face, crest, wings, tail, and underparts. ***Female*** shows little or no red.

Voice: Song is a liquid whistle, thinner and shorter than Northern Cardinal; call is a sharper *chink.*

Range: Fairly common in thorny brush, mesquite thickets, desert, woodland edges, and ranchlands. Casual north to Colorado and west to California.

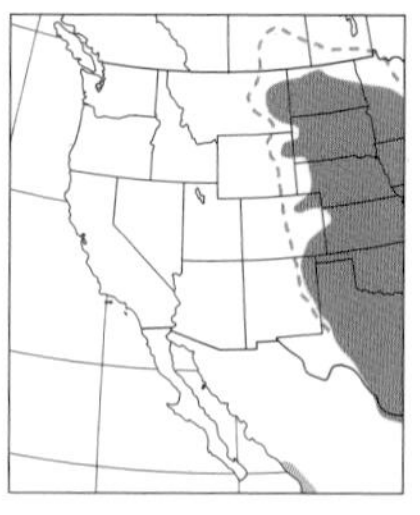

Dickcissel *Spiza americana L 6¼" (16 cm)*

Yellowish eyebrow, thick bill, and chestnut wing coverts are distinctive. ***Breeding male*** has black bib under white chin, bright yellow breast. ***Female*** lacks black bib, but has some yellow on breast; chestnut wing patch muted. Bib on ***winter adult male*** is less distinct. ***Immature*** is duller overall than adults, breast and flanks lightly streaked; female may show almost no yellow or chestnut. Compare with female House Sparrow.

Voice: Common call, often given in flight, is a distinctive electric-buzzer *bzrrrrt.* Song is a variable *dick dick dickcissel.*

Range: Breeds in open weedy meadows, grainfields, and prairies. Uncommon breeder in limited western range. Otherwise a rare to casual migrant in West. Casual in winter in California.

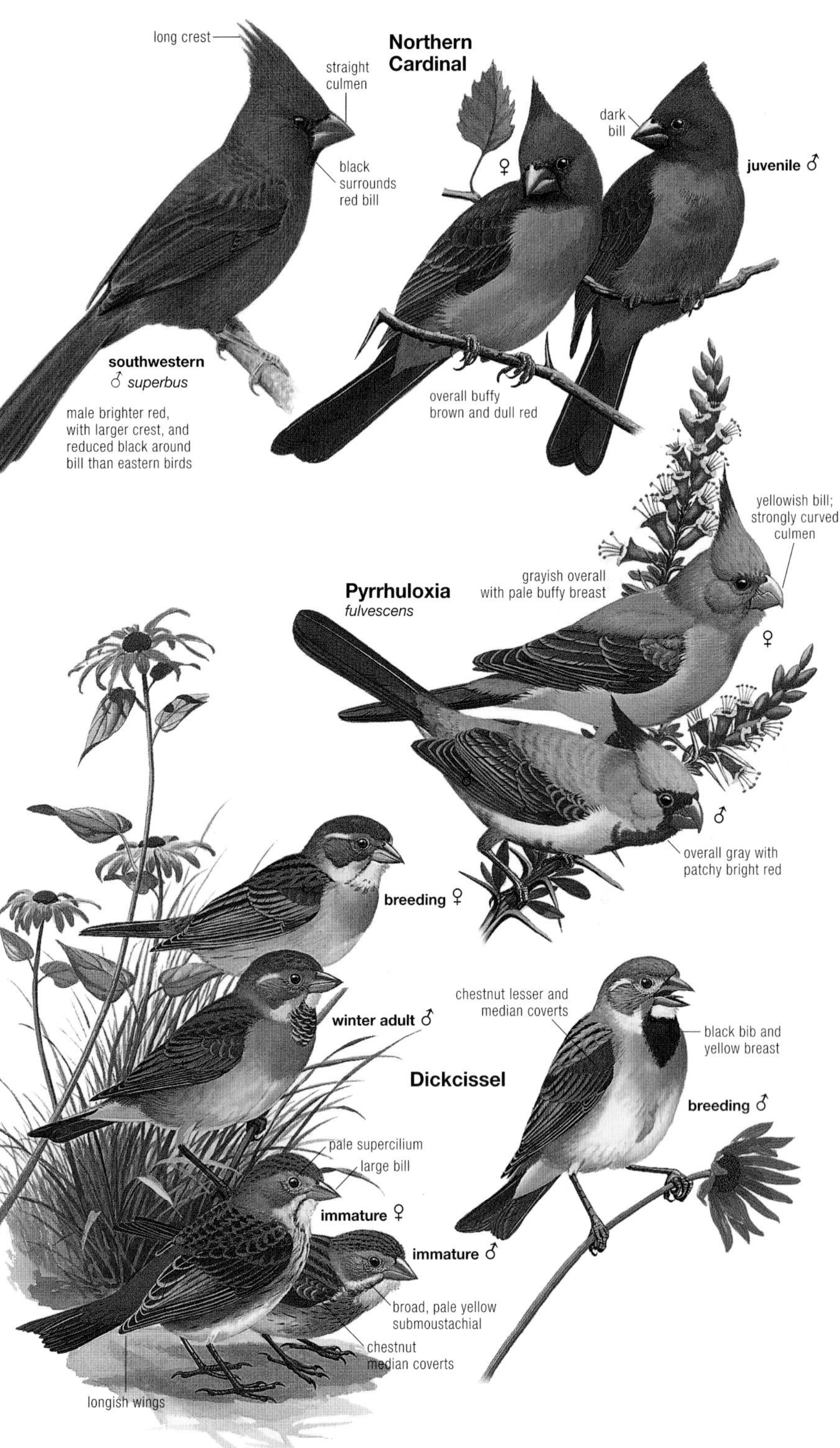

Northern Cardinal
long crest
straight culmen
black surrounds red bill
southwestern ♂ superbus
male brighter red, with larger crest, and reduced black around bill than eastern birds
♀
dark bill
juvenile ♂
overall buffy brown and dull red
Pyrrhuloxia
fulvescens
grayish overall with pale buffy breast
yellowish bill; strongly curved culmen
♀
♂
overall gray with patchy bright red
breeding ♀
winter adult ♂
Dickcissel
chestnut lesser and median coverts
black bib and yellow breast
breeding ♂
pale supercilium
large bill
immature ♀
immature ♂
broad, pale yellow submoustachial
chestnut median coverts
longish wings

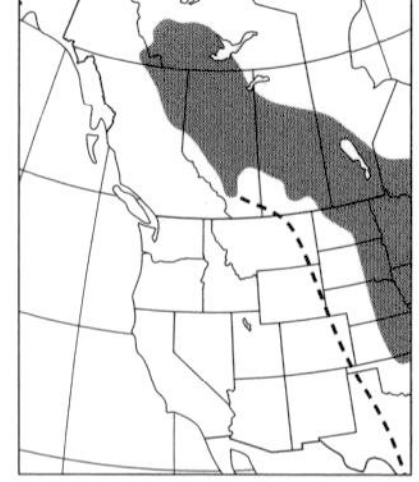

Rose-breasted Grosbeak *Pheucticus ludovicianus*
L 8" (20 cm) Large size; very large, triangular bill; upper mandible paler than Black-headed Grosbeak. ***Breeding male*** has rose red breast, white underparts, white wing bars, white rump. Rose red wing linings show in flight. Brown-tipped ***winter*** plumage is acquired before fall migration. ***Female***'s streaked plumage and yellow wing linings resemble female Black-headed, but underparts are more heavily and extensively streaked. Similar ***first-fall male*** is buffier above, with buffy wash across breast; often has a few red feathers on breast; red wing linings distinctive.
Voice: Rich, warbled songs of both species are nearly identical. Call, a sharp *eek*, is squeakier than Black-headed.
Range: Fairly common in limited western breeding range in deciduous woodlands. Rare migrant throughout West; accidental Alaska. Casual in winter in coastal California.

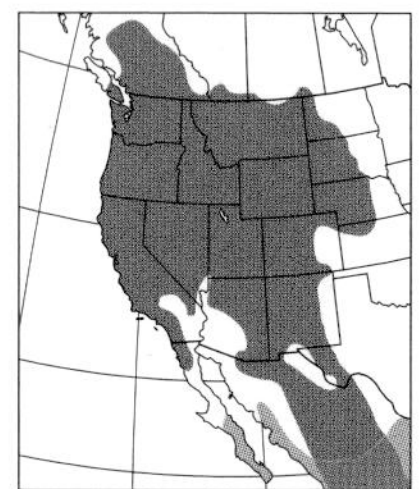

Black-headed Grosbeak *Pheucticus melanocephalus*
L 8¼" (21 cm) Large, with a very large, triangular bill, upper mandible darker than Rose-breasted Grosbeak. ***Male*** has cinnamon underparts, all-black head. In flight, both sexes show yellow wing linings. ***Female*** plumage is generally buffier above and below than female Rose-breasted, with the streaking below being both finer and more restricted to sides. ***First-fall male*** Black-headed is rich buff or butterscotch below, with little or no streaking.
Voice: Songs and calls of Rose-breasted and Black-headed are nearly identical, but Black-headed's call is lower-pitched.
Range: Common in open woodlands and forest edges. Very rare in winter on coastal slope of California; casual to western Oregon. Casual to Alaska and northwestern Canada. Hybridizes occasionally with Rose-breasted where ranges overlap on the Great Plains. Hybrids are rarely noted in the West.

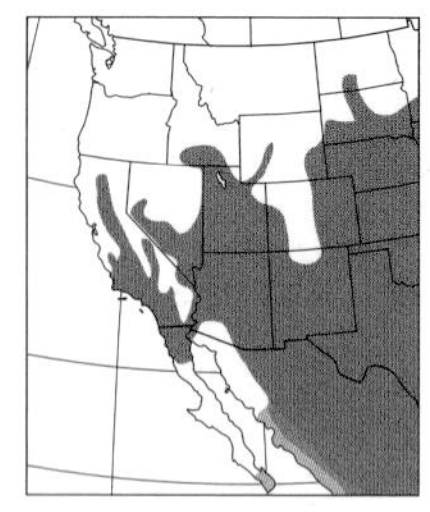

Blue Grosbeak *Passerina caerulea L 6¾" (17 cm)*
Wide chestnut wing bars, large heavy bill, and larger overall size distinguish ***male*** from male Indigo Bunting (next page). ***Females*** of these two species also similar; compare bill shape, wing bars, and overall size. Juvenile resembles female; in first fall, some ***immatures*** are richer brown than female. ***First-spring male*** shows some blue above and below; resembles adult male by second winter. In poor light, Blue Grosbeak resembles Brown-headed Cowbird (page 394); note Blue Grosbeak's bill shape and wing bars; also the habit of twitching and spreading its tail.
Voice: Listen for distinctive call, a loud, explosive *chink*. Song is a series of rich, rising and falling warbles.
Range: Fairly common; found in low, overgrown fields, streamsides, woodland edges, and hedgerows. Rare migrant (mostly fall) to coast of central and northern California. Casual from Oregon and British Columbia. Accidental to southeast Alaska. Accidental in winter in California and Arizona.

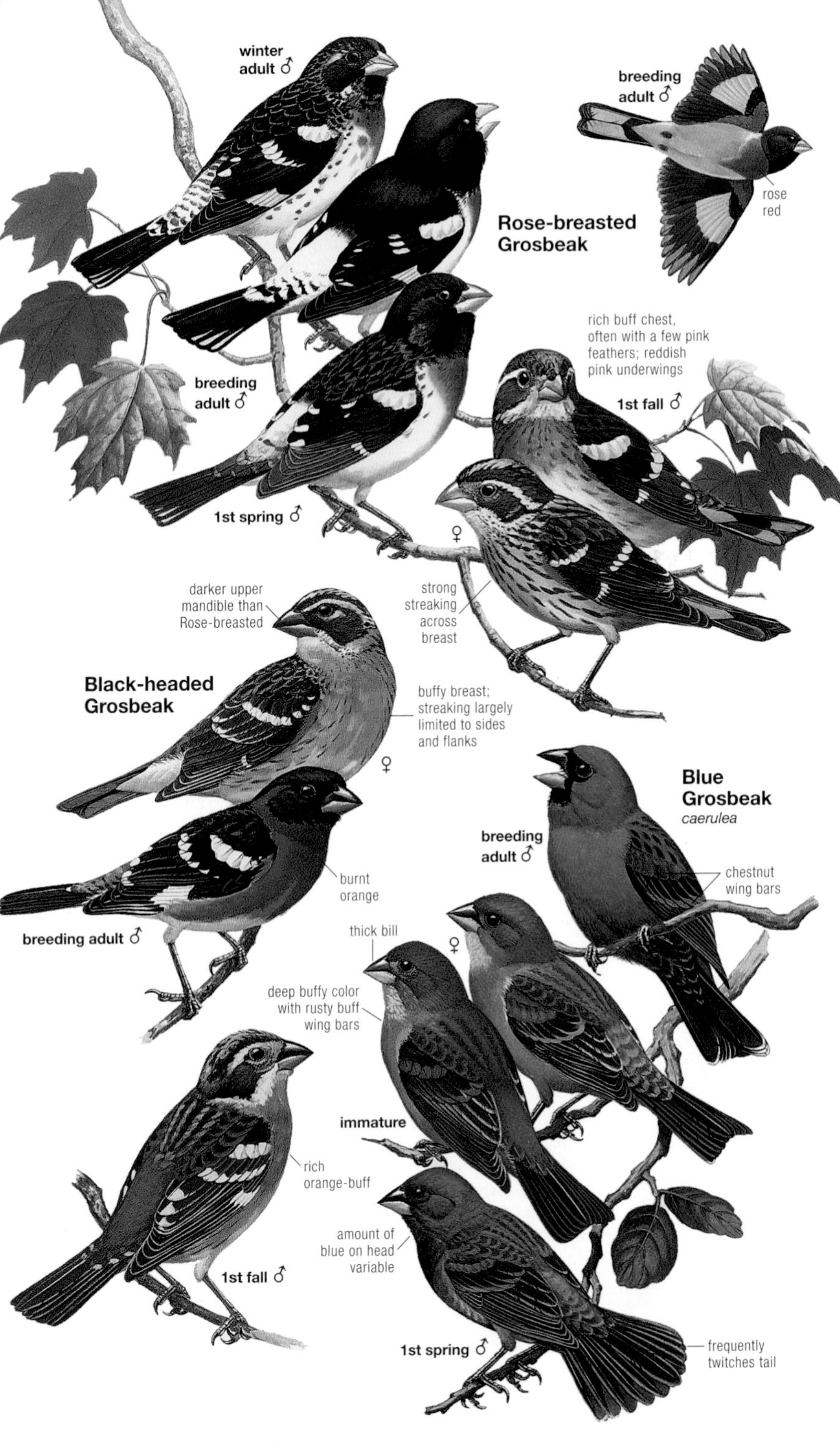

winter
adult ♂
breeding
adult ♂
rose
red
Rose-breasted
Grosbeak
rich buff chest,
often with a few pink
feathers; reddish
pink underwings
breeding
adult ♂
1st fall ♂
1st spring ♂
♀
darker upper
mandible than
Rose-breasted
strong
streaking
across
breast
Black-headed
Grosbeak
buffy breast;
streaking largely
limited to sides
and flanks
♀
Blue
Grosbeak
caerulea
breeding
adult ♂
chestnut
wing bars
burnt
orange
breeding adult ♂
thick bill
♀
deep buffy color
with rusty buff
wing bars
immature
rich
orange-buff
amount of
blue on head
variable
1st fall ♂
1st spring ♂
frequently
twitches tail

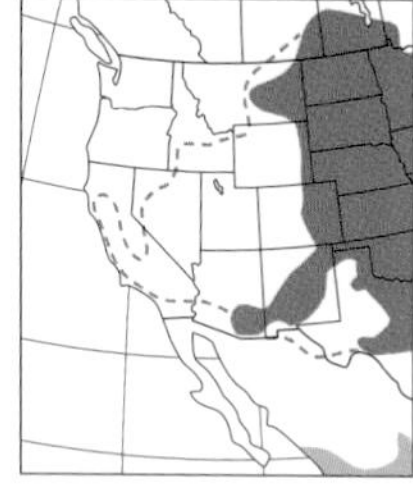

Indigo Bunting *Passerina cyanea* *L* 5½" (14 cm)
Breeding male deep blue. Smaller than Blue Grosbeak (previous page); bill much smaller; lacks wing bars. In ***winter*** plumage, blue is obscured by brown and buff edges. Female is brownish, with diffuse streaking on breast and flanks. Young birds resemble female.
Voice: Song is a series of varied phrases, usually paired. Calls include a sharp *pit* or *spik*.
Range: Uncommon to mostly rare in West in woodland clearings and borders and brushy hillsides. Casual to Alaska and in winter from Pacific states.

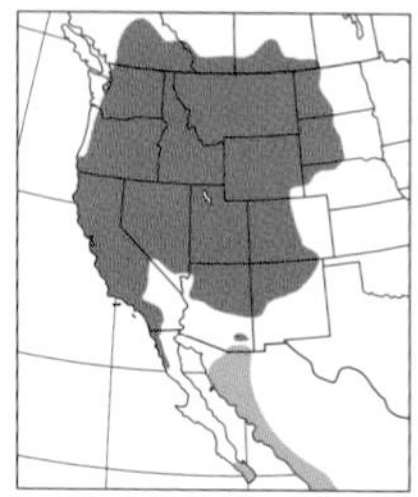

Lazuli Bunting *Passerina amoena* *L* 5½" (14 cm)
Adult male bright turquoise above and on throat; cinnamon across breast; thick white upper wing bars. ***Female*** is grayish brown above, rump grayish blue; whitish underparts with buffy wash across breast. Juveniles resemble female but have distinct fine streaks across breast; immature male is mostly blue by ***first spring.*** Winter adult male's blue color is obscured by brown edges.
Voice: Song is a series of varied phrases, sometimes paired; faster and less strident than Indigo Bunting.
Range: Found in open deciduous or mixed woodlands, brushy slopes, and chaparral, especially in areas near water. Occasionally hybridizes with Indigo. Casual north to Northwest Territories.

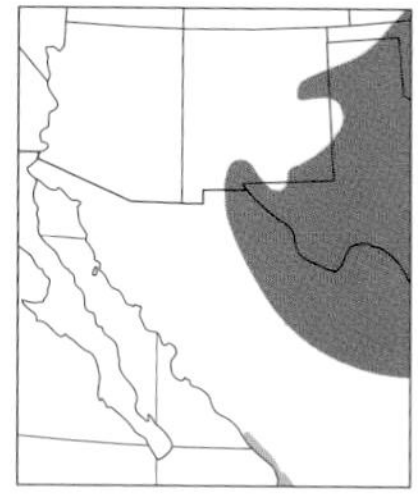

Painted Bunting *Passerina ciris* *L* 5½" (14 cm)
Adult male's gaudy colors are retained year-round. ***Female*** is bright green above, paler yellow-green below. ***Juvenile*** is much drabber, largely grayish; look for telltale hints of green above, yellow below. Fall molt in eastern nominate race takes place on breeding grounds; western *pallidior* molts on winter grounds. First-winter male resembles adult female; by spring, may show tinge of blue on head, red on breast.
Voice: Song is a rapid series of varied phrases, thinner and sweeter than Indigo Bunting. Call is a loud, rich *chip*.
Range: Fairly common summer resident in limited western breeding range in streamside brush and low thickets. Rare early fall (Aug.) migrant to southeastern Arizona. Very rare (mainly fall) to California. Otherwise casual in West. Some out-of-range birds may be escapes.

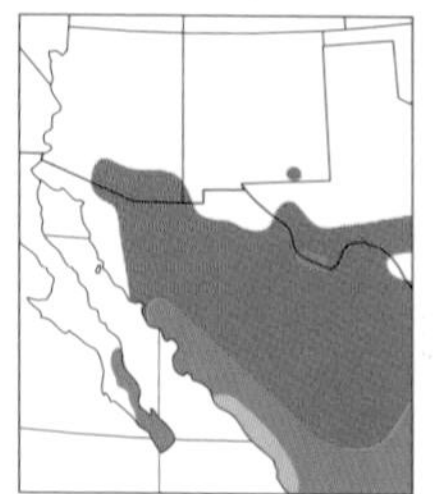

Varied Bunting *Passerina versicolor* *L* 5½" (14 cm)
Breeding male's plumage is colorful in good light; otherwise appears black. In ***winter,*** colors are edged with brown. ***Female*** is plain gray-brown or buffy brown above, slightly paler below; resembles female Indigo Bunting but lacks streaks and all wing markings; note also that Varied Bunting's culmen is slightly more curved. First-spring male resembles female.
Voice: Song is similar to Painted Bunting. Calls are similar to Lazuli and Indigo Buntings.
Range: Locally fairly common in thorny thickets in washes and canyons, often near water. Accidental to southeastern California.

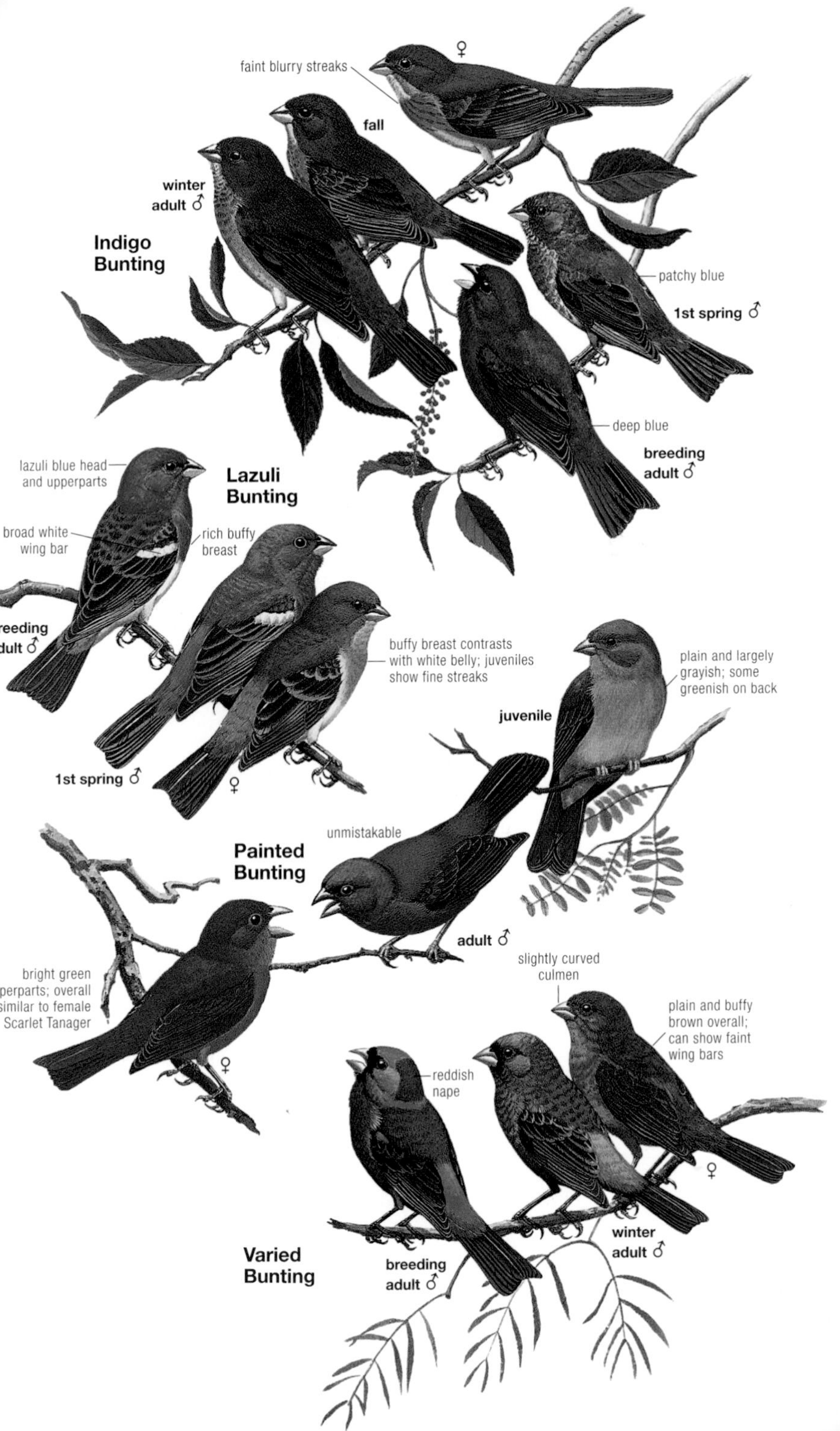

faint blurry streaks
♀
fall
winter adult ♂
Indigo Bunting
patchy blue
1st spring ♂
deep blue
breeding adult ♂
lazuli blue head and upperparts
Lazuli Bunting
broad white wing bar
rich buffy breast
reeding dult ♂
buffy breast contrasts with white belly; juveniles show fine streaks
1st spring ♂
♀
plain and largely grayish; some greenish on back
juvenile
unmistakable
Painted Bunting
adult ♂
bright green perparts; overall similar to female Scarlet Tanager
♀
slightly curved culmen
plain and buffy brown overall; can show faint wing bars
reddish nape
♀
winter adult ♂
Varied Bunting
breeding adult ♂

Blackbirds (Family Icteridae)

Strong, direct flight and pointed bills mark this diverse group.

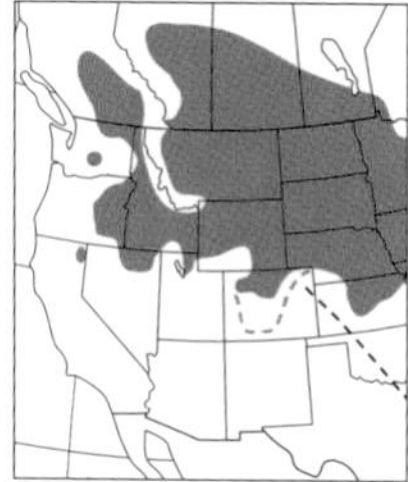

Bobolink *Dolichonyx oryzivorus L 7" (18 cm)*

Breeding male entirely black below; hindneck buff, fading to whitish by midsummer; scapulars, rump white. ***Breeding female*** buffy overall, with dark streaks on back, rump, sides; head striped with dark brown. ***Fall*** birds resemble female but rich yellow-buff below. In all plumages, note sharply pointed tail feathers.

Voice: Male's song is a rapid, loud, bubbling series of notes, often delivered in display flight. Calls include a low *chuck;* also a repeated whistled *ink* flight call.

Range: Nests primarily in hayfields, wet meadows. Most migrate east of the Great Plains. Rare to very rare migrant in West away from breeding grounds; on West Coast most are in fall. Accidental to Alaska, northwestern Canada; winters in South America.

Red-winged Blackbird *Agelaius phoeniceus*

L 8¾" (22 cm) Rounder wings and usually stouter bill than Tricolored. Glossy black ***male*** has red shoulder patches broadly tipped with buffy yellow. In perched birds, red patch may be hidden. ***Female*** brown above, heavily streaked below; sometimes shows a red tinge on wing coverts or pinkish wash on chin and throat. ***First-year male*** plumage distinguished from female Tricolored by reddish shoulder patch. Males in races of California's Central Valley and central coast region, known collectively as ***"Bicolored Blackbird,"*** nearly or totally lack the buffy band behind red shoulder patch. Females have darker bellies, like female Tricolored; but note chestnut-buff edging on feathers of upperparts, except when worn; rounder wings; stouter bill, except for *aciculatus* of Kern Basin in south-central California, which has a bill like Tricolored.

Voice: Song is a liquid, gurgling *konk-la-reee,* ending in a trill. Most common call is a *chack* note.

Range: Abundant; often found in immense flocks in winter. Generally nests in thick vegetation of freshwater marshes, sloughs, and fields; forages in open habitats.

Tricolored Blackbird *Agelaius tricolor L 8¾" (22 cm)*

More pointed wings and bill than Red-winged. Glossy (with slightly grayish sheen) black ***male*** has dark red shoulder patches, often hidden, broadly tipped with white; tips are buffy white in fresh fall plumage. ***Females*** usually lack any red on shoulder and never show pinkish on throat; plumage is sooty brown and streaked overall; darker than female Red-winged, particularly on belly; note more pointed wings and bill.

Voice: Calls are much like Red-winged's, but harsh, braying *on-ke-kaaangh* song lacks Red-winged's liquid tones.

Range: Gregarious; found year-round in large flocks in open country and dairy farms; nests in large localized colonies in marshes. Declining in parts of range.

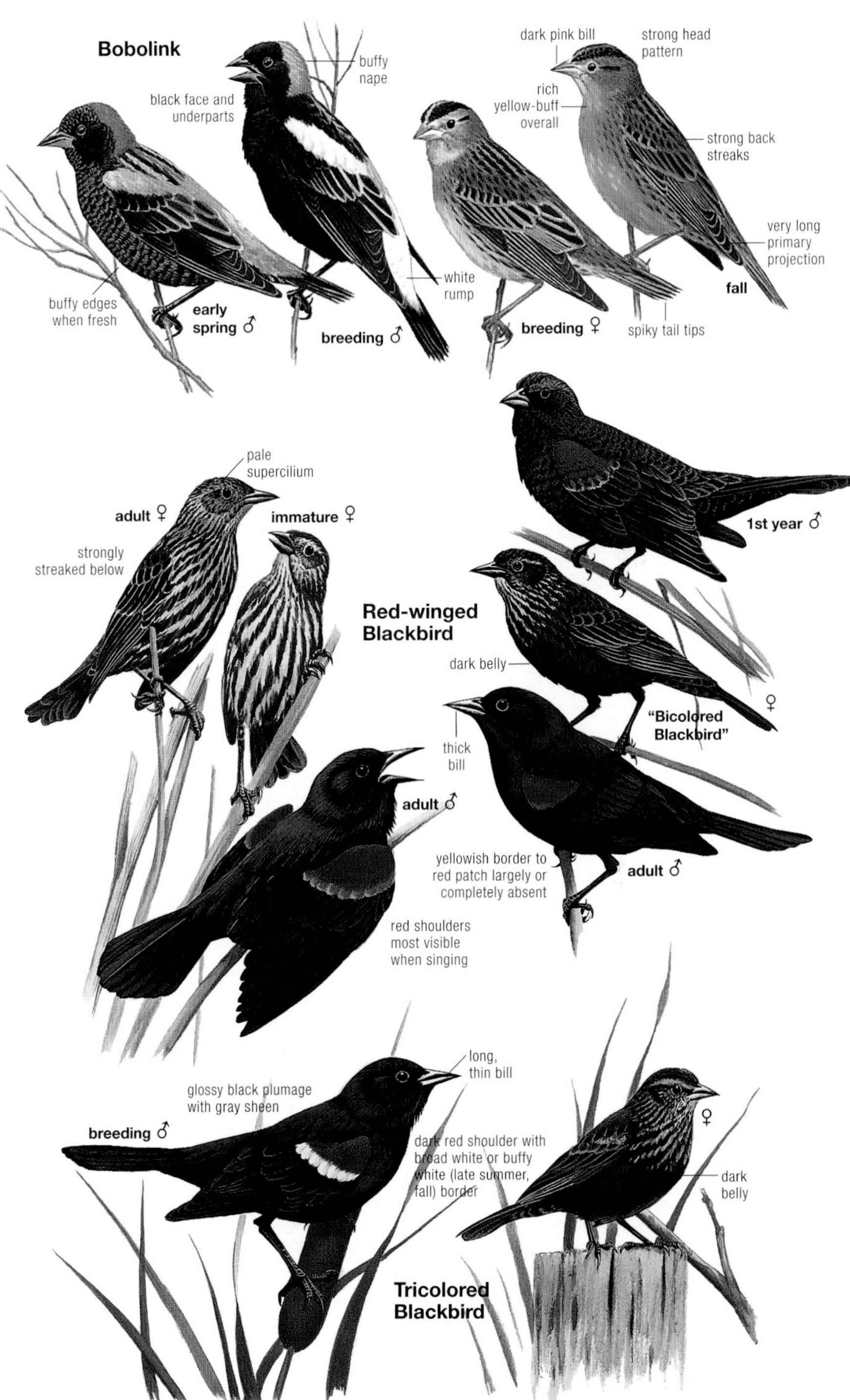
Bobolink
dark pink bill
strong head pattern
buffy nape
black face and underparts
rich yellow-buff overall
strong back streaks
very long primary projection
fall
white rump
buffy edges when fresh
early spring ♂
breeding ♂
breeding ♀
spiky tail tips
pale supercilium
adult ♀
immature ♀
1st year ♂
strongly streaked below
Red-winged Blackbird
dark belly
♀
"Bicolored Blackbird"
thick bill
adult ♂
yellowish border to red patch largely or completely absent
adult ♂
red shoulders most visible when singing
long, thin bill
glossy black plumage with gray sheen
breeding ♂
dark red shoulder with broad white or buffy white (late summer, fall) border
♀
dark belly
Tricolored Blackbird

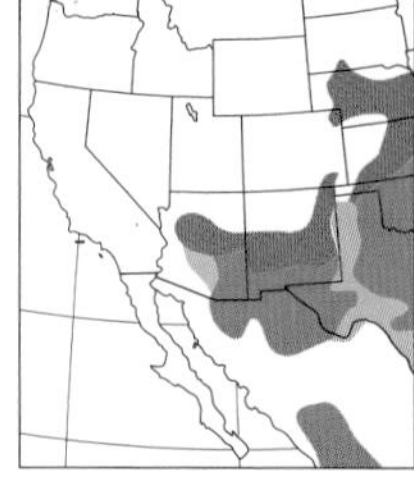

Eastern Meadowlark *Sturnella magna L 9½" (24 cm)*
Black V-shaped breast band on yellow underparts is characteristic of both meadowlark species after post-juvenal molt. In fresh ***fall*** plumage, birds are more richly colored overall, with partly veiled breast band and, on *magna,* rich buffy flanks. On Eastern females, yellow does not reach submoustachial area; barely reaches on males. Pale southwestern *lilianae* is the characteristic Eastern Meadowlark of the West. Best distinguished from Western Meadowlark by head and especially tail pattern. On northern nominate race, widespread in East, dark centers are visible on central tail feathers, uppertail coverts, secondary coverts, and tertials.
Voice: Song is a clear, whistled *see-you see-yeeer;* distinctive call is a high, buzzy *drzzt,* given in a rapid series in flight.
Range: Southwestern *lilianae* is fairly common in desert grasslands. Eastern *magna* is rare and irregular in summer in extreme northeastern Colorado in fields and meadows; casual elsewhere in eastern part of state.

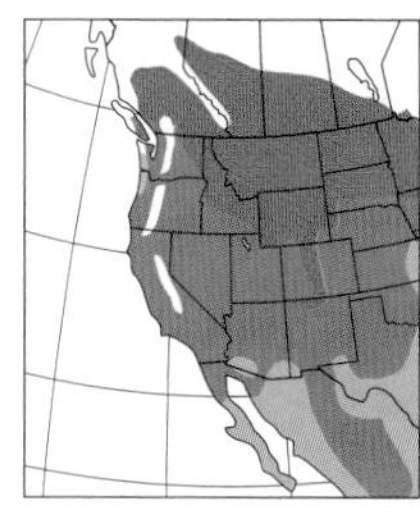

Western Meadowlark *Sturnella neglecta L 9½" (24 cm)*
Plumages similar to those of Eastern Meadowlark, but in ***spring*** and summer yellow extends well into the submoustachial area, especially in males; yellow often veiled in ***fall.*** Lack of dark centers to feathers of upperparts helps separate Western from more easterly races of Eastern, including *magna,* in areas where ranges overlap. Also, in fresh fall and winter plumage, Western's upperparts, flanks, undertail region much paler. Distinguished from pale Eastern *lilianae* by mottled cheeks, more mottled postocular and lateral crown stripes, less white in tail. Northwestern *confluenta* darker above, can show dark feather centers like Eastern.
Voice: Song is a series of bubbling, flutelike notes of variable length, usually accelerating toward the end. Sharp *chuck* note. Rattled flight call similar to Eastern, but lower pitched; also gives a whistled *wheet.*
Range: Overall common in grasslands and agricultural lands. Westerns are gregarious in winter; large flocks often gather along roadsides. Casual to Alaska and northwestern Canada.

IDENTIFYING: Meadowlarks Western Meadowlark is very widespread in the West; for most regions, it is the only Meadowlark species seen. Unlike Eastern Meadowlark, its appearance is pretty uniform throughout its range, although birds from the Northwest are somewhat darker (*confluenta*). In mid-elevation grasslands of the Southwest, a very pale Eastern subspecies (*lilianae*) is resident. Though largely absent as a breeder here, Western is of course widespread and numerous in winter. Separation of these birds is best done by head and tail pattern. Eastern has strong black head stripes and pale cheeks, whereas Western's head stripes are browner and more mottled auriculars. Eastern has extensive white on the outer tail feathers, so the effect is a dark wedge on Eastern and a dark triangular area on Western. Vocalizations, especially call notes (buzzy on Eastern, blackbird-like on Western), should be learned.

While essentially resident, Eastern *lilianae* has been collected on the Arizona side of the Colorado River. In the extreme eastern portion of the region in eastern Colorado, a few of the nominate race (*magna*) have occurred. Remarkably, this migratory subspecies has not yet been detected on the West Coast. Its tail pattern is different than *lilianae* and close to Western. In fresh fall and winter plumage, its sides and flanks are generously washed with rich buff; overall it's darker and more richly colored than Western.

Eastern Meadowlark

stiff, fluttery flight

short, broad triangular wings

extensive white in tail

spring
magna

more extensive white in tail in *lilianae* with only narrow rectangle of dark

southwestern spring
lilianae

pale cheek in all plumages with strongly contrasting black lateral and postocular lines

more like Western in overall coloration and in flank pattern and coloration, but note differences in head and tail patterns

spring
magna

whitish submoustachial

more richly colored above than Western, with stronger head pattern

fall
magna

juvenile
magna

strong side and flank streaks against rich buffy ground color when in fresh fall and winter plumage

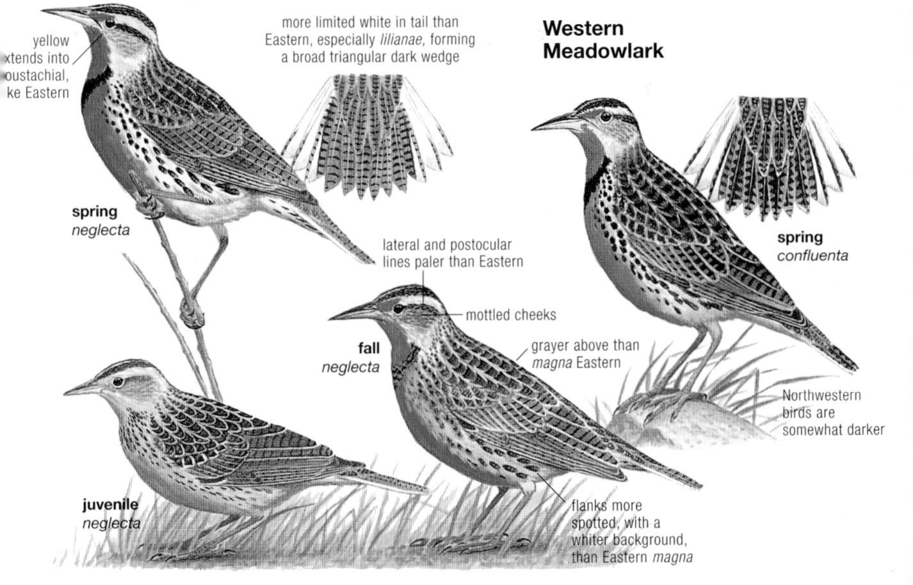

Western Meadowlark

yellow
xtends into
oustachial,
ke Eastern

more limited white in tail than Eastern, especially *lilianae,* forming a broad triangular dark wedge

spring
neglecta

spring
confluenta

lateral and postocular lines paler than Eastern

mottled cheeks

fall
neglecta

grayer above than *magna* Eastern

Northwestern birds are somewhat darker

juvenile
neglecta

flanks more spotted, with a whiter background, than Eastern *magna*

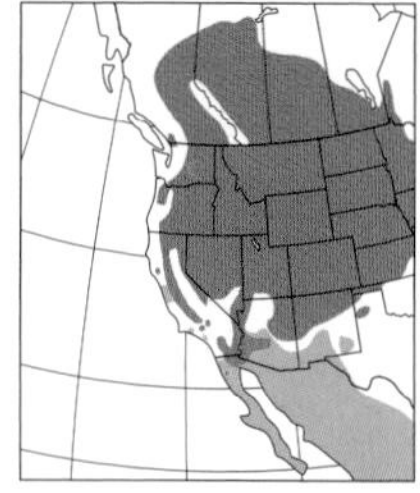

Yellow-headed Blackbird

Xanthocephalus xanthocephalus *L* 9½" (24 cm) ***Adult male***'s yellow head and breast and white wing patch contrast sharply with black body. ***Adult female*** is dusky brown, lacks wing patch; eyebrow, lower cheek, and throat are yellow or buffy yellow; belly streaked with white. ***Juvenile*** is dark brown with buffy edgings on back and wing; head mostly tawny. ***Immature male*** resembles female but darker; wing coverts tipped with white; acquires adult plumage by following fall.

Voice: Song begins with a harsh, rasping note and ends with a long, descending buzz. Call note is a rich *croak.*

Range: Locally common throughout most of range. Prefers freshwater marshes or reedy lakes; often seen foraging in nearby farmlands and feedlots. Overall rare on immediate West Coast; most recorded during migration. Casual in spring and fall as far north as southern Alaska and northwest Canada.

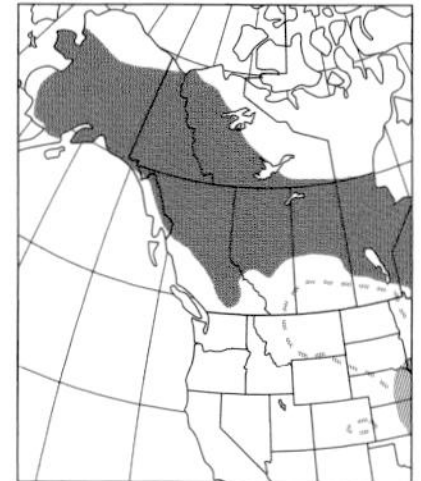

Rusty Blackbird *Euphagus carolinus* *L* 9" (23 cm)

Adults and fall immatures have yellow eyes. Fall adults and immatures are broadly tipped with rust; tertials and wing coverts edged with rust. ***Fall female*** has broad, buffy eyebrow, buffy underparts, gray rump. ***Fall male*** is darker; eyebrow fainter. Rusty feather tips wear off by spring, producing the dark ***breeding*** plumage. Juveniles have dark eyes. On all, note the long and very slender, spikelike bill.

Voice: Call is a harsh *tschak;* song is a high, squeaky *koo-a-lee.*

Range: Uncommon to fairly common in the eastern breeding range around marshes and ponds bordered by shrubs and usually some standing dead trees. But in range as a whole has sharply declined in recent decades. Otherwise casual to very rare in West mainly in late fall and winter. Casual also to the Bering Sea islands. Fall migrants are often solitary and found around aquatic habitats. Rare wintering Rustys often join Brewer's Blackbirds.

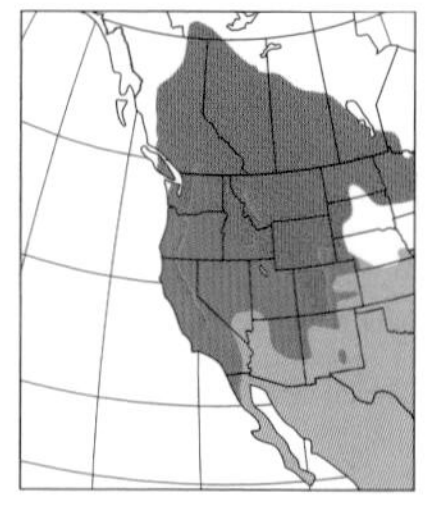

Brewer's Blackbird *Euphagus cyanocephalus*

L 9" (23 cm) ***Male*** has yellow eyes; ***female***'s are usually brown. Male is black year-round, with purplish gloss on head and neck, greenish gloss on body and wings. ***Immature males*** show variable buffy feather edgings, but never on tertials or wing coverts, as in Rusty Blackbird; note also the shorter, thicker bill. Female and juveniles are gray-brown.

Voice: Typical call is a harsh *check;* song is a wheezy *que-ee* or *k-seee.*

Range: Common in open habitats, including city parks; gregarious; often forages in parking lots. Casual north and west to the Yukon and Alaska.

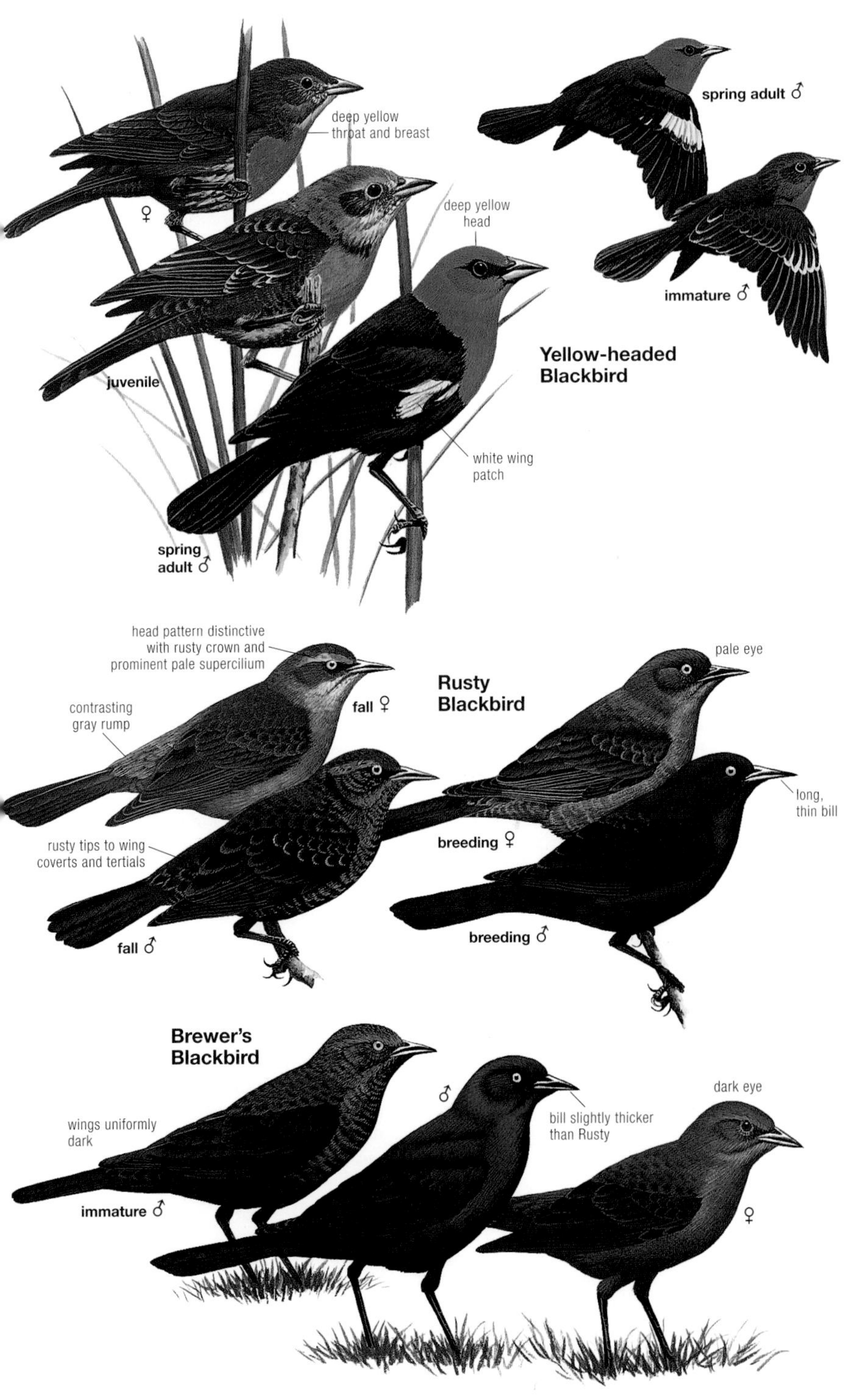
deep yellow
throat and breast
♀
deep yellow
head
juvenile
white wing
patch
spring
adult ♂
spring adult ♂
immature ♂
Yellow-headed
Blackbird
head pattern distinctive
with rusty crown and
prominent pale supercilium
contrasting
gray rump
fall ♀
Rusty
Blackbird
pale eye
long,
thin bill
rusty tips to wing
coverts and tertials
breeding ♀
fall ♂
breeding ♂
Brewer's
Blackbird
♂
bill slightly thicker
than Rusty
dark eye
wings uniformly
dark
immature ♂
♀

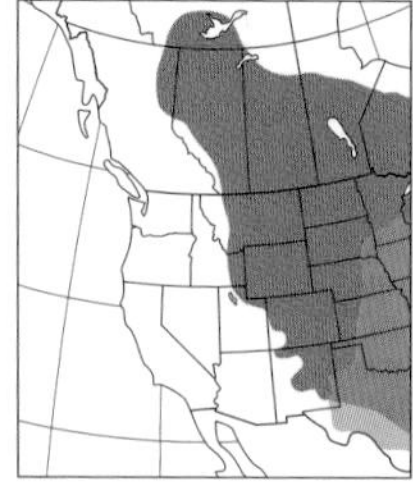

Common Grackle *Quiscalus quiscula L 12½" (32 cm)*
Long, keel-shaped tail; pale yellow eyes. Plumage appears all-black at a distance. In good light, ***males*** show glossy purplish blue head, neck, and breast. Widespread race *versicolor,* called "Bronzed Grackle," is the only race recorded from the West; it has a bronze back, contrasting with a blue head. Females are smaller and duller-bodied than males but still have purplish blue head. ***Juveniles*** are sooty brown, with brown eyes.
Voice: Song is a creaky *koguba-leek;* call note is a deep *chuck.*
Range: Fairly common in open fields, marshes, parks, and suburban areas. Casual to Arizona, Nevada, and the Pacific states north to Alaska.

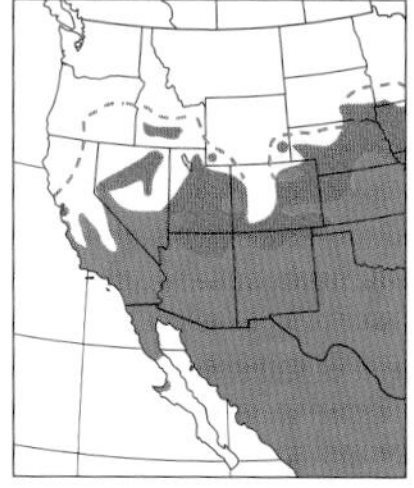

Great-tailed Grackle *Quiscalus mexicanus*
♂L 18" (46 cm) ♀L 15" (38 cm) Large, very long, keel-shaped tail, golden yellow eyes. ***Adult male*** iridescent black; purple sheen on head, back, underparts. ***Adult female***'s upperparts brown; underparts cinnamon-buff on breast. ***Juvenile*** like female but shows some streaking on underparts. Immature males duller, with shorter tails and darker eyes than adults by mid-fall. Females west of central Arizona smaller, paler below than *monsoni,* adjacent to the east.
Voice: Varied calls include clear whistles and loud *clack* notes.
Range: Common, especially in open flatlands with scattered groves of trees and in marshes and wetlands. Casual far north of breeding range; expanding north and west in western U.S.

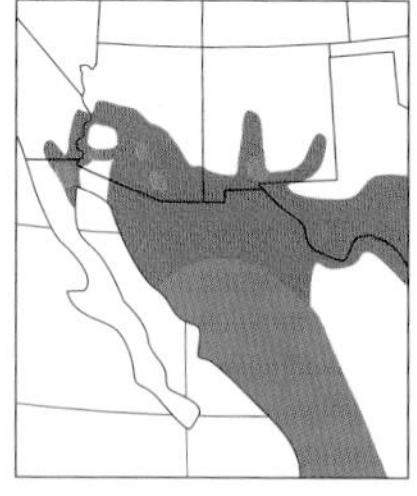

Bronzed Cowbird *Molothrus aeneus L 8¾" (22 cm)*
Red eyes distinctive at close range. Bill larger than Brown-headed Cowbird. ***Adult male*** is black with bronze gloss; wings and tail blue-black; thick ruff on nape and back gives a hunchbacked look. ***Adult female*** and juveniles in southwestern *loyei* are gray. In Texas nominate race (found regularly west to Pecos River), female is slightly duller but otherwise resembles male; juvenile is dark brown. Both races occur in west Texas.
Voice: Call is a harsh, guttural *chuck.* Song is wheezy and buzzy, often delivered in a spectacular "helicopter" display flight.
Range: Locally common in open country, brushy areas, and wooded mountain canyons; forages in flocks. Very local in winter. Casual north to Utah and Colorado.

Brown-headed Cowbird *Molothrus ater L 7½" (19 cm)*
Male's brown head contrasts with metallic green-black body. ***Female*** gray-brown above, paler below. ***Juvenile*** paler above, more heavily streaked below; pale edgings give its back a scaled look. Young males molting to adult plumage in late summer are a patchwork of buff, brown, and black. All cowbirds lay their eggs in nests of other species. Southwestern *obscurus* is distinctly smaller than eastern nominate *ater;* Rockies and Great Basin *artemisiae* is largest. Feeds with tail cocked up.
Voice: Male's song is a squeaky gurgling. Calls include a harsh rattle and squeaky whistles.
Range: Common; found in woodlands, farmlands, and suburbs. Rare visitor north to Alaska.

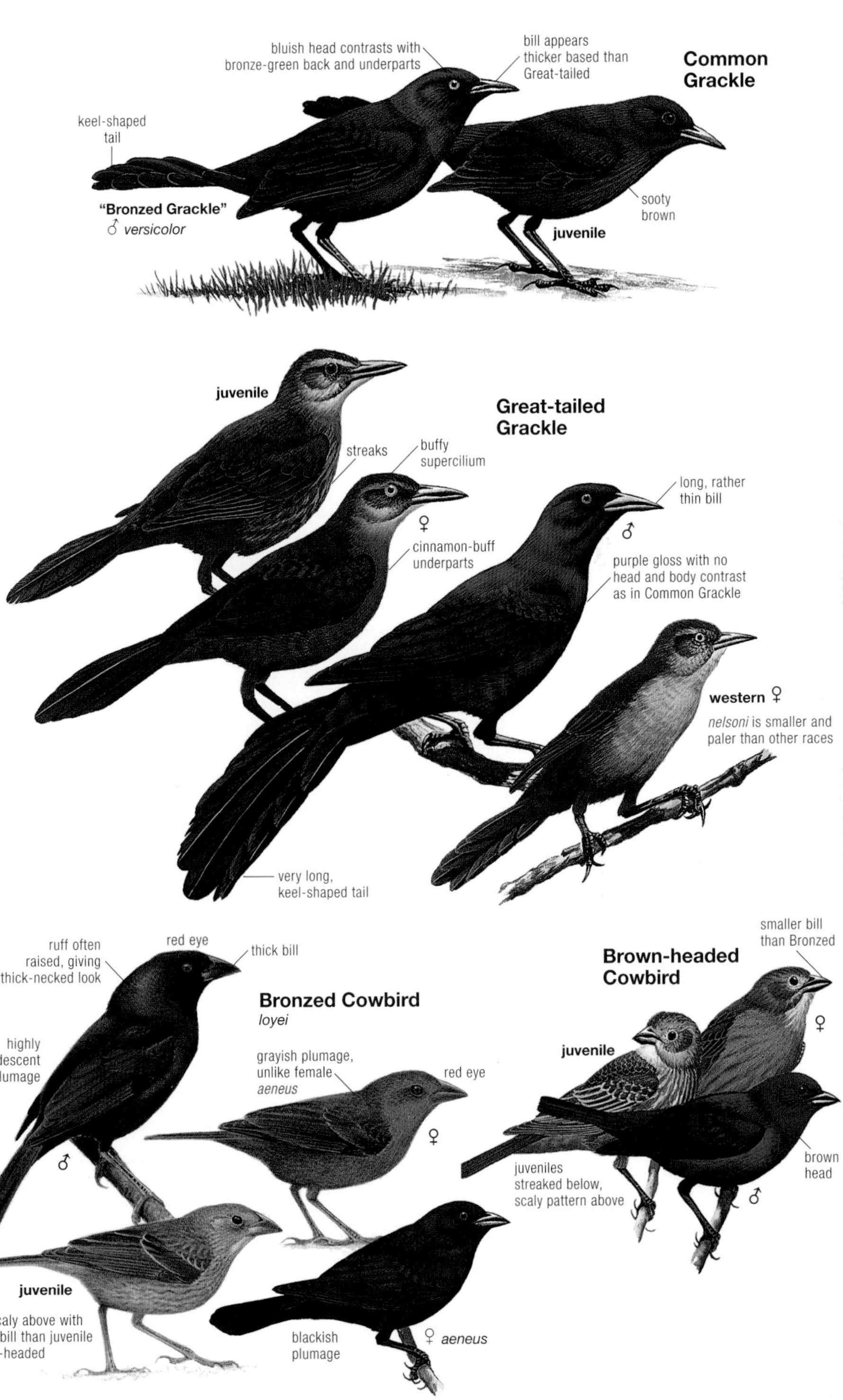
Common Grackle
bluish head contrasts with bronze-green back and underparts
bill appears thicker based than Great-tailed
keel-shaped tail
"Bronzed Grackle"
♂ versicolor
juvenile
sooty brown
Great-tailed Grackle
juvenile
streaks
buffy supercilium
♀
cinnamon-buff underparts
long, rather thin bill
♂
purple gloss with no head and body contrast as in Common Grackle
western ♀
nelsoni is smaller and paler than other races
very long, keel-shaped tail
Bronzed Cowbird
loyei
ruff often raised, giving thick-necked look
red eye
thick bill
highly
descent
plumage
♂
grayish plumage, unlike female aeneus
red eye
♀
juvenile
caly above with
bill than juvenile
-headed
blackish plumage
♀ aeneus
Brown-headed Cowbird
smaller bill than Bronzed
♀
juvenile
juveniles streaked below, scaly pattern above
brown head
♂

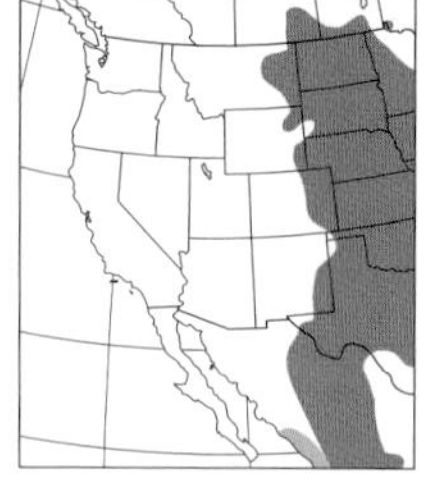

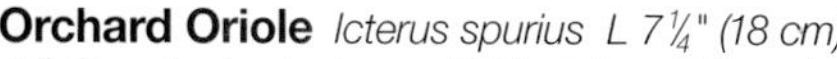

Orchard Oriole *Icterus spurius L 7¼" (18 cm)*

Adult male chestnut overall, black hood. ***Female*** olive above, yellowish below. Immature male resembles female; acquires black bib during winter; sometimes traces of chestnut by first spring. Smaller size, lack of orange tones or whitish belly, and thinner, more curved bill distinguish female and immature male from Baltimore and Bullock's Orioles. Compare especially to *nelsoni* Hooded Oriole.

Voice: Calls include a sharp *chuck*. Song is a loud, rapid burst of whistled notes, downslurred at the end.

Range: Locally common in suburban shade trees and orchards. Rare vagrant to Arizona and California in migration and winter; casual to Pacific Northwest; accidental to southeast Alaska.

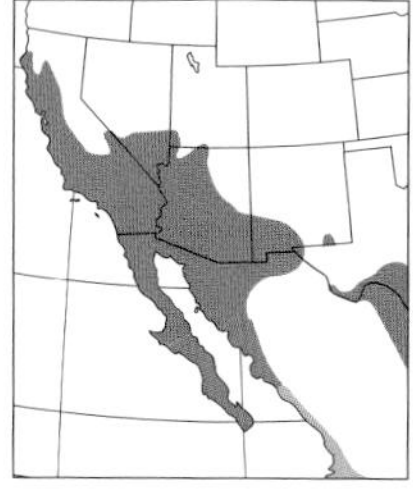

Hooded Oriole *Icterus cucullatus L 8" (20 cm)*

Bill long and slightly curved. ***Breeding male*** is orange or orange-yellow; note black patch on throat. Western birds (*nelsoni*) are yellower; they breed east locally to southeastern New Mexico and the El Paso region; nominate *cucullatus*, an uncommon and declining breeder along the Rio Grande in the Big Bend region of west Texas, is deeply orange—almost reddish orange—about the throat and has more black on the forehead than *nelsoni;* more numerous *sennetti* (not shown) just to the east is just slightly duller. All ***winter adult males*** have buffy brown tips on back, forming a barred pattern; compare with Streak-backed Oriole (page 431). Hooded ***female*** and immature male lack pale belly of Bullock's Oriole; bill is more curved. Compare *nelsoni* also with female and immature male Orchard Orioles, which are smaller with smaller bill (but juveniles have short bills too). Immature male acquires black patch on throat by winter.

Voice: Calls include a whistled, rising *wheet;* song is a series of whistles, trills, and rattles.

Range: Common in varied habitats, especially near palms. Breeding has expanded northward on West Coast. Very rare in winter in southern California. Casual to Pacific Northwest, Montana, and Colorado; accidental to the southern Yukon.

IDENTIFYING: Female-plumaged Orioles

Separating female-plumaged orioles is often tricky—particularly when telling Hooded Orioles from Orchard Orioles. Young male and female orioles in most species closely resemble each other; differences are more pronounced during winter. Vocalizations in all species can be critical for identification.

In the West, Bullock's Oriole is the widespread species and the one in which females have a white belly that contrasts with a lemon yellow breast. Bullock's shows dark "teeth" extending into the wing bars and a darkish eye line.

The similar-looking Baltimore Oriole—which is rare to very rare over most of the West—is more orangish overall, and its thicker wing bars lack the "teeth" found on Bullock's.

Hooded and Orchard have entirely yellow underparts. Structurally, they each have a graduated tail and appear rather long tailed overall. They can be very hard to tell apart, particularly in late summer when short-billed juvenile Hoodeds are seen. Orchard, which is indeed smaller, seems to twitch its tail more than other orioles.

Scott's Oriole is duller overall (more of an olive-green) with a straighter bill and dull streaks above.

Another species, Streak-backed Oriole, is a casual stray from western Mexico. It has a thick-based bill and a stippled back and is typically more orangish, especially about the head.

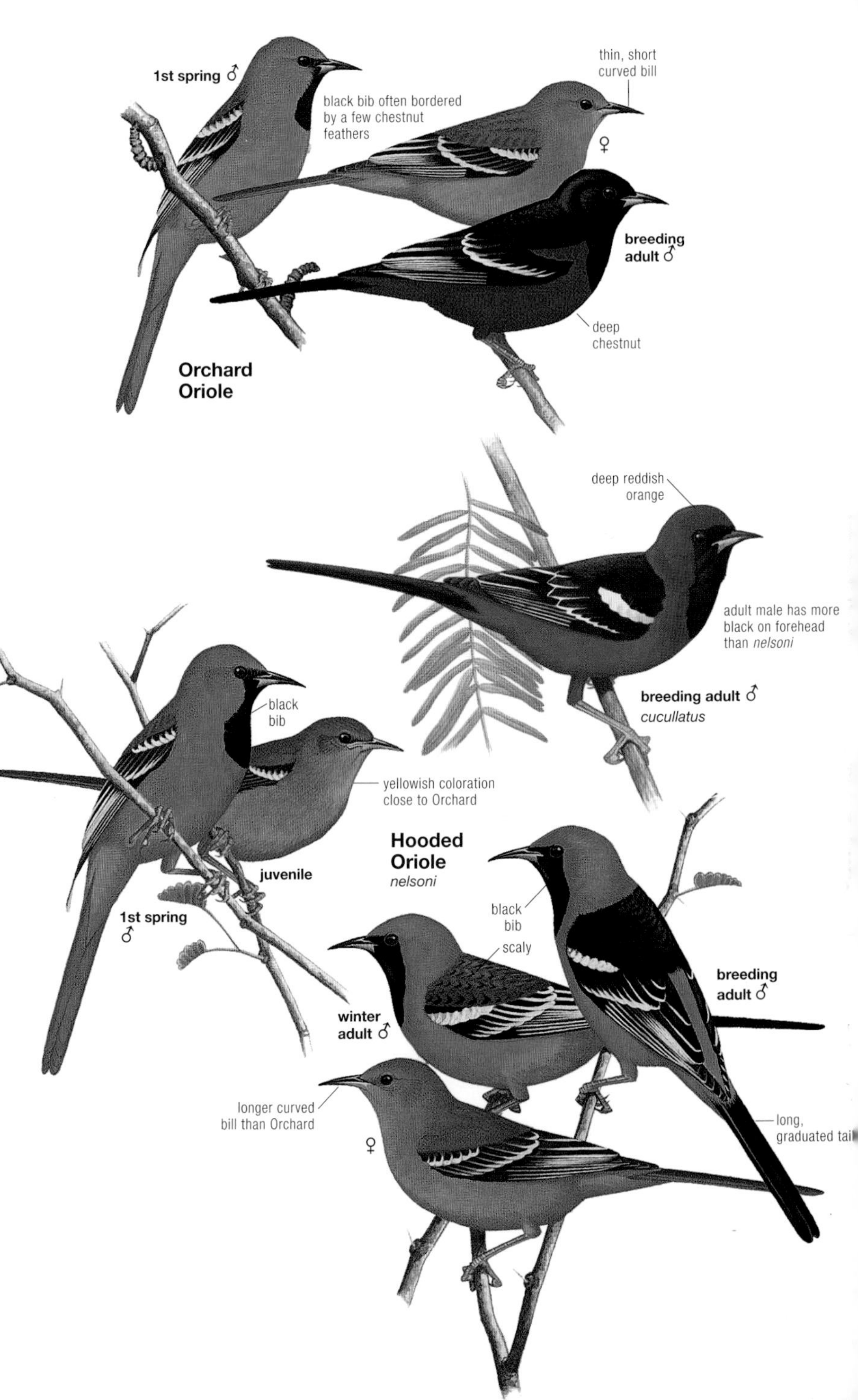
1st spring ♂
thin, short
curved bill
black bib often bordered
by a few chestnut
feathers
♀
breeding
adult ♂
deep
chestnut
Orchard
Oriole
deep reddish
orange
adult male has more
black on forehead
than nelsoni
breeding adult ♂
cucullatus
black
bib
yellowish coloration
close to Orchard
Hooded
Oriole
nelsoni
juvenile
1st spring
♂
black
bib
scaly
breeding
adult ♂
winter
adult ♂
longer curved
bill than Orchard
♀
long,
graduated tail

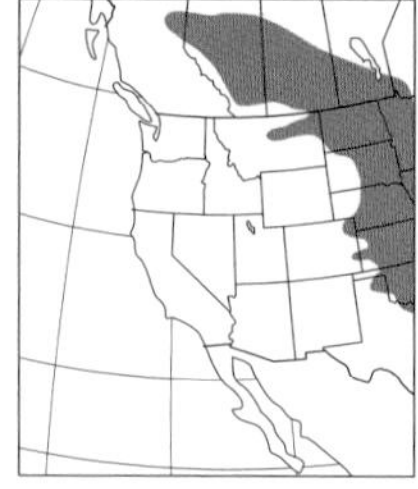

Baltimore Oriole *Icterus galbula L 8¼" (21 cm)*
Adult male has black hood and back, bright orange rump and underparts; large orange patches on tail. ***Adult females*** are brownish olive above and orange below, with varying amounts of black on head and throat; those with maximum black (shown) resemble first-spring males. Extent and intensity of color on underparts of ***fall immatures*** are highly variable; has distinctly contrasting wing bars and palish lores; no eye line or yellowish eyebrow.
Voice: Common call is a rich *hew-li;* also gives a series of rattles. Song is a musical, irregular sequence of *hew-li* and other notes.
Range: Fairly common in deciduous woodland in western breeding range. Rare to very rare otherwise in West; a few winter regularly in coastal California. Accidental to the Yukon.

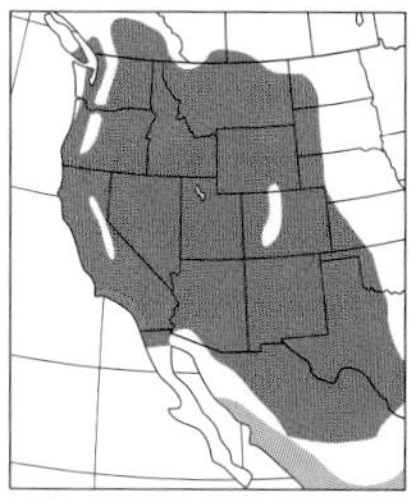

Bullock's Oriole *Icterus bullockii L 8¼" (21 cm)*
Formerly considered same species as Baltimore Oriole; some interbreeding on western Great Plains. ***Adult male*** has less black on head (crown, eye line, throat patch); note bold white patch on wing, entirely orange outer tail feathers. ***Females*** and ***immatures*** have yellow throat and breast, unlike extensive orange on most Baltimores (although the dullest Baltimores are difficult to separate from Bullock's); note Bullock's dark eye line, less contrasting wing bars, plainer back. Most birds show dark "teeth" intruding into white of median covert bar. By ***first spring,*** males have black lores and throat.
Voice: Song is a mix of whistles and harsher notes; call is a harsh *cheh* or series of same.
Range: Common breeder where shade trees grow. Small numbers winter in coastal California; casual elsewhere. Casual vagrant to Alaska, including to St. Lawrence Island (several records).

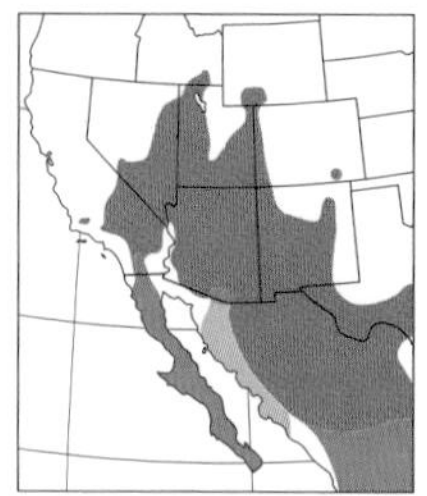

Scott's Oriole *Icterus parisorum L 9" (23 cm)*
Adult male's black hood extends to back and breast; rump, wing patch, and underparts bright lemon yellow. Adult female is olive and streaked above, dull greenish yellow below; throat shows variable amount of black. Immature male's head is mostly black by first spring. ***Females*** and immatures larger, grayer, more streaked above; have straighter bill than female Hooded Oriole (previous page).
Voice: Common call note is a harsh *shack;* song is a mixture of rich, whistled phrases, reminiscent of Western Meadowlark.
Range: Found in arid and semiarid habitats. Casual to northern California; accidental to Oregon and Washington. A few winter in coastal southern California.

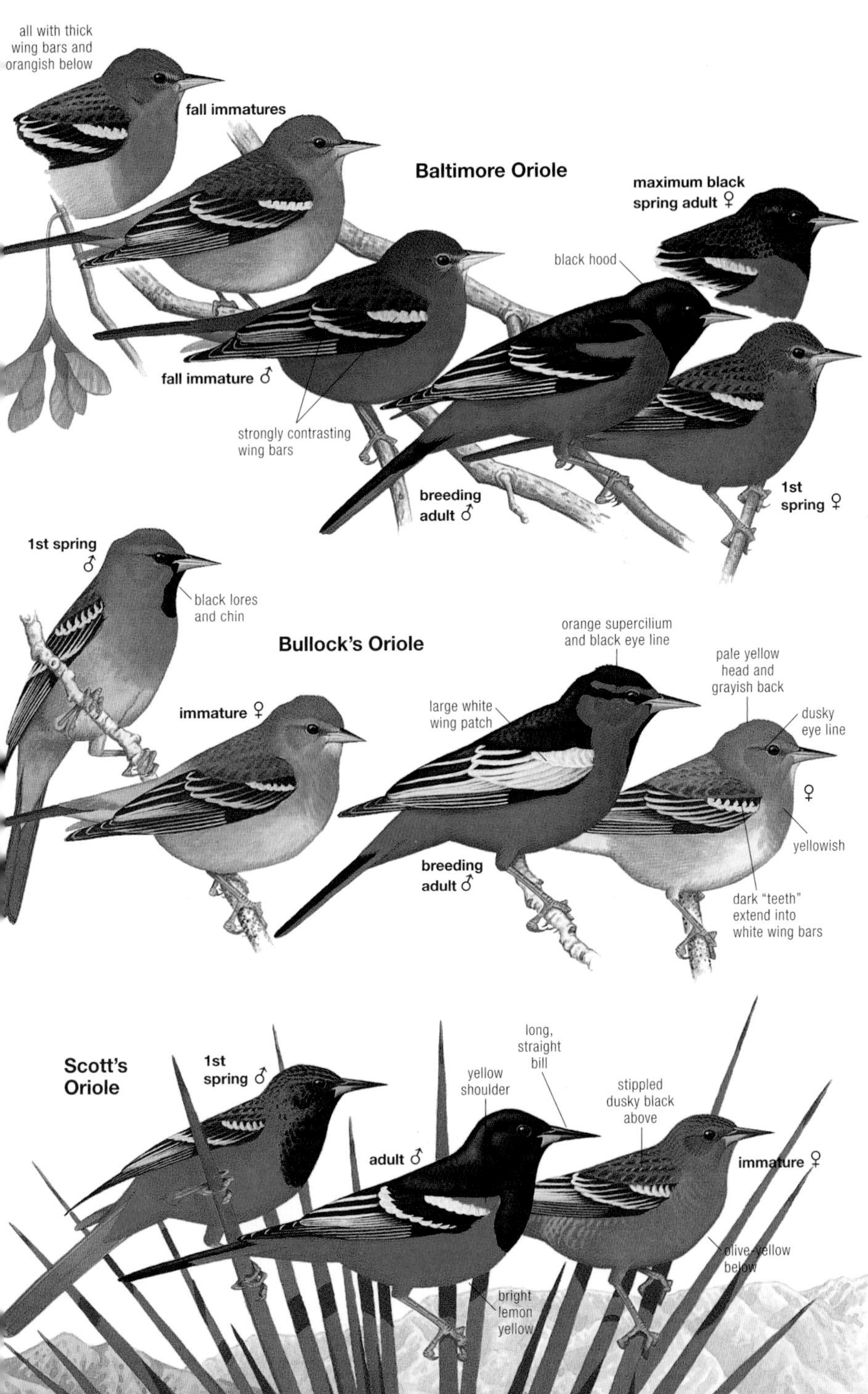

all with thick wing bars and orangish below
fall immatures
Baltimore Oriole
maximum black spring adult ♀
black hood
fall immature ♂
strongly contrasting wing bars
breeding adult ♂
1st spring ♀
1st spring ♂
black lores and chin
Bullock's Oriole
orange supercilium and black eye line
pale yellow head and grayish back
large white wing patch
dusky eye line
immature ♀
♀
yellowish
breeding adult ♂
dark "teeth" extend into white wing bars
Scott's Oriole
1st spring ♂
long, straight bill
yellow shoulder
stippled dusky black above
adult ♂
immature ♀
olive-yellow below
bright lemon yellow

Fringilline and Cardueline Finches, Allies
(Family Fringillidae)

These seedeaters fly with undulating flight. Many nest in the North; in fall, flocks of "winter finches" may roam south.

Brambling *Fringilla montifringilla L 6¼" (16 cm)*
Eurasian species. ***Adult male*** has tawny orange shoulders, spotted flanks; head and back fringed with buff in fresh fall plumage that wears down to black by spring. ***Female*** and juvenile have mottled crown, gray face, striped nape.
Voice: Flight call, a nasal *check-check-check;* also gives a nasal *zwee;* song consists of just a short buzzy note.
Range: Fairly common but irregular migrant on Aleutians; rare on Pribilofs and St. Lawrence Island; casual in fall and winter in western Canada and northern U.S.; recorded south to central California. Has nested on Attu Island (1996).

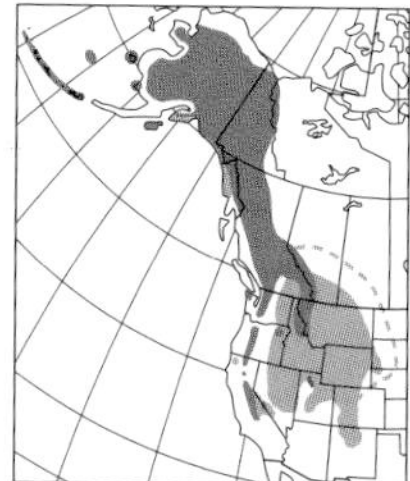

Gray-crowned Rosy-Finch *Leucosticte tephrocotis 5½-8¼" (14-21 cm)* Dark brown, with gray on head; pink on wings and underparts; underwings silvery. Female less pink, ***juveniles*** grayish. All have yellow bill in ***winter,*** black by spring. Western *littoralis,* ***"Hepburn's Rosy-Finch";*** much larger, darker Pribilofs *umbrina;* and Aleutians *griseonucha* show more gray on face than widespread nominate race (not illustrated)—which has plumage like *dawsoni* with narrow gray head band—and closely allied *dawsoni* from the Sierra Nevada and White Mountains.
Voice: All species of rosy-finches give a high, chirping *chew,* often given in courtship flight.
Range: Descends from higher elevations in winter. Both nominate *tephrocotis* and *littoralis* are migratory, migrating regularly as far south as the Sandia Mountains, New Mexico, and as far east as the Black Hills and Badlands of South Dakota. Casual on the western Great Plains; accidental to Arizona.

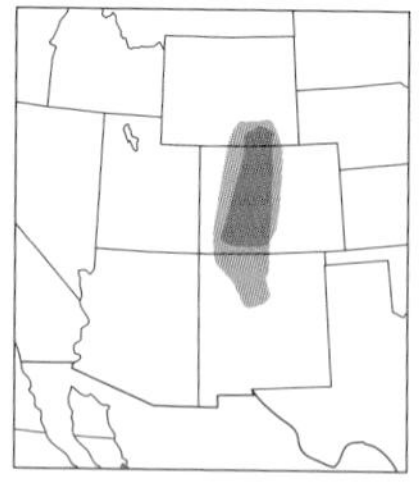

Brown-capped Rosy-Finch *Leucosticte australis L 6" (15 cm)* Plumages, behavior, and voice like Gray-crowned. Lacks gray head band of other North American rosy-finches. ***Male*** rich brown; darker crown; extensive pink on underparts. ***Female*** much drabber; some young female Gray-crowneds can be very similar.
Range: The least migratory of the rosy-finches. Migrates south to Sandia Mountains, but unrecorded away from Rocky Mountain region from southern Wyoming south to northern New Mexico.

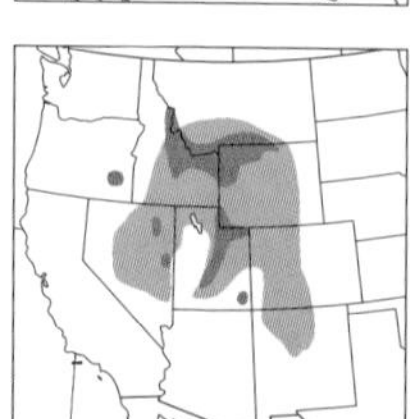

Black Rosy-Finch *Leucosticte atrata L 6" (15 cm)*
Plumages, behavior, and voice like Gray-crowned. Darkest rosy-finch. ***Male*** is blackish; in fresh plumage, scaled with silver gray; has gray head band; shows extensive pink. ***Female*** is blackish gray with no brownish tones and with little pink.
Range: Casual to eastern California, northern Arizona, and western Nebraska.

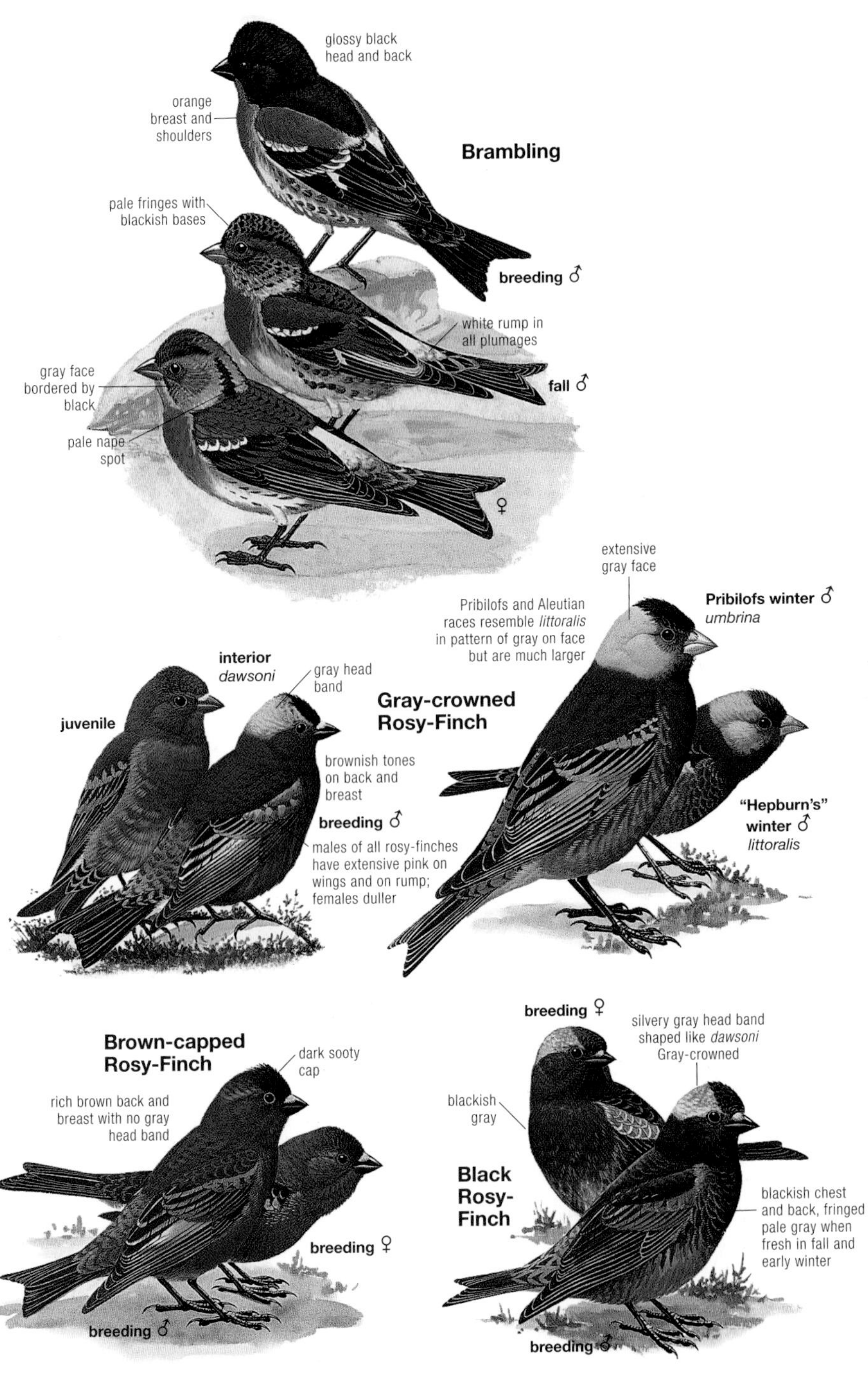
Brambling
glossy black head and back
orange breast and shoulders
breeding ♂
pale fringes with blackish bases
white rump in all plumages
fall ♂
gray face bordered by black
pale nape spot
♀
Gray-crowned Rosy-Finch
extensive gray face
Pribilofs and Aleutian races resemble *littoralis* in pattern of gray on face but are much larger
Pribilofs winter ♂ *umbrina*
interior *dawsoni*
gray head band
juvenile
brownish tones on back and breast
breeding ♂
males of all rosy-finches have extensive pink on wings and on rump; females duller
"Hepburn's" winter ♂ *littoralis*
Brown-capped Rosy-Finch
dark sooty cap
rich brown back and breast with no gray head band
breeding ♀
breeding ♂
Black Rosy-Finch
breeding ♀
silvery gray head band shaped like *dawsoni* Gray-crowned
blackish gray
blackish chest and back, fringed pale gray when fresh in fall and early winter
breeding ♂

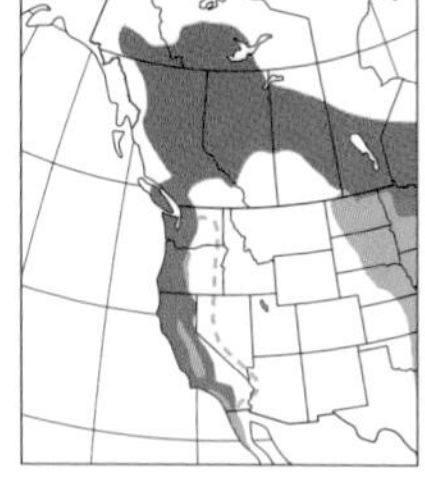

Purple Finch *Carpodacus purpureus* L 6" (15 cm)
Not purple, but rose red over most of ***adult male***'s body, brightest on head and rump. Rose color is acquired by second fall. Back is streaked; tail notched. Pacific coast race, *californicus,* is buffier below and more diffusely streaked than widespread *purpureus,* especially in female types. ***Adult female*** and immatures are heavily streaked below; closely resemble Cassin's Finch. Ear patch, whitish eyebrow, submoustachial stripe are slightly more distinct in Purple Finch; bill stubbier and more curved; undertail coverts are often not streaked. Compare also to female House Finch.
Voice: Calls include a musical *chur-lee* and, in flight, a sharp *pit,* a bit sharper in *californicus.* Song is a rich warbling, longer and more variable in *purpureus;* shorter than Cassin's Finch, lower and less strident than House Finch.
Range: Fairly common; found in coniferous or mixed woodland borders, suburbs, parks, and orchards; in the West Coast region, inhabits coniferous forests, oak canyons, and lower mountain slopes. Nominate race breeds across boreal forest of Canada west to northern British Columbia. Rare in migration and winter on western Great Plains south to New Mexico. Casual farther west, including Alaska, with multiple records on St. Lawrence Island. Pacific *californicus* breeds north to southwestern British Columbia. Casual in migration to western Great Basin.

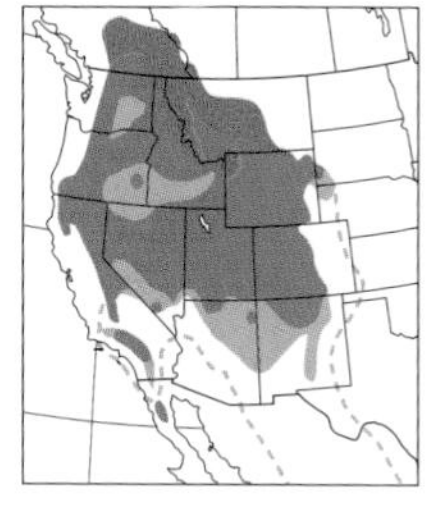

Cassin's Finch *Carpodacus cassinii* L 6¼" (16 cm)
Crimson of ***adult male***'s cap ends sharply at brown-streaked nape. Throat and breast paler than Purple Finch; streaks on sides and malar stripe more distinct. Red hues begin to appear late in second summer. Tail strongly notched. Undertail coverts always distinctly streaked, unlike many Purples. ***Adult female*** and immatures otherwise closely resemble Purple Finch. Cassin's facial pattern is slightly less distinct; culmen is straighter and longer; has longer primary projection.
Voice: Call is a dry *kee-up* or *tee-dee-yip.* Lively song, a variable warbling, is longer and more complex than Purple Finch, especially *californicus.*
Range: Fairly common in upper mountain forests, evergreen woodlands. Casual in fall and winter to West Coast. Very rare on western Great Plains.

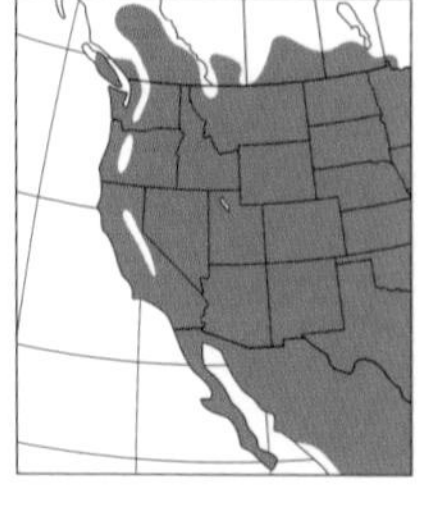

House Finch *Carpodacus mexicanus* L 6" (15 cm)
Male has brown cap; front of head, bib, and rump are typically red but can vary to orange or occasionally yellow. Bib is clearly set off from streaked underparts. Tail is squarish. ***Adult female*** and juvenile are streaked with brown overall; lack distinct ear patch and eyebrow of Purple and Cassin's Finches. Young males acquire adult coloring by first fall.
Voice: Lively, high-pitched song consists chiefly of varied three-note phrases; includes strident notes, unlike Purple Finch; usually ends with a nasal *wheer.* Calls include a whistled *wheat.*
Range: Common to abundant; found in lowlands and slopes up to about 6,000 feet. Range has expanded rapidly also in the West; especially numerous in towns; casual to Alaska.

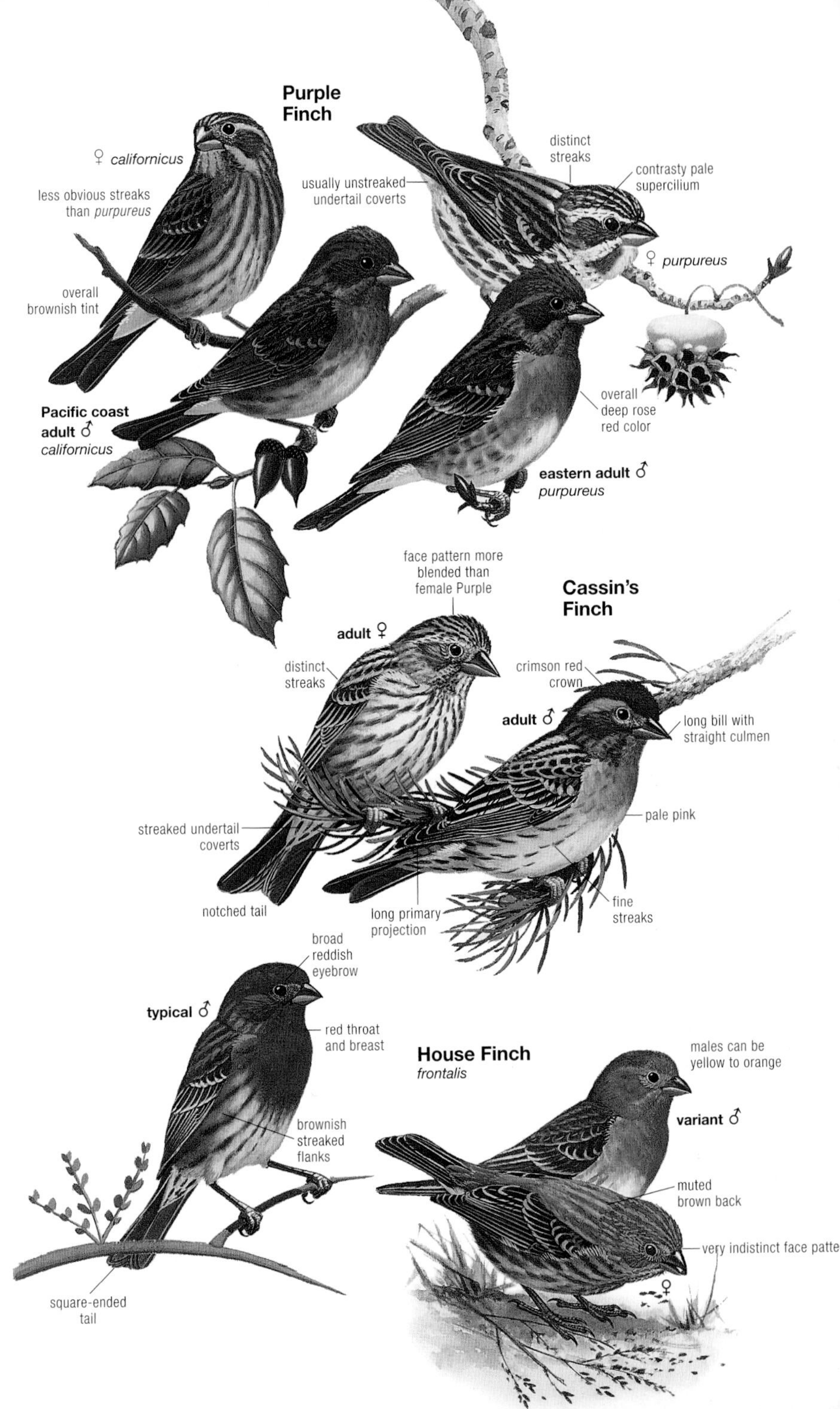
Purple Finch
♀ californicus
less obvious streaks than purpureus
overall brownish tint
Pacific coast adult ♂ californicus
usually unstreaked undertail coverts
distinct streaks
contrasty pale supercilium
♀ purpureus
overall deep rose red color
eastern adult ♂ purpureus
face pattern more blended than female Purple
Cassin's Finch
adult ♀
distinct streaks
crimson red crown
adult ♂
long bill with straight culmen
pale pink
streaked undertail coverts
notched tail
long primary projection
fine streaks
broad reddish eyebrow
typical ♂
red throat and breast
House Finch
frontalis
males can be yellow to orange
variant ♂
brownish streaked flanks
muted brown back
very indistinct face patte
♀
square-ended tail

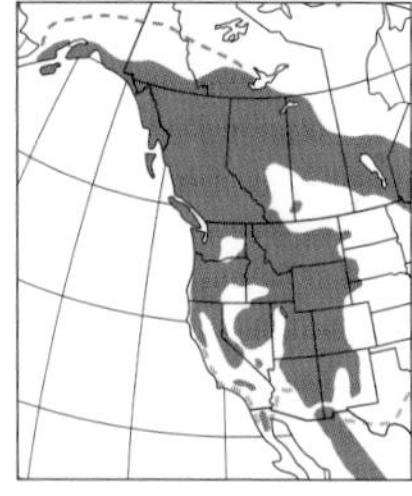

Red Crossbill *Loxia curvirostra* L 5½-7¾" (14-20 cm)
Bill with crossed tips identifies both crossbill species. Dark brown wings lack the bold white bars of White-winged Crossbill. Plumage highly variable. Most ***males*** are reddish overall, brightest on crown and rump, but may be pale rose or scarlet or largely yellow; always have red or yellow on throat. Most ***females*** are yellowish olive; may show patches of red; throat is always gray, except in a small northern subspecies where yellow extends to center, but not sides, of throat. ***Juvenile*** is boldly streaked; a few juveniles and a very few adult males show white wing bars, the upper bar thinner than the lower. Immatures are like the respective adult but juvenile wing is retained. All birds except adult males have olive edges on wings. Subspecies vary widely in size, including bill size; extremes shown here. All have their "home range." Distinct differences in vocalizations have led some authorities to believe that there may be a half dozen or more cryptic separate species in the Red Crossbill complex. All have large heads and short, notched tails.
Voice: Calls, given chiefly in flight, vary among subspecies. Song begins with several two-note phrases followed by a warbled trill.
Range: Fairly common. Inhabits coniferous woods. May nest at any time of year, especially in southern range. Dependent on cone crops. Irruptive migrant. Rare migrant outside mapped range but any race may turn up almost anywhere.

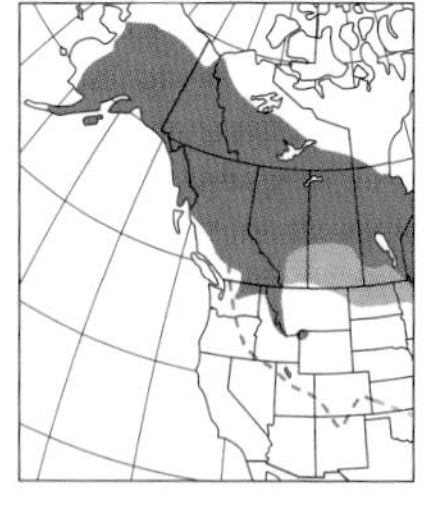

White-winged Crossbill *Loxia leucoptera* L 6½" (17 cm)
All ages have black wings with white tips on the tertials; two bold, broad white wing bars. Upper wing bar is often hidden by scapulars. ***Adult male*** is bright pink overall, paler in winter. ***Immature male*** is largely yellow, with patches of red or pink. ***Adult female*** is mottled with yellowish olive or grayish; rump pale yellow; underparts grayish olive, with yellow wash on breast and sides. ***Juvenile*** is heavily streaked; wing bars thinner than in adults.
Voice: Variable song, often delivered in display flight, combines harsh rattles and warbles; flight call is a rapid series of harsh *chet* notes.
Range: Inhabits coniferous woods. Highly irregular in its wanderings, dependent on spruce cone crops. Irruptive migrant. Casual in central Oregon, southern Utah, northern New Mexico.

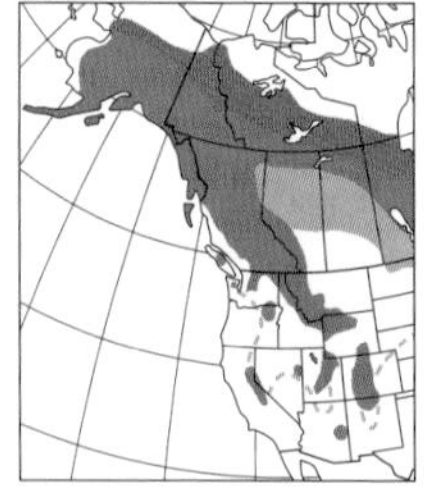

Pine Grosbeak *Pinicola enucleator* L 9" (23 cm)
Large and plump, with long tail. Bill is dark, stubby, strongly curved. Two white wing bars. ***Male***'s gray plumage is tipped with red on head, back, and underparts. ***Female*** and immatures are grayer overall; head, rump, and underparts variably yellow or reddish; some females and immature males are ***russet.***
Voice: Typical flight call is a whistled *pui pui pui;* alarm call, a musical *chee-vli.* Location call shows considerable geographic variation. Song is a rather short, musical warble.
Range: Uncommon to fairly common; inhabits open coniferous woods. Usually unwary and approachable. In West, Rockies *montana* is irruptive, casually reaching California, northern Arizona, and western Great Plains. Asian *kamtschatkensis* is casual to western Aleutians (Attu and Shemya Islands) in spring.

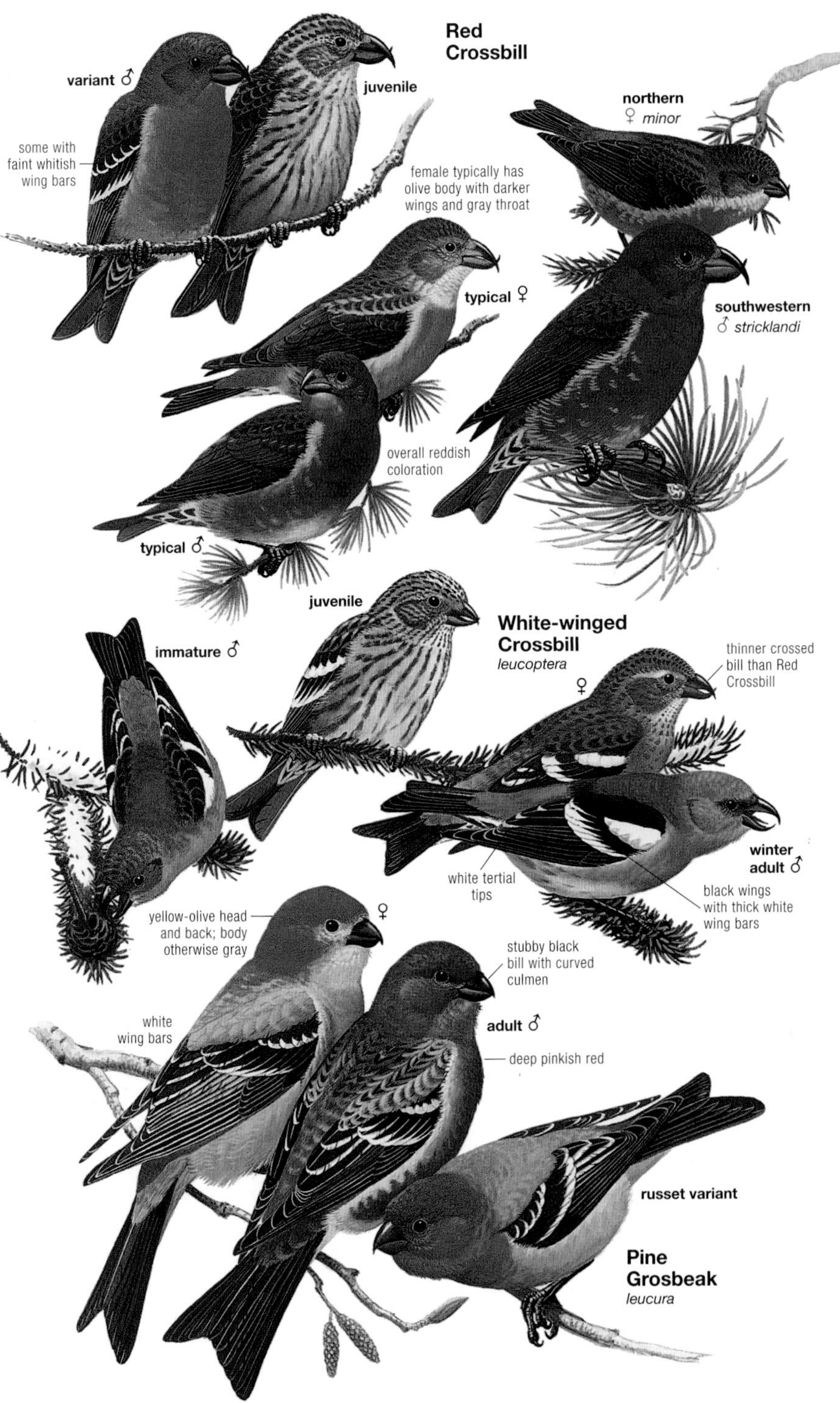

Red Crossbill
variant ♂
juvenile
some with faint whitish wing bars
northern ♀ minor
female typically has olive body with darker wings and gray throat
typical ♀
southwestern ♂ stricklandi
overall reddish coloration
typical ♂
juvenile
White-winged Crossbill
leucoptera
immature ♂
thinner crossed bill than Red Crossbill
♀
winter adult ♂
white tertial tips
black wings with thick white wing bars
yellow-olive head and back; body otherwise gray
♀
stubby black bill with curved culmen
white wing bars
adult ♂
deep pinkish red
russet variant
Pine Grosbeak
leucura

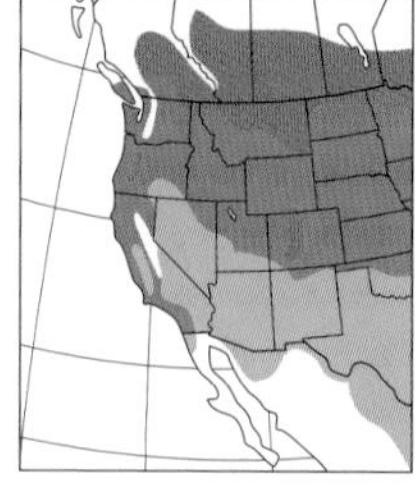

American Goldfinch *Carduelis tristis L 5" (13 cm)*
Breeding adult male is bright yellow with black cap; black wings have white bars, yellow shoulder patch; uppertail and undertail coverts white, with black-and-white tail. ***Female*** is duller overall, olive above; lacks black cap and yellow shoulder patch. White undertail coverts distinguish female from most Lesser Goldfinches. ***Winter adults*** and immatures are either brownish or grayish above; male may show some black on forehead. ***Juvenal*** plumage, which is held into Nov., has cinnamon-buff wing markings and rump.
Voice: Song is a lively series of trills, twitters, and *swee* notes. Distinctive flight call is *per-chik-o-ree.*
Range: Common and gregarious; found in weedy fields, open second-growth woodlands, residential areas (including gardens), and roadsides, especially in thistles and sunflowers. Casual north to southern Alaska and the Yukon.

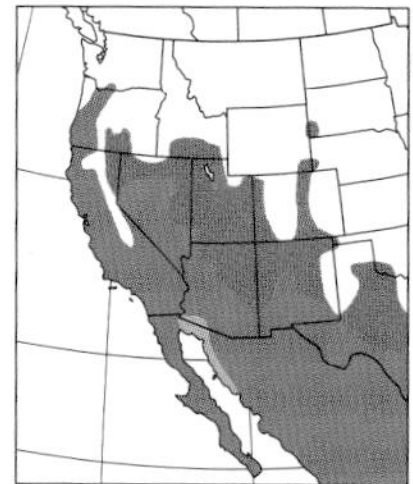

Lesser Goldfinch *Carduelis psaltria L 4½" (11 cm)*
All birds have a white wing patch at base of primaries. Entire crown black on ***adult male;*** back varies from black in eastern part of range to greenish in western birds. Most ***adult females*** are dull yellow below; except for a few extremely pale birds, they lack the white undertail coverts typical of American Goldfinch. ***Immature male*** lacks full black cap. Juvenile resembles adult female.
Voice: Call is a plaintive, kittenlike *tee-yee.* Song is somewhat similar to American Goldfinch. Frequently imitates other species.
Range: Common in dry, brushy fields, woodland borders, and gardens. Range expanding northward. Rare on western Great Plains, but increasing. Casual in central British Columbia and Montana; accidental to the Yukon.

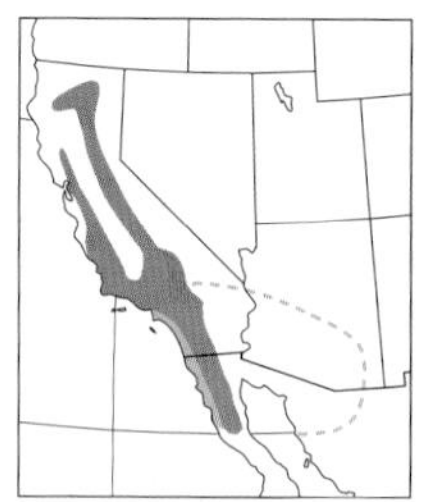

Lawrence's Goldfinch *Carduelis lawrencei*
L 4¾" (12 cm) Wings extensively yellow; upperparts grayish by spring; large yellow patch on breast. ***Male*** has black face and yellowish tinge on back. Fall and ***winter*** birds are browner above, duller below. ***Juvenile*** is faintly streaked, unlike other goldfinches.
Voice: Call is a bell-like *tink-ul.* Mixes *tink* notes into jumbled, melodious song. Lawrence's and Lesser Goldfinches often mimic other species' songs.
Range: Fairly common in spring and early summer; may sometimes flock with other goldfinches, but generally prefers drier interior foothills and mountain valleys; also western fringe of desert near watercourses. Erratic but usually uncommon at other seasons. Irregular fall movements to Southwest. In some winters, locally numerous in southeastern Arizona with fewer in southern New Mexico; absent in other winters. Casual as far east as west Texas and north to Nevada. Accidental to western Colorado.

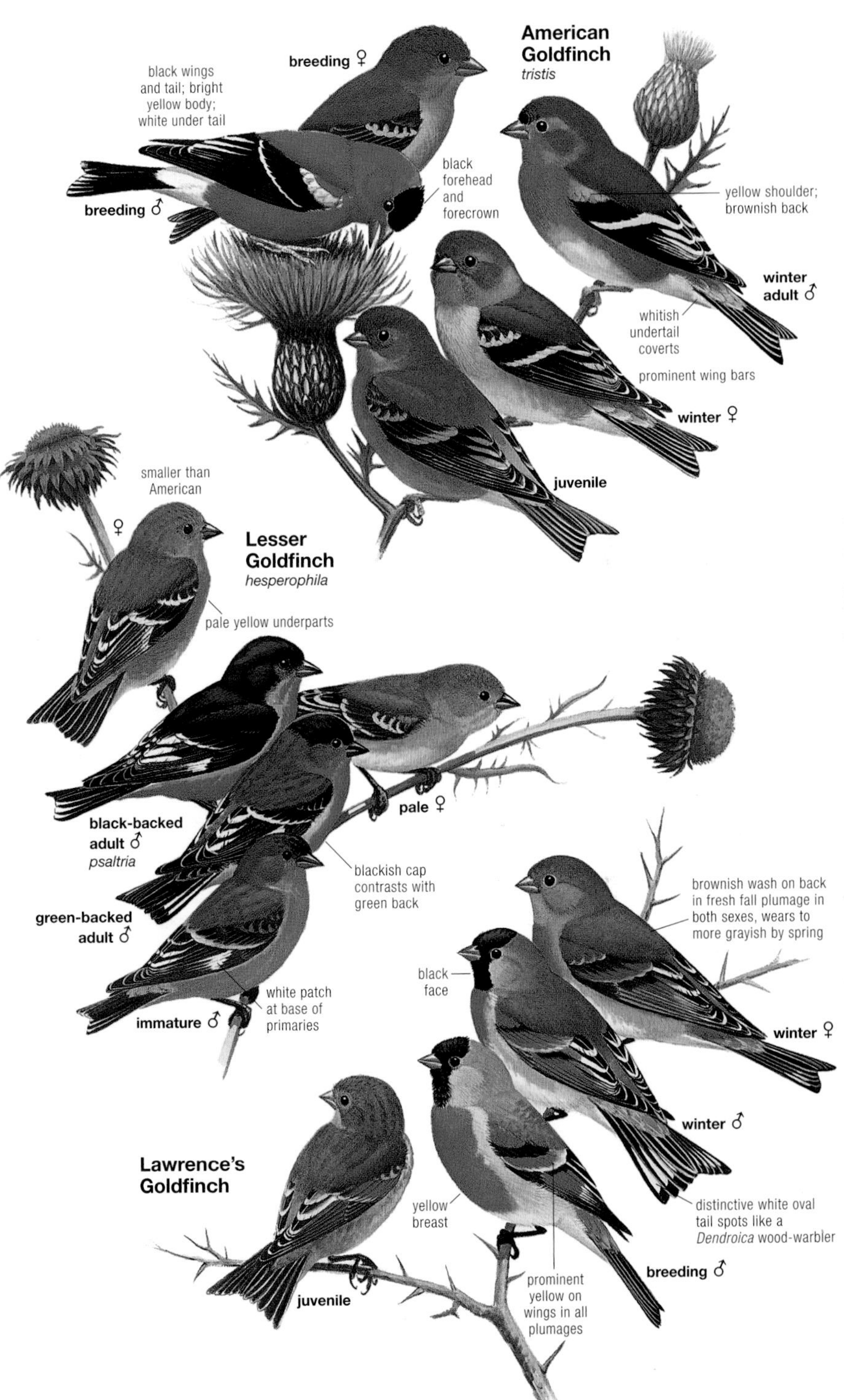
American
Goldfinch
tristis
breeding ♀
black wings
and tail; bright
yellow body;
white under tail
breeding ♂
black
forehead
and
forecrown
yellow shoulder;
brownish back
winter
adult ♂
whitish
undertail
coverts
prominent wing bars
winter ♀
juvenile
smaller than
American
♀
Lesser
Goldfinch
hesperophila
pale yellow underparts
pale ♀
black-backed
adult ♂
psaltria
blackish cap
contrasts with
green back
green-backed
adult ♂
white patch
at base of
primaries
immature ♂
brownish wash on back
in fresh fall plumage in
both sexes, wears to
more grayish by spring
black
face
winter ♀
winter ♂
Lawrence's
Goldfinch
yellow
breast
distinctive white oval
tail spots like a
Dendroica wood-warbler
breeding ♂
prominent
yellow on
wings in all
plumages
juvenile

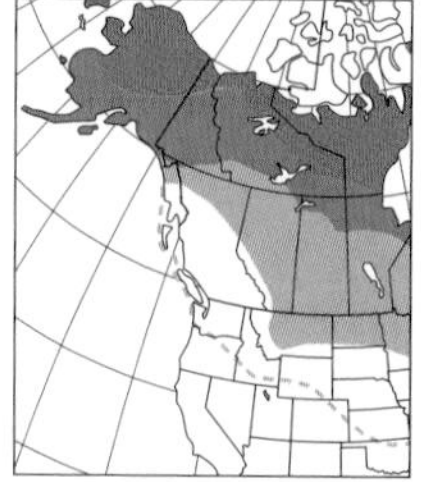

Common Redpoll *Carduelis flammea L 5¼" (13 cm)*
Red or orange-red cap or "poll," black chin. ***Male*** usually has bright rosy breast and sides. Both sexes buffier in winter. ***Juvenile*** lacks red cap until late-summer molt; males acquire pinkish breast by end of second summer. Extent of interbreeding with Hoary Redpolls is unknown.
Voice: When perched, gives a rising *swee-ee-eet* call; flight call is a dry, scratching single *chit* note or series of *chit* notes. Song combines trills and twittering.
Range: Fairly common; breeds in forests and tundra scrub. Gregarious. Favors brushy, weedy areas, also catkin-bearing trees. Irruptive migrant. Rather numerous to border states in some winters, especially east of Cascades; almost absent in others. Casual to northern California, Nevada, and northern New Mexico.

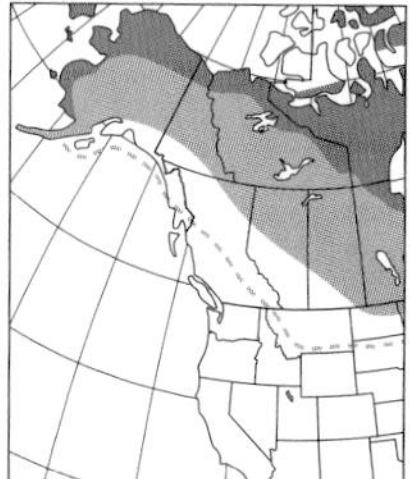

Hoary Redpoll *Carduelis hornemanni L 5½" (14 cm)*
Closely resembles Common Redpoll but is usually frostier and paler overall, with a slightly smaller bill. Streaking below and on rump and undertail coverts minimal or absent; fainter on sides and flanks. ***Male***'s breast is usually paler and pinker than Common; color does not extend to cheeks or sides.
Voice: Calls and song similar to Common.
Range: Fairly common; above Arctic tree line. The race *hornemanni,* of Canadian Arctic islands and Greenland, is larger and paler than more widespread *exilipes;* recorded once (Mar. 1964) from Fairbanks, Alaska. Rare sightings with Commons occur irregularly south of Canada in winter, south to Montana and northern Wyoming; casually to Washington and northeastern Oregon; accidental to Utah.

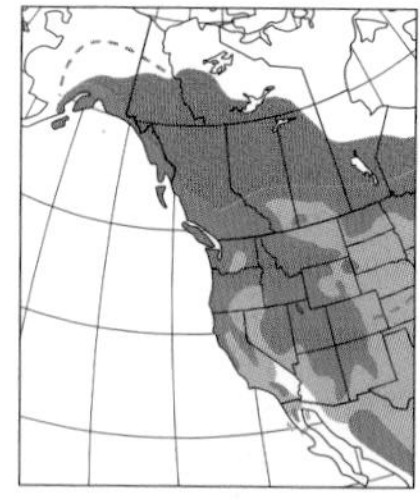

Pine Siskin *Carduelis pinus L 5" (13 cm)*
Prominent streaking; yellow at base of tail and in flight feathers conspicuous in flight; bill thinner than in other finches. ***Juvenile***'s overall yellow tint is lost by late summer.
Voice: Calls include a whiny, rough, rising *tee-ee* and, in flight, a harsh, descending *chee.* Song like American Goldfinch, but huskier.
Range: Gregarious; may flock with goldfinches in winter. Found in coniferous and mixed woods in summer; forests, catkin-bearing trees, shrubs, and fields in winter. Winter range is erratic. Casual to Bering Sea islands and throughout the Aleutians.

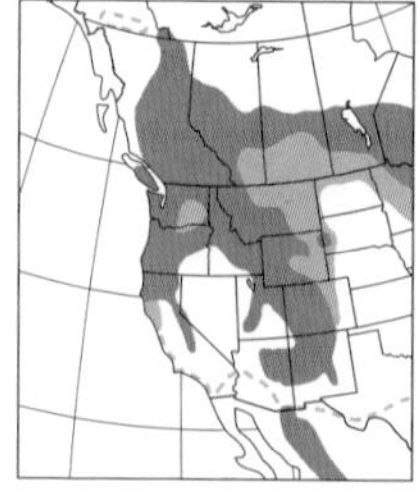

Evening Grosbeak *Coccothraustes vespertinus L 8" (20 cm)* Stocky, noisy finch. Big bill pale yellow or greenish by spring, whitish by fall; prominent white patch on inner wing. Yellow forehead and eyebrow on ***adult male;*** dark brown and yellow body. Grayish tan ***female*** has thin, dark malar stripe, white-tipped tail; second wing patch, on primaries, is conspicuous in flight. ***Juveniles*** have brown bills; female resembles adult female; male yellower overall, wing and tail like adult male.
Voice: Loud, strident call is *clee-ip* or *peeer.*
Range: Breeds in mixed woods; in the West, mainly in mountains; in migration and winter, varied wooded habitats. Numbers and range limits vary greatly. Casual to southeast Alaska.

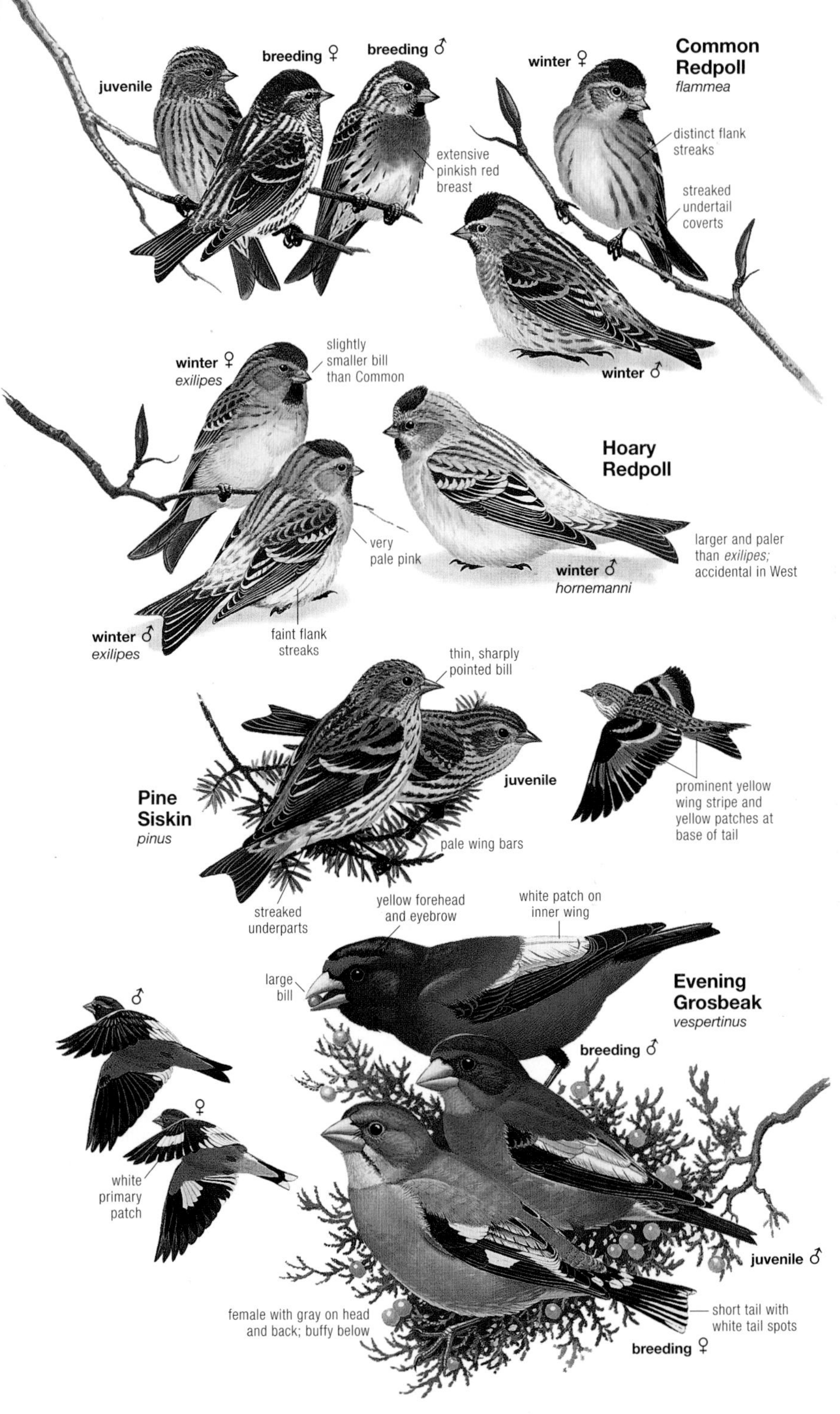

Common
Redpoll
flammea
juvenile
breeding ♀
breeding ♂
winter ♀
distinct flank streaks
extensive pinkish red breast
streaked undertail coverts
winter ♂
winter ♀
exilipes
slightly smaller bill than Common
Hoary
Redpoll
very pale pink
larger and paler than exilipes; accidental in West
winter ♂
hornemanni
winter ♂
exilipes
faint flank streaks
thin, sharply pointed bill
Pine
Siskin
pinus
juvenile
prominent yellow wing stripe and yellow patches at base of tail
pale wing bars
streaked underparts
yellow forehead and eyebrow
white patch on inner wing
large bill
Evening
Grosbeak
vespertinus
♂
breeding ♂
♀
white primary patch
juvenile ♂
female with gray on head and back; buffy below
short tail with white tail spots
breeding ♀

Old World Sparrows (Family Passeridae)

Gregarious, Old World family. Two species have become established in North America.

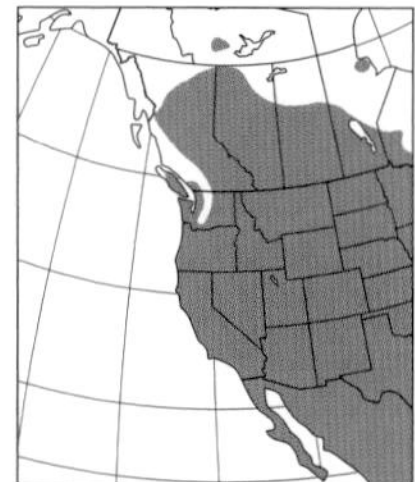

House Sparrow *Passer domesticus L 6¼" (16 cm)*
Breeding male has gray crown, chestnut nape, black bib, black bill. Fresh ***fall*** plumage is edged with gray, obscuring these markings; bill becomes brownish. ***Female*** is best identified by the combination of streaked back, buffy eye stripe, and unstreaked breast. Juvenile resembles adult female.
Voice: Calls include a sweet *cheelip* and monotonous chirps.
Range: Common and aggressive; common in populated areas. Gregarious in winter. Also known as English Sparrow. Casual to the Yukon and to southeast and western Alaska, the latter likely resulting from introductions in the Russian Far East.

Estrildid Finches (Family Estrildidae)

Most species in this large, Old World family (found from Africa to Australia and South Pacific islands) are small, with pointed tails. Related to weavers. Escapes or releases also seen.

Nutmeg Mannikin *Lonchura punctulata L 4½" (11 cm)*
Small, with heavy bill, pointed tail. ***Adults*** rich reddish brown above; scaly pattern below; thick bill black. Highly gregarious. Also widely known by another English name, Scaly-breasted Munia. ***Juveniles*** are tan; bill slate gray.
Voice: Song, *tiks* and whistles, is nearly inaudible; frequently given call is a loud *kibee.*
Range: Widespread in Southeast Asia, introduced or escaped in West. Found in greater Los Angeles area north to Santa Barbara; increasing. Favors grassy, weedy areas.

Weavers (Family Ploceidae)

Breeding males in this large, primarily African family are often highly colored. Weavers are known for their elaborate woven nests. Escapes or releases found locally in North America.

Orange Bishop *Euplectes franciscanus L 4" (10 cm)*
Breeding male is bright orange-red with black cap, breast, belly; long tail coverts obscure tail. ***Females,*** immatures, and winter birds are streaked above. Compare especially with Grasshopper Sparrow (page 366); note Orange Bishop's thicker, pinkish bill; short, blunt tail, often flicked open. Also known as Northern Red Bishop.
Voice: Complex song is high and buzzy. Calls include a sharp *tsip* and a mechanical *tsik tsik tsk.*
Range: Native to sub-Saharan Africa; widely introduced. Established in Los Angeles (1980s) and Phoenix (1998) areas, where it favors weedy areas, especially river bottoms.

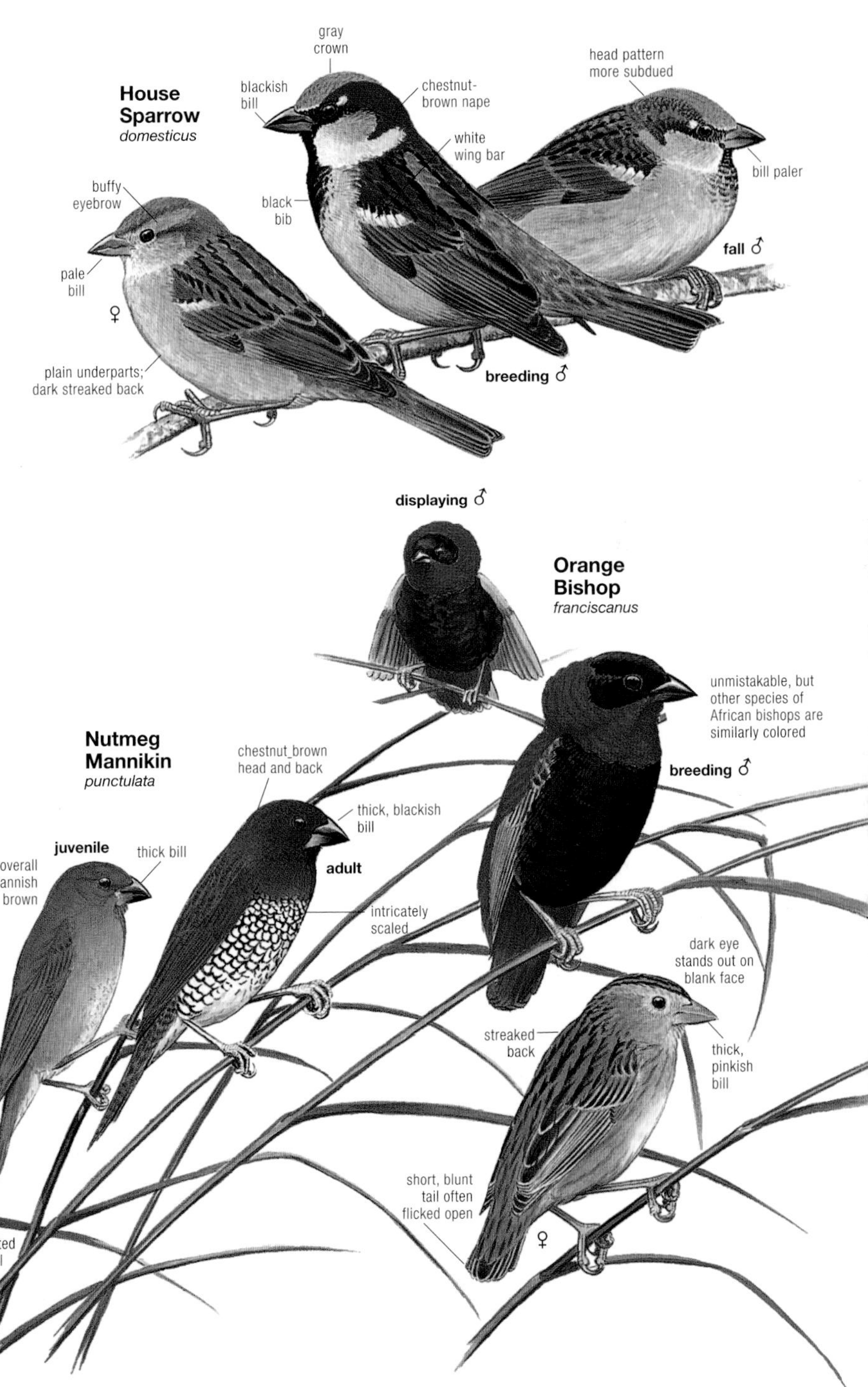
House
Sparrow
domesticus
gray
crown
blackish
bill
chestnut-
brown nape
head pattern
more subdued
white
wing bar
bill paler
buffy
eyebrow
black
bib
fall ♂
pale
bill
♀
plain underparts;
dark streaked back
breeding ♂
displaying ♂
Orange
Bishop
franciscanus
unmistakable, but
other species of
African bishops are
similarly colored
Nutmeg
Mannikin
punctulata
chestnut_brown
head and back
breeding ♂
thick, blackish
bill
juvenile
thick bill
overall
tannish
brown
adult
intricately
scaled
dark eye
stands out on
blank face
streaked
back
thick,
pinkish
bill
short, blunt
tail often
flicked open
♀
inted
tail

Rarities from Asia, Mexico, the Pacific Ocean

This appendix contains casual or accidental species that have been primarily recorded in the West or that are equally rare in both the West and the East. Most originate from Asia or are pelagic Pacific species. Illustrations not shown to scale.

adult *middendorffii*

Taiga Bean Goose *Anser fabilis*

L 30-35" (76-90 cm) WS 61-75" (155-191 cm) Eurasian species breeding on taiga from northern Scandinavia east to Anadyrland and wintering from northwest Europe to China and Japan. One specimen record from St. Paul Island, Pribilofs, on 19 Apr. 1946. A group of three were photographed on Shemya Island, Aleutians. from Sept. 2007 on into the winter. One, believed to be this species, was photographed in early winter 2007 from western Washington. Similar to immature Greater White-fronted Goose, but larger and with blackish base to long wedge-shaped bill with variable amounts of yellow-orange before tip. Within range, size increases clinally from west to east; eastern birds are largest and have been named *middendorffi*, but some treat the species as monotypic. Calls are loud and deep, very different from Greater White-fronted.

adults *serrirostris*

Tundra Bean Goose *Anser serrirostris*

L 28-33" (71-84 cm) WS 59-71" (150-180 cm) Eurasian species, breeding on tundra from Russian Northwest to Chukotski Peninsula, Anadyrland, and Koryakland, Russian Far East; winter range similar to Taiga Bean-Goose. Casual to the western Aleutians (two specimens, probably more regular), and there are specimens from the Pribilofs and St. Lawrence Island (photos too); one photographed in late Oct. 1999 from the southern Yukon. The majority of previous Alaska records of Bean Geese are now best left as unidentified. Similar to Taiga, but slightly smaller and with shorter and thicker based bill that is extensively black at base with a subterminal yellow-orange ring near tip. As with Taiga, size increases clinally from west to east. East Asian birds are nominate *serrirostris*, but some regard the species as monotypic. Calls are said to be higher pitched than Taiga.

adult

Lesser White-fronted Goose *Anser erythropus*

L 22-26" (55-66 cm) WS 47-53" (119-135 cm) Palearctic species. Specimen from Attu Island, Alaska, on 5 June 1994. Population is declining, especially from the Western Palearctic. Closely resembles Greater White-fronted Goose (page 14); but smaller, stockier, and with shorter neck and stubbier bill. The yellow orbital ring is conspicuous. It has a darker neck than Greater White-fronted (except for the *elgasi* and *flavirostris* subspecies of Greater).

Eastern Spot-billed Duck *Anas zonorhyncha*

L 22" (56 cm) Asian species, casual vagrant to Aleutians and Kodiak Island. Told from similar American Black Duck and female Mallard by pale tertials and sharply defined yellow tip of black bill. This recently split East Asian species lacks the red spots at base of bill for which this duck is named.

Shy Albatross *Thalassarche cauta*

L 35-39" (90-99 cm) WS 87-101" (220-256 cm) Casual off Pacific coast from Washington to northern California; once off Kasatochi Island, Aleutians. Only specimen (nominate *cauta*) off Washington in 1951; nine other records since 1996. Taxonomic opinions differ, but presently divided into four subspecies breeding in the following locations: *cauta* breeds on islands off Tasmania; nearly identical *steadi* breeds on Auckland, Antipodes, and Chatham Islands, New Zealand; *salvini* breeds on Snares and Bounty Islands off New Zealand, and on Iles Crozet in southwestern Indian Ocean; unrecorded *eremita* group (dark gray head) breeds on Chatham Island. Remaining nine North American records divided between those of *cauta/steadi* and those believed to be of *salvini* (including Aleutians record). Adults of *cauta/steadi* white-headed, unlike all ages of *salvini*, which have a grayish washed head; younger *cauta/steadi* head also grayish. Underwing pattern distinctive in all ages: primaries more extensively dark in *salvini* (and *eremita*); larger than Laysan, which has smaller, thinner, mostly pinkish bill. Note Shy's paler back, longer and grayer tail, more extensive white on the rump, more languid flight style; all ages show extensively white underwings, characteristic dark "thumb mark" at beginning of leading edge. Yellow-tipped bill in *cauta* adults (*steadi* very similar); grayer, darker tipped bill in all younger birds. Bill dusky with a dull yellow ridge and dark lower tip in adult *salvini*.

Light-mantled Albatross *Phoebetria palpebrata*

L 31-35" (79-89 cm) WS 72-86" (183-218 cm) A circumpolar species of the southern oceans that breeds on subantarctic islands. One individual at Cordell Bank, off northern California, on 17 July 1994. A very graceful flyer. ***Adult*** has dark head with prominent white eye crescents and strikingly pale mantle and body. The long, dark, wedge-shaped tail is distinctive. At close range, note bluish line of skin on the lower mandible (sulcus). Juvenile is browner overall, with less prominent eye crescents and gray sulcus.

Wandering Albatross *Diomedea exulans*

L 42-53" (107-135 cm) WS 100-138" (254-351 cm) Circumpolar in southern oceans. One onshore record at Sea Ranch, Sonoma County, California, 11 to 12 July 1967. Five European records. A polytypic species (5 to 7 subspecies), some authorities recognize up to five species. Huge size—wingspan reaches over 11 feet. Massive pinkish bill and white underwings with narrow dark trailing edge and primary tips. ***Adult*** extensively white above. Juvenile is dark chocolate brown with conspicuous white face. Maturation takes up to 15 years. Becomes white first on the mantle, body, and head, eventually spreading to upperwing coverts.

Great-winged Petrel *Pterodroma macroptera*

L 16" (41 cm) WS 38" (97 cm) Southern oceans species; two records (July-Aug., Oct.) off central California of presumed *gouldi* subspecies with whiter face. Similar to Murphy's, but browner (less gray); more uniform underwing; white more evenly distributed around bill; and dark legs and feet.

Hawaiian Petrel *Pterodroma sandwichensis* **E**
L 17" (43 cm) WS 39" (98 cm) Recently split from Galapagos Petrel (*P. phaeopygia*), which together were formerly known as Dark-rumped Petrel. The endangered Hawaiian Petrel nests only on Hawaiian Islands. Both species have mostly black crown that extends down sides of neck forming a partial collar. Both uniformly dark above, but may show a slight M-pattern and white on the uppertail coverts. Note underwing pattern. The two are not known to be separable with certainty in the field, but it has recently been proposed that Hawaiian has more of a capped look with an insertion of white into the dark shawl. Casual, recorded off California and Oregon from May to Oct., over 20 records, but no specimens; best documented birds thought to be Hawaiian.

Stejneger's Petrel *Pterodroma longirostris*
L 11" (28 cm) WS 23" (58 cm) Breeds on Juan Fernandez Islands off Chile. Casual well off the California coast, chiefly in fall. Resembles Cook's Petrel but distinct, dark half hood contrasts with grayish back and extensive white forehead; tail is longer and more uniformly colored, with less white in outer tail feathers.

Bulwer's Petrel *Bulweria bulwerii*
L10" (26 cm) WS 26" (66 cm) Bird of tropical and subtropical oceans; accidental summer visitor off Monterey, California (one photographed on 26 July 1998). Sooty brown overall with pale diagonal bar across secondary coverts. Long tail usually held in a point; wedge shape visible only when fanned. Flight is buoyant and erratic, long wings slightly bowed and held forward. Flies within a few feet of the water; flight, when it is windy, is more like gadfly petrels.

Parkinson's Petrel *Procellaria parkinsoni*
L 18" (46 cm) WS 45" (115 cm) Breeds on islands off New Zealand; ranges north in austral winter to east-central Pacific, north to southern Mexico. One certain record (1 Oct. 2005, about 18 miles off Point Reyes, California). Almost wholly blackish petrel; rather thick yellowish bill, with black lines and tip; feet and legs dark. Compare to similarly colored Flesh-footed Shearwater (page 76), note bill shape and color. Westland Petrel (*P. westlandica*) from South Pacific is similar but is even larger and thicker billed; unrecorded north of Equator.

Streaked Shearwater *Calonectris leucomelas*
L 19" (48 cm) WS 48" (122 cm) Asian species, casual off California (most records from Monterey Bay) in the fall, accidental inland in California's upper Central Valley and Wyoming. Head is variable, largely white to rather heavily streaked; often looks white at a distance. Pale fringes give upperparts a scaly look. White uppertail coverts form a pale "horseshoe," but can be absent. Bill color varies from pale gray to pale pink. Note the white axillaries and dark underwing primary coverts. Languid, soaring flight is typical of *Calonectris* shearwaters.

Wedge-tailed Shearwater *Puffinus pacificus*
L 18" (46 cm) WS 40" (101 cm) Polymorphic species from warm waters of Pacific and Indian Oceans. Casual in summer and fall to waters off central California; accidental on Salton Sea. Long tail held in a point; wedge shape visible only when fanned. Slender, grayish bill has darker tip. Head and upperparts of ***light morph*** grayish brown; mostly white with mottled brown below. Most sightings are of wholly brown ***dark morph,*** which has paler base to flight feathers. Languid flight with prolonged soaring on bowed wings angled forward.

Townsend's Shearwater *Puffinus auricularis*
L 13" (33 cm) WS 33" (83 cm) Two subspecies: nominate *auricularis* breeds on the Revilla Gigedo Islands off western Mexico; *newelli* with whiter undertail and longer tail breeds on the Hawaiian Islands. One record of *newelli*; turned into a rehab center after it had been attracted to a night construction worker's head lamp at Del Mar, California, on 1 Aug. 2007. Similar to Manx Shearwater (page 78) but more sharply black and white with more dark on the longest undertail coverts and a longer tail.

Ringed Storm-Petrel *Oceanodroma hornbyi*
L 8¼-9" (21-23 cm) South American species of the Humboldt Current from Chile to southern Ecuador; casual to Colombia. Nesting grounds unknown, but possibly in the central Andes. Recent well-documented record off San Miguel Island, California, on 2 Aug. 2005. Note large size and striking plumage pattern, including blackish cap and breast band; tail is deeply forked.

Wedge-rumped Storm-Petrel *Oceanodroma tethys*
L 6½" (17 cm) WS 13¼" (34 cm) Breeds on the Galápagos Islands (nominate *tethys*) and on islets off Peru (much smaller *kelsalli*). Casual off California coast from Aug. to Jan.; specimen (Jan.) is of *kelsalli*. Bold white triangular patch of uppertail coverts gives the appearance of a white tail with dark corners. Compare with the rounded rump band and white flanks of Wilson's (page 80).

Tristram's Storm-Petrel *Oceanodroma tristrami*
L 10" (25 cm) WS 22" (56 cm) Breeds on Leeward Hawaiian Islands and Volcano and southern Izu Islands off southern mainland Japan. One certain record, one photographed and measured on Southeast Farallon Island off central California on 22 Apr. 2006. Larger and grayer than Black Storm-Petrel (page 80) with paler carpal area and more deeply forked tail.

Red-tailed Tropicbird *Phaethon rubricauda*
L 37" (94 cm) WS 44" (112 cm) Species from tropical and subtropical Pacific and Indian Oceans. Very rare, usually well off California coast. Broadest winged tropicbird; flies with languid wingbeats. Flight feathers mostly white. ***Adult*** has red bill; red tail streamers, narrower than in other tropicbirds. ***Juvenile***'s all-white tail lacks streamers; upperparts barred; bill black, gradually changing to yellow and then red. Note also lack of black collar on nape.

Nazca Booby *Sula granti L 32" (81 cm) WS 62" (158 cm)*
Recently split from the Masked Booby, this eastern tropical Pacific endemic ranges north to Mexico. One debatable (on origin) record, an immature landed on a ship off northern Baja California and rode to San Diego (29 May 2001). Other records of immatures off southern and central California remain problematic. Similar to Masked Booby in all plumages; subtle shape differences include shorter and thinner bill, shorter legs, and longer wings and tail. Note ***adult***'s orange-pink bill and more orange (not yellow) iris. Juvenile averages paler than Masked, and pale collar is less marked or absent.

Great Frigatebird *Fregata minor*
L 37" (95 cm) WS 85" (216 cm) Extensive breeding range in Indian and Pacific Oceans. Two photographed records of adults off California (male in Monterey Bay on 13 Oct. 1979, and female Southeast Farallon Island on 14 Mar. 1992). Closely resembles Magnificent Frigatebird (page 82). Adult male distinguished from Magnificent by russet bar on upper wing coverts, pink feet and often by whitish scallops on axillaries. Note ***adult female***'s dark head with pale gray throat, rounder (less tapered) black belly patch, and red orbital ring. When fresh, juvenile has rusty wash to head and chest, and pink feet.

Lesser Frigatebird *Fregata ariel*
L 30" (76 cm) WS 73" (185 cm) Widespread in southwest and central Pacific and Indian Ocean; a few colonies in south Atlantic. One found dead and photographed (specimen discarded) near Basin, Wyoming, on 11 July 2003; and a subadult female photographed at Arcata, California, on 15 July 2007. Our smallest frigatebird, in all plumages a white spur extends from the flanks into the axillaries. Juvenile has pale, rusty head.

Yellow Bittern *Ixobrychus sinensis*
L 15" (38 cm) WS 21" (53 cm) Widespread Asian species. One specimen record from Attu Island, Alaska (17 to 22 May 1989). In ***adults*** (sexes similar), head and neck are buffy, cap and tail are black, and neck is streaked. Juvenile is more streaked overall. In flight, note black primary coverts and flight feathers. An Asian congener, Schrenck's Bittern (*Ixobrychus eurhythmus*), though scarce, is highly migratory and could occur in North America. It is slightly larger than Yellow Bittern, more cinnamon dorsally, and has a slate gray trailing edge to its wing.

Gray Heron *Ardea cinerea*
L 33-40" (84-102 cm) WS 61-69" (155-175 cm) Widespread Old World species. Two records from St. Paul Island, one on 1 Aug. 1999 and another on 1 and 2 Oct. 2007. Similar to Great Blue Heron (page 90), but smaller, with shorter legs and neck. In all plumages lacks rufous thighs of Great Blue; in flight leading edge of wing shows prominent white area, rather than rufous.

Intermediate Egret *Mesophoyx intermedia L 27" (69 cm)*
Widespread Old World species found in Africa and from India to Australia. Breeds north in Asia to Japan. One found dead (Asian nominate race) on Buldir Island, western Aleutians, on 30 May 2006, had likely arrived and died some days earlier. Similarly shaped and colored like the larger Great Egret (page 90), but with shorter bill with a distinct dark tip.

Chinese Egret *Egretta eulophotes*
L 27" (65 cm) WS 41" (104 cm) Threatened Asian species, breeding on islands off Korea, China, and perhaps the Russian Far East; winters in the Philippines and Borneo, some on coastal mainland of Southeast Asia. One specimen record from Agattu Island, Alaska, 16 June 1974. Shorter legs than Little Egret. In ***breeding*** plumage has shaggy crest, turquoise lores, entirely orange-yellow bill, and black legs with yellow feet. Nonbreeding birds lack crest; legs and feet are yellowish green and bill mostly dark.

Chinese Pond-Heron *Ardeola bacchus*
L 18" (46 cm) WS 34" (86 cm) Migratory East Asian species that occurs rarely, but with increasing frequency, to Japan and Korea. A breeding-plumaged adult was on St. Paul Island, Alaska, 4 to 9 Aug. 1996. Members of this genus are short and stocky and most have entirely white wings, rump, and tail (especially visible in flight); yellow legs and feet. ***Breeding male*** has bright chestnut head, neck, and upper breast, slaty lower breast, and blue-based bill. Breeding female lacks slaty lower breast. Immatures and nonbreeding adult is much duller with streaked neck and not separable from several other congeners from south and Southeast Asia.

Steller's Sea-Eagle *Haliaeetus pelagicus*
L 33-41" (84-104 cm) WS 87-96" (221-244 cm) Nests in northeastern Asia; casual in Alaska; recorded on Aleutians, Pribilofs, Kodiak Island, near Juneau. In flight, white shoulders show as white leading edge of wings; trailing edge of wing more curved than White-tailed or Bald Eagles. Immense yellow-orange bill; long, white, wedge-shaped tail; white thighs. ***Juvenile*** lacks white shoulders; end of tail is dark.

Eurasian Kestrel *Falco tinnunculus*
L 13½" (34 cm) WS 29" (74 cm) Casual on western Aleutians and in Bering Sea region; accidental in fall, early winter on the West Coast south to California. Resembles American Kestrel, but note larger size and single, not double, dark facial stripe. In flight, distinguished by wedge-shaped tail and two-toned upperwing, with back and inner wing paler. Hovers as it hunts. ***Adult male*** has russet wings, gray tail; female duller, often with gray rump. ***Juvenile*** similar to adult female, but dark barring heavier on upperparts and tail.

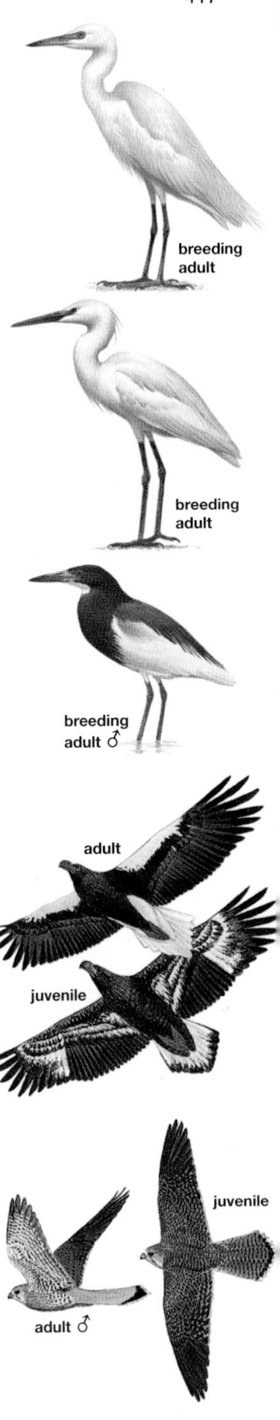

Eurasian Hobby *Falco subbuteo*

L 12¼" (31 cm) WS 30¼" (77 cm) Old World species. Casual between late spring and fall in Bering Sea region and on western Aleutians; an Oct. record from Seattle. Small, short-tailed falcon with long, slender wings; in folded wing, wing tips extend well past tip of tail. Graceful and powerful flier. White cheeks; thin, pale eyebrow; thin, dark moustachial stripe; heavily streaked below. ***Adult*** has rufous-red undertail coverts; is dark gray above. ***Juveniles*** are blackish brown above with buffy feather fringes; lack rufous below. By following spring some look like adults, others intermediate in appearance. Compare all ages carefully to Merlin and Peregrine Falcon (pages 114 and 116).

Common Crane *Grus grus*

L 44-51" (112-130 cm) WS 79-91" (202-231 cm) Eurasian species. Two records from central Alaska and a sight record from eastern New Mexico. Almost always with migrating flocks of Sandhill Cranes. ***Adult*** distinguished from Sandhill Crane by blackish head and neck marked by broad white stripe. ***Juvenile*** like juvenile Sandhill; may show trace of white head stripe by spring. In flight, in all ages, black primaries and secondaries show as a broad black trailing edge on gray wings.

Whooping Crane *Grus americana* **E**

L 52" (132 cm) WS 87" (221 cm) Sparse wild population breeds in freshwater marshes of Wood Buffalo National Park in Alberta/Northwest Territories, Canada, and winters in Aransas National Wildlife Refuge on Gulf Coast of Texas. A small population has been introduced in Florida. ***Adult*** is white overall, with red facial skin; black primaries show in flight. Juvenile bird is whitish, with pale reddish brown head and neck and scattered reddish brown feathers over the rest of its body. Call is a shrill, trumpeting *ker-loo ker-lee-loo.* Endangered: Wild population is now about 150, including introductions. Intensive management and protection seem to be slowly succeeding.

Greater Sand-Plover *Charadrius leschenaultii*

L 8½" (32 cm) Old World species. Only North American record is one that wintered at Bolinas Lagoon, California, from 29 Jan. to 8 Apr. 2001. Overall closely resembles Lesser Sand-Plover (page 130), but longer bill; longer pale legs, more greenish yellow. In flight, wing stripe broader and feet project beyond tail. In breeding plumage, colored breast band is not as dark or extensive.

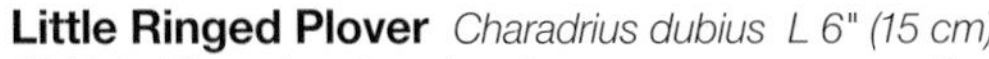

Little Ringed Plover *Charadrius dubius* *L 6" (15 cm)*

Old World species. Casual spring vagrant to western Aleutians. A small, slim plover with conspicuous yellow eye ring; legs rather dull color. In flight, note lack of wing bar. In ***breeding*** adult, white line separates brown forecrown from rear of head. On winter birds and ***juveniles,*** brown replaces black on head and breast, and eye ring is slightly duller; juvenile often shows yellow-buff tint to pale areas on head and throat. Rather solitary. Call is a descending *pee-oo* that carries a long way.

juvenile

breeding ♂ *curonicus*

Black-winged Stilt *Himantopus himantopus L 13" (33 cm)* Widespread in Old World. Two spring records from western Aleutians: Nizki Island from 24 May to 3 June 1983 and Shemya Island, 1 to 9 June 2003. One specimen record from St. George Island, Pribilofs, 15 May 2003. Similar to Black-necked Stilt (page 132), but paler on rear neck and lacks white spot above eye. ***Adults*** vary from entirely white head and neck to darker head and neck.

Green Sandpiper *Tringa ochropus L 8¾" (22 cm)* Eurasian species, casual in spring on western Aleutians, Pribilofs, and St. Lawrence Island. Resembles Solitary Sandpiper in plumage, behavior, and calls. Structure also similar, but a little plumper, straighter billed. Note white rump and uppertail coverts, with less extensively barred tail; lacks solidly dark central tail feathers of Solitary; upperparts and wing linings are darker. Similar Wood Sandpiper has more spotting above, more barring on tail, and paler wing linings. Call is like Solitary.

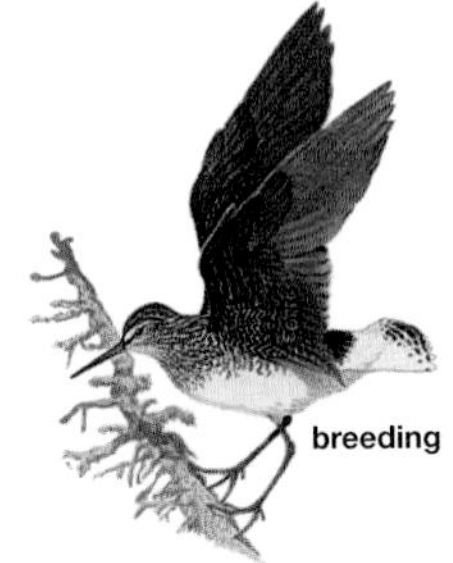

Marsh Sandpiper *Tringa stagnatilis L 8½" (21 cm)* Old World species. Common in Asia. Casual in central and western Aleutians (four fall records) and St. Paul Island. One wintered recently on Oahu. A small and slender *Tringa* with a long needle-like bill and disproportionately long, greenish legs; distinct supercilium in all plumages. Plumages overall suggestive of Common Greenshank. In ***breeding*** plumage, neck and sides are streaked and spotted with brown and mottled with black above. Juvenile is faintly streaked on sides of breast, brownish above with pale buff edges. ***Winter*** adult pale gray and uniform above and with long needle bill suggests a winter-plumaged Wilson's Phalarope; Marsh has much longer legs. In flight, white wedge extends up back; note long leg projection past tail. Call is a *tew* note, like call of Lesser Yellowlegs; often delivered in a series.

Little Curlew *Numenius minutus L 12" (30 cm)* Breeds in Russian Far East; winters mainly in northern Australia. Casual fall vagrant to coastal central California (four fall records involving both adult and juvenile birds) and one well-documented record in late spring for Gambell, St. Lawrence Island, Alaska. Also, an accepted spring record of a flyover in western Washington. Like a diminutive Whimbrel, with shorter and only slight curved bill; note mostly pale lores. Calls include a musical *quee-dlee* and a loud *tchew-tchew-tchew*.

Far Eastern Curlew *Numenius madagascariensis L 25" (64 cm)* Despite scientific name, found nowhere near Madagascar! Breeds in Russian Far East, winters in the Sunda Isles, New Guinea, Australia, New Zealand; a few on mainland Southeast Asia. Casual in spring and early summer on Aleutians and Pribilofs; accidental (Sept. 1984) from coastal British Columbia. Large, with a very long, downcurved bill. Closely resembles Eurasian Curlew, but overall browner, especially from lower belly to undertail coverts. In flight, underwings are heavily barred with dark; and upperparts, including rump, are uniform.

Great Knot *Calidris tenuirostris* *L 11" (28 cm)*
Asian species, casual in spring (once in fall) to western Alaska. Accidental in fall to Oregon. Larger than Red Knot, with longer bill. Compare to Surfbird and Rock Sandpiper (pages 144 and 146). In ***breeding*** plumage, shows black breast and black flank pattern. ***Juvenile*** has buffy wash and distinct spotting below; dark back feathers edged with rust. Resembles Red Knot in flight but primary coverts darker, wing bar fainter.

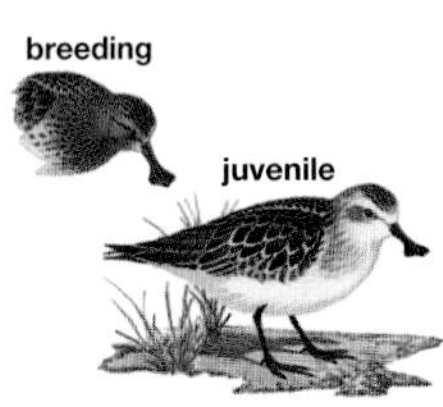

Spoon-billed Sandpiper *Eurynorhynchus pygmeus*
L 6" (15 cm) Globally threatened species. Recent estimated population on breeding grounds of between 400 and 600 individuals represents a greater than 50 percent reduction in the last 15 years. Breeds on coast of Russian Far East; winters coastal Southeast Asia; casual migrant (about six records) to western and northern Alaska. One record of a fall migrant, a breeding-plumaged adult, from Vancouver region, British Columbia (from 30 July to 3 Aug. 1978). Spoon-shaped bill is diagnostic and gives bill a longer look, but spoon is sometimes hard to see with clarity at a distance; beware of other small *Calidris* with mud on bill tip. In ***breeding*** plumage is easily mistaken for Red-necked Stint, apart from bill. ***Juvenile*** has darker cheek and more contrasting supercilium than Red-necked Stint. On winter grounds in Southeast Asia, feeds farther out into the water than Red-necked Stints; probes like Western Sandpiper but often with a side-to-side motion.

Broad-billed Sandpiper *Limicola falcinellus* *L 7" (18 cm)*
Eurasian species, casual fall migrant on western and central Aleutians. All sightings so far of juveniles. Plump body with short legs and long, broad-based bill with distinctive drooped tip give it a distinctive profile. Note also the distinctive split supercilium. Call is a dry and high-pitched buzzy trill; also shorter calls.

Jack Snipe *Lymnocryptes minimus* *L 7" (18 cm)*
Small, chunky Eurasian species. Two late fall records for California and recent report of two specimen records for Oregon; one spring record for Pribilofs. Secretive, reluctant to flush. Flight is low, short, fluttery, on rounded wings. Bobs while feeding. Pale base to short bill, pale split eyebrow stripes with no median crown stripe, broad buffy back stripes, streaked flanks, pale underparts.

Pin-tailed Snipe *Gallinago stenura* *L 10" (26 cm).*
Breeds in Siberia and Russian Far East; winters chiefly in Southeast Asia. Two specimen records from Attu Island, Aleutians (25 May 1991 and 19 May 1998). Chunkier, shorter billed, and shorter tailed than Common Snipe. On ground, note barred secondary coverts and even-width pale edges on inner and outer webs of scapulars for a scalloped look. In flight, note buffy secondary covert panel, uniformly dark underwings, no pale edge to secondaries, distinct foot projection past tail. Larger Swinhoe's Snipe (*G. megala*) from Asia (unrecorded in North America) perhaps not separable in field. In hand, razor-thin outer tail feathers are diagnostic. Call is high, ducklike *squak.*

Oriental Pratincole *Glareola maldivarum*
L 9" (23 cm) WS 23½-25½" (60-65 cm) Asian species. Winters south to Australia. Recorded twice in Alaska: a specimen from Attu Island, 19 to 20 May 1985; one at Gambell, St. Lawrence Island, 5 June 1986. Short-tailed pratincole with no white trailing edge to wing and chestnut underwings.

Belcher's Gull *Larus belcheri L 20" (51 cm) WS 49" (124 cm)*
Resident on west coast of South America; accidental to California, one near adult at the mouth of Tijuana River, near San Diego, from 3 Aug. 1997 to 2 Jan. 1998. Medium-size, three-year gull. Plumages and bill color similar to Black-tailed, but dark eyes, longer legs, thicker bill. ***Winter*** and second-winter birds have dark hood, red only on tip of bill. Adult has yellow orbital ring. ***First-winter***'s head and breast smoky brown; belly white; mottled above.

Black-tailed Gull *Larus crassirostris*
L 18½" (47 cm) WS 47¼" (120 cm) East Asian species, casual in coastal Alaska; accidental on West Coast south to California. Three-year or four-year gull, about size of Ring-billed Gull (page 172); bill and wings long; legs short. Distinctive white eye crescents except on breeding adult and third-winter bird. Adult has black ring near red tip of bill; yellow iris, red orbital ring. Mantle dark slate gray; tail has broad subterminal band. Head of ***winter adult*** heavily streaked. ***First-winter*** bird has white on face, otherwise heavily washed with brown.

Swallow-tailed Gull *Creagrus furcatus*
L 23" (58 cm) WS 52" (132 cm) Breeds on Galápagos Islands and on Isla Malpelo, Colombia. Otherwise, pelagic, ranging south to central Chile. Two California records, one at Pacific Grove and Moss Landing from 6 to 8 June 1985; another on 3 Mar. 1996, 15 miles west of Southeast Farallon Island. All plumages unmistakable. Much larger than Sabine's Gull (page 182) but with similar wing pattern in all plumages. Note very long drooped bill. ***Adults*** in breeding plumage have a slaty-gray hood with scarlet eye ring.

Oriental Turtle-Dove *Streptopelia orientalis L 13½" (34 cm)*
Asian species; casual to Aleutians and Bering Sea in spring and summer; accidental on Vancouver Island and California. Large and stocky; scaly pattern above with buffy, gray, and reddish fringes on black feathers; black-and-white streaked patch on neck. North American records are nominate *orientalis,* which is dark with gray rump and tail tip.

orientalis

tail

Thick-billed Parrot *Rhynchopsitta pachyrhyncha*
L 16¼" (41 cm) Declining species in northwestern Mexico. Former sporadic visitor primarily to Chiricahua Mountains, Arizona. Last valid record in 1938; recent New Mexico record (2003) not accepted (origin). Releases into Chiricahuas in 1980s were unsuccessful. ***Adult*** green with red forehead, eyebrow, thighs, marginal coverts; long, pointed tail. Yellow underwing bar; slow, shallow wingbeats. Immature's bill paler, no red on eyebrow and wing.

Oriental Scops-Owl *Otus sunia*
L 7½" (19 cm) WS 21" (53 cm) A small, nocturnal, insectivorous owl of eastern Asia. Multiple subspecies, northern ones are migratory. Two records (*japonicus*) of rufous morphs from Aleutian Islands, Alaska: a dried wing found on Buldir Island on 5 June 1977 and one found alive on Amchitka Island on 20 June 1979, subsequently died (specimen). Three color morphs: gray-brown, reddish gray, and ***rufous.*** Fine dark streaks on head; breast streaked vertically and horizontally with thin crossbars. Short ear tufts. Northern subspecies may be specifically distinct, calls differ.

Brown Hawk-Owl *Ninox scutulata L 12¼" (31 cm)*
East Asian species ranging north to Ussuriland, Korea, and Japan. Eleven subspecies recognized; darker northern breeding *japonica* is migratory. One record from St. Paul Island, Pribilofs, from 27 Aug. to 3 Sept. 2007. Overall slate-brown coloration with a round head and yellow eyes, and a long banded tail. Also widely known by an alternative English name, Brown Boobook.

jotaka ♂

Gray Nightjar *Caprimulgus indicus L 11-12¾" (28-32 cm)*
Asian species, formerly known as Jungle Nightjar. One desiccated specimen (*jotaka*) salvaged on Buldir Island, Alaska, on 31 May 1977. Overall color is grayish brown, patterned with black, buff, and grayish white. Note long wing-tip projection. Adult ***male*** has large white subterminal patch on inner primaries and white tips to all but central pair of tail feathers; on female, wing patch and tail tips more buffy. The two more northerly and migratory subspecies (*jotaka* and *hazarae*) have different vocalizations and are treated as a distinct species by some authors, *C. jotaka.*

White-throated Needletail *Hirundapus caudacutus*
L 8" (21 cm) Large Asian swift, four late May records on western Aleutians. Dark overall, with pale patch on back; white throat and undertail coverts. Tail short and stubby.

Common Swift *Apus apus L 6½" (17 cm)*
Breeds in Palearctic; winters in Africa. Two summer records from St. Paul Island, Pribilofs: specimen on 28 June 1950 and one photographed on 28 and 29 June 1986. Long, thin winged, dark, with paler throat, long forked tail. Pribilofs specimen of eastern race *pekinensis* is paler than nominate.

Fork-tailed Swift *Apus pacificus L 7¾" (20 cm)*
Asian species, casual to western Alaska's islands in spring and fall (once in fall on both St. Lawrence and Middleton Islands). White rump; long tail's fork not always apparent and appears as a long point. Also widely known as Pacific Swift.

Xantus's Hummingbird *Hylocharis xantusii*
L 3½" (9 cm) Endemic to southern Baja California, Mexico. Accidental vagrant to southern California and southwestern British Columbia. Plumages and calls similar to White-eared Hummingbird, but note buff on underparts and rufous in tail; ***male*** has black forehead and ear patches.

Cinnamon Hummingbird *Amazilla rutila*
L 4-4½" (10-12 cm) Resident in lowlands from Sinaloa and Yucatán Peninsula, south to Costa Rica. Two records from Southwest: 21 to 23 July 1992 at Patagonia, Arizona; 18 to 21 Sept. 1993 at Santa Teresa, New Mexico. Adults with cinnamon tail, underparts; black-tipped red bill. Immature similar but upperparts edged cinnamon when fresh, upper mandible mostly dark.

Plain-capped Starthroat *Heliomaster constantii*
L 5" (13 cm) Casual stray in summer and fall from Mexico to arid foothills and deserts of southeastern and central (once) Arizona. Broad white malar stripe, white eye stripe, and white patches on sides of rump are conspicuous. Throat shows variable amount of red; note also very long bill. Call is a sharp *chip*.

Bumblebee Hummingbird *Atthis heliosa*
L 2¾-3" (7-8 cm) Endemic to montane forests of Mexico north of the Isthmus of Tehuantepec. Two specimens taken on 2 July 1896 in Ramsey Canyon, Arizona. That two would be taken on the same date from one locality with no records since seems unlikely, but the specimens are extant and the records have not yet been refuted. A tiny hummingbird with a short bill and a short, rounded or double-rounded, rufous-based tail with white tips. ***Adult males*** have an elongated magenta-rose gorget. Females and immatures closely resemble female-type Calliope Hummingbirds, which have darker tails that fall shorter than or equal to wing tips; on Bumblebee, tail extends beyond wing tips.

Eared Quetzal *Euptilotis neoxenus L 14" (36 cm)*
Casual in mountain woodlands of southeastern Arizona, mostly in late summer and fall. Wary. Larger and thicker bodied than Elegant Trogon; bill is black or gray; lacks white breast band. Calls include a loud upslurred squeal ending in a *chuck* note; also a loud, hard cackling. Male's song is a long, quavering series of whistled notes that increase in volume.

Eurasian Hoopoe *Upupa epops L 10½" (27 cm)*
Widespread Old World species. One North American record, a specimen (*saturata*) from Old Chevak, Yukon-Kuskokwim Delta, Alaska, 2 to 3 Sept. 1975. Unmistakable: pinkish brown coloration; long crest (sometimes raised); long, thin, slightly downcurved bill. Striking black-and-white wing pattern in flight; wingbeats slow and floppy. The two races from equatorial Africa and farther south and from Madagascar are each treated as separate species by some authors.

Great Spotted Woodpecker *Dendrocopos major* *L 9" (25 cm)* Widespread in Eurasia. Casual to western Aleutians and Pribilofs; accidental in winter north of Anchorage. Large size with large white cheek and scapular patch and red undertail coverts. Female lacks red nape patch. Call, a sharp *kick.*

Tufted Flycatcher *Mitrephanes phaeocercus L 5" (13 cm)* Widespread tropical species; partially migratory at northern end of range (northern Mexico). Accidental in winter and early spring to west Texas and southeastern and western Arizona. Distinctive small, crested flycatcher with cinnamon underparts and face; brownish olive above with faint cinnamon wing bars. Behavior suggests pewees. Call, a whistled *tchurree-tchurree.* Sometimes given singly; also a soft *peek* like Hammond's Flycatcher.

Nutting's Flycatcher *Myiarchus nuttingi L 7¼" (18 cm)* Tropical species; found from northwestern Mexico to Costa Rica; three certain winter records from southeastern Arizona and coastal southern California. Similar to Ash-throated Flycatcher but belly yellower; slightly more olive above; rufous primary edges blend to yellow-cinnamon secondary edges. Dark on outer webs of outer tail feathers does not extend across tip as in Ash-throated; orange, not flesh-colored, mouth lining. Call, a rather sharp *wheep,* different from Ash-throated.

Piratic Flycatcher *Legatus leucophaius L 6" (15 cm)* Widespread tropical species. Accidental in West; Big Bend, Texas (Mar.) and twice in fall in eastern New Mexico. Dark olive-brown above; blurry olive streaking below. Distinct head pattern; dark malar streak; pale throat; stubby black bill. Black tail can show rufous edges. Often perches out in the open.

Brown Shrike *Lanius cristatus L 7½" (19 cm)* Asian species; casual in Alaska where there are spring and fall records from western Aleutians, St. Lawrence Island, and Anchorage. Two fall and winter records from California. ***Adult male***'s distinct white border above black mask extends across forehead; warm brown upperparts, often brighter on rump, uppertail coverts; warm buff wash along sides, flanks. Lacks white wing patches. Adult female similar, mask less solid; some barring below. ***Juvenile*** barred on sides, flanks; distinct dark subterminal edges above; dark brown mask, short whitish border above and behind eye. Much juvenal plumage retained into fall, some into winter. Compare all ages, plumages to much larger, longer billed immature Northern Shrike. Old World Red-backed Shrike (*L. collurio*) and Isabelline Shrike (*L. isabellinus*) considered close relatives.

Brown-chested Martin *Progne tapera L 6½" (16 cm)* South American species. Southern subspecies, *fusca,* is an austral migrant to northern South America. Accidental; one photographed at Patagonia Lake State Park, near Nogales, Arizona, on 3 Feb. 2006. Smaller than Purple Martin with brownish upper parts, white below with brown sides, and brown band across breast.

Common House-Martin *Delichon urbicum L 5" (13 cm)*
Old World species. Casual mainly in spring in western Alaska. Deep, glossy blue above; mostly white below with white rump; underwing coverts pale smoky gray. Female slightly grayer below; juvenile duller. Soars for long periods. Call, a rough scratchy *prrit*, somewhat similar to Rough-winged Swallow.

lagopoda

Middendorff's Grasshopper-Warbler
Locustella ochotensis L 6" (15 cm) Casual to western Aleutians, Pribilofs, Nunivak, and St. Lawrence Island, mostly in fall. Big, chunky warbler, wedge-shaped tail has whitish tips; hefty bill. Indistinct dark markings above; yellowish buff below with a faintly streaked breast, rustier above. Like all *Locustella* warblers, Middendorff's is very secretive.

fall

Lanceolated Warbler *Locustella lanceolata L 4½" (11 cm)*
Mainly Asian species. Casual in spring to western Aleutians. Bred on Buldir Island in June 2007. Accidental in fall in California. Resembles Middendorff's Grasshopper-Warbler but smaller; less broadly streaked above, including crown and rump, but streaks extend to feather tips; clear brown fringe on tertials. Breast, undertail coverts, and flanks are streaked. Highly secretive. Walks and runs; flicks its wings. Distinctive call, a metallic *rink-tink-tink*, delivered infrequently; also an explosive *pwit* and excited *chack* when disturbed. Song, a thin, insectlike reeling sound, like a fishing line makes.

adult

Sedge Warbler *Acrocephalus schoenobaenus*
L 4¾" (12 cm) A common Old World warbler breeding from northwestern Europe to western Siberia and northwestern China; winters sub-Saharan Africa. One immature photographed at Gambell, St. Lawrence Island, Alaska, on 30 Sept. 2007. Overall buffy-brown with a wedge-shaped tail and long primary projection. Distinctly patterned with long bold supercilium and dark lateral and complete eye stripe with paler median crown area, and a faintly streaked back. Immature faintly streaked across the breast.

1st fall

Willow Warbler *Phylloscopus trochilus L 4½" (11 cm)*
A highly migratory Old World species. Several fall records for St. Lawrence Island, Alaska. Like the similar Arctic Warbler (page 306) in overall coloration and long primary projection, but smaller, with smaller bill and a plainer wing. Whistled *hoo-eet* call note is very unlike Arctic's buzzy note.

adult
yakutensis

Wood Warbler *Phylloscopus sibilatrix L 5" (13 cm)*
Breeds in the western Palearctic; winters in tropical Africa. Two fall records for western Alaska: one collected on Shemya Island, western Aleutians, 9 Oct. 1978; one photographed on St. Paul Island, 7 Oct. 2004. A colorful *Phylloscopus* with yellow throat breast contrasting sharply with white belly; the yellow supercilium is well defined by a dark eye line; yellow-green edges to flight feathers and greater coverts; and dark centered tertials with sharply defined pale edges. Note very long primary projection.

fall
adult

Pallas's Leaf-Warbler *Phylloscopus proregulus* *L 3½" (9 cm)* A tiny kinglet-size Old World Warbler breeding from southwestern Siberia east to Ammurland, Ussuriland, and Sakhalin Island, Russian Far East. Winters primarily in southeastern China, northern Indochina. Frequent vagrant to northwestern Europe. One photographed at Gambell, St. Lawrence Island, on 25 and 26 Sept. 2006. Distinctive; deep yellow median crown stripe, supercilium; sides of crown quite dark. Distinct wing bars, tertial tips, yellow rump, often visible as species frequently hovers. Most now regard species as monotypic. Call is a soft, nasal rising *chuee.*

Yellow-browed Warbler *Phylloscopus inornatus* *L 4½" (11 cm)* Primarily breeds in the northeastern Palearctic region. Casual in fall from western Alaska; recorded Attu, St. Paul, and St. Lawrence Islands. Distinctly patterned with bold supercilium and two pale wing bars; tertials with sharply defined, pale edges. Note small and mostly dark bill. Call a distinctive upslurred *swee-eet,* not too unlike call of male Pacific-slope Flycatcher. Most authorities have now split the less migratory and more southerly breeding subspecies (*humei* and *mandellii*) as a separate species, Hume's Leaf-Warbler (*P. humei*).

Lesser Whitethroat *Sylvia curruca* *L 5½" (14 cm)* Old World species. Only record was one photographed at Gambell, St. Lawrence Island, Alaska, 8 to 9 Sept. 2002. Outer rectrices tipped with white; gray crown with a dark mask, brownish above, and whitish underparts with a tan wash on the sides and flanks. Call is a hard *tik,* often repeated. Multiple subspecies groups are treated by some Old World authorities as up to four species.

spring ♀

adult ♂

Narcissus Flycatcher *Ficedula narcissina* *L 5¼" (13 cm)* East Asian species; two spring records of males on Attu Island in the western Aleutians (from 20 to 21 May 1989 and 21 May 1984). ***Adult male*** overall black and yellow-orange; most orange on eyebrow and throat. Has yellow rump; white patch on inner secondary coverts. First-spring male similar, but duller. ***Female*** and first-fall male drab; brownish olive above, green on rump; contrasting uppertail coverts and tail tinged reddish; whitish throat; brownish mottling on breast. First-fall male similar to female.

1st year ♂

spring
sibirica

Mugimaki Flycatcher *Ficedula mugimaki* *L 5¼" (13 cm)* Highly migratory species of eastern Asia. Only record: Shemya Island, Alaska, 24 May 1985, supported by marginal photos. Note long wings. Adult male has blackish head and upperparts; white wing patch; short, broad downcurving white supercilium; extensively orange underparts. Female brownish above; burnt orange on throat, breast; two thin pale wing bars. ***First-year male*** closer to female, but with partial, broad, downcurving supercilium.

Dark-sided Flycatcher *Muscicapa sibirica* *L 5¼" (13 cm)* Asian species; casual to western Aleutians; four spring records for Pribilofs. Dark wash on sides, and flanks. Whitish half collar; brownish supraloral spot; short bill; long primary projection.

Asian Brown Flycatcher *Muscicapa dauurica*
L 5¼" (13 cm) Asian species; two spring records: one from Attu Island, the other from Gambell, St. Lawrence Island. Grayish brown above; largely whitish below; grayish wash across chest or, rarely, some diffuse streaks. Bill larger than Dark-sided or Gray-streaked, extensively flesh-colored at base of lower mandible; primary projection shorter; supraloral area paler.

Spotted Flycatcher *Muscicapa striata L 6" (15 cm)*
Widespread breeder in the Palearctic, east to about Lake Baikal; winters in Africa, south of the Sahara. One photographed from Gambell, St. Lawrence Island, Alaska, on 14 Sept. 2002. Grayish brown above, with fine streaking on crown, and indistinct whitish eye ring; lacks distinct malar and submoustachial markings; below indistinctly streaked, not spotted, across throat and breast. Juvenile is spotted with buff above and has dark mottling below.

Siberian Blue Robin *Luscinia cyane L 5½" (14 cm)*
Highly migratory Asian species. One certain North American specimen record from Attu Island, Alaska, 21 May 1985; an additional spring sighting of an adult male from the Yukon is disputed. Adult male is deep blue above, clear white below. ***Adult female*** brownish above with faint buffy eye ring; buffy wash across breast with faint stippling, and most have some bluish on tail (lacking on immature female). Immature male has some blue on scapulars, wings, and tail. Frequently vibrates tail.

Red-flanked Bluetail *Tarsiger cyanurus L 5½" (14 cm)*
Primarily Asian species; casual in spring and fall to western Aleutians and Pribilofs; one late fall record for Farallones, off California. Note bluish tail, often flicked down; orangish flanks. ***Adult male*** has bright blue upperparts, but much individual variation; brightest birds may be several years old. Immature male closely resembles ***female*** until second fall. Rather secretive. Calls include a *hueet* and dry *keck-keck.*

Stonechat *Saxicola torquatus L 5¼" (13 cm)*
Eurasian species; casual in spring and fall from scattered locations in Alaska; accidental in fall from California. All records from the eastern *maurus* group of races, known as "Siberian Stonechat." Compact body; pale spot on inner coverts; paler rump. Note pattern of black on head of ***adult male*** obscured by fresh pale feather tips in ***fall***; orange-buff wash on breast; extensive white on sides of neck, belly, and rump. Female and first-fall male have pale throat; pale buffy rump. Favors open country.

Blue Mockingbird *Melanotis caerulescens L 10" (25 cm)*
Mexican species; moves altitudinally. Casual in winter to southeastern Arizona. Records from coastal southern California and New Mexico of questionable origin. ***Adult*** deep slate blue with black mask and red eye. Immature slightly duller, brownish tinge to wings, darker eye.

Gray Wagtail *Motacilla cinerea L 7¾" (20 cm)*
Eurasian species. Very rare spring migrant on western Aleutians; casual on Pribilofs and St. Lawrence Island; accidental south to California. Gray above, with greenish yellow rump, yellow below; whitish tertial edges, but lacks wing bars. ***Breeding male*** has black throat. Female and winter birds have whitish throat, paler below. Distinctly longer tail and flesh-colored legs separate Gray from Eastern Yellow Wagtail (page 322). Call, a metallic *chink-chink.*

Tree Pipit *Anthus trivialis L 6" (15 cm)*
Palearctic breeding species, wintering mainly in Africa south of the Sahara and in India. Three records for western Alaska: a specimen from Cape Prince of Wales on 23 June 1978, and two photographed at Gambell, St. Lawrence Island, Alaska (6 June 1995; 21, 27 Sept. 2002). Resembles Olive-backed Pipit (page 324), but browner above and with distinct back streaks; face pattern more blended and no dark spot in rear of cheek; call similar.

Pechora Pipit *Anthus gustavi L5½" (14 cm)*
Asian species. Casual in spring on the western Aleutians and St. Lawrence Island (mostly fall). Shows distinct primary projection. Resembles immature Red-throated Pipit, but compare Pechora Pipit's richly patterned back plumage, extending onto the nape; black centers with dull rufous edges contrast with white lines, or "braces," on the sides. Also a yellowish wash across the breast contrasts with the whitish belly. Quite secretive. Call is a hard *pwit* or *pit,* but Pechora is often silent when flushed.

Gray Silky-flycatcher *Ptilogonys cinereus L 7½" (20 cm)*
Resident (some seasonal movement) from northern Mexico to Guatemala; largely montane. One accepted record from west Texas from 12 Jan. to 5 Mar. 1995 in El Paso. Four well-documented southern California records have been questioned on origin. Structured like Phainopepla. ***Adult males*** are gray with orange-yellow flanks and bright yellow undertail coverts; note white eye ring and white base of tail. Females and juveniles are similar, but duller.

Crescent-chested Warbler *Parula superciliosa*
L 4¼" (11 cm) Resident from northern Mexico to northern Nicaragua; casual to southeastern Arizona; one sight record for Chisos Mountains, Texas. Bluish gray head with broad white eyebrow; green back; no wing bars or white in tail. Chestnut crescent distinct on ***adult male;*** reduced on female and immature male; absent or an orange wash on ***immature female.***

Slate-throated Redstart *Myioborus miniatus L 6" (15 cm)*
Middle and South American species, casual in southeastern Arizona, southeastern New Mexico, and west Texas. Head, throat, and back are slate black, breast dark red. Chestnut crown patch visible only at close range. Lacks white wing patch of similar Painted Redstart; reduced white on outer tail feathers less extensive; tail strongly graduated. Call, a *chip* note, very different from Painted Redstart.

Fan-tailed Warbler *Euthlypis lachrymosa L 5¾" (15 cm)*
Tropical species; casual, mainly late spring, to southeastern Arizona; accidental to Big Bend, Texas (fall). Large, with long, graduated, white-tipped tail held partly open and pumped sideways or up and down. Head pattern distinct with broken white eye ring; white lore spot; yellow crown patch. Note tawny wash on breast. Song of rich, loud slurred notes; call, a penetrating *schree.* Found low in canyons; often walks on ground; secretive.

Worthen's Sparrow *Spizella worthenii L 5½" (14 cm)*
Critically endangered. Only extant populations are in northeastern Mexico in Coahuila and Nuevo Léon. Only U.S. record at Silver City, New Mexico, on 16 June 1884, the type specimen of the species; probably part of a small resident population, subsequently extirpated. Resembles *aranacea* Field Sparrow (page 362), but crown solidly rufous and rump grayish; vocalizations differ.

Pine Bunting *Emberiza leucocephalus L 6½" (17cm)*
Primarily an eastern Palearctic species. Two fall records from Attu Island, Alaska, both males: one photographed 18 to 19 Nov. 1995 and a specimen (nominate *leucocephalus*) on 6 Oct. 1993. Breeding male is rusty overall, with chestnut head, and bold white eyebrow and cheek patch; in winter, duller head lacks white crown patch. Female is duller still with a weak malar, but has a rusty eyebrow and at least a small white spot at rear of cheek.

Little Bunting *Emberiza pusilla L 5" (13 cm)*
Eurasian species, rare in fall to St. Lawrence Island. Casual on Pribilofs and western Aleutians and in California. Small, with short legs, short tail, a small triangular bill, bold creamy white eye ring, chestnut ear patch, and two thin, pale wing bars. Underparts whitish and heavily streaked; outer tail feathers white. In ***breeding*** plumage, shows chestnut crown stripe bordered by black stripes. Many ***males*** have chestnut on chin. ***Immatures*** and winter adults have chestnut crown, tipped and streaked with buff and black; compare with female Rustic and Reed Buntings. Call note is a sharp *tsick.*

Gray Bunting *Emberiza variabilis L 6¾" (17 cm)*
Asian species, casual spring vagrant on western Aleutians. A large, heavy-billed bunting; shows no white in tail. ***Breeding male*** is gray overall, prominently streaked with blackish above. ***Female*** is brown; chestnut rump is conspicuous in flight. Immature males through first spring are intermediate. Call is a sharp *zhii.*

Yellow-browed Bunting *Emberiza chrysophrys L 6" (15 cm)*
Breeds southeastern Siberia, winters in central and eastern China. One photographed at Gambell, St. Lawrence Island, Alaska, on 15 Sept. 2007. Distinctive with broad well-defined yellowish supercilium; pale spot in rear of ear coverts. The white outer tail feathers are characteristic of most other *Emberiza*, but not the vaguely similar, smaller and shorter tailed Savannah Sparrow (page 364). Often appears slightly crested. Call is a short *ziit.*

Yellow-throated Bunting *Emberiza elegans L 6" (15 cm)*
East Asian species. One record of a male photographed on Attu Island, Alaska, 25 May 1988. Note prominent crest. Yellow-and-black head pattern of ***adult male*** is striking. Female and immature male are similar, but duller, with brownish auriculars.

Yellow-breasted Bunting *Emberiza aureola L 6" (15 cm)*
A declining, mostly Asian species; casual to Alaska, mostly on western Aleutians in spring. White outer tail feathers, like most *Emberiza* buntings. ***Breeding male*** has rufous-brown upperparts, bright yellow underparts, white patch on lesser and median wing coverts. East Asian race, *ornata,* which has reached Alaska, has black on forehead and base of breast band. Winter adult male usually shows features of breeding plumage. ***Female*** and immature have striking head pattern: median crown stripe, ear patches with dark border, pale spot in rear. Yellowish underparts with sparse streaking; unmarked belly. Call is a *tzip,* similar to Little Bunting.

Pallas's Bunting *Emberiza pallasi L 5" (13 cm)*
Casual in spring and fall to northern Alaska, St. Lawrence Island, and western Aleutians. Compare with Reed Bunting. Note Pallas's smaller size, smaller two-toned bill with straighter culmen (except ***breeding male,*** which has black bill); grayish lesser wing coverts; less rufous wing bars; shorter tail. ***Female*** has more indistinct eyebrow and lateral crown stripes than female Reed; lacks median crown stripe. Call, a *cheeep,* recalls Eurasian Tree Sparrow, very unlike Reed's call.

♀

breeding ♂

Reed Bunting *Emberiza schoeniclus L 6" (15 cm)*
Eurasian species, casual vagrant on westernmost Aleutians in late spring; one fall record on St. Lawrence Island. All records are of pale East Asian *pyrrhulina.* Distinctive ***breeding male*** shows extensive rust. Other plumages more like Pallas's, but note heavier bill with curved culmen, dark lateral crown stripes with paler median, and chestnut lesser wing coverts, often obscured. Calls, a *seeoo,* falling in pitch; flight note, a hoarse *brzee.*

adult ♂

adult ♀

Yellow Grosbeak *Pheucticus chrysopeplus L 9¼" (24 cm)*
Mexican species, casual to southeastern Arizona and New Mexico, mainly in late spring to early summer, to low and middle elevations. ***Male*** distinguished by massive bill, yellow plumage. ***Female*** duller. Call and song like Black-headed's.

1st spring

adult
castaneopectus

Black-vented Oriole *Icterus wagleri L 8½" (22 cm)*
Resident northern Mexico to central Nicaragua; accidental: one at Rio Grande Village, Big Bend National Park, summers of 1969 and 1971; one at Patagonia Lake, southeast Arizona, 18 Apr. 1991. Long, narrow bill; long, graduated tail. ***Adult*** has black head, back, undertail coverts, tail, wings; yellow shoulders; chestnut border between breast and belly. ***First-spring*** has black lores and chin; streaked back. Juvenile lacks black bib. Call is a nasal *nyeh.*

Streak-backed Oriole *Icterus pustulatus* *L 8¼" (21 cm)*
Mexican species, casual mostly in fall and winter, in southeastern Arizona, southern California; accidental to New Mexico and Colorado. Distinguished from winter Hooded Oriole (page 396) by broken streaks on upper back; deeper orange head; and much thicker based, straighter bill. Also compare to first-spring male Bullock's Oriole (page 398). ***Female*** is duller than ***male.*** Immatures resemble adult female. *Wheet* call is softer than Hooded Oriole's call and does not rise in pitch. Chatter calls resemble those of Baltimore Oriole.

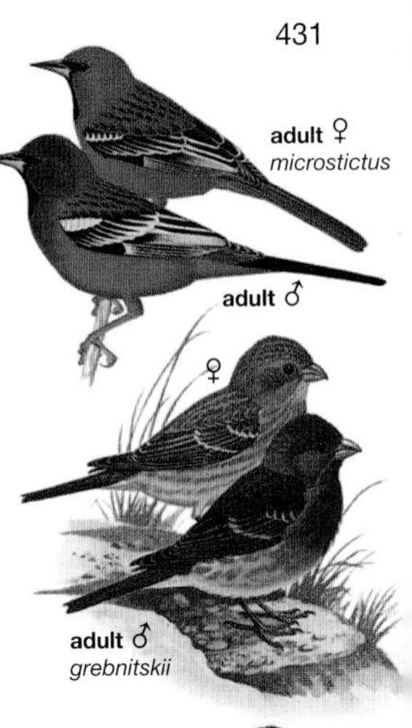

Common Rosefinch *Carpodacus erythrinus* *L 5¾" (15 cm)*
Eurasian species; very rare migrant, on the western Aleutians and other western Alaska islands; accidental from California (fall). Strongly curved culmen. Lacks distinct eyebrow. ***Adult male*** extensively red. ***Female*** and immatures diffusely streaked above and below except. Call is a soft, nasal *djuee.*

Oriental Greenfinch *Carduelis sinica* *L 6" (15 cm)*
Asian species. Casual migrant, mainly in spring, on outer Aleutians; one Pribilofs record. ***Adult male*** has greenish face and rump, dark gray nape and crown, bright yellow wing patch and undertail coverts. Adult female is paler, with a brownish head. Juvenile has same yellow areas as adults but is streaked overall.

Eurasian Siskin *Carduelis spinus* *L 4¾" (12 cm)*
Palearctic species. Two records of males from Attu Island: a specimen, 21 to 22 May 1993 and a sight record on 4 June 1978. ***Male*** is distinctive with black forecrown and chin, olive above, and extensively yellow below. ***Female*** is much duller, the yellow restricted to sides of breast, and a wash of yellow on face, eyebrow, and rump; juvenile duller still. Some Pine Siskins (page 408) are very similar, but wing coverts of Eurasian average darker.

Eurasian Bullfinch *Pyrrhula pyrrhula* *L 6½" (17 cm)*
Eurasian species. Casual migrant on Aleutians and Bering Sea islands; casual in winter on Alaskan mainland. Cheeks, breast, and belly intense reddish pink in ***male,*** brown in ***female.*** Black cap and face, gray back, prominent whitish bar on wing, distinct white rump. In profile, top of head and bill form unbroken curve. Juvenile resembles female, but with brown cap. Call is a soft, piping *pheew.*

Hawfinch *Coccothraustes coccothraustes* *L 7" (18 cm)*
Eurasian species. Rare spring stray on western and central Aleutians and on Pribilofs, casual to St. Lawrence Island and other islands of western Alaska. Stocky; yellowish brown above; pinkish brown below; has black throat and lores; shows conspicuous white band on extended wing. Big bill is blue-black in spring, yellowish in fall. Female resembles ***male,*** but is duller; has grayish secondaries and inner primaries. Walks with parrotlike waddle. Call is a loud, explosive *ptik.*

Rarities Primarily from Eastern North America

This unillustrated appendix contains species that are of casual or accidental occurrence in the West *but are more characteristic of the East.* Some, notably water birds, likely arrived from Mexico, farther south, or even the tropical Pacific; a few are widespread Eurasian species that have been recorded more regularly in the East. Most of the species in this appendix receive full treatment in our companion field guide to the East. For species recorded only once or twice in the West, the records are listed individually; otherwise, they are summarized. If states and provinces are listed, they are given in order from east to west and then from south to north.

American Black Duck *Anas rubripes* Casual: recorded MT, CO, CA, OR, ID, AB (has nested), NT, AK; introduced populations in WA, BC, disappeared by 2000

Least Grebe *Tachybaptus dominicus* Casual: recorded w. TX, s. AZ, se. CA

Cory's Shearwater *Calonectris diomedea* Accidental: recorded 25 mi. w. of Bodega Bay, CA, 9 Aug. 2003; one on Islas Coronados, Baja California, just sw. of San Diego, summer 2005, summer 2006

Greater Shearwater *Puffinus gravis* Casual: about six records off c. CA; accidental: Gulf of Alaska (summer)

White-tailed Tropicbird *Phaethon lepturus* Accidental: recorded Upper Newport Bay, Orange Co., CA, 29 May to 23 June 1964 (photograph); Scottsdale, near Phoenix, AZ, 22 Aug. 1980 (moribund specimen); both identified as greenish-billed Pacific subspecies *dorotheae*

Anhinga *Anhinga anhinga* Casual: recorded NM, CO, AZ, CA

Little Egret *Egretta garzetta* Accidental: recorded Buldir Is., Aleutians, AK, 27 May 2000 (specimen)

White Ibis *Eudocimus albus* Casual: recorded w. TX, NM, AZ, CA (several records); accidental: CO

Roseate Spoonbill *Platalea ajaja* Casual: recorded w. TX, NM, CO, UT, AZ, NV, CA, esp. late summer

Swallow-tailed Kite *Elanoides forficatus* Casual: recorded w. TX, CO, NM; accidental: c. CA

White-tailed Hawk *Buteo albicaudatus* Accidental: recorded Big Bend NP, w. TX. 11 May 1994; s. AZ, late 19th cent. (several records)

King Rail *Rallus elegans* Casual: recorded w. TX (has nested), NM, CO

Purple Gallinule *Porphyrula martinica* Casual: recorded w. TX, NM, CO, AZ, UT, NV, CA

Eurasian Coot *Fulica atra* Accidental: recorded St. Paul Is., Pribilofs, AK, 31 Oct. to 5 Nov. 1962 (specimen)

European Golden-Plover *Pluvialis apricaria* Accidental: recorded Ketchikan, AK, 13–14 Jan. 2001 (specimen)

Wilson's Plover *Charadrius wilsonia* Casual: recorded coastal s. CA; accidental: coastal c. CA, s. OR; Salton Sea, 1948 (nest record)

Northern Lapwing *Vanellus vanellus* Accidental: recorded Shemya Is., Aleutians, AK, 12 Oct. 2006 (specimen)

Eskimo Curlew *Numenius borealis* Probably extinct: nest records NT; specimen records AK (15+), AB , CO, 19th cent.

Purple Sandpiper *Calidris maritima* Accidental: specimen Pt. Barrow, AK, 29 Sept. 1990

American Woodcock *Scolopax minor* Casual: recorded w. TX, NM, CO, WY, MT, AB, s. CA

Great Black-backed Gull *Larus marinus* Casual: recorded e. CO (nearly annual), MT, AB, WA, BC, AK

Kelp Gull *Larus dominicanus* Accidental: recorded various spots e. CO, 17 Sept. to 3 Nov. 2003

Sooty Tern *Onychoprion fuscata* Casual: recorded coastal s. CA (nesting attempted); accidental: off c. CA, Attu Is., AK

Bridled Tern *Onychoprion anaethetus* Casual: recorded coastal s. CA (summer)

White-winged Tern *Chlidonias leucopterus* Casual: recorded AK; accidental: coastal n. and c. CA

Sandwich Tern *Thalasseus sandvicensis* Casual: recorded coastal s. CA (spring, summer), coastal c. CA (likely hybrids with Elegants)

Passenger Pigeon *Ectopistes migratorius* **EX** Extinct (by early 20th cent.); casual or accidental: specimens WY, AB, NT, BC, ID, NV, 19th cent. (formerly bred MT)

Groove-billed Ani *Crotophaga sulcirostris* Casual: recorded n. to NM, CO, AZ, s. NV, s. CA

Chuck-will's-widow *Caprimulgus carolinensis* Casual: recorded e. NM, NV, n. CA

White-collared Swift *Streptoprocne zonaris* Accidental: sight record Pt. St. George, Del Norte Co., CA, 21 May 1982

Green Violetear *Colibri thalassinus* Accidental: recorded w. TX, NM, CO, AB, CA

Eastern Wood-Pewee *Contopus virens* Breeds just e. of Pecos River, w. TX; casual: w. TX, NM, CO, WY, MT, AZ, CA, OR; only birds in full song can be considered identified with certainty

Acadian Flycatcher *Empidonax virescens* Breeds just e. of Pecos River, w. TX; accidental: recorded NM, AZ, BC

Great Kiskadee *Pitangus sulphuratus* Breeds just e. of Pecos River, w. TX; casual: recorded w. TX, NM, se. AZ

Couch's Kingbird *Tyrannus couchii* Breeds just e. (possibly a few just w.) of Pecos River, w. TX; casual: recorded w. TX (breeding record, Big Bend NP, 2007), NM; accidental: sw. AZ, s. CA, in winter

Gray Kingbird *Tyrannus dominicensis* Accidental: remarkable specimen record, Cape Beale, Vancouver Is., BC, 29 Sept. 1889

Fork-tailed Flycatcher *Tyrannus savanna* Accidental: recorded CA (twice), WA, ID, in fall

White-eyed Vireo *Vireo griseus* Casual: recorded w. TX, NM, CO, AZ, UT, NV, CA, WA

Black-capped Vireo *Vireo atricapillus* Breeds just e. of Pecos River, w. TX; probable rare breeder at Big Bend NP; accidental: recorded e.-c. NM, one w. of Melrose, 1–2 May 2004

Yellow-throated Vireo *Vireo flavifrons* Breeds just e. of Pecos River in w. TX; casual: recorded w. TX, NM, CO, WY, AB, AZ, NV, CA, WA

Wood Thrush *Hylochichla mustelina* Casual: recorded w. TX, NM, CO, WY, MT, UT, AZ, NV, CA, OR

Fieldfare *Turdus pilaris* Casual: recorded w. and n. Alaska; accidental: one recorded Port Coquitlam, BC, 28 Dec. 2004

Redwing *Turdus iliacus* Accidental: one recorded Olympia, WA, 21 Dec. 2004 to 14 Mar. 2005

Clay-colored Thrush *Turdus grayi* Accidental: one recorded Sam Nail Ranch, Big Bend NP, TX, 27 Dec. 2004 to 2 Apr. 2005

Long-billed Thrasher *Toxostoma longirostre* Casual: scattering of records w. TX, also a few records n. to NM, e. CO

Blue-winged Warbler *Vermivora pinus* Casual: recorded NM, CO, AB, AZ, NV, CA, OR, WA

Golden-winged Warbler *Vermivora chrysoptera* Casual: recorded w. TX, NM, CO, WY, MT, AB, ID, NV, AZ, CA, OR, WA

Tropical Parula *Parula pitiayumi* Casual: recorded w. TX, se. AZ; accidental: e. CO, one at Ft. Collins, 18 June to 4 July 2005

Golden-cheeked Warbler *Dendroica chrysoparia* Accidental: one recorded Chisos Mountains, Big Bend NP (photograph), w. TX, 29 June 2003; one collected Southeast Farallon Is., CA, 9 Sept. 1971

Yellow-throated Warbler *Dendroica dominica* Casual: recorded w. TX, NM, CO, WY, UT, AZ, NV, CA, OR, WA, BC; most *albilora*, but a few in late fall and winter nominate *dominica*

Cerulean Warbler *Dendroica cerulea* Casual: recorded NM, CO, AZ, NV, CA

Worm-eating Warbler *Helmitheros vermivorum* Casual: recorded w. TX, NM, CO, WY, ID, CA, OR

Swainson's Warbler *Limnothylypis swainsonii* Casual: a few records each w. TX, NM, CO; accidental: e. AZ

Kentucky Warbler *Oporornis formosus* Casual: w. TX, NM, CO, WY, MT, AB, AZ, UT, NV, CA, OR, WA

Golden-crowned Warbler *Basileuterus culicivorus* Accidental: one record w. of Melrose, NM, 8–10 May 2004

Eastern Towhee *Pipilo erythrophtalmus* Casual: recorded NM, e. CO (perhaps very rare), MT, AB, AZ

Henslow's Sparrow *Ammodramus henslowii* Accidental: one well-documented record (photograph) Clabber Hill Ranch, San Miguel Co., NM, 10–22 Oct. 2003; two sight records ne. CO

Art Credits

Jonathan Alderfer: Cover; title page; 8-Short-billed Dowitcher; 10; 11-Lark Sparrow; 12-goldeneye hybrid; 17-Brant; 35-flying Common Eiders; 37-*stejnegeri* White-winged Scoter; 41-goldeneye hybrid; 43-"Goosander"; 48-Common Eider; 57-displaying Sharp-tailed Grouse; 59-Gunnison Sage-Grouse; 69; 71-heads; 73; 75; 77-left Short-tailed Shearwater and heads; 79; 83-Masked Booby; 85; 87-breeding adult Brown Pelican, Neotropic Cormorant; 89; 127; 143-except flying Bar-tailed Godwit, flying Marbled Godwit; 145-flying Black Turnstone; 155-Stilt Sandpiper except flying figure; 157-Common Snipe, Wilson's Snipe; 159; 199-Black Guillemot, Thick-billed Murre, flying Common Murre; 201-flying winter Dovekie, Long-billed Murrelet; 205; 207-flying Rhinoceros Auklet; 209-Spotted Dove and Eurasian Collared-Dove with N. John Schmitt; 211-Mourning Dove and White-winged Dove with N. John Schmitt; 269-except Thick-billed Kingbird; 271-Rose-throat-ed Becard; 285-flying Chihuahuan Raven, flying Common Raven; 305-tail of female Blue-gray Gnatcatcher; 412-Eastern Spot-billed Duck; 413-except Great-winged Petrel; 414; 415-except Wedge-rumped Storm-Petrel and Red-tailed Tropicbird; 416-Nazca Booby, Gray Heron; 420-Jack Snipe, Pin-tailed Snipe; 421-Oriental Turtle-Dove with N. John Schmitt; 427-Blue Mockingbird; 428-Gray Silky-flycatcher. **David Beadle:** 8-Alder Flycatcher, Willow Flycatcher; 9-Hammond's Flycatcher; 257; 259; 261; 263; 269-Thick-billed Kingbird; 277-Philadelphia Vireo, Warbling Vireo; 287; 291-flying Cave Swallow; 301-*parkmanii* Winter Wren; 339-fall male Bay-breasted Warbler; 349-Red-faced Warbler; 363-Vesper Sparrow; 365-*canescens* Sage Sparrow; 375-"Oregon" Junco, "Pink-sided" Junco; 383-male *superbus* Northern Cardinal; 395-*loyei* Bronzed Cowbird; 413-Great-winged Petrel; 422-Gray Nightjar; 423-Cinnamon Hummingbird, Bumblebee Hummingbird; 424-Tufted Flycatcher, Brown-chested Martin; 428-Cresecent-chested Warbler; 429-Worthen's Sparrow. **Peter Burke:** 9-Western Tanager; 11-tails; 91-American Bittern, Least Bittern; 95-except Cattle Egret; 97-Glossy Ibis except flying figure, White-faced Ibis; 267; 275-Gray Vireo; 349-Rufous-capped Warbler, male Yellow-breasted Chat; 351-except Olive Warbler; 353; 355; 357-Spotted Towhee; 397; 399; 424-Nutting's Flycatcher, Piratic Flycatcher; 429-Fan-tailed Warbler; 430-Black-vented Oriole; 431-Streak-backed Oriole. **Marc R. Hanson:** 77-except left Short-tailed Shearwater and heads; 81; 123; 125-Common Moorhen, American Coot; 415-Wedge-rumped Storm-Petrel. **Cynthia J. House:** 8-scaup heads; 11-American Black Duck; 15; 17-*leucopareia, minima,* and *hutchinsii* Cackling Goose, *occidentalis* and flying Canada Goose; 19-except juvenile Whooper Swan; 21; 23; 25; 27; 29; 31; 33; 35-except flying Common Eider; 37-except *stejnegeri* White-winged Scoter; 39; 41-except goldeneye hybrid; 43-except "Goosander"; 45-except Egyptian Goose; 46; 47; 48-except Common Eider; 49; 412-Taiga Bean Goose, Tundra Bean Goose. **H. Jon Janosik:** 71-except heads; 83-Magnificient Frigatebird, Red-billed Tropicbird; 87-American White Pelican, Brown Pelican except breeding adult; 133-except *frazari* American Oystercatcher; 415-Red-tailed Tropicbird. **Donald L. Malick:** 13; 99; 101; 103-except third year Bald Eagle; 105-except flying figures; 107-perched juvenile Common Black-Hawk, perched adult Zone-tailed Hawk; 109-perched Short-tailed Hawk; 111-except perched *calurus,* flying *fuertesi,* and flying dark-morph *calurus* Red-tailed Hawk; 113-except flying dark-morph Ferruginous Hawk; 115-hovering American Kestrel, all perched figures except *suckleyi* Merlin; 117-except flight figures; 211-Common Ground-Dove, Ruddy Ground-Dove, Inca Dove; 219-Barn Owl; 221; 223; 225; 227; 229; 243-Belted Kingfisher, Green Kingfisher; 245; 247; 249; 251; 253-Hairy Woodpecker except *orius* male, American Three-toed Woodpecker, Black-backed Woodpecker, small comparison figures; 255. **Killian Mullarney:** 131-except flying figures, but including flying Mountain Plover from below; 141-standing Upland Sandpiper; 153-Pectoral Sandpiper except flying figure, Sharp-tailed Sandpiper except flying figure; 157-Ruff except flying figure, Buff-breasted Sandpiper except flying figure; 161; 164-phalaropes; 418-Little Ringed Plover. **Michael O'Brien:** 135-Willet; 293; 295; 297-Boreal Chickadee, Gray-headed Chickadee. **John P. O'Neill:** 243-Elegant Trogon; 297-Verdin, Bushtit; 423-Eared Quetzal. **Kent Pendleton:** 51-except flying Chukar; 53; 55; 57-except displaying Sharp-tailed Grouse; 59-except Gunnison Sage-Grouse; 61; 63-except Northern Bobwhite with white throat; 117; 118-flying figures; 119-except Red-shouldered Hawk; 120; 121. **Diane Pierce:** 91-Great Egret, Great Blue Heron; 93; 95-Cattle Egret; 97-flying Glossy Ibis, Wood Stork; 125-Sandhill Crane; 357-except Spotted To-whee; 359-Rufous-crowned Sparrow; 361; 363-except Vesper Sparrow; 365-except *canescens* Sage Sparrow; 367-Grasshopper Sparrow except fall *perpallidus,* Baird's Sparrow; 369-except juvenile Song Sparrow; 371; 373; 375-except "Oregon Junco," "Pink-sided Junco," and flying "Slate-colored Junco"; 377; 379; 381; 383-except *superbus* Northern Cardinal; 385; 387; 401; 403; 405; 407; 409; 418-Common Crane, Whooping Crane; 429-Little Bunting, Gray Bunting; 430-Pallas's Bunting, Reed Bunting, Yellow Grosbeak; 431-except Eurasian Siskin, Streak-backed Oriole. **John C. Pitcher:** 12-Greater Yellowlegs, Lesser Yellowlegs; 129-except flying figures; 135-except Willet; 137-except flying figures; 139-except flying Spotted Redshank; 145-except flying Black Turnstone; 147-Rock Sandpiper except flying figure; 149-except flying figures; 151-except flying figure; 153-White-rumped Sandpiper except flying figure, Baird's Sandpiper except flying figure; 419-Green Sandpiper; 420-Spoon-billed Sandpiper, Broad-billed Sandpiper. **H. Douglas Pratt:** 7-Gray Jay, Hermit Warbler; 209-Band-tailed Pigeon, Rock Pigeon; 217; 219-Common Cuckoo, Oriental Cuckoo; 235-Violet-crowned Hummingbird; 237; 239-except wings; 241; 265; 271-except Rose-throated Becard; 273-except flying figures; 275-except Gray Vireo; 277-Red-eyed Vireo, Yellow-green Vireo; 279; 281-Western Scrub-Jay, juvenile Mexican Jay, Pinyon Jay; 283; 285-except flying Chihuahuan Raven and Common Raven; 289-except flying female Purple Martin; 291-except flying Cave Swallow; 299; 301-except *parkmanii* Winter Wren; 303; 305-except tail of female Blue-gray Gnatcatcher; 307-Dusky Warbler, Artic Warbler; 309-Townsend's Solitaire; 311; 315-American Robin, Rufous-backed Robin; 317-except flying figure; 319-Brown Thrasher; 321-Eurpoean Starling; 323-except Siberian Accentor; 327; 329-except *ridgwayi* Nashville Warbler; 331-except Virginia's Warbler; 333-except Yellow Warbler; 335; 337; 339-except fall male Bay-breasted Warbler; 341-except Black-and-white Warbler; 343; 345; 349-Painted Redstart; 351-Olive Warbler; 389-except Bobolink; 393; 395-except *loyei* Bronzed Cowbird; 423-Plain-capped Starthroat; 425-Middendorff's Grasshopper-Warbler; 428-Gray Wagtail, Slate-throated Redstart. **David Quinn:** 12-Eurasian Hoopoe; 65; 67; 139-Spotted Redshank except flying figure; 307-Gray-streaked Flycatcher, Taiga Flycatcher; 309-Siberian Rubythroat, Bluethroat, Northern Wheatear; 315-Eyebrowed Thrush, Dusky Thrush; 323-Siberian Accentor; 325; 412-Lesser White-fronted Goose; 416-Yellow Bittern; 417-Intermediate Egret, Chinese Egret, Chinese Pond-Heron; 418-Greater Sand-Plover; 419-Black-winged Stilt, Marsh Sandpiper; 421-Oriental Pratincole; 422-Brown Hawk-Owl; 423-Eurasian 434 424-Great Spotted Woodpecker, Brown Shrike; 425-except Middendorff's Grasshopper-Warbler; 426; 427-except Blue Mockingbird; 428-Tree Pipit, Pechora Pipit; 429-Pine Bunting, Yellow-browed Bunting; 430-Yellow-throated Bunting, Yellow-breasted Bunting; 431-Eurasian Siskin. **Chuck Ripper:** 199-Common Murre except flying figure, Pigeon Guillemot; 201-Dovekie except flying winter figure, Marbled Murrelet, Kittlitz's Murrelet; 203; 207-except flying Rhinoceros Auklet; 231-Lesser Nighthawk; 233-Buff-collared Nightjar, Common Poorwill, tails of eastern Whip-poor-will. **N. John Schmitt:** 9-House Sparrow; 12-Eurasian Hobby; 17-*taverneri* and flying Cackling Goose, *parvipes* and *moffitti* Canada Goose; 19-juvenile Whooper Swan; 45-Egyptian Goose; 51-flying Chukar; 63-Northern Bobwhite with white throat; 103-third year Bald Eagle; 105-flying figures; 107-except perched juvenile Common Black-Hawk and perched adult Zone-tailed Hawk; 109-except perched Short-tailed Hawk; 111-perched *calurus*, flying *fuertesi* and flying dark-morph *calurus* Red-tailed Hawk; 113-flying dark-morph Ferruginous Hawk; 115-perched *suckleyi* Merlin, all flight figures except hovering American Kestrel; 119-Red-shouldered Hawk; 141-standing Bristle-thighed Curlew; 209-Spotted Dove and Eurasian Collared-Dove with Jonathan Alderfer; 211-Mourning Dove and White-winged Dove with Jonathan Alderfer; 213; 214; 215; 235-Black Swift, Chimney Swift, Vaux's Swift, White-throated Swift; 273-flying figures; 281-Island Scrub-Jay, adult Mexican Jay; 317-flying Northern Mockingbird; 319-except Brown Thrasher; 321-except European Starling; 367-except Baird's and Grasshopper Sparrows; 375-flying "Slate-colored" Junco; 411; 417-Steller's Sea-Eagle, Eurasian Kestrel; 418-Eurasian Hobby; 419-Little Curlew; 421-Oriental Turtle-Dove with Jonathan Alderfer, Thick-billed Parrot; 422-White-throated Needletail, Common Swift, Fork-tailed Swift. **Thomas R. Schultz:** 6; 7-Downy Woodpecker; 11-Common Tern; 133-*frazari* American Oystercatcher; 47-Red Knot except flying figure, Sanderling except flying figure; 155-Dunlin except flying figure, Curlew Sandpiper except flying figure; 167; 169; 171; 173; 175; 176; 177; 178; 179; 181; 183; 184; 185; 187; 189; 191; 193; 195; 197; 231-Common Nighthawk; 233-Whip-poor-will except tails; 253-Downy Woodpecker, *orius* Hairy Woodpecker; 289-flying female Purple Martin; 313; 329-*ridgwayi* Nashville Warbler; 331-Virginia's Warbler; 333-Yellow Warbler; 341-Black-and-white Warbler; 347; 349-Common Yellowthroat, female Yellow-breasted Chat; 359-except Rufous-crowned Sparrow; 367-fall *perpallidus* Grasshopper Sparrow; 369-juvenile Song Sparrow; 389-Bobolink; 391; 416-Great Frigatebird, Lesser Frigatebird; 418-Eurasian Hobby; 419-Little Curlew; 420-Great Knot; 421-Belcher's Gull, Black-tailed Gull, Swallow-tailed Gull; 422-Oriental Scops-Owl. **Daniel S. Smith:** 129-flying figures; 131-flying figures except Mountain Plover from below; 137-flying figures; 139-flying Spotted Redshank; 141-except standing Bristle-thighed Curlew and standing Up-land Sandpiper; 143-flying Bar-tailed Godwit, flying Marbled Godwit; 147-flying figures; 149-flying figures; 151-flying figure; 153-flying figures; 155-flying figures; 157-flying Ruff, flying Buff-breasted Sandpiper; 162; 163; 164-except phalaropes; 165; 419-Far Eastern Curlew. **Sophie Webb:** 233-tail of *arizonae* Whip-poor-will; 235-Lucifer Hummingbird; 239-wing figures; 423-Xantus's Hummingbird.

Acknowledgments

The editors and artists are indebted to the following individuals and institutions for their valuable assistance in the preparation of this book: Edward S. Brinkley; Paul A. Buckley; Burke Museum, University of Washington (Robert C. Faucett, Sievert Rohwer); Field Museum of Natural History (Mary Hennen, David Willard); Shawneen Finnegan; Jon S. Greenlaw; Marshall J. Iliff; Mark Lockwood; Los Angeles County Museum of Natural History (Kimball L. Garrett); Paul Mayer; Steve Mlodinow; National Museum of Natural History, Smithsonian Institution (James P. Dean); National Museums Liverpool, UK (Dr. Clemency Thorne Fisher, Tony Parker); Natural History Museum, Tring, UK (Mark Adams); Bill Pranty; Ripon College (William Brooks); Gary Rosenberg; Royal Ontario Museum (Glen Murphy, Mark Peck); Slater Museum of Natural History (Dennis Paulson, Gary Shugart); David Sonneborn; Bob Steele; John Sterling; University of Alaska, Fairbanks (Daniel D. Gibson); University of California, Los Angeles (Kathy C. Molina). Paul E. Lehman, in addition to being the Chief Map Researcher and Editor, read and commented on the entire text.

The editors and artists wish to thank the following individuals and institutions for their contributions to the *National Geographic Field Guide to the Birds of North America,* on which much of the current book is based: Mark Adams; David Agro; Thomas A. Allen; J. Phillip Angle; Jim Arterburn; Stephen Bailey; Lawrence G. Balch; Dr. Richard C. Banks; John Barber; Jon Barlow; Jen and Des Bartlett; Giff Beaton; Ken Behrens; Louis Bevier; Gavin Bieber; Eirik A. T. Blom; Daniel Boone; Jack Bowling; Edward S. Brinkley; Dawn Burke; Danny Bystrak; Richard Cannings; Steven W. Cardiff; Charles Carlson; John Carlson; Robin Carter; Allen Chartier; Graham Chisholm; Carla Cicero; Charles T. Clark; William S. Clark; Rene Corado; Marian Cressman; Ricky Davis; James P. Dean; Denver Museum of Natural History; Bruce Deuel; James Dinsmore; Donna L. Dittman; Robert Dixon; Peter J. Dunn; Peter Dunne; Cameron Eckert; Victor Emanuel; Richard Erickson; Doug Faulkner; Field Museum of Natural History; Dr. C. T. Fisher; Robert Fisher; John W. Fitzpatrick; David Fix; Rick Fridell; Kimball L. Garrett; Freida Gentry; Daniel D. Gibson; Peter Grant; Jon S. Greenlaw; John A. Gregoire; Britt Griswold; Dr. James L. Gulledge; Dr. George A. Hall; J. B. Hallett, Jr.; Robert Hamilton; Jo and Tom Heindel; Matt Heindel; Steve Heinl; Paul M. Hill; Chris Hobbs; Phill Holder; Steve N. G. Howell; Rich Hoyer; Rebecca Hyman; Frank Iwen; Greg Jackson; Alvaro Jaramillo; Joseph R. Jehl, Jr.; Ned K. Johnson; Colin Jones; Roy Jones; Lars Jonsson; Kenn Kaufman; Dan Kassebaum; Tom Kent; Wayne Klockner; Rudolf Koes; Lasse J. Laine; Daniel Lane; Dr. M. Largen; Greg Lasley; Paul E. Lehman; Nick Lethaby; Tony Leukering; Rich Levad; Mark Lockwood; Los Angeles County Museum of Natural History; Tim Loseby; Aileen Lotz; Louisiana State University Museum of Natural Science; Derek Lovitch; Rich MacIntosh; Bruce Mactavish; Laura Martin; Ron Martin; Guy McCaskie; Terry McEneaney; Mick McHugh; Ian McLaren; Doug McRae; Dominic Mitchell; Steve Mlodinow; Joseph Morlan; Killian Mullarney; Glen Murphy; Museum of Vertebrate Zoology, University of California, Berkeley; National Museum of Natural History, Smithsonian Institution; Natural History Museum, Tring, UK; Harry Nehls; Kenny Nichols; Michael O'Brien; Jerry Oldenettel; Gerald Oreel; Mike Overton; A. Parker; Tony Parker; John Parmeter; Michael Patten; Brian Patteson; Patuxent Wildlife Research Center (USGS); Dennis Paulson; Mark Peck; Paul Prior; Peter Pyle; David Quady; Betsy Reeder; Dr. J. V. Remsen; Robert F. Ringler; Don Roberson; Mark Robins; Gary Rosenberg; Philip D. Round; Bill Rowe; John Rowlett; Rose Ann Rowlett; Royal Ontario Museum; Will Russell; San Diego Natural History Museum; Larry Sansone; Santa Barbara Museum of Natural History; Rick Saval; Robert T. Scholes; Brad Schram; Thomas Schulenberg; Scott Seltman; Larry Semo; David Sibley; Ross Silcock; Mark Stackhouse; James Stasz; Rick Steenberg; Andrew Stepniewski; John Sterling; Mark Stevenson; Doug Stotz; Sherman Suter; Peder Svingen; Thede Tobish; Dr. John Trochet; Charles Trost; Laurel Tucker; Nigel Tucker; Bill Tweit; Philip Unitt; University of Alaska Museum; Arnoud van den Berg; T. R. Wahl; George Wallace; Western Foundation of Vertebrate Zoology; Mel White; Tony White; Hal Wierenga; Claudia P. Wilds; David W. Willard; Jeff Wilson; Chris Wood; World Museum Liverpool (UK); Alan Wormington; Louise Zemaitis; Barry Zimmer; Kevin Zimmer.

Index

The main entry for each species is listed in **boldface** type and refers to text page opposite the illustration.